The Reemergence of Self-Employment

THE REEMERGENCE
OF SELF-EMPLOYMENT

A COMPARATIVE STUDY OF
SELF-EMPLOYMENT DYNAMICS
AND SOCIAL INEQUALITY

Edited by
Richard Arum and Walter Müller

PRINCETON UNIVERSITY PRESS

PRINCETON AND OXFORD

Library of Congress Cataloging-in-Publication Data

The reemergence of self-employment : a comparative study of
self-employment dynamics and social inequality / edited by
Richard Arum and Walter Müller.
p.   cm.
Includes bibliographical references and index.
ISBN 0-691-11756-X (cl : alk. paper) — ISBN 0-691-11757-8
(pbk. : alk. paper)
1. Self-employed.   2. Equality.   3. Social status.   I. Arum,
Richard.   II. Müller, Walter, 1942–

HD8036.R44   2004
331.12—dc22   2003060700

British Library Cataloging-in-Publication Data is available

This book has been composed in Janson

Printed on acid-free paper. ∞

www.pupress.princeton.edu

Printed in the United States of America

10   9   8   7   6   5   4   3   2   1

Contents

Illustrations

Tables

Preface

THIS BOOK IS based on an international comparative research project examining recent developments in self-employment organized by Walter Müller at the Mannheim Center for European Social Research and Richard Arum at New York University. The project has involved researchers from eleven countries who have been meeting since August 1999 to develop and implement a unique analytical perspective that highlights inequalities both related to self-employment and found within self-employment.

Our cross-national research is informed by a social stratification perspective and provides new insights into both the character and determinants of recent cross-national growth in self-employment in advanced economies. Our project highlights the importance of distinguishing self-employment by occupational categories and gender, as well as appreciating the role of social class background and educational attainment in the structuring of labor market outcomes. Specifically, our research has four overall goals: (1) to distinguish among types of nonagricultural self-employment by applying an occupational categorization schema that distinguishes among professional (and managerial) self-employment, skilled nonprofessional self-employment, and unskilled nonprofessional self-employment; (2) to identify the relative weight of family background in the traditional inheritance of self-employment and the role of educational attainment in providing access to these various forms of self-employment; (3) to highlight the complex and dynamic character of self-employment by examining separately the process of self- employment entry and self-employment exit through use of event-history modeling; and (4) to examine the effects of national institutional settings (such as welfare state regimes and labor market regulations) on self-employment dynamics.

Our project provides detailed case-studies of eleven countries chosen to represent variation in national conditions. These papers are not a random collection of conference papers, but rather are a set of highly structured and comparable analyses that were commissioned to follow a common set of theoretical questions and methodological procedures. In particular, they use longitudinal panel and retrospective data on employment careers rather than relying on the limitations of cross-sectional data. These datasets represent the best available international sources to allow for a first-time systematic and large-scale comparative assessment of similarities and differences in the processes underlying entry and survival in self-employment.

The systematic character of the project allows the production of an explicitly comparative chapter that serves not just as a conclusion or summary of results, but rather as an original cross-national analysis made possible by the country-specific research. This chapter enables us to address the theoretical motivations informing the research. The combination of separate country-specific chapters and an explicitly comparative chapter allows a better understanding of both self-employment developments within countries and the overall changes in the phenomena.

Countries selected for the project represent various political, economic, and social ideal types. Western European corporatist economic states are represented by France, Germany, and the Netherlands. Australia, the United Kingdom, and the United States represent Anglo-American neoliberal economies. Societies that are characterized by the relative prominence of family-based social capital are represented by Italy, Japan, and Taiwan. Lastly, economies that are undergoing postsocialist transformations are represented by Hungary and Russia.

We have brought together prominent researchers from these eleven countries with expertise on their country's labor markets, stratification patterns, and local data. These researchers include Dominique Goux and Thomas Amossé from INSEE, France; Henning Lohmann and Silvia Luber, Mannheim University, Germany; Boris Blumberg, Maastrich University, and Paul M. de Graaf, Nijmegen University, Netherlands; Mariah Evans and Joanna Sikora, Canberra University, Australia; Nigel Meager and Peter Bates, University of Sussex, England; Paolo Barbieri, University of Milano, and Ivano Bison, University of Trento, Italy; Hiroshi Ishida, Tokyo University; Wei-hsin Yu, Academia Sinica, and Kuo-Hsien Su, National Taipei University, Taiwan; Péter Róbert, ELTE University, and Erzsébet Bukodi, Central Statistical Office, Hungary; and Ted Gerber, University of Wisconsin, with expertise on Russia.

The production of this volume was made possible by the cooperation of the scholars listed above. Upon their suggestion, we have dedicated all proceeds from sales of this volume to the Alan Kerckhoff and Aage Sorenson Fellowship Funds that support graduate student travel to meetings of the International Sociology Association's Research Committee on Social Stratification and Mobility (RC28).

In addition, the project was supported financially through a grant from the Fritz-Thyssen Foundation and institutionally through the support of the Mannheim Center for European Social Research and New York University's Department of Humanities and Social Sciences in the Professions. Henning Lohmann and Silvia Luber provided essential coordination of the project during their tenure at the Mannheim Center for European Social Research; Liz Anderson and Patricia Chow at New York University served as editorial assistants for the volume; Anita O'Brien at

Princeton provided excellent copy editing on the volume; and Ian Malcolm, sociology editor at Princeton University Press, provided encouragement and essential suggestions for direction on completing the final manuscript. We are grateful to these individuals and institutions that have made this project possible.

Richard Arum
Walter Müller

The Reemergence of Self-Employment

CHAPTER ONE

Self-Employment Dynamics in Advanced Economies

Walter Müller and Richard Arum

IN THE SECOND half of the twentieth century, social scientists typically viewed self-employment as an obsolete remnant of past forms of economic organization: its small-scale mode of production was expected to disappear under the dominating logic and competitive pressures of capital accumulation and mass production. Contrary to such predictions, recent developments have demonstrated that self-employment has resisted these pressures. Rather than diminishing its role in contemporary advanced societies, self-employment has grown in many national settings over recent decades. However, recent economic and social changes have not only reinvigorated self-employment, but also affected its character. Both developments require that social stratification researchers rethink their assumptions and reconceptualize their approach toward examining this activity.

Even if self-employment has merely persisted, it still represents a highly particular way to gain one's living in modern economic contexts. For most advanced societies, indeed, a cross-sectional picture immediately demonstrates that the self-employed constitute only a small fraction of the labor force. At any given time, only a minority fail to follow the normative practice of selling their labor capacity to an employer, but rather use their human, social, and economic capital for a business of their own and at their own risk. The first basic question then still is: *What are the factors leading individuals into self-employment and then inducing them to remain active in these kinds of endeavors?*

A self-employment rate of about 10 percent of the nonagricultural labor force is typically found in most advanced societies. However, in some societies this rate is much higher, in particular in the south of Europe and in Asian countries. In these countries, the rate of self-employment may be more than double the usual size, and in some national settings it accounts for 25 to 30 percent of the labor force. In earlier decades the high cross-national variation in the share of self-employment often was attributed to delays in economic development with convergence expected in the course of modernization. Today such explanations have lost much of their plausibility as even in economically highly advanced countries, such as Italy or Japan, self-employment has remained at very high levels. One should expect that societies with these widely varying levels of self-employment also vary in other ways, such as in the organization of work or even more generally in principles of social organization. *How, then, can we account for the continued strong variation between countries in the presence of self-employment today? What are the implications of different economic and social contexts for the level and character of self-employment?*

In the past, sociologists often assumed that self-employment to a large extent could be equated with the petty bourgeoisie, considered as a particular social class with its own specific social basis and principles of class formation and reproduction. Even though it has been characterized as the "uneasy stratum" (Bechhofer and Elliott 1981) and its internal heterogeneity has been widely acknowledged, it was assumed that this class mainly consisted of small proprietors, shopowners, skilled craftspeople, nonprofessional service providers, and others with similar working conditions who were running their own business. The bulk of the self-employed did indeed belong traditionally to these groups. Besides not working for wages or salaries, they shared a number of further common characteristics, notably a high level of intergenerational inheritance, a particular "moral economy" (Bechhofer and Elliott 1981:189), and specific political attitudes and orientations. Significant changes in the technology of production and the economic opportunity structure have recently occurred in many countries, including a revolution in computing and new communication technologies; expansion of female employment; the growth and persistence of mass unemployment; the decline in goods-producing industries and concentration of the distribution of goods in larger units; the rise of the service sector and increased professionalization; the growth of flexible production; and the spread of nontraditional work arrangements. For all these developments, arguments have been advanced that have repercussions on self-employment. *What has been the impact of economic change on the character of self-employment, the composition of the group, its internal homogeneity, and its economic strength and stability?*

Self-employment and small firm production have always constituted a context of work very different from employment in large, bureaucratically organized private companies or public administration. Specific social relations have usually been involved in the traditional petty bourgeois work unit: "The 'boss' works alongside his 'labour force.' Often the 'labour' is recruited from the networks of kinship, friendship and neighbourhood and thus there are 'non-contractual' elements in the relationship from the start." These authors also suggest that "in a society where large impersonal institutions mould much day-to-day living, this personalising of work relationships may be welcomed by both sides" (Bechhofer and Elliott 1981:194). Perhaps most significant in this traditional small-scale economic form of organization, and rather distinct in the modern context in which work tends to be separated and isolated from the family, has been the often intimate union of family and work in the self-employed venture. Indeed, self-employment has often been a family business, strongly dependent on the work of a married couple and their children. Women today, however, are more inclined to pursue their own independent careers and projects—even though to a varying extent in different societies—and children are certainly no longer easily kept as cheap family labor. *Has thus the family-embeddedness of self-employment eroded? Has the separation between spheres of life also invaded self-employment and transformed its social character? Is the varying extent to which individuals in different societies have access to family resources precisely one of the factors that lies behind the uneven level and character of self-employed activity?*

In research on social stratification, the family relatedness of self-employment has been particularly studied in the view of intergenerational inheritance of self-employment. It is regularly found that entry into self-employment is often a matter of directly inheriting a parental business, particularly so in agricultural self-employment where the family farm is passed from generation to generation. Also in this sense, self-employment has been characterized as a remnant of a social order, in which the intergenerational reproduction of social inequality still occurs primarily via direct inheritance, in contrast to access to positions of dependent work, where the transmission of advantage from generation to generation occurs mainly through socially unequal participation in education. *Is contemporary self-employment still characterized by the traditional mode of socially inherited reproduction, or have more recent forms of self-employment moved in a direction whereby acquired human capital resources have gained a significant role compared with both transmission of material capital and the provision of social capital?*

These are some of the core substantive questions that we pursue in this book with eleven national case studies on entry into and survival in self-employment. The national case studies provide both rich historical and contextual information to understand the specific nature of self-employment and the conditions of its recent development. The book concludes with a chapter presenting a comparative meta-analysis of cross-national results.

In this introductory chapter, we provide background information essential to understanding the topic, advance a theoretical framework for a cross-national study of self-employment dynamics, discuss the research design for the analysis, and present an outline of the structure of the book. In particular, we will discuss the reemergence of self-employment; the extent to which renewed analysis of self-employment is critical to understanding social inequality; the contemporary historical context of changes in work and employment relationships that have affected self-employment characteristics; a theoretical framework that emphasizes how resources, opportunities, and constraints structure individual-level decision making related to self-employment dynamics; and relevant dimensions of institutional and societal cross-national variation that affects self-employment outcomes.

SELF-EMPLOYMENT'S REEMERGENCE

Self-employment can no longer be dismissed as an economic activity on the verge of withering away in response to processes of capital accumulation or through competition with large firms. In the last quarter of the twentieth century, nonagricultural self-employment in most advanced economies reversed a historic pattern of decline and significantly increased its relative economic presence. In the United States, for example, the share of self-employment in the nonagricultural economy steadily declined from 12.0 percent in 1948 to 6.9 percent in 1970, before reversing course and increasing to 7.7 percent by 1993.[1] In many other countries, such as England and Japan, a relatively similar historic pattern occurred. An analysis of twenty-eight Organization for Economic Cooperation and Development (OECD) countries found not only that "self-employment has tended to increase its share of non-agricultural civilian employment over the past three decades," but that this was particularly true from 1979 to the early 1990s when self-employment grew in these countries at an average annual rate of 2.3 percent per year (compared to 1.4 percent for civilian employment in general), and the overall share of self-employment in nonagricultural employment increased on average from 9.8 to 11.9 percent. In many postsocialist countries, changes were even more dramatic: self-employment—a practice that at one time had been virtually prohibited—not only reemerged in many of these countries but often was actively encouraged by new state policies promoting an economic transition to capitalism.[2]

While specific estimates differ with respect to sources of data (e.g., individuals responding to government officials tend to underreport self-employment activity), results are fairly robust in supporting the substantive conclusion that following unanticipated increases in self-employment rates, particularly from the late 1970s through the early 1990s, the final part of the twentieth century was then characterized by relative stability in levels of this activity. From this recent pattern, there is thus no reason to anticipate an ever-expanding renaissance of self-employment; however, neither is there any longer a reason to expect a withering away of this economic form. Self-employment's unexpected reemergence and continued persistence in advanced economies thus demands renewed examination. Self-employment has returned: social scientist must now, once again, reckon with this resilient social form in our midst.

An increase in self-employment not only affects how researchers and policymakers evaluate this activity and how much attention is focused on it but, as importantly, has significant implications for understanding the life experiences and economic position of individuals more generally. Many current forms of self-employment are significantly less stable than traditional petty bourgeois activity of the past. Increased occupational instability and increasing overall rates of self-employment are associated with spells of self-employment becoming more common over an individual's life-course. For example, in the United States (where self-employment occurs at relatively modest levels), more than 40 percent of men by their early fifties have engaged in self-employment at some point in their past.[3] This figure is considerably higher than estimates from earlier periods, such as Lipset and Bendix's (1959: 102) estimate of "somewhere between 20 and 30 percent" of individuals. Given the high and apparently increasing propensity for self-employment activity to occur, the majority of individuals in advanced economies are related to, and likely to know well, individuals who have become self-employed.[4]

SOCIAL STRATIFICATION RESEARCH AND SELF-EMPLOYMENT

Studying self-employment's reemergence and internal transformations is particularly interesting to social stratification researchers in that these changes are closely related to several core intellectual concerns found within scholarship in this area. Social stratification researchers, for example, have long been interested in the character of employment activity in terms of inequality and stability, the social conditions associated with individuals engaging in nondependent enterprises (as this social status has historically had a disproportionate impact on political outcomes), and the extent to which an individual's educational achievement is capable of replacing direct ascriptive inheritance of occupational positions in modern societies.

Prior stratification researchers have paid varying attention to conceptualizing self-employment in occupational terms. Peter Blau and Otis Dudley Duncan's *The American Occupational Structure* (1967), for example, has three pages of indexed references to self-employment; David Featherman and Robert Hauser's *Opportunity and Change* (1978) has only two entries. Blau and Duncan identify self-employment as occurring in three of their seventeen occupational categories: self-employed professionals, proprietors, and farmers. Self-employed skilled and unskilled workers who associate with occupations other than proprietors (such as carpenters, bookkeepers, and drivers of motor vehicles) are subsumed into occupational categories dominated by dependent employees with similar skills.

European approaches within social stratification research differ from the Blau and Duncan classification schema in theoretical conceptualization of self-employment. Erikson, Goldthorpe, and Portocarero (1979) devised a now widely used class schema that assigns professional self-employment as well as self-employed large proprietors to occupational categories dominated by individuals associated with professional and managerial occupations in dependent employment.[5] Other self-employment is divided into small proprietors either with or without employees (IVa, IVb, respectively) and farmers (IVc). In most applications of the schema, categories IVa and IVb are collapsed into a common category of proprietors. The EGP schema thus in some respects inverts the Blau and Duncan classification system's treatment of self-employment by assigning professional self-employed to their related dependent occupational positions and defining the petty bourgeoisie as a residual category of nonprofessional and nonmanagerial self-employed.

In spite of these differences, however, both American and European approaches share the common feature of assigning certain forms of self-employment to class categories that include self-employment and dependent employees and that provide no explicit attention to "residual" self-employed occupational categories—that is, many forms of self-employment are simply excluded from focused analytical examination. In the Blau and Duncan classification, the nonprofessional self-employed are not considered; in the EGP schema, the professional self-employed are not identified as self-employed. Both these prior conceptualizations have thus become increasingly problematic as conceptual frameworks as self-employment has become increasingly heterogeneous: "the partial renaissance of self-employment"—as the OECD report cited above has labeled this economic phenomenon—is occurring precisely in those areas that have been analytically obscured by prior stratification work.

While social stratification researchers have differed in their conceptualization of self-employment as a category (e.g., in whether self-employed professionals or laborers should be included in this social grouping), there has been a general consensus among these scholars that the activity must be understood in some fashion as distinct from dependent employment. Self-employment differs from dependent employment in that it allows greater autonomy for individuals, but it also increases individual's exposure to the rewards and costs associated with direct involvement in and dependence on sales of products and services in a competitive and unstable market. As stratification researchers in particular are interested in inequality, they also should consider heterogeneity within self-employment—that is, not just mainly focus on traditional petty bourgeois craft production and proprietorship, but also take account of the potential growth of unskilled self-employment and self-employed professionals engaged in freelancing or other semi-autonomous jobs.

Although the self-employed as a social grouping have often been relatively small in terms of their demographic proportions, they have traditionally been the focus of inordinate attention as they have been recognized as possessing the potential to demonstrate a historically critical role in determining societal-level political outcomes. The autonomy and market insecurity of self-employed activity have been argued to combine to provide both greater freedom and motivation for this social grouping to attend to political matters. The material conditions associated with self-employment have thus been claimed to generate distinct social identities, economic interests, and political orientations relative to individuals in dependent employment (Bechhofer and Elliott 1985). Marx and Engels, for example, in the *Communist Manifesto* noted: "The lower middle class, the small manufacturer, the shopkeeper, the artisan, the peasant, all these fight against the bourgeoisie, to save from extinction their existence as fractions of the middle class. They are therefore not revolutionary, but conservative. Nay more, they are reactionary for they try to roll back the wheel of history."[6] Subsequent sociological research in general has tended to provide fairly similar evaluations. Seymour Martin Lipset, for example, argued that the petty bourgeoisie were the group "most prone to support fascist and other middle class extremist ideologies."[7] More recently the analysis by Michael Hout and colleagues of postwar U.S. voting suggested that "owners and proprietors moved from indifference to strong Republican support, especially since 1972."[8]

The political orientations of the self-employed have been understood as emerging from their contradictory class position in society. Erik Olin Wright, for example, theorized contemporary class location as involving several dimensions: a relationship to ownership, workplace authority, and education-based skills or credentials. While Wright's actual discussion of self-employment has tended to focus on the first two dimensions (ownership and workplace authority relationships associated with size of firm), consistent with this approach would be a consideration of whether the self-employed have professional qualifications and whether they are skilled or unskilled. Given that the self-employed vary along these three dimensions, it follows that their class interests are ambiguous or "contradictory": that is, their interests are only partially aligned with either capitalists or workers. In addition to occupying a contradictory class location with a potential for unpredictable political alliances and support for social movements, this social grouping has also been argued to take an active and disproportionately large role in the functioning of civil society through relatively high propensities for involvement with voluntary associations related to neighborhoods, ethnic groups, and economic advocacy organizations.

While the petty bourgeoisie have manifested a central role in contemporary political narratives, both Marxism and Modernity theories (e.g., Treiman 1970) have predicted the disappearance of this social activity and have emphasized how, as the traditional petty bourgeoisie disappear, so too does direct inheritance of occupational position. The declining presence of self-employment has thus been critical to stratification researchers' contention that education increasingly plays a critical role in mediating the relationship between origins and destinations. Blau and Duncan (1967: 41) note that self-employed occupational categories manifest the most intergenerational "occupational inheritance and self-recruitment"; the occupations are also assumed to have high degrees of stability over the life course due to "stronger occupational investment and commitment than mere employment." These arguments thus assume that self-employment is disappearing, that self-employment is stable over the life course, and that education is relatively unimportant for self-employment activity. The former assumption is clearly no longer valid, and, given the growing heterogeneity within self-employment, the latter two contentions require further empirical investigation.

In the past decade social stratification researchers, confronted with changing empirical realities, have begun to grapple anew with self-employment and to reconsider earlier assumptions about intergenerational inheritance of the status as well as the inevitable historical decline and disappearance of the activity. Robert Erikson and John Goldthorpe (1993: 222), for example, noted that "in the context of advanced industrialism this decline is often checked or indeed reversed" and that while "the petty bourgeoisie reveals a moderately strong propensity for intergenerational immobility, which we associate with the possibility of direct inheritance of property . . . in other respects, it must in fact be regarded as a rather open class."

Research in the past several years has also attempted even closer examination of assumptions about stability, inheritance, and homogeneity of the self-employed by separately studying paths into self-employment and factors related to survival in such enterprises (as opposed to identifying simple patterns of associations from cross-sectional data), as well as by distinguishing self-employment categories on the basis of occupational differences. Specifically, researchers have treated all self-employed as distinct from employees and have begun to distinguish among the self-employed in a clearer fashion. They have also adopted event-history modeling of longitudinal data estimating factors affecting entry and exit.

Arum (1997) proposed a simple occupational distinction between professional and nonprofessional self-employment for event-history analysis of this sector in the United States. Subsequently, self-employment has been further explored by distinguishing between professional and managerial proprietors, between skilled and unskilled nonprofessionals, as well as through examining the entry and exit dynamics of these and related occupational distinctions (see, e.g., Shavit and Yuchtman-Yaar 2001; Laferrère 2001; McManus 2000b).

We believe that an improved understanding of self-employment is possible, however, not simply by incorporating occupational differentiation more fully into an analytical framework, but more critically through explicitly recognizing individual-level decision-making processes whereby individual characteristics and structural factors affect choices related to entering and exiting self-employment. Specifically, involvement in self-employment implies a process whereby individuals actively *decide*—after considering the perceived relative costs and benefits attached to distinct paths—whether to enter self-employment or subsequently to remain self-employed (Abell 1996). We posit that most individuals in advanced economies begin their labor market activity with a "taken for granted" assumption of involvement in dependent employment. In almost all of the countries examined in this book (with the exception of Japan and Italy), the vast majority of self-employed individuals have not "inherited" self-employment from parents who were involved in similar enterprises. The decision to become self-employed in these settings thus must typically involve active consideration of relative incentives, resources, opportunities, and constraints, as would an individual's decision to remain self-employed. It is worth noting, however, that in most countries a significant percentage of employed individuals actually demonstrate an expressed preference for self-employment activity: in Italy and the United States, approximately 60 percent of employees claim that they would choose self-employment if given a choice between dependent employment and self-employment; in West Germany, Great Britain, and the Netherlands, the percentages of employees expressing a desire for self-employment are 47, 43, and 33 percent, respectively.[9] Through examining the structural factors affecting these choices, we are able to learn about self-employment dynamics and recognize factors that are related to producing changes in the characteristics of self-employment over time.

CHANGES IN WORK AND EMPLOYMENT STRUCTURE

While abstract theorizing about globalization has often been poorly connected to empirically observable social change and thus at times ill-suited as a basis for informing social stratification research (Goldthorpe 2001), concrete and identifiable changes to work arrangements have indeed occurred in many countries. Long-term employment contracts have in certain firms, industries, and countries often been replaced by nontraditional work arrangements (such as sub- and temporary employment contracting as well as other techniques that have redefined employer-employee relationships and commitments). While it is quite likely that these changes are related more to the spread of neoliberal economic policies than any actual increase in globalization of economic trade per se, these changes—regardless of their origins—manifest themselves particularly in, and at times emerge from, self-employment. Understanding the logic of self-employment and the contemporary character of it thus can also inform our understanding of the direction of social developments and inequality more generally. This study, by providing new insights into the growing variation in self-employment and the individual and institutional factors that have produced these changes, is suggestive of larger societal processes affecting social inequality more generally.

In related scholarship on regional economies and small business growth, researchers have advanced arguments about the advantages of small firm flexibility and raised expectations that self-employment and small businesses could have a critical role in job creation (e.g., Piore and Sabel 1984). Thus, entrepreneurship has been argued to be highly dynamic and critical for future economic growth. Because of these beliefs, governments have created specific policies affecting this sector in relationship to larger policies connected to labor market regulation. Ironically, as labor market regulation makes self-employment less attractive to enter (in terms of producing relatively high rewards within dependent employment), it simultaneously has created increased opportunities for entrepreneurial activity by producing significant incentives for employers to outsource production to increase flexibility and reduce internal labor costs. In addition, specific policies have been advanced to promote entrepreneurial behavior to stimulate job growth and utilize self-employment to reduce unemployment associated with labor market rigidities or economic downturns.

Structural conditions conducive to self-employment have also emerged from a broad related set of economic changes that are *sectoral* in character—i.e., declines in agriculture and manufacturing associated with technological change, increased productivity and the diffusion of manufacturing production away from localized domestic sources, and most importantly, the expansion of the service sector, where entry barriers into self-employment are lower than in capital-intensive manufacturing. These sectoral changes have led to increased individual opportunities for self-employment.

Several other developments, commonly related to increases in globalization and the spread of neoliberal policies, also contribute to a changing composition and character of self-employment, not simply the aggregate rate of this activity. Specifically, in many societies there has been an increase in marginalized forms of labor relationships and in labor market flexibility, and a decline in lifetime dependent employment relationships (Schizzerotto and Pisati 2003; Kim and Kurz 2003; Bernardi 2003). In attempts to increase flexibility, firms tend to reduce their stable workforce and often rely on subcontracting and outsourced self-employed or pseudo-self-employed labor, in particular to adapt to demand fluctuation. With such practices, there has been an increase in the number of self-employed professionals who rely on freelancing for income (e.g., Kallenberg, Reskin, and Hudson 2000; Hakim 1998) as well as in the number of individuals engaged in low-skilled self-employment found in construction or manual services (see chapter 5). Furthermore, in many countries immigration has expanded, with immigrant groups often having high rates of self-employment of a rather marginal kind, particularly when concentrated in ethnic enclaves.

The reemergence of self-employment has thus been associated with related changes in economic structure, technologies of production, and political market interventions (e.g., increases in professionalization, the rise of the service sector, business firm commitment to flexible production, growth of information technologies, and the introduction of policies promoting entrepreneurialism and small firm growth). These changes, however, imply that traditional forms of petty bourgeois self-employment (e.g., small shopkeepers, restauranteurs, skilled craftsworkers) quite likely have continued their declining historical presence and new forms of self-employment in both professional and unskilled occupation have been largely responsible for recent increases.

In addition, in many industrialized countries female self-employment in the past few decades has increased at significantly higher rates than male self-employment and has thus become an increasingly important component of overall self-employment (OECD 2000). During certain periods in their life course, women might be particularly drawn into various forms of self-employment activity that allow more flexible work arrangements. The growth of female self-employment is likely to have produced increased heterogeneity in self-employment overall as such activity has often been associated with simultaneous involvement with significant family commitments and has thus tended to be short-lived, part-time, or marginal in other ways. Increases in female labor force activity also likely produce growing demand for marginal domestically oriented self-employment, as women who enter the workforce outsource traditional domestic responsibilities to other women with fewer occupationally marketable skills (McManus 2001; Hochschild 1997; Connelly 1992).

Self-employment is likely not only increasingly heterogeneous within countries, but also probably more heterogeneous than dependent employment across industrialized societies as it is often directly embedded in family economic and social organization, not just market and state institutions. Family institutions, and in particular the share of women's work devoted to the family and labor market, considerably differ between countries, with such practices likely affecting the development of self-employment—an activity that has always been embedded in family relationships. As changes have occurred in family structure, women's educational attainment, female labor force participation, and forms of self-employment, research is needed to explore whether self-employment's relationship to the family has persisted. The relationship of family to self-employment should be considered in terms of both the effect of family participation on the act of self-employment and the direct intergenerational familial inheritance of self-employment positions.

Researchers have argued that a portion of the increase in self-employment has been concentrated in undesirable occupations and associated with an erosion of the social position of labor (see, e.g., Arum 2001, 1997; McManus 2000b; Kallenberg, Reskin, and Hudson 2000). Self-employment, particularly new forms of transitory and marginal self-employment in unskilled occupations, thus possibly is in part related to a "dark side of flexible production" (Harrison 1994). As a result one would expect that a growing proportion of self-employment has occurred in unskilled occupations with high entry and exit rates as well as strong associations with prior unemployment. On the other hand, self-employment increases have also been associated with the growing competitiveness of small firms and self-employed professionals who have taken advantage of changes in technology to identify specific market niches conducive to entrepreneurial success. In many locations, businesses have adopted strategies of flexible production, including outsourcing and the development of extensive network relationships with small firms and independent contractors (Reich 1991; Powell 1990). These changes have likely promoted a renaissance of small firms and increased possibilities for entrepreneurial success in some locations (Piore and Sabel 1984). While social science researchers have often focused on self-employment increases in both professional-managerial and unskilled occupations, they have also predicted and identified the decline of traditional petty bourgeois self-employment (e.g., Blau and Duncan 1967).

Resources, Opportunities and Constraints

For this project our analysis is guided by the assumption that individuals under conditions of bounded rationality consider existing and potential resources, opportunities, and constraints when choosing to enter or leave distinct self-employment occupational paths. Resources most salient to individuals in calculating the likelihood of self-employment success are education, family support (both inheritance and spousal assistance), and work experience (i.e., occupationally based human capital). The most significant opportunities and constraints to consider are related to the occupational structure an individual faces as well as his or her particular location in such a system. For example, an individual located in certain industrial sectors such as construction would have greater opportunities and fewer constraints to move into self-employment than an individual located in manufacturing. In a similar fashion, an unemployed individual who faces significant constraints in finding dependent employment is likely to assess opportunities in self-employment more favorably.[10]

Education

Education, particularly tertiary and vocational, provides individuals with human capital skills that are transferable between either self-employment or dependent employment. Prior research has suggested that in all countries education is related to self-employment, but research so far is inconsistent concerning the direction of educational effects. Generally, higher qualifications improve the likelihood of self-employment in a given area of work since self-employment compared with dependent work often requires qualifications in addition to the purely functional skills necessary for doing a given job well (such as management and planning skills, knowledge of financial affairs, understanding of market opportunities, ability in personnel guidance, and skills in public or customer relations). However, while several of these abilities can be trained, they often are not learned in schools and rather are acquired in family or other contexts. Prior research has found that in some countries, such as Germany and postsocialist Russia, education has a quasi-linear positive relationship to self-employment (Gerber 2001b, Luber et al. 2000). In other countries, such as the United Kingdom and Israel, education has more curvilinear effects, with both low and high levels of education associated with increased likelihood of self-employment activity (Shavit and Yuchtman-Yaar 2001; Luber et al. 2000; Meager, Kaiser, and Dietrich 1992). Meager et al. (1992) have also identified positive effects of vocational education on male self-employment in Germany.

While education in general is positively associated with self-employment entry, exceptions to this trend exist. Countries with high levels of self-employment, such as Italy, Portugal, and Greece, tend to have negative associations between education and self-employment, as much of self-employment is in low-skilled occupations (Blanchflower 2000). Research on national minorities and the prevalence of ethnic entrepreneurial enclaves has also suggested that self-employment can be used as an alternative strategy for social advancement when access to educational attainment is blocked or difficult to obtain (see, e.g., Wilson and Portes 1980; Aldrich and Waldinger 1990; Light 1992; Shavit and Yaar 2001). Individuals from lower social origins (e.g., ethnic minorities) or those who otherwise have less ability and aptitude for educational achievement, it has been argued, seek professional/managerial self-employment as an alternative route for acquiring successful occupational status given otherwise inadequate possession of educational credentials required for high attainment in dependent employment (Shavit and Yuchtman-Yaar 2001). From this perspective, individuals make a rational choice that, given their personal attributes, pursuing further educational attainment is unwarranted relative to labor force participation in a specific area (see, e.g., Breen and Jonsson 2000; Breen 1999; Manski 1993); related and supplementary factors can then lead these individuals into self-employment activity.

Work-Experience and Employment Position

Most individuals start their working life as wage or salary workers; very few work in autonomous enterprises when they first enter the labor market. They need work experience and must accumulate capital and financial resources for self-employment success, but they will also want to have sufficient years of expected future earnings to make initial investment in their self-employment projects worthwhile. Individuals at mid-career are therefore particularly likely to enter self-employment. Prior research suggests that work experience, given its association with skill acquisition, and knowledge of markets necessary for self-employment success—measured directly or indirectly through proxies such as age—have strong positive, curvilinear effects on self-employment likelihood in most advanced economies (Blanchflower 2000; Luber et al. 2000).

The early work career, however, and the characteristics of the position in the labor market an individual occupies at a given point are highly influential for the likelihood to enter self-employment and for the kind of self-employment entered because they define the opportunity structure and constraints that individuals face. Strohmeyer and Leicht (2000) show how training in a small firm strongly increases the probability of later becoming self-employed, most likely because the worker learns the skills required for operating a business. In terms of industrial sectors, we know from existing research that self-employment is particularly likely in certain industrial areas (e.g., construction and services) and less likely in sectors with large requirements for economic capital, such as manufacturing. We also expect that when individuals assess opportunities and relative incentives to become self-employed as opposed to remaining dependently employed, they will be unwilling or reluctant to move downward in terms of an occupational hierarchy. Individuals will utilize resources associated with their prior occupational position as much as possible to maintain or improve their occupational location. Unemployed individuals have a relatively higher likelihood to move into self-employment than dependent employees with similar characteristics as they are already actively on the market searching for employment positions. They must give up only the potential rewards of prolonging their job search to find even better alternatives in the future than those opportunities suggested by entering self-employment immediately. Employed individuals, on the other hand, must give up a job and continuous earnings tied to their present position when moving into self-employment. The opportunity costs will thus tend to be much higher for employed than for unemployed individuals, and the latter should be more likely to enter self-employment than the former. While unemployment likely affects an individual's decision to become self-employed, this does not necessarily imply a positive relationship between aggregate-level unemployment and self-employment rates. As the overall rate of unemployment increases, the pool of individuals particularly prone to entering self-employment rises; unemployment rates, however, also likely affect two other related phenomena—the likelihood of a dependent employee being willing to leave a job to start self-employed activity, and the likelihood that an existing self-employed enterprise will be able to sustain itself and survive in relatively undesirable market conditions.

Family Resources

Family support, in the form of both occupational inheritance and spousal assistance and involvement in the enterprise, is a significant individual-level resource that could affect a person's decisions both to become self-employed and to remain self-employed. Previous research in varied national settings has identified the effect of parental self-employment background on the likelihood of respondent's self-employment. Strong inheritance of self-employment is a common finding in most studies of intergenerational class mobility. Self-employment is more likely when parents have been similarly employed for a number of reasons. First, there are cases of direct inheritance of small family businesses. Second, parental involvement in self-employment could provide access to financial collateral and network contacts, thus reducing liquidity constraints (Laferrère 2001). Finally, and perhaps most importantly, familial involvement in self-employment provides "a taste for self-employment, a knowledge of enterprise from the inside" and a general "socialization of youths to the norms, values and skills ('entrepreneurial capital') that are particular to the self-employed class" (Laferrère 2001:22; Shavit and Yuchtman-Yaar 2000:61; Aldrich, Renzulli, and Langton 1998). The significance of family resources and traditions is bound not just to the intergenerational transmission of self-employment. Self-employment is often more generally embedded in familial relationships than is the case with dependent employment. Existing research has highlighted the degree to which self-employment frequently thus not only is inherited but often manifests itself as a family business involving the spouse, and sometimes children and relatives (Aldrich and Zimmer 1986). Family conditions, notably family status and self-employment of the spouse, thus also must be assessed as a significant determinant of self-employment dynamics.

Gender

Women—since they differ from men in their relative resources, opportunities, and constraints—will have distinctly different patterns and determinants related to self-employment. Researchers have long focused on the distinct character of male and female self-employment (see McManus 2001 for a review of this topic). Female self-employment tends to occur—like dependent employment—in sex-segregated occupations and particular industrial sectors, such as service branches (Lohmann and Luber 2000; Luber et al. 2000; Wharton 1989). Since family responsibilities are allocated unequally, pronounced differences appear in the effects of various family characteristics on male and female self-employment (McManus 2000a; Boden 1999; Carr 1996; Loscocco and Leicht 1993; Kallenberg and Leicht 1991). Female self-employment is of shorter duration and is typically less stable than male self-employment (Lin, Picot, and Compton 2000). Female self-employment is often part-time and has low income associated with it, although heterogeneity produces large variation in characteristics associated with this activity (Kallenberg, Reskin, and Hudson 2000; Manser and Picot 1999; Hakim 1998; Arum 1997; Devine 1994). Women with primary responsibility for childcare have incentives to utilize self-employment to supplement family income and thus tend to have greater involvement in marginal, part-time, or unskilled self-employment associated with flexible work arrangements.

CROSS-NATIONAL VARIATION

It is well known that the extent of self-employment varies between countries. We conjecture that such differences are not just a result of different levels of development and a country's economic modernization, but are conditioned by varying institutional arrangements that make entry and survival in self-employment more or less likely. Such conditions will also make self-employment more or less viable and attractive for different population groups. Countries will thus vary not only in the extent of self-employment but in the characteristics of self-employment as well. Through a dynamic and comparative design, this book contributes to a better understanding of both the general nature of self-employment and its variation in different institutional contexts.

Countries selected for the project differ in many socioeconomic and political aspects. In our discussion, we find it useful to focus on two illustrative dimensions of country-level differences: labor market regulation and family-based social capital. Figure 1.1 proposes how the eleven countries in our project might be theoretically placed within a two-dimensional chart based on these factors. We have operationalized labor market regulation by relying on a measure of employment protection legislation developed by the OECD. The measure is a composite index generated through examination of legislation affecting regular employment, temporary employment, and collective dismissals. Published information existed for nine out of the eleven countries in our study—Russia and Taiwan being the exceptions. For those two countries, authors of the relevant chapters consulted with colleagues who had expertise in the area of country-specific labor market regulation and generated estimates for this measure that approximated the values OECD researchers likely would have assigned if these countries had been included in the original study.[11] We have italicized these two countries in the figure to indicate that these are author-estimated values on the OECD Employment Protection Index, generated solely for comparative purposes in our project. In the figure, we have also used two arrows to identify three countries with rapidly changing regulatory regimes. Taiwan prior to 1996, during the period when observational data used for the case study described in this volume were collected, had only rudimentary employment protections in place; in the late 1990s the country implemented a range of new labor market regulations with the current Employment Protection Index now estimated at 1.9. A second arrow in the chart indicates the degree to which labor market regulations in both Russia and Hungary were significantly relaxed in the 1990s, as the economies underwent an economic transition, and again during the period under observation in the case studies.

We have operationalized family-based social capital very simply with a widely available—or easy to generate—measure: the percentage of adults aged 25–59 who are living in a household with their parents.[12] While adults live with parents in their households for a complex set of reasons (including not just cultural differences but economic necessity, housing shortages, and societal age structure), we believe this rudimentary measure is still useful for our purposes as it is suggestive of how intergenerational family relationships vary significantly across societies. Our concept of family-based social capital is distinct from broader notions of social capital that can be found in many aspects of social organization. While social capital in general has been utilized as a concept to discuss quite diverse phenomena both within our country-specific chapters and within the field of sociology more broadly, in our cross-national comparisons we are interested not in general social relationships associated with interpersonal networking or social integration of communities, but in a more narrow definition that serves to identify variation in the role of the family unit in societal economic organization.

It is worth cautioning readers that placement of countries in this figure is thus based on crude empirical measurement of our underlying concepts. Nevertheless, while the figure is not a definitive social mapping of these differences, the illustration is suggestive of a strategy useful for conceptualizing relevant factors related to cross-national variation. With these caveats in mind, the figure identifies variation along two dimensions, with countries farther to the right on the x-axis having increased labor market regulation and countries higher on the y-axis indicative of societies that are organized more extensively on principles of family-based social capital. Societies that have greater emphasis on family-based social capital would likely be characterized not just by a higher prevalence of adult children living at home with their parents, but also by the increased salience of extended kin networks and stronger family ties in general. We do not wish to reify these societal differences nor to imply that they are produced simply by national cultural differences as opposed to other economic, political, and institutional factors. Welfare-state policies, for example, likely emerge from and structure the extent to which family-based social capital is salient. Welfare-state regimes also vary in the degree to which they promote patriarchal family structures or, on the contrary, defamilialization (see, e.g., Esping-Andersen 1999). In addition, families in some countries serve to compensate for weak welfare states, but in other settings, individuals are left to the vagaries of market forces.

Labor market regulation also likely structures the prevalence and forms of self-employment activity across countries. Variation in labor market regulation is closely related to cross-national differences in how difficult it is to incorporate a self-employed business as well as the relative incentives to engage in self-employment that are associated with taxation policies. In the late 1990s the Union of Industrial and Employers' Confederations of Europe (UNICE) estimated differences across countries in the formal requirements associated with establishing a new business. Countries in our study, which were also included in the UNICE report, varied in terms of these requirements in a manner similar to our discussion of labor market regulation and political-economic ideal types. In the neoliberal economies of Australia, the United Kingdom, and the United States, new businesses could be established with one procedure in less than a week and with a minimum amount of financial costs associated with regulatory compliance. In the corporatist states of France, Germany, and the Netherlands, as well as Italy and Japan (the other countries in our study that are described as having higher degrees of labor market regulation), on average 8.4 procedures were required to establish a new business, the average time necessary to comply with regulations was 9.4 weeks, and administrative procedural costs on average were 5.7 times higher than in the neoliberal economies.[13]

Cross-national variation in institutional relationships affecting the establishment and regulation of small businesses also occurs through variation in taxation policies adopted by state authorities, which create incentives for the establishment and incorporation of businesses as well as for self-employment in general. Relevant tax policies to consider in this regard include differences in tax liability for unincorporated and incorporated businesses; variation in requirements for retirement and pension contributions (for employers, employees, and the self-employed); special tax regulations affecting family business inheritance and transfer; and variation in tax rates for individual, as opposed to corporate, income and profits.[14] While cross-national variation in regulatory procedures and taxation policies is significant, detailed discussion of these factors has been relegated to individual country-specific chapters. For purposes of cross-national comparison, we simplify the extraordinary legal and regulatory complexity of the institutional environment by discussing a summary measure of the degree of general labor market regulation affecting both self-employment and dependent employment in a society.

Three commonly discussed and distinct political-economic ideal types are clustered in figure 1.1. In the lower right-hand side of the illustration, Western European *corporatist states* with relatively high labor market regulation and comparatively low reliance on family-based social capital are represented by France, Germany, and the Netherlands. These societies have average scores of 2.5 on the OECD Employment Index and 4.5 percent of adults aged 25–59 living with parents in their households. The Anglo-American *neoliberal economies* of Australia, the United Kingdom, and the United States are clustered in the lower left-hand corner of the figure, being relatively low on both labor market regulation and family-based social capital (average score of only 0.9 on the OECD Employment Index and 3.6 percent of adults aged 25–59 living with parents in their households). In the middle of the figure, economies that are undergoing *postsocialist transformations* are represented by Hungary and Russia.

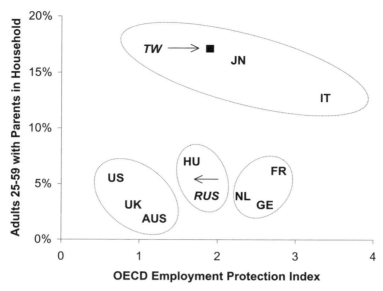

Figure 1.1: Cross-National Variation in Labor Market Regulation and Family-Based Social Capital

Individuals in these societies are relatively similar to corporatist and neo-liberal countries in terms of our measure of family-based social capital: on average, these two countries had 5.6 percent of adults aged 25–59 living with their parents. As discussed previously, labor market regulation in these postsocialist societies is in flux as governments introduce reforms promoting economic transition; these societies are increasingly embracing policies of labor market deregulation but remain, during the time of our analysis, more heavily regulated than Anglo-American neoliberal economies.

We examine three additional states—Taiwan, Italy, and Japan—that do not easily fit into any single political regime ideal type. Rather, we believe that these societies share a common reliance on social organization characterized by a high degree of family-based social capital but differ in the extent to which their economies are characterized by labor market regulation. Italy and Japan are known for high labor market regulation. Italy has the highest value (3.4) of any of our countries on the OECD Employment Protection Index; Japan is also relatively high. Small family-based firm growth in Italian and Japanese industrial regions has been argued, in particular, by past researchers to have resulted from extensive labor market regulation (Piore and Sabel 1984). Taiwan, however, is a rapidly developing country that historically has had only quite limited labor market regulation; significant changes in this *laissez faire* regulatory approach have emerged only with legislation in the late 1990s. In all three of these societies, though, one is likely to find evidence of social organization often structured around high degrees of family-based social capital, such as strong ties with extended kin and interdependence with parents throughout the life course. Our measure of adults aged 25–59 living with parents in their household, for example, was on average for these countries 15.4 percent, more than three times the average rate for other countries discussed in our analysis.

Given that incentives for self-employment activity are assessed relative to dependent employment, labor market regulation will likely manifest a curvilinear relationship, with pressures for self-employment highest at either end of the continuum. When labor market regulation and protection of workers in jobs are low, there are few incentives for workers to stay in dependent employment. Rather than staying in jobs with insecure prospects, workers may prefer to set themselves up in self-employment, where they may have better control of their future than in unprotected jobs. When labor market regulation is high, employers have greater incentives to outsource economic production, and this creates a niche for successful self-employment as well as barriers for gaining access to dependent employment. By raising the possibility that labor market regulation can have curvilinear effects, we again emphasize that individual decisions to become or remain self-employed are always evaluated relative to other activities, and most particularly individuals' assessments of possibilities for and conditions within dependent employment. In addition, marginal unskilled self-employment will likely be greatest in countries with lower levels of labor market regulation. In countries where labor market regulation is weak, dependent employment in unskilled manual and nonmanual work will be unprotected, insecure, and relatively undesirable. Unskilled self-employment in these economies will likely present itself as a reasonable alternative to the unattractive opportunities within dependent employment.

Cross-national variation also manifests itself along the dimension of family-based social capital. Societies with high levels of family-based social capital will likely have higher rates of self-employment, particularly traditional inherited petty bourgeois forms. The level of self-employment will thus be relatively larger in countries in the upper part of the figure (Taiwan, Italy, and Japan), as will self-employment in traditional nonprofessional skilled occupations. Family resources (such as direct inheritance of occupational position and spousal support) will likely have greater salience for self-employment entry and exit dynamics in societies with high levels of family-based social capital than in other societies; achievement effects (e.g., education and work experience), however, will be greater in countries with lower levels of family based social capital. While we have suggested that individuals will utilize whatever resources are available to them to facilitate movement into desirable forms of self-employment, certain resources will likely have greater salience in particular national settings. Achievement effects thus will be relatively lower in countries in the top half figure 1.1, as self-employment will be concentrated in areas where family resources have more direct influence on individual-level outcomes. Family resources will be important everywhere for entry and establishment of self-employment enterprises but are likely to remain particularly important for survival in countries in the upper half of the figure, where family-based relationships imply more long-term mutual dependence and responsibilities.

Postsocialist countries will also likely vary from other countries in their associations between age and self-employment. In economies undergoing postsocialist transformations, dependent employment in the short term has been constricted, with young individuals facing high entry barriers to finding initial desirable jobs in either established firms or remaining state enterprises. Younger individuals in these societies also likely have embraced more fully than older individuals preferences and tastes for entrepreneurial activity.

RESEARCH DESIGN AND ANALYTIC STRATEGY

The selection of countries for our study, while constrained by the availability of adequate longitudinal data allowing comparable estimation of models of self-employment dynamics, adequately represents significant variation in country-specific conditions that affect individual-level entry into and exit from self-employment activity—including political factors, such as labor market regulation, and social factors, such as the extent to which family-based social capital is an important organizing principle for structuring social activity. In each of the countries examined, individual researchers applied a common analytical and methodological framework, including similar occupational distinctions among the self-employed; presentation of descriptive statistics on self-employment heterogeneity and firm-size; identification of associations between self-employment and individual-level variables; estimation of survival rates of distinct self-employment states; and use of discrete-time event–history statistical models that capture the dynamic character of self-employment and include a set of co-variates operationalizing individual resources, opportunities, and constraints impinging on the likelihood of entering self-employment and subsequently remaining self-employed. Each chapter also provides a review of particular social, economic, legal, or other institutional conditions affecting the specific constraints and opportunities for self-employment to enable adequate interpretation of self-employment developments in each nation's wider social context.

Measuring Self-Employment

We examine heterogeneity within self-employment by categorically measuring self-employment in a manner distinct from either Blau-Duncan or an EGP occupational classification schema. This strategy derives from the premise that for most occupations, individuals basically have a choice to practice the occupation either as self-employed or in dependent employment, even though the opportunities and costs and benefits for such options may vary between occupational fields. Using a similar set of occupational classes for dependent and self-employed work allows us to identify the areas in which the choice for self-employment is most likely to be made. It also shows whether moves between both employment states occur in a basically horizontal way or involve mobility of a vertical kind, either upward or downward. Specifically, we distinguish among three categories of nonagricultural self-employment: professional managerial self-employment (equivalent to EGP professional and managerial categories I and II); traditional skilled and petty bourgeois self-employment (equivalent to EGP categories IIIa, V, and VI, as well as small shopkeepers and restauranteurs); and unskilled self-employment (equivalent to EGP categories IIIb and VII). Unlike the EGP schema, however, we do not necessarily assign self-employed with large numbers of employers to classes I and II, nor do we distinguish the rest of the self-employed by whether they employ others (IVa and IVb). Instead, our self-employment categories are based on the actual occupational identifications of survey respondents and largely ignore the distinction of whether individuals employ others.[15]

Individuals' occupational identification may vary somewhat between countries even if they hold similar social positions. An individual with a small business doing construction would be classified differently depending on whether he or she reports that his or her occupation is manager/proprietor of a small construction firm or carpenter or plumber who happens to employ others. In the first case the individual would be assigned to the professional-managerial class of self-employed; in the second case, to skilled self-employment. We believe, however, that such self-identification has social meanings attached to it that are related to how an individual perceives his or her own position within an existing social hierarchy. Regardless of whether distinctions in these self-identifications can appear somewhat arbitrary, individual perceptions, definitions, and self-reports of occupational position have social-psychological as well as political implications. For example, a German craftsman with a small business might take pride in identifying his or her occupation as being a skilled carpenter and dismiss the type of work that a typical American "managerial" contractor does as substandard *pfusch* work. In the United States, however, having one's own business might be considered more relevant than the presence or lack of any specific occupational skills. Such cross-national differences in self-identification are suggested by examination of variations in reported occupational classifications for individuals in the construction industry in Germany and the United States. While 6 percent of self-employed individuals in both Germany and the United States self-identify with unskilled occupations (such as laborer), the remaining portion of self-employed individuals in construction activities in these two countries dramatically differ in whether they self-identify with either professional-managerial occupations (30 percent in Germany compared with 55 percent in the United States) or skilled trade occupations such as carpentry, plumbing, and welding (64 percent in Germany compared with 38 percent in the United States).[16]

Event History Modeling of Self-Employment Dynamics

Existing cross-national research has relied largely on cross-sectional data and failed to distinguish adequately between types of self-employment (see McManus 2000b as an exception). While cross-sectional data can tell us much about factors associated with self-employment in general and when pooled over many years can usefully identify historic trends, such data fail to allow one to identify clearly the underlying mechanisms responsible for these observed patterns. Changes in the character of self-employment, with the decline of stable, inherited petty bourgeois activity, requires the reconceptualization of self-employment as involving distinct categories as well as the expansion of traditional stratification models to incorporate new methodologies allowing examination of dynamic processes over the life course. Only by examining determinants of self-employment entry and exit separately and by explicitly considering self-employment heterogeneity in one's research design is it possible to move toward a greater understanding of self-employment dynamics.

Therefore, all studies included in this volume systematically pursue such a dynamic approach by modeling separately the processes of entry into the three types of self-employment and by studying the factors affecting survival in self-employment once entered. In the comparative analysis of results in the concluding chapter, we often discuss effects of factors on both entry and exit processes concordantly to advance a more complete and accurate interpretation of self-employment determinants.

The event history models conducted separately for each country include a common set of covariates. We measured education using a categorical CASMIN schema modified appropriately to fit the specific national context. We operationalized social background to include measures of whether a father was self-employed, and whether the father's occupation was in professional-managerial, skilled, unskilled, or agricultural activities. We examined family status by identifying whether an individual had a nonemployed, self-employed, or dependent-employed spouse the prior year. In addition, we examined prior labor market activity by including in entry models whether an individual was unemployed, not-in-labor-force, type of occupation (professional-managerial, skilled, unskilled), type of industry, and a proxy for work experience that was available in all countries (age and age-squared). For exit models from self-employment activity, we included for labor market activity measures of work experience, type of industry, and years of self-employment. Ideally we attempted to run exit models separately for each distinct category of self-employment, as well as to identify all models separately for men and women. In certain countries, small sample sizes precluded such modeling, and gender or self-employment occupational categories were instead introduced as independent variables.

While country-specific chapters adopted similar measurement strategies and modeling techniques, the idiosyncratic character or inadequacies of local data sources required at times variation in country-specific measurement (see table 1.1 for description of data sources). A full accounting of differences in modeling occurs in individual country-specific chapters. Most of these variations were quite minor in character (such as collapsing various categories of education because of inadequate cases). A few variations, however, are significant enough that readers should be alerted to their presence: in two countries, Japan and the United Kingdom, no data on spouses were available for analysis; in two other countries, Russia and Australia, data were missing on both spousal characteristics and prior employment position of respondents. In addition, countries varied to the extent that retrospective data on job histories as opposed to longitudinal panel design data were used.[17] Given these data limitations, in the meta-analysis conducted at the end of this volume we are quite cautious not to overinterpret small differences in magnitudes of coefficients in our cross-national results; the general pattern identified in our findings and later discussion are pronounced, clear, and robust to alternative measurement specifications.

OUTLINE OF THE BOOK

The first three case studies in the book examine self-employment dynamics in corporatist states where labor market regulation tends to be higher and family-based social capital more limited. Chapter 2 presents

TABLE 1.1
Description of National Data Sources

Country	Dataset (date of collection)	Time period analyzed	Longitudinal/ retrospective design
Germany	German Socio-Economic Panel Study (1984–1998)	1984–1998	Longitudinal panel
France	Labor Force Surveys (1982–2002)	1980–2002	Longitudinal panel (partial)
Netherlands	Family Survey Dutch Population (1992, 1998)	1980–1998 (1932–1998)	Retrospective
United Kingdom	British Household Panel Survey (1990–2000)	1980–1999	Retrospective (1980–1989); longitudinal panel (1990–1999)
United States	Panel Study of Income Dynamics (1980–1992)	1980–1992	Longitudinal panel
Australia	International Social Science Surveys Australia (ISSSA) (1987–1999)	1980– 1998	Retrospective
Hungary	Social Mobility and Life-Course Survey; Hungarian Household Panel Survey (1992; 1992–1997)	1980–1997	Retrospective (1980–1992); longitudinal panel (1992–1997)
Russia	Survey on Employment, Income, and Attitudes in Russia (1998)	1991–1998	Retrospective
Italy	Italian Longitudinal Household Survey (1997)	1980–1997	Retrospective
Japan	Social Stratification and Social Mobility National Survey (1995)	1980–1995	Retrospective
Taiwan	Taiwan Social Change Survey (1996)	1980–1996	Retrospective

Henning Lohmann and Silvia Luber's exploration of self-employment in Germany and identifies how self-employment is becoming an increasingly heterogeneous category there since the 1980s. Even though a considerable core of traditional forms of self-employment linked to the "classical" determinants of inheritance and qualifications and to positive outcomes still exists, the proportion of skilled self-employed workers has declined since the 1980s. Highly regulated access to self-employment in Germany to a certain extent filters out potential precarious self-employment and leads to a relatively large percentage of high-quality and stable self-employment.

Chapter 3 examines self-employment in France where public disposals for helping people to start businesses are numerous. Thomas Amossé and Dominique Goux identify a decline in traditional self-employment that has been offset by three countervailing forces during the last twenty years: the development of self-employment in service occupations, partly due to the rise in subcontracting in manufacturing; the state's promotion of entrepreneurship; and the spread of the utilization of self-employment as a refuge to avoid the increased presence of unemployment.

Boris Blumberg and Paul de Graaf document in chapter 4 how the long-term trend of declining self-employment in the Netherlands has been reversed. In the Netherlands the general trend reversal took place around 1982 and has been particularly pronounced in certain sectors (e.g., service industries). Intergenerational effects are produced more as a result of occupational status than because of direct inheritance of self-employment per se in this national setting. Self-employment in general in the Netherlands has often been employed as a route to upward social mobility.

Following the three case studies of self-employment in corporatist states is an examination of three societies where neoliberal economic policies are prevalent. Nigel Meager and Peter Bates in chapter 5 suggest that the rapid growth of self-employment in the United Kingdom during the 1980s was the result of a combination of factors, some of which were specific to the country and have not persisted strongly in the 1990s. In particular, the 1980s saw deregulation of financial markets and easy access to capital for would-be entrepreneurs; the introduction of large-scale active labor market measures to support entry to self-employment from unemployment; a trend toward outsourcing and subcontracting of employment; and a particular development in the construction sector, leading to a significant growth of 'labor-only subcontracting' to avoid taxes and social costs. The evidence suggests, moreover, that some of the apparent shifts in the composition of self-employment in the 1980s—for example, faster increases in the self-employment rate among young people and women—have also not been durable ones.

Chapter 6 provides an analysis of the growing polarization and heterogeneity of self-employment in the United States. Self-employment in the United States has increased since the mid-1970s in close tandem with an overall growth in labor market inequality. This chapter argues that self-employment in the United States has a dual character. In one respect, self-employment has provided the possibility for the attainment of desirable professional and skilled occupations that leads to small-firm growth and relative occupational stability. On the other hand, much of the current increase in self-employment involves increases in male and female unskilled occupations. These unskilled positions are in occupations such as childcare, housecleaning, grounds-keeping, and motor vehicle operation. In the United States, these positions are particularly unstable, have low wages associated with them, and often involve the absence of guaranteed access to health care.

Our examination of case studies of neoliberal economies concludes in chapter 7 with a description of the resurgence of self-employment in Australia and its strong presence in the building trades, restaurants, small shops, motor vehicle repair services, domestic cleaning, and most recently, specialized niches of the information technology industry. Mariah Evans and Joanna Sikora note that women in Australia were less likely than men to enter self-employment but equally likely to stay if they arrived. Educational level and the academic and vocational orientation of one's education had important effects on entry, but not on exit.

The book next presents two case studies involving an examination of self-employment dynamics in postsocialist economies undergoing transitions to capitalism. In chapter 8, Péter Róbert and Erzsébet Bukodi analyze factors related to the increase of self-employment in Hungary before and after the collapse of state socialism. The increase of the service sector, decline of market regulations, shrinking of employment opportunities, appearance of unemployment, and changes in the political environment are taken into account for interpreting these developments. A large inflow into self-employment in Hungary has been combined with strong continuities and reproduction with respect to previous occupational status, education, and industrial location. The analysis also suggests that exits from self-employment increased in the 1990s, as the group of self-employed became less selective.

Ted Gerber in chapter 9 describes how self-employment is a new phenomenon in Russia. Other former Soviet-bloc countries such as Poland and Hungary permitted limited forms of small or individually operated enterprises during the 1970s and 1980s. Official proscriptions in the Soviet Union, however, relegated self-employment to the realm of the underground economy, until the Soviet regime collapsed at the end of 1991 and Russian President Boris Yeltsin adopted sweeping market reforms. In

Russia, specialized skills acquired through basic vocational education, as well as specialized secondary and tertiary schooling, are resources that facilitate success at self-employment. Human capital is an important ingredient in the recipe for self-employment survival; in contrast, Communist Party membership has no effect on survival in self-employment, and its effect on entry is initially positive, but turns negative after 1993. These findings suggest that where self-employment is concerned, "market transition" theory has more relevance for Russia than "power conversion" theory: human capital, not political connections or network ties, enhances both access to and survival in self-employment.

Our final three case studies involve our grouping of three societies with varied labor market regulation who share the common feature of a relatively high degree of family-based social capital. In Chapter 10, Paolo Barbieri and Ivano Bison's analysis of Italian data suggests high heterogeneity of self-employment, including the persistence of continued traditional and "premodern" activities. Self-employment in Italy is composed mainly of skilled and professional adult male workers with backgrounds of accumulated work experience who are embedded in relational circuits well endowed with social capital. Self-employment thus is not a marginal activity in Italy but is argued to take increasingly the forms of a crescent polarization—with a sustained growth of professionals counterbalanced by parallel increases in poorly qualified and unskilled self-employment. Such polarization appears strongly shaped by the traditional cleavages of social inequality, which therefore have not lost their causal importance in predetermining individuals' life chances.

Chapter 11 describes how in Japan, a second country in our comparative study with a high degree of both labor market regulation and family-based social capital, the self-employed and their family workers continue to play a substantial and dynamic role in the postwar economy. Hiroshi Ishida argues that a lack of clear effects of education in Japan is likely due to the generally high level and quality of educational attainment in the country. In Japan it is possible for even people with only compulsory education to be well equipped with basic work habits and skills that allow for self-employment entry and survival. Training offered in small firm settings also provides a significant alternative to formal schooling in preparing successful entrepreneurs. In addition, self-employment in Japan continues to rely heavily on direct intergenerational transmission.

Wei-hsin Yu and Kuo-Hsien Su in chapter 12 identify self-employment dynamics in Taiwan, a society characterized by little labor market regulation but a high degree of family-based social capital. The findings in Taiwan suggest that individuals can find self-employment activity a desirable alternative when there are not sufficient protections for low-skilled workers in the private sector. In addition, the Taiwanese case demonstrates the extent to which kinship networks and other personal ties related to social capital can play a significant role in fostering self-employment entry and survival. Recent changes in economic structure in Taiwan are argued likely to produce increased heterogeneity and polarization of self-employment over time.

We conclude the book with a meta-analysis of cross-national findings from the project. Specifically, in chapter 13 we identify similarity and variation in self-employment and advance a set of propositions about self-employment dynamics intended to guide further research in this area. Findings from the project suggest that self-employment is an increasingly heterogeneous activity, with growth occurring in professional-managerial and unskilled occupations as opposed to traditional skilled, craft-based self-employment. Self-employment, while increasingly common, is also highly unstable (particularly for women and in unskilled occupations that characterize a growing proportion of self-employment in many countries). Increases in self-employment coupled with (possibly growing) instability of the activity produce higher rates of individual involvement with self-employment over the life-course. Research in the book demonstrates that paths into self-employment today include not only traditional inheritance of the social position, but also attainment through educational achievement. Examination of effects of social background, education, and training on entry and exit into distinct types of self-employment identify the logic of dynamic processes that have produced observed cross-sectional patterns of association between self-employment and these variables. The chapter advances institutional explanations to explain the cross-national variation in self-employment dynamics across political-economic regime types and along the dimensions of labor market regulation and family based social capital. We identify implications of these finding for both social scientific research on self-employment as well as for state policy related to the sponsorship and regulation of this activity.

NOTES

The research described here is the result of the collaborative efforts of researchers from eleven countries: Thomas Amossé, Paolo Barbieri, Peter Bates, Ivano Bison, Boris Blumberg, Erzsébet Bukodi, Mariah Evans, Ted Gerber, Dominique Goux, Paul M. de Graaf, Hiroshi Ishida, Henning Lohmann, Silvia Luber, Nigel Meager, Péter Róbert, Joanna Sikora, Kuo-Hsien Su, and Wei-hsin Yu. Thanks to the Thyssen Foundation and the Mannheim Center for European Social Research for support of this project.

1. See John E. Bregger, "Measuring Self-Employment in the United States," *Monthly Labor Review* (January/February 1996): 3–9.

2. See the "Partial Renaissance of Self-Employment," *OECD Employment Outlook* (Paris: Organization for Economic Cooperation and Development, 2000): 156, 158.

3. Based on authors' analysis of men in the Panel Study of Income Dynamics with ten or more observations prior to 1992. Williams (2000), using an alternative data source, estimates the rate of young U.S. individuals ever being self-employed as 23 percent for men and 17 percent for women in a recent cohort aged 28–36 in 1993.

4. Lipset and Bendix (1959: 103) suggested this in the earlier American case.

5. Professional and large firm managerial self-employment is assigned to classes I/II of the EGP schema based on the theoretical assumption of substantial affinity between the respective groups of self-employed and their salaried counterparts—the salaried managers often having a substantial share of the enterprise in which they work, and the salaried professionals often combining independent practice and salaried work.

6. Karl Marx and Frederick Engels, *The Communist Manifesto* (New York: International Publishers, 1948): 19.

7. Seymour Martin Lipset, *Political Man: The Social Bases of Politics*, expanded edition (Baltimore: Johns Hopkins University Press, 1981): 105.

8. Michael Hout, Clem Brooks, and Jeff Manza, "The Democratic Class Struggle in the United States, 1948–1992," *American Sociological Review* (December 1995) 60:821.

9. David Blanchflower, "Self-Employment in OECD Countries," *Labour Economics* (2000) 7:474.

10. Besides resources, structural constraints, and opportunities, the individual option between dependent and self-employed work evidently also involves various other tradeoffs, often reflecting more subjective tastes and preferences, such as the evaluation of being independent and not working for someone else or the tradeoff between potentially higher income and higher risks and longer working hours. In the individual decision for self-employment, such concerns may be crucial, but they are less central in our attempt to identify the social structural factors shaping the choice between self-employed and dependent work.

11. See "Employment Protection and Labor Market Performance," *OECD Employment Outlook 1999* (Paris: Organization for Economic Cooperation and Development, 1999). The measure used is the Overall EPL Strictness Index, version 2 (a weighted measure from the late 1990s), p. 66.

12. Some measurement error occurs in identifying these values based on limitations to country-specific household survey data. Specifically, in some countries this measure is limited to whether the respondent reports that the parent in the household is the "head of household"; in other datasets, this restriction is not necessary. Small differences between these countries should thus not be overinterpreted. The difference between the three countries in the top half of the figure and the eight countries on the bottom, however, is indeed large and significant irregardless of these measurement issues.

13. As reported in *The OECD Small and Medium Enterprise Outlook* (Paris: Organization for Economic Cooperation and Development, 2000); p. 18. No data reported for Taiwan, Hungary, and Russia.

14. For detailed discussion of cross-national variation in taxation policies affecting self-employment and small businesses, see *Taxation and Small Businesses* (Paris: Organization for Economic Cooperation and Development, 1993).

15. This is not because we think the distinction is unimportant; rather it results from the fact that in several of the longitudinal databases used in the project, it is impossible to identify the points at which self-employed individuals work alone or employ others.

16. Unreported analysis conducted on U.S. Panel Study of Income Dynamics (see chapter 7) and German Mikrozensus 1996 data. Dependent employees in the construction industry had more similar occupational identifications: in Germany, 14 percent managerial and professional, 68 percent skilled, and 18 percent unskilled occupations; in the United States, 19 percent managerial and professional, 58 percent skilled, and 23 percent unskilled occupations.

17. The United States and Germany were the only two countries where annually collected longitudinal panel data was available. The United Kingdom and Hungary used data that combined repeated surveys with the collection of retrospective job histories; the rest of the countries in the sample used solely retrospective data. Retrospective data on job history tend to miss short-lived employment episodes; panel designs tend to be plagued with sample attrition problems.

REFERENCES

Abbott, A. 1988. *The system of professions: An essay on the division of expert labor.* Chicago: University of Chicago Press.

Abell, P. 1986. Self-employment and entrepreneurship: A study of entry and exit. In *James S. Coleman*, ed. Jon Clark, 175–205. London: Falmer Press.

Aldrich, H., L. Renzulli, and N. Langton. 1998. Passing on privilege: Resources provided by self-employed parents to their self-employed children. *Research in Social Stratification and Mobility* 16:291–317.

Aldrich, H., and R. Waldinger. 1990. Ethnicity and entrepreneurship. *American Review of Sociology* 16:111–35.

Aldrich, H., and C. Zimmer. 1986. Entrepreneurship through social networks. In *Population perspectives on organizations*, ed. H. Aldrich. Uppsala: Acta Universitatis Upsaliensis.

Arum, R. 1997. Trends in male and female self-employment: Growth in a new middle class or increasing marginalization of the labor force? *Research in Social Stratification and Mobility* 15:209–38.

———. 2001. Entrepreneurs and laborers: Two sides of self-employment activity in the United States. Manuscript prepared for the Self-Employment in Advanced Economies Project.

Arum, R., M. Budig, and D. Grant. 2000. Labor market regulation and the growth of self-employment. *International Journal of Sociology* 30:3–27.

Bechhofer, F., and B. Elliott, eds. 1981. *The petite bourgeoisie: Comparative studies of the uneasy stratum.* London: Macmillan.

———. 1985. The petite bourgeoisie in late capitalism. *Annual Review of Sociology* 11:181–207.

Bernardi, F. 2003. Globalisierung, Vermarktung der Arbeit und soziale Schichtung: Wandel der Erwerbskarrieren in Italien. In *Mehr Risiken—Mehr Ungleichheit? Abbau von Woglfahrtsstaat, Flexibilisierung von Arbeit und die Folgen*, ed. W. Müller and S. Scherer. Frankfurt/Main: Campus.

Blanchflower, D. 2000. *Self-employment in OECD countries*. NBER Working Paper 7486. Cambridge: National Bureau of Economic Research.

Blau, P., and O. Duncan. 1967. *The American occupational structure*. New York: Free Press.

Boden, R. 1999. Flexible working hours, family responsibilities and female self-employment: Gender differences in self-employment selection. *American Journal of Economics and Sociology* 58:71–84.

Breen, R. 1999. Beliefs, rational choice, and Bayesian learning. *Rationality and Society* 11:463–79.

Breen, R., and J. Jonsson. 2000. Analyzing educational careers: A multinomial transition model. *American Sociological Review* 65:754–72.

Carr, D. 1996. Two paths to self-employment? Women's and men's self-employment in the United States. *Work and Occupations* 23:26–53.

Connelly, R. 1992. Self-employment and providing childcare. *Demography* 29:17–29.

Devine, T. 1994. Changes in wage and salary returns to skill and the recent rise in female self-employment. *American Economics Review* 84:108–13.

Erikson, R., and J. Goldthorpe. 1993. *The constant flux: A study of class mobility in industrial societies*. Oxford: Oxford University Press.

Erikson, R., J. Goldthorpe, and L. Portocarero. 1979. Intergenerational class mobility in three Western European societies. *British Journal of Sociology* 30:415–41.

Esping-Andersen, G. 1999. *Social foundations of postindustrial economies*. New York: Oxford University Press.

Featherman, D., and R. Hauser. 1978. *Opportunity and change*. New York: Academic Press.

Frank, R., and P. Cook. 1996. *The winner take all society*. New York: Penguin Press.

Gerber, T. 2001a. Three forms of emergent self-employment in post-Soviet Russia: Entry and exit patterns by gender. Manuscript prepared for the Self-Employment in Advanced Economies Project.

———. 2001b. Paths to success: Individual and regional determinants of self-employment entry in post-Communist Russia. *International Journal of Sociology* 31:3–37.

Goldthorpe, J. 2001. *Globalization and social class*. Mannheimer Vorträge 9. Mannheim: Mannheimer Zentrum für Europäische Sozialforschung.

Hakim, C. 1998. *Social change and innovation in the labor market*. New York: Oxford University Press.

Harrison, B. 1994. *Lean and mean: Why large corporations will continue to dominate the global economy*. New York: Guilford Press.

Hochschild, A. R. 1997. *The time bind: When work becomes home and home becomes work*. New York: Metropolitan Books.

Kallenberg, A., and K. Leicht. 1991. Gender and organizational performance: Determinants of small business survival and success. *Academy of Management Journal* 34:136–61.

Kallenberg, A. L., B. F. Reskin, and K. Hudson. 2000. Bad jobs in America: Standard and nonstandard employment relations and job quality in the United States. *American Sociological Review* 65:256–78.

Kim, A., and K. Kurz. 2003. Prekäre Beschäftigung im Vereinigten Königreich und Deutschland. Welche Rolle spielen unterschiedliche institutionelle Kontexte? In *Mehr Risiken—Mehr Ungleichheit? Abbau von Wohlfahrtsstaat, Flexibilisierung von Arbeit und die Folgen,* ed. W. Müller and S. Scherer. Frankfurt/Main: Campus.

Laferrère, A. 2001. Self-employment and intergenerational transfers. *International Journal of Sociology* 31:3–26.

Light, I. 1992. The ethnic economy. In *Handbook of Economic Sociology,* ed. Neil Smelser. New York: Russell Sage.

Lin, Z., G. Picot, and J. Compton. 2000. The entry and exit dynamics of self-employment in Canada. *Small Business Economics* 15:105–27.

Lipset, S. M., and R. Bendix. 1959. *Social mobility in industrial countries.* Berkeley: University of California Press.

Lohmann, H. and S. Luber. 2000. Patterns of male and female self-employment: A comparison of France, Germany, Italy and the UK. Ms.

Loscocco, K., and K. Leicht. 1993. Gender, work-family linkages and economic success among small business owners. *Journal of Marriage and the Family* 55:875–87.

Luber, S., H. Lohmann, W. Mueller, and P. Barbieri. 2000. Male self-employment in four European countries. *International Journal of Sociology* 30:5–44.

Manser, M., and G. Picot. 1999. The role of self-employment in U.S. and Canadian job growth. *Monthly Labor Review* 122:10–25.

Manski, C. 1993. Adolescent econometricians: How do youth infer the returns to schooling? In *Studies of supply and demand in higher education,* ed. C. Clotfelter and M. Rothschild. Chicago: University of Chicago Press.

McManus, P. 2000a. Pathbreakers and traditionalists: Parental resources, career credentials and self-employment outcomes in the U.S. and Germany. Paper presented at the RC28 meeting, Libourne, France.

———. 2000b. Market, state and the quality of new self-employment jobs among men in the United States and western Germany. *Social Forces* 78:865–905.

———. 2001. Women's participation in self-employment in Western industrialized nations. *International Journal of Sociology* 31:70–97.

Meager, N., M. Kaiser, and H. Dietrich. 2000. *Self-employment in the United Kingdom and Germany.* London: Anglo-German Foundation for the Study of Industrial Society.

OECD. 1992. *Employment outlook.* Paris: OECD.

———. 2000. *Employment outlook.* Paris: OECD.

Piore, M., and C. Sabel. 1984. *The second industrial divide: Possibilities for prosperity.* New York: Basic Books.

Powell, W. 1990. Neither market nor hierarchy: Network forms of organization. *Research in Organizational Behavior* 12:295–336.

Reich, R. 1991. *The work of nations.* New York: Vintage.

Schizzerotto, A., and M. Pisati. 2003. Befristete Verträge in Italien. Ausgangspunkt für stabile Beschäftigung oder Falle? In *Mehr Risiken—Mehr Un-*

gleichheit? Abbau von Wohlfahrtsstaat, Flexibilisierung von Arbeit und die Folgen, ed. W. Müller and S. Scherer. Frankfurt/Main: Campus.

Shavit, Y., and E. Yuchtman-Yaar. 2001. Ethnicity, education and other determinants of self-employment in Israel. *International Journal of Sociology* 31:59–91.

Strohmeyer, R., and R. Leicht. 2000. Small training firms: A breeding ground for self-employment. *International Journal of Sociology* 30:59–90.

Treiman, D. 1970. Industrialization and social stratification. *Social Stratification: Research and Theory for the 1970s,* ed. E. O. Laumann. Indianapolis: Bobbs-Merrill.

Wharton, A. 1989. Gender segregation in private-sector, public-sector and self-employed occupations, 1950–1981. *Social Science Quarterly* 70:923–40.

Williams, D. 2000. Consequences of self-employment for women and men in the United States. *Labour Economics* 7:665–87.

Wilson, K., and A. Portes. 1980. Immigrant enclaves: An analysis of the labor market experiences of Cubans in Miami. *American Journal of Sociology.* 86: 295–319.

CHAPTER TWO

Trends in Self-Employment in Germany: Different Types, Different Developments?

Henning Lohmann and Silvia Luber

SELF-EMPLOYED INDIVIDUALS in West Germany in 1998 consisted of roughly 2.7 million people or 9.6 percent of the nonagricultural workforce.[1] Although the self-employed constitute a small group compared with the non-self-employed, they have gained increasing attention in the scientific and public debate for the last ten or fifteen years. Since 1980 the number of nonfarm self-employed has grown by about 50 percent. Current research trends are interested in the causes and consequences of this remarkable growth (Bögenhold 1985, Acs and Audretsch 1990, Leicht 1995). Self-employment is assumed to be linked to high jobcreation potential, not only for the self-employed themselves, but also for additional workers hired because of the establishment of new firms (Birch 1987; for Germany: Brüderl and Preisendörfer 2000). However, other research sees the increase in self-employment as being associated with the growth of marginal and insecure work (Döse et al. 1994, Kalleberg, Reskin, and Hudson et al. 2000). In Germany this argument has gained prominence in the discussion of so-called pseudo self-employment (*Scheinselbständigkeit*, see Dietrich 1998). The existing literature suggests that both developments are related to the rise of self-employment in Germany, and that self-employed work is becoming more manifold. Moreover, women account for an increasing share of the self-employed in Germany. However, it is arguable whether this growth runs parallel to the development of male self-employment or whether the mechanism of becoming self-employed differs between women and men and thus results in different outcomes (see McManus 2001b).

In this chapter we examine these assumed developments in self-employment over the time period 1984–1998, using longitudinal data from the German Socio-Economic Panel Study. We shall consider self-employment as a heterogeneous category. By focusing on the differences between distinct types of self-employment as well as on gender differences, we will analyze whether recent increases in self-employment are associated with growing variability and considerable change in the composition of self-employment.

CHARACTERISTICS OF SELF-EMPLOYMENT

A key characteristic of self-employment in Germany is its heterogeneity. Typically, this group of workers incorporates a variety of categories, for example, entrepreneurs and small business proprietors,[2] professionals and craft workers, as well as unskilled manual and nonmanual workers. In Germany, no legal definition of self-employment exists. Usually, it is defined in opposition to dependent employment, which is characterized by employees being subject to the directives of an employer concerning time, place, and content of work (Wank 1992). Self-employment is thus usually defined in terms of independence or autonomy, and the self-employed are those who work on their own account. Some of the above-mentioned groups of self-employed workers correspond quite well to the criterion of autonomy, while others might rather be so-called pseudo self-employed workers (Dietrich 1998).

The German national data sources on self-employment rely mainly on survey respondents' self-definition of their status, which may differ from their status as defined for purposes of employment law, taxation, or social security.[3] It is usually not possible to distinguish between these different kinds of self-employed workers in survey data. Some indications of the diversity can, however, be obtained by looking at the determinants of self-employment, as well as the sectoral and occupational patterns.

Previous research on the determinants of self-employment often gives an aggregate view of the composition of this group worldwide. It stresses the importance of different types of individual resources: financial, human, and social capital. Personal and family wealth increases the probability of self-employment entry (Lindh and Ohlsson 1996; Dunn and Holtz-Eakin 2000). The self-employed are more likely to possess higher levels of human capital in terms of education and work experience (Evans and Leighton 1990; Taylor 1996; Blanchflower 2000). Social capital, especially in the form of business networks, but also in terms of family resources, increases the probability of self-employment significantly (Brüderl and Preisendörfer 1998; Laferrère 2001).

Besides the general need for the aforementioned resources, the respective conditions for self-employment differ by country. Thus, recent research has found that in Germany a particularly strong influence of education on the probability of self-employment prevails (Luber et al. 2000) and is attributable to two mechanisms. First, Germany is characterized by a strong link between education and one's position in the labor market (Müller and Shavit 1998). In general, credentials are highly relevant. Second, and more closely related to self-employment, different effects of education are due to various qualificational entry barriers for self-employment in certain fields (Luber et al. 2000). For example, craft occupations require a specific vocational qualification, the "Meister" certificate.[4] Tertiary education is a prerequisite for self-employed professionals. These examples are two strictly regulated fields of self-employment, and they encompass about 40 percent of all self-employed jobs.[5] However, other areas of self-employment are less strictly regulated. For example, in contrast to the highly regulated core of the craft sector, other craft-related occupations require no qualificational preconditions.

Apart from educational qualifications, age is clearly a factor related to self-employment in Germany. In general, the self-employed are substantially older than their counterparts in wage and salary employment and thus possess on average more work experience. In Germany this difference is relatively pronounced, especially compared with countries such as the United Kingdom and Italy, where self-employment is already a frequent occurrence among younger workers (Meager 1993). On the one hand, this fact can be explained by the time that must be spent on the accumulation of qualifications and financial resources.[6] On the other hand, the transition from school to work is in general less problematic in Germany, and young workers are comparatively well integrated in the labor market (Scherer 2001). Therefore, in contrast to other countries, self-employment is less often used as an alternative entry path into the labor market, which results in a lower share of young self-employed.

Apart from individual resources, family-related resources have also been found to be crucial for self-employment. Parental self-employment is discussed in the context of social closure, but it is also seen as a source for social and specific human capital. Children of self-employed parents, especially males, have a higher propensity for being self-employed. Since social mobility is limited, following a father's employment status is relatively common (Müller 1986). Thus it is not surprising that in German studies, father's self-employment appears to be the strongest individual predictor for self-employment (Börsch-Supan and Pfeiffer 1992). Spousal self-employment is also important for determining one's own self-employment (Caputo and Dolinsky 1998).

Given that the profile of the self-employed worker is often one who is well qualified, has accumulated work experience, and also works in areas where competition is restricted due to entry barriers, the average outcome of self-employed work should be rather high. In fact, the average income of the self-employed tends to be higher than that of dependent workers. Whereas in some countries empirical evidence for considerable low-income self-employment exists (Sullivan and Smeeding 1997; Meager and Bates 2001), the evidence is comparatively small in Germany. McManus (2000) estimates that the proportion of newly self-employed men entering high-income jobs is 30 percent, whereas only 4 percent enter low-income jobs. The respective figures for the United States are 25 percent for high-income jobs and 17 percent for low-income jobs. But also in Germany, the income distribution of the self-employed is more extreme than the wage distribution (Merz 2000).

The notion that the largest part of self-employment in Germany is not precarious is further confirmed by a second quality measure: job stability, which in self-employment is usually higher than in dependent employment. Comparing Germany and the United States, one can observe that this holds true for both countries, but especially for Germany (McManus 2000). Here, 78 percent of the newly self-employed enter into stable jobs, while the share in the United States amounts to only 41 percent. Despite this large difference for stable self-employment, the figures for unstable self-employment are comparable (22 percent vs. 28 percent).[7] According to McManus (2000), the high stability of self-employed work in Germany can be attributed to two institutional features. First, the German labor market is very tightly structured: mobility of employed workers is generally very low, and job stability is on average very high. Second, the labor and social protection of dependent employed workers in Germany is comparatively all-encompassing. The transition from dependent employment to self-employment thus involves a loss of protections. The decision to enter self-employment due to this potential loss is more selective than in other countries, which results in a higher survival rate.

Besides these institutional factors, the stability of self-employment is also influenced by individual characteristics. The absence of individual resources such as experience, especially branch-specific experience, accelerates self-employment exit (Taylor 1998, 1999). The role of formal qualifications in the survival of self-employment is less clear. While studies on newly founded firms establish a positive relation between the educational level of the business founder and business success (Cressy 1996; Brüderl, Preisendörfer, and Ziegler 1992), evidence for such a relation in the process of self-employed workers staying in business is contested. McManus (2001a) finds no evidence for a positive influence of qualifications for self-employment survival in Germany. In contrast, variation in the probability of survival due to education could be established in the United States. She argues that the nonexistence of a preventive effect of education in Germany is due to the gatekeeping function of educational requirements necessary for entry into self-employment that automatically filter out potential failures.

Firm characteristics are generally more relevant than individual resources to the survival of the business. Size and capital are found to be decisive (Brüderl et al. 1992; Hinz 2000). Self-employed individuals with few or no employees have a higher risk of exiting self-employment than self-employed with many workers. Further, new businesses in the service sector more often fail than those in the industrial sector, and this is partly attributed to the smaller size of service businesses. In addition to this so-called liability of smallness, there is clear evidence for a "liability of new-ness"—the longer people stay in a self-employed business, the lower the exit rate from self-employment.

Gender Differences in Self-Employment

Male dominance is a main characteristic of self-employment. Although the number of self-employed women has continuously grown, the rates are still much lower than those for men. In Germany, as in most Western European countries (but deviating from developments in the United States), the growth of female self-employment is due mainly to the growth of female labor force participation, and not to an overpropor-tional increase in women's propensity for self-employment as compared to men's (Meager 1993; OECD 2000). Further, women are more likely to fail in self-employment. This is usually interpreted not as a lack of women's entrepreneurial skills but rather as an effect of different firm characteristics and gender-specific employment patterns (Jungbauer-Gans and Ziegler 1991; Jungbauer-Gans 1993). Besides the differences in business failures, a number of explanations for the persisting gender gap are discussed in the current literature. Recent research has shown that gender differences prevail in the structure of self-employment (for an overview, see McManus 2001b). Women work in different occupations and different industrial sectors. On average, the incomes of female self-employed are lower compared with both male self-employment and male dependent employment. Yet they are higher than that of female em-ployees (Jungbauer-Gans 1999). Also, the qualificational profile for self-employed men and women differs. Self-employed women tend to possess more often full tertiary education, whereas self-employed men more fre-quently have vocational education. In addition, the fields of study differ widely between self-employed men and women (Brush 1992; Watkins and Watkins 1986). Furthermore, intergenerational transmission of self-employment status is less marked for women than for men (Hartmann 1998). Thus, one can assume that women tend to possess on average a higher level of education, but less financial and social capital when enter-ing into self-employment.

CONDITIONS FOR SELF-EMPLOYMENT IN GERMANY, 1980s AND 1990s

The economic situation in West Germany since the beginning of the 1980s has been characterized by a persistent high unemployment rate and—compared with previous decades—rather moderate economic growth (Statistisches Bundesamt 2000). The relevance of the general economic development for self-employment has been extensively discussed, but the "unemployment push thesis" as well as the "economic upturn pull thesis" are contested (Bögenhold and Staber 1991, 1993; Meager 1992). A simple relationship between the level of unemployment or growth of GDP and the development of self-employment is hard to confirm (OECD 2000). What can be clearly linked to the general economic difficulties is the emergence of new or enlarged public promotion activities for new businesses and self-employment (Kulicke 1997). The initiatives were expected to offer, in addition to the assumed positive impacts of job creation and support for an economic upswing, a mechanism to reduce unemployment. Similar to many other countries, Germany introduced a program in 1986 to support the transition from unemployment to self-employment: the bridging allowance (*Überbrückungsgeld*). In terms of the number of participants, the program was quite successful (Meager 1993). The number of participants has been particularly high since 1994, when the formal requirements for participation were relaxed. Beyond the mere quantitative enrollments, the success of the program has been contested in the literature. Whereas Wießner (1998) reports high survival chances for self-employed workers who received the bridging allowance, Pfeiffer and Reize (2000) find a significantly lower chance of staying in business for these workers compared with other self-employed who did not participate in the program. At the very least, there is a clear effect of unemployment protection for the participants: the probability of becoming unemployed again is rather low (Reize 2000).

In addition to the growing inflow from unemployment into self-employment, general economic and labor market developments have contributed to the changing character of self-employed work in the 1980s and 1990s. Economic activities have shifted considerably away from manufacturing toward the service sector. This sectoral shift has contributed significantly to the growth of self-employment because it favors industries that offer good opportunities for self-employed work (Acs and Audretsch 1990; Leicht 1995). Related to this shift are significant changes in the labor market. On the one hand, an increase in knowledge-intensive, business-oriented service occupations has been established (Leicht 1995). Furthermore, the shares of occupational arrangements like franchise ownership (OECD 2000; Elsner 1996) or freelance work in cultural occupations (Gottschall 1999) have experienced marked growth. On the other hand, new forms of employment that are driven by the conversion of formerly dependent work into certain types of self-employment such as labor-only subcontracting have emerged (Döse et al. 1994). While the first trend mainly affects the highly skilled professional workforce, low-skill jobs are primarily affected by the latter. However, both are assumed to be related to a considerable increase in solo self-employment. Germany used to have very low numbers of self-employed working without employees: in 1984 the share was 38 percent (OECD 1986). This number has grown significantly, and it reached 47 percent in 1997 (OECD 2000). Although the share of employers is still higher than in other countries, there is clear evidence that the total increase in the number of self-employed workers in Germany during the 1990s is associated with an overproportional growth of solo self-employed (Leicht 2000). The described changes in self-employment have led to a widespread discussion in the 1990s about the potential marginalization and precariousness of self-employed work. In particular, the new forms of self-employment, which lack the crucial characteristic of autonomy (i.e., pseudo self-employment—*Scheinselbständigkeit*) are assumed to be related to poor economic and social prospects. As a result, a new law on pseudo self-employment was implemented in 1999. It aims to incorporate the pseudo self-employed into the social security system like dependent employed workers (BMA 2000; OECD 2000).[8]

The aforementioned developments indicate that self-employment is subject to change, and that this change is not unidirectional but consists of opposing processes driven by various factors. New opportunities for self-employment due to sectoral change, the emergence of new work arrangements, the growing number of solo self-employed, and the expanded inflow from unemployment might be interpreted as indicating growth at the two opposite poles of self-employment, and therefore as an increase in heterogeneity in this status group. Not only does this development reflect the contribution of a growth in the number of marginalized self-employed workers, but highly skilled occupations, such as free professions, can also be assumed to have contributed significantly to changes in self-employment.

The following analysis will provide an overview of the structure and development of self-employment during the last two decades in Germany, in order to explore whether the ongoing changes have led to an increase in heterogeneity within self-employment. Thus, three main questions are the focus of our empirical examination:

1. What determines who becomes self-employed in different fields of activity, and how is self-employment internally structured? We compare the socioeconomic profile of self-employed workers with that of dependent employed workers in order to find indications of the determinants of self-employment. Moreover, we differentiate between distinct forms of self-employed work and analyze their respective determinants and outcomes.
2. How has self-employed work developed in Germany since the 1980s? To address this question, we analyze the quantitative development of self-

employment between 1984 and 1998 to find empirical evidence of changes in the composition of self-employed work over time.

We assume that the answers to these two questions will differ considerably by gender, and thus, a third general question arises:

3. How does self-employment differ between men and women?

The empirical analyses consider the determinants of self-employment entry, survival, and exit. Examining the entries and exits will provide an encompassing picture of the changes in German self-employment over the last two decades.

Data and Variables

The analyses are based on longitudinal data from the German Socio-Economic Panel Study (GSOEP 1984–98).[9] The sample includes observations of persons living in West Germany (aged 18–60 years) who were interviewed in at least two consecutive waves. The analysis of survival in self-employment and the analysis of entry into and exit from self-employment are based on employment spells (i.e., spells in which the respondents did not change their employment status). We consider only the person's primary job. The construction of these spells is mainly based on information the GSOEP provides on job mobility.[10] Since we are considering shifts between (non)employment and self-employment, the job spells were collapsed into employment spells.

As argued above, self-employment must be regarded as a heterogeneous rather than a homogeneous category. We distinguish between three occupational categories, both for dependent employment and for self-employment. The classification we use is based on a collapsed EGP-class scheme (Erikson and Goldthorpe 1992).[11] Category I comprises professional, semiprofessional and higher managerial occupations (mostly EGP I and II). The second category consists of skilled and lower managerial occupations[12] (mostly EGP IIIa, V and VI). The third category includes all unskilled occupations (EGP IIIb and VIIa). This level of aggregation is still rather high. We therefore additionally use a more detailed classification scheme allowing for a finer distinction in line with the specific conditions for single groups of self-employment in Germany. In the refined classification, Category I is split into professionals/managers (more or less EGP I) and semiprofessionals (EGP II); Category II, into lower managerial and skilled occupations.

A look at the single occupations inside our three larger categories reveals clear gender differences.[13] While self-employed men in category I mainly work as general managers or as salespeople, women are more likely to work in professional occupations. Among the unskilled self-employed (category III), half of the men are motor vehicle drivers, while women work mainly in personal or household-related service occupations. If we look at only the most frequent occupations, the distribution in the skilled and lower managerial occupations (category II) seems to be rather similar for men and women. About 40–50 percent of the self-employed work as proprietors in wholesale and retail trade or catering and lodging. However, the largest part of the remaining self-employed work in craft occupations. Regarding these, again, clear gender differences can be established. While about a quarter of all women in this category work as hairdressers, men also work in production-related occupations.

Besides the occupational categories, we consider the following factors in the multivariate analysis: education, work experience, industrial sector, social origin, and partner support. Education is measured at the beginning of each spell by using the CASMIN-classification (see Brauns and Steinmann 1999). The classification ranges from compulsory or incomplete education (1ab) to full tertiary education (3b). Work experience is measured in a different way. As a general indicator, we use age, which is measured in years and years squared as time-dependent covariates. To analyze the effect of unstable work histories, we include the number of previous unemployment spells.

As an indicator of social origin, we use employment status of the respondent's father, referring to the situation when the respondent was 15 years old. We also analyze the influence of the employment status of the respondent's partner before the entry into or exit from self-employment. The information is included as a time-dependent covariate. Industrial sectors are included in the form of a strongly collapsed NACE-classification (seven sectors). Since we consider employment spells, which can include different jobs, the industrial sector and the occupation can also change over time in the analysis.

Results

Using two main steps, we will answer our three guiding questions about the structure and development of self-employed work in Germany. First, we examine the descriptive statistics for different determinants and outcomes of self-employment, especially in comparison with dependent employment. Second, we estimate multivariate discrete-time event-history models to predict self-employment entry and exits by individual resources. We use pooled data based on the yearly information of all panel waves from 1984 to 1998, or compare figures based on subsets of five-year periods to show changes during the observation period.

Descriptive Analyses

We begin by considering the quantitative development and gender differences in self-employment (table 2.1). Here, we use, in addition to the GSOEP, the larger Eurostat Labor Force Surveys (LFS). As expected, in both data sets, the female self-employment rate is much lower than the male one. Interestingly, the size of the gender gap is much smaller in the GSOEP sample than in the LFS. While male self-employment is less frequent according to the GSOEP figures, female self-employment rates are higher than in the LFS.[14] Since the number of self-employed in the GSOEP sample is small, especially for women, the LFS results are more reliable for a comparison over time. These figures show a growth of about 20 percent in the self-employment rate for men, as well as for women, during the observation period. At the same time, the female share in self-employment has increased from 25.6 percent to 27.9 percent. Since the growth of female and male self-employment rates is comparable, the increase in the female share of self-employed must be seen as a result of increased female labor force participation. As expected, there is no evidence of a decreasing gap in the level of female and male self-employment. At the end of the 1990s, women's propensity to be self-employed is still clearly lower than men's.

In addition to self-employment rates, table 2.1 contains indicators of the structure and characteristics of self-employment. For example, social origin and size of firm exhibit remarkable changes over time in the profile of the self-employed. As expected, a self-employed family background is a highly relevant factor for self-employment. The share of those with a self-employed father is much higher among the self-employed than among employees (inflow rates). This holds true especially for men. However, while in the 1980s more than a third of all male, and more than a quarter of all female self-employed had a self-employed father, this proportion declined in more recent years. Outflow rates also decrease (i.e., share of sons or daughters with self-employed fathers who become self-employed themselves), but compared with the inflow rates, the decline is less marked. This means that the mechanism of intergenerational transmission of self-employment status is still effective, but there is an increasing share of people who enter self-employment via paths other than from parental inheritance, and this is especially true for women. One reason for this is the lower share of self-employed in the parents' generation. In addition, especially in the 1990s, entries from unemployment into self-employment have gained importance. At the same time, the likelihood of working in solo self-employment has increased substantially, particularly among men. Whereas solo self-employment has expanded by about 46 percent among male self-employed, the growth amounts to only 33 per-

TABLE 2.1
Development of General Characteristics by Gender (in percent) in Germany

Period	Male			Female		
	1984–88	*1989–93*	*1994–98*	*1984–88*	*1989–93*	*1994–98*
Self-employment rate (SOEP)	8.6	9.3	10.6	7.3	6.6	7.2
Self-employment rate (EUROSTAT)	9.4	10.0	11.6	5.3	5.5	6.3
Inflow from self-employment origin						
Into self-employment	36	28	21	26	15	16
Into dependent employment	10	10	9	14	13	11
Outflow into self-employment						
From self-employment origin	26	23	21	12	7	10
From dependent employment origin	6	8	10	6	6	7
Share of solo self-employed of all self-employed	24	25	35	42	44	56
Inflow from unemployment into new self-employment	10	7	15	7	4	8
Distribution by occupational categories: self-employed						
Professional/managerial	40	46	56	36	34	45
Skilled	53	46	34	53	59	45
Unskilled	7	8	10	11	6	10
Distribution by occupational categories: employees						
Professional/managerial	28	30	34	24	25	27
Skilled	44	43	41	33	30	33
Unskilled	29	27	25	43	45	39

Source: SOEP 1984–98 (pooled data, weighted), Eurostat LFS.
Note: Some distributions do not add up to 100% due to rounding.

cent among female self-employed. Yet male self-employed more often employ others than do women.

Changes are furthermore reflected in the development of the occupational distribution in self-employment. In the lowest section of table 2.1, we compare the distribution of self-employed and dependent workers across the three occupational categories and show their development over time. The occupational structure of self-employed and employees differ noticeably. Some 40–50 percent of the self-employed are in professional and managerial occupations, while the respective share of the dependent workforce is much smaller. Also, the share of skilled workers is higher in self-employment than in dependent employment, while the share of unskilled self-employment is much lower (10 percent or less). This statement is valid for all five-year observation periods. Nevertheless, some changes are worth mentioning. First, there is a general trend in dependent as well as in self-employment toward a higher share of professional and managerial occupations. Second, among employees, the number of unskilled workers has decreased. This development is not paralleled in self-employment. In contrast, especially in male self-employment, the share of unskilled occupations has grown. But since this growth started at a very low level, the share of unskilled self-employed is still much lower than the share of unskilled employees. Thus, the rise of professional, managerial, and unskilled self-employment takes place at the expense of skilled self-employment. These changes in the structure of self-employed work can be seen as further indications of a potential trend of growing numbers of new, or rather "nontraditional," forms of self-employment.

Having shown the patterns of change, we now look more closely at the distinct forms of self-employed work and how they differ from each other and from dependent work in terms of determinants and outcomes (table 2.2). In general, the self-employed are older than typical employees. The share of young workers (18 to 30) is smaller.[15] Hence, as expected, there is not much evidence of young workers entering into self-employment due to a lack of alternatives in the labor market.

Furthermore, the educational profile of the two groups differs substantially. Although considerable differences between self-employed and dependent employed workers in each occupational category exist, the variation between the occupational groups comes out more clearly. Whereas professional and managerial occupations are characterized by tertiary education, workers in skilled and unskilled jobs more often have either vocational or only compulsory education. The proportion of vocational education is particularly high in male skilled occupations—over 80 percent (CASMIN 1c, 2a, or 2c voc.). Nevertheless, remarkable differences between self-employed and employees within each occupational category obtain. Unskilled self-employed women are relatively well qualified in

TABLE 2.2
Profile of Self-Employed vs. Employees by Occupational Categories (in percent) in Germany

	Male						Female					
	I		II		III		I		II		III	
	S.-e.	Empl	S.-e.	Empl	S.-e.	Empl	S.-e.	Empl	S.-e.	Empl	S.-e.	Empl
Age in years												
18–30	11	12	12	30	20	30	17	30	9	35	7	26
31–45	60	50	43	40	44	36	57	45	49	38	51	34
46–60	29	37	45	30	36	33	26	25	42	27	42	40
Education (CASMIN)												
1ab	5	2	6	9	21	24	4	3	17	9	20	39
1c	16	24	63	57	45	59	20	16	41	32	49	42
2a	19	18	22	21	25	10	25	25	15	39	19	12
2b	1	0	0	1	0	3	1	3	3	6	2	3
2c gen.	6	2	0	1	1	2	1	2	3	2	5	1
2c voc.	9	8	4	6	3	2	15	12	2	10	2	2
3a	14	14	3	2	1	1	9	8	12	2	2	0
3b	31	33	1	3	3	0	24	31	6	2	1	1
Share of father self-employed	26	13	31	8	19	7	18	14	19	14	16	11
Share of solo self-employed	34		18		45		55		43		52	
Job satisfaction in scale units: 1–10												
Mean	7.32	7.36	7.58	7.25	7.21	7.02	7.69	7.53	7.66	7.34	7.82	6.90
s.d.	1.94	1.84	1.92	1.93	2.38	2.16	1.71	1.90	1.92	2.00	1.83	2.11
Average monthly personal net income in DM												
Mean	5,280	4,448	4,075	3,038	3,377	2,671	3,868	2,791	2,581	2,264	2,114	1,783
s.d.	3,024	2,048	2,419	1,192	1,935	871	2,593	1,325	1,751	922	1,732	720

Source: SOEP 1984–98 (pooled data, weighted) and Mikrozensus 1996.
Note: Some distributions do not add up to 100% due to rounding.

comparison with their employee counterparts. Similarly, unskilled self-employed men possess comparatively more vocational qualifications at the secondary level. However, the self-employed are not better qualified in all categories. The high share of self-employed skilled women with only compulsory education or less is noticeable, and in professional and managerial occupations, the dependent workforce tends to be slightly better qualified. This is particularly pronounced among women, where about a third of employees have a full university degree compared with only a quarter of the self-employed (CASMIN 3b).

As discussed earlier, parents' self-employment status is one of the most crucial determinants for self-employment according to occupational group. The skilled self-employed have the highest inflow rate; 31 percent of all male self-employed in this group have a self-employed father, while the respective share of employees is only 8 percent. The share is much lower among female skilled self-employed (19 percent). Parental self-employment is also important for professional and managerial self-employment, but considerably less so for unskilled self-employed. For all occupational categories, the self-recruitment rates in self-employment are higher for sons than for daughters.

The distinct types of self-employed work are linked to the differing individual resources necessary to become self-employed in different fields of activity. Are these distinct forms connected with different outcomes in terms of the size of the firm, income, and job satisfaction? With regard to firm size, the share of solo self-employment differs considerably among the three types of self-employed work, and the variation is greatest among men. While more than half of all female professional, managerial, and unskilled self-employed are solo self-employed, the highest share of male solo self-employment can be found among unskilled workers (45 percent). This is the direct opposite of the skilled self-employed. In the latter group, 82 percent of male self-employed are employers, and more than half of self-employed women are employers as well.

Regarding the remuneration of self-employed workers, further differences can be observed. In general, the income figures establish a quite orderly pattern. Considering only full-time workers' monthly net income, the self-employed earn more money than employees. There are obvious rewards for skills for both the self-employed and employees. Additionally, there is a clear gender income gap, again for both types of employment. Male self-employed in professional and managerial occupations earn the most, while female self-employed in unskilled occupations earn the least. In each occupational category, self-employed women earn more than female employees but less than male employees. Regarding the size of the gender income gap, the evidence is ambiguous. The "reward" for being male is higher in skilled and unskilled self-employment than in the respective dependent categories. In contrast, female earnings in professional and managerial self-employment are relatively high, so that the earnings gap is smaller than the wage gap.

Although women earn less, they are more satisfied with their work, especially when they are self-employed. Men are also more satisfied when they are self-employed, but the differences are less marked. One could interpret this result as a consequence of the higher degree of autonomy in self-employment, which is valued particularly highly by women. The only group of self-employed who are not more satisfied than their dependent counterparts are the male managers and professionals. This finding might be due to their already high autonomy.

Entry into Self-Employment

While the descriptive analysis has given a general overview of the composition and profile of the group of self-employed workers, the following analyses will examine those determinants that are crucial to the process of entry into self-employment. We shall start with general models in order to give an overview of these determinants. Next, we will consider gender differences, and finally move into a more detailed consideration of the relevance of the previously discussed determinants for self-employment in the different occupational categories. All models consider the probability of entering self-employment instead of remaining in one's actual employment status (dependent employment, unemployment, or out of labor force).

Model 1 in table 2.3 examines all entries into self-employment. Our analyses confirm for the most part the findings of previous research. Therefore, we will discuss these results only briefly. Education is a highly relevant resource in the process of becoming self-employed, and here we find a quasi-linear relationship. Workers with only compulsory education are the least likely to move into self-employment. Vocational or secondary education increases the probability of self-employment entry. The effect is strongest for tertiary education. The fact that we find a clear educational pattern in the entry model whereas we did not see equally strong differences between dependent and self-employed workers of the same occupational category in the descriptive analyses reveals that the positive influence of education is due to the composition of self-employment in Germany—relatively more self-employed than employees are working in professional or skilled occupations, which are clearly related to higher education, while the share of unskilled workers is small. Hence, the highly skilled groups determine the predominant educational pattern.[16]

Furthermore, work experience is important, which is partly captured by the parameters for age. The relationship between the probability of entering into self-employment and age is curvilinear. Older age increases the likelihood of becoming self-employed in the younger years, but as one grows older, this influence flattens out or decreases. A clear confirmation of previous research can also be observed concerning the relevance of social origin and partner support. Self-employed family background increases the likelihood of becoming self-employed, as does having a self-employed partner. Apart from individual resources, opportunities set by industrial branches also play an important role for self-employment entry. People previously engaged in traditional services such as distribution, catering, and lodging are more likely to enter into self-employment than people engaged in the industrial sector. Similarly, people working in the construction sector are more likely to become self-employed than workers from other sectors. The negative sign for "other services" is mainly due to the public sector that is included in this category. Self-employment entries from the public sector are extremely rare.

Entry into self-employment is a frequent transition into employment for those previously unemployed or not in the labor force. The parameters of these two groups in comparison with dependent workers are clearly higher. Despite the high values, these effects do not imply a general propensity of the unemployed to enter into self-employment, but rather they show higher mobility rates compared with other workers. Only after 1994 can a considerable increase in the number of unemployed people entering into self-employment in Germany be established, which coincides with the described changes in the respective promotion programs.[17] For those who reentered the labor market, no rise comparable to the one established for the unemployed could be observed. Hence, the development seems not to be linked to a higher degree of labor market closure that forces previously unemployed into self-employment due to a lack of alternatives, but rather it is a result of the enlarged promotion of such transitions. In model 2 (table 2.3), we find more evidence that people in a more precarious situation in the labor market are more likely to move into self-employment. The propensity to enter into self-employment increases with the number of unemployment spells, which we use as an indicator for unstable work histories. Workers in skilled occupations are least likely to enter into self-employment.

In addition to the models reported in table 2.3, we studied the interactions between all of the covariates and time (1980s vs. 1990s). The results (not reported) show that despite the changes we observed in the structure of self-employment, there is hardly any change over time in the central mechanisms of self-employment entry.

The previously discussed general model confirms that women, even when controlling for individual characteristics, are less likely to enter into self-employment: the parameter for women is negative. Like other

TABLE 2.3
Coefficient Estimates for Entry into Self-Employment in Germany

	M1	M2	M3 (women)	M3 (men)
Gender (ref: male)				
Female	−0.719**	−0.723**		
	(0.112)	(0.112)		
Education (CASMIN) (ref: 1ab/2b or 3ab)				
1ab			−1.387**	−0.630*
			(0.372)	(0.275)
1c	0.264†	0.268†	−0.807*	−0.542*
	(0.140)	(0.139)	(0.330)	(0.261)
2a	0.390*	0.405*	−0.779*	−0.329
	(0.163)	(0.163)	(0.346)	(0.268)
2c (gen.)	0.441*	0.473*	−0.560	−0.278
	(0.220)	(0.219)	(0.443)	(0.335)
2c (voc.)	0.590**	0.604**	−0.435	−0.197
	(0.205)	(0.205)	(0.395)	(0.304)
3ab	0.861**	0.883**		
	(0.224)	(0.223)		
Age (minus 18)				
Age in years	0.139**	0.132**	0.163**	0.117**
	(0.020)	(0.020)	(0.030)	(0.028)
Age in years (squared)	−0.004**	−0.004**	−0.005**	−0.004**
	(0.001)	(0.001)	(0.001)	(0.001)

Social origin *(ref: father employee)*			
Self-employed	0.359*	0.054	0.507**
	(0.155)	(0.281)	(0.190)
Farmer	0.086	0.011	0.104
	(0.267)	(0.412)	(0.350)
Not working	−0.766*	−0.756	−0.797*
	(0.308)	(0.516)	(0.384)
Previous employment status *(ref: skilled employee)*			
Employee (cat. I)	0.547**	0.420	0.638**
	(0.177)	(0.355)	(0.212)
Employee (cat. III)	0.307†	0.356	0.346†
	(0.161)	(0.319)	(0.187)
Unemployed	1.089**	0.778†	1.244**
	(0.216)	(0.411)	(0.253)
Out of labor force	0.653**	0.537	0.470†
	(0.185)	(0.328)	(0.277)
Previous industrial sector *(ref: mining, manufacturing, energy, and not working)*			
Construction	0.457*	dropped	0.636**
	(0.211)		(0.216)
Traditional services	0.784**	0.298	1.004**
	(0.163)	(0.285)	(0.195)
Other services	−0.191	−0.405	−0.113
	(0.154)	(0.272)	(0.189)

TABLE 2.3 (continued)

	M1	M2	M3 (women)	M3 (men)
Employment of partner (ref: employee)				
Self-employed	0.755**	0.754**	0.446	1.184**
	(0.214)	(0.214)	(0.301)	(0.306)
Not working	−0.261'	−0.272'	−0.046	−0.249
	(0.154)	(0.155)	(0.391)	(0.173)
No partner	0.092	0.069	0.112	0.102
	(0.140)	(0.140)	(0.211)	(0.191)
Previous unemployment (ref: never unemployed)				
Number of unempl. spells		0.223**		
		(0.085)		
Intercept	−6.476**	−6.462**	−7.460**	−6.243
	(0.255)	(0.254)	(0.438)	
Number of observations	96,554	96,554	49,701	47,655
Number of events	473	473	182	291
Chi²	348.5	358.98	142.09	250.11
Pseudo R^2	0.058	0.059	0.051	0.062
Degrees of freedom	24	25	22	23

Source: SOEP 1984–98 (pooled data).

Note: Standard errors in parentheses. Discrete-time event-history analysis (binomial logit model).

' $p < 0.10$ * $p < 0.05$ ** $p < 0.01$

central characteristics of self-employment, this result is also stable over time. A more detailed perspective on gender differences is given in model 3 (women/men, table 2.3). From the general model we know that the propensity to move into self-employment is highest for workers with a tertiary degree, which we now use as a reference category.[18] The negative signs for all education parameters clearly show that this holds true for women as well as for men. The main difference is seen among those with incomplete or only compulsory education. Women of this group are much less likely to move into self-employment than their male counterparts. Furthermore, in contrast to women, men with vocational education, especially those with a secondary degree, are quite likely to move into self-employment. In sum, tertiary education is of specific relevance for women, while for men the differences between tertiary education and other degrees are less marked.

As expected, there are also differences in the relevance of father's employment status. For men, we see the typical finding of a clear transmission of the self-employment status. In contrast, father's self-employment has no significant effect on the likelihood of women's self-employment. The bivariate association between female self-employment and self-employed family background, present in the descriptive analyses, is not reproduced in the multivariate estimations. Thus, all effects of parental self-employment on daughters' entry into self-employment are mediated through individual resources such as education. Gender differences can also be observed in the relevance of a self-employed partner. For both men and women, self-employment entry is more likely when the partner is self-employed. However, this effect is much stronger and more significant for men.

The discussed models considered entry into all types of self-employment. Now we turn to a multinomial model that gives insights into the differences among self-employment in the three occupational categories (table 2.4).[19] It is noticeable that education, which was found to be highly relevant in the general model, does not have any effect for skilled or unskilled self-employed. Compared with workers with compulsory education or less, we see no statistically significant difference for bearers of higher-level qualifications. Concerning unskilled self-employment, the parameters of higher-level qualifications are negative. The missing impact of education in skilled occupations is probably due to the heterogeneous character of this category. We will explore this assumption further below. With regard to the professional and managerial occupations, we do find the expected statistically significant effect of higher education. Workers with tertiary education are particularly likely to enter into professional or managerial self-employment.

The effects of previous occupations on the likelihood of entering into

TABLE 2.4
Coefficient Estimates for Entry into Self-Employment by Occupational
Categories in Germany

	Prof./manag.	Skilled	Unskilled
Gender (ref: male)			
Female	− 1.020**	− 0.620**	− 0.822**
	(0.196)	(0.183)	(0.256)
Education (CASMIN) (ref: 1ab/2b)			
1c	0.681*	0.003	0.268
	(0.294)	(0.184)	(0.308)
2a	1.235**	− 0.001	0.050
	(0.302)	(0.236)	(0.410)
2c (gen.)	0.633	− 0.226	− 0.161
	(0.423)	(0.440)	(0.598)
2c (voc.)	1.749**	− 0.172	− 1.313
	(0.328)	(0.381)	(1.017)
3ab	1.795**	− 0.203	− 0.641
	(0.375)	(0.484)	(1.082)
Age (minus 18)			
Age in years	0.131**	0.136**	0.129**
	(0.035)	(0.030)	(0.049)
Age in years	− 0.004**	− 0.004**	− 0.005**
(squared)	(0.001)	(0.001)	(0.001)
Social origin (ref: father employee)			
Self-employed	0.425^{c}	0.366	0.147
	(0.240)	(0.288)	(0.439)
Farmer	− 0.413	0.406	0.146
	(0.584)	(0.366)	(0.609)
Not working	− 0.428	− 0.536	− 1.572
	(0.455)	(0.465)	(1.023)
Previous employment status (ref: skilled employee)			
Employee (cat. I)	1.698**	− 0.314	0.258
	(0.335)	(0.298)	(0.636)
Employee (cat. III)	0.219	− 0.322	1.665**
	(0.444)	(0.213)	(0.387)
Unemployed	2.173**	0.291	1.699**
	(0.418)	(0.304)	(0.582)
Out of labor force	1.761**	− 0.226	1.183*
	(0.389)	(0.263)	(0.522)

TABLE 2.4 (*continued*)

	Prof./manag.	Skilled	Unskilled
Previous industrial sector *(ref: mining, manufacturing, energy, and not working)*			
Construction	0.538	0.343	0.586
	(0.425)	(0.276)	(0.545)
Traditional services	0.467	0.989**	0.712ᵗ
	(0.360)	(0.226)	(0.381)
Other services	0.416ᵗ	−1.117**	0.342
	(0.250)	(0.305)	(0.351)
Employment of partner *(ref: employee)*			
Self-employed	0.628	1.191**	−0.717
	(0.411)	(0.277)	(1.024)
Not working	−0.311	−0.183	−0.485
	(0.283)	(0.225)	(0.366)
No partner	0.463*	−0.232	−0.252
	(0.228)	(0.242)	(0.331)
Constant	−9.104**	−6.403**	−7.969**
	(0.540)	(0.365)	(0.594)
Number of observations		97,658	
Number of events		437	
Chi²		551.99	
Pseudo R^2		0.084	
Degrees of freedom		72	

Source: SOEP 1984–98 (pooled data).

Note: Standard errors in parentheses. Discrete-time event-history analysis (multinomial logit model).

ᵗ $p < 0.10$ * $p < 0.05$ ** $p < 0.01$

self-employment show quite a regular pattern. Employees are very likely to become self-employed in the same occupational category in which they were previously employed. For workers in unskilled occupations, entry into self-employment is not connected to mobility into higher, qualitatively better occupational categories. Conversely, those workers in professional, managerial, or skilled occupations are least likely to enter into unskilled self-employment. Differences between the occupational categories can also be found with regard to the importance of a self-employed partner. Having a self-employed partner is most important for the skilled self-employed. This category is dominated by crafts, retail, catering, and lodging businesses, which are rather likely to be run as family businesses.

In sum, this model has already shown that the disaggregation of the group of self-employed reveals certain variations by occupational group.[20] However, mainly due more to the lack of clear educational effects, it seems appropriate to use a detailed classification in which we separate semiprofessionals from professional and managerial self-employment, and proprietors in distribution, catering, and lodging ("lower managerial") from skilled occupations.[21] In doing so, we find remarkable differences between occupational categories (table 2.5). Professional and higher managerial self-employment is clearly linked to higher, especially tertiary, education. Also for semiprofessionals, tertiary education is important, but to a lesser degree. Entry into skilled self-employment, which is dominated by craft occupations, is strongly connected to lower degrees plus vocational qualifications. These are the typical requirements for the "Meister" degree. Self-employment in lower managerial or unskilled occupations is definitely not related to a higher degree of education. The probability of entry is similar for all educational categories. Bearers of vocational qualifications are even less likely to move into lower managerial self-employment than those with only compulsory education. These findings clearly reflect institutional regulation of access to self-employment in specific fields of activity.

Regarding the previous job, we find for all occupational categories that self-employment entry is clearly structured by occupations: the probability to move into a certain self-employment category is highest when already working in the same occupational group. In contrast, when we look at the relevance of entries from unemployment, there are remarkable differences among the five types of self-employment. It is unlikely for an unemployed worker to move into skilled self-employment. Again, this can be attributed to the effectiveness of educational requirements. To become self-employed in this sector requires work experience and specific vocational training. The probability of entering self-employment increases with the number of unemployment spells mainly in occupations that are characterized by low institutionalized requirements or by a high share of freelance activities, as in semiprofessions. In this category, the most frequent jobs are commercial artists, translators, and therapists.

The transmission of father's self-employment is strongest in skilled occupations. It is also rather strong for professionals and higher managerial self-employed. But as the results from additional models show (not controlling for education and/or previous occupation), the transmission of parental employment status in this category is more strongly imparted via education. Although less predominant, this result also holds true for semiprofessionals. In contrast, in the lower managerial and unskilled occupations, no such mediation of parental class through education or previous employment is found.

Exit from Self-Employment

As with entry into self-employment, we also assume differences between genders and occupational categories for exit from self-employment. The survival functions in figure 2.1 support the previously reported result that the prospects for women are significantly worse than for men. Less than half of self-employed women (42 percent) remain self-employed after five years. For men, the respective figure is 63 percent. However, with regarding to occupational categories, we cannot find the assumed differences. The differences between the three larger occupational categories are very small five years after self-employment entry. A bit more than half of the workers in each group are still in self-employment (57 percent of professional and higher managerial, 57 percent of skilled and lower managerial, and 55 percent of unskilled). However, as figure 2.2, which is based on the refined classification, shows, the lack of difference is due to the aggregation of groups that are fairly different with regard to employment stability. As in the entry analysis, the largest differences can be found between the lower managerial and skilled self-employed. Whereas 69.3 percent of the skilled are still in business after five years, only 48.9 percent of the lower managerial self-employed survive. The same difference can be observed among the professionals. Semiprofessionals are as likely as lower managerial workers to quit self-employment, but professional and higher managerial self-employment is almost as stable as skilled self-employment. The low survival rates of lower managerial workers can be explained by the fact that they are mostly proprietors of businesses in the service sector, which is characterized by higher exit rates than other sectors. The high share of exits in semiprofessional occupations is probably linked to flexible forms of work. The self-employed workforce in this occupational category works in occupations that are often executed on a freelance basis. Furthermore, there is an effect of entry barriers. Survival is highest in the areas which are subject to rather strict qualificational entry barriers (professionals, skilled), while in all other occupational categories it is significantly lower. However, despite these differences, overall survival in self-employment is relatively high. This can be attributed to the specific conditions in the German labor market that reduce general mobility (see above). Also, over time (comparing the 1980s with the 1990s), no significant change in the chance of survival could be observed. On the one hand, the proportions of both rather stable (i.e., professionals) and unstable (i.e., semiprofessionals and unskilled) forms of self-employment are growing. On the other hand, not only are stable forms of self-employment (i.e., skilled) affected by a decline, but also unstable lower managerial occupations. Thus, despite the fact that the composi-

TABLE 2.5
Coefficients Estimates for Entry into Self-Employment by Occupational Categories in Germany (extract of results)[1]

	Professional/ managerial	Semiprofessional	Lower managerial	Skilled	Unskilled
Education (CASMIN) *(ref: 1ab/2b)*					
1c	0.127	0.865*	−0.562*	1.267**	0.244
	(0.546)	(0.354)	(0.238)	(0.399)	(0.307)
2a	1.069*	1.313**	−0.726*	1.355**	0.047
	(0.539)	(0.371)	(0.332)	(0.441)	(0.412)
2c (gen.)	1.463*	0.064	−0.620	0.759	−0.121
	(0.689)	(0.596)	(0.608)	(0.702)	(0.596)
2c (voc.)	2.062**	1.566**	−0.293	0.601	−1.303
	(0.567)	(0.407)	(0.477)	(0.678)	(1.021)
3ab	2.253**	1.309*	−0.424	0.435	−0.688
	(0.659)	(0.538)	(0.574)	(1.069)	(1.122)
Social origin *(ref: father employee)*					
Self-employed	0.549	0.424	−0.281	0.859*	0.146
	(0.387)	(0.305)	(0.537)	(0.352)	(0.439)
Self-employed[2]	0.637†	0.491	−0.301	0.874*	0.091
	(0.378)	(0.307)	(0.540)	(0.344)	(0.434)
Self-employed[3]	0.786*	0.542†	−0.249	0.848*	0.089
	(0.375)	(0.303)	(0.535)	(0.345)	(0.433)

Employment status before self-employment entry *(ref: skilled employee)*

	Model 1	Model 2	Model 3	Model 4	Model 5
Professional/ managerial	3.217** (0.803)	−0.176 (0.817)	1.625** (0.556)	###	0.536 (0.845)
Semiprofessional	###	1.699** (0.379)	1.159* (0.560)	−1.110ᵗ (0.605)	−0.031 (0.786)
Lower managerial	###	###	2.476** (0.734)	###	###
Unskilled	1.466 (0.906)	−0.346 (0.547)	1.192** (0.405)	−1.703** (0.506)	1.561 (0.388)
Unemployed	3.222** (0.928)	1.741** (0.475)	1.410** (0.481)	−0.390 (0.528)	1.588* (0.573)
Number of unempl. spells	−0.251 (0.454)	0.336ᵗ (0.181)	0.262ᵗ (0.155)	0.163 (0.212)	0.314** (0.182)
Number of observations	91,621	97,130	97,343	94,384	97,110
Number of events	56	102	112	86	81
Chi²	245.59	189.92	184.76	134.24	117.56
Pseudo R^2	0.207	0.096	0.084	0.103	0.090
Degrees of freedom	24	25	26	24	25

Source: SOEP 1984–98 (pooled data)

Notes: ###: Estimates omitted due to insufficient number of cases. Discrete-time event-history analysis (multinomial logit model). Standard errors in parentheses.

[1] Models include all variables as in the models reported in table 2.5 except when otherwise indicated.

[2] Models without controlling for education.

[3] Models without controlling for education and previous employment status.

ᵗ $p < 0.10$ * $p < 0.05$ ** $p < 0.01$

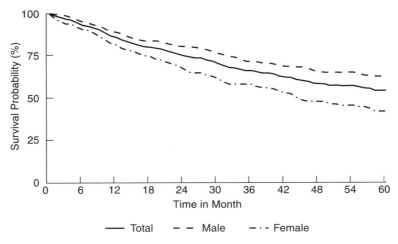

Figure 2.1: Survival Rates of Self-Employed by Gender in Germany

tion is subject to change, in the aggregate, the stability of self-employment is not affected.

In addition to the general picture given by the analysis of survival curves, the question of how far survival is influenced by the individual resources of the self-employed and by the characteristics of the business

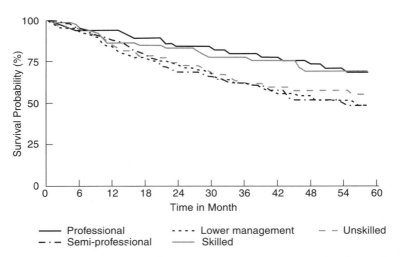

Figure 2.2: Survival Rates of Self-Employed by Occupational Categories in Germany

will be assessed in the multivariate analysis. Table 2.6 contains the results from the multivariate exit models. First we examine the joint models for men and women (models 1 and 2). The figures clearly show that education, compulsory or full tertiary, has no preventive effect for self-employment exit. As we have shown, education strongly affects entry into self-employment but is not decisive for survival. Even distinguishing different occupational categories did not result in significant education effects (models not reported). These findings fit into explanations of the gate-keeping function of education in highly regulated fields of activity as already filtering out potential failures. However, education also has no preventive effect on exits in less regulated occupational groups. Controlling for occupational category (model not reported) does not alter this pattern and reproduces the results already seen in the analyses of survival curves.

As with education, father's self-employment does not contribute to a worker's survival in self-employment. A more important factor is the age of the worker. The curvilinear pattern of the influence of age can be interpreted as caused by the relevance of previous work experience, since we control for the duration of the current self-employment spell. The duration that people are in self-employed businesses also diminishes the risk of exiting. Especially in the first years, businesses have a high failure rate, but the probability of leaving self-employment decreases significantly with time. Hence, our results support the thesis of the "liability of newness" discussed in the literature. In contrast, the results do not support the "liability of smallness" hypothesis. Entrepreneurs who are running larger firms (twenty or more employees) are the most likely to exit self-employment. This result is probably caused by coding errors such as freelancers who work only short periods in self-employment and erroneously indicate the size of the client's firm rather than the size of their own firm. This is plausible since a large share of the workers "employing" twenty or more people work in typical freelance occupations, and large year-to-year changes in the size of the firm are quite frequent.[22] However, comparing only solo-self-employed and employers with not more than nineteen employees, the latter are more likely to survive in self-employment, which can be interpreted as only weak and insignificant support for the "liability of smallness" hypothesis.

As in the entry analysis, we have run models separated by gender in the exit analysis. The joint model established a rather strong effect of being female on the likelihood of exit, which was only partly mediated by gender differences in other covariates.[23] The separated models show that all parameters for men and women point in the same direction, although their strength varies somewhat. The strongest differences can be observed for age and unstable work histories (previous unemployment

TABLE 2.6
Coefficient Estimates for Exit from Self-Employment in Germany

	M1	M2
Gender *(ref: male)*		
Female	0.567**	0.557**
	(0.140)	(0.142)
Education (CASMIN) *(ref: 1ab/2b)*		
1c	0.126	0.140
	(0.209)	(0.209)
2a	0.015	0.009
	(0.235)	(0.234)
2c (gen.)	−0.024	−0.076
	(0.417)	(0.392)
2c (voc.)	−0.174	−0.188
	(0.325)	(0.333)
3ab	−0.055	−0.106
	(0.303)	(0.310)
Age (minus 18)		
Age in years	−0.143**	−0.148**
	(0.034)	(0.034)
Age in years (sq.)	0.003**	0.003**
	(0.001)	(0.001)
Social origin *(ref: father employee)*		
Self-employed	−0.161	−0.122
	(0.201)	(0.202)
Farmer	0.305	0.303
	(0.351)	(0.363)
Not working	0.286	0.263
	(0.377)	(0.370)
Duration in current self-employment status		
Duration in years	−0.041**	0.200**
	(0.013)	(0.014)
Previous unemployment *(ref: never unemployed)*		
Number of unempl. spells		−0.162ᵗ
		(0.107)
Firm size *(ref: no employees or more than 19)*		
1–19 employees		−0.269
		(0.150)
20+ employees		0.646**
		(0.247)
Intercept	−0.913**	−0.908
	(0.332)	(0.347)
Number of observations	3,824	3,824
Number of events	182	182
Chi^2	89.7	103.9
Pseudo R^2	0.055	0.061
Degrees of freedom	13	16

Source: SOEP 1984–1998 (pooled data).
Note: Standard errors in parentheses. Discrete-time event-history analysis (binomial logit model).
ᵗ $p < 0.10$ * $p < 0.05$ ** $p < 0.01$

M3 (women)	M3 (men)	M4 (women)	M4 (men)
−0.111	0.246	−0.078	0.266
(0.322)	(0.282)	(0.327)	(0.284)
−0.128	0.089	−0.113	0.051
(0.359)	(0.326)	(0.355)	(0.333)
−0.592	0.232	−0.569	0.121
(0.838)	(0.486)	(0.823)	(0.451)
−0.211	−0.105	−0.152	−0.123
(0.483)	(0.455)	(0.485)	(0.461)
0.274	−0.380	0.249	−0.468
(0.415)	(0.458)	(0.438)	(0.453)
−0.102^t	−0.180**	−0.117*	−0.179**
(0.057)	(0.044)	(0.058)	(0.045)
0.002	0.003**	0.002	0.003**
(0.001)	(0.001)	(0.001)	(0.001)
−0.350	−0.054	−0.257	−0.035
(0.340)	(0.252)	(0.349)	(0.250)
0.669	−0.073	0.825	−0.218
(0.598)	(0.512)	(0.596)	(0.537)
0.208	0.517	0.136	0.476
(0.558)	(0.513)	(0.588)	(0.504)
−0.070*	−0.029^t	−0.064*	−0.028^t
(0.028)	(0.016)	(0.028)	(0.016)
		0.330^t	0.110
		(0.179)	(0.141)
		−0.020	−0.265
		(0.240)	(0.196)
		0.371	0.798*
		(0.405)	(0.320)
−0.411	−0.773^t	−0.447	−0.717
(0.560)	(0.416)	(0.580)	(0.437)
1,070	2,754	1,070	2,754
90	92	90	92
25.6	52.2	31.9	64.3
0.052	0.047	0.058	0.057
12	12	15	15

spells). In the baseline model, there is no clear influence of age for women, while it is rather strong for men (model 3 women/men, table 2.6). The first result changes when controlling for unstable work histories in supplementary analyses (model 4 women/men, table 2.6). Women with generally unstable work histories are also more likely to exit from self-employment early, while this association cannot be found for men. Regarding the "liability of smallness" hypothesis, as in the general model, we face problems with the firm size measure. However, it seems that the firm size is a more important predictor for men than for women. Moreover, education does not have a preventive effect for either men or women. Hence, the higher risk of women leaving self-employment is not due to differences in the qualifications between men and women but may be attributed to differences in firm-specific characteristics and the generally less stable careers of women.

Conclusion

In this article we analyzed the developments of self-employed work during the last two decades by examining different aspects of self-employment in order to answer three main questions: What determines who becomes self-employed in different fields of activity and how is self-employment structured internally? How has self-employed work developed in Germany since the 1980s? And how does self-employment differ between men and women?

Germany is characterized by self-employment growth during the observed period. However, this growth does not affect all types of self-employed work in the same way. Increases in professional and managerial as well as unskilled self-employment point to a growth at the two opposite poles of self-employed work, rather than in the traditional core. This can be interpreted as an increase in heterogeneity in self-employment. Remarkable changes in the structure of self-employment are further indicated by the increasing number of self-employed practicing typical freelance activities, and the growing number of solo self-employed and the expanded inflow from unemployment. Hence, the growth in self-employment in Germany is primarily based on increases in new, or rather nontraditional, forms of self-employed work. However, marginalized self-employment is of only limited relevance in Germany. Nevertheless, the traditional entry path based on the intergenerational transfer of self-employment has lost importance. But the overall pattern of mechanisms determining the entry into self-employment is stable over time. In particular, age and education are crucial factors in this respect.

There are distinct forms of self-employment which differ considerably from each other in terms of their underlying determinants and outcomes. The overall empirical picture that emerges is that each of these forms is related to a specific socioeconomic profile that can be partially traced back to institutional regulation of access. A clear pattern of entry paths to almost every occupational category can be found. People become self-employed in the same occupational category they previously worked in as employees. Entry into lower managerial jobs in traditional services, a sector without strict entry barriers, does not follow this pattern as clearly. However, the number of these workers has decreased. In contrast, entries from unemployment are becoming more frequent. In addition, unstable work histories increase the probability of entry into self-employment, particularly in occupations characterized by low institutionalized requirements or a high share of freelance activities. These results further strengthen the assertion that nontraditional entries related to divergent determinants are contributing to the ongoing change in self-employment. Nevertheless, all types of self-employment activities are related to positive outcomes in terms of income and satisfaction. Concerning stability, considerable differences between the distinct forms of work were present.

Furthermore, self-employment differs considerably by gender. The extent and structure of self-employed work varies between men and women, and these differences are stable over time. Women move less often into self-employment and are more likely to exit. Thus, on the basis of flow data, there is no empirical evidence for a narrowing of the gender gap in the extent of self-employed work. However, despite the quantitative differences in mobility rates, the determinants of entry and exit do not differ substantially by gender apart from the relevance of father's self-employment. Furthermore, men and women differ only slightly in their qualificational profile (vocational training vs. tertiary education). Regarding the differences in the probability of exit, we cannot identify one crucial factor for why women are more likely to exit. Besides firm characteristics, the different character of male and female career patterns is also an important factor and one that we could not adequately model.

Taken together, we found that self-employed work in Germany has become increasingly heterogeneous since the 1980s. Even though developments in nontraditional and new forms of self-employment have for the most part caused the respective growth, indications for increasing marginalization or precariousness of own-account workers are rather weak. On the contrary, a considerable core of traditional forms of self-employment linked to the "classical" determinants of inheritance and qualifications and to positive outcomes still exists, although the proportion of skilled self-employed workers has declined since the 1980s. The outcomes in terms of income and satisfaction related to self-employed work are on average better than those related to dependent employment. This could be attributed to the highly regulated access to self-employment in Germany, which to a certain extent already filters out potentially precarious self-employment. The stability of self-employment is relatively high in Germany and is not subject to major change, due to the fact that both stable and unstable forms of self-employment are growing. Future research must show whether the observed trends are going to continue. Will self-employment in Germany continue to be related to relatively positive outcomes, or will the proportion of marginalized and low-quality self-employment increase? We surmise that maintenance of strict institutional regulations will prevent a marginalization of large parts of German self-employment.

Notes

Revised version of a paper originally prepared for the Workshop on Self-Employment in Advanced Economies, Mannheim, Germany, November 17–19, 2000. This paper has benefited from detailed comments and many helpful suggestions by Walter Müller and Richard Arum in response to early drafts. All errors remain our own. The authors also gratefully acknowledge financial support from the Fritz-Thyssen Stiftung.

1. Since self-employment in agriculture involves different dynamics, we shall discuss only nonagricultural self-employment. Due to the specific conditions present in East Germany after reunification, we will further restrict our analysis to West Germany. For analysis of self-employment in East Germany, see, e.g., Hinz (1998).

2. Normally this category also includes owner-managers of incorporated businesses (OECD 2000).

3. For an overview of these different kinds of definitions in Germany, see, e.g., Bieback (1999); Petersen (1998).

4. To achieve the "Meister" certificate, one needs to pass an exam following specific vocational training courses and several years of work experience (Klinge 1990).

5. The share of craft businesses amounts to about 20 percent of all self-employed (for the number of craft businesses, see ZDH 2000). Additionally, in 1996, about 16.9 percent of all self-employed worked as professionals (Oberlander et al. 1997, Institut für Freie Berufe 1993).

6. A study by Logotech (1997) compares the conditions for self-employment in different countries in Europe and comes to the conclusion that in Germany

administrative procedures are quite time-consuming and financial requirements are rather high.

7. The relative stability has been estimated for specific aggregated occupation-industry-employment status categories resulting in three groups: high, medium, and low stability. In Germany, no occupation-industry group in self-employment was classified as medium stable (McManus 2000, 881ff.).

8. Since in Germany social security is based mainly on employment status, for the majority of the self-employed no obligatory social security system exists, unlike for dependent employees (Fachinger and Oelschläger 2000).

9. For detailed information on the data, see Haisken-DeNew and Frick (1998).

10. Each year the respondents are asked about their current work status and potential job changes in the course of the actual and previous year. If a change has taken place in the previous months, the respondents are asked to indicate the month and the type of change. This information was used to construct job spells on a monthly basis. In some cases, the annual employment status information and the retrospective employment calendar were used to define the status of the spell. Some inconsistencies were brought into line by the use of a weighted imputation method.

11. The self-employed of class IV are assigned to a category according to their occupational codes.

12. This means the managers of small service enterprises in distribution, catering, and lodging (ISCO-68 410, 510).

13. The three most frequent occupations in the single categories according to gender are, for men, category I: general managers (14.8 percent), insurance, real estate, and securities salespeople (11.2 percent), medical doctors (6.8 percent); for women, category I: commercial artists and designers (11.6 percent), physiotherapists and occupational therapists (11.4 percent), insurance, real estate, and securities salespeople (9.4 percent). For men, category II: working proprietors in wholesale and retail trade (22.2 percent) or in catering and lodging (16.9 percent), hairdressers (7.9 percent); for women, category II: working proprietors in wholesale and retail trade (36.9 percent) or in catering and lodging (13.3 percent), hairdressers (26.4 percent). For men, category III: motor vehicle drivers (52.8 percent), structural metal preparers and erectors (9.3 percent), salespeople, shop assistants, and demonstrators (7.2 percent); for women, category III: salespeople, shop assistants, and demonstrators (24.4 percent), maids and related housekeeping service workers (15.5 percent), launderers, dry cleaners, and pressers (8.5 percent).

14. We can only speculate about the reasons for the difference between the two data sources: On the one hand, the rates especially for women might differ because the number of self-employed in the GSOEP sample is rather small. On the other hand, there could be differences as to how the questionnaires classify marginal types of employment or self-employment. Yet general patterns are comparable, although the level of self-employment differs. To further check the reliability of the sample, we examined the distribution of the main indicators used (e.g., occupational categories, age, and education) of the German Mikrozensus 1996 (the scientific usefile contains about 500,000 cases). Differences in the distribution of these variables between the GSOEP and the German Mikrozensus

were surprisingly low. Therefore, we are, despite the differences in the level of self-employment, quite convinced of the accuracy of the data.

15. The size of the youngest age group is especially small in male professional and managerial self-employment. But the respective proportion is also low in dependent employment, probably due to the long duration of education.

16. To check whether this is an effect of the differences in the data structure (stock vs. flow data) or rather due to differences in the survival rates by education, we also looked at the educational distribution of the new self-employment entrants vs. employees by occupational categories. As in the descriptive results presented above, there are no signs of a clearly better qualified group of self-employed entrants.

17. Comparing self-employment rates by the status the year before results in the following figures: The rates among those workers who were unemployed the year before are 6.0 percent (1984–88) and 5.5 percent (1989–93), which are clearly lower than the rate of those workers who were already working the year before (about 8 percent). In contrast to the previous periods, in 1994–98 the rate of the previously unemployed jumped to 10.3 percent, while the rate of those working the year before increased only to 9.3 percent. Thus, the unemployed really are more likely to be self-employed compared with those who were working the year before.

18. We have chosen to use CASMIN 3ab as a reference category in the gender-specific analysis because from descriptive analyses (not documented here) we saw that the entry rates of bearers of a tertiary degree were almost equal for women and men.

19. The risk set in this model is, as before, workers in dependent employment, the unemployed, and those out of the labor force. The estimation looks at the probability of entering a given category of self-employment.

20. We also ran this model separately for women and men, but for women the model collapsed due to the small number of cases. The results for men reveal, apart from minor changes in the size of some effects, no major differences from the general model. The strongest differences can be observed for skilled self-employed. For men, the parameters for having a self-employed father and the construction sector are significant (10 percent level), which fits into the picture of a male-dominated traditionally oriented crafts sector.

21. See also the section above on data and variables.

22. The group of self-employed with more than nineteen employees consists of about 45 percent of salespeople, authors, commercial artists, journalists, and teachers, occupations that are often executed on a freelance basis. This assumption is strengthened by the fact that there is a relevant share of workers in this group who report large year-to-year changes in the number of employees (e.g., solo self-employed who indicate a firm size of more than 200 workers the next year).

23. Most of the covariates do not explain much of the gender differences (e.g., effect "female" without any covariates but duration: 0.583). The strongest reduction is obtained by the factors tertiary education and professional occupation (which are clearly interrelated). The gender differences in the stability of self-employment are highest for the professionals.

REFERENCES

Acs, Z. J., and D. B. Audretsch. 1990. *The economics of small firms: A European challenge.* Dordrecht: Kluwer Academic Publishers.

Bieback, K. 1999. Neue Selbständigkeit und soziale Sicherung—Notwendigkeit einer Neurorientierung. *Sozialer Fortschritt* 48:166–74.

Birch, D. L. 1987. *Job creation in America: How our smallest companies put the most people to work.* New York: Free Press.

Blanchflower, D. G. 2000. *Self-employment in OECD countries.* NBER Working Paper 7486. Cambridge: National Bureau of Economic Research.

Brauns, H., and S. Steinmann. 1999. Educational reform in France, West Germany and the United Kingdom: Updating the CASMIN educational classification. *ZUMA Nachrichten* 23:7–44.

Brush, C. G. 1992. Research on women business owners: Past trends, a new perspective and future directions. *Entrepreneurship Theory and Practice* 17:131–54.

Brüderl, J., and P. Preisendörfer. 1998. Network support and the success of newly founded businesses. *Small Business Economics* 10:213–25.

Brüderl, J., and P. Preisendörfer. 2000. Fast-growing businesses: Empirical evidence from a German study. *International Journal of Sociology* 30:45–70.

Brüderl, J., P. Preisendörfer, and R. Ziegler. 1992. Survival chances of newly founded business organizations. *American Sociological Review* 57:227–42.

Bundesministerium für Arbeit und Sozialordnung (BMA). 2000. *Scheinselbständigkeit und arbeitnehmerähnliche Selbständige.* Berlin: BMA.

Bögenhold, D. 1985. *Die Selbständigen: Zur Soziologie dezentraler Produktion.* Frankfurt: Campus Verlag.

Bögenhold, D., and U. Staber. 1991. The decline and rise of self-employment. *Work, Employment and Society* 5:223–39.

———. 1993. Notes and issues. Self-employment dynamics: A reply to Meager. *Work, Employment and Society* 7:465–72.

Börsch-Supan, A., and F. Pfeiffer. 1992. Determinanten der Selbständigkeit in der Bundesrepublik Deutschland. In *Herausforderungen an den Wohlfahrtsstaat im strukturellen Wandel*, ed. R. Hujer, H. Schneider, and W. Zapf, 257–87. Frankfurt: Campus.

Caputo, R., and A. Dolinsky. 1998. Women's choice to pursue self-employment: The role of financial and human capital of household members. *Journal of Small Business Management* 36:8–17.

Cressy, R. 1996. Are business startups debt-rationed? *Economic Journal* 106:1253–70.

Dietrich, H. 1998. *Erwerbsverhalten in der Grauzone von selbständiger und abhängiger Erwerbsarbeit.* Nuremberg: Institut für Arbeitsmarkt- und Berufsforschung der Bundesanstalt für Arbeit.

Dunn, T., and D. Holtz-Eakin. 2000. Financial capital, human capital, and the transition to self-employment: Evidence from intergenerational links. *Journal of Labour Economics* 18:282–305.

Döse, A., A. Höland, P. Schallhöfer, and T. Roethe. 1994. *Neue Formen und Bed-*

ingungen der Erwerbsarbeit in Europa: Eine rechtssoziologische Untersuchung. Baden Baden: Nomos.

Elsner, S. 1996. Franchising, Scheinselbständigkeit, Sozialdumping. *Zeitschrift für ausländisches und internationales Arbeits- und Sozialrecht* 10:83–91.

Erikson, R., and J. H. Goldthorpe. 1992. *The constant flux: A study of class mobility in industrial societies.* Oxford: Oxford University Press.

Evans, D. S., and L. S. Leighton. 1990. Some empirical aspects of entrepreneurship. In *The economics of small firms: A European challenge,* ed. Z. J. Acs and D. Audretsch, 79–97. Dordrecht: Kluwer Academic Publishers.

Fachinger, U., and A. Oelschläger. 2000. *Selbständige und ihre Altersvorsorge: Sozialpolitischer Handlungsbedarf.* ZeS Working Paper. Bremen: Zentrum für Sozialpolitik.

Gottschall, K. 1999. Freie Mitarbeit im Journalismus: Zur Entwicklung von Erwerbsformen zwischen selbständiger und abhängiger Beschäftigung. *Kölner Zeitschrift für Soziologie und Sozialpsychologie* 51:635–54.

Haisken-DeNew, J. P., and J. R. Frick. 1998. *DTC—Desktop Companion to the German Socio-Economic Panel Study (GSOEP).* Berlin: Deutsches Institut für Wirtschaftsforschung.

Hartmann, P. H. 1998. Intergenerationale berufliche Mobilität in West- und Ostdeutschland. In *Blickpunkt Gesellschaft: Soziale Ungleichheit in Deutschland,* ed. M. Braun and P. Mohler. Opladen: Westdeutscher Verlag.

Hinz, T. 1998. *Betriebsgründungen in Ostdeutschland.* Berlin: Edition Sigma.

———. 2000. Good times, bad times? Periods of market entry and survival chances of newly founded businesses. *International Journal of Sociology* 30:28–58.

Institut für Freie Berufe. 1993. *Freie Berufe in Europa. Daten, Fakten, Informationen.* Bonn: Institut für freie Berufe.

Jungbauer-Gans, M. 1993. *Frauen als Unternehmerinnen.* Frankfurt: Peter Lang.

———. 1999. Der Lohnunterschied zwischen Frauen und Männern in selbständiger und abhängiger Beschäftigung. *Kölner Zeitschrift für Soziologie und Sozialpsychologie* 51:364–90.

Jungbauer-Gans, M., and R. Ziegler. 1991. Sind Betriebsgründerinnen in der Minderheit benachteiligt? *Kölner Zeitschrift für Soziologie und Sozialpsychologie* 43:720–38.

Kalleberg, A. L., B. F. Reskin, and K. Hudson. 2000. Bad jobs in America: Standard and nonstandard employment relations and job quality in the United States. *American Sociological Review* 65:256–78.

Klinge, G. 1990. *Niederlassungs- und Dienstleistungsrecht für Handwerker und andere Gewerbetreibende in der EG.* Baden Baden: Nomos.

Kulicke, M. 1997. Förderung junger Technologieunternehmen in Deutschland. In *Technologieunternehmen im Innovationsprozeß: Management, Finanzierung und regionale Netze,* ed. K. Koschatzky, 109–26. Heidelberg: Physica-Verlag.

Laferrère, A. 2001. Self-employment and intergenerational transfers. *International Journal of Sociology* 31:3–26.

Leicht, R. 1995. *Die Prosperität kleiner Betriebe: Das längerfristige Wandlungsmuster von Betriebsgrößen und—strukturen.* Heidelberg: Physica-Verlag.

———. 2000. Die 'neuen Selbständigen' arbeiten alleine: Wachstum und Struktur der Solo-Selbständigen in Deutschland. *Zeitschrift für Klein- und Mittelunternehmen* 48:75–90.

Lindh, T., and H. Ohlsson. 1996. Self-employment and windfall gains: Evidence from the Swedish lottery. *Economic Journal* 106:1515–26.

Logotech. 1997. *International comparison of the formal requirements and administrative procedures required for the formation of SME's of any legal status in the E.U. and other major countries.* European Innovation Monitoring System (EIMS) Publication 58, commissioned by the European Commission.

Luber, S., H. Lohmann, W. Müller, and P. Barbieri. 2000. Male self-employment in four European countries. *International Journal of Sociology* 30:5–44.

McManus, P. A. 2000. Market, state and the quality of new self-employment jobs among men in the United States and western Germany. *Social Forces* 78:865–905.

———. 2001a. Pathways into self-employment in the United States and Germany. *Vierteljahrshefte zur Wirtschaftsforschung* 70.

———. 2001b. Women's participation in self-employment in Western industrialized nations. *International Journal of Sociology* 31:70–97.

Meager, N. 1992. The fall and rise of self-employment (again): A comment on Bögenhold and Staber. *Work, Employment and Society* 6:127–34.

———. 1993. *Self-employment and labour market policy in the European Community.* Discussion Paper FS I 93, 201. Berlin: Wissenschaftszentrum Berlin für Sozialforschung.

Meager, N., and P. Bates. 2001. The self-employed and lifetime incomes: Some UK evidence. *International Journal of Sociology* 31:27–58.

Merz, J. 2000. The distribution of income of self-employed, entrepreneurs and professionals as revealed from micro income tax statistics in Germany. In *The personal distribution of income in an international perspective*, ed. R. Hauser and I. Becker, 99–128. Heidelberg: Springer Verlag.

Müller, W. 1986. Soziale Mobilität: Die Bundesrepublik im internationalen Vergleich. In *Politische Wissenschaft und politische Ordnung*, ed. M. Kaase, 339–54. Opladen: Westdeutscher Verlag.

Müller, W., and Y. Shavit. 1998. The institutional embeddedness of the stratification process: A comparative study of qualifications and occupations in thirteen countries. In *From school to work. A comparative study of educational qualifications and occupational destinations*, ed. W. Müller and Y. Shavit, 1–48. Oxford: Clarendon Press.

Oberlander, W., U. Fraenk, G. Glahn, and M. Kräuter. 1997. *Neue freiberufliche Dienstleistungen—Potentiale und Marktchance.* Köln: Deutscher Ärzte Verlag.

OECD. 1986. Self-employment in OECD countries. In *Employment Outlook*, 43–65. Paris: OECD.

———. 2000. The partial renaissance of self-employment. In *Employment Outlook*, 155–99. Paris: OECD.

Petersen, U. 1998. Die rechtliche Definition der selbständig Tätigen in der Bundesrepublik Deutschland. In *Soziale Sicherheit und die Entwicklung der selbständigen Erwerbstätigkeit außerhalb der Landwirtschaft*, ed. Internationale Vereinigung für Soziale Sicherheit, 145–51. Paris: European Regional Meeting.

Pfeiffer, F., and F. Reize. 2000. From unemployment to self-employment—public promotion and selectivity. *International Journal of Sociology* 30:71–98.

Reize, F. 2000. *Leaving unemployment for self-employment: A discrete duration analysis of determinants and stability of self-employment among former unemployed.* Discussion Paper 00-26. Mannheim: Zentrum für Europäische Wirtschaftsforschung.

Scherer, S. 2001. Early career patterns: A comparison of Great Britain and West Germany. *European Sociological Review* 17:119–44.

Statistisches Bundesamt. 2000. *Datenreport 1999.* Bonn: Bundeszentrale für politische Bildung.

Sullivan, D. H., and T. M. Smeeding. 1997. *All the world's entrepreneurs: The role of self-employment in nineteen nations.* Luxembourg Income Study Working Paper 163. Luxembourg: Centre d'Etudes de Population, de Pauvreté et de Politiques Socio-Economiques.

Taylor, M. P. 1996. Earnings, independence or unemployment: Why become self-employed? *Oxford Bulletin of Economics and Statistics* 58:253–66.

———. 1998. *Self-employment survival, exit and bankruptcy in Britain.* Discussion Paper 98-24. Colchester: Institute for Labour Research.

———. 1999. Survival of the fittest? An analysis of self-employment duration in Britain. *Economic Journal* 109:140–55.

Wank, R. 1992. Die 'neue' Selbständigkeit. *Arbeits-/Sozialrecht* 45:90–93.

Watkins, J. M., and D. S. Watkins. 1986. The female entrepreneur: Her background and determinants of business choice—some British data. In *The survival of the small firm*, ed. J. Curran, J. Stuwarth, and D. Watkins, 220–32. Aldershot: Gower.

Wießner, F. 1998. Bridging allowance as an instrument of labour market policy— a provisional appraisal. *IAB Labour Market Research Topics* 30:1–23.

Zentralverband des Deutschen Handwerks (ZDH). 2000. *Daten und Fakten zum deutschen Handwerk.* www.zdh.de (accessed 7/25/2001).

CHAPTER THREE

Entries and Exits from Self-Employment in France over the Last Twenty Years

Thomas Amossé and Dominique Goux

IN FRANCE THERE has been a long-run decline in job security, expressed through a secular rise in contingent jobs within firms, as well as a rise in the risk of involuntary job losses for both high- and low-seniority workers (Givord and Maurin 2001; DiPrete et al. 2002). This decline is particularly pronounced in high-tech firms open to international trade and is plausibly driven by the force of globalization, and by the rapid diffusion of new information technologies. At the same time, the wage profiles within firms are becoming flatter, suggesting that the role of seniority is declining, and that employment relationships no longer strengthen as time goes on (DiPrete et al. 2002).

Most research on the impact of globalization on employment security is concerned with the weakening relationships between employers and employees. In this chapter, we focus on another potential effect of the new economic and technological environment, namely, the emergence of new forms of self-employment. We speculate that the growing complexity of the economic environment increases the demand for highly skilled professionals with a high level of expertise in legal or organizational issues. At the same time, the persistence of a high level of unemployment may increase the number of low-skilled candidates creating small businesses in the service sector. As far as France is concerned, these hypotheses have not been tested, and many questions remain unanswered. Who are the new self-employed workers? Has there been any change in the nature of self-employment? Are social background and technical skills still crucial assets for entering self-employment and successfully running a business? Have there been any changes in the degree of job stability for self-employed workers (i.e., in the rate of entry into and exit from self-employment)?

To address these issues, we use the Labor Force Surveys (LFS) conducted by the French National Institute for Statistics and Economics Studies (INSEE) between 1982 and 2002. These surveys contain information about self-employment status at the time of the survey and one year before, which allows analysis of entry into self-employment. The data allow us to differentiate three types of self-employment: unskilled nonprofessional, skilled nonprofessional, and professional.

A multivariate logit regression will identify the determinants of entry into skilled, unskilled, and professional self-employment, and their evolution over the last twenty years. Starting from 1990, the LFS provides month-by-month information on employment status. This makes it possible to measure the duration of self-employment. Thus, our analysis of exit from self-employment relies on a sample of self-employment spells, representative of the durations of self-employment for those entering self-employment during the 1990–2000 period. Duration models are fitted to the determinants of exit from self-employment.

Our main findings are as follows. We find that the proportions of both low-skilled self-employed and highly skilled professionals within total self-employment are steadily rising, to the detriment of traditional skilled self-employed workers in the construction and manufacturing sectors. The increasing complexity of the economic and legal environment, combined with a persisting high level of unemployment, has deeply modified the structure of self-employment. We also find that having a self-employed father is becoming less of an asset for entering self-employment. One plausible explanation is the speed of technical change, such that the economic environment has changed, and it is now less important to have a self-employed father. Another explanation is that the new small businesses require initial investments that are on average less costly than two or three decades ago, which could be a consequence of the rapid diffusion of new information technologies. Furthermore, we find that being a low-skilled person is less of a handicap for creating a new firm, now that new small firms in the service sector require fewer technical skills than traditional self-employment activities in the construction or manufacturing sectors. Lastly, we do not detect any structural changes in the rate of entry into and exit from self-employment. The job security of new self-employed workers seems neither higher nor lower than what it was two decades ago.

The study is organized in the following manner. First, we describe French legislation concerning self-employment. There are two kinds of enterprise: the individual firm, which is the more common status of new firms, and the company. Subsidies to encourage the starting of a new business are numerous; we describe the most important ones. We also present the data, the annual Labor Force Surveys. The main trends in self-employment activity are presented next. The final section is dedicated to a scrutiny of self-employment entries and exits. Entries into self-employment are analyzed for the 1984–2002 period. Due to the lack of pertinent information on the 1982–1989 Labor Force Surveys, exits from self-employment are analyzed only for the 1990–2000 period.

Institutional Context and Data

Self-Employed Categories

In France, the type of activity of the firm determines whether the owner is a craftsperson (*artisan*), shopkeeper (*commerçant*), or professional (*profession libérale*). There is an official list of all crafts and professional activities. Most of the professional activities are also regulated: a certain degree is necessary to set up in these activities, and in some cases there is even a restricted intake (*numerus clausus*).

The simplest, but riskiest, legal status is the individual firm (*entreprise individuelle*). No distinction is made between the capital of an individual firm and the capital of the entrepreneur. Almost two-thirds of created firms are individual firms, but they represent a smaller percentage of the stock of firms.

The other possible legal status is the company (*société*). There are three categories of companies: the Société à Responsabilité Limitée (SARL), the Entreprise Unipersonnelle à Responsabilité Limitée (EURL), or the Société anonyme (SA). All separate the capital of the firm from the capital of the entrepreneur.[1] They correspond to different numbers of partners (one for the EURL, at least two for the SARL and at least seven for the SA) and to different levels of capital invested. Consequently, they correspond to firms of very different sizes. On average, the SAs employ between thirty and forty people, ten times more than the EURLs or the SARLs. In 1998 around 41 percent of the stock of French firms were companies. Among them, 15 percent were EURLs, 16 percent SAs, and 69 percent SARLs (Cordellier 2000).

Due to the relative complexity of administrative formalities, it is quite difficult to set up a business in France. Even though in the recent years legal procedures have been simplified, low-skilled workers, such as childcare providers or gardeners, are still mostly wage earners (with multiple employers), not self-employed. This specific context must be taken into account when comparing France with other countries.

Government Subsidies

Before dealing with the econometric analysis, we give a broad outline of the institutional context of business creation in France. Government subsidies for starting a new business are numerous. In 1996 around thirty official programs offered aid for firm creation (Commissariat Général du Plan 1996), but only six types of aid concerned more than ten thousand firm creations each year. The others often do not benefit more than a few hundred firms. The purposes of the aids are quite diverse and include information, training, financial subsidies, tax cuts, reduced rate loans, social security contribution cuts, and so forth. We list only the most important financial subsidies.

Since 1980 the French government has provided transfer payments to the unemployed who attempt to start businesses. At that time self-employment was seen as a safety valve where the unemployed could find jobs. The program has been extended because the authorities believe that firm creation is an efficient solution for placing workers without jobs. The Aide aux Chômeurs Créateurs ou Repreneurs d'Entreprise (ACCRE, subsidy for unemployed who create or rescue a firm) applies to unemployed who have been registered at the National Office for Employment (ANPE) for six months or more, or who benefit from the Minimum Guaranteed Income (RMI).[2] It consists of a lump sum payment (32,000 francs from 1994 to 1996)[3] and free social insurance taxes during the first year of the firm. There is an interval of no more than one month between the date of application and the acceptance (or rejection) by the administration.

The ACCRE has been in place since 1980, following a three-year period of experiment (1977–80). However, access conditions and implementation have regularly changed (for a detailed presentation of the ACCRE, see Aucouturier, Cealsi, and Charpail 1996). The share of firm creations that benefit from the ACCRE increased from 18 percent in 1990 to 37 percent in 1995 (Aucouturier and Charpail 1997). Because of restriction placed on applicants, the number of firms benefiting from the ACCRE has been decreasing since 1995 (Lamontagne and Thirion 2000). The ACCRE is not the only subsidy encouraging individuals to set up new businesses, but it is by far the most important. The Enterprise Allowance Scheme started in 1982 in Britain, and other, similar programs have been put in place in many other European countries (André 1995; Bendick and Egan 1987). More recently, the United States established similar government programs to encourage unemployed to set up businesses (Blanchflower 2000). The *Défi Jeunes* subsidy, created in 1987, provides grants to young people, aged 18 to 28, who start original businesses or businesses with social utility. In 2000 the grant ranged from 10,000 to 50,000 francs. *Défi Jeunes* also assists young people with the required legal and administrative procedures. The Prime Régionale à la Création d'Entreprise (PRCE) is paid by some regional councils (*conseils régionaux*) when the firm creates jobs in the short term. In 2000 the subsidy could not exceed 150,000 francs (200,000 francs in some regions).

Data

We used the annual Labor Force Surveys, conducted by INSEE between 1982 and 2002. The following standard information is compiled for each respondent: age, gender, nationality, labor-market status (employed, unemployed, out of the labor force), occupation, and educational attainment. Self-employed people are identified according to their own reports. We systematically excluded from self-employed status those working in agriculture, as well as family workers. Managers who receive a salary or wages (*salariés chefs d'entreprise*) are usually considered self-employed in France, as they earn income directly from their own business, trade, or profession and are their own employers. The problem is that the 1982 to 1989 French Labor Force Surveys do not allow us to identify wage earners who are also their own employer. In these surveys, the total number of self-employed is therefore incalculable. Thus, we are forced to exclude self-employed who receive wages from their own business from our sample of self-employed. This narrow definition of self-employed will be used in the following analysis because it is the only one that allows a 1982–2002 comparison.

To analyze exit from self-employment, we will rely on a specific and representative sample of spells in self-employment. The nine Labor Force Surveys from 1990 to 1998 give a total sample of 2,800 spells of self-employment; 880 of these end during the observation period and 1,920 are right-censored (for a detailed presentation of the data, see appendix 3.1).

For the analysis of entry into self-employment, we used data drawn from all of the surveys. Indeed, each survey contains information on the employment status of each respondent at the time of the survey and one year before (including for the respondents who were not in the LFS sample the previous year). We have used these data to calculate entry rates and to analyze the determinants of entry into self-employment. We concentrated on the 1984, 1987, 1990, 1993, 1996, 1999, and 2002 surveys. Since the sample is renewed by one-third each year, we can thus limit individuals from being present twice in our analysis sample. There are about 630,000 individuals, aged between 18 and 60 years in the year prior to the survey, who were unemployed, out of the labor force, or employed, but not self-employed, the year before the survey. We also excluded those who were farmers or family workers the year prior to the survey (see appendix 3.1 for more details).

We distinguish professional self-employment from nonprofessional self-employment. For nonprofessional self-employment, we distinguish between skilled and unskilled self-employment, according to EGP crite-

TABLE 3.1
Correspondence between French PCS Code and Skill Level

Skill level	Profession	PCS code
Unskilled	Retail food shopkeepers	2212, 2213, 2233, some 2247
	Small restaurant, hotel, and café managers	2221, 2222, 2224, some 2247
	Taxi drivers and truck drivers	2171, 2181, 2182
	Household childcare workers	5631
	Craftspeople not elsewhere classified	2174
Skilled	Food processing craftspeople	2101 to 2107
	Building craftspeople	2151 to 2157
	Craftspeople in wood, textile, leather or printing	2121 to 2143
	Craftspeople in mechanics or in metal	2111 to 2113, 2161 to 2163, some 2247
	Personal services workers	2172, 2173, 2245, some 2247
	Retail shopkeepers, except food retailers	2210, 2211, 2214 to 2218, some 2247
	Trade intermediaries and wholesale shopkeepers; intermediate restaurant, hotel, and café managers	2231 to 2236, some 2247
Professionals	Managers of businesses with 10 or more employees	2310, 2320, 2331, 2332, 2333, 2334
	Legal, technical, and business professionals; architects	3121 to 3128, some 2247
	Health professionals	3111 to 3116
	Nurses, physiotherapists, chiropodists	4316, 4321, 4323
	Education and social services workers	4232, 4233, 2246
	Communication and art professionals	3511, 3512, 3531, 3532, 3533, 3534, 3535, 4631, 4632, 4633, 4635, 4637, 2244
	Brokers, finance, real estate agents	2241, 2242, 2243, some 2247
	Associate professionals, technicians	4324, 4326, 4795

Note: See INSEE 1994 for the meaning of the PCS codes.

ria, as well as according to criteria prevalent in the French PCS (*categories socioprofessionnelles*) classification scheme for wage earners. Table 3.1 shows how we classified the self-employed professions. The other variables of interest are described in appendix 3.1.

THE IMPORTANCE OF SELF-EMPLOYMENT AND ITS STRUCTURE

In 2002, 1.6 million workers were self-employed, representing 6.7 percent of the total workforce. This figure excludes farmers, family workers, and self-employed who receive wages from their business, according to our definition of self-employment.[4] The rate of self-employment is significantly lower in France than in the United Kingdom, Japan, Spain, or Italy. The French rate is very close to the rates observed in Germany, the United States, Canada, and Sweden (Blanchflower 2000).

What our figures show is a slight increase in the self-employment rate over the 1980s, followed by a constant decline since the mid-1990s (fig. 3.1). The decline is weaker than the increase because it is explained in part by the massive increase in employment between 1997 and 2002.[5] Thus, the number of self-employed in 2002 is approximately the same as in 1982, but their employment share decreased by about 1 percent. These shifts correspond to both a persisting decline in traditional self-employment in the construction and manufacturing sectors and a more favorable evolution of both highly skilled professionals and low-skilled self-employment in the service sector.

The composition of self-employment has changed substantially in recent decades (fig. 3.2). The share of professionals has increased, especially in health care (nurses, physicians, etc.) and legal and business services (lawyers, brokers, etc.), while skilled self-employment, the historical core of self-employment, has been persistently losing jobs (more than 200,000 jobs over the last ten years). The share of unskilled self-employment in total employment remains stable.

THE INDIVIDUAL DETERMINANTS OF SELF-EMPLOYMENT

In 2002, 8.9 percent of men were self-employed, compared with 4.2 percent of women.[6] As in most OECD countries, the probability of being self-employed is higher among men than among women (Blanchflower 2000). The probability of being self-employed is higher for individuals with upper-tertiary-level diplomas than for less educated individuals (see table 3.2). This reflects the fact that one needs such a diploma to become a professional. Vocationally oriented postsecondary degrees, such as nurse or physiotherapist, have promoted self-employment, especially for women. Interestingly, individuals with vocational education (1c or 2a) are not more likely to become self-employed than average. This holds for

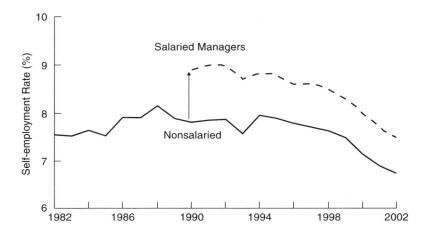

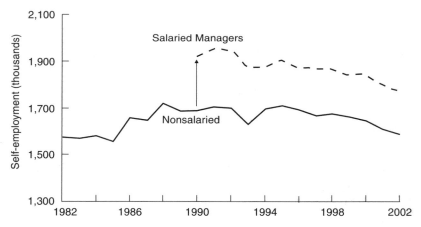

Figure 3.1: Long-Term Evolution of Employment and Self-Employment in France.
Source: Labour Force Surveys, 1982–2002, INSEE.
Note: Individuals in employment, aged 18–60 years.

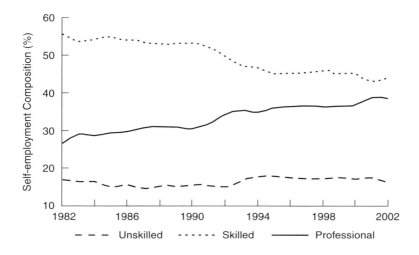

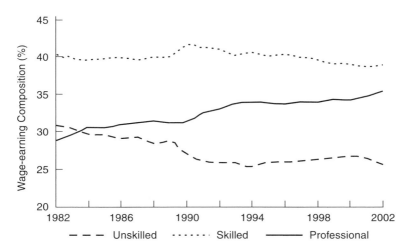

Figure 3.2: Long-Term Evolution of Unskilled, Skilled, and Professional Employment in France.

Note: Individuals in employment, aged 18–60 years.

Source: Labour Force Surveys, 1982–2002, INSEE.

TABLE 3.2
Self-Employment in Employment Stock in France, 1982 and 2002 (in percent)

	Male	Female	Total
Educational level			
1a	7.1 *(−1.2)*	2.8 *(−0.8)*	5.2 *(−1.2)*
1b	7.2 *(−1.5)*	3.8 *(−0.2)*	5.5 *(−0.8)*
1c	9.6 *(−1.2)*	3.7 *(−0.6)*	7.4 *(−1.0)*
2a	7.4 *(−4.2)*	3.8 *(−2.2)*	5.8 *(−3.6)*
2bc	7.3 *(−3.6)*	3.4 *(−1.3)*	5.1 *(−1.8)*
3a	8.0 *(−0.6)*	5.6 *(+0.3)*	6.7 *(+0.0)*
3b	13.1 *(−4.9)*	6.7 *(−2.6)*	10.1 *(−5.0)*
Industry			
Manufacturing	4.2 *(+0.0)*	2.3 *(+1.0)*	3.7 *(+0.3)*
Construction	19.0 *(+0.3)*	5.4 *(+3.3)*	17.7 *(+0.3)*
Service	9.4 *(−3.3)*	4.6 *(−0.8)*	6.8 *(−2.1)*
Father's occupation			
Self-employed	20.8 *(−6.0)*	8.8 *(+0.8)*	15.4 *(−1.0)*
Not self-employed	7.0 *(−2.0)*	3.5 *(+0.0)*	5.5 *(+0.0)*
Potential experience			
0–4 years	1.7 *(−1.5)*	1.3 *(−0.7)*	1.5 *(−1.2)*
5–9 years	4.1 *(−1.8)*	3.0 *(+0.4)*	3.6 *(−0.9)*
10–19 years	8.2 *(−1.8)*	4.7 *(+0.5)*	6.7 *(−0.2)*
20 or more years	11.5 *(−1.9)*	4.9 *(−0.4)*	8.5 *(−1.4)*
All	8.9 *(−1.5)*	4.2 *(+0.0)*	6.8 *(−1.1)*

Source: Labour Force Surveys, 1982 and 2002, INSEE.

Notes: Individuals in employment in March 2002. Self-employment excludes farmers and family workers, aged 18 to 60 years. In 2002, 19% of men working in the construction industry were self-employed, compared with 18.7% in 1982 [19.0 − 0.3 = 18.7]).

both men and women and reflects the fact that vocational education in France is primarily for those who have failed in the general track, rather than for those who have actually chosen a vocational career. Blanch-flower (2000) found some evidence that self-employment is more prevalent at the tails of the education distribution, especially for the least educated. With the United Kingdom, France seems to be an exception, where the most educated have the highest probability of becoming self-employed.

One-fifth of men whose father was self-employed are themselves self-employed, three times more than those whose father was not self-employed (odds ratio of 3.1).[7] For women, the difference in the probability

TABLE 3.3
Employees of Self-Employed in France, 2002 (in percent)

Size of firm (number of wage-earners)	Male	Female	Total
1–2	69.8	80.0	72.5
3–5	14.1	11.2	13.4
6–9	8.3	4.5	7.2
10–19	4.3	1.6	3.6
20–49	2.2	1.6	2.0
50 and over	1.3	1.1	1.3
Total	100	100	100

Source: Labour Force Survey, 2002, INSEE.

Notes: Individuals self-employed in March 2002, aged 18 to 60 years. Self-employment excludes farmers and family workers. In 2002, 2.0% of self-employed individuals supported between 20 and 49 workers in their firm.

TABLE 3.4
Twelve Most Common Self-Employed Professions in France

Profession	2002				1982	
	Number	%	Number	%	Number	%
Building craftspeople	241	13.8	233	14.7	286	18.1
Health professionals	155	8.8	155	9.8	127	8.1
Legal, technical, and business professionals; architects	119	6.8	108	6.8	228	14.5
Managers of businesses with 10 or more employees	117	6.7	98	6.2	90	5.7
Small restaurant, hotel, and café managers	113	6.4	58	3.7	89	5.6
Retail shopkeepers, except food retailers	110	6.3	106	6.7	134	8.5
Nurses, physiotherapists, chiropodists	104	5.9	104	6.6	44	2.8
Craftspeople in mechanics or in metal	103	5.9	97	6.1	49	3.1
Retail food shopkeepers	92	5.3	83	5.2	81	5.1
Communication and art professionals	81	4.6	78	4.9	47	3.0
Trade intermediaries and wholesale shopkeepers; intermediate restaurant, hotel, and café managers	77	4.4	61	3.8	48	3.0
Food processing craftspeople	65	3.7	63	4.0	101	6.4
Total self-employment	1,752	100	1,586	100	1,577	100

Source: Labour Force Surveys, 1982 and 2002, INSEE.

Notes: Numbers are in thousands. In 2002, there were 233,000 building craftspeople self-employed in France, representing 14.7% of total (nonagricultural) self-employment, compared with 286,000 in 1982.

of being self-employed between those whose father was self-employed and those whose father was not is smaller (8.8 percent vs. 3.5 percent, with an odds ratio of 2.7). For both men and women, social background remains a very important asset when creating a new business. The majority of self-employment for both men and women occurs in small enterprises with no or few other additional employees (see table 3.3).

THE OCCUPATIONAL STRUCTURE OF SELF-EMPLOYMENT AND ITS CHANGES

Almost one-fifth of men employed in the construction industry are self-employed. Construction is the industry where self-employment is the most prevalent. The service industry has lower rates of self-employment, and the manufacturing industry has even lower ones.

Self-employed workers can be divided into three main subgroups. In spite of its continuous decline, the share of skilled self-employment is still the largest. In 2002 it still represented 44.4 percent of the total. In contrast, professional self-employment has been continuously increasing and now represents 38.9 percent of the total. The share of unskilled self-employment is 16.6 percent.

In 2002 the largest self-employed occupations were the following (table 3.4): around 16 percent of self-employed were health professionals (9.8 percent were physicians, dentists, or veterinarians and 6.6 percent were nurses, physiotherapists, or chiropodists). The aging of the French population and progress in medicine have both increased supply and demand for care. These occupations represented only 11 percent of self-employment at the beginning of the 1980s. In 2002, 15 percent of self-employed were building craftsworkers (bricklayers, plumbers, roofers, carpenters, joiners, or painters). They were the largest group twenty years ago (18 percent). In the face of competition from larger units, smaller, independent retail shopkeepers (12 percent in 2002) are losing ground: their share in self-employment decreased by one-third in the last twenty years. The increase in the number of meals taken outside the home and the development of tourism have compensated for the competition of chains in the hospitality industry: small hotel, restaurant or café owners with less than three employees constituted 6.7 percent of self-employed in 2002. The last point worth noting is that the share of legal, technical, and business professionals has doubled in the last twenty years (6.1 percent vs. 3.1 percent). The composition of the nonagricultural self-employed population has changed significantly over the last two decades (fig. 3.2). In 2002 the share of professionals in total self-employment was more than one and one-half times higher than in 1982 (39 percent vs. 27 percent).

In contrast, traditional skilled self-employment has strongly declined, while the share of unskilled self-employment has remained stable. First, this stability in the relative importance of low-skilled positions is specific to self-employment. Over the same period, the percentage of low-skilled workers in total payroll employment fell from 31 percent to 26 percent (Chardon 2001). Self-employment provides low-skilled persons with positions that are more and more difficult to obtain within firms. Second, the rise in the share of professionals is much stronger in self-employment than in wage-earning employment. All in all, the skill composition of self-employed and of wage earners has become very similar, with a relatively low proportion of unskilled persons, and relatively high proportions of professional or skilled persons.

ECONOMETRIC ANALYSIS OF ENTRIES AND EXITS

Entry into Self-Employment

Entries into self-employment are studied for the 1982–2002 period. We analyze the probability of entry into self-employment, and its evolution, by estimating three logit models: over the 1980s, over the 1990s and over the entire period (table 3.5a). We also analyze the probability of entry into the three different categories of self-employment—professional, skilled, and unskilled—using a multivariate logit model (table 3.5b).

The first important finding is that we do not observe any long-run upward or downward trend in the rate of entry into self-employment. However, there is a clear link between the propensity to enter self-employment and the business cycle, especially for traditional, skilled self-employment. Entries into self-employment were more frequent in 1986–87, a period of rapid restructuring in the French manufacturing industries, and in 2001–02. In the mid-1980s, creating one's own firm was a way to avoid long-term unemployment. In 2001–02, the number of job creations fell, and unemployment began to increase again. Thus, creating one's own firm allowed one to avoid unemployment. In contrast, during the 1997–98 economic upturn, entries into self-employment diminished.

THE EFFECTS OF EDUCATION, EXPERIENCE, GENDER, AND SOCIAL BACKGROUND

Men are more likely to enter self-employment than women are, especially in skilled self-employment. Indeed, skilled self-employment corresponds mostly to positions in the construction sector, which are traditionally held by men. Differences between men and women are as significant in the nineties as in the eighties.

Men and women are more likely to enter self-employment in the mid-

TABLE 3.5A
Logit Regression Estimates of the Determinants of Entry into Self-Employment

	1984–1987– 1990	1996–1999– 2002	All the period
Intercept	−6.56 (0.14)	−7.12 (0.16)	−6.45 (0.11)
Gender			
Men	1.13 (0.07)	−1.11 (0.07)	1.08 (0.04)
Women	* *	* *	* *
Age			
Age simple	0.14 (0.01)	0.13 (0.01)	0.13 (0.01)
Age squared*100	−0.45 (0.03)	−0.32 (0.03)	−0.36 (0.02)
Year			
1984			−0.25 (0.07)
1987			−0.13 (0.07)
1990			−0.28 (0.07)
1993			−0.46 (0.07)
1996			−0.60 (0.07)
1999			−0.63 (0.07)
2002			* *
Educational level			
1ab	* *	* *	* *
1c	0.40 (0.07)	0.29 (0.07)	0.36 (0.05)
2a	0.43 (0.14)	0.46 (0.12)	0.33 (0.09)
2bc	0.46 (0.12)	0.24 (0.12)	0.27 (0.08)
3a	0.64 (0.12)	0.53 (0.10)	0.57 (0.07)
3b	0.85 (0.11)	0.61 (0.10)	0.64 (0.07)
Father's occupation			
Unemployed or unknown	−0.15 (0.12)	−0.22 (0.15)	−0.17 (0.09)
Agricultor	−0.02 (0.11)	0.19 (0.11)	0.11 (0.07)
Professional self-employed	0.80 (0.15)	1.29 (0.12)	1.07 (0.09)
Skilled or unskilled self-employed	0.82 (0.08)	0.82 (0.08)	0.82 (0.05)
Professional wage earner	0.42 (0.08)	0.31 (0.08)	0.36 (0.05)
Skilled or unskilled wage earner	* *	* *	* *
Spouse's occupation			
No spouse	* *	* *	* *
Unemployed or unknown	0.51 (0.08)	0.73 (0.08)	0.63 (0.05)
Agricultor	−0.32 (0.51)	0.22 (0.46)	−0.09 (0.32)
Professional self-employed	1.00 (0.19)	1.40 (0.17)	1.27 (0.12)

TABLE 3.5A (*continued*)
Logit Regression Estimates of the Determinants of Entry into Self-Employment

	1984–1987– 1990	*1996–1999– 2002*	*All the period*
Skilled or unskilled self-employed	1.11 *(0.14)*	1.64 *(0.12)*	1.37 *(0.09)*
Professional wage earner	0.17 *(0.10)*	0.52 *(0.09)*	0.35 *(0.06)*
Skilled or unskilled wage earner	−0.04 *(0.09)*	0.27 *(0.09)*	0.13 *(0.06)*
Prior labor market position			
Unemployed	1.62 *(0.10)*	1.59 *(0.10)*	1.63 *(0.07)*
Out of the labour market	0.59 *(0.11)*	0.13 *(0.12)*	0.38 *(0.07)*
Professional	−0.43 *(0.12)*	−0.34 *(0.11)*	−0.31 *(0.07)*
Skilled	0.23 *(0.10)*	0.20 *(0.10)*	0.21 *(0.07)*
Unskilled	* *	* *	* *

Source: Labour Force Surveys, 1984, 1987, 1990, 1993, 1996, 1999, 2002, INSEE.

dle of their careers. The highest probability is between 34 and 38 years old. Earlier and later in life, people are much less likely to enter self-employment. Some labor market experience seems necessary to enter self-employment. Through work experience, workers acquire a better knowledge of their abilities and increase their skill. They may thus feel more confident about taking on the responsibilities of self-employment (Laferrère and McEntee 1995). Age also allows the gathering of the necessary amount of capital (borrowing is possible, but only for those with sufficient collateral to provide security for a loan). Another explanation is that it can take time to find an opportunity to start a business (Evans and Leighton 1989). Conversely, older people may be more reluctant to start a business because their risk aversion is higher than that of younger people.

Generally speaking, there is a strong link between education and the probability of entering self-employment. This reflects the fact that many self-employment occupations require a specific degree (*CAP* for most crafts, tertiary education for most free professions). Interestingly, those with a technical or vocationally oriented degree (1c and 2a) have a greater probability of entering skilled and unskilled self-employment than those without a degree. This suggests that there is a minimum level of education required for entering self-employment. Surprisingly, the level of vocational qualification has no impact on the propensity to enter skilled or unskilled self-employment; differences between possessing only the *baccalauréat* (2a) versus short-course vocational training (1c) are not significant. This suggests that the new vocational tracks provide students not so much with specific skills as with some general knowledge about how to create and run a new business.

The association between educational level and the propensity to enter self-employment is weaker during the 1990s than during the 1980s, for both men and women. This perhaps reflects the fact that the new self-employed activities require skills different from those that one acquires at school (most notably, the "interactive" skills that are necessary in trade and service activities).

Men and women whose fathers were self-employed have a higher probability of entering self-employment, especially skilled and unskilled self-employment. The association is weaker for entries into professional self-employment. It seems that for the latter, a higher degree is a better asset than a self-employment background, while for entries into skilled and unskilled self-employment, having a self-employed father is more efficient than a degree. This is not the only dimension of social background that affects self-employment entry probabilities. Generally speaking, men and women who have a father who worked in professional occupations are more likely to enter self-employment as opposed to agricultural or unskilled occupations. The effect of social background on entry into self-employment has increased over the last twenty years. The increase is particularly strong for the effect of having a professional self-employed father.

PARTNERS AND SUBSIDIES

Those who have a partner have a higher probability than singles of entering self-employment, especially skilled and unskilled self-employment. Among those who have a partner, those who have a working partner have a higher probability of entering self-employment, and the probability is even higher when this partner is also self-employed. The presence of a partner can be helpful in two ways: if she or he is a wage earner, especially if she or he holds an indefinite term-contract, then she or he brings a permanent source of income to the household. In such a case, the partner represents a kind of insurance against the risks of bankruptcy. The partner can also be involved as a family worker or associate. In such a case, the partner does not represent insurance, but cheap or unpaid labor.

The probability of entering self-employment is higher for the unemployed than for those out of the labor market or the dependently employed. It is perhaps the consequence of the main public subsidy for

TABLE 3.5B
Multinomial Logit Regression Estimates of the Determinants of Entry into
Self-Employment

	Professional	Skilled	Unskilled
Intercept	−8.71 *(0.28)*	−7.32 *(0.15)*	−7.52 *(0.21)*
Gender			
Men	0.88 *(0.08)*	1.40 *(0.07)*	0.72 *(0.09)*
Women	* *	* *	* *
Year			
1984	−0.27 *(0.13)*	−0.15 *(0.10)*	−0.38 *(0.14)*
1987	−0.16 *(0.12)*	0.09 *(0.09)*	−0.64 *(0.15)*
1990	−0.42 *(0.13)*	−0.09 *(0.10)*	−0.54 *(0.15)*
1993	−0.37 *(0.12)*	−0.46 *(0.10)*	−0.56 *(0.14)*
1996	−0.69 *(0.13)*	−0.50 *(0.10)*	−0.67 *(0.14)*
1999	−0.64 *(0.12)*	−0.61 *(0.10)*	−0.64 *(0.14)*
2002	0.00 *	0.00 *	0.00 *
Age			
Age simple	0.12 *(0.02)*	0.12 *(0.01)*	0.17 *(0.02)*
Age squared*100	−0.35 *(0.04)*	−0.34 *(0.03)*	0.43 *(0.04)*
Educational level			
1ab	* *	* *	* *
1c	0.04 *(0.13)*	0.50 *(0.06)*	0.23 *(0.10)*
2a	0.68 *(0.18)*	0.39 *(0.12)*	0.20 *(0.20)*
2bc	0.91 *(0.14)*	0.08 *(0.12)*	0.16 *(0.17)*
3a	1.53 *(0.12)*	0.02 *(0.12)*	−0.03 *(0.20*
3b	1.74 *(0.11)*	−0.47 *(0.16)*	−0.54 *(0.25)*
Father's occupation			
Unemployed or unknown	−0.19 *(0.17)*	−0.19 *(0.12)*	−0.15 *(0.18)*
Agricultor	−0.24 *(0.17)*	0.23 *(0.09)*	0.12 *(0.14)*
Professional self-employed	1.07 *(0.13)*	1.05 *(0.15)*	1.07 *(0.22)*
Skilled or unskilled self-employed	0.59 *(0.11)*	0.91 *(0.07)*	0.89 *(0.11)*
Professional wage earner	0.42 *(0.09)*	0.32 *(0.08)*	0.25 *(0.13)*
Skilled or unskilled wage earner	* *	* *	* *
Spouse's occupation			
No spouse	* *	* *	* *
Unemployed or unknown	0.19 *(0.11)*	0.78 *(0.08)*	0.76 *(0.12)*
Agricultor	−0.07 *(0.59)*	−0.12 *(0.51)*	−0.06 *(0.60)*
Professional self-employed	1.52 *(0.15)*	1.05 *(0.24)*	−0.88 *(0.73)*

Table 3.5B (continued)

	Professional	Skilled	Unskilled
Skilled or unskilled self-employed	0.93 (0.19)	1.51 (0.13)	1.49 (0.16)
Professional wage earner	0.33 (0.10)	0.42 (0.10)	0.04 (0.16)
Skilled or unskilled wage earner	0.00 (0.12)	0.30 (0.08)	−0.04 (0.12)
Prior labor market position			
Unemployed	2.34 (0.21)	1.93 (0.10)	1.04 (0.11)
Out of the labour market	1.24 (0.21)	0.61 (0.11)	−0.18 (0.13)
Professional	0.99 (0.20)	−0.60 (0.13)	−1.63 (0.19)
Skilled	0.55 (0.22)	0.69 (0.09)	−0.79 (0.12)
Unskilled	* *	* *	* *

Source: Labour Force Surveys, 1984, 1987, 1990, 1993, 1996, 1999, 2002, INSEE.

starting a new business, the ACCRE, that applies exclusively to the unemployed. There is no equivalent subsidy for those who work or are out of the labor force. For employees, the probability of entering self-employment depends on the occupation and the sector in which they work. Those employed in the low-skilled service sector have a relatively high probability of entering self-employment (estimations not reported). This is doubtless the sector where the differences in required abilities (and assets) between employed and unemployed are the least important.

The Survival Rate in Self-Employment

Exits from self-employment are analyzed for the 1990–2000 period. Figures 3.3 and 3.4 show the three-year nonparametric survival curves. Women fail more quickly than men do. The difference in survival probabilities between men and women is weak, but significantly different from zero. Three years after the beginning of the self-employed activity, 42 percent of men and 46 percent of women have exited self-employment. Our figures are quite close to figures from independent firm surveys. According to the System of Information on New Enterprises (SINE) survey, 41 percent of firms created in 1994 failed before their third birthday, regardless of the gender of the entrepreneur (Lamontagne and Thirion 2000).

For men, there are no significant differences in the survival rates according to skill level (fig. 3.3). In contrast, for women, skilled and professional self-employment are more stable than unskilled self-employment (fig. 3.4).

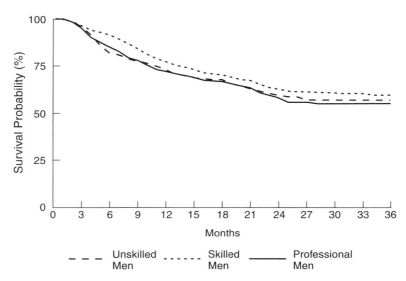

Figure 3.3: Nonparametric Survival Curves of Self-Employment Spells in France

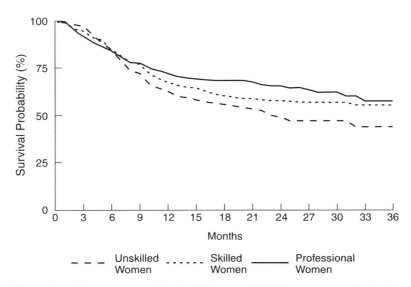

Figure 3.4: Nonparametric Survival Curves of Self-Employment Spells in France

This nonparametric analysis shows that the hazard function is not constant over the first three years of self-employment. Therefore, to get a clearer picture of the determinants of exit from self-employment, we used a Cox semiparametric model (Cox 1972), which is less data-demanding than a nonparametric approach but nevertheless allows hazard functions to vary over time. Table 3.6 shows separate analyses for men, women, and the overall population. In the early 1990s, a period of deep recession, the propensity to exit self-employment in the first three years was higher than in the late 1990s. This confirms that the business cycle does impact the probability of survival.

Furthermore our estimates reveal that, ceteris paribus, there is no net effect of gender on the probability of failure during the first three years in business. The fact that the gross survival rates are smaller for women than for men is only a composition effect. Similarly, the smaller rate of self-employment among women is due only to the smaller propensity to enter self-employment.

The absence of any net effect of gender differs strongly from what is observed in most other Western countries, where men are, ceteris paribus, less likely to exit self-employment than women. This is perhaps due to the fact that women's selection to enter self-employment is stronger in France than in other countries. Men and women are more likely to create a successful business in the middle of their career. The effect of age on the survival rate shows a pronounced peek in the hazard rate between 36 and 39 years old. On a sample of U.S. male business owners, Bates finds similar results: U.S. entrepreneurs between 45 and 54 year old are the most likely to see their own business survive (Bates 1990). The middle of the career is a period when entries are more likely and, for those who enter self-employment, a time when the probability of persistence in self-employment is also higher.

For men, a high level of education (3b) is related to a high survival rate in the first three years. In contrast, for women, postsecondary degree holders are not more likely to survive than dropouts are. Short-course vocational training diplomas (1c) are good assets for success in business, for both men and women.

Social background has little effect on the probability of survival. The probability of three-year survival does not depend on father's occupation. The only significant effect (at the 10 percent level) is that women with a self-employed father survive their first three years in self-employment more often than other women. All in all, there is no clear evidence that the specific human capital transmitted from father to child increases the stability of self-employment. However, the data allow only the analysis of the survival in self-employment during the first three years. It is possible

TABLE 3.6
Cox Model Estimates of the Determinants of Exit from Self-Employment in France

	Total		Male		Female	
	Estimate	Standard error	Estimate	Standard error	Estimate	Standard error
Gender (male omitted)						
Female	−0.08	(0.07)				
Year (1995–2000 omitted)						
1989–1994	0.20	(0.09)	0.37	(0.11)	−0.06	(0.14)
1992–1997	0.06	(0.09)	0.20	(0.11)	−0.20	(0.14)
Age						
Age simple	−0.11	(0.01)	−0.12	(0.02)	−0.09	(0.02)
Age squared*100	0.28	(0.03)	0.32	(0.04)	0.21	(0.05)
Educational level (lab omitted)						
1c	−0.39	(0.08)	−0.43	(0.10)	−0.35	(0.15)
2a	−0.26	(0.15)	−0.23	(0.19)	−0.32	(0.26)
2bc	−0.65	(0.17)	−0.72	(0.22)	−0.57	(0.28)
3a	−0.51	(0.14)	−0.55	(0.19)	−0.34	(0.22)
3b	−0.55	(0.14)	−0.81	(0.18)	−0.13	(0.24)
Self-employed as (unskilled omitted)						
Professional	0.10	(0.11)	0.22	(0.14)	−0.22	(0.19)
Skilled	−0.21	(0.09)	−0.19	(0.12)	−0.21	(0.14)

(continued)

TABLE 3.6 (continued)

	Total		Male		Female	
	Estimate	Standard error	Estimate	Standard error	Estimate	Standard error
Father's occupation (unemployed omitted)						
Agriculture	0.11	(0.19)	0.07	(0.23)	0.20	(0.32)
Professional	0.11	(0.17)	0.02	(0.22)	0.30	(0.30)
Skilled or unskilled	0.02	(0.16)	−0.02	(0.20)	0.10	(0.28)
Father self-employed						
Yes	−0.07	(0.08)	−0.01	(0.11)	−0.27	(0.15)
Partner's occupation (no partner omitted)						
Agriculture	0.38	(0.31)	1.07	(0.51)	0.18	(0.40)
Professional	−0.40	(0.23)	−0.42	(0.24)	−0.42	(0.72)
Family worker	−0.01	(0.10)	−0.04	(0.14)	0.02	(0.16)
Skilled or unskilled	0.14	(0.08)	0.09	(0.10)	0.18	(0.15)
Partner self-employed						
Yes	−0.05	(0.12)	0.01	(0.18)	−0.13	(0.17)
Number of spells	2,800		1,856		944	
% of censored spells	68.6		70.0		65.7	

Source: Labour Force Surveys, 1990–2000, INSEE.

that social background plays very little role during this first three-year period but becomes significant later on.

Traditional skilled self-employment is more stable than the two other types of self-employment. This is probably not due to the type of education or skills that one requires, but rather because self-employment in the construction sector corresponds to more stable activities than self-employment in the service sector.

Those who reported having partners who are family workers are less likely to exit self-employment than those without such partners. Other family characteristics did not have any impact on self-employment stability.

Conclusion

This chapter has described the changes in the skill composition of self-employment over the last two decades and identified the factors responsible for these changes. The first finding is that the secular decline in the share of self-employment that had stopped during the 1980s resumed in the 1990s: in 2002 the number, as well as the share, of self-employed was at a historical low. The second result is that the composition of self-employment changed dramatically over the last two decades: the share of professional self-employment increased by 50 percent, while the share of skilled self-employment—the traditional core of self-employment—lost 12 points. Unskilled self-employment has remained marginal, representing about 15 percent of total self-employment. The increasing complexity of firms' economic and legal environment has been a driving force in the very rapid upskilling of self-employed jobs. The skills of self-employed jobs are now very close to the average.

Regarding entries into and exits from self-employment, three main results can be observed: (1) Being a low-skilled person is becoming less of a handicap to creating a business. Our interpretation is that new firms are more likely to be created in the service sector, which decreases the average skill requirement for entering self-employment. (2) Having a self-employed father is becoming more of an advantage in entering self-employment. finally, (3) we do not find any deep change in the rate of entry into nor exit from self-employment over the last ten to twenty years. The new forms of self-employment are neither more nor less stable than the traditional ones.

APPENDIX 3.1: DATA

This study uses the annual Labor Force Surveys conducted by the National Institute for Statistics and Economics Studies between 1982 and 2002. The surveys take place in March of every year. The 1990 and 1999 surveys were moved to January and the 1982 survey to April because of the population census. The survey sample is representative of the population aged 15 and over. The sampling fraction is on average 1/300. The following standard information is compiled for each respondent: age, gender, nationality, labor-market status (employed, unemployed, out of the labor force), occupation, and educational attainment. The survey also gives information on employment status: self-employed, wage earner, or family worker.

The first advantage of the LFS is that since 1990 it provides information on the monthly labor-market status and employment status for the previous year of the survey. In other words, for each of the twelve months preceding the survey, we know whether the respondent was a wage earner, self-employed, unemployed, a student or in another situation (retired, etc.). We are thus able to identify individuals who were self-employed for at least one month over a twelve-month period.

The second advantage of the LFS is that only one-third of the sample is renewed each year. One can thus track the career of a portion of the sample for three years. The analysis of individual spells of self-employment will be based on the subsample of individuals who respond three times consecutively. Thus, two categories of individuals are excluded from the sample studied: (1) those who have moved to a new address in the second and the third years of the survey, and (2) those who are not joinable or who do not answer the second or the third survey. The sample is thus a partial selection of individuals who could at some point in their life become self-employed. Survival mechanisms are diverse and probably dependent on self-employment occurrence. However, we will neglect this selection issue.

Descriptive analysis of the prevalence of self-employment in the total employed population by gender, age, or educational level will rely on the whole LFS sample, avoiding any selection issues. It will use previous versions of the LFS, conducted between 1982 and 1989. These surveys give almost the same information as the more recent ones, except that they do not provide information on the monthly labor-market status and employment status for the year preceding the survey. For this reason, they cannot be used for the analysis of exit from self-employment.

Self-employed are identified according to their own reports. We also excluded from the self-employed farm workers and family workers, following Müller, Lohmann, and Luber guidelines.

ANALYSIS OF EXITS FROM SELF-EMPLOYMENT

To analyze exit from self-employment, we rely on a specific and representative sample of spells in self-employment. Here we describe the construction of the spells of self-employment sample for the 1998 LFS, the most recent survey that can be used in our analysis. In the 1998 survey, 34,144 individuals aged between 19 and 61 years were interviewed for the first time.[8] A total of 27,905 of them were interviewed a second time in 1999 (81.7 percent), and 22,938 were interviewed a third time in 2000 (67.2 percent). These 22,938 individuals form the basis for the construction of our spells of self-employment sample. They were aged between 18 and 60 in March 1997, the date of the beginning of the observation window. Over the three-year period during which we can follow month by month the career of these individuals, we identified 1,730 spells of self-employment. Among them 1,000 are left-censored, meaning that the self-employment began in March 1997, the first month of observation. To avoid stock sampling bias, we delete these spells from our analysis. This makes a total of 730 spells of self-employment that begin sometime between April 1997 and March 2000. We then cleaned the sample, eliminating spurious observations: inconsistent annual declaration and retrospective declaration, inconsistent seniority in the firm at the date of the survey and retrospective declaration, and so on. This makes a total of 311 usable spells. The skill level of self-employment can be determined for only 272 of these. The 39 spells eliminated are all short spells, of less than eleven months. We also suspect them to be spurious spells of self-employment, due to errors in data capture at the time of the survey. Thus, 272 spells of self-employment can be used in the analysis.

Following the hypothesis that the selection of individuals answering the LFS three times is random, our 272 spells of self-employment should represent around 135,000 effective spells of self-employment beginning sometime between April 1997 and March 1998. The official number of firm creations for 1998 is 250,000 (Cordellier 2000). This figure includes 160,000 creations de novo (*créations pures*), but also 40,000 ongoing firms (*reprises*) and 50,000 boosts (*réactivations*) of firms. According to our sources, these firm creations concerned 135,000 individuals who were not self-employed before.

The same procedure done on the nine LFSs from 1990 to 1998 yields a total sample of 2,800 spells of self-employment; 880 of these end during the observation period, and 1,920 are right-censored (68.6 percent).

ANALYSIS OF ENTRIES INTO SELF-EMPLOYMENT

The analysis of entry into self-employment raises specific difficulties. The potential population at risk is all people who are not self-employed. If we consider the sample of people who have left school and who are not self-employed at the date of the survey, people who have a high seniority out of self-employment are overrepresented. Ideally, one would need to follow a representative sample of individuals who have just left school over their life-course. We do not have any survey of that kind, but the LFS allows us to follow such individuals during their very first three years after leaving school. These analyses give information on transitions into self-employment, which occur at the beginning of the working life. However, self-employment entries do not occur only at the beginning of the career (Tabourin, Debard, and Parent 2001), and analyzing only entries into self-employment over the first three years of the career would give a distorted picture of entries into self-employment in general. To obtain more representative samples for analyzing self-employment entries, we used data drawn from the total samples of the LFSs. Indeed, each LFS contains information on the employment status of each respondent at the date of the survey and one year before (including for the respondents who were not in the LFS sample the previous year). We have used these data to calculate entry rates and to analyze the determinants of entries into self-employment. We concentrated on the 1984, 1987, 1990, 1993, 1995, 1999, and 2002 surveys. With the sample being renewed by one-third each year, we limit that way the cases of individuals who are present twice in our analysis sample. This yields about 630,000 individuals, aged 18 to 60 in the year preceding the survey, who were unemployed, out of the labor force, or employed but not self-employed in that year. We also excluded those who worked as farm and family workers that year.

INDIVIDUAL CHARACTERISTICS

The self-employed are a disparate group. We use a three-class schema to differentiate them. First, we distinguish professional self-employment from nonprofessional self-employment. Professional self-employment includes physicians, chemists, managers of firms with ten employees or more, lawyers, engineers, and all occupations that would be classified in EGP categories I or II.[9] For nonprofessional self-employment, we distinguish among skilled and unskilled self-employment, according to EGP criteria, as well as according to criteria prevalent in the French PCS classification for wage earners. The distinction between skilled and unskilled self-employment is not straightforward in the French context. The French professional code differentiates between craftspeople and shopkeepers (petty bourgeoisie) but even in its most detailed level does not separate skilled from unskilled professions. Table 3.1 shows how we classify self-employed professions.

We used the CASMIN schema to describe qualifications. We defined each class from the French system of education as follows: (1a) no degree at all or *Certificat d'études primaires* (CEP), a primary-school leaving diploma, now abolished; (1b) *Brevet d'Etudes du Premier Cycle* (BEPC) or *Brevet élémentaire* (BE), some lower secondary-school leaving diplomas; (1c) short-course vocational training diplomas, gathering essentially *Certificat d'Aptitude professionnelle* (CAP) and *Brevet d'Enseignement Professionnel* (BEP); (2a) technical and professional *Baccalauréat*, which is the advanced high-school leaving diploma, a prerequisite for admission to almost all postsecondary education; (2b, 2c) general *Baccalauréat*; (3a) postsecondary degrees corresponding to two years of education beyond the *Baccalauréat*, gathering essentially *Brevet de Technicien Supérieur* (BTS), *Diplôme Universitaire Technologique* (DUT), which are vocationally oriented, the first university cycle (DEUG), and social and paramedical degrees; (3b) postsecondary degrees corresponding to strictly more than two years of education beyond the *Baccalauréat*: *Grandes écoles, écoles d'ingénieur*, doctor's degrees, bachelor's degrees, thesis, Ph.D, etc.

The LFS gives two pieces of information about the father's background: whether or not the father was self-employed, and the two-digit PCS coding of the father's occupation, allowing us to distinguish among professional, skilled, and unskilled occupations. A small proportion of the respondents did not report their father's occupation. However, we retained them in our analysis and introduced a dummy variable indicating that father's occupation was unknown.

The labor market situation of the partner and his or her occupation is included in the analyses.[10] The other independent variables are gender, age, and potential job experience. Potential job experience is measured by the number of years between leaving school and the survey date.

NOTES

1. There are at least two other legal statuses for companies, but they represent less than 1 percent of firms: the *association "loi de 1901"* and the *Société Coopérative de Production* (SCOP).

2. Since 1995 it has also applied to jobseekers who have been registered at the ANPE for more than six out of the past eighteen months.

3. The lump sum payment was stopped in 1997. Before 1993 the amount of the lump sum payment had been determined by the worker's previous unemployment insurance contributions (from 5,000 to 90,000 francs until 1983; from 10,000 to 43,000 francs at the end of the 1980s).

4. If we add self-employed who receive wages, 1.8 million workers were self-employed in March 2002, representing 7.5 percent of the total workforce.

5. The addition of self-employed who receive a wage, which is possible over the 1990–2002 period, does not change these trends: the share of self-employment under the wider definition is stable between 1990 and 1994 and decreases regularly from 1995 to 2002.

6. If we include self-employed who earn wages, 10 percent of men were self-employed in 2002, compared with 4.7 percent of women.

7. If we include self-employed who earn wages, father's self-employment status becomes even more important: one quarter of men whose fathers were self-employed (under the wider definition) are themselves self-employed, which corresponds to an odds ratio of 3.7.

8. Thus they were aged between 18 and 60 at the beginning of the observation window.

9. They are also professions that are classified as *cadres, professions intermédiaires,* or *chefs d'entreprise* in the French PCS code (codes beginning with 23, 3, or 4).

10. Our definition of partner includes official spouses and consensual union partners.

REFERENCES

André, V. 1995. L'emploi non salarié dans les pays européens de 1983 à 1994. *Premières Synthèses* 116.

Aucouturier A., R. Cealsi, and C. Charpail. 1996. *Itinéraires du chômeur créateur d'entreprise.* Cahier Travail et Emploi. Paris: La documentation française.

Aucouturier, A. and C. Charpail. 1997. Les créateurs d'entreprises: les chômeurs aidés et les autres. *Premières Synthèses* 35.

Bates, T. 1990. Entrepreneur human capital inputs and small business longevity. *Review of Economics and Statistics* 72:551–59.

Bendick, M., Jr., and M. L. Egan. 1987. Transfer payment diversion for small business development: British and French experience. *Industrial and Labor Relations Review* 40:528–42.

Blanchflower, D. 2000. *Self-employment in OECD countries.* NBER Working Paper 7486. National Bureau of Economic Records.

Chardon, O. 2001. Les transformations de l'emploi non qualifié depuis vingt ans. *Insee Première* 796.

Charpail, C. 1995. L'aide aux chômeurs créateurs ou repreneurs d'entreprise en 1994. *Premières Synthèses* 106.

Commissariat Général du Plan. 1996. *Evaluation des aides à la création d'entreprise.* Commission headed by B. Larrera de Morel. Paris: La documentation française.

Cordellier, C. 2000. Créations et cessations d'entreprises: sous la stabilité, le renouvellement. *Insee Première* 740.

Cox, D. R. 1972. Regression models and life tables. *Journal of the Royal Statistical Society, Series B*, 34:187–202.

DiPrete, T., D. Goux, E. Maurin, and A. Quesnel-Vallée. 2002. Insecure employment relationships in flexible and regulated labor markets: A comparison of distribution and consequences in the United States and France. Paper prepared for the Oxford RC28 meeting.

Estrade, M., and N. Missègue. 2000. Se mettre à son compte et rester indépendant. *Economie et Statistique* 337–38:159–78.

Evans, D. S., and L. S. Leighton. 1989. Some empirical aspects of entrepreneurship. *American Economic Review* 79:519–35.

Givord, P., and E. Maurin. 2001. *Changes in job stability and their causes: An empirical analysis method applied to France, 1982–2000.* Document de travail CREST 2001–07.

INSEE. 1994. *Nomenclature des professions et catégories socioprofessionnelles PCS.* Paris: INSEE.

Laferrère, A. 1998. Devenir travailleur indépendant. *Economie et Statistique* 319–20:13–28.

Laferrère, A., and P. McEntee. 1995. Self-employment and intergenerational transfers of physical and human capital: An empirical analysis of French data. *Economic and Social Review* 27:43–54.

Lamontagne, E., and B. Thirion. 2000. Création d'entreprises: les facteurs de survie. *Insee Première* 703.

Marchand, O. 1998. Salariat et non-salariat dans une perspective historique. *Economie et Statistique* 319–20:3–11.

Tabourin, R., P. Debard, and M. Parent. 2001. Jeune, diplômé et créateur d'entreprise. *Insee Première* 814.

CHAPTER FOUR

Dutch Self-Employment between 1980 and 1997

Boris F. Blumberg and Paul M. de Graaf

BETWEEN 1945 AND THE early 1980s, both the absolute and the relative number of self-employed declined in countries with advanced economies. Since the beginning of the 1980s, this downward trend has turned or at least come to a halt in most of these countries. Figure 4.1 shows the development of the Dutch self-employment rate between 1980 and 1996. Since 1983, the share of self-employed among the working populations has grown continuously, and one can speak of a trend reversal. In this chapter, we will investigate Dutch self-employment between 1980 and 1998 along two lines. Our first line looks at more macro-oriented explanations for the recent trend in self-employment, with attention to differences in self-employment between different industrial sectors and social classes. The second line focuses on the micro level, again with an emphasis on the social background and environment. Our main focus is on analyses of the micro level, investigating determinants of entry into and exit out of self-employment.

The chapter is organized as follows. The following section is subdivided into three subsections. The first provides some explanations for the observed trends in self-employment in the Netherlands. In the second subsection, we discuss the sociological and economic literature on the decision to become self-employed and the role social classes play. The third subsection concentrates on the exit decision and discusses some literature on firm survival. Then we provide descriptive analyses for self-employment in the Netherlands in 1985 and 1997 to illustrate the recent trends in Dutch self-employment. In the following section, we describe the datasets used, and the measurement and operationalization of the relevant variables. Section four presents the analysis and results. To analyze entry and exit we apply event-history models, an appropriate advanced technique for investigating life events such as the decision to become self-employed. We also explain the particularities of the statistical models used. The last section provides conclusions.

Favoring and obstructing environmental conditions and characteristics of the potential founder, such as social background, human capital, and personality traits, explain many self-employment trends. The former focuses on the macro level, while the latter attempts to answer the question of why a person becomes self-employed.

Trend Explanations of Self-Employment

A large number of studies have explained developments and changes in self-employment rates at the macro level. Several studies have found a negative relationship between economic development and the self-employment rate (Blau 1987; Loutfi 1991; Schaffner 1993). In more developed countries, people with entrepreneurial capabilities are more likely to become paid managers, since high real wages increase the opportunity costs of self-employment (Lucas 1978). Iyigun and Owen (1998) argue similarly that less people are willing to incur the risk of self-employment if the returns from paid labor are safe and high.

However, in a comparative study of twenty-three OECD countries and thirty-three less developed countries, Acs, Audretsch, and Evans (1992) report that self-employment rates actually rise with economic development, and they hold the major shift of employment opportunities from the capital-intensive manufacturing sectors to the service sector responsible for this trend reversal. Others (e.g., Piore and Sabel 1984; Jensen 1993) see the last quarter of the twentieth century as a phase of creative destruction à la Schumpeter (1950), caused by globalization and the information revolution. The enormous developments in information and communication have reduced the importance of scale economies in many sectors and have even allowed smaller companies to enter markets dominated by large companies. Furthermore, small firms seem to be better at adapting to changing conditions and implementing new technologies. Jovanovic (1993) argues that advances in information technology reduce market coordination costs to close to the level of coordination costs within a hierarchy, and as a result, firm size and diversification declines. Many firms restructured and concentrated on their core businesses by deinvesting and forming independent entities out of their peripheral business units. Another explanation for this trend reversal emphasizes changing consumer preferences in developed countries. First of all, the demand for services increases with an increasing per capita income. The service sector is in turn characterized by a small average firm size and low entry barriers. Second, higher incomes and the multicultural influences of globalization create individualized and specialized demands, which are better met by many small firms rather than one large firm (Carrol and Hannan 2000). Finally, governments recognized that small firms create the most new jobs and economic growth dynamics. Consequent changes in economic policies, such as more flexible labor laws, lower corporate taxes, and deregulation facilitated the startup of and success chances of new businesses.

Certainly, some of the explanations provided above will have only temporary effects on the self-employment rate. The push for starting up new businesses in deregulated industries will fade, as recent concentration processes (e.g., in the telecommunication sector) already signal. Other explanations, however, point to stable higher levels of self-employment. The information revolution reduced the coordination costs associated with economic transactions and thereby allowed the forming of networks of small and large firms. Further, the more specialized and individualized demand of consumers with high incomes results in a greater diversity of products and services. Consequently, scale economies become less important, and the competitive advantage of larger firms diminishes, allowing smaller firms to operate successfully in these markets.

Why Do People Become Self-Employed?

Many aspects of the macro explanation above refer to specific settings, which facilitate the startup and survival of new businesses. But despite all of these favorable conditions, people who decide to become self-employed are still needed. Therefore, the question "why do people become self-employed" has piqued the interest of many scholars in the social sciences.

Although higher expected earnings are one of the motives for entering self-employment, empirical studies find only weak or no evidence for the hypothesis that the decision to become self-employed is determined by a comparison of the expected lifetime earnings in paid labor and self-employment. For the United Kingdom, Rees and Shah (1986) and Dolton and Makepeace (1990) report that the earnings of self-employed are not significantly different from what they would have earned if they had been in paid labor. De Wit and van Winden (1989) come to the same conclusion in an analysis of Dutch data. Small effects from the earning differential are however reported by Gill (1988) and Taylor (1996). These poor results with respect to the impact of the earning differential are probably caused by uncertainty and bounded rationality (Simon 1957). Individuals will find it hard to recognize and assess all possible business and employment opportunities. Further, the estimation of expected lifetime incomes requires a far-reaching foresight, which amounts to more than forty years for younger people. If individuals are unable to calculate their future earnings, their decision to become self-employed is more likely to depend on an assessment of their current success chances. Those who believe themselves to possess the resources and capabilities to become self-employed successfully will enter self-employment. The others will prefer a paid job, or will rely on unemployment benefits if no job is available.

Penrose (1959) identified four qualities of a successful entrepreneur: ambition, fund-raising ingenuity, versatility, and good judgment. Especially in psychology, researchers have tried to identify personal traits that distinguish the entrepreneur from the employee. Traits that have been investigated include the need for achievement (McClelland 1961), locus of control (Rotter 1966), and risk aversion. However, partly due to research design deficiencies, such as selection bias, ill-defined populations, small samples, and missing control groups, it is not clear whether these traits identify entrepreneurs or successful people in general (see, e.g., Amit, Glosten, and Muller 1993). Furthermore, one can question the direction of the causal relationship, since the difficult start conditions of new businesses may force an entrepreneur to show high levels of achievement (Sandberg 1986).

In sociological as well as economic studies on self-employment, human capital is often used to explain self-employment trends. The general argument for the influence of human capital on entry into self-employment is that higher human capital results in higher productivity, and consequently higher profits and better success chances. General education and years of working experiences are commonly used indicators for human capital. However, different empirical studies sketch an unclear picture of the relationship between such indicators and entry into self-employment. Most studies report nonsignificant effects for education (see, e.g., Carroll and Mosakowski 1987; Taylor 1996; de Wit and van Winden 1989). An exception is Rees and Shah (1986), who find that a higher education increases the chance to become self-employed. With respect to work experience, the picture is even fuzzier. Evans and Leighton (1989) as well as de Wit and van Winden (1989) find a negative relation, while Carroll and Mosakowski report a nonsignificant effect, and Dolton and Makepeace (1990) and Evans and Jovanovic (1989) observe a positive relationship.

There are several reasons for these inconsistent results. First, a higher education and more work experience are partly endogenous with self-employment. The decision to continue schooling or to obtain more work experience postpones the decision to become self-employed. Second, one can doubt whether formal education teaches the skills crucial for successful self-employment. Hence, human capital obtained through education does not necessarily increase one's productivity as an entrepreneur. Third, the self-employed are a rather heterogeneous group. Uncle Tom, who keeps the gardens of our college friend Ernesto, who inherited a manufacturing firm, and our niece Tosca, who started a fast-growing software company after graduating, are all called self-employed. Hence, an analysis of entry into self-employment should account for different class departure points.

The self-employment of one's parents is the factor that is most strongly correlated with entry into self-employment (see, e.g., Blanchflower and Oswald 1998; Blau and Duncan 1967; Carroll and Mosakowski 1987; Luijkx and Ganzeboom 1989; Taylor 1996; de Wit and van Winden 1989), even if one excludes those individuals who took over a family business (Blumberg and Pfann 2001). The strong effect of the parents' employment status points to the issue of intergenerational mobility.

Social class–oriented research on self-employment investigates the intergenerational mobility flows into and out of self-employment (see, e.g., Goldthrope 1980; Hout 1983), as well as the social mobility within an individual's career. Empirical studies show that entry into self-employment is positively related with the father's socioeconomic status (Mayer and Carroll 1987). Two mechanisms explain the movements into self-employment from a social mobility perspective. First, it is intriguing how much larger the chance to become self-employed is for children with self-employed parents. In general, this fact is explained by socialization and the inheritance of capital. Children of the self-employed obtain during their upbringing values and skills that are useful for self-employment. Further, they might get more direct and indirect support when they decide to become self-employed themselves. One can easily imagine that the son of a family that has been employed in the civil service for generations will meet more reluctance from his parents than a daughter of a successful self-made man. On average, the self-employed have an income advantage compared with people in paid labor. For the Netherlands, one can state that this advantage is around 40 percent in the 1980s and 1990s (CBS 1999). Thus, children with self-employed parents are likely to inherit more and are also more able to obtain financial support from their family to start a business. Finally, some of the younger self-employed enter this class by taking over the family business. Given that the survival chances of an established business are much higher than those of a new business (see, e.g., Freeman, Carroll and Hannan 1983; Preisendörfer and Voss 1990), those who take over a family business enter self-employment with much less risk than those who start from scratch.

Self-employment can also be a route to upward mobility. Often people are restrained from moving up the social ladder because they lack the formal educational requirements for better-paid jobs or are confronted with prejudices concerning their social and ethnic origin. For these groups, self-employment provides an opportunity to achieve a higher socioeconomic status. Recent empirical studies that investigate self-employment among ethnic minorities support this argument. Bates (1997) investigates self-employment among immigrants in the United States. He concludes that Korean and Chinese immigrants in particular cannot fully utilize their human and social capital on the labor market and therefore choose self-employment. However, as Fairlie and Meyer (1996) have pointed out, one should recognize that the self-employment rates of ethnic minorities differ considerably, and African Americans, for example, are far less likely to enter self-employment.

Exit from Self-Employment

Understanding the complete dynamics of self-employment requires more than just investigating who chooses self-employment and why. In addition to entry movements, we need to analyze exit movements. Thus, the other question is: who leaves self-employment, and for what reasons? The two most important reasons for leaving self-employment are: (1) the self-employed stop because their businesses are economically not able to survive, or even go bankrupt, and (2) the self-employed find better opportunities on the labor market and switch to paid work.

Most economic and sociological studies investigate exit from self-employment from the firm's perspective, and not from the self-employed individual's perspective. These studies address the survival chances of firms and thereby focus at least implicitly on the first reason for leaving self-employment. Brüderl, Preisendörfer, and Ziegler (1992) use an approach that combines human capital theory and organizational ecology to explain the survival rates of young business firms in Upper Bavaria (Germany). Their main conclusion is that individuals with higher human capital have better survival chances. Thus, the straight argument that high levels of human capital increase productivity and survival chances holds. Additionally, selection effects are present; individuals with higher levels of human capital start larger businesses with higher a priori survival chances (see, e.g., Hannan and Freeman 1989).

SELF-EMPLOYMENT IN THE NETHERLANDS

In the Dutch laws and regulations, definitions for entrepreneur, self-employed, and employee differ largely due to the different objectives specific laws have. For example, the definition for self-employment in social security laws is narrower than in tax regulations. The distinction between self-employed and dependently employed is especially trouble-some for the estimated 100,000 self-employed without personnel, who are predominately active in the sectors of construction, business, and per-sonal services. Statistics Netherlands uses a rather broad definition of self-employed, which includes the self-employed without employees, as well as owner/managers of incorporated and limited companies. Our de-scriptive analyses are based on data from Statistics Netherlands and use their broad definition. The later analyses of self-employment determi-nants make use of the Family Survey Dutch Population, in which the respondents self-reported their employment status, presumably also by applying a rather broad definition of self-employment.

In the Netherlands, the long-term trend of a declining self-employ-ment rate has been reversed as in many other Western countries, such as Belgium, Germany, Ireland, Italy, Spain, and the United Kingdom (Lu-ber and Gangl 1997). In the Netherlands, the nonagricultural self-employment rate started to rise in 1980 but dropped in the late 1980s. Since 1990, the self-employment rate has again increased (see fig. 4.1). However, it must be noted that the trend differs between industrial sec-tors. Table 4.1 gives an overview of the self-employment rates in differ-ent sectors for men and women in 1985 and 1997. Between 1985 and 1997, the overall self-employment rate for men increased from 10.6 per-cent to 12.3 percent, and for women from 4.0 percent to 8.3 percent. The table shows clearly that the increase takes place in specific sectors, while other sectors have retained a declining rate. For men, we observe a sharp increase in self-employment in the sectors of manufacturing, con-struction, transport, education, and other services. The sectors of retail, hotel and restaurants, and health and agriculture show declining male self-employment. For women, we observe a rising self-employment rate between 1985 and 1997 for all sectors except hotels and restaurants. However, the rise is relatively small in the sectors of retail, business ser-vices, and health.

In the Netherlands, more than three hundred different subsidies are offered to foster entrepreneurship. However, it should be noted that the vast majority of these subsidies were implemented in the late 1990s and therefore do not affect most of the self-employment decisions analyzed in this chapter. The Dutch government distinguishes six policy areas that affect entrepreneurship: (1) administrative requirements; (2) tax policy; (3) the Bankruptcy Act; (4) startup costs; (5) governance structure; and (6) infrastructure (Ministry of Economic Affairs 2002). Until 2001, regis-tering a business required a certificate for entrepreneurship. Although this law was not enforced very strictly, as it was common practice to register the business if the business starter promised to obtain the certifi-cate in the future, it can still be considered as a major obstacle to the

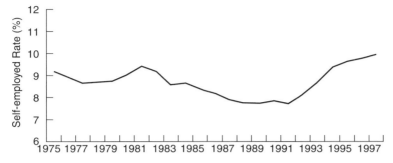

Figure 4.1: Self-Employment Rate between 1975 and 1997 (Excluding Agriculture) in the Netherlands

self-employment of less educated persons. Starting a business also involved other administrative obligations and expenses, depending on the sector. In more regulated sectors, these burdens are considerable. For example, the administrative costs for a starting painter are about € 1,000, and for an electrician around € 3,000 (Zevenbergen 2000). Concerning the nominal and effective corporate tax tariffs (35 percent and 30 percent in 1999), the Netherlands occupies a middle position in Europe. The

TABLE 4.1

Self-Employment Rates by Industrial Sector and Sex in the Netherlands, 1985 and 1997 (in percent)

	1985		1997	
Industrial sector	*Men*	*Women*	*Men*	*Women*
Manufacturing	2.1	1.8	4.1	5.5
Construction	7.1	1.9	13.4	8.3
Retail and wholesale	20.1	6.9	15.9	8.2
Hotels and restaurants	37.5	11.5	18.9	9.8
Transport and communication	3.0	1.5	6.5	2.3
Financial services	4.1	0.8	7.2	1.7
Business services	15.6	8.6	18.7	9.1
Education	2.3	1.0	4.4	3.9
Health	16.7	3.5	12.5	4.1
Other services	3.1	3.3	6.6	12.4
Agriculture	58.9	8.8	56.2	36.1
Total, including agriculture	10.6	4.0	12.3	8.3
Total, excluding agriculture	7.8	3.9	10.5	7.7

Source: Labor Force Surveys Statistics Netherlands, AKT85 and EBB97.

Dutch Bankruptcy Act is rather strict compared with other countries, and the possibility to suspend payments (surséance) does not work well, since 73 percent of such arrangements still end in bankruptcy.

The Netherlands is ahead of even other advanced economies with respect to the usage of information technology. Recent figures show that in the Netherlands there are 201 personal computers per 1,000 inhabitants, as compared to 134 in France or 165 in Germany (UNESCO 1998). The only European country with more personal computers is Switzerland (348 computers per 1,000 inhabitants). The information revolution has led to an increase in self-employment because it creates an additional demand for professional services, which is efficiently done in smaller firms. Furthermore, developments in the information and communication technology reduced coordination costs. Thus, it became viable to outsource business activities that can be easily separated from the core process. Forming independent business entities for such separable activities has the advantage of enhanced monitoring and control through higher financial transparency, and higher flexibility with respect to changes in market demand. For example, the rise in self-employment in financial services can be ascribed to the fact that many banks and insurance companies outsourced the selling of their products to independent intermediaries. These developments have even seeped through to the manufacturing sector. In this sector, the rise in self-employment takes place in those industries related to information and communication technology, while other, more traditional industries, such as metal or food, experience lower levels of self-employment. Higher self-employment rates in the educational sector seem to mirror the growing importance of lifetime learning, and the derived demand for professional training. In sectors where labor costs form a large part of total expenditures (e.g., construction), firms have an incentive to transfer risks and payments associated with social security to their self-employed subcontractors, especially if demand is seasonal, and work disabilities are likely. The changes in the self-employment rates in retail and hotel and restaurants can be ascribed to sector-specific changes in the economic organization of labor and institutions. Vertical or horizontal integration of smaller businesses allows the realization of economies of scale and thereby reduces the self-employment rate. The strong concentration process in retailing is easily visible if one walks down the main shopping streets of any Dutch city. Shops owned by local businesspeople have decreased enormously and been replaced by chain retailers, who realize scale advantages in marketing and procurement. Similar processes can also be observed in the hotel and restaurant sector, where large hotel chains have taken over formerly privately owned hotels, and breweries have expanded by opening pubs and restaurants. Finally, the role of agriculture has diminished in the

TABLE 4.2

Self-Employment Rates by Educational Attainment and Sex in the Netherlands, 1985 and 1997, Excluding Agriculture (in percent)

	1985		1997	
Educational level	*Men*	*Women*	*Men*	*Women*
1ab: elementary	5.8	3.1	9.0	6.6
1c: lower vocational	4.1	3.0	7.0	6.5
2a: intermediate vocational	11.6	4.9	11.4	6.9
2b: intermediate general	5.1	1.6	8.7	5.6
2c: higher general	4.6	1.4	9.3	5.2
3a: higher vocational	5.5	5.1	10.2	8.4
3b: university	11.1	8.6	15.8	10.2

Source: Labor Force Surveys Statistics Netherlands, AKT85 and EBB97.

Dutch economy. Cost-efficient production requires large investments in capital goods, which only large farms can afford. Furthermore, subsidies and legislation from the European Council seem to favor larger farms.

Table 4.2 shows how the Dutch self-employment rates differ between educational levels for men and women in 1985 and 1997. The educational level is ranked according to the CASMIN schema (Müller et al. 1989) applied to the Dutch educational system (de Graaf and Ganzeboom 1993). Overall, it can be stated that self-employment increased across all educational levels for both men and women between 1985 and 1997. As mentioned before, it is unclear to what extent formal education teaches entrepreneurial skills. Therefore, a relationship between educational level and self-employment rates is neither expected nor found. People with a university degree have above-average rates of self-employment. This is certainly partly caused by self-employment in free professions, such as doctors and lawyers, which require a university degree. Furthermore, one could argue that vocational education is likely to provide more practical skills close to the actual tasks done on the job. Yet only individuals with an intermediate vocational education show higher self-employment rates, not people with lower and higher vocational education. However, the narrowing gap between the total self-employment rate and the rate for higher vocational education might indicate that individuals with vocational education are better equipped to enter self-employment.

The concept of social classes as an explanation for entries into and exits out of self-employment plays an important role in this paper. We apply multivariate analyses to elucidate movements into and out of self-employment by looking at the previous social class of the self-employed

TABLE 4.3

Self-Employment Rates by Skill Level and Sex in the Netherlands, 1985 and 1997 (in percent)

Skill level	1985		1997	
	Men	Women	Men	Women
Professionals and managers	8.2	5.8	13.4	10.7
Skilled	9.3	4.5	9.8	4.7
Unskilled	2.5	0.5	4.3	7.0

Source: Labor Force Surveys Statistics Netherlands, AKT85 and EBB97.

and the father's social class. In social class research, the self-employed are usually treated as distinct social classes (Erikson and Goldthorpe 1992). Applying a social mobility perspective to investigate self-employment requires that social classes be defined independently from employment status. Therefore, we use a collapsed schema of three classes: professional/ managerial, skilled, and unskilled. In each of these three classes one can be either dependently employed or self-employed (see below for more details on the definitions of the three classes).

Table 4.3 shows the self-employment rates with respect to social classes in 1985 and 1997. The general rise of the self-employment rate since 1985 is caused by increased self-employment in the professional/ managerial and the unskilled classes. In the unskilled class, the female self-employment rate rose higher than the male rate in 1997. However, in the two other classes, the self-employment rates of men still exceed those of women, and the gap has even increased in the investigated period. A look at the distribution of self-employment (upper panel of table 4.4) over the different classes reveals some interesting shifts. In 1985 most self-employed men and women were self-employed in the skilled class, but in 1997 the dominant class for self-employed people was the professional/managerial class. Comparing the upper and lower panels of table 4.4, which show the class distribution for self-employed and for paid employees, allows us to infer the heterogeneity of self-employment and paid labor. Between 1985 and 1997, the largest class changed from skilled to professional/managerial for people in paid labor as well. Furthermore, we observe that the share of the unskilled class is much larger for paid employees than for self-employed. This finding is in line with the lower self-employment among less educated people and indicates that entering self-employment often requires a minimum level of education and skills.

We complete our sketch of Dutch self-employment with a look at the three most common occupations of self-employed men and women in

Table 4.4
Skill Level by Employment Status and Sex in the Netherlands, 1985 and 1997 (in percent)

	1985		1997	
Skill level	Men	Women	Men	Women
Self-employed				
Professionals and managers	33.5	36.8	55.5	48.6
Skilled	60.9	60.1	38.1	30.5
Unskilled	5.6	3.1	6.4	20.9
Paid employees				
Professionals and managers	31.7	24.2	42.1	31.1
Skilled	49.8	51.9	41.0	47.7
Unskilled	18.6	23.9	16.8	21.2

Source: Labor Force Surveys Statistics Netherlands, AKT85 and EBB97.

the three different social classes for 1985 and 1997. Overall, we observe that in 1997 occupations related to business and personal services, such as insurance and real estate agents, commercial, and care professions enter the top three occupations in all three classes. In the skilled and unskilled class, more traditional professions, such as tailor, hair stylist, and hotel or restaurant owner fall behind. This mirrors the increasing self-employment in all service sectors. In 1997 technicians are the largest occupation in the professional/managerial class, reflecting the rising importance of the information, communication and technology sector, where many small (consulting) firms were founded in the last decade of the twentieth century. Furthermore, construction workers are the most common occupation in the skilled class. For both sexes, medical professions form a large group in the professional/managerial class in 1985 and 1997, and for women this also holds for artists. In the skilled class, male and female shopkeepers belong in both years to the top three occupations. Differences between the sexes can be observed in the unskilled class. In 1985 and in 1997, the most popular male unskilled occupations are drivers and janitors, while female unskilled self-employed have mostly administrative occupations.

Data, Models, and Measurement

We use data from two retrospective life course surveys, the Family Survey Dutch Population 1992 (FSDP92; Ultee and Ganzeboom 1992) and the Family Survey Dutch Population 1998 (FSDP98; De Graaf et al.

2002). The design of the two surveys is similar: primary respondents are a sample of the Dutch population between 21 and 64 years old (FSDP92) or between 18 and 70 years old (FSDP98). Both samples include an over-sample of people living with a spouse, married or unmarried. Primary respondents and their spouses were interviewed with similar (FSDP92) or equal (FSDP98) questionnaires. We use both primary respondents and their spouses as respondents in our analysis, which brings the total number of cases to 3,827 (1,800 in 1992 and 2,027 in 1998).

Respondents and their spouses were interviewed on many aspects of their life course, including their residential, demographic, educational, and occupational careers. This design allows us to study the complete employment careers of the respondents in our two samples, but for comparative purposes we will also present separate analyses on the careers of persons who were between 18 and 60 years old in the period since 1980. In these latter models, we observe twelve years of employment history for respondents interviewed in 1992, and eighteen years of employment history of respondents interviewed in 1998. Given the age distributions of the sample in the survey years, we have a bias toward younger age groups in earlier years. This is especially the case in the analyses for the whole sample, when we extend our analyses to employment histories during the 1960s and 1970s. For this period, we have only observations of people younger than 35–45 years. In addition, we limited our sample to people who do not have an agricultural occupation or who worked in the agricultural industry. In our analysis, we have data on 3,777 respondents who were at risk to enter self-employment; 326 of them entered self-employed at least one time. In the period since 1980, 3,677 respondents were at risk to enter self-employment, 203 of whom experienced a transition to self-employment once or more.

Altogether, we observe 350 entries into self-employment, 177 of which entered into professional/managerial self-employment, 132 into skilled self-employment, and 27 into unskilled self-employment (for 14 cases, there is no valid information on the occupational level of the self-employment). For the period since 1980, these numbers are somewhat lower: 209 total entries into self-employment (118, 76, and 8 transitions, respectively, and 7 missing information on occupational level). Furthermore, we have data on 160 exits from self-employment, of which 105 are observed in the period since 1980.

We use discrete event history analysis (Allison 1984; Yamaguchi 1991) to estimate competing risk models of determinants of entry into self-employment and exit from self-unemployment. Discrete time models allow the use of covariates that change over time, are flexible in the type of duration dependency, and require a data matrix, which is easy to construct (i.e., a person-period file). We have constructed a person-year file, in which for all respondents the variables are observed for every observed year (i.e., the situation on January). Logistic regression models can be used to estimate the effects on entry into self-employment and exit from self-employment. We present three models:

1. A simple logistic regression model in which the dependent variable is the entry into self-employment. At risk are both those who were employed and those without jobs. This last group includes unemployed and disabled persons, persons in education, and housewives. Data limitations prevent these groups from being distinguished in the analysis.
2. A multinomial logistic regression model in which the entry into self-employment is divided in two categories: professional/managerial and skilled occupation. Lacking data prevent transitions to self-employed in unskilled jobs from being analyzed. These events will be treated as censored cases in the analysis. This is a competing risk model in which the third category (no entry into self-employment) is the reference category. The risk group is the same as in the first model.
3. A simple logistic regression model in which the dependent variable is exit out of self-employment. At risk are people in self-employed jobs in the year preceding the event.

Determinants of entry into self-employment and exit from self-employment are:

Age and age squared	Age is transformed into (age-18). Age is a time-dependent covariate.
Survey 1998	A dummy variable with 0 = FSDP92 and 1 = FSDP98.
Sex	A dummy variable with 0 = female and 1 = male.
Education	A set of three dummy variables: low education (CASMIN 1abc), medium education (CASMIN 2abc), and high education (CASMIN 3ab). The reference group is low education.
Origin status	A set of four time-dependent dummy variables: an employed job in EGP class I or II (labeled professionals/managers), an employed job in EGP class IIIa, IV, V, VI, or VIIa (labeled skilled work), an employed job in EGP class IIIb or VIIb (labeled unskilled work), or no job (Erikson and Goldthorpe 1992). The group "no job" includes persons who are out of the labor market (more than 95 percent) and persons who are unemployed. The reference group is the unskilled class.

Industry	The industrial sectors are coded in five groups: mining/manufacturing, construction, traditional services (including hotels and trade), business services (including finance, transport, communication), and other services. Mining/manufacturing is the reference category.
Spouse information	We have complete information on the labor market history of the current spouse (married or unmarried). We do not have information on previous spouses. A set of four time-dependent dummies is created: spouse has no job, spouse is employed, spouse is self-employed, and no spouse information. The category "no spouse information" includes episodes of respondents who are single (largest group) and respondents who entered self-employment while living with a former spouse. The reference group is "spouse has no job."
Father's class	Father's class has the same categories as the respondent's.
Origin status	Professionals/managers, skilled work, and unskilled work based on the EGP class scheme. Father's class is based on the occupational title of the job he had at respondent's age 15. Unskilled work is the reference category.
Father's self-employment	An indicator whether the respondent's father was self-employed or not at respondent's age 15.
Unemployment rate	Before the 1970s the percentage of the labor force population unemployed in the Netherlands was less than 2 percent, but in the 1970s it increased to double-digit figures. The unemployment rate decreased from 13.2 to 6.0 percent between 1980 and 1998.
Solo self-employment	One additional variable in the analysis of transition out of self-employment will be an indicator of solo self-employment. The self-employed with employees have value 0; those without have value 1.
Personality	One of the two surveys (FSDP98) includes information on the big five personality traits: extraversion, agreeableness, conscientiousness, emotional stability, and openness or creativity (Eysenck 1947). These personality dimensions are self-assessed by the respondents (five items for each dimension, according to the procedure developed by Gerris [1998]).

Although the data include information on previous self-employment or previous unemployment, effects of these interesting aspects of the work career could not be included in the analysis due to very small numbers of individuals who reported such previous events. The person-period file is constructed on a yearly base and gives the variables on January first of each year. In the models, some variables are lagged one year, ensuring the correct time order of independent variables and transitions. These lagged variables are age, origin status, industry, and spouse information.

Analysis and Results

In this section we first analyze entry into self-employment, and then exit from self-employment, with event history models. The analysis of both movements is organized as follows. First, we inspect the Kaplan-Meier survival functions, and then we proceed with an event history analysis of entries and exits, which includes covariates on the characteristics of the respondent, the respondent's social background, environment and industries. Then we extend these models with an indicator for the macroeconomic conditions (i.e., the national unemployment rate and the psychological characteristics of the respondents). Finally, we conduct a competing risk event-history analysis for entries into the three distinct categories of self-employment.

Entry into Self-Employment

In the following analyses we estimate the time it takes to become self-employed. The estimation of this time requires the definition of a starting and an end point. The end point is naturally when someone becomes self-employed. The starting point is defined by the first time a person becomes at risk (i.e., could become self-employed). Our starting point is the end of education. All people who have a paid job, are unemployed, or are out of the labor force are at risk. Persons who are still in education and switch directly from being in education to self-employment are not considered in the analysis. First, we inspected the Kaplan-Meier survival function for all entries into self-employment. The relative number of entries into self-employment is rather constant for the first twenty-five years of the labor market career, and only in the last third of a career do movements into self-employment occur less frequently.

Table 4.5 shows the results of an event-history analysis for entries into self-employment. In the first model, only the 209 entries between 1980 and 1998 are considered. In the second model, entries prior to 1980 are also included. The number of entries thus increases to 350. We include

TABLE 4.5
Effects on Entry into Self-Employment in the Netherlands[a]

	Entries since 1980	All entries
Respondent's characteristics		
Male	0.313~	0.428**
Age	0.163**	0.133**
Age (squared)	−0.005**	−0.004**
Education: medium[b]	0.592**	0.509**
Education: high[b]	0.816**	0.656**
Origin: professional manager[c]	0.087	−0.203
Origin: skilled[c]	0.101	−0.067
Origin: unemployed/not in labor force[c]	−0.541*	−0.538*
Social background and environment		
Father professional/manager[d]	0.352~	0.428**
Father skilled[d]	0.167	0.049
Father self-employed	0.304*	0.544**
Spouse: employed in paid labor[e]	0.261	0.218
Spouse: self-employed[e]	1.027*	1.148**
No Spouse[e]	0.505~	0.342*
Industrial sector		
Construction[f]	0.886*	0.836**
Traditional services[f]	0.932**	1.062**
Business services[f]	−0.459	0.023
Other services[f]	−0.396	−0.185
Business cycle		
Unemployment rate	−0.037	−0.005
Control variable		
Survey 1998	−0.139	−0.459**
Intercept	−7.673**	−7.361**
Number of events	209	350
Number of cases (persons * years)	50,239	85,059
−2 Log Likelihood	2,586	4,339
Chi^2	122.6	205.1
Degrees of freedom[g]	25	25

Source: Family Survey Dutch Population, 1992/93 and 1998.
[a] Logistic regression; reference category is no entry into self-employment
[b] Reference category: low education
[c] Reference category: unskilled
[d] Reference category: unskilled
[e] Reference category: spouse no job
[f] Reference category: manufacturing industry
[g] The effects of indicator variables representing a missing value on respondent's education, skill level, father's skill level and self-employment, and industrial sector are included in the model but are not reported.
** $p < 0.01$ * $p < 0.05$ ~ $p < 0.10$

the second model to check whether the effects found for entries between 1980 and 1998 are stable. This is necessary since the number of observed entries (209) is rather small given the number of effects to be estimated. Although some coefficients change in magnitude, the overall picture does not differ for all entries and entries since 1980.

What determines entry into self-employment? First of all, males are more likely to enter self-employment. The significant coefficients of age and age squared indicate a ∩-shaped relationship between age and the chance to become self-employed. This result reflects the age dependency of an individual's productivity. On the one hand, productivity rises with the experience an individual acquires over time. On the other hand, productivity decreases with age because a person's physical capabilities deteriorate over time. Given that higher productivity increases the success chances of self-employment and thereby also the chance that someone will become self-employed, entry into self-employment becomes age dependent.

With respect to the educational level of the respondent, we find that the chance to enter self-employment is significantly larger for high and medium educational levels. This finding corresponds neither with findings in previous studies, which report no effect (see, e.g., de Wit and van Winden 1989; Dolton and Makepeace 1990; Taylor 1996), nor with the self-employments across educational levels as shown in table 4.2. An explanation for this result might be that we collapsed the CASMIN educational categories into three major categories. The coefficients for the educational dummies used show only that self-employment is more likely in the two upper levels compared with the low educational level. A finer distinction of educational levels would likely result in a much less obvious relation between education and self-employment.

The skill level of the previous occupation has no impact on the self-employment decision. Only people who are currently out of the labor force or are unemployed have a significantly lower chance of becoming self-employed. The relation between social class and entry into self-employment is ambiguous. On the one hand, higher-skilled people are more productive, and therefore more likely to succeed in self-employment because they can generate higher profits. Thus, one might expect that skill level is positively related to self-employment. On the other hand, higher-skilled people usually already occupy well-paid jobs, which often include the supervision of others. Employees supervising others have to start firms with employees to remain in the highest social class and therefore not only face higher startup costs, but also higher opportunity costs in terms of income and control losses. Thus, highly skilled people are less likely to become self-employed.

With respect to social background and environment, we look at the respondent's father and spouse (if present). The coefficients of the father's status variables clearly show that the chance of becoming self-employed is positively related to the father's social class. People with a father who has been a professional or manager have significantly higher chances to enter self-employment. Whether the father himself has been self-employed has a positive significant effect, but this effect is smaller and less significant for entries since 1980 than for all entries. Surprisingly, in our study, the effect of father's self-employment is not as strong as in many previous studies (see, e.g., Blanchflower and Oswald 1998; Carroll and Mosakowski 1987; Lindh and Ohlsson 1996; Taylor 1996; de Wit and van Winden 1989). We estimated an additional model in which father's social class is not included. In this model the effect of father's self-employment is not significant, and even less than the effect in the model with controls for father's social class. The less significant coefficient for entries since 1980 suggests that in the Netherlands, the impact of father's self-employment has decreased due to changes in the social and economic structure (deregulation and growing importance of service sector). Apparently, becoming self-employed is facilitated by entrepreneurial values and attitudes transferred from a self-employed father, but it is facilitated even more by the higher levels of general human capital and wealth in the higher classes. The coefficients of the spouse effects indicate that not having a spouse, or having a self-employed spouse, significantly increases the chance to become self-employed. However, people who have a spouse with a paid job are not more likely to enter self-employment than people with a nonworking spouse. Thus, an additional secure income source from the spouse does not compensate for the higher income uncertainty of self-employment. The positive coefficients of the variables "spouse: self-employed" and "no spouse" point to other factors than the financial effect of the spouse. Self-employed without a spouse have in general fewer responsibilities, because they do not have to care for other dependent family members. Given the lower level of responsibility, they are better able to incur the risks of becoming self-employed. For self-employed spouses, we cannot distinguish whether the spouse has a separate business or is a partner in the respondent's business. Still, in both cases, a self-employed spouse is likely to support self-employment through shared values and attitudes.

We included four dummies for the previous industry of the respondent and used the manufacturing sector as a reference category. Thus, our industry dummies control for industry-specific experiences that influence one's possibility of becoming self-employed. For both samples, the coefficients of the variables of construction and traditional services are positive and significant, while the coefficients for business and other services are negative, but not significant. The positive effect of the construction variable supports the notion that in the last two decades the economic organization of labor has changed in the construction industry, and construction employees have become increasingly self-employed. Employers in construction have shifted the risks associated with demand fluctuations and work disabilities to (solo) self-employed subcontractors. Limited promotion possibilities in the traditional service sector, and especially within restaurants and small shops, explain the positive coefficient for this sector. Finally, we included a control variable for the survey year, which is negative and significant for the sample with all entries. Thus, based on all entries, respondents of the 1998 survey are less likely to become self-employed. This significant coefficient is not caused by an age-related bias of our samples and may stem from problems with regard to measurement comparability.

The models of table 4.5 also include the general unemployment rate as a predictor of entry into self-employment, to account for the macro-economic situation. The coefficient of the unemployment rate is not significant at all. This is not unexpected, since this effect is not very clear theoretically. On the one hand, a favorable economic climate might facilitate self-employment because firms realize higher profits more easily, and more opportunities for new businesses arise. On the other hand, the opportunity costs for self-employment rise as well, because in a booming economy, demand for labor increases, and consequently the offered wages and salaries rise.

In table 4.6 we distinguish two kinds of entry into self-employment: entry into self-employment in a professional or managerial occupation and in a skilled occupation. Due to the very few entries into unskilled self-employment (only twenty since 1980, and only forty-seven for all entries), it is not possible to estimate a model distinguishing all three kinds of entries. Applying a competing risk event-history model sheds some light on intergenerational and interpersonal patterns of social mobility. In the discussion of the results, we will focus on the effects of education, class of the respondent's occupation prior to self-employment, and father's class. We will also highlight differences between the two kinds of self-employment entry.

As reported in the previous analysis, education is related to entry into self-employment. People with an intermediate educational level are much more likely to enter skilled and professional self-employment. Furthermore, individuals who have obtained higher education choose self-employment in occupations of the professional class. None of the effects of the class associated with the previous occupation are significant, and all point in different directions. Thus, by and large, entry into self-employment in distinct classes is not influenced by the previous occupation and class. The mostly nonsignificant negative effects of the variable "ori-

TABLE 4.6
Effects on Entry into Professional/Managerial and Skilled Self-Employment in
the Netherlands

	Entries since 1980		All entries	
	Professional/ managerial	Skilled	Professional/ managerial	Skilled
Respondent's characteristics				
Male	0.494*	0.078	0.666**	0.205
Age	0.160**	0.201**	0.136**	0.191**
Age (squared)	−0.005**	−0.006**	−0.004**	−0.006
Education: medium[a]	0.588~	0.712*	0.631**	0.664**
Education: high[a]	1.483**	−0.156	1.387**	−0.084
Origin: professional manager[b]	0.342	−0.551	−0.093	−0.290
Origin: skilled[b]	0.161	0.034	−0.207	0.473
Origin: unemployed/ not in labor force[b]	−0.344	−0.826~	−0.434	−0.455
Social background and environment				
Father professional/ manager[c]	0.261	0.742~	0.541*	0.465~
Father skilled[c]	−0.272	1.137**	−0.237	0.651**
Father self-employed	0.225	0.428~	0.515**	0.484**
Spouse: employed in paid labor[d]	0.369	−0.056	0.370	−0.136
Spouse: self-employed[d]	0.144	1.430*	0.804~	1.087*
No spouse[d]	0.582~	0.352	0.350	0.348
Industrial sector				
Construction[e]	0.744	1.251*	0.226	1.812**
Traditional services[e]	0.809*	1.137*	0.797**	1.765**
Business services[e]	−0.458	−0.516	−0.220	0.367
Other services[e]	−0.755*	0.150	−0.697*	0.833~
Business cycle				
Unemployment rate	−0.067	−0.023	−0.005	−0.013
Control variable				
Survey 1998	−0.030	−0.300	−0.185	−0.696**
Intercept	−8.288**	−9.139**	−8.482**	−9.374**
Number of events	118	76	177	132
Number of cases (persons * years)	50,231		85,032	

Table 4.6 (continued)

	Entries since 1980		All entries	
	Professional/ managerial	Skilled	Professional/ managerial	Skilled
−2 Log Likelihood	2,763		4,156	
Chi^2	196.7		302.7	
Degrees of freedom[f]	50		50	

Source: Family Survey Dutch Population, 1992/93 and 1998.
[a] Reference category: low education
[b] Reference category: unskilled
[c] Reference category: unskilled
[d] Reference category: spouse no job
[e] Reference category: manufacturing industry
[f] The effects of indicator variables representing a missing value on respondent's education, skill level, father's skill level and self-employment, and industrial sector are included in the model but are not reported.
** $p < 0.01$ * $p < 0.05$ ~ $p < 0.10$

gin: unemployed / not in labor force" support the notion that people are not forced into self-employment because they would otherwise not be able to make a living. While the social class of the previous occupation does not restrict entry into self-employment, intergenerational mobility does play a role. Entry into self-employment is most likely to occur in the same class as the father's occupation. Respondents with a father in the skilled class are likely to enter skilled self-employment, and less likely to enter the professional class. Respondents with a father working in the class of professionals and managers have a significantly higher chance of entering self-employment in the professional class, but also in the skilled class.

With respect to the other variables, some differences between entry into skilled and professional self-employment come to light. In the overall analysis of entry into self-employment, we observed a significant positive effect of a self-employed spouse. Distinguishing two kinds of self-employment reveals that this effect is significant only for entry into skilled self-employment. Thus, individuals who enter skilled self-employment profit more from a self-employed spouse. The coefficient for the construction sector is also significant only for skilled self-employment. Apparently, people who had a paid job in construction predominantly became self-employed in the skilled class. This is further evidence for our thesis that the increased self-employment in construction is caused by structural changes in the construction industry, where former construction employees become self-employed subcontractors. Finally, we observe that previous employment in other services slightly increases the chance of becoming self-employed in the skilled class but decreases the chance of becoming self-employed in the professional class. The composition of the sector is very heterogeneous (including government organizations as well as personal services, such as cleaning and hairdressing) and impedes a strong interpretation of the coefficients.

Exit from Self-Employment

Figure 4.2 shows Kaplan-Meier survival functions for exits from self-employment during the first ten years of self-employment, separately for exits from professional/managerial self-employment and for exits from skilled self-employment. There are too few exits from unskilled self-employment in the data to include them in this figure. The figure shows slight differences between exits from professional/managerial and exits from skilled self-employment spells, and it shows that most exits occur in the first few years. After ten years, about 30 percent of the self-employed in our retrospective life-course dataset have left self-employment. This is a low figure when compared with estimates from prospective panels, and it might be the result of underreporting of short self-employment spells or short episodes between two self-employment spells.

Now we turn to movements out of self-employment. The first model in table 4.7 shows the results for exits of those who entered self-employment between 1980 and 1998; the second model, for all observed exits. A glance at the table shows that exits from self-employment are less well explained by our determinants on the micro level than entries to self-employment. In the first model, no coefficients are significant, with the exception of age effects. Therefore, the following discussion focuses on the model for all entries. The effects of the age variables show a U-shaped relationship between age and exit. Experience accumulated over one's lifetime reduces the failure chances of new businesses. The significant positive effect of the quadratic term can be ascribed to the elderly who exit the labor force and retire early. Furthermore, we observe that people who are self-employed without having employees are more likely to leave self-employment. This result coincides with results from firm survival studies, which find a positive relationship between firm size and survival. The educational level and the skill level of the self-employed have no effects on exit.

With respect to a respondent's social background, only father's self-employment is negatively related to exit. The intergenerational transfer of entrepreneurial skills from the father to his offspring furnishes the self-employed with abilities that facilitate survival in self-employment. We have seen that father's social class is positively related to entry, but

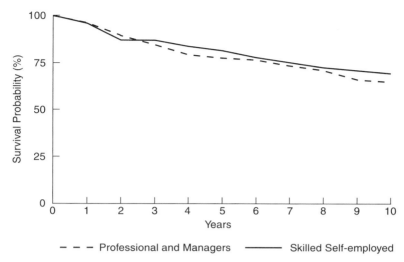

Figure 4.2: Kaplan-Meier Function for Survival in Self-Employment, for Professionals/Managers and for Skilled Self-Employed in the Netherlands

we now observe that it has no effect on exit. This suggests that the financial capital of fathers in the professional class is more important than their human or social capital. Wealthy fathers can support entry into self-employment by providing necessary starting capital but are unable or unlikely to sponsor an unprofitable business permanently. If the human and social capital acquired from a father in a higher class facilitated self-employment, one would expect a lasting effect of these forms of capital, and consequently negative effects on exit. Analogous to the entry analysis, only a self-employed spouse has an effect in our exit analysis.

None of the industry dummies is significant, although the dummy for the traditional service industry is on the edge of significance ($p = 0.120$). In the descriptive section on self-employment in the Netherlands, we illustrated the changes in self-employment in different sectors. These dynamics in self-employment are caused mainly by increased entries into specific sectors, and less by exits. It should be noted that agricultural self-employment is not considered in the current analysis. Macroeconomic conditions did not have an influence on the entry decision but do influence exit, at least when all entries (before and after 1980) are analyzed simultaneously. In unfavorable economic conditions (i.e., a high unemployment rate), more self-employed are forced to give up. These findings suggest that exit is not necessarily an autonomous decision of the self-employed, but that market forces urge people to leave self-employment.

TABLE 4.7
Effects on Exit from Self-Employment in the Netherlands

	Exits since 1980	All exits
Respondent's characteristics		
Male	−0.322	−0.180~
Age	−0.128**	−0.130**
Age (squared)	0.002*	0.002**
Education: medium[a]	−0.345	−0.264
Education: high[a]	−0.049	−0.020
Origin: professional manager[b]	0.122	−0.016
Origin: skilled[b]	−0.028	−0.204
Origin: solo self-employment	0.111	0.354~
Social background and environment		
Father professional/manager[c]	0.419	0.120
Father skilled[c]	0.363	0.141
Father self-employed	−0.260	−0.327~
Spouse: employed in paid labor[d]	−0.357	−0.338
Spouse: self-employed[d]	−0.791	−0.214
No spouse[d]	0.029	0.074
Industrial sector		
Construction[e]	−0.705	−0.261
Traditional services[e]	0.489	0.517
Business services[e]	−0.227	−0.217
Other services[e]	−0.032	0.240
Business cycle		
Unemployment rate	0.014	0.049~
Control variable		
Survey 1998	−0.279	−0.266
Intercept	−1.498	−1.943**
Number of events	105	160
Number of cases (persons * years)	2,170	3,357
−2 Log Likelihood	797	1,217
Chi^2	44.0	69.0
Degrees of freedom[f]	26	26

Source: Family Survey Dutch Population 1992/93 and 1998

[a] Reference category: low education

[b] Reference category: unskilled

[c] Reference category: unskilled

[d] Reference category: spouse no job

[e] Reference category: manufacturing industry

[f] The effects of indicator variables representing a missing value on respondent's education, skill level, father's skill level and self-employment, industrial sector, and solo self-employment are included in the model but are not reported.

** $p < 0.01$ * $p < 0.05$ ~ $p < 0.10$.

The Effects of Personality on Entry and Exit

The survey in 1998 included information on the so-called big-five personality traits (Digman 1990) of the respondent. In psychological research, it has been suggested that entrepreneurship is related to specific personal characteristics, such as need for achievement, locus of control and risk attitude. However, it should be noted that empirical evidence on the relationship between personality traits and entrepreneurship is weak and inconsistent (Miner 1997). In table 4.8 we present the effects of these big-five personality traits on self-employment entry and exit. These effects stem from models in which all predictor variables of the previous models are included. Interestingly, the variable for openness and creativity and the variable for conscientiousness have significant effects on the chance of becoming self-employed. The positive effect of openness and creativity is in line with the well-known description of Schumpeter's entrepreneur. According to Schumpeter (1950), an entrepreneur is an innovator and creator whose activities initiate and cause dynamics in an economy. The negative coefficient of conscientiousness indicates that precision and carefulness are personal characteristics not conducive to self-employment. This finding suggests that people who quickly decide on the basis of some rough information are more likely to become self-employed. We do not find any effects of personality on exit from self-employment.

TABLE 4.8
Effects of Personality Traits on Entry into and Exit from Self-Employment in the Netherlands[a]

Personality trait	All entries	All exits
Extraversion	0.135	0.029
Agreeableness	−0.176	−0.273
Conscientiousness	−0.284**	−0.031
Stability	0.060	−0.015
Openness	0.382**	−0.010
Number of events	158	59
Number of cases (persons * years)	45,323	1,318
−2 Log Likelihood	1984	450
Chi^2	119.5	32.3
Degrees of freedom[b]	29	28

Source: Family Survey Dutch Population, 1998
[a] All effects from tables 4.5 and 4.7 are included in the models.
[b] Degrees of freedom are not consistent due to empty missing value indicators.
** $p < 0.01$ * $p < 0.05$

Conclusions

The landscape self-employment in the Netherlands has changed over the last two decades. Since 1990, overall self-employment has risen from a low point of 8 percent to the current rate of 10 percent, but we can observe considerable differences. Sectors that have known traditionally high rates of self-employment (retail, hotels, and restaurants) show declining rates of self-employment and are outrun in absolute and relative numbers by the sectors of business services and construction for both genders, and the sector of other services for women. Thus, the general shift from an industrial economy to a service economy is also reflected in Dutch self-employment. Self-employment in distinct social classes has been the focus of this paper. Such a distinction among the self-employed reveals some interesting results. While self-employment among male and female skilled people has remained rather constant between 1985 and 1997, self-employment rose considerably among unskilled as well as professional/managerial people in this period. Although a deeper investigation of this polarization is beyond the scope of this paper, it is clear that the parallels of this result and recent discussions about the shifting of risks from the society back to the individual are deceptive. At the upper end of the societal ladder, those who possess the necessary resources to bear additional risks are willing to take them, and have the chance to achieve higher profits. Further down this ladder, unskilled people—especially women—might have to bear risks such as no social security and no payment during sickness, because the regular labor market has no job openings for these kinds of work.

In this study we investigated self-employment in the Netherlands between 1980 and 1998 on a micro level. We considered in particular social mobility issues, which have been neglected by other studies on entry into self-employment in the Netherlands (de Wit and van Winden 1989; Blumberg and Pfann 2001). Our results show that the impact of social background differs if the self-employment of different social classes is distinguished. As is known from general stratification studies, intergenerational mobility is also an issue among the self-employed. Self-employment is most likely to occur in the same class the father belongs to. Our analysis shows clearly that self-employment is not a route for upward social mobility. Contrarily, we observe that self-employment in the skilled class is often entered by people with a father in the professional class. Furthermore, we find evidence that a self-employed father increases the chance of entering self-employment, although this effect is less apparent for entries since 1980. Entering self-employment also does not promote improving one's class position with respect to one's previous job. Overall, we do not find any relation between class of previous job and class of self-employment. However, when we look at the effects of education, we find that people with a medium educational level have increased chances to enter skilled and professional/managerial self-employment. This finding suggests that self-employment allows those individuals to exploit valuable capabilities that are not honored or recognized by the educational system or the paid labor market. People who obtain higher education usually enter professional/managerial self-employment and are less likely to enter skilled self-employment.

We were much better able to explain entry into self-employment than exit. Exit from self-employment seems to be less determined by the considered characteristics of a self-employed individual. The significant effects of solo self-employment and the national unemployment rate in our exit analysis suggest that factors related to the firm and the macroeconomic environment are more relevant determinants of exit. This also suggests that the invisible hand of the market mechanism is able to sort out unsuccessful business owners, but not to detect promising entrepreneurs. However, it should be noted that we were not able to distinguish voluntary exits (e.g., selling of the firm or switching to better opportunity in the paid labor market) and forced exits (e.g., unprofitable business or even bankruptcy). One would expect voluntary exits to be more related to the characteristics of the respondent, and forced exits to the characteristics of the firm and macroeconomic conditions.

REFERENCES

Acs, Z. J., D. B. Audretsch, and D. S. Evans. 1992. *The determinants of variations in self-employment rates across countries over time*. Discussion Paper FS IV 92-3. Berlin: Wissenschaftszentrum für Sozialforschung.

Aldrich, H., and R. Waldinger. 1990. Ethnicity and entrepreneurship. *Annual Review of Sociology* 16:111–35.

Allison, P. 1984. *Event history analysis: Regression for longitudinal regression analysis*. Beverly Hills: Sage.

Amit, R., L. Glosten, and E. Muller. 1993. Challenges to theory development in entrepreneurship research. *Journal of Management Studies* 30:815–34.

Bates, T. 1997. *Race, self-employment and upward mobility*. Baltimore: Johns Hopkins University Press.

Blanchflower, D. G., and A. J. Oswald. 1998. What makes an entrepreneur? *Journal of Labor Economics* 16:26–60.

Blau, D. M. 1987. A time series analysis of self-employment. *Journal of Political Economy* 95:445–67.

Blau, P. M., and O. D. Duncan. 1967. *The American occupational structure*. New York: Wiley.

Blumberg, B. F., and G. A. Pfann. 2001. *Social capital and uncertainty reduction for self-employment.* IZA Discussion Paper Nr. 303. Bonn: Institute for Labor Studies.

Borjas, G. J. 1987. Self-selection and the earnings of immigrants. *American Economic Review* 77:531–53.

Brüderl, J., P. Preisendörfer, and R. Ziegler. 1992. Survival chances of newly founded business organizations. *American Sociological Review* 57:227–42.

Carroll, G. R., and M. T. Hannan. 2000. *The demography of corporations and industries.* Princeton: Princeton University Press.

Carroll, G. R., and E. Mosakowski. 1987. The career dynamics of self-employed. *Administrative Science Quarterly* 32:570–89.

CBS [Statistics Netherlands]. 1999. *Tijdreeksen arbeid en sociale zekerheid* [Time series labor and social security]. Voorburg: CBS.

de Graaf, N. D., P. M. de Graaf, G. Kraaykamp, and W. Ultee. 2002. *Codebook Family Survey Dutch Population 1998.* ICS Codebook 54. Nijmegen: University of Nijmegen, Department of Sociology.

———. 2003. *Family Survey Dutch Population 1998.* ICS Codebook 55. Nijmegen: University of Nijmegen: Department of Sociology.

de Graaf, P. M., and H. Ganzeboom. 1993. Family background and educational attainment in the Netherlands of birth cohorts 1891–1960. In *Persistent inequality: Changing educational attainment in thirteen countries,* ed. Y. Shavit and H. P. Blossfeld, 75–99. Boulder: Westview Press.

de Wit, G., and F. A. van Winden. 1989. An empirical analysis of self-employment in the Netherlands. *Small Business Economics* 1:263–72.

Digman, J. M. 1990. Personality structure: Emergence of the five factor model. *Annual Review of Psychology* 41:417–40.

Dolton, P. J., and G. H. Makepeace. 1990. Self-employment among graduates. *Bulletin of Economic Research* 42:35–53.

Erikson, R., and J. C. Goldthorpe. 1992. *The constant flux: A study of class mobility in industrial societies.* Oxford: Clarendon Press.

Evans, D. S., and B. Jovanovic. 1989. An estimated model of entrepreneurial choice under liquidity constraints. *Journal of Political Economy* 97:808–27.

Evans, D. S., and L. S. Leighton. 1989. Some empirical aspects of entrepreneurship. *American Economic Review* 79:519–35.

Eysenck, H. J. 1947. *Dimensions of personality.* London: Kegan Paul, Trench, Trubner & Co.

Fairlie, R. W., and B. D. Meyer. 1996. Ethnic and racial self-employment differences and possible explanations. *Journal of Human Resources* 31:757–93.

Freeman, J., G. R. Carroll, and M. T. Hannan. 1983. The liability of newness: Age dependence in organizational death rates. *American Sociological Review* 48:692–710.

Gerris, J. 1998. *Parents, adolescents and young adults in Dutch families: A longitudinal study.* Nijmegen: Nijmegen University Institute of Family Studies.

Gill, A. M. 1988. Choice of employment status and the wages of employees and the self-employed: Some further evidence. *Journal of Applied Econometrics* 3:229–34.

Goldthorpe, J. C. 1980. *Social mobility and class structure in modern Britain.* Oxford: Clarendon Press.

Hannan, M. T., and J. Freeman. 1989. *Organizational ecology*. Cambridge: Harvard University Press.

Hout, M. 1983. *Mobility tables*. Beverly Hills: Sage Publications.

Hout, M., and H. S. Rosen. 1999. *Self-employment, family background, and race*. NBER Working Paper 7344. Cambridge: NBER.

Iyigun, M. F., and A. L. Owen. 1998. Risk, entrepreneurship and human capital accumulation. *American Economic Review, Papers and Proceedings* 88:454–57.

Jensen, M. C. 1993. The modern industrial revolution, exit, and the failure of internal control systems. *Journal of Finance* 68:831–80.

Jovanovic, B. 1993. The diversification of production. *Brookings Papers: Microeconomics 1993*, 197–235.

Lindh, T., and H. Ohlsson. 1996. Self-employment and windfall gains: Evidence from the Swedish lottery. *The Economic Journal* 106:1515–26.

Loutfi, M. F. 1991. Self-employment patterns and policy issues in Europe. *International Labour Review* 130:1–19.

Luber, S., and M. Gangl. 1997. *Die Entwicklung selbständiger Erwerbsarbeit in Westeuropa und den USA 1960–1995*. [Development of self-employment in Western Europe and the U.S. 1960–1995]. Mannheimer Zentrum für Europäische Sozialforschung, Working Paper 16.

Lucas, R. E. 1978. On the size distribution of firms. *Bell Journal of Economics* 9:508–23.

Luijkx, R., and H. Ganzeboom. 1989. Intergenerational class mobility in the Netherlands between 1970 and 1985. In *Similar or different: Continuities in Dutch research on social stratification and social mobility*, ed. W. Jansen, J. Dronkers, and K. Verrips, 5–30. Amsterdam: SISWO.

McClelland, D. 1961. *The achieving society*. New York: Free Press.

Mayer, K. U., and G. R. Carroll. 1987. Jobs and classes: Structural constraints on career mobility. *European Sociological Review* 3:14–38.

Miner, J. B. 1997. *A psychological typology of successful entrepreneurs*. Westport: Quorum Books.

Ministry of Economic Affairs. 2002. *Toets op het concurrentievermogen 2002* [Test of the competitive capabilities 2002]. Den Haag: Ministry of Economic Affairs.

Müller, W., P. Luttinger, W. König, and W. Karle. 1989. Class and education in industrial nations. *International Journal of Sociology* 19:3–29.

Penrose, E. 1959. *The theory of the growth of the firm*. 3d ed. Oxford: Oxford University Press.

Piore, M. J., and C. F. Sabel. 1984. *The second industrial divide: Possibilities for prosperity*. New York: Basic Books.

Preisendörfer, P., and T. Voss. 1990. Organizational mortality of small firms: The effects of entrepreneurial age and human capital. *Organization Studies* 11:107–29.

Rees, H., and A. Shah. 1986. An empirical analysis of self-employment in the UK. *Journal of Applied Economics* 1:95–108.

Rotter, J. B. 1966. General expectancies for internal versus external control of reinforcement. *Psychological Monographs* 80, 609.

Sandberg, W. R. 1986. *New venture performance: The role of strategy and industry structure*. Lexington: Lexington Books.

Schaffner, J. A. 1993. Rising incomes and the shift from self-employment to firm based production. *Economic Letters* 41:435–40.

Schumpeter, J. A. 1950. *Capitalism, socialism and democracy*. New York: Harper and Row.

Simon, H. A. 1957. *Models of man*. New York: Wiley.

Taylor, M. P. 1996. Earnings, independence or unemployment: Why become self-employed? *Oxford Bulletin of Economics and Statistics* 58:253–66.

Ultee, W., and H. B. Ganzeboom. 1992. *Family survey Dutch population 1992 [machine readable data-set]*. Nijmegen: University of Nijmegen, Department of Sociology.

UNESCO. 1998. *World culture report: Culture, creativity and markets*. Paris: UNESCO.

Yamaguchi, K. 1991. *Event history analysis*. Newbury Park: Sage.

Zevenbergen, P. 2000. Good preparation is half the work. In *Entrepreneurship in the Netherlands: Opportunities and threats to nascent entrepreneurship*, ed. Ministry of Economic Affairs, 17–32. Den Haag: Ministry of Economic Affairs.

CHAPTER FIVE

Self-Employment in the United Kingdom during the 1980s and 1990s

Nigel Meager and Peter Bates

A KEY FEATURE of self-employment in the United Kingdom, as in other countries, is its diversity. Typically, most national data sources on self-employment rely on survey respondents' self-definition of their status as self-employed, which may differ from their status as defined for purposes of taxation, social security, or employment law.[1] Traditionally, in UK employment law, the key distinction is between a *contract of service*, which is an employment contract under which an employer buys the right to a worker's service, and a *contract for services*, under which the organization is buying not the right to the worker's service, but rather the right to the end product of his or her labor. A contract for services is not an employment contract, and a worker who is engaged under such a contract will not be entitled to the protection of statutory employment rights and will be self-employed rather than employed. In practice, there is no hard-and-fast test of which kind of contract applies in any given circumstance. Employment tribunals and courts decide the status of individuals according to a series of criteria, which include factors such as whether individuals makes their own decisions about the way in which they perform the work; whether they have more than one client; whether they have the final say in the way the business is run; whether they provide their own tools and equipment; whether they risk their own money in the business; whether they are free to hire other workers on their own terms; and whether they have to correct unsatisfactory work at their own time and expense. Similar tests apply in deciding whether an individual is self-employed for tax and social security purposes.

Although these basic principles determining employment status are, in principle, constant over time, in practice, the emphasis placed in interpreting the various criteria may vary from time to time, as may the ways in which the legal measures embodying those definitions are enforced. It remains unclear how far such changes affect the numbers and kinds of people who report themselves as self-employed in survey data, but it is likely that there is such an effect. We discuss below, for example, how measures to reduce the number of employees in the construction sector claiming self-employment status for tax purposes are likely to have had an effect on the reported trends in self-employment in this sector. Another important recent development in the UK has been the introduction of new tax regulations in 1999, in response to the growth in "personal service companies" (one-person businesses set up by specialist consultants or freelancers, often selling services to organizations for whom they had previously worked as employees). The new regulations aim to treat such people, for tax purposes, as if they were employees, rather than self-employed (Peel 1999). As yet, it is unclear how far this changing legal framework will have reduced the numbers of such companies in existence, on the one hand, and how far it will have reduced the numbers of such individuals reporting themselves as self-employed in survey data, on the other hand.

Most survey data sources, including those used in the present chapter, usually define self-employment in terms of independence or autonomy (i.e., the self-employed are those who see themselves as working on their own account rather than for an employer in a conventional employment relationship: see Bryson and White [1997] for discussion of this kind of definition). The group of people satisfying this definition is, however, an extremely heterogeneous one, incorporating a variety of categories of work with differing degrees of autonomy and independence, which, at a minimum, include:

- Entrepreneurs and small business proprietors (whether these are recorded as "self-employed" may also depend on whether or not their business is incorporated—see Hakim [1989])
- Independent professional workers (in the liberal professions and the arts, for example)
- Skilled manual and craftworkers
- Farmers
- Some categories of home workers or "outworkers"
- "Labor only" subcontractors (e.g., in the construction industry)

Some of these groups correspond more closely to the autonomous model of the genuinely self-employed, whereas others (particularly the last two) include people who are self-employed in name only, and who might be better regarded as "disguised employees."

AGGREGATE TRENDS IN SELF-EMPLOYMENT

In the UK, as in many advanced economies, the previous decline in self-employment, which had been evident for several decades, came to a halt and was reversed in the 1980s. Indeed, during that period, the UK was one of the countries in which the growth in self-employment was one of the fastest and most dramatic. The decade of 1979–89 was a period of historically unprecedented growth in self-employment. Data from the Labour Force Survey (LFS) for Great Britain[2] show that over this period, self-employment almost doubled, from 1.77 million to 3.43 million, and the self-employment rate (i.e., the proportion of all those in employment who are self-employed) grew from 7.3 to 13.1 percent.

This apparent resurgence of self-employment brought with it a corresponding resurgence of interest in self-employment among social scientists and policymakers. The former, having previously dismissed self-employment as a somewhat archaic petty bourgeois segment of the labor market, composed largely of artisans and farmers and doomed to decline in numbers with continued industrialization, rapidly turned to look for explanations for its reappearance. Interest among the latter was driven more by a belief (or hope) that this growth reflected a flowering of "entrepreneurism" and that the growing numbers of self-employed constituted an army of small dynamic businesses that would reinvigorate declining economies and create employment for workers whose jobs were lost in traditional sectors in the recessions of the 1970s and early 1980s.[3]

The subsequent experience in the 1990s showed, however, that some of the more dramatic claims that the self-employment growth of the previous decade represented a fundamental shift in the structure of the UK labor market may have been premature. Self-employment increased every year in the 1980s and did not follow the economic cycle. In the 1990s, however, until the latter part of the decade (around 1997), self-employment moved more closely with the overall level of employment, falling in the recession of the early 1990s, and then recovering from 1994 onward. Some commentators argued that self-employment had re-established a procyclical pattern in the 1990s, following the exceptional period of the 1980s (Campbell and Daly 1992; Moralee 1998). In the latter part of the 1990s, however, any link between aggregate self-employment and the overall cycle appears to have been broken once more, with self-employment once again falling during the period of economic growth from 1997 to 2000. Indeed, if we look at the share of self-employment in overall employment (the self-employment rate), figure 5.1 shows that in contrast to the 1980s, the trend for most of the 1990s was downward, to the extent that by 2000 the aggregate self-employment rate in the UK had fallen back to almost the same level as in 1984 (11.3 percent and 11.2 percent, respectively).

RECENT CHANGES IN THE COMPOSITION OF SELF-EMPLOYMENT

Similarly, it also appears that some of the compositional shifts in self-employment that occurred in the 1980s may not have represented sustained trends.

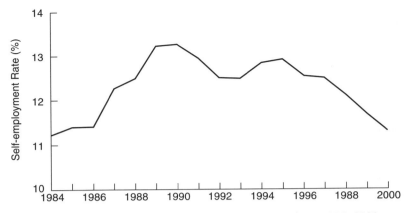

Figure 5.1: Self-Employment Rate in the United Kingdom, 1984–2000

Gender

Looking first at the gender composition of self-employment, as Campbell and Daly (1992) noted, although female self-employment grew pro-
portionately faster than male self-employment during the 1980s, most of
this difference occurred in the first half of the decade. Since 1984, the
rates of growth of male and female self-employment have been broadly
similar to the rates of growth of male and female employment in total.
Thus the female share of self-employment grew slightly over the period
(from 24 percent in 1984 to 27 percent in 2000), but the faster growth of
female self-employment compared with male self-employment was broadly
in line with the overall growth in women's labor force participation. The
net effect is that, by 2000, the female self-employment rate remained at
just under half the male self-employment rate, the same as it was in 1984.
There is, therefore, no strong evidence of sustained differential growth
in women's self-employment in the UK.

Age

Turning to age, there has also been a recent reversal of the trends recorded in the 1980s. As in many other countries, the UK data suggest
that the likelihood of being self-employed (and the likelihood of entry to
self-employment) increases with age (see Meager 1993 and below). This
is consistent with the hypothesis that an accumulation of both human
and financial capital may be both a precondition for self-employment
entry and a factor that enhances survival chances in self-employment.
LFS data for the UK show that self-employment rates increase dramati-

cally with age, and that the highest self-employment rate is found among people older than the normal state retirement age. The literature contains various explanations for this pattern. First, it is clear that the self-employed do not have a fixed retirement age and therefore have the option of continuing employment into old age, which is often denied to their counterparts in waged employment. Second, it is also clear that some people move from employee to self-employed status in later life, as a route into retirement (the self-employed may have greater scope than wage employees to vary their labor input as they age). Finally, however, there is also some evidence (see, for example, Meager, Court, and Moralee 1996) that there is a significant group of self-employed people who face low incomes and poor pension entitlements in later life, and who may, therefore, be less able to afford to retire at a given age than their employee counterparts. In the 1980s, however, there was some evidence that age differences among the self-employed were beginning to narrow, and that self-employment had grown relatively fast among young people in the 20–34 age group (Meager 1991). Meager (1993) noted, moreover, that by 1989 the age profile of self-employment rates was flatter in the UK than in most other EU countries and argued that the advantage conferred by age (in terms of assets, experience, and qualifications) may have been less marked in the UK than elsewhere, for institutional and regulatory reasons. It is interesting to note, however, that any flattening of the age profile of self-employment that occurred in the UK during the 1980s appears to have reversed during the 1990s. Thus, figure 5.2 shows clearly that compared with the position at the beginning of the 1990s, by 2000 self-employment rates had increased among the older groups (55 plus) and fallen among those in the younger age ranges.

Sectoral and Occupational Patterns

We have noted above the heterogeneity of the groups who are likely to be recorded as self-employed in the survey data discussed here, and the possible differences between survey definitions of self-employment and official definitions for the purposes of tax or social security law, for example. It is not possible, in any reliable way, to distinguish "degrees of self-employment" from the aggregate survey data. Some picture of the diversity of self-employment, and the differential trends occurring within the overall group, can, however, be obtained by looking at sectoral and occupational data. Figure 5.3 shows that there have been very different trends at a sectoral level in the propensity to be self-employed. In some sectors, particularly those with low or medium self-employment rates, there has been little change over the period 1984–2000, or at most a slight upward trend. This is the case, for example, in manufacturing, public administra-

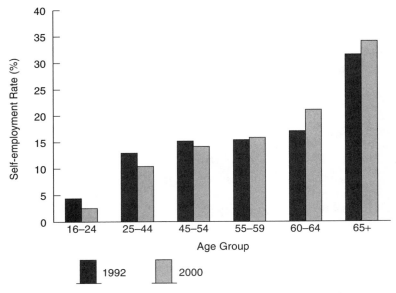

Figure 5.2: Self-Employment Rates by Age in the United Kingdom, 1992–2000

tion, education and health, transport and communication, and business and financial services (thus, although the business and financial services sector has shown the strongest *absolute* growth over the period, with the numbers of self-employed doubling, this growth has been broadly in line with the growth of overall employment in this sector).

In the remaining sectors, the patterns are varied. In the "other services" category, which includes a range of community, social, and personal services activities, there has been some growth in self-employment rates over time, but with clear cyclical fluctuations (the self-employment rate fell back during the recession of the early 1990s).

In the distribution, hotels, and restaurants sector, however, the trend has been clearly downward throughout the period. This is a relatively large sector, in which overall employment has grown but self-employment has declined, in both absolute and relative terms. This trend has had some influence on the aggregate rate of self-employment, since traditionally this sector has accounted for a significant share of the self-employed (in 1984, 29.9 percent of the self-employed were found in distribution, hotels, and restaurants; by 2000, this had fallen to 18.7 percent). This pattern reflects shifts in the overall economic structure of the sector, which has been characterized by growing concentration, and the gradual displacement of small family-owned establishments by large retail and catering chains.

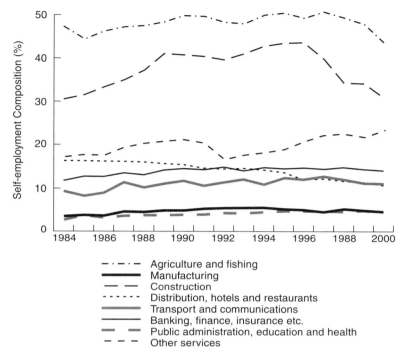

Figure 5.3: Self-Employment Rates by Sector in the United Kingdom, 1984–2000

Agriculture is a small and declining sector in overall employment terms, and despite its high rate of self-employment, trends in this sector have little influence on the overall pattern of self-employment in the UK. In the 1980s and 1990s, agricultural self-employment appears to have held up relatively well, with job loss in agriculture concentrated more on employees than on the self-employed. By the late 1990s, this pattern had changed slightly, however, with the continuing decline in agricultural employment also hitting the level and rate of self-employment. It seems likely that whereas the initial response to crisis in the agricultural sector occurred through the laying off of wage employees, more recent years have seen a growth in the number of farm closures and sales and corresponding reductions in the number of self-employed farm owners.

Finally, and perhaps of most significance in explaining trends in aggregate self-employment in the UK, is the pattern of change in the construction sector. The massive growth in construction self-employment during the 1980s and early 1990s played a significant role in the overall growth of self-employment during this period, although there is evidence that much of the growth consisted of bogus self-employment, with construction firms moving their workforces into self-employed status for reasons associated with avoidance of tax and social costs. This period saw the emergence of large numbers of self-employed construction workers (operating as "labor-only subcontractors"), and the balance of evidence suggests that many of these represented "disguised employment," or self-employment in name only (see Nisbet 1997; Winch 1998). Particularly striking from figure 5.3 is the rapid absolute and relative decline in self-employment in this sector after 1996, such that by 2000, the rate of self-employment in construction had fallen back to its mid-1980s' level of around 30 percent.

There is, as yet, no hard evidence on the factors underlying this reversal of the trend, but the main reason is likely to be measures introduced since 1997 by the taxation and social security benefits authorities in the UK (the Inland Revenue and the Contributions Agency, respectively). These measures aimed to clamp down on construction workers who had been claiming self-employed status for tax purposes, while in reality their status was that of regular employees. The measures did not represent a change in the regulations, but rather a change in the approach to their implementation, which shifted the responsibility to construction companies to determine the true employment status of their employees.

It is also possible that some large construction employers have recently begun to discover the hidden costs of an excessive use of self-employed labor. Thus Winch (1998) argues that the growth of self-employment in construction in the 1980s (a trend that had been in evidence since 1977) represented a strategic choice by construction companies to emphasize flexibility over productivity as a source of competitive advantage. He concludes that the ability of the sector to increase productivity and quality has been compromised due to the ways in which labor-only subcontracting and self-employment hinder training and innovation. Indeed, it seems likely that the impact on the stock of skills in construction had begun to bite by the late 1990s. This impact was not evident in the early years of expanding self-employment, when the industry was operating with an already trained skilled workforce who were increasingly being shifted to self-employed status. The effects of self-employment growth became more severe only as those skills aged and were not updated (the data suggest that in construction, as in other sectors, the self-employed are much less likely to engage in further training than their employee counterparts), and as the declining supply of new apprentice-trained young wage employees became apparent. It seems likely that the capacity of the sector to absorb a higher proportion of self-employed workers was reached by the early 1990s, at which point one of the most distinctive features of UK self-employment compared with other European countries may have begun to disappear.

Turning to recent trends in UK self-employment rates by occupation (as reported, for example, in Knight and McKay 2000), the most notable feature is the sharp and fairly continuous fall in managerial self-employment rates over the 1990s. This is a relatively large group: around a quarter of self-employed people in the UK report themselves as "managers or administrators." As previous authors have noted, this may reflect their perceptions of themselves as owner-proprietors of their own businesses, rather than the nature of their main occupation. For example, a craftsperson who moves from dependent employment to self-employment may appear as a "manager" in self-employment, although the real nature of his or her activity has changed little or not at all. Nevertheless, the falling numbers of self-employed in this category represent a marked trend, which is observable in several of the main UK datasets. One hypothesis is that this reflects increasing diversity in the self-employed population, with a relative decline in the proportion of self-employed who see themselves as small business proprietors or entrepreneurs in the traditional sense, and a growth in the proportion who see themselves as working in their own occupation or profession, but on "their own account" rather than for an employer.

Explaining Recent Trends — Evidence to Date

Attempts to explain aggregate self-employment trends in the UK (as in other countries) face two key difficulties. The first of these stems from the extreme heterogeneity of self-employment, discussed above. The "self-employed" include individuals engaged in very different activities, with varying degrees of autonomy, and the growth or decline of each of these groups is influenced by a range of different factors. This heterogeneity makes it unlikely that one can successfully model trends in self-employment as a single aggregate.

The second difficulty stems from the fact that the aggregate trends discussed above are trends in the *stock* of self-employment. It is clear that movements in the stock of self-employment are themselves the outcome of separate movements in *inflows to* and *outflows from* self-employment, and that these flows may themselves be subject to different influences. A clear illustration of this difficulty can be seen in the debate about the role of unemployment and the economic cycle in influencing self-employment. Much of the earlier, inconclusive literature on this subject (see Bögenhold and Staber 1991; Storey 1991) argued for a countercyclical relationship between unemployment rates and self-employment on the basis of stock data, interpreting any observed relationship as indicating a "push" into self-employment in the context of declining opportunities for wage employment. However, as the present author and others have pointed out (Meager 1992), this is an argument about inflows. When it comes to outflows from self-employment, it is arguable that they will also move in a countercyclical fashion (increasing in a recession as business conditions deteriorate), and the net impact of these two influences on self-employment stocks is indeterminate. The experience of the UK in the 1980s (see below) is a very clear example of the difficulty of identifying a robust relationship between aggregate self-employment and the economic cycle (for a more recent analysis, see Cowling and Mitchell [1997], who provide interesting econometric evidence to the effect that it is not the overall stock of unemployment but its duration structure that is most important in leading to changes in self-employment).

The new analysis presented below, in common with the analyses for other countries in this volume, begins to address both of these difficulties. It not only disaggregates self-employment by certain key characteristics to allow for the heterogeneity of the concept but also develops distinct explanatory models for entry to and exit from self-employment. Before turning to these models, however, it is worth briefly looking at what the previous literature offers us in terms of explanations for the UK.

Unusual Self-Employment Developments in the 1980s

Most of the explanatory effort to date has been devoted to interpreting and explaining the exceptionally fast growth in self-employment levels and rates experienced in the UK during the 1980s. A common conclusion of the research covering this period (see, for example, Acs, Audretsch, and Evans 1992; Meager 1992; Meager 1993) is that no single factor can adequately account for these developments. Rather, to explain the differential experience of European countries and the unusual developments in the UK despite a generally convergent macroeconomic environment and a common policy stance supportive of self-employment growth, we must take account of several interrelated influences.

The first such influence is the economic cycle. As noted above, growing unemployment may have opposing impacts on self-employment entry and exit, and the net impact on aggregate self-employment is not predictable a priori. The evidence suggests that the "unemployment push" effect may have predominated in the early 1980s (when the UK experienced higher rates of inflow from unemployment to self-employment than did most other European countries—Meager 1993). In contrast, it seems that the effect of economic growth predominated in the late 1980s, the net result being that self-employment grew throughout the decade, in a period of deep recession for the first half of the decade followed by strong economic growth in the second half.

A second influence on self-employment developments in the UK has been structural change. The shift in the overall structure of employment from sectors with relatively low densities of self-employment (such as manufacturing—see above) to sectors with higher rates of self-employment (especially service sectors) was particularly marked in the UK (and more rapid than in some other countries such as Germany) during the 1980s, and this shift more than outweighed the impact on self-employment of the ongoing decline in agricultural employment. (As we have already noted, agriculture, although having a high rate of self-employment, has relatively little weight in the overall picture of employment in the UK.)

Third, a commonly cited influence is that of changing working and contractual patterns. Thus, in addition to the unusual developments in the construction sector noted above, the 1980s saw a trend toward the "contracting out" of service functions by large employers and the growth of franchising, and these shifts in the contractual organization of work further contributed to self-employment growth.

These three influences were, however, also present to a greater or lesser extent in other countries where self-employment did not increase, or not as rapidly as in the UK, during the 1980s. Further country-specific factors need also to be taken into account, therefore, and the literature on this period suggests that a second range of factors, more specific to the UK situation, were also important (see Meager 1993; Campbell and Daly 1992; Bryson and White 1997).

Key among this second group of influences is the regulatory framework for business startup, which, it has been argued, was considerably looser in the UK than in some other European countries (such as Germany—see Meager 1992), such that self-employment may have been more responsive in the UK than elsewhere to some of the short-term economic and structural influences identified above.

Further, it is clear that the structure and regulation of the market for financial capital facing the self-employed is likely to have played a role. There is some evidence that the UK capital market regime was less strict during the 1980s than in some other countries and underwent a considerable relaxation as a result of financial deregulation in the 1980s. This, coupled with factors, such as growing home ownership and massive house price appreciation (and associated equity withdrawal from the housing market), generated an environment characterized by easy access to loan capital for potential self-employed people (Cowling and Mitchell 1997).

Finally, it is also worth noting the role of active labor market policies aimed at encouraging people, especially the unemployed, to enter self-employment. The UK's Enterprise Allowance Scheme (EAS) was among the largest in the European countries during this period. While the evaluation evidence (Meager, Court, and Moralee 1996; Metcalf 1998) suggests that the effectiveness of such schemes in creating sustainable self-employment opportunities for unemployed people was limited at best, they undoubtedly contributed to the short-term inflow to self-employment during the late 1980s.

Other factors identified in the literature appear to have been less important in the UK's case. In particular, despite arguments by many contemporary commentators to the effect that the Thatcher government's emphasis on the "enterprise culture" led to a more positive attitude toward self-employment among the workforce, the evidence from attitude surveys conducted during this period (see Blanchflower and Oswald 1990) does not support this argument.

The 1990s and the Fall-Back in Self-Employment

We have seen (fig. 5.1) that since 1990, the relationship between self-employment and overall employment has once again changed in the UK. In place of the continuous rise of self-employment, the 1990s saw fluctuations in the levels and rates of self-employment, and after the middle of that decade self-employment fell back, such that at the end of the decade the rate of self-employment was back to the position last seen in the mid-1980s. In the recession at the beginning of the 1990s, self-employment fell along with total employment (a marked contrast to the experience of the previous recession in the early 1980s—see also Cowling and Mitchell 1997). As employment picked up after 1993, so initially did self-employment (but less rapidly), before declining in the second half of the decade.

It remains unclear whether the experience of the 1980s was an aberration, and whether self-employment levels will, in future, be more sensitive to overall economic conditions, or even resume their earlier (pre-1980s) historical downward trend. There is, to date, little conclusive research evidence on what happened to UK self-employment in the 1990s, but it is possible to develop some hypotheses for the different experiences of the 1980s and 1990s by drawing on the existing evidence on the factors influencing inflows to and outflows from self-employment in the UK (see Bryson and White 1997).

First, it seems that some of the specific factors contributing to self-employment growth in the 1980s did not persist to the same extent in the subsequent decade. Thus, for example, in the case of "outsourcing," there were fewer "non-core" support activities left within many organizations to subcontract during the 1990s. In the construction sector, in particular, even by the early 1990s it was clear that the potential for further self-employment growth was limited and, as we have already noted, the

Self-Employment in the United Kingdom • 147

changes in the enforcement of the income tax regime in this sector from 1996 onward removed much of the incentive for self-employment. As a result, self-employment in construction declined dramatically.

Similarly, some institutional factors supporting self-employment growth were less present in the 1990s; the capital market for start-up finance was clearly tighter than during the credit boom of the 1980s, and a more sluggish housing market in the early part of the 1990s also affected the net personal wealth of many individuals. The policy environment also shifted, and the scale of the various initiatives supporting self-employment entry was reduced, with a shift in policy emphasis toward sustaining existing small businesses rather than stimulating start-ups (although there remained a policy interest in the latter, and the New Deal for Young People, the key active labor market program of the post-1997 UK Labour government, included a subsidized self-employment option for participants).

Second, it seems likely that the recession of the early 1990s may have had different implications for the volume and composition of self-employment than its predecessor in the early 1980s. The 1990s' recession led to significant job loss in service sectors (containing high concentrations of the self-employed), whereas the impact of the 1980s' recession was greatest in the manufacturing industries. While the overall shift from manufacturing to services continued during the 1990s and was reinforced in the latter part of that period by the strength of the British pound against European currencies (which hit manufacturing exports), it was less marked than in the 1980s. There may also have been other structural shifts militating against self-employment. Figure 5.3 showed, for example, a recent acceleration in the decline in self-employment rates in retailing and catering (due to a shift toward larger organizations), which offset the impact of overall expansion of this sector on the aggregate self-employment rate.

Third (see also Meager and Bates 2001), the 1980s' growth in self-employment included large numbers of people who did not fit the profile of the traditional self-employed entrepreneur or small business owner. The inflows of "new self-employed" during this period were more likely to be young, more likely to be female, and more likely to be drawn from the ranks of the unemployed than were their predecessors (and, as noted above, some of these trends did not persist in the 1990s). Self-employed people with these characteristics were more likely to enter highly competitive service-sector activities with low capital requirements and low barriers to entry, often with a poor chance of survival or a high risk of displacing existing businesses (Meager, Court, and Moralee 1996). As Bryson and White (1997) point out, the existing research does not adequately disentangle the relative influence on self-employment survival of characteristics such as age, gender, and previous unemployment, on the one hand, and the nature of the self-employment entered, on the other hand (but see the new analysis of these issues in the current chapter, below). Nevertheless, the changing composition of the newly self-employed during the 1980s raises the clear possibility that they included people with personal or business characteristics associated with lower survival rates (a possibility consistent with the rapid fall in self-employment as the economy entered recession after 1990).

Self-Employment Dynamics and Income Levels

The current evidence, therefore, remains inconclusive as to whether, taking the 1980s and 1990s together, the UK's experience represents a reversal of the previous secular decline in self-employment, or whether the 1980s in particular represented a short-term deviation from that decline that has now resumed.

Whatever conclusion we reach about trends in the overall size of the self-employment *stock*, however, the limited evidence to date does suggest that there have been changes in the dynamics of self-employment. Meager and Bates (2001), for example, present evidence for the UK that suggests that there have been increases in the transition rates between labor market states, including self-employment, and that the stock of self-employment considerably understates the prevalence of self-employment. It would appear, therefore, that a much larger proportion of the workforce experiences self-employment during their working lives than is suggested by the stock data alone, and that this proportion is tending to increase. Traditional notions of self-employment as a distinct and declining labor market segment, whose occupants are drawn from a narrow social stratum, with little mobility between that segment and the rest of the labor market, may, therefore, be breaking down (this kind of hypothesis is consistent also with the clear evidence of a persistent decline in the share of the self-employed who report themselves as "managers"—see above).

Thus, even if the stock of self-employment has not grown dramatically, self-employment itself is more pervasive in the sense that more people, and different types of people in different types of jobs, are experiencing self-employment during their working lives. The evidence from the UK suggests, moreover, that these changes may have important implications for the incomes and economic well-being of those experiencing self-employment (Meager and Bates 2001). Thus the data indicate not only that the self-employed have more polarized incomes than do employees (i.e., self-employed people have a higher probability of falling in either extreme of the income distribution), but that this pattern carries

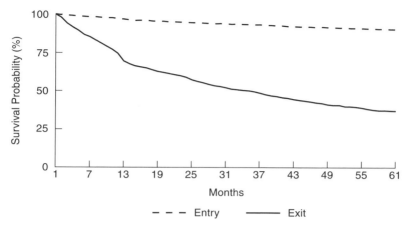

Figure 5.4: Survival Curves for Entry to and Exit from Self-Employment in the United Kingdom, 1980–95

over into the income levels of older people *who have previously been self-employed*. Further, when other personal and job-related characteristics are controlled for in multivariate analysis, it seems that self-employment experience significantly increases a person's likelihood of falling in the lowest decile of earned income, both while they are self-employed and in later life (by contrast, the relationship between self-employment and the likelihood of high incomes is explicable by other factors, such as education, gender, or occupational experience, and there is no distinct role of self-employment). Meager and Bates discuss various explanations for these findings, including the possibility that social security and pensions provision are not adequately adjusted to a growth in self-employment among segments of the population who have not traditionally experienced self-employment. One implication of a widening experience of self-employment among the working population, therefore, is a higher potential risk of the development of a group of low-income, self-employed workers, and particularly of a group with low incomes in old age, due to an inability of some types of self-employed people to accumulate pensions rights, personal savings, and other assets. It is this dispersion of experience (perhaps associated with the extreme heterogeneity of the self-employed as a category), including a group for whom self-employment leads clearly to lower levels of income and assets, that characterizes self-employment as compared with dependent employment. This issue of dispersion of outcomes and the particular association of self-employment with an increased probability of poor outcomes is not fully taken into account by those who have argued, for the UK, using work history data, that there is *"no evidence that experience of self-employment led to low income in retirement"* (Knight and McKay 2000, 91). The latter analysis is based on observations showing that the *average* income levels of the self-employed (and ex-self-employed) differ little from the *average* income levels of employees (and ex-employees) and does not take into account the different dispersions of income levels and the findings from multivariate analyses that self-employment increases the chance of lower income levels.

MULTIVARIATE ANALYSIS

We now turn to the preliminary findings of our new analysis of self-employment flows, using panel data and an analytical framework common to that adopted for other advanced countries and reported in the companion chapters in this book.[4] We use data from the British Household Panel Survey (BHPS). The BHPS is a nationally representative panel survey of over ten thousand individuals, which began in 1990. In each subsequent year (wave), the respondents were reinterviewed about changes in their personal and occupational circumstances during the preceding twelve months. The data were supplemented in waves 2 and 3 with retrospective information on respondents' employment history in previous decades.

The issue of "recall error," relating to the start and end dates of various labor market episodes, makes the process of combining these data sets somewhat problematic. Harpin (1997), however, linked the panel waves with the retrospective work history data, and we use two of the combined files created by Harpin. The data used here are, therefore, based on waves 6 to 9, together with Harpin's aggregation of:

- Waves 1 to 5 panel surveys
- Waves 1 to 5 historic records of the last twelve months' employment
- Wave 2 retrospective data on economic status since leaving school
- Wave 3 data on employment status since leaving school

As some of the information used in these models was collected only in wave 1, the analysis is restricted to those who took part in the initial survey.

Our primary unit of observation is an individual per unit of time. As there are repeated observations of individuals across time, we have corrected the standard errors within the multivariate analysis accordingly.

Figure 5.4 contains survival curves for entry to and exit from self-employment using the same data set as contained in the multivariate analysis below.[5]

Transitions into Self-Employment (1980–99)

Table 5.1 presents three models of entry into self-employment: for men and women separately, and for men and women taken together. Looking at the global model, it is clear that being female significantly reduces the likelihood of entering self-employment compared with being male. Table 5.2, which presents separate models for entry into self-employment by occupational group, shows that this gender pattern is consistent across all occupational groups, but the strength of the effect is weaker in higher occupational groups. Thus the "disadvantage" of being female is smallest in entry to professional self-employment and greatest in entry to unskilled self-employment.

The role of age is consistent and statistically significant in all of the models in tables 5.1 and 5.2 and reflects well-known patterns from previous research. The relationship between age and the likelihood of becoming self-employed is a curvilinear one, with the likelihood increasing with age from the youngest groups, before peaking and then declining again among those in the oldest categories.

Educational background emerges as an important influence on entry probabilities. Looking first at the models for all occupations (in table 5.1), in all three cases (all respondents, males, and females), compared with those in the lowest reference category (CASMIN 1a/1b), all those with higher levels of qualification have a higher likelihood of becoming self-employed, although in the case of the next highest level of qualification (CASMIN 1c/2a) the difference is not statistically significant at conventional levels. It is interesting to note, however, that there is not a monotonically increasing probability of self-employment entry with educational level. In all three of the models, the highest likelihood of entering self-employment is recorded among those with a general or vocational qualification below higher education level (CASMIN 2b), and the entry probability among higher education graduates is slightly lower.

When we look separately at the role of education in entry to self-employment in different occupations, however, a clearer and more intuitive set of relationships emerges (table 5.2). Thus, as far as entry into professional self-employment is concerned, there is a clear and monotonically increasing relationship with educational level: the more qualified someone is, the more likely they are to enter professional self-employment. Turning to skilled self-employment, the highest likelihood of entry occurs among those with intermediate qualifications (CASMIN 2c). Finally, when we look at entry into unskilled self-employment the pattern is very different. Thus, compared with the poorly qualified reference group, those with higher educational qualifications have a *lower* probability of self-employment entry, and the only group recording a statis-

TABLE 5.1
Logit Model of Entry into Self-Employment in the United Kingdom, 1980–99

	All		Male		Female	
	Coef.	*s.e.*	*Coef.*	*s.e*	*Coef.*	*s.e*
Gender *(ref: male)*						
Female	−0.748***	(0.078)	N/a	(N/a)	N/a	(N/a)
Age						
Age (yrs, age 18 = 0)	0.060***	(0.011)	0.049***	(0.013)	0.090***	(0.019)
Age squared	−0.001***	(0.000)	−0.001***	(0.000)	−0.002***	(0.000)
Education (CASMIN) *(ref: 1ab)*						
1c/2a	0.017	(0.252)	0.700	(0.591)	0.075	(0.279)
2b	0.351***	(0.100)	0.437***	(0.126)	0.260	(0.167)
2c	0.618***	(0.121)	0.500***	(0.152)	0.878***	(0.199)
3a	0.490***	(0.102)	0.369***	(0.129)	0.712***	(0.167)
3b	0.481***	(0.138)	0.320*	(0.170)	0.785***	(0.230)
Employment status before self-employment entry *(ref: unskilled employee)*						
Professional employee	0.099	(0.111)	−0.040	(0.129)	0.517**	(0.226)
Skilled employee	−0.081	(0.100)	−0.234**	(0.118)	0.290	(0.201)
Unemployed	1.467***	(0.116)	1.609***	(0.137)	1.016***	(0.245)
Economically inactive	0.526***	(0.115)	0.495***	(0.166)	0.588***	(0.203)
Industrial sector before self-employment entry *(ref: primary, manufacturing, utilities; also includes those not in labor market)*						
Construction	1.212***	(0.134)	1.332***	(0.144)	0.457	(0.575)
Traditional services	0.439***	(0.109)	0.632***	(0.137)	0.186	(0.192)
Transport and communication	0.081	(0.177)	0.125	(0.197)	−0.096	(0.423)
Financial and business services	0.453***	(0.123)	0.649***	(0.152)	0.078	(0.223)
Other services	−0.005	(0.112)	−0.048	(0.158)	−0.204	(0.187)

TABLE 5.1 (continued)

	All		Male		Female	
	Coef.	s.e.	Coef.	s.e	Coef.	s.e
Father self-employed (ref: father not self-employed)						
Self-employed	0.335***	(0.094)	0.343***	(0.118)	0.347**	(0.153)
Social background of father (ref: father unskilled employee) Professional						
employee	0.134	(0.097)	0.048	(0.125)	0.215	(0.156)
Skilled employee	.049	(0.084)	0.158	(0.103)	−0.140	(0.144)
Other	0.034	(0.126)	0.063	(0.162)	−0.047	(0.202)
Constant	−5.411***	0.147	−5.282***	0.178	−6.534***	0.277
Number of observations	103,564		44,682		58,882	
Wald χ^2 (degrees of freedom)	481.88$_{(21)}$		274.61$_{(20)}$		109.70$_{(20)}$	
Pseudo R^2	0.042		0.040		0.026	
Log likelihood	−5910.37		−3452.01		−2423.90	

* $p < 0.10$ ** $p < 0.05$ *** $p < 0.01$

tically significant higher probability than the reference group is the group with intermediate general qualifications (i.e., high school qualifications gained at age 16).

Prior unemployment is a strong influence on self-employment entry (compared with the reference category of an unskilled employee). This pattern is observed in all the entry models of tables 5.1 and 5.2. Similarly (also compared with unskilled employees), those who are economically active are also more likely to enter self-employment (although this effect is weaker overall than the impact of unemployment and is also found only in the model for entry into skilled self-employment).

Occupational status prior to self-employment entry is an important influence (table 5.2). Thus professional employees are significantly more likely to enter professional self-employment than are skilled or unskilled employees, skilled employees are more likely to enter skilled self-employment than are professional or unskilled employees, and both professional and skilled employees are significantly less likely to enter unskilled self-employment than are unskilled employees. This suggests that

TABLE 5.2
Multinomial Logit Model of Entry into Self-Employment by Occupational Group in the
United Kingdom, 1980–99

	Professional		Skilled		Unskilled	
	Coef.	s.e	Coef.	s.e	Coef.	s.e
Gender (ref: male)						
Female	−0.326***	(0.115)	−0.827***	(0.124)	−1.545***	(0.193)
Age						
Age (yrs, age 18 = 0)	0.067***	(0.017)	0.053***	(0.016)	0.084***	(0.026)
Age squared	−0.001***	(0.000)	−0.002***	(0.000)	−0.002***	(0.001)
Education (CASMIN) (ref: 1ab)						
1c/2a	0.582	(0.394)	0.046	(0.334)	−0.588	(0.717)
2b	0.866***	(0.195)	0.171	(0.154)	0.423**	(0.181)
2c	1.366***	(0.213)	0.526***	(0.178)	0.199	(0.260)
3a	1.321***	(0.187)	0.370**	(0.161)	−0.088	(0.224)
3b	1.562***	(0.220)	−0.356	(0.294)	−1.360**	(0.628)
Employment status before self-employment entry (ref: unskilled employee)						
Professional employee	0.689***	(0.173)	−1.158***	(0.306)	−2.119***	(0.362)
Skilled employee	−0.576***	(0.189)	0.739***	(0.179)	−1.636***	(0.222)
Unemployed	1.181***	(0.217)	1.886***	(0.210)	0.592***	(0.230)
Economically inactive	0.125	(0.209)	0.996***	(0.217)	−0.079	(0.240)
Industrial sector before self-employment entry (ref: primary, manufacturing, utilities; also includes those not in the labor market)						
Construction	0.305	(0.286)	1.438***	(0.175)	1.138***	(0.321)
Traditional services	0.456***	(0.166)	0.029	(0.202)	0.571**	(0.239)
Transport and communication	0.120	(0.261)	−1.530***	(0.589)	0.469	(0.295)
Financial and business services	0.455***	(0.151)	−0.126	(0.292)	0.853***	(0.312)
Other services	−0.399***	(0.156)	0.082	(0.179)	0.220	(0.295)

TABLE 5.2 (*continued*)

	Professional		Skilled		Unskilled	
	Coef.	s.e	Coef.	s.e	Coef.	s.e
Father self-employed (*ref: father not self-employed*)						
Self-employed	0.215**	(0.130)	0.445***	(0.158)	0.415*	(0.219)
Social background of father (*ref: father unskilled employee*) Professional						
employee	0.369***	(0.140)	0.109	(0.173)	− 0.509**	(0.259)
Skilled employee	0.068	(0.138)	0.179	(0.133)	− 0.169	(0.169)
Other	0.021	(0.210)	0.170	(0.198)	− 0.186	(0.255)
Constant	− 7.220***	(0.286)	− 6.225***	(0.238)	− 5.681***	(0.311)
Number of observations			94,082			
Wald χ^2 (degrees of freedom)			$994.69_{(69)}$			
Pseudo R^2			0.080			
Log likelihood			− 6642.10			

* $p < 0.10$ ** $p < 0.05$ *** $p < 0.01$

self-employment does not generally operate as a mechanism for social or occupational mobility within an individual's working life.

For men, but not for women, the sector of employment prior to self-employment is an influence on self-employment entry, although it is not clear how far this reflects sector-specific experience accumulated by the individuals in question, or whether it is also due to particular opportunities to become self-employed that are more available to employees in certain sectors. It is, however, clear that compared with men who are outside the labor market or who are employed in the primary or manufacturing sector, men employed in financial and business services, traditional services, and (especially) construction are more likely to enter self-employment. The strong effect in the construction sector is unsurprising and is consistent with the particular characteristics of UK construction, noted above.

Table 5.2 shows, again as expected, that the construction effect is concentrated among skilled and unskilled workers, whereas professional employees are most likely to enter self-employment in traditional services or financial services.

As previous studies have shown, parental self-employment (in this case the self-employment of the father) is a significant factor influencing self-employment entry and is consistent with the notion of intergenerational transmission of self-employment propensities. This transmission may have a cultural dimension, as well as a structural/financial one. Someone brought up in a culture of self-employment is more likely to acquire the attitudes, skills, networks, and so forth leading to self-employment entry. Equally, they may be more likely to inherit a business or to join the "family firm." This effect is evident for both men and women (table 5.1), but it is interesting to note (table 5.2) that it applies only to entry to skilled and (to a lesser extent) unskilled self-employment. There is no effect of parental self-employment on entry to professional self-employment. The latter does, however, appear to be influenced by the broader social background of the father (i.e., there is also some intergenerational transmission of occupational status), and table 5.2 shows that having had a father who is a professional employee is a positive influence on the likelihood of entry to professional self-employment (and a negative influence on the likelihood of entry to unskilled self-employment).

Exits from Self-Employment (1980–99)

Tables 5.3 and 5.4 present a similar analysis of the dynamics of exit from self-employment, again distinguishing between different occupational categories, and between men and women.

In these models the effect of gender is marked, at least for professional and skilled self-employment. Self-employed women in these occupations are more likely than their male counterparts to exit self-employment. Taken together with the lower likelihood of female entry to self-employment, this greater instability of female self-employment reinforces the picture revealed in the LFS data (above) which suggests no strong trend toward long-term growth in female self-employment (other than that due to the growth in female labor market participation more generally).

In all of the models, the effect of age on exit propensity is the obverse of that observed for the entry models (i.e., the propensity to exit generally declines with age), although the relationship is curvilinear and after a certain point begins to increase again (this may, of course, simply be a retirement effect). Taken together with the results for self-employment entry, it appears that stability of self-employment increases with age; as they get older (up to a certain age at least), people are more likely to enter self-employment and more likely to stay self-employed.

There is a positive impact of qualification level on the likelihood of exit, although this effect appears to be present mainly among professional occupations (i.e., there is increasing dynamism of professional self-employment with increasing educational level); the least well qualified are least likely to enter this kind of self-employment but most likely to remain in it when they do. It is clear from the other countries examined in this volume that the UK is unusual in this respect. One hypothesis might be that the nature of self-employment among highly qualified people in the UK is less stable than elsewhere and may be associated with the deregulation and "flexibilization" of some professional labor markets; it might, for example, reflect the growth of professional freelancers (e.g., in information technology–related occupations, or in media jobs), who may move frequently between self-employment and wage employment. If this were the case, however, we would expect this to be reflected in exit rates by occupation as well as by qualification. The occupational data suggest, however, that professional self-employment as a whole is indeed more stable than the other occupations. Thus, looking at all self-employed (table 5.3) and at male self-employed (table 5.4), we can see that those in professional self-employment are significantly less likely to exit than those in unskilled or skilled occupations.

As far as sector is concerned, compared with primary, manufacturing, and construction self-employment, employment in the other sectors (services of various types) is less stable, with higher exit rates.

Parental (father's) self-employment not only increases the chances of entry to self-employment, it also improves the likelihood of "success" in self-employment (at least as measured by exit probabilities). This effect is significant for all self-employed, for self-employed men, and for self-employed professionals. Over and above this effect of a self-employed father, however, there seems to be no effect of the father's social or professional status on the likelihood of exit.

Changes in Entry to and Exit from Self-Employment between the 1980s and 1990s

Our analysis of the Labour Force Survey (see above) has shown a clear shift in the behavior of the aggregate stock of self-employment between the 1980s (when self-employment was on a strong upward trend, apparently independent of the economic cycle) and the 1990s (when self-employment levels and rates fluctuated around a declining trend). Our BHPS data set, containing, as it does, information on transitions into and out of self-employment throughout this period, enables us to look further at the apparent changes that occurred between the 1980s and 1990s. In particular, it enables us to examine whether and to what extent the observed changes in the aggregate stock of self-employment reflect

TABLE 5.3
Logit Model of Exit from Self-Employment by Occupational Group in the United Kingdom, 1980–99

	All		Professional		Skilled		Unskilled	
	Coef.	s.e.	Coef.	s.e	Coef.	s.e	Coef.	s.e
Gender (ref: male)								
Female	0.509***	(0.080)	0.634***	(0.109)	0.512***	(0.168)	0.331	(0.229)
Age								
Age (yrs, age 18 = 0)	−0.070***	(0.014)	−0.071***	(0.022)	−0.055***	(0.022)	−0.088***	(0.028)
Age squared	0.002***	(0.000)	0.002***	(0.000)	0.001***	(0.000)	0.002***	(0.001)
Education (CASMIN) (ref: 1ab)								
1c/2a	0.374	(0.232)	0.021	(0.356)	0.424	(0.330)	1.036**	(0.480)
2b	0.287***	(0.096)	0.217	(0.192)	0.324**	(0.141)	0.202	(0.186)
2c	0.538***	(0.109)	0.572***	(0.186)	0.632***	(0.164)	0.454	(0.309)
3a	0.268***	(0.089)	0.262	(0.163)	0.220	(0.147)	0.306	(0.224)
3b	0.444***	(0.135)	0.464***	(0.184)	0.448	(0.352)	−0.243	(0.947)
Occupation in current self-employ-ment (ref: unskilled)								
Professional	−0.330***	(0.118)	N/a	(N/a)	N/a	(N/a)	N/a	(N/a)
Skilled	−0.070	(0.112)	N/a	(N/a)	N/a	(N/a)	N/a	(N/a)

Industrial sector of current self-employment spell *(ref: primary, manufacturing, utilities; also includes those not in the labor market)*

	(1)		(2)		(3)		(4)	
Construction	0.118	(0.115)	1.092***	(0.424)	−0.018	(0.144)	0.108	(0.271)
Traditional services	0.386***	(0.116)	0.478**	(0.196)	0.728***	(0.201)	0.135	(0.266)
Transport and communications	0.649***	(0.183)	0.620	(0.529)	0.868	(0.607)	0.527**	(0.249)
Financial and business services	0.646***	(0.134)	0.792***	(0.206)	0.585**	(0.268)	0.621	(0.392)
Other services	0.317***	(0.116)	0.459**	(0.195)	0.308	(0.192)	0.076	(0.341)
Father self-employed *(ref: father not self-employed)*								
Father self-employed	−0.200***	(0.081)	−0.370***	(0.120)	−0.025	(0.136)	−0.024	(0.218)
Social background of father *(ref: father unskilled employee)*								
Father professional employee	−0.017	(0.093)	−0.074	(0.131)	−0.100	(0.179)	0.093	(0.275)
Father skilled employee	0.065	(0.080)	−0.133	(0.144)	0.116	(0.121)	0.283	(0.177)
Father other	−0.100	(0.110)	−0.136	(0.211)	−0.070	(0.167)	−0.185	(0.233)
Constant	−1.708***	(0.192)	−2.106***	(0.332)	−2.036***	(0.271)	−1.235***	(0.376)
Number of observations	9,356		4,213		3,633		1,510	
Wald χ^2 (degrees of freedom)	162.23$_{(19)}$		80.52$_{(17)}$		84.36$_{(17)}$		35.16$_{(17)}$	
Pseudo R^2	0.024		0.029		0.031		0.027	
Log likelihood	−3639.43		−1620.15		−1357.27		−638.73	

* $p < 0.10$, ** $p < 0.05$ *** $p < 0.01$

Table 5.4

Logit Model of Exit from Self-Employment by Gender in the United Kingdom, 1980–99

	Male		Female	
	Coef.	s.e.	Coef.	s.e
Age				
Age (in yrs; age 18 = 0)	−0.070***	(0.016)	−0.073***	(0.024)
Age squared	0.002***	(0.000)	0.001***	(0.001)
Education (CASMIN) (ref: 1ab)				
1c/2a	1.123**	(0.559)	0.188	(0.265)
2b	0.320***	(0.112)	0.161	(0.185)
2c	0.676***	(0.127)	0.245	(0.197)
3a	0.292***	(0.108)	0.188	(0.162)
3b	0.517***	(0.166)	0.246	(0.234)
Occupation in current self-employment (ref: unskilled)				
Professional employee	−0.539***	(0.139)	0.022	(0.220)
Skilled employee	−0.190	(0.125)	0.200	(0.224)
Industrial sector of current self-employment spell (ref: primary, manufacturing, utilities; also includes those not in the labor market)				
Construction	0.087	(0.127)	1.011*	(0.559)
Traditional services	0.411***	(0.143)	0.371*	(0.208)
Transport and communications	0.510***	(0.203)	1.399***	(0.357)
Financial and business services	0.603***	(0.166)	0.851***	(0.250)
Other services	0.501***	(0.167)	0.247	(0.177)
Father self-employed (ref: father not self-employed)				
Self-employed	−0.202**	(0.099)	−0.166	(0.145)
Social background of father (ref: father unskilled employee)				
Professional employee	−0.026	(0.118)	−0.025	(0.159)
Skilled employee	0.010	(0.093)	0.215	(0.158)
Other	−0.118	(0.130)	−0.054	(0.196)
Constant	−1.653***	(0.223)	−1.279***	(0.376)
Number of observations	6,835		2,521	
Wald χ^2 (degrees of freedom)	95.43$_{(18)}$		49.06$_{(18)}$	
Pseudo R^2	0.020		0.020	
Log likelihood	−2451.65		−1174.50	

* $p < 0.10$ ** $p < 0.05$ *** $p < 0.01$

changes in inflow and/or outflow rates. Thus, for example, the data enable us to ask whether the leveling off and then decline in aggregate self-employment levels after the beginning of the 1990s are due to a slowing of inflow rates and/or to a growth in outflow rates.

To do this, we have extended the inflow and outflow models of tables 5.1 and 5.3 to include a new independent variable, which takes the value 0 if the spell in question occurred during the 1980s, and the value 1 if it occurred during the 1990s. These models are presented in table 5.5 (entry) and table 5.6 (exit). It is interesting to note that the coefficients on this variable are positive and highly significant in all the models examined (i.e., the models suggest that, other things being equal, *both* entry rates and exit rates were higher in the 1990s than in the 1980s). Compared with the 1980s, then, it would seem that this segment of the labor market exhibited even greater "dynamism" and turbulence during the 1990s. Entry rates to self-employment were even higher in the 1990s than in the 1980s, but durations of self-employment were also shorter, so that exit rates grew as well.

Given that the logit models in tables 5.5 and 5.6 are nonlinear in their parameters, we cannot directly compare the values of the coefficients on the new variables between the models. We cannot, therefore, conclude from the finding that the coefficients in all the exit models are considerably larger than their counterparts in the corresponding entry models that exit rates grew by more than entry rates between the 1980s and the 1990s. Taking the findings from tables 5.5 and 5.6 together with the earlier evidence on trends in aggregate self-employment, however, it is clear that the two sets of evidence (i.e., higher rates of entry and exit, and a fall in the overall stock of self-employment) are at least consistent with such an interpretation.

CONCLUDING REMARKS

This chapter has examined a number of aspects of recent developments in UK self-employment. We have looked at aggregate trends in self-employment and the changing composition of self-employment at an aggregate level, and we have then undertaken a micro-level analysis of the determinants of entry to and exit from self-employment.

Our analysis suggests, first, that the rapid growth in self-employment in the UK during the 1980s, a growth that considerably exceeded that in most comparable countries, was the result of a combination of factors, some of which were specific to the UK and did not persist in the 1990s (or were much weaker influences during this later period). In particular, the 1980s saw deregulation of financial markets and easy access to capital

TABLE 5.5
Logit Model of Entry into Self-Employment in the United Kingdom, 1980–99, Version 2

	All		*Male*		*Female*	
	Coef.	*s.e.*	*Coef.*	*s.e*	*Coef.*	*s.e*
Gender (*ref: male*)						
Female	−0.727***	(0.078)	N/a	(N/a)	N/a	(N/a)
Age						
Age (yrs, age						
18 = 0)	0.057***	(0.011)	0.046***	(0.014)	0.085***	(0.019)
Age squared	−0.001***	(0.000)	−0.001***	(0.000)	−0.002***	(0.000)
Education (CASMIN)						
(*ref: 1ab*)						
1c/2a	0.008	(0.252)	0.687	(0.591)	0.069	(0.280)
2b	0.312***	(0.100)	0.410***	(0.126)	0.210	(0.167)
2c	0.556***	(0.121)	0.460***	(0.152)	0.793***	(0.202)
3a	0.459***	(0.102)	0.348***	(0.130)	0.674***	(0.167)
3b	0.434***	(0.138)	0.292*	(0.170)	0.715***	(0.230)
Employment status before self-employment entry (*ref: unskilled employee*) Professional						
employee	0.092	(0.111)	−0.042	(0.129)	0.504**	(0.228)
Skilled employee	−0.083	(0.100)	−0.231**	(0.118)	0.282	(0.203)
Unemployed	1.433***	(0.117)	1.563***	(0.140)	1.072***	(0.249)
Economically inactive	0.492***	(0.116)	0.451***	(0.169)	0.581***	(0.205)
Industrial sector before self-employment entry (*ref: primary, manufacturing, utilities; also includes those not in the labor market*)						
Construction	1.212***	(0.136)	1.323***	(0.145)	0.444	(0.575)
Traditional services	0.410***	(0.111)	0.606***	(0.138)	0.159	(0.195)
Transport and communications	0.059	(0.178)	0.105	(0.198)	−0.149	(0.424)
Financial and business services	0.415***	(0.125)	0.622***	(0.153)	0.019	(0.227)
Other services	−0.033	(0.113)	−0.066	(0.158)	−0.240	(0.191)

TABLE 5.5 (*continued*)

	All		Male		Female	
	Coef.	*s.e.*	*Coef.*	*s.e*	*Coef.*	*s.e*
Father self-employed (*ref: father not self-employed*)						
Self-employed	0.337***	(0.093)	0.345***	(0.117)	0.351**	(0.152)
Social background of father (*ref: father unskilled employee*) Professional						
employee	0.128	(0.097)	0.043	(0.125)	0.211	(0.156)
Skilled employee	0.051	(0.084)	0.159	(0.103)	− 0.142	(0.144)
Other	0.029	(0.126)	0.063	(0.162)	− 0.058	(0.202)
At risk in 1980 or 1990s (*ref: 1980s*)						
At risk in 1990s	0.337***	(0.062)	0.214***	(0.079)	0.469***	(0.107)
Constant	− 5.508***	(0.150)	− 5.330***	(0.179)	− 6.673***	(0.282)
Number of observations	103,564		44,682		58,882	
Wald χ^2 (degrees of freedom)	$523.93_{(22)}$		$289.67_{(21)}$		$123.88_{(21)}$	
Pseudo R^2	0.045		0.041		0.031	
Log likelihood	− 5895.58		− 3448.35		− 2489.64	

*$p < 0.10$ ** $p < 0.05$ *** $p < 0.01$

for would-be entrepreneurs; the introduction of large-scale active labor market measures to support entry to self-employment from unemployment; a trend toward outsourcing and subcontracting of employment; and a particular development in the construction sector, which involved employees being made self-employed to avoid tax and social costs.

None of these trends persisted to the same extent in the 1990s, and indeed some of them were reversed (access to start-up capital became harder, for example, and the tax authorities introduced a much stricter regime for labor in the construction sector). As a result, self-employment rates, by the end of the 1990s, had fallen back to the levels of the mid 1980s, and UK self-employment is no longer following a significantly different trajectory from that in other advanced countries. Indeed, it seems likely that aggregate self-employment in the UK is subject mainly

TABLE 5.6
Logit Model of Exit from Self-Employment in the United Kingdom, 1980–99, Version 2

	All		Male		Female	
	Coef.	s.e.	Coef.	s.e	Coef.	s.e
Gender (ref: male)						
Female	0.518***	(0.081)				
Age						
Age (yrs, age 18 = 0)	−0.096***	(0.014)	−0.094***	(0.017)	−0.102***	(0.025)
Age squared	0.002***	(0.000)	0.002***	(0.000)	0.002***	(0.001)
Education (CASMIN) (ref: 1ab)						
1c/2a	0.272	(0.256)	1.304***	(0.498)	0.067	(0.286)
2b	0.121	(0.095)	0.145	(0.111)	0.006	(0.186)
2c	0.304***	(0.109)	0.440***	(0.127)	0.018	(0.203)
3a	0.101	(0.092)	0.125	(0.110)	−0.001	(0.170)
3b	0.237*	(0.138)	0.352**	(0.165)	0.009	(0.238)
Occupation in current self-employment (ref: unskilled)						
Professional self-employed	−0.272**	(0.121)	−0.454***	(0.144)	0.044	(0.223)
Skilled self-employed	−0.120	(0.114)	−0.213*	(0.129)	0.127	(0.229)
Industrial sector of current self-employment spell (ref: primary, manufacturing, utilities; also includes those not in the labor market)						
Construction	0.040	(0.118)	0.005	(0.131)	0.628	(0.521)
Traditional services	0.337***	(0.121)	0.343**	(0.146)	0.341	(0.221)
Transport and communications	0.395**	(0.180)	0.275	(0.199)	0.997***	(0.380)
Financial and business services	0.438***	(0.139)	0.415***	(0.169)	0.566**	(0.264)
Other services	0.141	(0.119)	0.254	(0.168)	0.100	(0.188)
Father self-employed (ref: father not self-employed)						
Self-employed	−0.164**	(0.080)	−0.135	(0.098)	−0.191	(0.147)

Table 5.6 (*continued*)

	All		Male		Female	
	Coef.	*s.e.*	*Coef.*	*s.e*	*Coef.*	*s.e*
Social background of father (*ref: father unskilled employee*) Professional						
employee	−0.043	(0.094)	−0.080	(0.116)	0.012	(0.164)
Skilled employee	0.043	(0.082)	−0.006	(0.094)	0.185	(0.163)
Other	−0.112	(0.111)	−0.145	(0.131)	−0.046	(0.196)
At risk in 1980 or 1990s (*ref: 1980s*)						
At risk in 1990s	1.654***	(0.077)	1.747***	(0.099)	1.470***	(0.122)
Constant	−2.233***	(0.205)	−2.262***	(0.244)	−1.646***	(0.392)
Number of observations	9,356		6,835		2,521	
Wald χ^2 (degrees of freedom)	607.76$_{(20)}$		403.93$_{(19)}$		177.69$_{(19)}$	
Pseudo R^2	0.096		0.095		0.081	
Log likelihood	−3374.53		−2264.06		−1100.86	

* $p < 0.10$ ** $p < 0.05$ *** $p < 0.01$

to influences (such as the ongoing shift to the service sector) that are also found in other economies.

The evidence suggests, moreover, that some of the apparent shifts in composition of self-employment in the 1980s (e.g., faster increases in the self-employment rate among young people and among women) have also not been durable ones, and again (contrary to the conclusions drawn by some earlier researchers), it does not appear that by the end of the 1990s there was any notable shift in the age or gender composition of self-employment.

This is not to say, however, that there have been no recent or ongoing changes in the nature or composition of self-employment in the UK. Indeed there have been, and these changes are consistent with a model suggesting that some traditional boundaries of self-employment are breaking down. Self-employment, we hypothesize, is increasingly a labor market state that more people in the UK experience during their working lives than used to be the case. Self-employment is less of a distinct labor market segment, affecting only certain types of people (in certain occupations, sectors, and social classes). This hypothesis is borne out by work history data (see also Meager and Bates 2001), which show that many more people experience spells of self-employment over a given period than is suggested by stock data alone. It is also borne out by the data in the present chapter on the changing occupational composition of self-employment, particularly the rapid recent decline in the share of self-employment that is accounted for by the group "managers," which is consistent with the argument that the traditional picture of the self-employed person as an entrepreneur or small business owner is now less universal, with growing numbers of self-employed people who now identify themselves as independent professionals, craftworkers, or service providers, rather than business "managers."

Similarly, the changing sectoral composition of self-employment would appear to be contributing to this greater flexibility and turbulence within self-employment. In particular, our analysis of aggregate self-employment trends shows that to an increasing extent, UK self-employment is concentrated in the service sectors. When we look at flows data, however, we also find that service-sector self-employment is significantly less stable, recording higher exit rates than self-employment in other sectors.

Taking self-employment as a whole, also striking is the finding that even within the period of analysis considered in this paper (the 1980s and 1990s), the dynamism of this segment of the labor market continued to increase, with significantly higher overall rates of entry to and exit from self-employment in the 1990s than in the 1980s.

We have also argued, here and in previous work (Meager and Bates 2001; Meager, Court, and Moralee 1996) that these developments may have important implications for the quality of working life, particularly when earnings are taken into account. Many commentators have noted that the self-employed are, on average, better off in earnings terms than employees, and that in retirement, those who have been self-employed are, on average wealthier than those who have only been employees. These data, however, fail to take into account the much wider distribution of incomes among the self-employed (and in retirement, among the ex-self-employed) than among employees (and ex-employees). Our analysis suggests that a significant proportion of the self-employed are found to have very low incomes (and similarly that a significant proportion of the ex-self-employed are poor in old age). More importantly, however, it suggests that being self-employed per se contributes to the likelihood of very low incomes, controlling for other factors, but does not contribute to the likelihood of very high incomes. This analysis raises important questions about the welfare implications of a growth in new or "non-traditional" forms of self-employment.

Our dynamic analysis conducted with panel data, replicating similar analysis undertaken in the other countries reported in this volume, reinforces the findings of previous research. In particular, it shows persistent gender effects, in the sense that women are less likely than men to enter self-employment, and that female self-employment is less stable than male self-employment. Similarly, age patterns are found that confirm or reinforce those found in previous studies. Generally speaking, entry propensities increase and exit propensities decrease with age; this is consistent with arguments that suggest that the accumulation of financial and human capital with age is a factor facilitating entry into self-employment and protecting against exit. The results in the present chapter suggest, however, that the relationships are both curvilinear. That is, after a certain age, the increasing propensity to enter self-employment flattens off and declines, and similarly, the propensity to leave self-employment ceases to decline after a certain age and then increases as retirement age approaches.

The findings that relate to social mobility, class, and educational background are interesting. At an aggregate level (i.e., taking all the self-employed together), the familiar relationship found in previous studies is observed, namely, that parental self-employment is a significant predictor both of entry to self-employment and of "success" within self-employment (measured by lower probabilities of exit). This intergenerational transmission of skills, attitudes, and possibly also financial resources has long been given as an explanation for the presumed homogeneity and stability of the petty bourgeois self-employment segment. Our analysis is, however, distinguished by a disaggregation of the self-employed by occupational category, and it is at this level that more heterogeneity emerges. Thus it is notable that having had a self-employed father is a predictor only of entry into unskilled and skilled self-employment, but *not* into professional self-employment. For the latter, it is parental social background more generally that is influential (i.e., having had a professional father, irrespective of whether he was self-employed, and having a higher-level qualification both increase the likelihood of professional self-employment and reduce the likelihood of unskilled self-employment).

For certain types of self-employment at least, therefore, it would seem that the influence of parental self-employment is moderated by other aspects of social and educational background. In other words, professional self-employment would appear to be a labor market segment that is "open" to those without a family background of self-employment, if they nevertheless have a high level of education and/or a professional family background. It is much less clear that self-employment is a vehicle for upward or downward social mobility, either between or within generations. We have seen that parental social background is a strong influence on entry to professional self-employment. Equally, looking at an individual's own trajectory, although there is some evidence that those with intermediate qualification levels also have higher probabilities of entering professional self-employment than those with no qualifications, it is also clear that there is a very strong relationship between an individual's prior occupational status and his or her occupational status in self-employment.

Notes

1. See Casey and Creigh (1988), who compare LFS estimates of self-employment with those derived from administrative sources based on social security or tax records.
2. Published data from the LFS prior to 1984 exclude Northern Ireland. LFS data presented elsewhere in this chapter for the period 1984 onward, however, cover the UK as a whole (i.e., including Northern Ireland).
3. See Meager (1993) and Meager and Bates (2001) for further discussion of these issues.
4. We have excluded the agricultural sector from the data used for the multivariate analysis to ensure consistency with the data used for the other countries in the study. In practice, excluding agriculture makes very little difference to the findings, due to the small size of agricultural employment and self-employment in the UK.
5. The survival curves have been constructed only for the subperiod 1980–95, for which Harpin has created continuous time rather than discrete time data.

References

Acs, Z., D. Audretsch, and D. Evans. 1992. *The determinants of variations in self-employment rates across countries and over time*. Discussion Paper FS IV 92-3. Berlin: Wissenschaftszentrum Berlin für Sozialforschung.

Blanchflower, D. G., and A. J. Oswald. 1990. Self-employment and Mrs. Thatcher's enterprise culture. In *British Social Attitudes: The 1990 Report*. Aldershot, England: Gower.

Bögenhold, D., and U. Staber. 1991. The decline and rise of self-employment. *Work, Employment and Society* 5:223–39.

Bryson, A., and M. White. 1997. *Moving in and out of self-employment*. PSI Report 826. London: Policy Studies Institute.

Campbell, M., and M. Daly. 1992. Self-employment: Into the 1990s. *Employment Gazette* (June), 269–92.

Casey, B., and S. Creigh. 1988. Self-employment in Great Britain. *Work, Employment and Society* 2(3).

Cowling, M., and P. Mitchell. 1997. The evolution of UK self-employment: A study of government policy and the role of the macroeconomy. *The Manchester School* 65:427–42.

Hakim, C. 1989. Workforce restructuring, social insurance coverage and the black economy. *Journal of Social Policy* 18:471–503.

Knight, G., and S. McKay. 2000. *Lifetime experiences of self-employment.* DSS Research Report 120. London: Department of Social Security.

Meager, N. 1991. *Self-employment in the United Kingdom.* IMS Report 205. Brighton: Institute of Manpower Studies.

———. 1992. Does unemployment lead to self-employment? *Small Business Economics* 4:87–103.

———. 1993. *Self-employment and labour market policy in the European Community.* Discussion Paper FSI 93-901. Berlin: Wissenschaftszentrum Berlin für Sozialforschung.

Meager, N., and P. Bates. 2001. The self-employed and lifetime incomes: Some UK evidence. *International Journal of Sociology* 31:27–58.

Meager, N., G. Court, and J. Moralee. 1996. Self-employment and the distribution of income. In *New inequalities: The changing distribution of income and wealth in the United Kingdom*, ed. J. Hill. Cambridge: Cambridge University Press.

Metcalf, H. 1998. *Self-employment for the unemployed: The role of public policy.* Research Report 47. London: Department for Education and Employment.

Moralee, L. 1998. Self-employment in the 1990s. *Labour Market Trends* (March), 121–30.

Nisbet, P. 1997. Dualism, flexibility and self-employment in the UK construction industry. *Work, Employment and Society* 11:459–80.

Peel, M. 1999. One-man bands may be forced to look for pastures new. *Financial Times*, 9 November.

Storey, D. 1991. The birth of new firms—does unemployment matter? A review of the Evidence. *Small Business Economics* 3:167–78.

Winch, G. 1998. The growth of self-employment in construction. *Construction Management and Economics* 16:531–43.

CHAPTER SIX

Entrepreneurs and Laborers: Two Sides of Self-Employment Activity in the United States

Richard Arum

SELF-EMPLOYMENT IN the United States has increased since the mid-1970s in close tandem with an overall growth in labor market inequality. Self-employment activity both reflects the larger trend toward economic polarization—since it involves both successful entrepreneurs and economically marginal laborers—as well as presents itself as a special case of this phenomenon (that is, it is a more advanced form of the general trend of states not just tolerating, but fostering, greater divergence in what is considered acceptable labor market outcomes). Self-employment occupies this peculiar social position because the activity occurs in an economic niche where state, familial, and market forces interact in uniquely formative ways. In modern economies, self-employment generally occurs when individuals have incentives to engage in entrepreneurial activities and/or firms have incentives to subcontract with individuals or small enterprises in networked forms of production (rather than when businesses subsume these services into internal hierarchies). Self-employment dynamics are thus the product of the interaction between macro-level opportunity structures and micro-level individual attributes (Aldrich and Waldinger 1990).

Because self-employment occurs in relatively unregulated economic niches within a larger context of more pronounced state regulation, it is dependent on how states manage and shape labor market activity (Arum, Budig, and Grant 2000; Blau 1987; Brock and Evans 1986). Self-employed individuals face economic markets in the relative absence of protections and safeguards provided by modern state and bureaucratic organization. In the absence of these safety nets, existing inequalities flourish. Women and racial minorities often thus face greater obstacles and risks in attempting to establish and maintain successful self-employment enterprises than do white men. Ethnic entrepreneurs in the United States often are able to sustain themselves in these climates only by relying on differentiated business strategies, such as situating themselves in "ethnic enclaves," acting as "minority middlemen," or utilizing unpaid (or underpaid) family labor. Since self-employment is relatively unregulated and full of risks, most individuals either fail as entrepreneurs or occupy relatively undesirable self-employment positions; for the few who are successful, however, the rewards of self-employment activity in the United States can be quite large.

STATE REGULATION AND SELF-EMPLOYMENT

Self-employment flourishes when the incentives for the activities are greater—for example, when state regulation has simultaneously created high costs and rigidities for firms relying on long-term labor contracts relative to the benefits and opportunities associated with subcontracting to small firms, entrepreneurs, or marginal laborers. The United States relative to most continental European countries has relatively low levels of labor market regulation with subsequently fewer incentives for firms to outsource production. In the United States, private firms have wide discretion in choosing appropriate forms to manage their relationships with employees: not only is government regulation weak, but so too are the constraints imposed by professional associations and unions. By the early 1990s, the unionization rate of nongovernment workers had declined to a post–World War II low. In the 1980s, U.S. firms faced few difficulties in implementing reorganization plans that laid off large numbers of workers and midlevel managers to increase profits and respond to global economic competition. Bluestone and Harrison (1988:36–37) estimate that from 1980 to 1986, employment declined 17 percent in the textile industry, 30 percent in primary metals, and 40 percent in steel— plant closings and permanent layoffs in manufacturing also led to lost jobs for 780,000 managers and professionals, according to the Bureau of Labor Statistics.

While the United States overall has low levels of labor market regulation relative to many continental European countries, labor market regulation of large employers in the United States has been increasing. Although politicians have often embraced a rhetoric of deregulation, state and federal officials in the 1980s and early 1990s expanded many workplace rights, such as right-to-know laws concerning toxic materials, remedy-for-wrongful-discharge statutes, and legislation protecting workers who apply for worker's compensation (Edwards 1993). Firms have responded to new legislation, regulation, and threats of litigation by expanding due process rights and altering the internal structure of firms to comply—at least symbolically—with these policy changes (Guthrie and Roth 1998; Sutton et al. 1994; Edelman 1992). The federal character of the U.S. system of government grants individual states great latitude to determine the level of regulation in local labor markets (Eisinger 1988).

In the context of growing regulation, states significantly vary in the extent to which they are regulated (Grant 1996, 1995). In recent years, self-employment activity increased most dramatically in those states that had highly regulated labor markets or were increasing their level of regulation (Arum, Budig, and Grant 2000). Economic settings with strong state regulation of large businesses—such as Italy (Barbieri 2001; Piore and Sabel 1984)—provide the strongest incentives for businesses to outsource production to individuals engaged in self-employment or small-firm activity.

In the United States, individuals are involved in self-employment under varying legal designations for the activity and with quite different tax implications, financial incentives, and economic risks (such as personal liability) associated with the chosen designation. Many self-employed individuals simply identify themselves as "sole proprietors"—a legal status that requires only an easily obtainable tax identification number: as this designation does not involve the creation of a new separate legal entity, the business is technically considered simply an extension of the individual, who therefore assumes full personal liability for all business obligations. Other self-employed individuals choose to organize their activities as incorporated businesses for tax and other purposes (such as greater flexibility in possibilities for transferring rights to third parties). Evidence suggests that "incorporation has definitely been on the upswing in the United States," with a progression from 1.8 percent of total employment in the mid-1970s to 2.8 percent by the early 1980s (Bregger 1996:8). While increasing numbers of self-employed individuals find reasons to incorporate themselves, it is important to note that these individuals are not considered self-employed in official U.S. government labor market statistics. Rather, although they report to government surveyors that they are self-employed, since 1967 they have been reclassified as wage and salary workers—i.e., employees of their own businesses—if they respond positively to the prompt: "Is this business incorporated?" Official estimates of U.S. self-employment thus often have underreported this activity, even before considering the phenomenon of nonreported, informal self-employment activity (Bregger 1996).

GROWING INEQUALITY AND ECONOMIC MARGINALIZATION

The increase in self-employment activity in the United States occurred concurrently with a dramatic growth in economic inequality. Since the mid-1970s, the gini-coefficient measuring inequality in individual incomes rose from 0.395 to 0.435 in 1992 (Ryscavage 1995). Social scientists have identified various causes for this growth in inequality but largely agree that state policy has exacerbated these trends (Fischer et al. 1996). One important cause of growing inequality is the decline of U.S. labor unions (Freeman 1993; Card 1992). While the wages of less-educated male workers have stagnated since the mid-1970s, top executives have won increasingly generous pay packages. The compensation of the average chief executive officer in the United States rose 5.2 percent per year in the 1980s and is now at least seventy times larger than the wages of the average adult male—a difference much larger than in other countries (Levy 1998:123). CEO compensation in the United States has increasingly been tied to short-term profits and fluctuations in the price of company securities. This change has coincided with the ascendancy of a management philosophy based on short-term "financial conceptions of control" that implicitly questions managerial commitment to long-term investments such as employee development (Fligstein 1990).

Instead of establishing a stable, well-trained workforce, corporate management has embraced a philosophy of developing greater flexibility through relying on temporary contingent laborers whenever possible. While contingent workers sometimes establish formal employment relationships with firms specializing in temporary assignment, often these firms are bypassed and workers are simply hired as "independent contractors" without associated employee benefits or employment protections. In February 1995 the U.S. government added a special supplementary battery of questions on contingent labor activity to the monthly Current Population Survey (CPS) to generate estimates of the characteristics of this growing segment of the workforce.

The February 1995 CPS assigned individuals to categories based on both their employment arrangements as well as the degree to which their employment was considered contingent (Polivka 1996). Some 8.3 million workers, approximately 6.7 percent of the total workforce, were assigned to the category "independent contractor" (which included also consultants and freelance workers), the vast majority of whom also indicated that they were self-employed. An additional 3.7 million workers, 3.1 percent of the U.S. workforce, were involved in alternative employment arrangements (e.g., they were on-call workers, employed by temporary agencies, or entirely subcontracted out on an intrafirm basis). The CPS reported that 76 percent of "independent contractors" had no employees and 17 percent had tenures of one year or less (Cohany 1996). Kalleberg, Reskin, and Hudson (2000) used these data to document the extent to which these nonstandard employment arrangements were associated with negative outcomes such as low earnings and the absence of pension and health insurance benefits.

Variation in earnings associated with self-employed occupations is much greater than variation in earnings associated with dependent employment. In the United States, the extent to which self-employment includes not just successful entrepreneurs, but a large number of marginalized laborers has been identified in past research. In the 1980s, 29 percent of men and 34 percent of women in nonprofessional self-employment reported that their involvement with self-employment was "supposed to be temporary" (compared with 20 percent of men and 23 percent of women in nonprofessional dependent employment). In the United States, where individuals have no guarantee of health care coverage, 31 percent of men in nonprofessional self-employment in 1980 had no health care insurance compared with 11 percent of men in nonprofessional dependent employment. Hourly earnings also reflect the marginalization of this type of labor activity. In 1980, hourly earnings of $10.40 for men and $5.70 for women were reported by individuals in nonprofessional self-employment compared with $13.80 and $8.40 for men and women in nonprofessional dependent employment (Arum 1997). In comparative perspective, McManus (2000) recently demonstrated that the United States has a larger proportion of low-paying and unstable self-employment jobs for men than does Western Germany.

INDUSTRY AND OCCUPATIONAL CHARACTERISTICS

The heterogeneity within self-employment makes analysis of its character rather difficult. Research on the topic has often been facilitated by distinguishing among self-employment on the basis of either occupational categories or industrial classifications. In terms of occupation, researchers have in the past distinguished between professional and other forms of nonprofessional self-employment (e.g., skilled and unskilled nonprofessional occupations). In the United States in recent years, nonprofessional self-employment has been growing at a greater rate than professional self-employment, particularly for women (Arum 1997).

The extent to which self-employment is associated with particular industrial sectors is also well documented in the United States. Self-employment rates are particularly high and growing in the construction industry. Self-employment is also slightly higher than average in the service sector, an area of the economy that is dramatically increasing in both size and relative importance in the overall economy. Steinmetz and Wright (1989:1003) have concluded from these trends that in the United States, "self-employment is growing much more rapidly in the traditional core of industrial society than within the newer post-industrial services." Labor economists examining recent changes in patterns of self-employment have also highlighted the extent to which changes in the characteristics of industrial structure and the technologies of production have contributed to the resurgence of self-employment. David Blau (1987: 449), for example, has used time-series analyses to highlight the extent to which "the most important causes of rising self-employment in the past decade are changes in industrial structure and technology."

ETHNICITY, GENDER, AND FAMILY DETERMINANTS

There is a large body of research in the United States on the extent to which self-employment is associated with individual attributes, such as ethnic minority status, gender, and family status. These individual-level attributes structure the incentives and disincentives provided by self-employment activity. While immigrants in the United States as a whole do not have significantly higher rates of self-employment than the general population,[1] certain immigrant groups have particularly high rates of self-employment. Self-employment is particularly prevalent among Korean, Chinese, Japanese, Russian, and Middle Eastern immigrants to the United States. This concentration of self-employment among particular immigrant groups, rather than as a response to shared attributes related to immigrant status per se, distinguishes the United States from other societies with large migration streams, such as Israel (Shavit and Yuchtman-Yaar 2001). Researchers attribute these high rates of self-employment among particular immigrant ethnic groups to differences in social networks, familial relations, educational attainment, and entrepreneurial experience (Aldrich and Waldinger 1990; Portes and Rumbaut 1990; Kim and Hurh 1985; Min 1984).

Self-employment activity is also structured by gender and family status. Occupational sex segregation is pronounced in the United States within both self-employment and dependent employment (Wharton 1989). Men have significantly higher rates of self-employment than women, although the rate of female self-employment is increasing dramatically (Arum 1997). Men and women are affected differently by family responsibilities, with women's self-employment success negatively affected by family commitments (Loscocco and Leicht 1993; Hisrich and Brush 1986). Self-employment for women is often more precarious than male self-employment and concentrated in more economically marginal occupational roles (Arum 1997).

DATA AND METHODS

This study relies primarily on 1980–92 annual data from the Panel Study of Income Dynamics (PSID), with brief discussion of supplementary descriptive results based on data from the 1983, 1992, and 2000 Current Population Surveys. The two sets of results are not strictly comparable. In the body of the text, I focus on PSID estimates due to difference in occupational and industrial coding—PSID uses 1970 and CPS relies on 1980 classifications—and greater problems of self-employment under-reporting in government-collected micro data.[2]

The PSID is a longitudinal study of U.S. families that is based on an initial oversampling of low-income families and the later inclusion into the study of families formed by individuals exiting the original set of families and creating new autonomous households. Weights are used in this study to adjust estimates for the nonrepresentativeness of the sample. All analysis is based on individuals between the ages of 18 and 60 who are not involved in agricultural activity and is conducted separately by gender.

The research relies on the utilization of a variety of units of analysis appropriate to the specific measurement task. The unit of analysis for generating survival curves is an individual spell of self-employment that begins between 1980 and 1987. Descriptive findings identifying the size of firm are based on individual reports from 1985 (the only year that PSID provides such data). Descriptive analysis of the prevalence of self-employment by age, education, industry, parental background, and time period relies on pooled 1980–92 data where the unit of analysis is therefore the person-year. All multivariate analyses of paths into and out of self-employment also use the person-year as the unit of analysis.

Analysis follows the research design protocols specified in project guidelines proposed by Mueller, Lohmann, and Luber (1999, 2000). Self-employment throughout the research is defined as nonagricultural self-employment and is differentiated through the application of a three-category schema that extends my earlier research utilizing simply a professional and nonprofessional distinction to identify separately skilled and un-skilled nonprofessional self-employment occupations (Arum 1997). Professional self-employment in this schema includes all individuals who, based on their occupations, would ordinarily be classified in EGP categories I or II, with the notable exception of restauranteurs, hoteliers, shop-keepers, and retail-trade proprietors who have been reassigned to the skilled self-employment category.[3] "Traditional" skilled self-employment is the category utilized for individuals who, based on their occupations, would have been assigned EGP categories IIIa, V, and VI or reassigned as discussed above from professional self-employment based on their in-dustrial activity. Unskilled self-employment is the category for occupa-tional codes associated with EGP categories IIIb or VII (Erikson and Goldthorpe 1992). Note that our classification schema will assign indi-viduals who employ others into either skilled or unskilled self-employ-ment if the individual identifies with an occupation associated with those classes and does not simply report being a proprietor or manager of a small business.

For men the most common occupational codes in the various categories of self-employment are as follows. Professional self-employment—managers and administrators not elsewhere classified (50.1 percent), lawyers (6.2 percent), accountants (5.3 percent); skilled self-employment—managers and administrators not elsewhere classified who were in retail trade or service industries (30.0 percent), carpenters (9.5 percent), automobile mechanics (7.4 percent), wholesale trade sales representatives (6.6 percent), construction and maintenance painters (4.3 percent); and unskilled self-employment—truck drivers (23.4 percent), taxicab drivers and chauffeurs (10.0 percent). For women, quite distinct self-employment occupations were prevalent. Professional self-employment—managers and administrators not elsewhere classified (23.7 percent), real estate agents and brokers (10.7 percent), painters and sculptors (7.9 percent); skilled self-employment—managers and administrators not elsewhere classified who were in retail trade or service industries (23.4 percent), hairdressers and cosmetologists (20.3 percent), bookkeepers (11.9 percent), secretaries not elsewhere classified (6.3 percent); and unskilled self-employment—nonprivate household childcare workers (46.3 percent), private household maids and servants (12.6 percent), private household childcare workers (7.0 percent). Self-employment in the United States is profoundly sex-segregated. Only the indistinct "managers and administrators not elsewhere classified" category appears as both a common male and female self-employment occupation.[4]

While the methodology follows the research project design protocols wherever possible, it is worth noting two important exceptions to the comparability of the analysis required by anomalies present in the PSID data structure. First, inadequate specification of educational experience in the data required that along with CASMIN categories ED1, ED2a, ED2b, ED3a, and ED3b, an *additional vocational education* measure be included. The additional vocational education measure identifies individuals who report having received vocational training and who did not also report receiving exactly twelve years of education (in which case they were classified as ED2a). Individuals are assigned to the ED1 category if they have not completed twelve years of schooling. ED2a is the category for individuals who report twelve years of education and vocational training. Individuals with some postsecondary training, but who have not completed a degree, are assigned to ED3a; individuals with sixteen or more years of education completed are assigned to ED3b (for discussion of CASMIN, see Arum and Hout 1998; Mueller et al. 1989). Second, father's background was identified in the data simply on the basis of one-digit coding that collapses occupation and self-employment into the response category "self-employed businessman." This analysis therefore codes father's background as being uniquely one of the following five categories: professional, skilled, unskilled, agricultural, or self-employed.

Additional differences in the U.S. analysis reflect either the particularities of U.S. society (e.g., race) or the flexibility granted country-specific researchers. Race is classified in this study as *white, African American*, and *other nonwhite race*. Work experience was measured simply as prior years of work experienced for the analysis of paths into self-employment; for paths out of self-employment, work experience was measured as length of *self-employment spell* and *work experience prior to spell*. Difficulties in translating U.S. census industry codes into corresponding Economic Activities in the European Union (NACE) industrial codes led to the collapsing of all service-sector industries into one common category. Prior year employment, occupation, and family characteristics are measured (with the latter including dummy variables for *spouse employed, spouse nonemployed*, and *spouse self-employed* in prior year, with the omitted category being no spouse).

The analysis proceeds as follows. First, survival curves of distinct types of self-employment are generated. Second, the prevalence of self-employment over the life-course is identified. Third, the proportion of self-employed by education, industry, parental background, and time period is reported. Fourth, the size of firms associated with self-employed entrepreneurs is examined. Fifth, competing risk event history is conducted identifying factors associated with entry into the three distinct categories of self-employment. The risk set for the analysis originally includes all individuals who are not self-employed in the prior year; supplementary analysis is conducted on a risk set that is restricted to those who were active in the labor market the prior year. Sixth, event-history analysis is conducted on the factors associated with self-employment exit. Analysis here is conducted separately for each distinct category of self-employment. The risk set for the analysis is defined in two ways: as all individuals who were self-employed in the prior year; as well as a supplementary analysis where the risk set is restricted to include only those individuals who were self-employed in the prior year and whose self-employment spell began after 1980. For the event-history analysis, missing data on social background, family characteristics, and prior work experience are handled by the mean substitution method with (unreported) dummy variables added to the analysis to adjust for the substitution.

DESCRIPTIVE FINDINGS

Figure 6.1 presents five-year survival curves for professional, skilled, and unskilled self-employment separately by gender. To avoid the possibilities

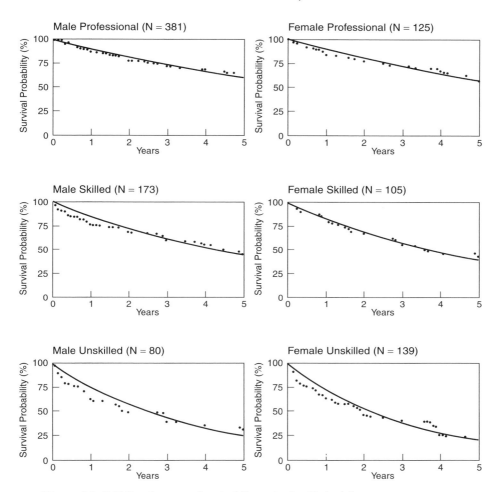

Figure 6.1: Self-Employment Survival Rates in the United States

of any duration bias, the survival curves are conservatively estimated based on self-employment spells beginning between 1980 and 1987 (the start dates allow five years of subsequent observation for all spells).[5] The survival curves are generated based on a fitted exponential function with deviations from the predicted values indicated by marked points off the curves. The survival curves overall highlight the inherent instability of self-employed activity as well as suggesting pronounced differences between professional and nonprofessional self-employment.

Professional self-employment not surprisingly is the most stable form examined. Even in professional self-employment (where subsequent analysis will demonstrate that there is a concentration of individuals with high levels of human capital), many aspiring entrepreneurs fail. Five years after the beginning of the activity, 36 percent of men and 45 percent of women have ceased their involvement with self-employment.

Skilled and unskilled survival rates are much lower. For men in skilled self-employment, 25 percent have exited by the end of the first year and 56 percent have left by year five; for men in unskilled self-employment, 38 percent have exited by the end of year one and 69 percent by year five. Women also have extraordinarily low rates of survival in nonprofessional self-employment: 57 percent of women have left skilled self-employment by year five, and 80 percent of women have left unskilled self-employment before the end of the five-year observation period.

While figure 6.1 suggests that individual self-employment spells are at high risk of failure, figure 6.2 identifies the prevalence of self-employment over the life course. When comparing male and female results, pronounced gender differences are evident. While men demonstrate relatively constant rates of skilled and unskilled self-employment activity from their late twenties to age 60, male professional self-employment increases dramatically up to age 48 where it peaks at 14 percent. Women exhibit relatively stable rates of self-employment from their early thirties onward, with professional self-employment activity approximating 3.5 percent throughout this latter life-course stage. These descriptive results raise an important question to consider subsequently when examining the results of the multivariate analysis: why is age more closely associated with male professional self-employment than with either female professional self-employment or self-employment in nonprofessional occupations?

Tables 6.1A and 6.1B provide descriptive statistics on the occupational distribution of self-employment and dependent employment by education, industry, parental background, and time period, separately for men and women. Rates are based on nonagricultural labor market participation. Inspecting first the associations between self-employment and education, two interesting patterns emerge. First, there is a strong relationship between educational qualifications and whether an individual is likely engaged in either professional or unskilled self-employment. Men are likely in unskilled self-employment only if they have not completed secondary education or if they completed secondary education without the addition of any vocational training. Women are more likely engaged in unskilled self-employment if they have twelve years or less of educational attainment. Unsurprisingly, professional self-employment is more likely if individuals have completed four years of a postsecondary degree. Overall, the association between education and male self-employment is quasi-linear and approximates more the pattern past research has identi-

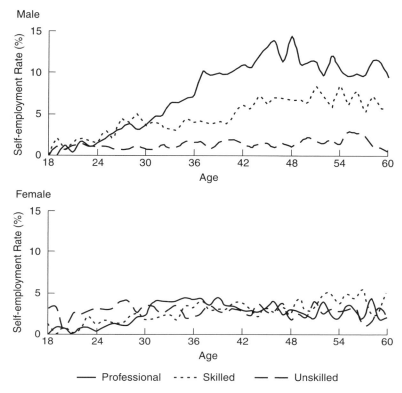

Figure 6.2: Self-Employment over the Life Course in the United States

fied with Germany and postcommunist Russia than the curvilinear pattern identified in the United Kingdom and Israel (Gerber 2001; Shavit and Yuchtman-Yaar 2001; Luber et al. 2000).

The second notable association between education and self-employment is the significance of vocational education. Men and women are significantly more likely in skilled self-employment if they are high school graduates with vocational training (ED2a) than otherwise. Additional vocational education training other than Ed2a is also moderately related to skilled self-employment for men and women.

Table 6.1 also highlights the associations between self-employment and specific industrial branches of activity. Professional and skilled self-employment is particularly concentrated in the construction industry (NACE F), where instability of seasonal and economic cycles produces large incentives for work to be organized by flexible, network-based production strategies. The construction sector also provides moderate levels

TABLE 6.1A
Male Occupational Distributions by Education, Industry, Parental Background, and Time Period in the United States (in percent)

	Male self-employment				Male dependent employment			N of row[a]	
	Professional	Skilled	Unskilled	All S.E.	Professional	Skilled	Unskilled		(% in row)
Education (CASMIN)									
Ed. 1	3.6	4.2	2.9	10.7	7.1	37.3	44.9	4,936	(13)
Ed. 2a	4.5	6.9	0.9	12.3	20.0	40.6	27.1	1,856	(5)
Ed. 2b	4.8	5.1	1.9	11.7	13.0	35.7	39.7	7,408	(20)
Ed. 3a	6.5	6.0	1.1	13.7	32.8	32.9	20.6	11,034	(30)
Ed. 3b	12.6	3.2	0.6	16.4	63.8	13.2	6.6	11,622	(32)
Add. Voc. Ed.	7.6	4.8	1.5	13.9	30.1	34.7	21.4	7,604	(21)
Industry (NACE classification)									
NACE C/D/E	2.6	0.5	0.8	3.8	30.9	35.3	30.0	11,560	(32)
NACE F	17.6	11.9	1.9	31.3	12.4	41.3	14.9	3,931	(11)
NACE G/H	4.5	14.8	2.0	21.3	25.4	25.5	27.9	7,363	(20)
NACE I	1.9	0.4	5.1	7.4	28.0	31.7	32.9	2,761	(8)
NACE J/K	19.3	1.0	1.0	21.3	56.0	9.9	12.7	2,883	(8)
NACE L	11.0	1.2	0.1	12.3	53.5	19.0	15.3	7,817	(22)
Parental background									
Self-employment	14.9	9.6	1.2	25.7	40.6	20.9	12.7	1,747	(5)
Other-employment	7.2	4.5	1.4	13.1	34.2	28.6	24.2	35,109	(95)
Time period									
1981–82	6.3	4.3	1.0	11.6	34.0	31.3	23.0	5,270	(14)
1991–92	8.5	5.0	1.4	15.0	34.5	26.5	24.2	6,231	(17)
All	7.6	4.7	1.4	13.7	34.5	28.2	23.6	36,856	(100)

Note: PSID, pooled data, ages 25–60.
[a]N refers to pooled observations, not individual cases.

TABLE 6.1B

Female Occupational Distributions by Education, Industry, Parental Background, and Time Period in the United States (in percent)

	Female self-employment				Female dependent employment			N of row[a]
	Professional	Skilled	Unskilled	All S.E.	Professional	Skilled	Unskilled	(% in row)
Education (CASMIN)								
Ed. 1	0.8	2.4	4.2	7.4	7.2	19.8	65.7	3,986 (12)
Ed. 2a	2.9	4.6	4.9	12.3	26.6	35.6	25.6	1,679 (5)
Ed. 2b	1.4	2.9	3.2	7.5	14.6	40.4	37.5	9,468 (29)
Ed. 3a	2.9	2.9	2.6	8.4	35.2	36.3	20.1	10,138 (31)
Ed. 3b	5.1	1.9	1.9	8.9	69.0	14.1	8.0	7,938 (24)
Add. Voc. Ed.	3.6	4.1	2.7	10.4	37.9	28.9	22.8	6,218 (19)
Industry (NACE classification)								
NACE C/D/E	2.2	0.5	1.0	3.6	18.8	35.1	42.5	5,845 (18)
NACE F	8.3	7.6	1.8	17.7	19.5	41.3	21.5	714 (2)
NACE G/H	0.6	6.4	8.4	15.3	17.0	27.8	39.9	6,799 (21)
NACE I	0.9	1.0	1.0	2.9	28.9	42.6	25.7	1,324 (4)
NACE J/K	7.6	1.7	1.0	10.3	37.1	42.4	10.3	3,592 (11)
NACE L	2.8	2.1	1.8	6.7	48.4	24.2	20.7	14,102 (44)
Parental background								
Self-employment	6.7	4.0	1.9	12.6	48.0	24.0	15.4	1,649 (5)
Other-employment	2.5	2.6	3.0	8.1	32.9	30.5	28.6	31,560 (95)
Time period								
1981–82	2.1	2.0	1.7	5.9	31.4	34.8	28.0	4,199 (13)
1991–92	3.0	2.8	3.6	9.4	36.0	29.9	24.6	5,938 (18)
All	2.8	2.7	2.9	8.3	33.6	30.2	27.9	33,208 (100)

Note: PSID, pooled data, ages 25–60.
[a] N refers to pooled observations, not individual cases.

of unskilled self-employment opportunities for men. The overall U.S. self-employment rate in the construction industry is significantly higher than the rate in Germany, although lower than in England (Luber et al. 2000). The financial business service sector (NACE J/K), whose role in the economy has been expanding in recent decades, has higher than average rates of self-employment—particularly professional—for both men and women. Unskilled self-employment is particularly prevalent in the transportation and communication sector (NACE I) for men and in the traditional service sector (NACE G/H) for women. Women and men also have higher rates of skilled self-employment in the traditional service sector (NACE G/H) than in general.

Individuals whose fathers were "self-employed businessmen" were particularly likely to end up in professional self-employment. Men and women were more than twice as likely to be professionally self-employed if their fathers were self-employed than otherwise. The magnitude of these associations is remarkably similar to rates reported for France (Laferrère 2000). Men with a self-employed father were also more than twice as likely to be present in our category of skilled self-employment that includes traditional small proprietors. The background of having a father who was a "self-employed businessman" was not as strongly related to other forms of self-employment with the exception that women were more likely to report skilled self-employment and less likely to report unskilled self-employment activity.

Lastly, table 6.1 reports growth in self-employment from the early 1980s to the early 1990s.[6] In just a brief decade's time, there is clear evidence of overall self-employment increases for men from 11.6 to 15.0 percent and for women from 5.9 percent to 9.4 percent. While all categories of self-employment are increasing, the growth is most pronounced in the unskilled self-employment category. Over the decade, the incidence of male unskilled self-employment increased by 40 percent (from a rate of 1 to 1.4 per hundred), and female unskilled self-employment more than doubled (from a rate of 1.7 to 3.6 per hundred). Since unskilled self-employment is related to low earnings, pronounced job instability, and the lack of health care, the dramatic increase of this type of marginalized labor has troubling implications for those concerned with trends of growing economic inequality in the United States.[7]

Table 6.2 provides descriptive data on the size of enterprise associated with individual self-employment. While self-employment is often simply equated with the entrepreneurial promotion of jobs (see, e.g., Birch 1987), the results suggest that self-employment activity is not uniformly associated with such employment creation. Of the categories examined, only the majority of individuals in male professional and skilled self-employment have any workers in their enterprises at all. Only approximately 5

TABLE 6.2
Self-Employment by Firm Size (1985) in the United States (in percent)

Size of enterprise	Male				Female			
	Professional	Skilled	Unskilled	All	Professional	Skilled	Unskilled	All
1	32.2	49.0	74.3	42.5	61.5	71.3	91.8	76.0
	(72)	(72)	(32)	(176)	(52)	(70)	(97)	(219)
2	9.8	15.6	20.1	13.0	7.9	8.9	2.7	6.3
	(22)	(23)	(9)	(54)	(7)	(9)	(3)	(18)
3–4	19.1	10.2	5.6	14.6	8.5	4.5	1.5	4.6
	(43)	(15)	(2)	(60)	(7)	(4)	(2)	(13)
5–9	18.8	11.1	0	14.1	14.2	6.4	4.0	7.7
	(42)	(16)	(0)	(59)	(12)	(6)	(4)	(22)
10–24	12.3	10.2	0	10.3	0	4.4	0	1.5
	(28)	(15)	(0)	(43)	(0)	(4)	(0)	(4)
25–49	5.5	3.4	0	4.2	4.0	3.1	0	2.2
	(12)	(5)	(0)	(17)	(3)	(3)	(0)	(6)
50+	2.3	1.0	0	1.4	3.9	1.5	0	1.7
	(5)	(1)	(0)	(6)	(3)	(2)	(0)	(5)
Total	100	100	100	100	100	100	100	100
	(225)	(148)	(43)	(416)	(84)	(99)	(106)	(289)
Column Percent (N)								

Note: Self-employment in family owned firms results in exaggeration of entrepreneurial job creation (e.g., in the 50+ employee category, only one women independently ran her own firm; the others reported occupations such as "office manager" and "bookkeeper" in firms where husband reported occupational positions with greater authority).

percent of self-employed individuals support more than twenty-five individuals in their firms.

Table 6.3 provides descriptive statistics on all other variables used in the multivariate analysis. Means on the dependent variables provide information that suggests the dynamic character of self-employment activity. On an annual basis, entry rates into male self-employment range from 14.2 individuals per thousand in professional self-employment to 4.3 per thousand in unskilled self-employment. Entry rates into female self-employment range from 6.8 per thousand in skilled self-employment to 12.1 individuals per thousand in unskilled self-employment.

Mean statistics on paths out of self-employment suggest the highly unstable character of these enterprises. Annual exit rates from self-employment range from a low of 14.6 percent per year for male skilled self-employment to a high of 37.4 percent per year for female unskilled self-employment. When the risk set on paths out of self-employment is

TABLE 6.3
Descriptive Statistics of Variables from Multivariate Analysis in the United States

	Males			Females		
	N	Mean	S.D.	N	Mean	S.D.
Individual characteristics						
African American	45,790	0.101	0.301	49,887	0.139	0.334
Other nonwhite race	45,790	0.025	0.157	49,887	0.021	0.138
Age	45,790	36.850	11.500	49,887	37.438	10.102
Age squared (in thousands)	45790	1.490	0.902	49,887	1.511	0.794
Social background						
Father prof. occupation	45,790	0.173	0.378	49,887	0.141	0.348
Father skilled occupation	45,790	0.469	0.498	49,887	0.443	0.480
Father agr. occupation	45,790	0.103	0.304	49,887	0.111	0.303
Father self-employed	45,790	0.043	0.203	49,887	0.048	0.206
Family characteristics						
Spouse employed	45,790	0.333	0.471	49,887	0.450	0.480
Spouse non-employed	45,790	0.336	0.472	49,887	0.087	0.272
Spouse self-employed	45,790	0.045	0.208	49,887	0.106	0.297
Human capital/work experience						
Ed2a	45,790	0.047	0.211	49,887	0.045	0.200
Ed2b	45,790	0.203	0.402	49,887	0.293	0.439
Ed3a	45,790	0.291	0.454	49,887	0.284	0.435
Ed3b	45,790	0.293	0.455	49,887	0.213	0.395
Additional voc. training	45,790	0.208	0.406	49,887	0.176	0.367
Self-employment spell (years)	3,333	8.638	9.510	1,611	5.265	6.203
Work experience prior to spell (years)	3,333	10.704	10.432	1,611	6.394	8.137

TABLE 6.3 (*continued*)

	Males			Females		
	N	*Mean*	*S.D.*	*N*	*Mean*	*S.D.*
Prior labor market position						
Unemployed	45,790	0.048	0.214	49,887	0.041	0.192
Not in labor force	45,790	0.133	0.340	49,887	0.318	0.450
Professional occupation	45,790	0.360	0.480	49,887	0.222	0.402
Skilled occupation	45,790	0.102	0.302	49,887	0.238	0.411
Construction industry (F)	45,790	0.077	0.267	49,887	0.018	0.129
Trad. service industry (G&H)	45,790	0.057	0.231	49,887	0.131	0.325
Trans./comm. industry (I)	45,790	0.057	0.231	49,887	0.029	0.162
Fin./bus. services (J&K)	45,790	0.058	0.234	49,887	0.071	0.248
Other services (L − Q)	45,790	0.162	0.368	49,887	0.273	0.430
Dependent variables						
Path into self-employment	39,901			43,060		
Professional entry		1.42%			0.68%	
Skilled entry		1.00%			0.74%	
Unskilled entry		0.43%			1.21%	
Path out of professional self-employment	1,635	0.153	0.433	458	0.200	0.493
Path out of skilled self-employment	1,280	0.146	0.391	554	0.196	0.453
Path out of unskilled self-employment	418	0.278	0.445	599	0.374	0.497

restricted to those who started their self-employment post-1980 (i.e., when the long-term self-employed successes are excluded from the analysis), the rates of self-employment exit are increased to a high of 40.8 percent departures per year in the case of female unskilled self-employment.[8]

MULTIVARIATE ANALYSIS

Table 6.4 provides results for competing risk event-history analysis of paths into professional, skilled, and unskilled self-employment. African Americans are relatively unlikely to enter self-employment compared with whites. The age of individuals is also significantly related to self-employment entry in a complex curvilinear pattern that is discussed in detail below. Father's occupation is also associated with self-employment entry. Men with a self-employed and/or professional father were more likely to move into professional self-employment than were men with a father who worked in unskilled occupations. Women with a self-employed father were more likely to move into skilled self-employment. Interestingly, skilled self-employment entry was also elevated for women with a father from an agricultural background. Further analysis (based on unreported cross-tabulations of skilled self-employed occupations by social background) suggests that individuals with a father from an agricultural occupation relied upon particular sets of skills that were transferable to the process of entering skilled self-employment. Specifically, women from these backgrounds were more likely working as bookkeepers than otherwise expected.

The effects of family characteristics on self-employment entry vary significantly by gender. Men who have a spouse who was employed the previous year were less likely to enter self-employment than men who were not cohabiting. Women who have an employed spouse the previous year have higher rates of entering unskilled self-employment; women with a self-employed spouse the previous year were particularly likely to move into self-employment themselves. Women with a spouse who was self-employed the previous year are predicted to enter professional self-employment at a rate of 1.4 per hundred, skilled self-employment at a rate of 3.3 per hundred, and unskilled self-employment at a rate of 2.3 per hundred (compared with average rates of 0.7, 0.7, and 1.2 per hundred, respectively). While spouses who work can provide financial resources to facilitate entry into self-employment, the results for men suggest that this is not necessarily the case. Women's dramatically higher rates of entering self-employment are partially a reflection of the extent to which successful male self-employment often involves the utilization of family members in the firm (see discussion of results on firm size above).

Educational attainment is associated with self-employment entry, particularly for women (results on education will be discussed in greater depth below). Vocational training in high school (Ed2a) and additional vocational training in postsecondary institutions encourage self-employment for women in professional and skilled occupations.

TABLE 6.4

Event-History Analysis of Paths into Discrete Categories of Self-Employment in the United States

	Male self-employment entry			Female self-employment entry		
	Professional	*Skilled*	*Unskilled*	*Professional*	*Skilled*	*Unskilled*
Intercept	−11.944**	−7.816**	−7.805**	−10.669**	−8.889**	−3.566**
	(0.742)	(0.711)	(1.017)	(1.116)	(0.981)	(0.627)
Individual characteristics						
African American	−0.753**	−0.622**	−0.496	−0.537*	−0.636*	−0.511**
	(0.231)	(0.206)	(0.260)	(0.268)	(0.258)	(0.161)
Other nonwhite race	−0.301	−0.464	0.212	−0.711	−1.069	0.137
	(0.340)	(0.404)	(0.425)	(0.632)	(0.788)	(0.273)
Age	0.284**	0.127**	0.157**	0.197**	0.098*	−0.053
	(0.035)	(0.036)	(0.053)	(0.055)	(0.048)	(0.033)
Age squared (×100)	−0.316**	−0.142**	−0.179**	−0.254**	−0.125*	0.041
	(0.042)	(0.045)	(0.068)	(0.069)	(0.061)	(0.043)
Social background						
Father prof. occupa-tion	0.439*	0.106	−0.960*	0.201	1.121**	0.020
	(0.210)	(0.227)	(0.407)	(0.252)	(0.311)	(0.182)
Father skilled occu-pation	0.180	0.105	−0.067	−0.090	0.680	−0.229
	(0.197)	(0.187)	(0.223)	(0.234)	(0.286)	(0.142)
Father agr. occupa-tion	0.116	0.399	−0.336	−0.966*	1.189**	0.071
	(0.236)	(0.224)	(0.323)	(0.378)	(0.305)	(0.177)
Father self-employed	0.496*	0.588*	0.021	0.374	1.270**	−0.254
	(0.251)	(0.267)	(0.462)	(0.290)	(0.339)	(0.261)
Family characteristics						
Spouse employed	−0.249*	−0.293*	−0.492*	0.184	0.173	0.485**
	(0.121)	(0.142)	(0.213)	(0.157)	(0.167)	(0.116)
Spouse nonemployed	0.228*	−0.038	−0.145	0.211	0.102	−0.255
	(0.115)	(0.133)	(0.192)	(0.267)	(0.271)	(0.214)
Spouse self-employed	0.188	0.450*	−0.352	0.809**	1.686**	0.705**
	(0.203)	(0.225)	(0.482)	(0.186)	(0.173)	(0.161)
Human capital/work experience						
Ed2a	−0.427	0.257	−0.292	1.341**	0.583	0.971**
	(0.364)	(0.242)	(0.353)	(0.426)	(0.327)	(0.176)
Ed2b	0.096	0.083	−0.274	0.763*	0.620**	0.024
	(0.213)	(0.169)	(0.209)	(0.336)	(0.200)	(0.127)
Ed3a	0.588**	0.211	−0.310	1.164**	0.094	−0.201
	(0.187)	(0.159)	(0.219)	(0.328)	(0.217)	(0.149)
Ed3b	0.713**	−0.124	−0.925**	1.923**	0.308	−0.246
	(0.191)	(0.190)	(0.324)	(0.326)	(0.231)	(0.176)
Additional voc. training	−0.059	0.172	−0.312	0.424**	0.873**	0.252
	(0.113)	(0.131)	(0.222)	(0.152)	(0.162)	(0.142)

(*Table continues on p. 190*)

TABLE 6.4 (*continued*)

	Male self-employment entry			Female self-employment entry		
	Professional	*Skilled*	*Unskilled*	*Professional*	*Skilled*	*Unskilled*
Prior labor market position						
Unemployed	0.754**	1.189**	0.980**	0.462	0.471	0.016
	(0.226)	(0.226)	(0.296)	(0.260)	(0.244)	(0.182)
Not in labor force	0.966**	0.153	0.387	1.045**	0.217	0.549**
	(0.213)	(0.236)	(0.319)	(0.255)	(0.206)	(0.159)
Professional occupation	0.825**	−0.371*	−1.862**	0.721**	−1.261**	−1.302**
	(0.125)	(0.149)	(0.402)	(0.250)	(0.254)	(0.219)
Skilled occupation	0.810**	0.250	0.206	0.303	−0.239	−0.858**
	(0.160)	(0.163)	(0.243)	(0.259)	(0.179)	(0.167)
Construction industry (F)	1.462**	1.400**	0.132	0.060	1.110**	0.061
	(0.181)	(0.188)	(0.353)	(0.486)	(0.374)	(0.406)
Traditional service industry (G&H)	0.390*	1.385**	0.838**	−0.532	1.332**	0.781**
	(0.173)	(0.164)	(0.243)	(0.338)	(0.270)	(0.200)
Transport/communication industry (I)	0.438*	−0.216	0.684*	−0.474	0.103	−0.388
	(0.218)	(0.323)	(0.302)	(0.509)	(0.505)	(0.441)
Finance/business service industry (J&K)	1.334**	0.246	−0.191	0.635*	0.231	0.244
	(0.161)	(0.310)	(0.555)	(0.269)	(0.384)	(0.302)
Other services (L − Q)	0.773**	−0.232	−0.518	−0.192	0.508	0.415*
	(0.142)	(0.240)	(0.394)	(0.239)	(0.282)	(0.199)
Pseudo R^2		0.078			0.078	

Note: N = 39,689 (men); N = 45,926 (women)

* $p < 0.05$ ** $p < 0.01$

Labor market position for the prior year also structures paths into self-employment. Men were particularly likely to begin self-employment spells if they were unemployed in the previous year. Men who were unemployed the previous year are predicted to move into professional self-employment at a rate of 2.9 per hundred, skilled self-employment at a rate of 3.1 per hundred, and unskilled self-employment at a rate of 1.1 per hundred (compared with average rates of 1.4, 1.0, and 0.4 per hundred, respectively). Men who reported being not in the labor force the prior year were also more likely to move into professional self-employment. Male entry into professional and skilled self-employment was particularly likely when previous year employment was located in the construction sector. Men employed in the construction industry the prior year are predicted to move into professional self-employment at a rate of 5.3 per hundred and into skilled self-employment at a rate of 3.6 per hundred.

Women were more likely to enter professional self-employment if they were unemployed or not in the labor force the previous year. Women who were not in the labor force the prior year were also particularly likely to enter unskilled self-employment (a predicted rate of 1.8 per hundred relative to the average rate of 1.2 per hundred). Women were more likely to move into skilled self-employment if they were previously employed in the construction or traditional service industry compared with the manufacturing industry.

Because of the large number of women who were not-in-the-labor-force the prior year and the significant association of not in the labor force activity with paths into self-employment, separate supplementary models were run restricting the risk set solely to those who were active in the labor market the previous year (i.e., employed or unemployed) to explore possible bias in the analysis. Several statistically significant differences emerge in the results. The restrictions on the risk set in the supplementary analysis generate evidence of a strong and significant association between previous-year unemployment and paths into unskilled self-employment for women, a result that was otherwise obscured by covariation in the earlier analysis.[9]

Table 6.5 presents results for a set of separate event-history analyses of paths out of the distinct categories of self-employment. The risk set for these analyses includes all individuals who were self-employed after 1980. African American men were at a higher risk of leaving skilled self-employment than whites; other nonwhites in the United States face high rates of exit from male unskilled self-employment. Age again has strong curvilinear effects on professional self-employment exit—first decreasing the likelihood of exit, until a point in middle age where the likelihood of exit begins to increase (the effects of age on self-employment dynamics will receive greater attention below).

Social background also affects self-employment stability. Men are more likely to remain professionally self-employed if their father was employed in a professional or skilled occupation, compared with if their father was employed in an unskilled occupation. Men who reported having a father who was a self-employed businessman were much more likely to exit unskilled self-employment: 61 percent of men in unskilled self-employment who reported having a father who was a self-employed businessman were predicted to exit during a given year (compared with an average exit rate of 28 percent). In spite of the fact that the PSID measure of social background relies on father's occupation and has no information on mother's employment, strong intergenerational effects on women are evident. Women are much less likely to leave professional self-employment if their father was involved in an agricultural occupation as opposed to an unskilled occupation. Women who came from a family

TABLE 6.5
Event-History Analysis of Paths out of Discrete Categories of Self-Employment in the United States

	Male Self-Employment Exit			Female Self-Employment Exit		
	Professional	Skilled	Unskilled	Professional	Skilled	Unskilled
Intercept	6.536**	3.689**	4.927*	0.749	−1.093	4.524**
	(1.331)	(1.378)	(2.424)	(2.487)	(1.958)	(1.597)
Individual characteristics						
African	0.337	1.200**	0.349	−0.206	1.213*	0.967*
American	(0.369)	(0.373)	(0.570)	(0.553)	(0.582)	(0.400)
Other nonwhite	−0.247	−1.436	4.528**	1.387	−0.541	1.041
race	(0.437)	(1.014)	(1.675)	(0.750)	(0.873)	(0.729)
Age	−0.304**	−0.173**	−0.263*	−0.217	0.133	−0.280**
	(0.062)	(0.066)	(0.122)	(0.113)	(0.096)	(0.081)
Age squared	0.310**	0.212**	0.338*	0.310*	−0.218	0.338**
(×100)	(0.069)	(0.080)	(0.147)	(0.136)	(0.118)	(0.101)
Social background						
Father prof.	−1.273**	0.466	−1.019	0.513	−0.188	0.777*
occupation	(0.279)	(0.365)	(0.880)	(0.524)	(0.594)	(0.391)
Father skilled	−1.068**	0.562	−0.570	1.068*	−0.318	0.836**
occupation	(0.265)	(0.307)	(0.472)	(0.485)	(0.546)	(0.322)
Father agr.	0.089	0.393	−0.452	−2.275*	−1.030	0.679
occupation	(0.313)	(0.346)	(0.567)	(0.952)	(0.584)	(0.374)
Father self-	−0.420	0.198	1.444*	−0.051	−0.484	0.138
employed	(0.333)	(0.390)	(0.736)	(0.630)	(0.625)	(0.692)
Family characteristics						
Spouse	0.232	−0.745**	0.160	0.283	−0.484	−0.843**
employed	(0.188)	(0.233)	(0.486)	(0.295)	(0.625)	(0.264)
Spouse	−0.005	−0.489*	0.325	−0.734	0.857	−1.589**
nonemployed	(0.193)	(0.228)	(0.447)	(0.668)	(0.789)	(0.510)
Spouse self-	−0.381	−0.826**	−0.090	0.021	−0.255	−1.335**
employed	(0.254)	(0.280)	(0.568)	(0.326)	(0.314)	(0.330)
Human capital/ work experience						
Ed2a	0.512	−0.885*	0.225	0.710	−0.807	0.568
	(0.392)	(0.399)	(0.814)	(1.129)	(0.542)	(0.408)
Ed2b	−0.423	−0.258	−0.538	0.561	0.220	0.412
	(0.322)	(0.263)	(0.362)	(1.073)	(0.402)	(0.305)
Ed3a	−0.003	−0.701**	−0.178	−0.882	−0.662	0.192
	(0.273)	(0.250)	(0.440)	(1.093)	(0.385)	(0.315)
Ed3b	−0.217	−0.114	−0.073	0.405	0.212	−0.274
	(0.278)	(0.279)	(0.456)	(1.076)	(0.434)	(0.356)
Additional voc.	−0.061	0.452*	−1.481**	0.878**	−0.095	−0.298
training	(0.159)	(0.201)	(0.457)	(0.300)	(0.316)	(0.295)

Table 6.5 (*continued*)

	Male Self-Employment Exit			Female Self-Employment Exit		
	Professional	*Skilled*	*Unskilled*	*Professional*	*Skilled*	*Unskilled*
Work experience prior to spell (years)	0.039* (0.016)	−0.020 (0.021)	−0.017 (0.028)	−0.007 (0.019)	0.002 (0.020)	−0.021 (0.018)
Self-employment spell	−0.032 (0.018)	−0.068** (0.023)	−0.151** (0.036)	−0.068* (0.027)	−0.057* (0.026)	−0.127** (0.028)
Prior labor force position						
Construction industry (F)	−1.129** (0.240)	−0.792* (0.342)	0.649 (0.509)	1.001 (0.610)	−0.312 (0.566)	2.002 (1.000)
Traditional service industry (G&H)	−0.964** (0.272)	−1.281** (0.328)	0.283 (0.415)	−0.497 (1.033)	−1.214* (0.480)	0.749 (0.530)
Transport/communication industry (I)	−0.117 (0.431)	−0.626 (0.737)	0.116 (0.410)	0.966 (0.954)	0.239 (0.753)	2.696** (1.009)
Finance/business service industry (J&K)	−0.355 (0.226)	−0.792 (0.564)	0.239 (0.663)	0.734 (0.463)	−0.956 (0.565)	0.474 (0.751)
Other services (L − Q)	−0.060 (0.211)	−2.386** (0.646)	0.644 (1.077)	0.986* (0.444)	−0.647 (0.489)	1.001 (0.558)
Pseudo R^2	*0.081*	*0.142*	*0.253*	*0.097*	*0.142*	*0.147*
N of regression	1,614	1,270	416	458	553	599

* $p < 0.05$ ** $p < 0.01$

with a professional or skilled father were more likely to exit unskilled self-employment occupations.

The stability of self-employment experience is also strongly associated with family characteristics of individuals. Men are much less likely to exit skilled self-employment if they have a spouse, while women are much less likely to exit unskilled self-employment if they are married or otherwise cohabitating.

Education has weaker and less consistent effects on self-employment exit than it does on entry. Men are less likely to exit skilled self-employment if they had vocational experience in high school (Ed2a) or unskilled self-employment if they had reported additional vocational education. Additional vocational education increases the likelihood of female professional self-employment and male skilled self-employment exit.

Gender differences exist on the effects of work experience on self-employment exit. Work experience prior to the beginning of self-employment is positively related to male professional self-employment departures but not related to female professional self-employment exit. The duration dependence of self-employment is evident in the coefficients on the measure of self-employment spell. Male skilled and unskilled self-employment are strongly duration dependent as are all categories of female self-employment.

The sector in which self-employment occurs also influences the stability of the activity. The construction and traditional service sector have low rates of male professional and skilled self-employment exit. Women's self-employment is less sensitive to industrial sector than is male self-employment. Skilled female self-employment in traditional and finance/business service sectors is particularly stable. Many of the effects of industrial sector on male and female professional self-employment exit are also significantly different.

Supplementary analyses of self-employment exit were conducted with the risk set restricted to individuals who began their self-employment spell after 1980. The restriction significantly reduces the sample size in the analysis and (by omitting the existing long-term successful enterprises) further highlights the unstable character of self-employment.[10] The supplementary analyses identify stronger effects of duration dependence—this result reconfirms that there are dramatic differences between the survival odds of an enterprise in its first compared to its fifth year, but less differences between the fifteenth and twentieth years. Such findings are consistent with results identified in survival curves presented earlier. Few other significant differences emerged in this alternative analysis.[11]

FINDINGS ON EDUCATION AND AGE

While the event-history analysis utilized in this research has the methodological advantage of better capturing the dynamic character of self-employment activity, discussion of results is complicated by the necessity of simultaneously considering entry and exit findings, as well as the challenge of translating logistic regression coefficients into more readily interpretable results. These obstacles to adequate interpretation are overcome in detailed discussion below of associations of education and age with self-employment—the former factor being of particular interest to comparative social stratification researchers; the latter factor emerging as an enigma in the earlier discussed descriptive results of U.S. self-employment prevalence over the life course.

Figure 6.3 identifies the predicted effects of education on self-employment entry and exit. The results presented are the odds ratio of CASMIN education categories Ed2a–Ed3b relative to Ed1. The odds

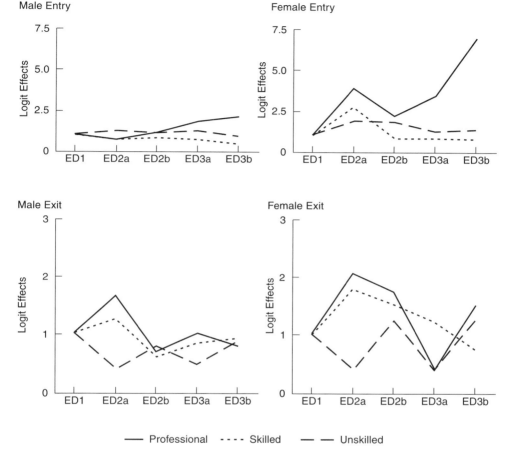

Figure 6.3: Effects of Education on Self-Employment Entry and Exit in the United States

ratios are calculated here simply as the exponential value of the relevant coefficient. Examining the effects of education on male entry in the top left panel, one identifies a rather straightforward set of associations: increased educational attainment in general is related to a greater likelihood of entry into professional self-employment and a decreasing likelihood of entry into skilled and unskilled self-employment; the only exception to this is Ed2a and Ed3a, which encourage skilled self-employment. The odds ratios for male exit in the bottom left panel highlight the extent to which the dynamic character of self-employment leads to different effects of education on entry and exit probabilities. The strongest educational associations identified in the exit odds ratios are related to secondary vocational education (Ed2a). Men with secondary vocational education have noticeably lower odds of exit from skilled self-employment and higher odds of exit from other forms of self-employment, particularly professional.

The effects of education on female self-employment are larger and more variable. While tertiary education facilitates female professional self-employment entry, Ed3b does not discourage other forms of self-employment activity. Entry into all categories of self-employment for women is also strongly associated with secondary vocational education (Ed2a). The effects of education on female professional self-employment exit are somewhat counterintuitive. The results suggest that women with little education who have established themselves in the category of professional self-employment by creating and managing small firms (rather than in having attained credentials that allow them into the liberal professions) will demonstrate particular tenacity in working to ensure their firm's survival.[12]

Figure 6.4 presents graphic representation of the curvilinear effects of age on self-employment entry and exit rates. The particularly high overall rates of male professional self-employment in an individual's mid- to late forties are identified here as primarily the product of the associations between age and entry. The curvilinear effects of age on male professional self-employment entry are particularly pronounced and peak at the same life-course period when male professional self-employment is highest. The exit rates of male professional self-employment have less of a pronounced curvilinear character.

Male unskilled self-employment, which early in the life course is quite low and then increases slightly in an individual's late twenties before again flattening out, is understood as a product of complex opposing entry and exit dynamics. Early and late in the life course, men are unlikely to enter unskilled self-employment, and if they are in the state they are likely to leave. In the middle of the life course, men are more likely to enter, but the increase fails to produce an overall greater likelihood of unskilled self-employment because men in this state are unlikely to remain involved in such activities as they grow older. Male skilled self-employment rates are largely flat across the life course because entry and exit rates move in the same general direction, causing variation in turnover rates, but not affecting the overall prevalence of the activity.

Recalling results from the earlier analysis of female self-employment over the life course, self-employment rates were largely constant after a gradual increase in professional and skilled self-employment up to a woman's early thirties. Examination of the self-employment associations between age and self-employment entry and exit suggests that this is due

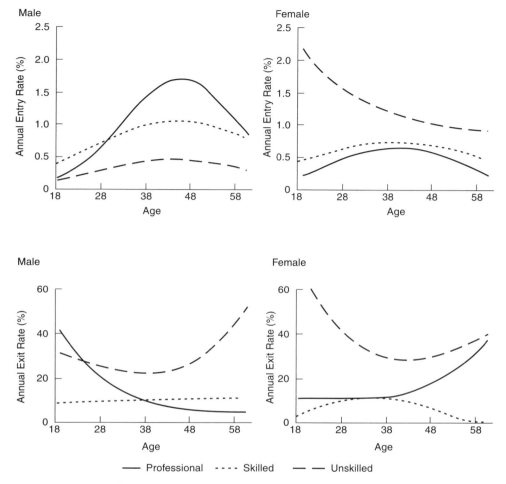

Figure 6.4: Effects of Age on Self-Employment Entry and Exit in the United States

once again to age being associated with similar movements in both entry and exit likelihood. Specifically, as women move past their middle thirties, they become less likely either to enter professional self-employment or to leave the activity if they are in it. The results suggest that female professional self-employment later in life has little turnover and is also a relatively stable activity.

Conclusions

The results presented here highlight the distinct character of U.S. self-employment. U.S. self-employment increasingly has a dual character that mirrors the growing economic polarization in the larger society. In one respect, self-employment provides the possibility of attainment of desirable professional and skilled occupations that can lead to the generation of small firms and relative occupational stability. The rewards for successful professional self-employment can indeed be extraordinarily high with large incomes attached or, particularly for women, the attainment of high hourly earnings but with greater flexibility in controlling and limiting the amount of hours worked than in traditional dependent employment (Arum 1997). Even in professional self-employment, however, outcomes are uncertain, with 36 percent of men and 45 percent of women ending their involvement in such activities in the first five years.

Much of the current increase in self-employment in the United States, however, has involved increases in male and female unskilled self-employment. Descriptive results suggest that unskilled self-employment is the category of self-employment increasing at the greatest rate. These unskilled positions are in occupations such as childcare, housecleaning, grounds-keeping, and motor vehicle operation. In the United States, these positions are particularly unstable, have low wages associated with them, and often involve the absence of access to health care. If we hope to understand U.S. self-employment in comparative perspective, these two sides of self-employment activity in the United States must be recognized.

While U.S. self-employment has been demonstrated to manifest increasingly a dual character, it is important to recognize the historical, political, and institutional context for these developments. The United States in general during this time period has faced growing economic polarization and relatively dramatic economic restructuring as a product of multiple factors, including the implementation of neoliberal economic policies, changes in industrial structure, and the emergence of technologies stimulating greater flexibility in production processes. In such a context, self-employment involves both an increase in the lure of potential rewards and the threat of negative consequences—depending on an individual's resources and success in adapting economic activities to the changing environment.

Notes

1. Self-employment likelihood is quite low among immigrants from Mexico and Central America (Arum 1997: n. 5).

2. Underreporting of self-employment in government-collected micro data is likely to occur, for example, when individuals are engaging in self-employment activity that is not being reported to other government agencies (such as welfare, unemployment, and tax collection offices). As an example of this underreporting, the CPS in 1992 identifies out of 61,614 individuals only 102 private household childcare workers and 242 private household cleaners and servants (occupational codes 406 and 407, respectively), none of whom report being self-employed. In the nongovernmental collected PSID data from the same year, 25 percent of unskilled nonprofessional self-employment occurs in these two categories. While the CPS uses 1980 and PSID uses the 1970 occupational coding classifications, the example used here is unaffected by this difference since these occupational categories were similarly defined in both decades.

3. Reclassification was made by assigning self-employed individuals in EGP categories I and II who were in activities associated with industry codes in retail trade (607–699) or personal services (777–797) to the "traditional" skilled self-employment category.

4. The "managers and administrators not elsewhere classified" category is used in U.S. occupational codes for proprietors and self-employed businesspeople who run their own firms and who have not provided other, more specific occupational information.

5. To be included in the analysis, a spell had to exist for a measurable amount of time (i.e., the analysis excludes individuals who report during an interview that they are self-employed but are unable to generate a start date of the spell prior to the interview, nor do they later mention being self-employed for any length of time in subsequent interviews).

6. Occupational data for 1980 were reported in two-digit codes, while 1981–92 data were provided in three-digit census codes. To avoid any possible coding bias, I present 1981–82 data as the earlier time here. Since self-employment activity is influenced by business cycles, it is worth noting that the 1981–82 data occur in the beginning of a deeper recession than the 1991–92 data. Unemployment rates range from 7.2 to 10.8 percent in the initial period, while they range from 6.4 to 7.8 percent in the latter (Bureau of Labor Statistics 2000).

7. In supplementary analysis a similar pattern is not identified in government-collected CPS data. In particular, analysis of these data suggests much more over-time stability in overall patterns of self-employment (results available upon request). Changes in the welfare system and the tax system (e.g., the creation of an Earned Income Tax Credit) during this time period, however, create variation in the incentives to not report self-employment activity to government authorities. No definitive conclusions thus can be drawn from the differences in CPS and PSID self-employment trends. Caution in interpretation and the need for further research on these trends, however, are clearly warranted.

8. For this and other reasons, I am quite skeptical of restricting the risk set in this way. I present results here that apply such a restriction for comparative purposes only. I also provide an alternative specification that does not use this restriction in defining the risk set.

9. Coefficients and standard errors are 1.772 (0.540); significant at the $p < .01$ level.

10. The supplementary analysis, while accurately capturing the dynamic character of self-employment, does so at the cost of distorting the analysis of the factors related to actual self-employment exits between 1980 and 1992. The analysis in table 6 focuses on the dynamics of survival of new enterprises, rather than the dynamics of the survival process occurring for self-employment enterprises in general during this historic period of self-employment expansion. Because both models control for first-order self-employment duration dependence, however, the results are largely similar.

11. Notable exceptions are significantly larger effects of father's professional occupation on male professional self-employment exit, and construction industry location on male unskilled self-employment exit.

12. They also likely have fewer alternative opportunities available to them in dependent employment.

REFERENCES

Aldrich, H., and R. Waldinger. 1990. Ethnicity and entrepreneurship. *Annual Review of Sociology* 16:111–35.

Arum, R. 1997. Trends in male and female self-employment: Growth in a new middle class or increasing marginalization of the labor force. *Research in Stratification and Mobility* 15:209–38.

Arum, R., M. Budig, and D. Grant. 2000. Labor market regulation and the growth of self-employment. *International Journal of Sociology* 30:3–27.

Arum, R., and M. Hout. 1998. The early returns: The transition from school to work in the United States. In *From School to Work: A Comparative Study of Educational Qualification and Occupational Destinations*, ed. Y. Shavit and W. Mueller, 471–510. New York: Oxford University Press.

Barbieri, P. 2001. Self-employment in Italy: Does labor market rigidity matter? *International Journal of Sociology* 31:38–69.

Birch, D. 1987. *Job creation in America*. New York: Free Press.

Blau, D. 1987. A time-series analysis of self-employment in the United States. *Journal of Political Economy* 95:445–67.

Bluestone, B., and B. Harrison. 1988. *The great U-turn: Corporate restructuring and the polarizing of America*. New York: Basic Books.

Bregger, J. E. 1987. Measuring self-employment in the United States. *Monthly Labor Review* 110:3–9.

———. 1996. Measuring self-employment in the United States. *Monthly Labor Review* (January/February): 3–9.

Brock, W., and D. Evans. 1986. *The economics of small businesses: Their role and regulation in the U.S. economy*. New York: Holmes and Meier.

Bureau of Labor Statistics. 2000. *Labor force statistics from the current population survey: Unemployment rate civilian labor force, 16 years and older*. Series ID: LFS21000000.

Card, D. 1992. *The effects of unions on the distribution of wages*. Working Paper 4195, National Bureau of Economic Research.

Cohany, S. 1996. Workers in alternative arrangements. *Monthly Labor Review* 118:31–45.

Edelman, L. 1992. Legal ambiguity and symbolic structures: Organizational mediation of civil rights law. *American Journal of Sociology* 97:1531–576.

Edwards, R. 1993. *Rights at work: Employment relations in the post-union era.* Washington, DC: Brookings.

Eisinger, P. 1988. *The rise of the entrepreneurial state: State and local economic development policy in the United States.* Madison: University of Wisconsin Press.

Erikson, R., and J. Goldthorpe. 1992. *The constant flux: A study of class mobility in industrial societies.* Oxford: Clarendon Press.

Evans, D. S., and L. Leighton. 1989. Some empirical aspects of entrepreneurship. *American Economic Review* 79:519–35.

Fischer, C., et al. 1996. *Inequality by design: Cracking the bell curve myth.* Princeton: Princeton University Press.

Fligstein, N. 1990. *The transformation of corporate control.* Cambridge: Harvard University Press.

Freeman, R. 1993. How much has de-unionization contributed to the rise in male earning inequality? In *Uneven tides: Rising inequality in America*, ed. S. Danzinger and P. Gottschalk, 133–63. New York: Russell Sage Foundation.

Gerber, T. 2001. Paths to success: Individual and regional determinants of self-employment entry in post-communist Russia. *International Journal of Sociology* 31:3–37.

Grant, D. S. II. 1995. The political economy of business failures across the American states, 1970–1985: The impact of Reagan's new federalism. *American Sociological Review* 60:851–73.

———. 1996. The political economy of new business formation across the American states, 1970–1985. *Social Science Quarterly* 77:28–42.

Guthrie, D., and L. M. Roth. 1998. The states, courts and maternity policies in U.S. organizations. *American Sociological Review* 64:41–63.

Hisrich, R., and C. Brush. 1986. *The woman entrepreneur.* Lexington, MA: Lexington Books.

Kalleberg, A., B. Reskin, and K. Hudson. 2000. Bad jobs in America: Standard and nonstandard employment relations and job quality in the United States. *American Sociological Review* 65:256–78.

Kim, K. C., and W. M. Hurh. 1985. Ethnic resource utilization of Korean immigrant entrepreneurs in the Chicago minority area. *International migration review* 19/1:82–111.

Laferrère, A. 2000. Self-employment and intergenerational transfers: Liquidity constraints and family environment. *International Journal of Sociology* 30.

Levy, F. 1998. *The new dollars and dreams: American incomes and economic change.* New York: Russell Sage.

Loscocco, K., and K. Leicht. 1993. Gender, work-family linkages and economic success among small business owners. *Journal of Marriage and the Family* 55:875–87.

Luber, S., H. Lohmann, and W. Mueller. 2001. Male self-employment in four European countries: The relevance of education and experience across industries. *International Journal of Sociology* 30.

Luber, S., H. Lohmann, W. Müller, and P. Barbieri. 2000. Male self-employment in four European countries: The relevance of education and experience across countries. *International Journal of Sociology* 30:5–44.

McManus, P. 2000. Market, state, and the quality of new self-employment jobs among men in the U.S. and western Germany. *Social Forces* 78:865–905.

Min, P. G. 1984. From white-collar occupations to small business: Korean immigrants' occupational adjustment. *Sociological Quarterly* 25:333–52.

Mueller, W., H. Lohmann, and S. Luber. 1999. *Self-employment in advanced economies: Project summary.* Mannheim: University of Mannheim.

———. 2000. Minutes from First Workshop on Self-Employment in Advanced Economies, Libourne, France, 10 May.

Mueller, W., et al. 1989. Class and education in industrial nations. *International Journal of Sociology* 19:3–39.

Piore, M., and C. Sabel. 1984. *The second industrial divide: Possibilities for prosperity.* New York: Basic Books.

Polivka, A. 1996. A profile of contingent workers. *Monthly Labor Review* 118:10–21.

Portes, A., and R. Rumbaut. 1990. *Immigrant America: A portrait.* Berkeley: University of California Press.

Ryscavage, P. 1995. A surge in growing income inequality. *Monthly Labor Review* 118:51–61.

Shavit, Y., and E. Yuchtman-Yaar. 2001. Ethnicity, education and other determinants of self-employment in Israel. *International Journal of Sociology* 31:59–91.

Steinmetz, G., and E. Olin Wright. 1989. The fall and rise of the petty bourgeoisie: Changing patterns of self-employment in the postwar United States. *American Journal of Sociology* 94.

Sutton, J., et al. 1994. The legalization of the workplace. *American Journal of Sociology* 99:944–71.

Wharton, A. S. 1989. Gender segregation in private sector, public sector, and self-employed occupations, 1950–1981. *Social Science Quarterly* 70:923–40.

CHAPTER SEVEN

Self-Employment in Australia, 1980–1999

M.D.R. Evans and Joanna Sikora

SELF-EMPLOYMENT REPRESENTED a small but nontrivial niche in the Australian workforce over the last two decades of the twentieth century. In the mid-1980s, 12 to 14 percent of the Australian workforce was self-employed. In the late 1990s,[1] about 15 percent was self-employed. Among men, the proportion of self-employed has fluctuated without trend. Among women, self-employment has grown slightly;[2] but that still leaves women only a small fraction of the self-employed. Self-employment is strong in agriculture, the building crafts, restaurants, small shops, motor vehicle repairs, domestic cleaning, the liberal professions, and, recently, in specialized niches of the information technology industry. Overall, there has been little change in the level of self-employment within most industries. At the end of the 1990s, small businesses with fewer than twenty employees (most of which are headed by a self-employed person or family) accounted for 60 percent of all private companies and provided employment to 47 percent of the private-sector workforce (Surry 2000).

This relative constancy in self-employment has occurred in the context of a rapidly changing labor market. This same period has seen substantial deregulation of the labor market, with a "subsidiarity" policy on pay increasingly removing wage negotiations from the once mighty central Arbitration Commission to more local bargaining. Over this period, unemployment rose to a historically unusual high of around 8 percent and has been stuck near that figure for the past decade. Pay inequalities widened within occupations as well as between them.

This chapter begins by describing the institutional setting of self-employment in Australia. Then it summarizes prior research on self-employment in Australia and shows how our analysis builds on that research. We then detail our data, methods, and measures. Next, we provide a descriptive account of self-employment in Australia, investigating bivariate links of key social variables with the probability of being self-employed. Following that, we examine the dynamics of self-employment, describing them via survival curves and modeling them using multivariate event-history models. Finally, we reflect on the key findings of the analysis in light of the themes of marginalization and gender differentiation.

Institutional Setting

Governmental taxation levels and arrangements can influence the "packaging" of many businesses. In Australia, self-employment can be "packaged" for the tax office as either an incorporated or an unincorporated business. In the past, most disputes were settled via regulation, but with the opening of the market and the replacement of arbitration with courtroom disputes, the limited liability that comes with incorporation has become more attractive, and it is thought that most medium to large businesses are now incorporated. A question that arises in connection with taxation arrangements is whether self-employment offers an opportunity to avoid taxes. Studies indicate that self-employed Australians tend to spend more than their official incomes, and thus it is possible that opportunities for minimization of taxable reported income are a factor that allows the poorer self-employed to enjoy a higher standard of living, complemented by government-provided social assistance (Bradbury 1997a). On the other hand, low income non-self-employed also tend to spend more than their reported incomes, so it may be that the discrepancy simply reflects income smoothing, with people using credit during hard times.

In the late 1990s, as a part of the Goods and Services Tax (GST) reform, the Australian Taxation Office began changing its rules to make business taxation more efficient. For example, it introduced the Simplified Tax System to streamline procedures for small (a turnover of less than AUD 1 million) businesses. These new procedures are thought to have induced a wave of applications for business incorporations (Surry 2000). These are sometimes interpreted as representing an efflorescence of self-employment, but given the IsssA evidence of rather little change in self-employment, we are inclined to think that a great many of them represent the incorporation of existing small enterprises. Moreover, the efficacy of some of these measures is open to question. Some observers viewed the provisions of this legislation as generous and facilitating small business operations, but others criticized its complexity and cost-inefficiency for small-scale entrepreneurs (Wolfers and Miller 2001). While it is assumed that the introduction of GST has been beneficial for large businesses, its impact on small business is harder to evaluate because the evidence is contradictory. On the one hand, the number of businesses (measured as the number of individuals who registered for an Australian Business Number, a document required by the Australian Taxation Office) reached 2.5 million. But on the other hand, this figure exceeds the estimates of ABS by a factor of two and so probably includes many hoped for as well as actual businesses. Thus it cannot be treated as an indicator of tax reform success in providing incentives for small business. Our best guess at this stage is that the tax changes largely shifted small businesses from the unincorporated to the incorporated category, rather than inducing a new flow of entrants.

Also relevant are governmental programs to encourage people to start small businesses. Such programs include the Small Business Professional Development Programme, funded by the Commonwealth Department of Education, Training and Youth Affairs, and special educational resources encouraging female self-employment, like the Office of Small Business's Women's Web Resource Centre. Other government initiatives aimed at stimulating self-employment in general and as a remedy to unemployment are the New Enterprise Incentive Scheme, which includes income maintenance and training, and the Self Employment Development scheme, which allows the unemployed to spend three months on benefits, trying to develop a business (OECD 2001).

Access to welfare benefits or social security payments from the government could also influence the attractiveness of self-employment. In Australia the self-employed are eligible for the same social security payments as wage and salary earners and are subject to the same income and assets tests. The previously self-employed have full access to age pensions, various forms of disability pensions, and sickness and carer allowances. Moreover, self-employment history makes no difference to access to child support payments and rent assistance. Thus, the low-income self-employed are not in any way disadvantaged when it comes to accessing these services. Moreover, special social assistance programs target farmers and nonfarm self-employed to provide free training and financial support in various transition periods (into self-employment—New Enterprise Incentive Scheme—or from one form of self-employment to another—e.g., Dairy Exit Program) (Centrelink 2002). Income-tests and assets-test thresholds are relatively generous (e.g., asset limits vary from about AUD 150,000 to 500,000), and arguably the self-employed can lower their taxable income through deducting from their reported incomes various work-related expenses that are not deductible from the earnings of wage and salary earners.

Retirement income arrangements in Australia have changed over the past several decades, from nearly exclusive reliance on a nearly universal age pension, to the rise of individually held shares in tax-advantaged funds known as "superannuation funds." In terms of retirement funds, the incorporated self-employed in Australia have better access to the increasingly important personal retirement funds called "superannuation." These funds are increasingly important because the Australian government is largely phasing out the age pension by declining to raise assets-tests thresholds. At present, over 70 percent of senior Australians receive at least a partial age pension, but this will decline steeply over the coming decades, unless governmental policy changes. Because the incorporated self-employed are treated for tax purposes as waged employees covered by employment protection legislation, they have access to employer-provided Superannuation Guarantee payments currently at about 9 percent of gross annual income (ABS 2001). "Superannuation" is a form of tax-advantaged deferred compensation, whereby the money going into the account escapes contemporary income tax (when one would normally be in a high tax bracket because one is working) and is taxed only at withdrawal (when, as one is no longer working, one is normally in a lower tax bracket). There are some exceptions to superannuation requirements (i.e., employers may not have to pay superannuation contributions for employees under age 18 who are working less than thirty hours a week, or for employees with low earnings) (ABS 2001). An ABS survey in 2001 estimated that the proportion of owner-managers of unincorporated enterprises with no superannuation was 35 percent, compared with 12 percent of owner-managers of incorporated enterprises (ABS 2002). It is not clear to what extent this represents greater financial stress among the unincorporated, and to what extent it represents choice. Survey evidence shows that superannuation is the least-favored form of investment among the Australian public at large, perhaps because superannuation members feel they have little say in the choice of investments (Webster and Valenzuela 2002).

Prior Research

The place of self-employment in the Australian stratification system has long intrigued researchers. A key finding has been that, throughout the twentieth century, men growing up in families where the father was self-employed have been more likely than their peers with an employee father to take up self-employment themselves (Broom et al. 1980; Kelley 1990), and that this is true among immigrants as well as people born in Australia (Kelley and McAllister 1984). It seems likely that this reflects the skills and tastes acquired in the family of origin rather than a marginalized underclass forced into unwilling self-employment generation after generation. This interpretation is reinforced by the fact that father's occupational status has no effect on son's self-employment (Broom et al. 1980; Kelley 1990), whereas the marginalization hypothesis implies that coming from a family at the bottom of the occupational hierarchy would increase one's risk of self-employment.

Education has a small positive or nil total effect on self-employment, both among the population at large (Broom et al. 1980; Kelley 1990;

Kidd 1993) and among immigrants (Evans 1989; Kidd 1993; Le 2000). The positive impact is transmitted through occupation, and the residual direct effect of education net of occupation is nil or even negative (Evans 1989; Le 2000). There is very little research on the impact of different types of education on the probability of self-employment. Vocational qualifications had no effect on immigrant self-employment, net of a number of other education measures (Le 2000).[3] A small-scale study of female self-employment found that many had a business education background rather than a general education (Bennett and Dann 2000). Altogether, these studies do not suggest a prominent role for education in becoming self-employed, but it is possible that a more detailed investigation of separate types and levels of education, as is undertaken in this paper, might bear more fruit.

A repeated finding is that the self-employed are widely scattered throughout the social hierarchy. The self-employed do not come from especially privileged backgrounds, but neither do they come primarily from underprivileged backgrounds. More specifically, the effects of parents' education and father's occupational status on the chances of being self-employed are small or nil (Broom et al. 1980; Kelley 1990). Moreover, a man's own occupational attainment seems to have only a small positive effect on self-employment, both among the population at large (Broom et al. 1980; Kelley 1990) and among immigrants (Evans 1989). Studies that have looked for the effects of specific occupational groups rather than a continuous hierarchical measure of occupational status have produced conflicting results. A study of young adults found that skilled manual workers were particularly likely to move to self-employment (Blanchflower and Meyer 1994), but managerial and upper sales occupations were found to be the most conducive to self-employment among all age groups taken together (Le 2000). Using a finer occupational classification, Kelley and Sikora (2001) show that in the nonfarm workforce, self-employment reaches its maximum at 26 percent in the "higher sales" group of occupations, with semiskilled manual occupations and administrative and managerial occupations tied for second place; followed by professionals, routine sales, and higher service tied for third place; semiprofessional, skilled manual, unskilled manual, routine service, and higher clerical tied for fourth place; and routine clerical last, with just 4 percent self-employed.

With regard to the marginalization question, the key finding is that those at the bottom of the occupational hierarchy in the routine service and unskilled manual occupations have rather low self-employment rates, but the pattern of effects as one proceeds up the occupational hierarchy seems quite variable, with pockets of low self-employment fairly far up the occupational ladder.

Prior research on industrial trends in self-employment has concentrated on unincorporated self-employment because trend data are available from the Australian Bureau of Statistics (ABS 2000b), and because the ABS is the only source with large enough surveys to enable investigation of trends in small industries. However, it needs to be remembered that these probably represent only the self-employed running smaller enterprises. Unincorporated self-employment has been highest mainly in two industry groups: (1) construction and (2) agriculture, forestry, and fishing, with owner-managers comprising about one-fifth of the workforce in these industries. Over the last fifteen years, unincorporated self-employment has either remained steady or declined in other industries, except for in communication and transportation services, where it rose. Changes in self-employment within industries have moved in the same direction and been of the same size for both men and women (Sikora 2001a, 2001b). Because the only other long-term source on self-employment, the International Social Science Survey/Australia (IsssA), shows that self-employment (including both incorporated and unincorporated) in the nonfarm sector grew over the period (see descriptive section below), at least some of the apparent industry-specific declines observed in the ABS data probably represent shifts from unincorporated to incorporated businesses.

The rewards of self-employment have also been a focus for research. Findings on earnings from self-employment are mixed, with results from the 1970s and 1980s indicating that the self-employed—solo self-employed as well as heads of businesses that employ others—earn more than comparable employees (Broom et al. 1980; Kelley and McAllister 1984; Evans and Kelley 1991). An analysis of earnings within Goldthorpe's service class in Australia in the 1980s found that even in this restricted upper segment of the workforce, the self-employed earned more than comparable employees (Kelley 1990:38). However, at least for immigrants, returns may be lower in the 1990s (Le 1999; McDonald and Worswick 1999).[4] Concentrating on the potentially poor, a study of working age people receiving a particular form of welfare, "additional family payments,"[5] found that the average living standards of low-income self-employed families in the mid-1990s were higher than those of comparable employee families (Bradbury 1997b). The relative prosperity of the self-employed through the 1980s is evidence against their occupying marginal positions, but the evidence for the 1990s is more ambiguous. Note also that prosperity today does not imply prosperity tomorrow for the self-employed: in 1998, 84 percent of unincorporated owner-managers reported that earnings varied substantially (ABS 2000a:10).

The existing evidence on the role of gender in self-employment is rather patchy. In the late 1990s, about 30 percent of the self-employed were female (ABS 2000a:14).[6] In the early 1980s, Evans (1984) found that stratification characteristics made little difference to the self-employment of women, but that family characteristics mattered a good deal, and they mattered differentially in different immigrant and native-born groups. Much research on women and self-employment is based on very small, unrepresentative samples, so the following findings should be regarded more as hypotheses than as firmly established facts. Some believe that Australian women may exit waged employment to seek ultimate career fulfillment in self-employment, but others argue that serious marginalization risks are involved in such a step (Still 1993). In this vein, it has been contended that self-employment results in less deferred earnings in the form of "superannuation" coverage (Murphy 1995),[7] although self-employed immigrant women do not seem to be disadvantaged in current pay compared with other, comparable women (Evans 1984). Thus, at the lower end of the occupational hierarchy, self-employment for women may reflect necessity more than choice, due to a dearth of sufficiently attractive waged employment, but alternatively it may be part of an immigrant family strategy of social betterment achieved by tremendous reinvestment rates in patriarchically organized family businesses (Bottomley 1974). Along these lines, Bennett and Dann's (2000) small-scale study pointed out that reasons for female entrepreneurs to establish small businesses vary substantially, ranging from personal and family needs to general business needs. In terms of family links, self-employed, home-based work may be attractive to Australian women because it enables them to operate a business while their children are at home (Holmes, Smith, and Cane 1997).[8]

A great many studies of self-employment in Australia have focused on immigrant groups. These studies have tended to be gender-specific and focused on comparisons between immigrant groups. They find, for example, that female immigrants from the Mediterranean region were more likely to be in self-employment (mostly in family businesses) than were women coming to Australia from English-speaking countries or the formerly communist nations of Eastern Europe (Evans 1984). Studies in this literature also demonstrate that the size of the ethnic market and of the linguistically isolated labor force available to a potential entrepreneur influence the probability of self-employment, even net of individual characteristics, in both the 1980s (Evans 1987, 1989) and the 1990s (Le 2000). Good skills in the dominant language also facilitated entrepreneurship for immigrant women (Evans 1984) and men (Evans 1989) in the 1980s, and continued to do so in the 1990s (Le 2000).[9] Immigrant returns to entrepreneurship seem to have been identical to the returns of the native-born in the 1970s and 1980s (Kelley and McAllister 1984; Evans 1984; Evans and Kelley 1991) but may be lower in the 1990s (Le 1999;

McDonald and Worswick 1999), so there may be a whiff of increasing marginalization here. In-depth interviews (with a small, nonrepresentative sample) suggest that the desire for independence and the desire to earn more by working longer than standard hours were important motives for immigrant business ownership, at least in the past when there was more labor market regulation of working hours (Tait et al. 1989). The desire for independence contrasts with the consistent practice of deferential behavior and ability to tap into patronage, which are important for promotion in public-sector organizations in Australia (Matheson 1999).

Another frequent theme in studies of self-employment in Australia is its growth with age or labor force experience. In the 1980s, immigrants' chances of being self-employed increased nonlinearly with the duration of Australian labor force experience (Evans 1989), and that probably continued to be true in the 1990s (Le 2000). Concerning the impact of foreign work experience, there are mixed results, probably depending on the details of model specification (Evans 1989; Le 2000).

The labor market context of self-employment has changed drastically over this period. Governments of both the Left and the Right have moved strongly in the direction of decentralizing and decollectivizing negotiations over pay, with some issues devolved to more local negotiations of union and management groups and others devolved all the way to individual workplace "enterprise bargaining" (Campbell 1999; Wooden 2000). In the latter half of the 1990s, Australia's Liberal (pro-market) government has striven to introduce individual contracts between each worker and his or her boss without trade union mediation, but these have not yet won widespread acceptance (Evans and Kelley 2001c). The decentralization of pay negotiations potentially could undermine the niche advantages for self-employment where national wage negotiations had previously required pay and conditions too expensive for conventional businesses (Wooden 2000). For example, restaurants open in the evening or on weekends had to pay "penalty wages" for employment outside "normal" weekday daytime working hours. However, several potentially countervailing social forces may have increased either the motivation or the opportunity for self-employment. Beginning in the late 1980s, there was a very strong trend of organizational downsizing in Australia, with large private firms and government expelling large numbers of employees who had previously been entitled to very high job security and other union-negotiated benefits (Jensen and Littler 2000). The fraction of the workforce whose employing firm was downsizing increased from 18 percent in 1985 to a peak of 29 percent in 1995 and then fell back to 19 percent in 2001 (Evans and Kelley 2001d). Importantly, downsizing firms shed people throughout the occupational hierarchy (Evans and Kelley

2001d), so a wide variety of skills were suddenly in the market. Partly in response to this flood of experienced senior workers into the market, and partly in response to persistent relatively high unemployment, which averaged around 8 percent in the latter decades of the twentieth century[10] (Borland and Kennedy 1998, fig. 1), the Australian government initiated a range of programs intended to encourage self-employment.[11] On the other hand, the introduction of the new GST (similar to a European value added tax), with its onerous reporting requirements, may have discouraged some, especially less educated, potential entrepreneurs from starting businesses.

This chapter extends prior research in several ways. First the inclusive *scope* of the project means that we consider jointly and comparatively many groups that have previously largely been assessed in isolation—we include a wide span of the working ages, both genders, all levels of education, and all occupations, except farming and ranching. Second, existing studies of the *intergenerational transmission of self-employment* are based on the male labor force as a whole. It is known that there is a great deal of intergenerational transmission of self-employment in agriculture, but prior studies have not focused on the nonagricultural labor force, so this study extends prior research by investigating whether parental self-employment also encourages self-employment in the nonagricultural sector. Third, on *education*, existing studies have used either continuous measures or broad categories, so the fine-grained categories used in this research have the potential to reveal previously unnoticed effects. Fourth, on *occupation*, previous studies have not examined the possibility that self-employment entry and exit processes work differently within different groups of occupations, but that is one of the foci of this research. Fifth, prior research has generally focused on either men or women, but ours will include both *genders*, not only examining both men's and women's experiences, but assessing the degree to which the impact of the causal variables differs between men and women, and extending to research on women questions such as intergenerational transmission, which have heretofore been explored only for men. Finally, most of the existing research focuses on the chances of being self-employed in one's current workforce status, but equal chances could be generated by a variety of processes of entry and exit. Accordingly, this research examines the dynamics of self-employment in more detail than has heretofore been done for Australia, using event-history models that are more appropriate to the subject than the point-in-time logistic and ordinary least squared (OLS) regressions used in most prior research.

The design of the statistical analyses in this chapter follows the guidelines proposed by Mueller, Lohmann, and Luber (1999, 2000), so our results should be readily comparable with those from other chapters.

Data and Methods

The most comprehensive available data on self-employment in Australia are those from the pooled IsssA for 1984–99. The IsssA surveys are based on simple random samples of Australian citizens drawn from the compulsory electoral rolls, so no weighting factors are required and no adjustments for sample clustering are needed. Response rates run a little over 60 percent, and the surveys closely match the census on all characteristics available for comparison (Bean 1991; Sikora 1997; Evans and Kelley 2002, chap. 28; Kelley and Evans 1999). Since 1987, the IsssA has collected employment histories on which 15,311 individuals gave us complete information.[12] To make our analysis comparable to those of other countries in this book, we restrict the analysis to respondents between 18 and 60 years of age[13] working outside of agriculture and restrict the window of observation to the period 1980–98. With those restrictions, there are histories for 1,005 self-employed men and 566 self-employed women, as well as histories for 6,764 men and 6,976 women in dependent employment.

Using the employment histories, we constructed a person-year file recording the employment status of each person aged 18 to 60 in each year in the observation window 1980–98, together with data on their fixed and time-varying characteristics. There were 85,946 person-year observations. Treatment of censored observations and definitions of "at risk" groups follow the specifications for the *Self-Employment in Advanced Economies Project*, as set out elsewhere in this book, so (1) all eligible persons not in self-employment at a given time are at risk of entering it,[14] and (2) only those self-employed at a given time are at risk of exiting it.

For comparability, measurement also follows the definitions for the *Self-Employment in Advanced Economies Project*, as set out elsewhere in the book. *Self-employment* is based on a direct question asking whether the respondent worked in his or her "own business, farm, or professional practice," as an employee of a private business, and so forth. In Australia, as elsewhere in the world, the distinction between wage employment and self-employment is often blurred. For example, franchising is a form of employment that shares many characteristics with both self-employment and waged employment and has probably been on the increase in Australia, as in other industrialized countries, but we have no quantitative information on that. Our qualitative work suggests that franchise holders are likely to report themselves as self-employed. Perhaps more crucially, there is the question of whether entrepreneurs running incorporated businesses report themselves as "self-employed" or as "employees." On the one hand, ordinary language usage in Australia would clearly make them "self-employed." On the other hand, for tax and governmental reporting purposes, they must report themselves as waged or salaried employees of their firms (ATO 2002). It seems likely that the IsssA estimates must miss some of the incorporated self-employed, but the IsssA estimates the percentage who are self-employed at about 16 percent in the late 1990s, compared with about 17 percent for the Australian Bureau of Statistics data (both restricted to the nonfarm population), so the number missed probably amounts to 1 percent of the labor force, or about 6 percent of the truly self-employed. On the other hand, if "gray" self-employed workers are more likely to report themselves to a nongovernmental survey, then the observed parity between the aggregate percentages self-employed may conceal a larger-than-apparent loss to the IsssA of reporting of entrepreneurs labeled as employees of their own businesses. There are also other important ambiguities of definition of self-employment in Australia, perhaps most notably the problem of the "contractor." Over the past decade, large corporations and government have increasingly contracted out their services, and this seems to have taken place throughout the occupational hierarchy from janitors to lawyers and researchers (Surry 2000). The ambiguity is most extreme in the case of a contractor who has just one client. The Australian Tax Office has shifted in the direction of treating them as employees, but whether they report themselves as self-employed or as employees on censuses and surveys is an issue that research has not yet explored. These questions can only be resolved by future research.

Because some of the other data sets in the study are working from panel data on employment arrangements at given points in time, we here mimic that type of data and so, for example, do not count transitions occurring within a single year from one self-employed business to another as entries or exits. *Father's self-employment* is an indicator (dummy) variable also based on a direct question. *Previous self-employment* is an indicator variable scored one for those with any prior self-employment experience and zero for others.

Education follows CASMIN definitions. Some CASMIN categories are quite rare in Australia, so we use the following groups: (1) for the reference (omitted) category of "compulsory" education, we combine CASMIN categories 1a, 1b, and 2b, which jointly represent the most basic education available to most adults in most of the cohorts represented in these data. There are too few people in category 1a to analyze them separately. The amount of education that is compulsory has risen across these cohorts. (2) CASMIN 1c and 2a comprise "compulsory + vocational." (3) CASMIN 2cGen is secondary school completed. (4) CASMIN 2cVoc is "secondary + vocational." (5) CASMIN 3a is "lower tertiary," and (6) 3b is "higher tertiary." Australian educational levels have increased substantially over time (Evans and Kelley 2002, chap. 3), and several qualifications have changed from a vocational to an academic basis (for example, nurses' training was entirely hospital-based until the 1980s when it became university-based), so there are some ambiguities. In these cases, qualifications are coded according to their current content.

Age is in single years. For technical reasons, age squared is age minus 44 quantity squared.[15] *Unemployment rate* is the national annual average unemployment rate for the year in question.

Several sets of *time-varying* measures are created from the employment and life histories, including self-employment in previous spell, occupation in previous spell, duration of current spell, age in current year, and unemployment rate in current year. The unemployment rate and the time period were collinear over this short span, so we have omitted the time period, as the theoretical urgency of the unemployment context in connection to the marginalization theme was greater. Education, sex, and father's occupation are taken as fixed rather than time varying.

We estimate discrete-time models of probabilities of self-employment entry and exit using logistic regression and multinomial logistic regression. Because respondents contribute multiple observations and we have measured only a limited array of the variables that may affect self-employment, it is necessary to correct the standard errors using some form of multilevel analysis. Accordingly, we treat the person-years for each individual as a "cluster" of observations and estimate Huber-White standard errors using the Stata program. For the exit analyses, there is always the problem of what to do about the spells that began before our delimited period; we provide an analysis that excludes them, which is more closely comparable to the panel analyses of many other studies in this book. An alternative analysis that includes them (which has a larger case base, and hence, all else equal, more precise estimates) is available from the authors upon request.

DESCRIPTIVE ANALYSES

This section first describes the background characteristics of the self-employed. Next, it investigates the scale of the enterprise, the origins of self-employment, and the educational endowments of the self-employed and of employees among the three occupational groups. Finally, it sketches the work characteristics of the self-employed and of employees within each of the three occupational groups.

The Australian self-employed tend to be about four years older than employees, with a mean age of 41 compared with 37 (table 7.1). This

TABLE 7.1

Background Characteristics of Self-Employed and Employees within Same
Classes, Australians Age 18–60

	Age (mean years)	Married (%)	Male (%)
All	38	74	51
Professionals and managers (EGP 1, 2)			
Employee	39	75	56
Self-employed	42	86	71
Skilled (EGP 3a, 5, or 6)			
Employee	37	71	45
Self-employed	41	84	61
Unskilled (EGP 3b, 7a)			
Employee	37	70	43
Self-employed	41	83	59

Source: International Social Science Surveys Australia (IsssA), 1984–1999/2000.

holds in all three occupational groups: professional and managerial occupations, skilled occupations, and unskilled occupations.

The self-employed are also more likely to be married (or to live in informal marriages) than are employees. 85 percent of all self-employed live in marital relationships, compared with 72 percent of employees. This tendency is similar across all three occupational groups. Self-employed women are significantly more likely to be married than are women working for employers,[16] even net of age (not shown in table 7.1), and are even more likely to be wed than are self-employed men.

Women's self-employment increased between the 1980s and 1990s, yet towards the end of the 1990s women still made up under one-third of the Australian self-employed (table 7.1 and Sikora 2001b). Women's self-employment is often part-time: our data show that about 40 percent of self-employed Australian women worked part-time, whereas the proportion of part-time workers among self-employed men oscillated between 5 and 10 percent during that period (not shown in table 7.1). The gender gap is similar across professional, skilled, and unskilled occupations. For example, among professionals and managers, 71 percent of the self-employed are men,[17] compared with only 56 percent among employees.

Roughly half of all Australian self-employed were employers, and half solo entrepreneurs, in the 1980s and 1990s: 55 percent compared to 45 percent (table 7.2). However, the balance between solo self-employed and employers differs substantially by gender and occupation. Men (table

Table 7.2
Type of Self-Employment, Father's Self-Employment, and Educational Profile of Australian Self-Employed and Dependent Employees

	Self-employed						Dependent-employed					
	Prof./man		Skilled		Unskilled		Prof./man		Skilled		Unskilled	
	1980s	1990s	1980s	1990s	1980s	1990s	1980s	1990s	1980s	1990s	1980s	1990s
Men (N)	(210)	(181)	(251)	(182)	(106)	(75)	(1,727)	(1,471)	(1,351)	(788)	(857)	(570)
% all employed men	5	6	6	6	2	2	38	45	30	24	19	17
Self-employed (solo)	30[aB]	42[aB]	45[B]	45[B]	63	71						
Father self-employed	31[C]	29[C]	33[C]	26[C]	32[bc]	35[BC]	20[C]	19[C]	19[C]	16[C]	19[C]	17[C]
Ed1a	2	1	3	1	8	3	1	1	3	2	7	7
Ed1b + 2b	17[b]	12	34[AB]	21[AB]	48[b]	39	18	14	33	22	56	40
Ed1c + 2a	15[bc]	10	42[B]	48[Bc]	24[BC]	29	14[c]	14	34	41[c]	14[C]	23
Ed2c(vocational)	11	12	6	9	5	4	10	9	7	9	3	5
Ed2c(general)	11[C]	9	7	8[c]	9	11	12[C]	11	15	16[c]	14	15
Ed3a14	15	2	3[B]	5	8	12	13	25	25			
Ed3b	31	41	5	10[Bc]	2	6	33	39	5	5[c]	4	6

Women (N)	(69)	(94)	(148)	(127)	(75)	(53)	(1,272)	(1,235)	(1,581)	(1,007)	(1,117)	(764)
% all employed women	2	3	3	4	2	2	30	38	37	31	26	23
Self-employed (solo)	80^{aB}	62^{aB}	59^B	62^B	73	73						
Father self-employed	23	27	35^C	19	19^b	8^B	23	25	20^C	15	18	16
Ed1a	1	1	3^c	0	9	2	1	0	1	1	5	2
Ed1b + 2b	29^{abC}	15^a	60^{AB}	43^{AB}	65^b	51	16^C	12	57	46	65	53
Ed1c + 2a	4^b	10	12^{AB}	24^{AB}	7^{AB}	31^{AC}	8	12	11	19	7	16^C
Ed2c(vocational)	9	11	10	11^C	3	4	13	7	6	5^c	5	5
Ed2c(general)	13	5	10	10^c	11	12	8	8	17^c	16^c	12	14
Ed3a	9	19	5	10^{Bc}	5	0	21^c	17	4	6^c	3	5
Ed3b	35	39	1	2^{Bc}	0	0	33	44	3	8^c	2	5

Source: International Social Science Surveys Australia (IsssA), 1984–1999/2000.

[A] Significantly different over time $p < 0.01$, [a] significantly different over time $p < 0.05$

[B] Significantly different between men and women $p < 0.01$, [b] significantly different between men and women $p < 0.05$

[C] Significantly different between self-employed and employees $p < 0.01$, [c] significantly different between self-employed and employees $p < 0.05$

7.2, upper panel) are much more likely than women (lower panel) to have employees in their businesses. Pooling occupational classes, the proportion of employers among women probably did not change over the period (no significant change). By contrast, for men the proportion of employers dropped from 54 percent to 48 percent (a statistically significant decline). This might suggest a glacial convergence in the scale of self-employment between men and women. Nonetheless, within occupational groups, there are large and significant differences between men and women in the prevalence of solo entrepreneurship (row labeled "Self-employed (Solo)"). The more skilled the self-employed men are, the greater the likelihood that they employ others. The pattern of solo self-employment among Australian women is different: the proportion of solo entrepreneurs among female professionals and skilled workers is significantly greater than among men. Concerning differences in the scale of self-employment between men and women, the only significant changes over time are a general decrease in the proportion of male employers, and an increase in the proportion of employers among self-employed female professionals.

In Australia, a significantly larger percentage of the self-employed than of employees have a self-employed father, a difference that did not change between the 1980s and the 1990s. However, the difference is highly gender differentiated. Self-employed men in each occupational category are around 10 percentage points more likely than their employee counterparts to have a self-employed father,[18] but paternal self-employment is not significantly more common among self-employed women compared with female employees in the same occupations.[19]

The educational experiences of the self-employed and of employees are broadly similar, with both groups in all occupations showing educational upgrading in the 1980s and 1990s (for details on educational trends in Australia more generally, see Kelley and Evans 2002).

In professional and managerial occupations, the self-employed mostly did not differ significantly from their employee peers in their educational profile in the 1980s, among both men and women. Importantly, both self-employed men and women in this occupational group are maintaining educational parity with their employee peers into the 1990s.

In the skilled occupational group, the bulk of people had either just compulsory education (Ed1b + 2b of CASMIN) or compulsory plus a basic vocational qualification (Ed1c + 2a), for both employees and the self-employed, and for both men and women. For men, several differences emerge in the 1990s: the self-employed are becoming more likely than their employee peers to hold basic vocational qualifications or upper tertiary qualifications, but less likely to have completed secondary general education as their highest qualification. For women, other differences between self-employed and employees emerge in the 1990s. Self-employed and employee women do not differ in their representation in the lower educational qualifications, rather their distributions differ within the higher range of qualifications. Self-employed women in the skilled occupations are more likely than their employee peers to have upper vocational (Ed2c, vocational) qualifications, less likely to have completed secondary school (Ed2c, general), more likely to have lower tertiary qualifications (Ed3a), and less likely to have upper tertiary qualifications (Ed3b). Overall, these differences for women are small, even though statistically significant, but they may indicate that completing the upper levels of vocationally oriented education[20] increases women's chances of entering self-employment in the skilled occupational group.

In the unskilled occupational group, by far the largest educational category is compulsory education (Ed1b + 2b of CASMIN) for both men and women, but especially for women in the 1980s. Between the 1980s and 1990s, there may be a shift toward having compulsory education plus a basic vocational qualification (Ed1c + 2a) particularly among women, but this is not statistically significant.[21] Importantly, there is certainly no increase in the representation of the lowest educational qualifications among either self-employed women or men in this occupational group.

All in all, do vocational qualifications enhance chances of engaging in self-employment in Australia? The data suggest that vocational qualifications only enhance the likelihood of running one's own business in some occupations, a tendency that, moreover, varies by gender and time (Ed1c + 2a and Ed2c [vocational]). Throughout the period, men with vocational qualifications are more likely to be self-employed than are women with corresponding qualifications.

Turning to the rewards of self-employment, the self-employed in all three occupational groups are significantly more satisfied with their jobs than are employees in similar occupations (table 7.3). Professional and managerial work is the most satisfying both for the self-employed (mean of 77 points out of 100) and for employees (71 points). The gap is somewhat larger among people in the skilled occupational group: job satisfaction averages 74 points among the self-employed, compared with only 65 points for skilled employees. Enhanced job satisfaction of the self-employed is also evident among the unskilled, averaging 67 points among the self-employed and 62 points among employees.

Australian self-employment is more concentrated in small business than is dependent employment (table 7.3, column 2). In Australia, the self-employed labor market sector is mostly the domain of very small firms. Two-thirds are unincorporated enterprises, which tend to be smaller, often solo firms.[22]

Another feature of the work situation is how much time it takes—how

TABLE 7.3
Work Characteristics of Self-Employed and Employees within Same
Occupational Group, Australians Age 18–60

	Job satisfaction (0–100)	Company size	Weekly hours (mean)	% Long hours	% Long year	Occupational status (0–100)
All	68	1,484	31	16	9	51
Professionals and managers (EGP 1, 2)						
Employee	71	2,049	35	19	10	77
Self-employed	77	177	39	41	26	78
Skilled (EGP 3a, 5, or 6)						
Employee	65	1,762	29	8	4	45
Self-employed	74	50	40	39	28	45
Unskilled (EGP 3b, 7a)						
Employee	62	1,095	24	8	4	25
Self-employed	67	232	36	32	24	25

Source: International Social Science Surveys Australia (ISSSA), 1984–1999/2000

Notes: "Job satisfaction" is a seven-point rating on the widely used "delighted-to-terrible scale," here rescored at equal intervals from 0 to 100 to facilitate interpretation. Company size is the number of people who work in respondent's firm. "Long hours" are 45 hours or more in a typical working week. A "long year" is 2,500 hours or more worked in the year (that is, hours actually worked rather than hours paid; it does not include holidays, sick leave, or any other paid nonworking time). Occupational status is a hierarchical assessment of occupational position, here measured by Kelley's Worldwide Status Scores, which range from 0 to 100 (Kelley 1990: 344–46).

many hours are actually devoted to work. We investigated three facets of work time—average weekly hours, the percentage of workers on long hours of forty-five hours or more a week, and the percentage working a long year (2,500 hours or more a year). On all three indicators, the self-employed in each occupational group work longer hours than do their employee peers.

Turning next to the kinds of jobs undertaken by the self-employed, among male self-employed professionals and administrators, 8 percent work in the modal occupation, business professional NEC (ISCO 2419). Among their employee peers, only 5 percent work as business professionals (ISCO 2419). Among self-employed female professionals and managers, the most common occupation is private teacher at 8 percent. By contrast, female professionals in dependent employment are most likely to work in nursing and midwifery (19 percent).

Turning to men in the skilled occupational group, the self-employed are highly concentrated, with 19 percent working in the modal occupation, running small businesses mainly in education, healthcare, recreational, cultural, or sporting facilities (ISCO 1319). Skilled male employees are most likely to be machinery mechanics (9 percent). Self-employed women in the skilled occupational group are most likely to be accounting and bookkeeping clerks (22 percent). By contrast, skilled female employees are most likely to work as stenographers or typists. In our sample, one-fifth of all dependent employed skilled women perform such jobs.

In the unskilled occupational group, the most common occupation of male entrepreneurs is driving heavy trucks and lorries: 25 percent. Unskilled men working for an employer are also likely to be truck drivers (16 percent).

Of self-employed unskilled women, over one-third work in retail trade, close to one-fifth as domestic workers or helpers and cleaners,[23] and 8 percent care for other people's children. Among their employee peers, work in retail trade (ISCO 5220) was also the most frequently reported occupation at 27 percent, followed by 12 percent house cleaners and domestic helpers working for an employer, and 9 percent helpers and cleaners of offices, hotels, and other establishments.

Turning to the level or hierarchical placement of the work people are doing, within each occupational group, the self-employed and employees are working at jobs with the same average socioeconomic status (table 7.3, last column). There are huge differences between the occupational groups, of course, but within those groups, the self-employed and employees are working in jobs of the same caliber, on average.

The labor turnover process is important in many aspects of work, so we begin to explore this area here with Kaplan-Meyer estimates depicting the exit process over time (figure 7.1).[24] About 10 percent self-employment spells ended before the second year of self-employment, and 20 percent of spells ended before the third year, so the concentration of exits is high in the first couple of years, with relatively fewer cases with longer histories of self-employment.[25] Rates of exit from self-employment increase almost linearly with time. Professional and administrative occupations have somewhat greater holding power (Evans and Laumann 1983) than do occupations in the skilled or unskilled categories, but the difference is not great.

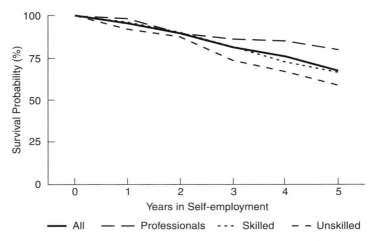

Figure 7.1: Kaplan-Meier Estimates of Survival Rates in Self-Employment in Australia

MULTIVARIATE ANALYSES

Following the general plan of the comparative project, we present results from (1) logistic regression models predicting entry into any form of self-employment, (2) multinomial logistic regression models predicting entry into occupational clusters of self-employment, and (3) logistic regression models predicting exit from self-employment. More details on the modeling strategy are in the Data and Methods section above.

One of our themes throughout this section will be whether the causal processes underlying entry into self-employment work differently for men and women, but it is also worth noting that women are, in general, significantly less likely to enter self-employment, net of the various family background and labor market characteristics built into our model.[26]

Entry into Self-Employment

Beginning with effects rooted in the socialization stage of life, father's self-employment significantly enhances the chances of entry into self-employment for both men and women (table 7.4).[27] These findings show that the bivariate connection between father's self-employment and offspring's later self-employment is a direct one not mediated by labor market assets such as education, which are controlled in the model. This is consistent with an interpretation stressing tastes and preferences for self-employment, rather than a marginalization interpretation.

TABLE 7.4

Logistic Regression Entry Analysis: Entry into Any Self-Employed Job in Australia, 1980–98

	Men (1)		Women (2)	
Basic Model				
Panel A: Summary statistics				
Number of person-years	40,313		45,633	
Wald chi^2(14)	108.4		102.1	
Pseudo R^2	0.02		0.02	
Log likelihood	−3237.9		−2705.0	
Panel B: Coefficients	*Coef.*	*Std. Err.*	*Coef.*	*Std. Err.*
Demographic variables				
Age in years	0.093**	(0.014)	0.128**	0.016
Age squared[a]	−0.003**	(0.000)	−0.004**	0.000
Father's work				
Father's occupation (dummies)				
Unskilled (reference)	0	—	0	—
Professional	0.243*	(0.121)	0.108	(0.138)
Skilled	0.037	(0.114)	−0.002	(0.126)
Farmer	0.253[t]	(0.146)	0.023	(0.158)
Father's occupation missing	−0.030	(0.191)	−0.222	(0.209)
Father self-employed	0.277**	(0.104)	0.273*	(0.110)
Education (dummies)				
CASMIN 1ab2b: compulsory (reference)	0	—	0	—
CASMIN 1c2a: compulsory + vocational	0.484**	(0.114)	0.458**	(0.135)
CASMIN 2cGen: secondary general	0.106	(0.166)	0.400**	(0.149)
CASMIN 2cVoc: secondary vocational	0.437**	(0.163)	0.199	(0.194)
CASMIN 3a: lower tertiary	0.522**	(0.157)	0.048	(0.168)

TABLE 7.4 (*continued*)

	Men (1)		Women (2)	
	Coef.	*Std. Err.*	*Coef.*	*Std. Err.*
CASMIN 3b: higher tertiary	0.189	(0.131)	0.021	(0.141)
Constant	− 5.056**	(0.166)	− 5.327**	(0.173)
Extended Model[b]				
Previous self-employment	0.997**	(0.111)	0.820**	(0.152)
Unemployment rate	0.004	(0.027)	− 0.031	(0.032)

[a] Precisely: (age-44)**2
[b] Basic model variables controlled but not shown.
[c] $p < 0.10$ * $p < 0.05$ ** $p < 0.01$

Father's occupation also influences the probability of self-employment for men: having a father in the professional and administrative occupational group significantly increases a man's chances of entering self-employment in adulthood, even net of the father's self-employment status. Prior studies on other countries generally report positive significant effects of father's occupational status on point-in-time self-employment for men (e.g., Robinson and Kelley 1979:45), so Australia appears to conform to a more general pattern in this. The effects are nonsignificant for women, which probably reflects a gender difference in the process, rather than deficiency of sample size.

Importantly, the results do not match the prediction of a marginalization hypothesis—namely, that having an unskilled father would increase one's chances of entering self-employment. Nor do they match a polarization variant in which growing up in a home at the top of the occupational hierarchy (the professional and managerial group) or at the bottom of the educational hierarchy (the unskilled occupational group) would exacerbate one's chances of entry into self-employment compared with peers from the middle (the skilled occupational group).

Father's employment effects are mixed when it comes to the hypothesis of gender differentiation. On the one hand, the propensity toward self-employment is equally strongly transmitted intergenerationally from father to son and from father to daughter. On the other hand, father's occupational group also influences sons' but not daughters' chances of entering self-employment.

Moving toward more proximate influences, consider education (table 7.4). Compared with those who exit the educational system upon completion of compulsory schooling, men who supplement compulsory schooling with a basic vocational qualification have significantly higher rates of entry into self-employment. This makes sense because a good deal of traditional vocational training in Australia was strongly oriented toward providing young men with the repertoire of skills they would need to practice a craft independently.[28] By contrast, men who complete an academic secondary school curriculum are no more likely than those with just compulsory education to start their own business. Yet those who complete a blended curriculum of academic secondary school plus a vocational qualification are much more likely than those with just compulsory education to enter self-employment. The effect of lower tertiary education is similar, but men with higher tertiary education are no more likely to enter self-employment than are those at the opposite end of the educational spectrum with just compulsory education. In sum, vocational education at all levels seems to substantially encourage entry to self-employment among men.

Educational influences on women's self-employment opportunities are somewhat different. Women with basic vocational training are more likely to enter self-employment than women with only compulsory schooling. This is also true for women who completed secondary school, but not for those who did a vocational course in conjunction with their secondary schooling, those who completed lower tertiary education, or those who completed upper tertiary education. It may be that women are more likely than men to pursue higher vocational and lower tertiary qualifications that are especially oriented toward assisting professionals and managers (e.g., dental technicians).

The hypothesis that self-employment is a marginal condition does not seem to apply to the pattern of educational effects for either gender. The marginalization hypothesis would suggest that self-employment propensities should be especially strong among those who exited the educational system immediately after completing compulsory education. But they are, in fact, among the least likely to enter self-employment (for both men and women). Nor does the polarization variant fit—it predicts elevated rates of entry to self-employment at both the top and the bottom of the educational hierarchy, but the pattern we find looks nothing like that, for either men or women.

Youth are famous for risk-taking, but they do not rush into self-employment. Rather, when multivariate analysis controls for the effects of other potentially confounding variables, rates of entry into self-employment rise gradually with age across young adulthood and then flatten (as shown by the large significant positive linear term and small significant negative quadratic term for age: table 7.4, columns 1 and 2). This is consistent with results showing a strong effect of labor force experience on point-in-time self-employment in 1981 Australian Census data (Evans

1989). This holds for both men (column 1) and women (column 2), with no significant difference between them. Recall that prior experience of self-employment is controlled in the model, so the increasing propensity to enter self-employment as one's career progresses is independent of the accumulation of self-employment experience.

Previous self-employment has a significant positive effect on entry into self-employment for both men and women, as shown in the extended model in table 7.4. This is all the more notable because many of these prior self-employment episodes were failures. Although some were successful businesses that were sold at handsome profits, others were operations involving little capital that were simply wound down when other activities and interests intervened. In considering these results it is also worth remembering that most successful self-employed people are not "at risk" of self-employment in this analysis, because we are examining only transitions from non-self-employment to self-employment.

The positive effect of prior self-employment is evidence against the marginalization thesis. One can imagine prior self-employment as part of a lifetime of economic desperation for people washing windshields on street corners when they are unable to get jobs as day laborers, but that seems very unlikely to be the case in Australia. The fact that people find self-employment more satisfying than corresponding jobs as employees, and repeatedly go into self-employment, suggests tastes and preferences, perhaps the "triumph of hope over experience," rather than marginalization.

Turning to the larger context, consider next the effect of the unemployment rate (at the time of exposure to the risk of self-employment). The national unemployment rate has no statistically significant effect either for men or for women, as shown in the extended model in table 7.4. Thus, contrary to the marginalization thesis, macroeconomic contraction does not seem to thrust people into self-employment.

Do these patterns hold for entry into self-employment in the three occupational groups when considered separately? To find out, we conducted a multinomial logistic regression analysis, as described in the Data and Methods section. Note that, net of the other variables in the model, women are significantly less likely than men to enter self-employment in the professional and managerial occupational group,[29] and also, to a lesser extent, in the "unskilled" group. In contrast, in the "skilled" group, women are as likely as men to enter self-employment. The fact that there is no gender difference once education and other characteristics are controlled for may suggest that it may be men's concentration in basic vocational training that accounts for their overrepresentation among the self-employed in the skilled occupational group.

When we consider the chances of entry into self-employment in each of the three occupational groups, the effects of paternal self-employment on entry are only significant for men in skilled self-employment and for women in professional self-employment. It may be that tastes and family resources significantly enhance chances of entering self-employment in typically male craft and trade occupations. For women, a family environment with exposure to running a business results in greater chances of entry into professional but not skilled or unskilled self-employment. Entry into self-employment in other occupational groups is unrelated to father's self-employment (table 7.5).

Similarly, father's occupational group has largely mixed, unstable, and nonsignificant effects on entry into the three separate occupational groups of self-employment for both men and women (table 7.5, columns 1 and 2). The only exception is a strong link between father's professional occupation and son's professional self-employment.

Turning to education, acquiring basic vocational qualifications substantially facilitates entry of men into skilled self-employment but has no effect on entry either into professional or unskilled self-employment (row CASMIN 1c2a). General (academic) secondary education (compared with basic education without vocational training) encourages entry of men into professional and managerial self-employment, but not into skilled or unskilled self-employment. Vocational secondary education also facilitates entry for men into self-employment in professional and managerial or skilled occupations (row 2cVoc). Lower tertiary education also facilitates entry for men into self-employment in professional and managerial occupations (row 3a), perhaps because a number of lower tertiary qualifications allow people to work as technicians or assistants servicing a variety of professionals,[30] but is neutral with respect to self-employment in the skilled and unskilled groups. Similarly, upper tertiary education significantly facilitates men's entry into self-employment in professional and managerial occupations (row CASMIN 3b). Upper tertiary education is neutral with respect to men's self-employment in skilled occupations and discourages men from undertaking unskilled self-employment.

For women, basic vocational qualifications substantially facilitate entry into skilled self-employment but do not affect entry into either professional or unskilled self-employment (row CASMIN 1c2a). General secondary education has a positive impact on entry into self-employment in professional and managerial occupations, but not for the skilled or unskilled occupational groups. Completing secondary school jointly with vocational training has no effect on women's likelihood of entering self-employment in any of the occupational groups. Lower tertiary education enhances women's self-employment chances in professional and administrative occupations, as does upper tertiary education. Thus, the patterns

TABLE 7.5
Entry Analysis: Self-Employed in Australia by Occupational Categories (multinomial logit)

	Men (1) Self-employment entry			Women (2) Self-employment entry		
	Professional	Skilled	Unskilled	Professional	Skilled	Unskilled
Basic Model						
Age in years	0.129**	0.091**	0.037	0.173**	0.116**	0.165**
	(0.027)	(0.022)	(0.031)	(0.047)	(0.023)	(0.036)
Age squared[a]	−0.003**	−0.003**	−0.002[c]	−0.004**	−0.004**	−0.005**
	(0.001)	(0.001)	(0.001)	(0.001)	(0.001)	(0.001)
Father's occupation (*ref: unskilled*)						
Professional	0.752**	−0.023	−0.146	0.146	0.078	−0.146
	(0.246)	(0.212)	(0.272)	(0.353)	(0.207)	(0.283)
Skilled	0.327	0.080	−0.503	0.115	0.121	−0.230
	(0.248)	(0.183)	(0.249)	(0.340)	(0.183)	(0.262)
Farmer	0.213	0.387	−0.011	−0.110	0.089	−0.404
	(0.342)	(0.233)	(0.316)	(0.443)	(0.232)	(0.371)
Father's occupation missing	−0.003	−0.011	−0.892	0.051	−0.262	−0.827
	(0.432)	(0.302)	(0.528)	(0.509)	(0.311)	(0.533)
Father self-employed	0.122	0.326*	0.127	0.614*	0.003	0.161
	(0.208)	(0.167)	(0.250)	(0.252)	(0.170)	(0.253)

Education						
CASMIN 1ab2b compulsory (reference)						
CASMIN 1c2a: compulsory + vocational	0.000 (0.337)	0.976** (0.182)	0.206 (0.238)	0.378 (0.447)	0.484* (0.192)	0.235 (0.290)
CASMIN 2cGen: secondary, general	1.261** (0.313)	−0.351 (0.334)	−0.418 (0.385)	0.890* (0.414)	0.301 (0.216)	0.128 (0.318)
CASMIN 2cVoc: secondary + vocational	0.909** (0.360)	0.591** (0.263)	0.442 (0.340)	0.545 (0.557)	0.418 (0.261)	−0.020 (0.441)
CASMIN 3a: lower tertiary	1.496** (0.301)	0.267 (0.267)	0.092 (0.379)	1.303** (0.361)	−0.231 (0.277)	−1.192* (0.594)
CASMIN 3b: higher tertiary	1.603** (0.266)	−0.261 (0.264)	−1.252** (0.422)	1.513** (0.327)	−0.217 (0.223)	−0.342 (0.319)
Constant	−7.695** (0.397)	−6.131** (0.267)	−5.577** (0.332)	−8.520** (0.479)	−5.855** (0.248)	−6.802** (0.384)
Extended Model[b]						
Previous self-employment	0.639** (0.223)	0.716** (0.195)	1.229** (0.250)	0.034 (0.468)	1.085** (0.202)	0.251 (0.458)
Unemployment rate	−0.015 (0.052)	0.047 (0.046)	−0.075 (0.068)	−0.006 (0.081)	−0.036 (0.046)	−0.020 (0.072)
Summary statistics for extended model						
Number of year-persons	40,313			45,633		
Wald chi^2(14)	246.1			155.2		
Pseudo R^2	0.04			0.03		
Log likelihood	−3223.3			−2680.5		

[a] Precisely: (age−44)**2.

[b] Basic model variables controlled but not shown.

* $p < 0.10$ * $p < 0.05$ ** $p < 0.01$

of educational effects on self-employment in particular occupational groups are closely similar for men and women.

Age strongly differentiates men's rates of entry into self-employment in the professional and managerial group. Entry into self-employment rises gradually with age across young adulthood and then flattens (as shown by the large significant positive linear term and small significant negative quadratic term for age). The same pattern holds, albeit in weakened form for men's entry into self-employment in the skilled occupations, but age fails to have a significant effect on men's entry into unskilled occupations. Women, too, are increasingly likely to enter self-employment in professional and managerial occupations as they move from young adulthood into maturity, with the increase leveling off. This same pattern holds for women's entry into both skilled and unskilled occupations. The growing likelihood of entering self-employment as one's career progresses is independent of the accumulation of entrepreneurial experience, because previous self-employment is controlled in the model.

Prior self-employment significantly increases the chances of men's entering self-employment in all three occupational groups (table 7.5). There is a fairly marked gender difference here, with prior self-employment significantly increasing women's likelihood of entering self-employment in the skilled occupational group, but not affecting their self-employment chances in the other occupational groups.

Macroeconomic troubles, as indexed by the national unemployment rate, do not significantly affect men's chances of entering self-employment in any of the occupational groups. Nor do they influence women's chances.

Exit from Self-Employment

Thus far, we have focused on factors influencing entry into self-employment, but the dynamics of self-employment involve exits as well, so it is to influences on the departure process that we turn next.[31] We focus on the post-1980 results but refer to the full sample analysis (not reported here in detail) for clarification when the results of the analysis with the larger number of cases are different.

Table 7.6 provides the results of simple discrete-time logistic models predicting exit from self-employment. There were a sufficiently large number of cases to conduct separate analyses by gender, but not by occupation and gender, so occupation is included as a set of dummy variables in the model.[32] Note that women and men do not differ significantly in their chances of exiting self-employment.[33]

Father's self-employment does not have a significant effect on exit

Table 7.6
Logistic Regression Exit from Self-Employment: Version 1 Left Truncated
Spells Excluded in Australia

	Men (1)		Women (2)	
Basic Model				
Panel A: Summary statistics				
Number of year-persons	3,167		2,360	
Wald chi²(14)	106.6		94.2	
Pseudo R^2	0.06		0.07	
Log likelihood	−917.4		−700.6	
Panel B: Coefficients				
	Coefficient	Std. Error	Coefficient	Std. Error
Age in years	−0.087**	(0.030)	−0.043	(0.036)
Age squared[a]	0.002**	(0.001)	0.000	(0.001)
Father's occupation				
Unskilled (reference)	0	—	0	—
Professional	−0.065	(0.228)	0.384	(0.264)
Skilled	−0.082	(0.204)	0.199	(0.244)
Farmer	−0.015	(0.256)	0.274	(0.292)
Father's occupation missing	−0.121	(0.314)	0.058	(0.368)
Father self-employed	0.120	(0.167)	0.093	(0.199)
Education				
CASMIN 1ab2b: compulsory (reference)	0	—	0	—
CASMIN 1c2a: compulsory + vocational	0.343	(0.191)	−0.108	(0.254)
CASMIN 2cGen: secondary, general	0.439	(0.314)	−0.576**	(0.252)
CASMIN 2cVoc: secondary + vocational	0.163	(0.265)	0.240	(0.393)
CASMIN 3a: lower tertiary	0.741**	(0.251)	−0.146	(0.306)
CASMIN 3b: higher tertiary	0.236	(0.265)	0.246	(0.260)

Table 7.6 (*continued*)

	Men (1)		Women (2)	
	Coefficient	Std. Error	Coefficient	Std. Error
Occupation while self-employed				
Unskilled (reference)	0	—	0	—
Professional	−0.948**	(0.245)	−1.115**	(0.302)
Skilled	−0.528**	(0.189)	−0.855**	(0.202)
Occupation missing	−0.043	(0.231)	−0.549**	(0.245)
Years of self-employment in this spell so far	0.482**	(0.088)	0.539**	(0.091)
Years of self-employment squared	−0.034**	(0.011)	−0.040**	(0.011)
Constant	−2.147**	(0.382)	−2.122**	(0.419)
Extended Model[b]				
Unemployment rate	−0.094*	(0.047)	0.024	(0.054)

[a] Precisely: (age-44)**2.
[b] Basic model variables controlled but not shown.
[t] $p < 0.10$ * $p < 0.05$ ** $p < 0.01$

rates for men in the self-employment spells since 1980. The same results hold for women. Nor is father's occupation a significant predictor of men's exits from self-employment. Moreover, in the analyses with left-truncated spells excluded, father's occupational characteristics also do not matter for predicting exit from self-employment for men. The same is true of women.

Educational qualifications are not significant predictors of exit from self-employment for either men or women. There are a few significant coefficients for CASMIN educational categories in table 7.6, but they are scattered and nonsystematic, so we are inclined to regard them as random false positives.

In contrast, there are important differences in the holding power of self-employment in different occupational groups. Compared with the unskilled self-employed, self-employed men in professional and managerial occupations are much less likely to exit, and self-employed men in skilled occupations are somewhat less likely to exit. Both of these effects are statistically significant. This same pattern also holds for women.[34]

Turning to age, men's rates of exit from self-employment decrease with age. They fall steeply at first and then flatten out (as shown by the large linear term and small quadratic term). In contrast, there seems to be no significant effect of age for women in the spells begun since 1980.

The results on the duration of the current spell of self-employment are unclear. We do not feel confident making any firm statement about the impact of duration because the effects vary hugely between estimates excluding left-truncated spells (table 7.6) and the estimates including them (not reported here).

The effects of the national unemployment rate are also unclear, although we think that in general, the best verdict on the available evidence is "probably no effect." The unemployment rate has a negative effect on exit rates for men in the sample of self-employment spells since 1980, but no effect on them in the full sample of spells,[35] and nonsignificant effects for women in both the post-1980 subsample of spells, and in the full sample.

Discussion

Nearly all the prior research on Australia has focused on point-in-time self-employment and hence ignores the dynamics of self-employment. As a result, it is worth considering to what degree our analysis of exits and entrances confirms or runs counter to results from prior research. We do that in this section.

Prior research on Australia has consistently found that the sons of self-employed men are more likely to be self-employed than are the sons of employees (Broom et al. 1980; Kelley and McAllister 1984; Kelley 1990). Our analyses of the dynamics of self-employment confirm this result, and moreover show that the same result holds for women (table 7.4). We also find that the influence of self-employed fathers is limited to encouraging entry: growing up in a self-employed family does not provide men or women with special skills to avert exit from self-employment (table 7.6).

Prior research suggested that father's occupational status, although influential in many other spheres of life, has little or no effect on son's self-employment (Broom et al. 1980; Kelley 1990). Our analysis of the dynamics of self-employment divides father's occupation into four groups, rather than employing the continuous measure used in prior research, and finds that father's professional employment encourages professional self-employment of men, but other than that we find no significant effects. None of the other effects of father's occupation on men's and women's entry into self-employment, entry into occupation-specific types of self-employment, or exit from self-employment is significant (tables 7.4, 7.5, and 7.6).

Prior research found little or no effect of education on self-employment (Broom et al. 1980; Evans 1989; Kelley 1990; Kidd 1993; Le 2000), but our findings reveal complex patterns of effects, with particular educational pathways enhancing chances of entry into some, but not all, self-employment niches. We find that entry into self-employment in the unskilled occupational group is unrelated to education for either men or women. In contrast, pretertiary vocational training (whether accompanied by secondary school completion or just by compulsory schooling) substantially enhances men's rates of entry into self-employment (table 7.5). The results for women are ambiguous. Secondary school (i.e., academic or general schooling, not vocational training) and tertiary study increase the likelihood of entering self-employment in the professional and managerial occupations for both men and women. Education appears largely unrelated to exit from self-employment for both men and women (table 7.6). In sum, our evidence on self-employment dynamics suggests that education does affect entry into self-employment; that these effects are partial and contingent; and that education does not affect exit from self-employment.

The timing of self-employment in work careers is another topic that prior research has touched on, although usually in the framework of workforce experience rather than age per se. We find that rates of entry into self-employment for both men and women increase nonlinearly with age—more steeply early in the career (table 7.4). This finding parallels prior research on the prevalence of point-in-time self-employment by workforce experience (Evans 1989). We also found that this same pattern holds within occupational zones (professional and managerial, skilled, and unskilled) for both sexes. The exception is that entry into self-employment in unskilled occupations for men is not age differentiated (table 7.5). The results on exit rates are more ambiguous: they decline significantly with age among men, but not among women (table 7.6).

The preponderance of prior evidence on the rewards for self-employment is positive, but somewhat mixed (Broom et al. 1980; Evans and Kelley 1991; Kelley and McAllister 1984; Kelley 1990; Le 1999; McDonald and Worswick 1999). Our contribution is to show that the self-employed report higher levels of job satisfaction than do employees, and that this holds within occupational groups as well as in the labor force as a whole (table 7.3).

CONCLUSIONS

In this section, we consider the conceptual implications of our findings for themes of globalization/marketization, marginalization, gender differentiation, and inherited advantage.

Globalization and marketization have indisputably occurred in Australia over the past couple of decades, with tariff barriers crumbling and centralized labor market regulation and arbitration shriveling. It seems reasonable to say that these changes have neither generally expanded nor generally shrunk the range of opportunities for self-employment, because self-employment as a fraction of the workforce appears to be holding steady. What is happening instead is an important shrinkage in the unskilled occupations and a large expansion in the professional and managerial occupations. These changes are in tandem with what is happening in the workforce as a whole, which has been undergoing a major upgrading of education and occupation. Thus, self-employment has changed greatly, but these changes have been moving with the times, in parallel with educational and occupational shifts in the employee population. Moreover, continuity is evident in the balance between solo and employer self-employed over time, suggesting that solo self-employed are not being squeezed out by increased competitiveness. The deregulation of entry, if indeed it really has occurred, has not brought in any evident flood of previously thwarted entrepreneurs. Thus, the evidence for Australia is that the globalization and marketization of the past two decades has not increased the marginalization of self-employment and has been creating new opportunities as fast as it has been destroying old ones.

That said, it is still worth asking whether the self-employed are marginalized in Australia. Evidence of marginal status would include (1) signs that self-employment is shunned when people have the option to choose and (2) signs that self-employed work is less rewarding. According to the marginalization hypothesis, the children of fathers with the worst jobs, having fewer options, are more likely to be forced into self-employment, but in fact, self-employed people come from families throughout the occupational hierarchy, with, if anything, a slight over-representation of families at the top. The marginalization hypothesis would also predict that less educated people, having fewer options, would be especially likely to take up self-employment. But the data show that they are not. Instead, advanced academic education and several forms of specialized vocational training promote entry into self-employment. Furthermore, the marginalization hypothesis would suggest that women with little education ought to be especially vulnerable and hence would be especially likely to be forced into self-employment. But this is not the case either. Moreover, if self-employment were marginalized, then exit rates should be higher among the highly educated, among those in higher-ranking occupations, and among those whose father worked in professional and managerial occupations, but they are not, for either men or women. In addition, if self-employment were marginal, and toward the bottom of people's lists of work options, then it ought to rise when times are hard, as necessity then forces people into less preferred alternatives. But the estimates show that entry into self-employment is unrelated to macroeconomic conditions as indicated by the unemployment rate. Finally, in terms of reward, the self-employed report higher job satisfaction not only in the workforce as a whole but even within occupational groups (as in many other countries, see Blanchflower 2000). According to all of these indicators, self-employment is not marginal in Australia.

What is the connection between self-employment and the gender differentiation of work? One possibility is that self-employment would allow women to escape the gender stereotyping they would experience as employees. The evidence on this point is not supportive. Instead, women tend to be concentrated in caring and service occupations—nursing and midwifery, teaching, cleaning,and the like—regardless of whether they are employees or self-employed, so self-employment does not lead to less (or more) gender segregation of occupations. On the other hand, women's self-employment rates have traditionally been below men's but have been rising over the past two decades, which could be taken as evidence of gender convergence. Another hypothesis concerning the connection between gender and self-employment, the "family friendliness" hypothesis, is that self-employment would be especially attractive to women because it would facilitate the blending of work and family responsibilities. If this hypothesis were correct, then we would expect to find that age patterns of entry for women would be intensely concentrated in the young adult ages (the key ages for family formation). But in fact, the effects of age on entry into self-employment for women are identical to those for men, and both show a midcareer rather than an early career peak. The fact that self-employed women are more likely than female employees to be married might be seen as suggesting that self-employment is especially compatible with the traditional female role, except that self-employed men are also more likely than their employee peers to be married. Thus, the evidence on the dynamics of self-employment casts doubt on two prominent hypotheses about gender and self-employment: the gender convergence hypothesis receives mixed support (yes on form, no on content), and the family friendliness hypothesis receives no support.

The fourth question concerns inherited advantage. Our evidence does not concern the direct inheritance of particular businesses or professional practices, but rather more generalized transfer of resources and, perhaps, skills, tastes, and preferences. Certainly there is a tendency toward intergenerational resemblance in self-employment among men: the percentage of men with self-employed fathers is higher among self-employed in all three occupational groups than among their employee peers, and the intergenerational link is still evident in the multivariate analysis. But fathers play little or no role in the self-employment dynamics of women. This is evidence against an "advantage" interpretation, since women's stratification outcomes tend to be even more strongly influenced by family background than men's. Moreover, if self-employment were an important channel of resources and privileges from one generation to the next, then we would expect that having a father further up the occupational hierarchy would be an advantage in entering self-employment. Here again, the evidence is positive for men and negative for women. From a slightly different angle, if self-employment enhanced the intergenerational transmission of advantage, one would expect to find that within occupational groups, the self-employed occupy the better jobs. But in reality, the occupational status of their jobs is equal, on average, to that of employees in the same occupational groups. In addition, with regard to the inherited advantage hypothesis, one would expect that those with fathers in more advantageous labor market positions would be better able to maintain themselves in self-employment, but our analysis shows that father's occupation has no impact on the risk of exiting from self-employment for either men or women. Although these pieces of evidence are not unanimous, the balance of this evidence is against intergenerational advantage.

In addition to these hypotheses, consider the possibility that self-employment is largely a matter of tastes and preferences as well as educational and family resources rather than marginalization. The fact that the self-employed throughout the occupational hierarchy are more satisfied with their work (despite longer hours and fewer holidays) than are their employee peers suggests that they are finding substantial subjective rewards in their work. In addition, the finding that previous self-employment is one of the most potent predictors of entry into self-employment suggests an important role of tastes and preferences in undertaking self-employment. Moreover, the age profiles of entry into self-employment—low in early adulthood, and rising toward a midcareer plateau—are consistent with the view that self-employment is a desired goal toward which many young men and women work for some years as employees before being able to achieve. Further, the strong connections between vocational education and skilled self-employment and between tertiary education and self-employment in the professional and managerial group suggest that at least some of the goal setting comes even earlier, with those planning self-employment choosing appropriate educational pathways toward their goals. In sum, the evidence from our analyses supports the interpretation that tastes and preferences play a role in entry into self-employment.[36]

NOTES

1. These figures are from survey data from the International Social Science Survey/Australia (IsssA) using the usual sociological concept of self-employment

and comparable with data in other chapters of this book. We prefer these to alternative figures based on census data because the definition of self-employed used by the Australian Bureau of Statistics for the Census (ABS) is not comparable to the sociological concept of self-employment, as the ABS treats owners in incorporated businesses as wage and salary earners and thus groups them together with employees. Therefore the ABS estimates of Australian self-employment are necessarily somewhat deflated. The trends in unincorporated self-employment in the ABS data and in total self-employment in the IsssA data are similar until the end of the 1990s, when the unincorporated self-employed show a downturn (ABS 2000a), but the total self-employed do not. Whether this represents a shift from unincorporated to incorporated self-employment or some other divergence between the two data sources is not yet known. Recently, the ABS began collecting information on both incorporated and unincorporated self-employment through its "Forms of Employment" survey, and its estimates of total self-employment combining these two forms closely approximate the IsssA figures for the late 1990s (further details in the Data and Methods section below), but these are not available for earlier years.

2. The same picture largely holds among the unincorporated self-employed in the ABS (2000a) data, except that the ABS finds a marked drop in female self-employment between 1996 and 1999, which is not evident in IsssA data.

3. These include education in years, in Australia and overseas, represented by both linear and quadratic terms.

4. Among employees, earnings of immigrants have been shown to match those of comparable long-established Australians in the 1970s and early 1980s, except for Mediterranean immigrants, who earn more than their native-born peers at low levels of education and in low-status occupations, but who earn less than their native-born peers at high levels of education or in high status jobs (Kelley and McAllister 1984; Evans and Kelley 1991). A relatively crude analysis contrasting the native-born with all groups of immigrants lumped together finds no difference in earnings between immigrants and native-born employees in the early 1990s (Le 1999). These findings of equality of earnings are consistent with the level of discrimination in hiring reported by immigrants (Evans, Jones, and Kelley 1988).

5. Australian welfare comes under a variety of particular program names. "Additional family payments" in the period under consideration were normally not sole support payments, but were available to working people on low incomes who form the focus of Bradbury's (1997b) analysis. They would normally be combined with an unemployment allowance or a disability allowance to support people out of work.

6. This figure is from the 1998 "Forms of Employment" survey conducted by the Australian Bureau of Statistics, which unlike earlier ABS data was intended to include as self-employed people who, formally, are employees of businesses they own, as well as people who run their own unincorporated business, farm, or professional practice. This makes it consistent with the sociological definition, which is also used in the empirical analyses later in this chapter. Traditionally, there has been less pressure to incorporate a small business in Australia than in the United States because many disputes were resolved inside a regulatory framework rather

than by court cases, so liability was less of an issue. That is probably changing now with deregulation, but tracing this development in detail is beyond the scope of this study.

7. Superannuation is Australia's form of forced and encouraged individual savings for old-age support. It is tax-advantaged in the sense that the amounts saved into it are taken from pretax earnings and required employer contributions, but one is presumably in a lower tax bracket after retirement, so savings withdrawn from a superannuation fund will be taxed at a lower rate than if one had enjoyed them while one was working. The system was introduced during the 1980s. Although this sounds attractive, Australians remain distrustful of it, and when asked what forms of investment they would choose if they had some extra money to save, superannuation comes a long way behind shares in the stock market, savings accounts, investment properties, and other possible investments (Webster and Valenzuela 2002). In general, superannuation coverage and holdings are lower for both men and women in the heavily self-employed occupations of the manual crafts ("trades" in Australian English) and plant and machinery operators and drivers, but it is not clear whether this is because they are short of money or because they prefer other investments (Webster and Valenzuela 2002).

8. A family-centered focus is not implausible for Australian women, given gender role attitudes that are conservative by international standards both among women in general (Evans 2000) and among mothers in particular (Evans and Kelley 2001a).

9. This greater facility in the dominant language means immigrant entrepreneurs may be somewhat overrepresented in English-language surveys such as the IsssA, on which our subsequent analysis is based.

10. This is in contrast to an average of 2 percent from the 1940s through the 1960s.

11. See the Institutional Setting section above.

12. We collect full information on up to three businesses, so we very slightly underestimate the probability of entering self-employment late in life among people who have previously had several failed businesses. We collect abbreviated information on other aspects of employment histories.

13. Work at higher ages is not rare for Australian men: 26 percent of Australian men between the ages of 60 and 64 are still in employment, compared with around 20 percent in the other English-speaking countries and Norway; highly variable rates among the ex-communist European countries; and 10 percent or less in the German-speaking countries (Evans 1999, table 1). In contrast, work careers for women in Australia have well and truly finished by age 60.

14. This means, for example, that we do not count people who change businesses within a year, or who add a second business to their portfolio, as entering self-employment because they are not in the risk set of the non-self-employed in the prior year.

15. The subtraction performed reduces rounding error that would otherwise occur in the computations involving the large age-squared terms, which are of a hugely larger magnitude than the values of the other variables in the model, but leaves predicted values unchanged (Mosteller and Tukey 1977:285).

16. In the 1980s, 86 percent of self-employed women were married, compared

with 71 percent of female dependent employees. This trend held well into the 1990s, with 89 percent of self-employed women living with spouses or partners, compared with only 73 percent of women working for employers. Self-employed women are also a little more likely to be married than are self-employed men: in the 1980s, 81 percent of self-employed men were married; in the 1990s, the figure was 83 percent.

17. Our estimates are very close to the estimates of the Australian Bureau of Statistics on the gender balance of self-employment. The ABS's survey of Forms of Employment (ABS 2000a), conducted in 1998, found that 69 percent of the self-employed in Australia are men.

18. Paternal self-employment was also significantly more common among self-employed men than among unemployed men or men not in the labor force, statuses relatively rare in Australia, and often socially deviant in these ages for men (results not shown in table 7.2).

19. There is just one significant difference, with paternal self-employment being significantly more common among self-employed women in the skilled occupations than among female employees in these same occupations in the 1980s. But the difference is not repeated in the 1990s or in any other group. Note also that self-employed women, unemployed women, and housewives were approximately equally likely to have a self-employed father, a pattern quite different from that for men (results available upon request from the authors).

20. Lower tertiary education has a strongly vocational orientation in Australia.

21. We suspect that this is probably due to the relatively small sample sizes in this occupational group rather than to a genuine null effect.

22. Some of this is a fairly technical matter of definition, depending on how one counts the firm size of franchisees and the like, so reports of average firm size can vary widely among reliable sources.

23. There are rather few (under a hundred) unskilled self-employed women in our sample, so these estimates are only tentative.

24. Figure 7.1 shows Kaplan-Meyer estimates of proportions of self-employed who remain in self-employment after each consecutive year in the observation window between 1980 and 1998. Only people with at least five years of observational histories are included, and we focus on their first five years in each self-employment spell.

25. These proportions correspond to ABS estimates of employment duration in current business or with current employer (ABS 2000a:10).

26. This effect is from a pooled model (not shown), just like that shown in table 7.4, except that it is run on the pooled sample of men and women, and gender is included as a variable in the model.

27. But the effects are not perfectly stable and failed significance tests in some of the sensitivity models we estimated.

28. These include both the manual skills to get the job done and the teamwork skills required when, as in the construction business, a number of self-employed people with different specialties coalesce temporarily on a project.

29. This finding is from a model identical to that depicted in table 7.5, but estimated on the pooled sample of men and women, and including gender as a predictor variable. The finding in the next sentence also comes from this analysis.

30. On the other hand, a number of lower tertiary qualifications have specifically involved training to be professionals' assistants and hence were traditionally thought of as "employee" occupations, but this may have shifted in part with the expansion of contractor roles.

31. We conducted two parallel analyses of exits from self-employment, one in which the risk set consisted of self-employment spells commenced since 1980 (comparable to the analyses of panel data elsewhere in this book: see table 7.6), and one in which the risk set is all spells of self-employment experienced by respondents, including those before 1980 (which has a larger number of cases). The full details of analysis including the left-truncated spells are not reported here due to space limitations but are available from the authors upon request.

32. This leaves open the possibility that some of the processes differ among educational groups, but we were unable to test for this systematically, as the standard errors were simply too large due to the relatively small numbers of cases.

33. This conclusion is based on a logistic model like that in table 7.6, except that gender is included as a causal variable. This model is estimated once on the risk set pooling the self-employment spells of men and women that began after 1980 and is estimated again on all pooled self-employment spells of both genders regardless of their start date.

34. This is true both in the estimates omitting the left-truncated spells and in the estimates including them.

35. Results available upon request from the authors.

36. A number of social theorists have been calling for a more systematic incorporation of tastes and preferences into the sociology of work. This is explicit in the work of Hakim (2000), and implicit in the postmaterialist/postmodernist hypotheses of Inglehart (1977, 1997) and Beck, Giddens, and Lash (1994). Our particular results suggesting that tastes and preferences are an influential social force on entry into self-employment can be seen as supporting their general claims for the importance of tastes and preferences in labor market processes.

REFERENCES

Australian Bureau of Statistics (ABS). 2000a. *Forms of employment*. ABS Cat. No. 6359.0. Canberra: ABS.
———. 2000b. *Time-series tables: Labour force*. ABS Cat. No. 6291.0.40.001. Canberra: ABS.
———. 2001. *Employment arrangements and superannuation*. Canberra: ABS.
———. 2002. *Forms of Employment*. Canberra: ABS.
Australian Taxation Office. 2002. *Tax basics for small business*. Canberra: ATO.
Bean, C. S. 1991. Comparison of National Social Science Survey data with the 1986 census. *National Social Science Survey Report* 2:12–19.
Beck, U., A. Giddens, and S. Lash. 1994. *Reflexive modernization*. Cambridge: Polity Press.
Bennett, R., and S. Dann. 2000. The changing experience of Australian female entrepreneurs. *Gender, Work and Organization* 7:75–83.

Blanchflower, D. G. 2000. Self-employment in OECD countries. *Labour Economics* 7:471–505.

Blanchflower, D. G., and B. D. Meyer. 1994. A longitudinal analysis of the young self-employed in Australia and the United States. *Small Business Economics* 6: 1–19.

Borland, J., and S. Kennedy. 1998. *Dimensions, structure and history of Australian unemployment.* Centre for Economic Policy Research Discussion Paper 388. Canberra: Australian National University.

Bottomley, G. 1974. Some Greek sex roles: Ideals, expectations and action in Australia and Greece. *The Australian and New Zealand Journal of Sociology* 10: 8–16.

Bradbury, B. 1997a. The living standards of the low income self-employed. *Australian Economic Review* 30:374–89.

———. 1997b. Social security and the self-employed. *SPRC Newsletter* 64:8–9.

Broom, L., et al. 1980. *The inheritance of inequality.* London: Routledge & Kegan Paul.

Campbell, I. 1999. Labour market deregulation in Australia: The slow combustion approach to workplace change. *International Review of Applied Economics* 13:353–94.

Centrelink, Commonwealth of Australia. 2002. *Are you self-employed or responsible for a farm? A guide to your options and our services.* Canberra: Centrelink.

Evans, M.D.R. 1984. Immigrant women in Australia: Resources, family and work. *International Migration Review* 18: 1063–90.

———. 1987. Language skill, language usage and opportunity: Immigrants in the Australian labour market. *Sociology* 21: 253–74.

———. 1989. Immigrant entrepreneurship: Effects of ethnic market size and isolated labor pool. *American Sociological Review*: 950–62.

———. 1999. Men's working hours. *Australian Social Monitor* 2:23.

———. 2000. Women's participation in the labour force: Ideals and behaviour. *Australian Social Monitor* 3: 49–57.

Evans, M.D.R., F. L. Jones, and J. Kelley. 1988. Job discrimination against immigrants: Perceptions, personal experience, norms and reality. In *Australian attitudes: Social and political analyses from the National Social Science Survey*, ed. J. Kelley and C. Bean, 111–27. Sydney: Allen and Unwin.

Evans, M.D.R., and J. Kelley. 1991. Prejudice, discrimination and the labor market: Attainments of immigrants in Australia. *American Journal of Sociology* 97:721–59.

———. 2001a. Employment for mothers of pre-school children: Evidence from Australia and 23 other nations. *People and Place* 9:28–46.

———. 2001b. How many trade union members? *Australian Social Monitor* 3:88.

———. 2001c. *Sources of attitudes towards industrial relations in Australia, 2001.* Report to the Department of Employment, Work Relations and Small Business, Canberra.

———. 2001d. Downsizing: Employees' experiences. *Australian Social Monitor* 4:27–32.

———. 2002. *Australian economy and society 2001: Volume 1, Education, work and welfare.* Sydney: Federation Press.

Evans, M.D.R., and E. O. Laumann. 1983. Professional commitment: Myth or reality? *Research in Social Stratification and Mobility* 2:3–40.

Hakim, C. 2000. *Work-lifestyle choices in the 21st Century*. Oxford: Oxford University Press.

Holmes, S., S. Smith, and G. Cane. 1997. Gender issues in home-based business operation and training: An Australian overview. *Women in Management Review* 12:68–73.

Inglehart, R. 1977. *The silent revolution*. Princeton: Princeton University Press.

———. 1997. *Modernization and postmodernization*. Princeton: Princeton University Press.

Jensen, B., and C. Littler. 2000. Downsizing in Australia. *Australian Social Monitor* 2:134–38.

Kelley, J. 1990. The failure of a paradigm: Log-linear models of social mobility. In *John Goldthorpe: Consensus and controversy*, ed. J. Clarke, S. Modgil, and C. Modgil, 319–46. London: Falmer Press.

Kelley, J., and M.D.R. Evans. 1999. Australian and international survey data for multivariate analysis: The IsssA. *Australian Economic Review* 32:298–302.

———. 2002. Trends in educational attainment in Australia. In *Australian Economy and Society 2001: Volume 1, Education, work and welfare*, ed. M.D.R. Evans and J. Kelley, 31–38. Sydney: Federation Press.

Kelley, J. and I. McAllister. 1984. Immigrants, socio-economic attainment and politics in Australia. *British Journal of Sociology* 35:387–405.

Kelley, J. and J. Sikora. 2001. Self-employment and occupation. *Australian Social Monitor* 3:105.

Kidd, M. P. 1993. Immigrant wage differentials and the role of self-employment in Australia. *Australian Economic Papers* 32:92–115.

Le, Anh T. 1999. Self-employment and earnings among immigrants in Australia. *International Migration* 37:383–412.

Le, Anh T. 2000. The determinants of immigrant self-employment in Australia. *International Migration Review* 34:183–214.

McDonald, J. T., and C. Worswick. 1999. The earnings of immigrant men in Australia: Assimilation, cohort effects and macroeconomic conditions. *Economic Record* 75:49–62.

Matheson, C. 1999. The sources of upward mobility within public sector organizations: A case study. *Administration & Society* 31:495–524.

Mosteller, F., and J. W. Tukey. 1977. *Data analysis and regression*. Sydney: Addison-Wesley.

Mueller, W., H. Lohmann, and S. Luber. 1999. *Self-Employment in Advanced Economies Project Summary*. Mannheim: University of Mannheim.

———. 2000. Minutes from First Workshop on Self-Employment in Advanced Economies. Libourne, France, 10 May.

Murphy, J. 1995. Superannuation coverage of women from a non-English-speaking background. *Australian Bulletin of Labour* 21:208–20.

OECD. 2001. The institutional set-up of labour market policy and employment services. In *Innovations in Labour Market Policies: The Australian Way*, 87–114. Paris: OECD.

Robinson, R. V., and J. Kelley. 1979. Class as conceived by Marx and Dahrendorf:

Effects on income inequality and politics in the United States and Great Britain. *American Sociological Review* 44:38–57.

Sikora, J. 1997. A comparison of 1994/1995 International Survey of Economic Attitudes Data with censuses. WwA: *Worldwide Attitudes* 1997. 12.21:1–12.

———. 2001a. Gender and self-employment. *Australian Social Monitor* 4:22.

———. 2001b. Self-employment by industry, 1984–1999. *Australian Social Monitor* 4:50–51.

Still, L. V. 1993. Quo vadis, women in management? *Women in Management Review* 8.

Surry, M. 2000. Love it, or hate it. *Asian Business* 36:65.

Tait, D., et al. 1989. Understanding ethnic small business: A case study of Marrickville. *Australian Journal of Social Issues* 24:183–98.

Webster, E., and R. Valenzuela. 2002. Householders' preferences for superannuation. In *Australian economy and society 2001: Volume 1, Education, work, and welfare*, ed. M.D.R. Evans and J. Kelley, 290–95. Sydney: Federation Press.

Wolfers, L., and J. Miller. 2001. The simplified tax system: Is this governmentspeak for 'Complex'? *Taxation in Australia* 35:374–77.

Wooden, M. 2000. *The transformation of Australian industrial relations*. Sydney: Federation Press.

ACKNOWLEDGMENT

Portions of this research were supported by the Australian Commonwealth Government's Department of Family and Community Services (FaCS) Social Policy Research Contract 011 "Neighbourhood and family influences on employment" with the University of Melbourne's Melbourne Institute of Social and Economic Research. FaCS neither endorses nor censors the views taken by contracting researchers, so the opinions and interpretations provided in this paper do not necessarily represent those of FaCS. We thank Jonathan Kelley for his comments.

CHAPTER EIGHT

Winners or Losers? Entry and Exit into Self-Employment in Hungary: 1980s and 1990s

Péter Róbert and Erzsébet Bukodi

RECENT STUDIES PROVIDE evidence that self-employment has become an increasingly important and relevant option to dependent employment. Despite the general tendency toward globalization in the world economy and the growing power of large multinational corporations in both production and service, self-employment appears to remain an alternative for ensuring an adequate standard of living for individuals and families. In searching for explanations for this phenomenon, a broad variety of "pulling" and "pushing" mechanisms have been considered and empirically tested (see, e.g., Arum 1997; Müller, Lohmann, and Luber 2001).

This chapter investigates the problem by putting some of these mechanisms, both conceptually and empirically, into the context of the economic and political developments of Hungary, a formerly communist country, in the 1980s and 1990s. First, we will provide a general overview of the shifting evaluation and political environment of self-employment in Hungary. We will discuss how changes started in the communist era and became more pronounced in the 1990s, under the conditions of emerging capitalism. The economic conditions of self-employed small businesses were also markedly different before and after 1990, as we will describe. In general, both the political and the economic transformation in Hungary have made the pushing and pulling mechanisms more relevant to the understanding of the transition to self-employment. After explaining the Hungarian context, we will present our data and the statistical models for estimating entry into and exit out of self-employment. The chapter ends by discussing and interpreting the results of the empirical analysis.

THE CHANGING POLITICAL AND ECONOMIC ENVIRONMENT OF SELF-EMPLOYMENT IN THE 1980s: PUSH AND PULL

As a communist country, state ownership and a state planning system dominated the economy in Hungary. The proportion of self-employed during the communist era was approximately 3 percent of the labor force. In the 1970s, however, Hungary began to deviate from the "baseline" of communism established in previous years. In a previous study on transition to self-employment, which focused on historical continuities and discontinuities over five decades in Hungary, the application of spline regression provided evidence for the significance of the economic changes brought on by the introduction of the so-called New Economic Mechanism (NEM) in 1968 (Róbert and Bukodi 2000). The main goal of NEM was to establish and bring market elements in a basically planned economy. As a consequence, from the 1970s on, the strength and rigidity of the planning system began to decline, giving way to a new system called *plan bargaining* (Bauer 1978). The proportion of self-employment did not increase in the 1970s if self-employment is limited to one's primary occupation. Instead, entrepreneurial activity appeared to a growing extent as a side job, occasional part-time work, or moonlighting after finishing a full-time job as an employee. The phenomenon, labeled the "second economy" (Gábor 1989), became widespread first in agriculture (Szelényi 1988) and in construction in the countryside (Sik 1988). From 1982 on, workers had the legal opportunity to establish so-called business work partnerships (known in Hungary by the acronym GMK) within the state companies, especially in manufacturing and construction (Laky and Neumann 1992; Burawoy and Lukács 1986). In the beginning of the 1980s, the proportion of those households that benefited financially from the second economy was estimated to be as great as 70 percent (Kolosi 1988). Although financial or material shortages were indicative of communist economies generally (Kornai 1980), this was less recognizable in Hungary, due to the second economy. This fact strongly contributed to the legitimization of private initiatives.

As the political environment became increasingly liberal in the 1980s, participants in the second economy, the part-time entrepreneurs, began to move to full-time self-employment. The aforementioned GMKs were small cooperatives, a form of joint private initiative, practically devoid of financial assets. Since their members took the profit as extra personal income, capital accumulation did not take place. In this sense, part-time participation in the second economy served as a stepping-stone for increasing self-employment in Hungary under communism and after 1990. Nearly half of the respondents from a snowball sampling technique survey, carried out among high-level business officials in Hungary in 1997, reported that they had participated in the second economy before 1990 (Kolosi and Sági 1998). It is reasonable to assume that these people, after having spent several years in the second economy and having worked under quasi market conditions, could accumulate the relevant skills, knowledge, social contacts, and even financial assets necessary to start an individual full-time business. At the same time, some experts argue that the second economy in Hungary was so entrenched in the formal and official forms of production that accumulated skills or experiences were hardly useful and convertible for entrepreneurial activity in a market economy (Laki 1993). In any case, emerging self-employment in Hungary was clearly an outcome deeply rooted in the historical developments of the society. It was a path-dependent process in line with the general thesis outlined by Stark (1992).

In sum, the pull factors of the political environment are probably the dominant influence for entry into self-employment in Hungary in the 1980s. At the same time, one could also argue that a push effect, namely, the low financial compensation in the state sector, additionally pushed people into the second economy and self-employment.

Mechanisms Influencing Entry and Exit after the Collapse of Communism

Privatization as a Main Driving Force

The collapse of communism brought significant political and economic changes to Hungary. Among these changes, privatization was the most important development that served as a driving force for the entry into self-employment. Privatization resulted in substantial change within the organizational structure of economic enterprises and led to a significant proportion of state employees becoming employees in the private sector. Employment in the state sector was already less than 60 percent in 1992, and the Hungarian Household Panel carried out by TÁRKI reported a further decline to 40 percent by 1997.

In connection with privatization, the structure of economic organizations was considerably reshaped. Soon after 1990, the large state-owned enterprises, which typically had hundreds or thousands of workers and employees, could not be privatized in their original form because of a lack of both interest and private capital. Instead, the number of enterprises and firms substantially increased, and their size, as measured by the number of employees, strongly decreased. The dramatic nature of this process may be seen from the following figures: in 1988, 72 percent of state-owned industrial firms had more than 1,000 employees, and 20 percent had more than 5,000. By 1991, less than half of the firms employed more than 1,000 people, and only 10 percent employed more than 5,000 (Economic Survey of Europe 1994, table 5.4.5).

To some extent, the downsizing of economic organizations was due to the economic potential of different actors who actively participated in privatization. Two groups, the GMKs and small cooperatives, as well as the earlier managers, were well connected to the centralized economy. However, their economic potential was limited. Consequently, management buyout became the typical form of privatization, leading to the division of large firms. According to the previously mentioned survey of key business officials (Kolosi and Sági 1998), 43 percent of the sample reported having held high managerial positions before 1990, and 25 percent participated in the privatization of the company. (For further details about privatization see, e.g., Estrin [1994], especially chapter 9 for Hungary.)

The Decline of the Labor Force and the Role of Unemployment

Since the private economy worked more efficiently and rationally than the centralized economy with respect to employment, a general shrinking of the labor market was a further consequence of privatization. The safety of lifetime jobs persisted only in the public sector, whereas the uncertainty of employment increased in the private sector, where privatization of firms was usually followed by a "rationalization" of the workforce. The expectation that people who had lost their jobs in privatized state firms would find new ones in other segments of the growing private sector was not satisfied.

The proportion of the registered unemployed was only 0.3 percent in 1989 and 1.7 percent in 1990, but it increased to 7.8 percent by 1991. The rate was the highest in 1992, at 13.2 percent. In the second part of 1990s, the rate was around 10 percent, and it declined to a one-digit figure by the end of the decade (Vukovich and Harcsa 1999, table 3). Since manufacturing and construction were the economic branches most affected by the transformation, and the risk of unemployment became especially high in these segments, which had a male-dominated workforce, the (official) unemployment rate was higher for men than for women in Hungary, unlike in most Western countries.

Unemployment may be considered a possible pushing factor into self-employment. On the other hand, some previous research on this question reveals that the social composition of self-employed coming from unemployment was closer to the social characteristics of self-employed individuals than of unemployed individuals (Pfeiffer and Reize 2000). If entries into self-employment from unemployment have occurred, this move probably resulted in unskilled self-employment. For exit from self-employment, we assume that this transition is also more likely for the unskilled self-employed who were often forced into self-employment as an activity of last resort.

The Increase of the Service Sector

The growing service sector in modern postindustrial societies is another explanatory mechanism for the increase of self-employment. It is usually considered a pull factor because the service sector provides more opportunity for small private businesses. The increase in the service sector in Hungary is shown by the census: in 1970, 32 percent of the labor force worked in the service sector; in 1980, the same proportion was 39 percent; and the 1990 census reported 46 percent. As a consequence of the economic transformation, the service sector increased more rapidly in the 1990s, growing to 59 percent by 1997.

In line with the aforementioned issues regarding overproportioned manufacturing and construction, branches that were in an economic crisis during the 1980s, we assume that employment in these industrial sectors would push people to self-employment. On the other hand, it is also reasonable to believe that transition to self-employment occurs within the same economic branch with the highest probability. Thus, employment in the service sector was probably a good background for an entry into self-employment in the service sector. With respect to exit from self-employment, self-employment activity in the service sector has better financial and market prospects, while self-employment in manufacturing or construction has a higher risk of failure.

Juridical and Fiscal Environment of Self-Employment

For characterizing the changing environment around self-employment in Hungary, we cannot leave out the juridical and fiscal elements that are part of the pulling mechanisms. First, juridical barriers and constraints disappeared after 1990. Second, different measures aiming to support self-employment, to establish new business, and to channel the unemployed back to the labor force were introduced. For supporting new business activities, government funds were established to provide special bank loans with low interest rates.

The tax system worked as a pushing factor as well. In Hungary, only business owners can deduct costs in their tax declaration or apply for the return of VAT. This regulation has possibly contributed to motivating people to move to self-employment as "own account workers." In Hungary, companies also have to pay roughly 30 percent in social security taxes for their employees. Consequently, firms are less motivated to hire permanent staff who are paid employee salaries and benefits. These firms hire potential employees as self-employed individuals who are paid by submitted invoices. Therefore, "false" self-employment in order to reduce taxes paid by companies and individuals is present in Hungary as well. With regard to social security law, the self-employed have to pay a monthly amount for their retirement fund, like dependent workers do, in order to be eligible for old-age pension. However, they cannot be registered unemployed if their business fails.

Nonmonetary Capital Accumulation

The accumulation of financial capital, which people could use for starting a private business, was relatively limited in Hungary. As a result, the available stock of nonmonetary resources, human capital, and social assets have played a relatively large role in facilitating transitions to self-employment. As far as human capital investments, the Hungarian school system is similar to the German one in having both academic and vocational tracks with part of the vocational training carried out in firms. Our earlier research revealed a reversed U-curve for the effect of a vocational track on transition to self-employment, while the impact of an academic track increased first and leveled off later over time (Róbert and Bukodi 2000). This pattern may vary, however, if we distinguish between various types of self-employment, and may be different from other postcommunist countries. For example, Gerber (2001) found that the influence of education increases linearly on the hazard of transition to self-employment in Russia. Higher educational level can also decrease the probability of exit from self-employment.

Work experience, accumulated social capital, degree of activity in the labor market, and position in the network system play significant roles in the transition to self-employment. Prior employment position before moving into self-employment activity can be a proxy for these effects. Since the character and magnitude of the necessary human and social capital that people had to accumulate in their previous position before entering into self-employment differ, we expect service-class people to have higher odds of becoming self-employed professionals, and skilled workers to have higher odds of becoming self-employed skilled workers. On the same grounds, we suppose that exit from self-employment is more probable for people with fewer accumulated assets and with a shorter duration in self-employment.

Social Background, Inheritance, and Transition to Self-Employment

As advocates of interrupted enbourgeoisement theory argue, the collapse of communism brings about the opportunity for families with the appropriate habitus, ambition, and material capital to return to self-employment after many decades of state employment by the communist government where they were forced to stay in a "parking lot" (Szelényi 1988). Indeed, stronger achievement orientation, risk taking, and the high value placed on independence, which are emphasized as important personal characteristics for entrepreneurship (cf. McClelland 1987), were prevalent in the 1990s in Hungary. Accordingly, social origin as a proxy for socialization in a family characterized by the psychological factors mentioned above can be an important push factor. In fact, in our previous analysis on Hungary we found a slight increase in the impact of father's self-employment on the odds of moving into any private business after 1980 (Róbert and Bukodi 2000). We also assume that transition to self-employment is combined with class reproduction in line with the affinity terms defined by Erikson and Goldthorpe (1992). On similar grounds, advantageous social origin can decrease the odds of exit from self-employment.

Party Membership

In a postcommunist country like Hungary, previous political participation can be considered as a determinant of transition to self-employment. The conversion of political capital into economic assets was a well-known hypothesis applied to the postcommunist transformation (cf. Hankiss 1990; Staniszkis 1991). Previous research in Hungary found evidence for only a moderate support of the "political capitalism" thesis. Even if former party membership turned out to have a positive impact on transition to self-employment, this effect did not persist when one controlled for other determinants, especially for education (Róna-Tas 1994). Our previous analysis showed that party membership influenced entry into self-employment in a declining manner over time, but the length of time spent in the party turned out to be a better predictor (Róbert and Bukodi 2000). In comparison, Gerber (2001) found only a very small effect of former party membership in Russia.

DATA AND MODELS

Two separate data sets have been pooled together in this chapter for analyzing entry into self-employment as well as exit from self-employment in Hungary over two decades. The first one, the Social Mobility Survey, covers the period of 1980 to 1992. This data was collected in 1992 by the Hungarian Central Statistical Office (CSO) and contains the full retrospective occupational history of the respondents, with job titles, employment status (employee, self-employed, etc.), and economic branch, as well as information on their education, social origin, and communist party membership. Since the unit of sample selection was the household and all adult members of the household were interviewed, data on spouses were also available.[1]

The second data set covers the period of 1992 to 1997. These data come from the Hungarian Household Panel Survey (HHP), which had six waves during this period and was carried out by the TÁRKI Social Research Center, together with the Department of Sociology of the University of Economics, Budapest. The data file contains information on the exact job title, employment status, and economic branch for each year as well as on education, social origin, and party membership. This survey was also based on a household sample, and data on the spouses are available, as well. Full retrospective occupational history, however, is not available in this file, but certain information is present for different points in time (first job, job in 1980, 1988, 1990).

Information from the retrospective occupational history in the CSO file was available for each year between 1980 and 1992. These data were handled as a "quasi" panel where the same respondents were "followed" during this period. Transition to self-employment is analyzed during a thirteen-year period (between 1980 and 1992), and for the age range of 18–60 years. Respondents from the "true" panel of the HHP file were then added to the CSO file. On the HHP file, transition to self-employment is analyzed during a six-year period (between 1992 and 1997) and restricted to the age range of 18–60 years.

The definition of self-employment in the surveys was based on a series of questions about employment status (employee/self-employed/member of producers' cooperative/unpaid family worker), number of subordinates, and sector of company (private/public). Normally, own-account workers are persons who classify themselves as self-employed without employees, and employers are those who classify themselves as self-employed with employees, but this distinction has not been made in our analysis. Member of producers' cooperatives and unpaid family workers do not belong to the group of self-employed according to our definition. In practice, respondents can have ownership and be a manager with employee status in the same company. In Hungary, these people tend to classify themselves on the grounds of their ownership proportion in the enterprise. Consequently, a part of them appears as self-employed in our study, while the other part appears as employees. Since information on the ownership share was not available in the data, we are not able to provide more details on this.

The individual files were transformed into event-history files following the method suggested by Blossfeld, Hamerle, and Mayer (1989). First, all jobs in the occupational history were considered as separate episodes. Second, the method of episode splitting was applied with the job episodes divided into years, the smallest time unit in the data set. The unit of observation was changed from individuals to spells (in years) derived from the job episodes. All analyses are carried out on these person-year files (cf. also Yamaguchi 1991).

For analyzing entry into self-employment, first the general hazard of this event is investigated. Estimates from discrete time event-history analyses are presented for both sexes pooled and for men and women separately. In the next step, the process is examined in a competing risks framework. The effects of the independent variables on the hazard of entry into the three different groups of self-employment are contrasted relative to remaining an employee or being out of the labor force. For analyzing exit from self-employment, discrete time event-history analyses were performed again for both sexes pooled and for men and women separately.

RESULTS

This section is divided into three parts. First, we identify trends of entry into self-employment as well as those of exit from self-employment between 1980 and 1997. Second, we turn to the analysis of entry into self-employment. Finally, we present the results from the analysis of exit from self-employment.

Trends of Transition into and out of Self-Employment between 1980 and 1997

Trends of transition into self-employment in Hungary between 1980 and 1997 are displayed by historical years in figure 8.1 for men and women, respectively. These figures indicate that 1990, the formal year of the collapse of communism, did not represent a turning point for this process. Although entry into self-employment was less frequent in the 1980s and became much more common in the 1990s, this trend was more pronounced for men than for women. A somewhat stronger rise had already started by 1986–87, especially for male skilled self-employment.

Further gender differences for entry into self-employment were evident, including more overall frequency for men than for women. The most characteristic transition for men was entry into skilled self-employment as indicated by its continuous rise after 1987. The male self-employed skilled workers are cabinet-makers, bricklayers, painters, shoemakers, locksmiths, electricians, plumbers, mechanics, restaurant owners, shopkeepers, and retail-trade proprietors. Entry into professional self-

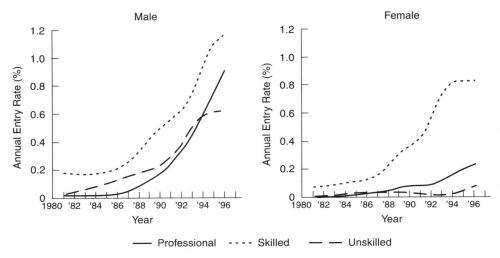

Figure 8.1: Observed Rate of Entry into Self-Employment by Historical Year in Hungary

employment was rare before 1987, but it started to grow steeply thereafter. Lawyers and building engineers are the typical male occupations in this category. From 1994 on, the transition into professional self-employment became more frequent for men than entry into unskilled self-employment. The majority of the male unskilled self-employed jobs are in sales and catering, but there are also many truck drivers among them. Entry into these jobs was quite steep in the 1980s. It increased after 1990 but came to a halt after 1994.

For Hungarian women, transition to professional and unskilled self-employment lags, especially compared with the same moves for men. Entry into unskilled self-employment (unskilled service refers to jobs in sales, catering, or cleaning) indicated only a moderate increase between 1980 and 1997. More inflow occurred into professional self-employment, where typical female jobs are artist or translator. Skilled self-employment among women started to grow already in the second part of the 1980s. It increased in the first part of 1990s but halted thereafter. Typical jobs in this field are hairdresser, tailor, and shopkeeper.

Figure 8.2 shows the trends for entry into self-employment by age, for men and for women. The profiles of these curves reveal that entry into self-employment tends to occur in the twenties, and that men tend to be somewhat younger than women. The pattern is more pronounced for male and female skilled self-employment, as well as for male unskilled self-employment. The shape of the curves for entry into professional

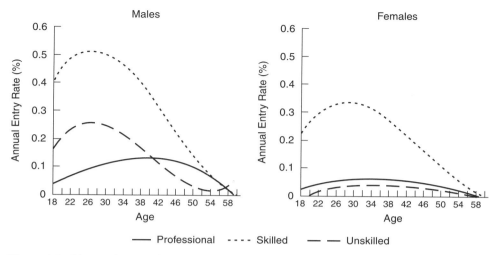

Figure 8.2: Observed Rate of Entry into Self-Employment by Age in Hungary

and managerial self-employment indicates that this event occurs at an older age, evidently because more time is needed to accumulate the necessary capital for this transition.

Figure 8.3 displays the trends for exit from self-employment in Hungary between 1980 and 1997 for men and women together. The investigated event was quite rare in the 1980s when self-employment was low in Hungary, and it was a highly selected group. Consequently, exit from self-employment was not frequent between 1980 and 1991. However, exit from self-employment started to increase after 1992, and we can observe a steep rise in this respect. More women left self-employment in this period than men. The growing exit from self-employment in the 1990s is probably a consequence of the fact that many of these people were forced to move into self-employment due to economic reasons, and they left this state when they could find a job as an employee.

Figure 8.4 shows exit from self-employment from the viewpoint of the other time component of the event, the length of time spent in self-employment. As the survival curves reveal, more than half of the self-employed remain in private business. For the first four or five years in self-employment, there is no difference for exit between men and women: about 20 percent of them left their private business. Later, exit from self-employment increases more steeply for men than for women. In fact, the data indicate that only slightly more than 30 percent of women left self-employment, while the same proportion is nearly 50 percent for men. The result is not surprising because, as we have discussed

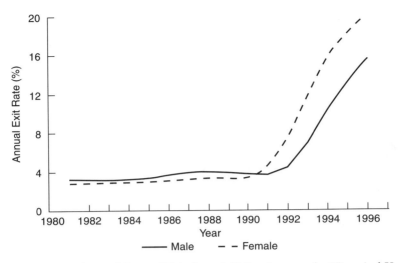

Figure 8.3: Observed Rate of Exit from Self-Employment by Historical Year in Hungary

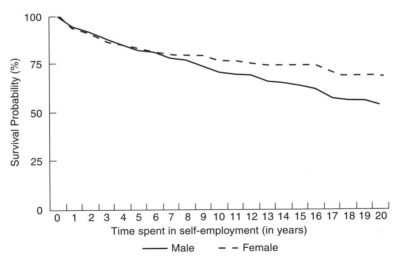

Figure 8.4: Survival Curves for Exit from Self-Employment in Hungary

above, self-employed women constitute a smaller and more selective group compared with men who enter into self-employment more frequently and in larger numbers.

To provide a more comprehensive view of Hungarian self-employment, we collected additional descriptive information on the social standing of the self-employed. We present further information in the appendix to this chapter (table 8.A1), which includes social characteristics about the self-employed (as defined by the group of skilled craftsworkers and tradespeople), in comparison with other occupational groups. We do not present data on income level because these data are unreliable. However, official statistics make it possible to provide information on possessing various household items and durable goods, even from the perspective of change over time, and this is a good indicator of material circumstances. The living conditions of skilled self-employed appear to be better than the conditions of skilled or unskilled employees, although the self-employed were in a more advantageous situation in this respect in the 1980s than in the 1990s. When applied to professional employees, the living conditions of self-employed are roughly similar, although they own more material items (color television, video). Data on other aspects of social standing (cultural participation, holidays) are only partly available for recent times. In this respect, it seems that the position of the self-employed is better in comparison with skilled or unskilled workers but worse in comparison with professionals. For cultural participation, the relative situation of the self-employed seems to have improved in contrast to the other social groups between 1982 and 2000.

Entry into Self-Employment between 1980 and 1997

Results of the multivariate analysis of the transition to self-employment are presented in table 8.1, for both sexes (first column) and for men and women separately (second and third columns, respectively). For predictor variables, we have social origin, education, prior class, and prior economic branch before self-employment, party membership, and spouse's occupational status. The effects of historical changes and age are relevant for entry into self-employment, as discussed above, but controlling for them did not influence the impact of the other determinants, so these controls were omitted.

Estimates of the first model indicate that the probability of entry into self-employment is 1.95 times greater for men than for women, keeping all other explanatory variables at a constant level. This is in line with our descriptive findings as well.

For social origin, a father with a professional or managerial position increases the probability of entry into self-employment the most, but

TABLE 8.1
Social Determinants of Entry into Self-Employment between 1980 and 1997 in Hungary[a]

Explanatory variables	All self-employed	Self-employed men	Self-employed women
Gender (male = 1)	0.666**		
	(0.076)		
Social origin			
Professional, manager	0.449**	0.470**	0.363*
	(0.108)	(0.139)	(0.172)
Skilled worker	0.260**	0.270*	0.201
	(0.089)	(0.113)	(0.143)
Farmer	− 0.428*	− 0.409*	− 0.549+
	(0.175)	(0.208)	(0.325)
Agricultural worker	− 0.087	− 0.128	− 0.045
	(0.113)	(0.145)	(0.181)
Unskilled worker	0	0	0
Father self-employed	0.103	0.003	0.231
	(0.135)	(0.178)	(0.208)
Education			
High tertiary	1.383**	1.139**	1.695**
	(0.181)	(0.238)	(0.281)
Low tertiary	1.208**	1.253**	1.062**
	(0.177)	(0.232)	(0.274)
Secondary	1.323**	1.369**	1.254**
	(0.116)	(0.155)	(0.175)
Vocational	1.288**	1.163**	1.595**
	(0.112)	(0.147)	(0.174)
Primary	0	0	0
Origin (prior) position			
Professional, manager	− 0.405**	− 0.493**	− 0.145
	(0.123)	(0.164)	(0.190)
Skilled worker	− 0.279**	− 0.314**	− 0.091
	(0.094)	(0.119)	(0.158)
Unemployed	1.680**	1.400**	2.229**
	(0.232)	(0.309)	(0.354)
Out of labor force	− 0.818**	− 1.020**	− 0.353+
	(0.128)	(0.165)	(0.203)
Unskilled worker	0	0	0
Sector of employment			
Mining, manufacturing (not in labor force)	0	0	0

TABLE 8.1 (*continued*)

Explanatory variables	All self-employed	Self-employed men	Self-employed women
Construction	0.574**	0.582**	0.747**
	(0.132)	(0.151)	(0.285)
Traditional services	0.780**	0.872**	0.660**
	(0.112)	(0.155)	(0.165)
Transport, communication	0.414**	0.524**	− 0.042
	(0.128)	(0.146)	(0.308)
Business, personal services	1.158**	1.357**	0.962**
	(0.126)	(0.163)	(0.199)
Health, education, public,	0.013	0.290$^+$	− 0.224
administration	(0.129)	(0.174)	(0.193)
Ever in Communist Party	− 0.564**	− 0.609**	− 0.467
	(0.136)	(0.155)	(0.286)
Spouse's status			
Employee	− 0.355**	− 0.274**	− 0.492**
	(0.073)	(0.094)	(0.119)
Self-employed	1.185**	1.253**	1.107**
	(0.144)	(0.227)	(0.190)
Out of labor force	0.408**	0.442**	0.318
	(0.143)	(0.167)	(0.279)
No partner/no informa-			
tion	0	0	0
Intercept	− 6.654**	− 5.966**	− 6.701**
	(0.135)	(0.171)	(0.200)
− 2 Log likelihood	10599.728	6240.949	4312.780
Degree of freedom	23	22	22
Number of events	889	544	345
Number of spells	200,809	91,867	108,942

Source: Social Mobility and Life History Survey 1992 (Central Statistical Office) and Hungarian Household Panel Survey, 1992–97 (TÁRKI) pooled data-file.

[a] Unstandardized estimates from discrete time logistic model, standard errors in parentheses.

** $p < 0.01$ * $p < 0.05$ $^+$ $p < 0.1$

having a father who was a skilled worker also has a significant positive impact compared with having an unskilled worker father. The pattern is more pronounced for men than for women. Father's self-employment does not turn out to be significant for entry into self-employment.

Education has the strongest influence on transition into self-employment. Having a university diploma increases the odds of entry into self-employment nearly three times compared with having a primary level of education. The effect is similar for men and for women. In fact, the parameter estimates for education are greater than the coefficients for the other factors listed in table 8.1. It is not surprising that human capital investments are the most important precondition for transition to self-employment in Hungary because the accumulation of financial capital was probably more difficult during the socialist era.

Occupational position before self-employment and level of education are strongly correlated. This explains the "strange pattern" in our study. For example, the odds of entry into self-employment are significantly lower for those who were professionals, managers, or skilled workers than for those who were unskilled workers. If this was simply taken at face value, the findings of several previous studies on Hungary would be challenged. However, when the impact of prior class is examined without controlling for education (and social origin), previous managerial, profes-sional, or skilled employment increases the probability for entry into self-employment.[2] Another interesting finding is that the odds for transition to self-employment are significantly higher for those who were unem-ployed. This result can be understood in light of the special institutional context of the emerging private economy in Hungary. An unemployment period between employment and self-employment provided the oppor-tunity to take advantage of the special financial measures offered by the postcommunist government for establishing private businesses.[3] Finally, data on prior class indicates that entry into self-employment is signifi-cantly less probable from an out-of-the-labor-force state, as compared with being an unskilled worker. People in this position have obviously less possibility for accumulating the capital needed for self-employment.

Mining and manufacturing were the sectors most affected by the col-lapse of communism. Employment in this sector definitely offered very few opportunities for capital accumulation usable in a future self-employ-ment career. Prior employment in construction (another crisis sector af-ter communism), however, increases the probability of entry into self-employment. The odds are even higher for the traditional service sphere (transportation and communication) and especially for business and per-sonal services. Prior employment in health, education, or public adminis-tration did not increase the chances for a move into self-employment. This pattern is similar for both men and women.

Unlike predictions derived from the hypothesis of "political capital-ism," former Communist Party membership does not increase the odds of entry into self-employment. On the contrary, in a multivariate anal-ysis, when estimates are controlled for education and class of employ-ment before self-employment, Communist Party membership even decreases the probability of a transition into self-employment. Evidence shows that party membership in Hungary was overrepresented among those with a tertiary education and those in a managerial position (Szelényi 1987). The negative effect appears only for men.

The influence of spouse's status is the last independent variable we will discuss in the model. The estimates confirm the "self-employment comes in couples" theory. A self-employed partner increases the odds for an entry into self-employment for both sexes. If the spouse is an employee, however, the odds of becoming self-employed are lower. This holds more for women than for men. If the wife is not working, there is a significantly higher chance of the husband entering self-employment. This pattern is not present for the opposite sex.

We now distinguish among three types of self-employment: professionals/managers, skilled, and unskilled workers, using the same predictor variables. Parameter estimates are presented in table 8.2, separately for men and women.

The effects for social origin reveal a pattern of strong intergenerational class inheritance for professionals/managers or skilled workers, where respondents tend to stay self-employed in the "same class" as that of their father. For men, a professional or managerial father makes one 1.8 times more likely to enter into professional or managerial self-employment, while a skilled worker father makes the individual 1.37 times more likely to enter into skilled self-employment, both relative to an unskilled father. The pattern is less pronounced for women. Interestingly, father's managerial or professional position has a significant positive impact on entry into unskilled self-employment as well. These results indicate that transition to self-employment is a mobility process combined, at least partly, with class reproduction, as we assumed.

A similar pattern emerges for the influence of education. High and low tertiary levels of education, as well as secondary level of education, increase the odds of entry into the group of self-employed managers and professionals. For the transition to skilled and unskilled self-employment, secondary level of education and vocational training (apprenticeship) are the strongest predictors. Skilled self-employment requires these levels of education to a greater extent. Education in general has a stronger effect for women than for men, except into unskilled self-employment.

As we have seen, prior employment position seems to have less of an influence on becoming self-employed in a multivariate perspective. The more detailed model in table 8.2 refines the previous picture so that male skilled workers have significantly less of a chance to move into professional self-employment, but they do move into skilled self-employment. Unskilled self-employed, however, is mainly composed of former unskilled employees, as one can indirectly read through the significant neg-

TABLE 8.2
Social Determinants of Entry into Different Categories of Self-Employment between 1980 and 1997 in Hungary[a]

	Men			Women		
Explanatory variables	Self-employed professional and manager	Skilled self-employed	Unskilled self-employed	Self-employed professional and manager	Skilled self-employed	Unskilled self-employed
Social origin						
Professional, manager	0.589*	0.194	0.708*	0.730$^+$	0.323	−0.331
	(0.284)	(0.202)	(0.288)	(0.417)	(0.207)	(0.603)
Skilled worker	0.017	0.314*	0.268	0.302	0.285$^+$	−0.567
	(0.296)	(0.145)	(0.230)	(0.413)	(0.163)	(0.477)
Farmer	−2.322$^+$	−0.303	−0.218	x	−0.226	x
	(1.237)	(0.270)	(0.353)	x	(0.332)	x
Agricultural worker	−0.681	−0.040	−0.110	−0.530	0.094	−0.685
	(0.482)	(0.185)	(0.273)	(0.680)	(0.201)	(0.572)
Unskilled worker	0	0	0	0	0	0
Father self-employed	−1.435$^+$	0.311	−0.235	−0.274	0.387$^+$	−0.983
	(0.759)	(0.209)	(0.393)	(0.663)	(0.224)	(1.270)
Education						
High tertiary	2.694**	0.902*	x	3.524**	1.470**	x
	(0.553)	(0.384)	x	(0.791)	(0.359)	x
Low tertiary	2.850**	0.879*	0.010	2.532**	1.042**	−0.582
	(0.549)	(0.392)	(0.603)	(0.807)	(0.333)	(1.048)
Secondary	2.098**	1.616**	0.890**	2.463**	1.242**	0.568
	(0.501)	(0.222)	(0.267)	(0.702)	(0.197)	(0.539)
Vocational	0.438	1.427**	1.003**	0.948	1.746**	0.488
	(0.587)	(0.211)	(0.233)	(0.927)	(0.191)	(0.599)
Primary	0	0	0	0	0	0

Origin (prior) position						
Professional, manager	−0.358	−0.236	−1.202**	0.178	−0.426+	0.241
	(0.347)	(0.245)	(0.380)	(0.502)	(0.233)	(0.627)
Skilled worker	−1.674**	0.439**	−1.442**	−0.346	0.013	−0.770
	(0.471)	(0.165)	(0.229)	(0.505)	(0.175)	(0.582)
Unemployed	2.567**	1.327**	0.988+	x	2.474**	1.928+
	(0.628)	(0.508)	(0.517)	x	(0.377)	(1.163)
Out of labor force	−0.269	−0.578*	−2.091**	−1.726*	−0.114	−0.880
	(0.434)	(0.230)	(0.328)	(0.745)	(0.225)	(0.698)
Unskilled worker	0	0	0	0	0	0
Sector of employment						
Mining, manufacturing (not in labor force)	0	0	0	0	0	0
Construction	1.478**	0.620**	−0.196	0.547	0.696+	1.201
	(0.415)	(0.184)	(0.380)	(0.606)	(0.359)	(0.737)
Traditional services	1.397**	1.256**	−0.452	0.060	0.869**	−0.365
	(0.416)	(0.189)	(0.412)	(0.453)	(0.187)	(0.681)
Transport, communication	0.408	0.307	0.797**	−0.220	−0.108	0.351
	(0.498)	(0.208)	(0.232)	(0.713)	(0.387)	(0.746)
Business, personal services	1.856**	1.231**	1.404**	0.043	1.252**	−1.194
	(0.419)	(0.219)	(0.307)	(0.563)	(0.220)	(1.467)
Health, education, public, administration	0.899*	0.204	−0.019	−0.276	−0.396	0.195
	(0.361)	(0.255)	(0.420)	(0.394)	(0.248)	(0.552)
Ever in Communist Party	−0.085	−0.912**	−0.575+	−2.097+	−0.208	−0.407
	(0.264)	(0.237)	(0.348)	(1.250)	(0.311)	(0.927)

TABLE 8.2 (continued)

Explanatory variables	Men			Women		
	Self-employed professional and manager	Skilled self-employed	Unskilled self-employed	Self-employed professional and manager	Skilled self-employed	Unskilled self-employed
Spouse's status						
Employee	−0.115	−0.295*	−0.287	−0.586*	−0.474**	−0.461
	(0.229)	(0.124)	(0.183)	(0.300)	(0.136)	(0.422)
Self-employed	1.226*	1.581**	−0.119	0.996*	1.019**	1.955**
	(0.500)	(0.269)	(0.837)	(0.492)	(0.222)	(0.544)
Out of labor force	0.828*	0.504*	0.019	−0.630	0.517⁺	x
	(0.381)	(0.216)	(0.375)	(1.258)	(0.289)	x
No partner/no information	0	0	0	0	0	0
Intercept	−8.576**	−7.153**	−6.246**	−9.102**	−7.178**	−7.668**
	(0.556)	(0.252)	(0.275)	(0.717)	(0.232)	(0.507)
−2 Log likelihood	6653.298			4489.022		
Degree of freedom	66			66		
Number of events	98	313	133	52	265	28
Number of spells	92,411	92,411	92,411	109,287	109,287	109,287

Source: Social Mobility and Life History Survey 1992 (Central Statistical Office) and Hungarian Household Panel Survey, 1992–97 (TÁRKI) pooled data-file

[a] Unstandardized estimates from discrete time multinomial logistic model, standard errors in parentheses.

** $p < 0.01$ * $p < 0.05$ ⁺ $p < 0.1$

ative estimates for the other origin states. For women, this pattern does not hold. But (as shown before) unemployed persons had significantly higher odds (as compared to unskilled workers) for entering into self-employment. In many respects, both male and female skilled and unskilled self-employed seem to "continue" in activities similar to their previous job. These results underline again that mobility into self-employment occurs "within the class" where people worked as employees, and where they accumulated the various forms of necessary capital.

The influence of the sector of prior employment is stronger for men than for women. As compared to mining and manufacturing (and being out of the labor force), construction, traditional services, business, and personal services all provide appropriate background for entering into professional/managerial or skilled self-employment. Self-employed unskilled workers come, however, from transportation and communication. Employee positions in health, education, or public administration were also backgrounds that facilitated entry into self-employed professional and managerial activity.

For party membership, the estimates confirm our previous findings. Although descriptive statistics (not presented here due to size constraints) indicate a high proportion of former members of the Hungarian Socialist Workers Party among male self-employed professionals and managers, the impact of former party membership is not significant for this entry. With regard to male transition to skilled self-employment, a significant negative effect was found for prior Communist Party membership.

Finally, for spousal influence, the odds of entry into professional/managerial or skilled self-employment are higher for men if their wife is also self-employed. The same pattern emerges for women, especially if they move into unskilled self-employment. For men, the probability of entry into private business is also higher if the wife does not work. We can assume that in such cases the wife helps her husband's business as an "unpaid family worker." One more important gender difference appears in the descriptive statistics: half of the self-employed professional and managerial women have no spouse, while the corresponding figure for men is only slightly higher than one-third.

Exit from Self-Employment between 1980 and 1997

In principle, this analysis refers to two groups of self-employed: those who started their business after 1980, and those who were already self-employed in 1980, the earliest year in our observation window. In Hungary, the second group is not much larger than the first one, and the exit process does not differ much for the two groups, with respect to the

TABLE 8.3
Social Determinants of Exit from Self-Employment between 1980 and 1997
in Hungary[a]

Explanatory variables	All self-employed	Self-employed men	Self-employed women
Gender (male = 1)	0.191		
	(0.200)		
Social origin			
Professional, manager	−0.167	−0.267	0.119
	(0.281)	(0.366)	(0.498)
Skilled worker	0.242	0.018	0.687+
	(0.224)	(0.286)	(0.400)
Farmer	−1.294*	−0.908	−8.276
	(0.595)	(0.619)	(26.811)
Agricultural worker	0.214	0.246	0.217
	(0.264)	(0.325)	(0.497)
Unskilled worker	0	0	0
Father self-employed	−0.775+	−0.334	−7.724
	(0.406)	(0.425)	(18.949)
Education			
High tertiary	0.019	0.073	−0.716
	(0.464)	(0.618)	(0.819)
Low tertiary	0.565	0.429	0.701
	(0.398)	(0.514)	(0.737)
Secondary	0.373	0.433	−0.331
	(0.271)	(0.367)	(0.452)
Vocational	0.081	−0.094	0.207
	(0.278)	(0.353)	(0.521)
Primary	0	0	0
Self-employment			
Professional, manager	−1.482**	−1.215**	−1.639**
	(0.302)	(0.422)	(0.483)
Skilled worker	−2.170**	−1.800**	−2.838**
	(0.219)	(0.296)	(0.412)
Unskilled worker	0	0	0
Sector of self-employment			
Mining, manufacturing	0	0	0
Construction	0.101	0.081	0.357
	(0.297)	(0.324)	(1.299)
Traditional services	−0.665**	−.884*	−0.065
	(0.256)	(0.358)	(0.414)

TABLE 8.3 (*continued*)

Explanatory variables	All self-employed	Self-employed men	Self-employed women
Transport, communication	− 1.942**	− 1.904**	− 0.128
	(0.320)	(0.393)	(0.654)
Business, personal services	− 0.845**	0.224	− 1.779*
	(0.297)	(0.368)	(0.692)
Health, education	0.983**	0.988*	1.296**
	(0.320)	(0.464)	(0.498)
Duration of self-employment	− 0.176**	− 0.146**	− 0.266**
	(0.046)	(0.054)	(0.095)
Spouse's status			
Employee	− 0.345⁺	− 0.398⁺	− 0.214
	(0.187)	(0.237)	(0.327)
Self-employed	− 0.214	0.503	− 1.536⁺
	(0.372)	(0.427)	(0.889)
Out of labor force	− 0.374	− 0.740⁺	0.481
	(0.345)	(0.419)	(0.677)
No partner/no informa-tion	0	0	0
Intercept	− 1.023**	− 1.048*	− 0.549
	(0.326)	(0.437)	(0.548)
− 2 Log likelihood	1153.360	757.423	356.276
Degree of freedom	21	20	20
Number of events	159	100	59
Number of spells	3,936	2,506	1,430

Source: Social Mobility and Life History Survey 1992 (Central Statistical Office) and Hungarian Household Panel Survey, 1992–97 (TÁRKI) pooled data-file.

[a] Unstandardized estimates from discrete time logistic model, standard errors in parentheses.

** $p < 0.01$ * $p < 0.05$ ⁺ $p < 0.1$

social determinants of the end. Consequently, we decided to focus only on the non-left-truncated cases, who entered into self-employment after 1980. An advantage of this choice is that we have a more accurate measure for the duration of the private business, which we intend to use as a predictor. Other independent variables in the statistical model are social origin, education, type, and sector of self-employment and spouse's occupational status. As we do not distinguish between different kinds of destinations after leaving self-employment, so the dependent variable is dichotomous. The estimates are presented in table 8.3, for both sexes (first column) and for men and women separately (second and third columns, respectively).

Despite the results displayed by the survival curves (fig. 8.4), the effect of gender in the first model does not reveal any significant difference between men's and women's chances of exiting self-employment. As further results indicate, the odds for exit from self-employment are not much dependent either on social origin or on level of education in Hungary. Self-employed offspring of farmer fathers have higher chances for survival. Father's self-employment also increases the probability of remaining self-employed. Although higher levels of education increased the odds of entry into self-employment, it does not decrease the odds of exit. In fact, the descriptive statistics show that those who exit from self-employment are somewhat better educated, but the difference does not turn out to be significant in a multivariate perspective.

Compared with self-employed unskilled workers, self-employed skilled workers have significantly lower probabilities of closing their businesses. The odds for leaving self-employment are also lower for professionals and managers. Consequently, the least stable group in the private sector is unskilled self-employment. But professionals/managers also move more easily into employee jobs than the skilled self-employed, who are probably less flexible and own businesses that are less transferable. The whole pattern is more pronounced for women.

Sector of self-employment is also a strong predictor for the survival of a private business. Compared with mining and manufacturing, self-employed people in traditional services, transportation, communication, business, and personal services have higher odds of staying in self-employment. A self-employed job in traditional services or transportation and communication decreases the odds of exit for men, while a self-employed job in personal services decreases the odds of exit for women. Self-employment in health or education increases the odds of exit for both sexes, but especially for women.

As expected, longer duration in a private business decreases the odds of exit from self-employment. One more year of experience in the private sector decreases the probability of exit by 1.8 times for men and by 1.3 times for women, keeping all other determinants constant. The degree of embeddedness in the market is probably higher for those private enterprises that existed longer and had more time for the accumulation of necessary social or financial capital.

The influence of spouse's employment status is smaller on exit from self-employment, compared with entry. Having a wife who is an employee decreases the probability of exit for a husband, probably because the employee position of the wife provides some stability and safety for the household. But the same effect is even greater if the wife is not working, because in this case the man is the only "official" breadwinner in the family (although it may be noted that the wife may contribute to the family income). This pattern is more marked for women: the odds of exit from self-employment are lower for women if their husband is also self-employed (i.e., the whole family is in the private business), as the "self-employment comes in couples" theory suggests.

Discussion

This chapter investigated transition to and from self-employment in Hungary between 1980 and 1997, in a period when the political and economic environment changed rapidly with respect to emerging pushing and pulling mechanisms that influence private business enterprises. In the 1980s, the second economy provided an important background and stepping stone for private initiatives under communism. This was, in fact, a situation where individuals had strong incentives to engage in part-time entrepreneurial activities in order to earn extra money to supplement their relatively low salaries in state firms. At the same time, firms had strong incentives to subcontract with new private cooperatives of individuals to improve the low effectiveness of their production in a state-controlled and planned economy. Thus, capitalism began to grow surreptitiously ("under the grass") in Hungary.

The rise of full-time self-employment was rather moderate in the 1980s, but it increased in the last two years of the decade. A higher rise of entrepreneurship was observable in the 1990s, although with certain variations for types of self-employment and gender. The pattern of change over time for leaving self-employment was relatively similar. Exit from the highly selected group of the self-employed was low in the 1980s, but increased in the 1990s when a large part of the growing self-employed population was, in fact, forced to engage in self-employment as a last resort.

We took into consideration the effect of life course as well, examining by age structure those who moved into self-employment. Our results confirm a well-known pattern: transition to self-employment does not occur immediately after entry into the labor force. Individuals need some time for accumulating the various types of capital required for private business. However, if someone spends an extended period in an employee position, the likelihood of entry into entrepreneurship begins to decrease. This pattern was more pronounced for men than for women. In addition, entry into professional self-employment also occurs at an older age in Hungary than entry into other forms of self-employment.

Various mechanisms were expected to influence these processes, including social inheritance and accumulation of human capital or other assets from a previous employee status. Social origin was reproduced in the process of transition into self-employment. Coming from a professional or managerial background increased the odds of entry into professional self-employment. Similarly, if one's father was a skilled worker, the individual had an increased probability of entering skilled self-employment. At the same time, intergenerational transmission of self-employment did not turn out to be a strong variable in Hungary. This may be a consequence of the fact that self-employment in the parental generation was low due to the communist nationalization program and the dominance of state ownership. Thus, we still think that it is a valid assumption that socialization with respect to individualistic habitus, ambition, achievement orientation, and so forth has considerable effects on entry into self-employment. We suppose that this type of socialization was characteristic of, and became an effective pull, when the historical, political, and economic changes in Hungary allowed them to operate. In fact, in this respect, our analysis provided some confirmation for the affinity hypothesis of class inheritance proposed by Erikson and Goldthorpe (1992). At the same time, social origin did not influence exit from self-employment.

Previous accumulation of capital as well as conversion of accumulated capital are two crucial mechanisms for recruitment into self-employment. Since accumulation of financial assets was scarce in Hungary under communist rule, human capital investments and social capital played strong roles in determining transition to self-employment. The importance of human capital investment is clearly demonstrated by the estimates for education in the statistical models. The pattern is obvious in this respect: the higher the educational level, the higher the likelihood for entry into the group of self-employed professionals and managers. The vocational track was especially useful for moving into skilled self-employment. On the other hand, higher education does not prevent anybody from leaving self-employment. Odds for exit from self-employment were not affected by human capital investments in Hungary.

Turning to further determinants of transition to self-employment, the previous position in employment was considered as a proxy for accumulated work experience and social capital that are required for success in private business. In this respect, our results provided further evidence for the existence of marked continuities within the process of transition to self-employment. We expected that managerial or professional employee positions would increase the likelihood of a move into the group of self-employed professionals and managers. Significant estimates did not appear in the models, due to the strong effect of education and the multicollinearity between these two sets of predictors. However, our competing risks model revealed that the previous skilled worker position is a strong and significant predictor of entry into skilled self-employment, at least for men.

The rising unemployment level in the 1990s was also an expected push factor into self-employment, especially considering the financial measures that were introduced by the state to help establish private businesses. The analysis supported this assumption as well; unemployment as a prior position turned out to increase the odds of transition into self-employment. Another pushing effect was expected for employment in manufacturing and construction, on the grounds that the decline of communism in the 1980s and the collapse of communism after 1990 affected these branches most. Traditional services, transportation, communication, business, and personal services, on the other hand, were expected to be pulling forces because these spheres offered better opportunities for private businesses. Our models revealed a stronger impact of economic branches on transition to self-employment for men than for women. Prior employment in construction and services turned out to increase the odds of entry into self-employment as compared to manufacturing. At the same time, having a business in the service sector decreased the chances for exit from self-employment.

Former Communist Party membership is another example of the use or conversion of accumulated capital. According to our analyses, it did not increase the chances of self-employment. Thus, the results for Hungary did not support Staniszkis's (1991) hypothesis of "political capitalism." To understand the contradiction between our present and previous findings in this respect, we have to emphasize that the dichotomous measure of whether an individual was ever a Communist Party member is less specific than the length of time spent in the party, which was the measure used in our previous analysis (Róbert and Bukodi 2000). Furthermore, Communist Party membership in this model controlled for prior employment in managerial or professional position as well, but these positions and party membership were strongly correlated.

In this analysis, we did not look at the transition into self-employment as a fully individual event, but rather we assumed that it occurred in a family context, where the employment status of the spouse also mattered. Indeed, we found evidence that self-employment does tend to "come in couples." A self-employed spouse increased the odds of starting a private business for both sexes and decreased the odds of exit from self-employment, at least for women.

We conclude that the features of transition into self-employment in Hungary can be at times unique, but is in other respects quite common to those in other advanced societies. To some extent, the accelerated speed of the transitions in the last decade is an outcome of the general political and economic transformation and, consequently, a historical push-and-pull effect is present. However, the general push-and-pull effects, like the shift from an industrial economy to a postindustrial service economy, or the role of unemployment, are also present and effective in Hungary. Yet, we can isolate two special features of Hungarian self-employment: the self-employed group is heterogeneous, perhaps more mixed than in the developed marked economies, and part of the self-employed population definitely belongs to the "winners" (i.e., those who most benefited economically and socially from the postcommunist transformation). The political collapse of communism created a historical opportunity for transition for people who possessed the necessary capital, either inherited or achieved. The other half of the self-employed population, however, consists of the less fortunate players in the country's transformation, those who have lost the safety of life-long state employment. These people neither inherited nor accumulated assets to draw upon, and the changing economic conditions forced them into self-employment. It is not a surprise that many of them exited self-employment quickly.

This dual character of self-employment is emphasized by the odds of exit from self-employment. Compared with the most recently established private enterprises, business activities with a longer duration have a higher chance of survival. This is especially true for the skilled self-employed, who are able to keep their business viable longer than the unskilled self-employed. Additionally, the likelihood of exit is smaller for the professional and managerial self-employed. However, this group is quite heterogeneous, including a wide range of activities. Certain professional occupations, such as artist, translator, or engineer, do not require much financial capital, and these jobholders can easily move between employed and self-employed positions, following their labor market interests.

All in all, significant changes with respect to self-employment are combined with a high level of continuity and reproduction of inequalities. Successful entrepreneurs are offspring of self-employed or service-class families. They have high levels of competitive educational credentials and accumulated a large stock of social capital in managerial and professional positions before the collapse of communism. The other fraction of self-employed may also come from self-employed families but are usually less educated, or with a less marketable education, and they have less accumulated resources and capital. For those in forced self-employed positions, which occur as a result of displacement from unemployment, not much of a positive change in status was found for this group. The present inner stratification of the petty bourgeoisie in Hungary mirrors the previous social standing of individuals prior to their involvement in this activity.

TABLE 8.A1
Aspects of Social Standing of Self-Employed and Other Occupational Groups in Hungary

	Head of household				
	Skilled self-employed	*Skilled worker*	*Professional*	*Unskilled worker*	*Total*
Percent having household items					
Automatic washing machine					
1986	56.0	28.7	70.4	7.3	26.8
1993	71.4	52.9	78.7	24.9	38.6
1999	86.7	69.8	92.4	39.4	54.4
Freezer					
1986	30.2	13.6	31.3	6.8	13.7
1993	75.3	68.1	64.7	40.0	56.2
1999	77.2	71.7	66.8	52.7	63.5
Microwave					
1993	29.4	16.1	29.5	6.2	12.4
1999	72.5	52.0	67.2	25.4	38.6
Color television					
1986	52.3	24.8	54.5	8.3	24.6
1993	93.0	87.0	93.9	56.1	69.7
1999	98.1	96.2	95.6	85.6	89.3
Video player					
1986	6.7	1.5	3.2	—	1.2
1993	57.1	45.9	54.5	25.3	27.1
1999	78.4	63.6	70.3	37.3	42.7
Personal Computer					
1986	1.5	0.8	6.2	0.5	1.1
1993	16.2	8.7	22.5	2.1	6.4
1999	32.0	19.9	55.3	7.4	16.5
Cultural participation, 1982 and 2000					
Average number of books					
1982	133	148	419	88	164
2000	427	244	1,017	118	315
Average number of CDs, 2000	25	11	31	2	12

Table 8.A1 (*continued*)

	Head of household				
	Skilled self-employed	Skilled worker	Professional	Unskilled worker	Total
Cultural participation in the last 12 months					
Percent of theatre visits					
1982	13	22	55	10	23
2000	38	14	53	6	22
Percent of museum visits					
1982	14	21	56	9	21
2000	38	23	69	8	28
Percent of concert visits					
1982	4	9	27	4	10
2000	15	5	30	1	9
Percent of cinema visits, 2000	38	23	46	10	27
Leisure and holiday, 2000					
Percent not on holiday in last 5 years	46	60	20	83	60
Percent having holiday abroad in last 5 years	30	14	48	4	18

Sources: A háztartások tartós javai (Durable goods in the households), Central Statistical Office, Budapest, 2000; Stratification Model Survey, 1982; TÁRKI Monitor Survey, 2000

Notes

During the preparation of the final version of this chapter, the first author was holding a fellowship at the Hanse-Wissenschaftskolleg, Delmenhorst, Germany.

1. We used the same data for a previous analysis on the same topic (Róbert and Bukodi 2000), but some differences should be underlined for the present study: (1) the observation window is narrower—we go back only to 1980, so a left-censoring is applied; (2) self-employment is defined in a more refined manner, making distinction between self-employed professionals and managers, skilled self-employed, and unskilled self-employed in contrast to employees and individuals

being not in labor force; (3) the set of explanatory variables is also wider, predicting entry into self-employment by origin state (previous class prior to self-employment) as well as economic branch, and spouse's employment status in addition to social origin, father's self-employment, education, and party membership.

2. Due to lack of space, this model is not presented. It is available from the authors upon request.

3. Despite the significant coefficients in the model, estimates are based on a relatively small number of cases.

REFERENCES

Arum, R. 1997. Trends in male and female self-employment: Growth in a new middle class or increasing marginalization of the labor force? *Research in Social Stratification and Mobility* 15:209–38.

Bauer, T. 1978. Investment cycles in planned economies. *Acta Oeconomica* 21:243–60.

Blossfeld, H., A. Hamerle, and K. U. Mayer. 1989. *Event history analysis*. Hilsdale: Erlbaum.

Burawoy, M. and J. Lukács. 1986. Mythologies of work: A comparison of firms in state socialism and advanced capitalism. *American Sociological Review* 50:723–37.

Economic survey of Europe in 1993–1994. New York: United Nations Economic Commission for Europe.

Erikson, R. and J. Goldthorpe. 1992. *The constant flux*. Oxford: Clarendon Press.

Estrin, S., ed. 1994. *Privatization in Central and Eastern Europe*. London: Longman.

Gábor, R. I. 1989. Second economy and socialism: The Hungarian experience. In *The underground economies*, ed. E. L. Feige, 339–60. Cambridge: Cambridge University Press.

Gerber, T. P. 2001. Paths to success: Individual and regional determinants of self-employment entry in post-communist Russia. *International Journal of Sociology* 31:3–37.

Hankiss, E. 1990. *East European alternatives*. Oxford: Oxford University Press.

Kolosi, T. 1988. Stratification and social structure in Hungary. In *Annual Review of Sociology*, ed. W. R. Scott and J. Blake. Palo Alto: Annual Review, Inc.

Kolosi T., and M. Sági. 1998. Top entrepreneurs and their social environment. *Acta Oeconomica* 49:335–64.

Kornai, J. 1980. *Economics of shortage*. Amsterdam: North-Holland.

Laki, M. 1993. Chances for the acceleration of transition: The case of Hungarian privatization. *East European Politics and Societies* 7:440–51.

Laky, T., and L. Neumann. 1992. Small entrepreneurs of the 1980s. In *Social Report 1990*, ed. R. Andorka, T. Kolosi, and Gy. Vukovich. Budapest: TÁRKI.

McClelland, D. C. 1987. Characteristics of successful entrepreneurs. *Journal of Creative Behaviour* 3:219–33.

Müller, W., H. Lohmann, and S. Luber, eds. 2000–2001. Self-employment in advanced economies I–III. *International Journal of Sociology* 30–31.

Pfeiffer, F., and F. Reize. 2000. From unemployment to self-employment—public promotion and selectivity. *International Journal of Sociology* 30:71–99.

Róbert, P., and E. Bukodi. 2000. Who are the entrepreneurs and where do they come from? Transition to self-employment before, under and after communism in Hungary. *International Review of Sociology* 10: 147–71.

Róna-Tas, Á. 1994. The first shall be last? Entrepreneurship and communist cadres in the transition from socialism. *American Journal of Sociology* 100:40–69.

Sik, E. 1988. Reciprocal exchange of labour in Hungary. In *On work*, ed. R. E. Pahl. Oxford: Basil Blackwell.

Staniszkis, J. 1991. "Political capitalism" in Poland. *East European Politics and Societies* 5:127–41.

Stark, D. 1992. Path dependence and privatization strategies in East Central Europe. *East European Politics and Societies* 6:17–54.

Szelényi, I. 1988. *Socialist entrepreneurs: Embourgeoisement in rural Hungary.* Madison: University of Wisconsin Press.

Szelényi, Sz. 1987. Social inequality and party membership: Patterns of recruitment into the Hungarian Socialist Workers' Party. *American Sociological Review* 52:559–73.

Vukovich, Gy., and I. Harcsa. 1999. The Hungarian society reflected by facts. In *Social Report 1998*, ed. T. Kolosi, I. Gy. Tóth, and Gy Vukovich. Budapest: TÁRKI.

Yamaguchi, K. 1991. *Event history analysis.* Newbury Park: Sage Publications.

CHAPTER NINE

Three Forms of Emergent Self-Employment in Post-Soviet Russia: Entry and Exit Patterns by Gender

Theodore P. Gerber

SELF-EMPLOYMENT IS a new phenomenon in Russia. Other former Soviet-bloc countries such as Poland and Hungary permitted some limited forms of small or individual enterprise during the 1970s and 1980s (Szelényi 1988; Róbert and Bukodi 2000; Kolodko 2000). But in the Soviet Union official proscriptions relegated self-employment to the realm of the underground economy. Only when the Gorbachev regime implemented the "Law on Cooperatives" in the middle of 1988 could Russians openly take up self-employment. Even then, cooperatives faced tight official constraints on their size, property form, activities, and capacity to hire employees (Jones and Moskoff 1991). Not until the Soviet regime collapsed at the end of 1991 and Russian President Boris Yeltsin adopted sweeping market reforms in January 1992 did the doors open for unrestricted self-employment.

The very novelty of self-employment there makes post-Soviet Russia an especially interesting case for comparative analysis of the social determinants of who becomes and remains self-employed in advanced economies. A strong argument can be made for the universality of processes shaping access to and success in self-employment if they operate in Russia as they do in developed capitalist societies, despite the long legacy of Soviet-style socialism and the rampant uncertainties of the post-Soviet transition. Moreover, the self-employed represent, as we shall see, a rare group of "winners" in the market transition process. They clearly owe their victory, such as it is, to the process of market transition: without market transition, they would not have had access to this particular path of success. By determining how variables such as gender, age, education, employment status, occupation, industry, and regional characteristics influence entry to and exit from self-employment, we thus gain insight into how market transition affects stratification processes.

Controversy has surrounded several theories proposing general accounts of the impact of market transition on stratification in former state socialist countries like Russia. According to *market transition theory*, the spread of market institutions increases returns to human capital and entrepreneurial skill, while decreasing returns to political position, because markets reward productivity while state socialist institutions reward redistributive power (Nee 1996; Cao and Nee 2000). This theory, originally developed in reference to China, has been challenged on empirical and theoretical grounds (Xie and Hannum 1996; Walder 1996; Gerber and Hout 1998; Gerber 2002b). *Power conversion theory* claims that Communist Party cadres use their superior positions within powerful networks to preserve, even enhance, their material advantages after market transition (Róna-Tas 1994). While former Communist Party members enjoy higher earnings, net of other variables, this may reflect unobserved human capital rather than social capital (Gerber 2000a, 2001c). The present study of self-employment addresses these debates by examining whether the self-employed enjoy higher earnings in contemporary Russia (as predicted by market transition theory) and assessing the effects of education and Communist Party membership on entry to and survival in self-employment.

PREVIOUS FINDINGS AND NEW QUESTIONS

In an earlier study (Gerber 2001b), I found that the self-employed—both with and without employees—earn more, have higher subjective material satisfaction, and support market reforms to a greater extent than all classes of dependent employees. These distinctive characteristics obtain even when other determinants of earnings, subjective material well-being, and views on market reforms are statistically controlled (Gerber 2002a). Many of the factors shaping entry to self-employment in advanced capitalist societies exert similar effects in post-Soviet Russia. However, education, age, gender, and family background operate somewhat differently in the Russian context. Other effects on entry to self-employment, such as membership in the Communist Party of Soviet Union (CPSU), distinguish Russia from capitalist countries, though they may operate similarly in other former state-socialist societies.

This chapter expands the earlier analyses in three ways, each pursued in accordance with the common approach applied in this volume. First, I adopt the distinction among professional, qualified, and unqualified forms of self-employment and examine differences in these forms, both in the levels of socioeconomic standing they imply and in the factors that shape entry to them. Second, I estimate separate models of entry to self-employment for women and men. The findings show evidence of gender differences in the mechanisms shaping access to self-employment. Finally, I consider the factors shaping exit from self-employment, a topic the earlier study did not take up.

Fewer but Better Off? Obstacles to Self-Employment in Russia

One might have expected self-employment to take off rapidly in Russia in the wake of the January 1992 market reforms, which effectively removed legal barriers. But several factors have retarded the growth of individual enterprise (Barkhatova 2000; Gerber 2001a; Radaev 2002). Lack of capital poses one major barrier to entry: the commercial banking sector has not developed adequately and has been especially deficient in providing financing to indigenous small enterprises.

Although reformers declared that private property would revitalize the Russian economy (Boycko, Shleifer, and Vishny 1995) and officials have often announced plans to help small businesses (Barkhatova 2000), actual reform policies have emphasized macroeconomic stabilization and privatization of the state sector rather than the growth of a new private sector (Blasi, Kroumova, and Kruse 1997; Kolodko 2000). High taxes that come in a bewildering variety, changing tax rates, and inconsistent applications of tax law have placed undue burdens on small firms. Excessive and changing regulatory regimes and licensing requirements have also discouraged potential entrepreneurs and expanded the opportunities for corrupt officials to demand bribes. Weak legal institutions increase transaction costs, jeopardize property rights, and permit organized criminal groups to demand protection payoffs from new firms and self-employed individuals. Altogether, the Russian legal and regulatory context has been extremely unfavorable toward small businesses.

The Russian Labor Code—at least prior to its substantial reform in 2001—placed heavy restrictions on the use of fixed-term contract workers by both state and private enterprises, effectively discouraging the practice of requiring employees to become self-employed contractors. Given the general weakness of enforcement mechanisms, these restrictions may not have prevented the practice from spreading, as enterprise managers sought greater flexibility and lower labor costs (in the form of mandatory social security payments and severance pay for open-term employees) in the recessionary context of transition-era Russia (Gimpelson and Lippoldt 2001). The evidence is sketchy, however, on exactly how widespread the "informal" use of fixed-term contracts became during the 1990s. In small firms, which accounted for 13 percent of overall employment, ratio of fixed-term to open-term employees was 0.46 in mid-1995, implying that 31.5 percent of employees were contractors (Russell and Hanneman 2000). But the numbers were surely smaller in medium-size and larger firms: a survey of managers of forty large firms

(Shelomentsev 2001) indicates that almost none used contractors until after the August 1998 financial crisis, which is subsequent to the period covered by the survey data analyzed herein, January 1991 to March 1998). In fact, 16 percent of individual self-employment spells in the survey data are characterized by contract work for a firm—only 2 percent for firms with more than fifty employees.[1] This suggests that contract work for large employers does not represent a driving force behind individual self-employment in Russia. Finally, it is possible—though difficult to establish empirically—that there are greater cultural barriers to self-employment in Russia than in other developed countries, including the former communist countries of Eastern Europe. The communist system was in place for nearly seventy-five years in Russia, long enough that few living Russians ever experienced life in a capitalist system, where self-employment is lauded rather than condemned.

These factors help explain why self-employment has grown more slowly in Russia during the 1990s than in Hungary, Poland, and the Czech Republic, and why the self-employment rate remains much lower than in most Western capitalist societies (Aslund 1995; Kolodko 2000). Nonetheless, by January 1, 2000, there were 890,600 privately owned small businesses operating in Russia, according to official figures (Goskomstat Rossii 2000:158).[2] At the start of 1998, the end-point for the period covered by the survey data analyzed herein, there were 861,100 such enterprises employing roughly 6.5 million workers in the Russian Federation (Goskomstat Rossii 1998:326), implying a rather modest net gain of approximately 29,500 small businesses during 1998 and 1999. These figures nonetheless indicate that the self-employed have established a firm toehold in the new social structure that has emerged in transition-era Russia.

According to official documents, the individually self-employed are legally considered to be small business owners, whether or not they register as a "legal subject" (Goskomstat Rossii 1999). Therefore, the various tax, registration, licensing, and regulatory burdens apply in theory to the individually self-employed as well. As a result of these onerous burdens, a great deal of self-employment takes place informally—that is, many individually self-employed and small business owners do not register as such. However, because we identify spells of self-employment among our survey respondents based on their self-identification as self-employed (with or without employees), we have a more accurate view than can be gleaned from official data. We cannot, on the other hand, distinguish between those self-employed who register their businesses and those who do not.

But the question naturally arises: do the individually self-employed have much in common with small proprietors, or are they more accurately viewed as desperate workers, displaced by structural changes in the economy, who take up individual work activity as a survival strategy of last resort? Hanley (2000) found that in Poland, Hungary, and the Czech Republic, the individually self-employed are equivalent to marginalized, informal workers in former state-socialist societies, while small proprietors represent an entrepreneurial elite. My earlier work (Gerber 2001b) suggests that in Russia the situation is different: employers rank substantially higher than the individually self-employed on earnings and subjective material satisfaction, but the individually self-employed are still better off than all classes of dependent employees (with the partial exception of managers).

One possible reason why the individually self-employed fare better in Russia than in Eastern European countries is selection: the barriers to self-employment appear to be higher in Russia, as evinced by the fact that fewer enter self-employment there. Thus, the relatively small number who are able to surmount the barriers—even to become individually self-employed—have qualities that make them especially successful at self-employment. This explanation is plausible, but there is another explanation that can be tested empirically with the data at hand: it may be that the key distinction in Russia is not between employers and the individually self-employed, but between unqualified and professional self-employment, with qualified self-employment representing an intermediate category. Arum's work (1997; this volume; Arum, Budig, and Grant 2001) suggests that the difference between professional and unqualified forms of self-employment carries greater weight, with the latter group representing a marginalized portion of the labor force in the United States. Before we can conclude that self-employment as such represents a path to success in Russia, we must determine whether the distinction among professional, qualified, and unqualified self-employment has the same significance there.

The Gender Gap in Russian Self-Employment

In contrast to the situation in many advanced capitalist countries, where women have gained on men with respect to access to self-employment, women's disadvantages appear to have remained stable in Russia (Gerber 2001b). This has serious consequences for gender inequality in contemporary Russia, because self-employment provides relatively rare opportunities for material success. Perhaps women's access to self-employment depends on a different set of factors than men's access, and these differences may account for some of the gender gap in self-employment.

Russia's gender gap in self-employment may be reinforced by gender differences in the rate of survival in self-employment. Some research on the United States indicates that women exit self-employment at higher rates than men (Wharton 1989; Loscocco and Robinson 1991). But the evidence on this point is mixed (see, e.g., Kalleberg and Leicht 1991; Loscocco and Leicht 1993). More generally, it is of interest whether survival in self-employment is affected by the same variables in Russia as in other countries: age, duration in self-employment, human capital, and industry (a proxy for product market conditions). Communist Party cadres appear to be more successful entrepreneurs than nonparty members in Hungary (Róna-Tas 1994). The same may hold for Russia, but no empirical work has examined the variables affecting exit from self-employment there.

In sum, this chapter addresses three important questions left unanswered in my previous analyses of self-employment in Russia: (1) How similar are the three forms of self-employment, in terms of their living standards, composition, and paths of entry? (2) Are there gender differences in the effects of the key variables of interest—age, education, employment status, occupation, industry, and regional characteristics—on access to self-employment? (3) What variables influence exit from self-employment?

DATA

The data are from the Survey of Employment, Income, and Attitudes in Russia (SEIAR), given to a nationally representative sample of 4,818 in January and March 1998.[3] A battery of questions traced respondents' labor market activities, including entry to and exit from self-employment *as their main activity*, since December 1990. I prepared employment/activity histories spanning January 1991 to January/March 1998 based on these questions. To perform the discrete-time analysis called for in the protocol for this volume, I then transformed the continuous spell file into a person-year file, using the employment status and occupation of the respondent at the outset of the year to define their origin state for the remainder of the year.

Aggregating the continuous histories into person-year units entails some loss of information and introduces some measurement error. Changes in employment status or occupation during a year are not reflected until the following year. Thus, a respondent who begins the year as a professional employee, then becomes unemployed, then takes up self-employment before the start of the following year is treated as moving from the origin state of professional employment to self-employment. However, this problem is not so serious, so long as the dependent variable is understood as the probability of entering a particular form of self-employment during a particular year, conditional on employment status and occupation at the outset of that year. There were no cases of multiple transitions to self-employment in one year. The use of retrospective data also introduces recall errors. But there are no panel data sets from Russia covering the period in question with measures that would permit the analyses presented herein.

I was able to code the vast majority of self-employment spells into one of the three categories using accompanying occupation information. However, the occupation variable was missing for 34 of the self-employment spells (out of a total of 201). For these spells I imputed the form of self-employment from current income and preceding occupation.

The risk set for entry to self-employment consists of person-years formed from respondents aged 18–60 in a given year who (at the start of the year) are working as dependent employees in the nonfarm sector, unemployed, or not in the labor force (NLF). The NLF category includes students in their final year of schooling, those in compulsory military service, and voluntary nonparticipants (e.g., housewives). Person-years corresponding to respondents who (at the start of the year) are already self-employed or retired are excluded from the risk set for entry to self-employment, as are agricultural employees, students not in their final year of schooling, and women on maternity leave.[4] These risk-set restrictions yield a weighted sample of 8,753 male person-years and 9,877 female person-years.[5] In all models, robust standard errors are obtained, with correction for the clustering of person-years within respondents.

The risk set for exit from self-employment consists of person-years formed from respondents in the eligible age window who either began the year in nonagricultural self-employment or entered self-employment during the year.[6] I do not divide the risk set by gender or by form of self-employment because the sample is too small. Although there are 534 weighted person-years, these represent only 185 respondents, and the standard errors are corrected for the clustering of observations within respondents. I re-estimated the preferred model after excluding observations from left-truncated self-employment spells—that is, those that began before the outset of the observation window. This did not change the pattern of effects at all but did increase the standard errors and pushed some t-statistics below the critical value. The increase in standard errors reflects the drop in sample size. Thus, I report only the models estimated on the full sample.

Variables

Baseline models for entry to self-employment include the variables specified by the project guidelines: age, age-squared, education, current occupation type and employment, father's occupation, and industry of dependent employment.[7] Although the data support classification of education by the full set of CASMIN categories, I aggregate 1ab, 1c, 2a, and 2b into the omitted category in the entry models. Preliminary analyses showed no significant differences among these four categories in any entry rate.[8] Furthermore, zero cells require special efforts to estimate the education and occupation effects in the competing risk models for women.[9] Father's occupation does not include a dummy variable for self-employment because the data have information only on father's occupation, not on father's employment status. In any case, only the very youngest respondents could have had a self-employed father at the age of 14, the age at which father's occupation was ascertained. Industry effects are specified using dummy variables for employment in trade/catering/personal services and in construction.[10]

I expand the baseline model with measures for other effects found to influence self-employment entry in Russia (Gerber 2001b)—time, membership in the CPSU, and place of residence—to see whether they vary by gender and form of self-employment. CPSU membership initially had a positive net effect on the hazard of entry to self-employment, but the effect diminished monotonically in magnitude and reversed sign in 1993. In the interest of parsimony, I include a one-degree-of-freedom measure of this time-varying CPSU effect in the models for entry to self-employment, which is the product of a dummy variable for CPSU membership and a *reversal* variable, which is monotonic rescaling of year corresponding to the partial effect of CPSU membership on the logged hazard of self-employment entry estimated in Gerber (2001b).[11]

I test three measures of location effects: the annual rate of unemployment in the respondent's *oblast* of residence, the annual logged value (adjusted for inflation using regionally specific deflators) of services sold in the respondent's *oblast*, and the logged size of the respondent's city of residence.[12] Some error is built into the regional measures, since the survey did not determine whether and when respondents changed their region (or locality) of residence during the period under study, as some respondents undoubtedly did. They are nonetheless preferable to nationwide measures of macrolevel effects because of the great regional variation in economic conditions and policies in transition-era Russia (Van Selm 1998; Gerber 2000b). Despite the poor quality of the measures, my earlier studies found several contextual effects consistent with theory: higher rates of entry to self-employment prevail in tighter regional labor markets, where dependent employment is a less viable alternative, and in areas with more rapid service-sector growth, because self-employment is heavily concentrated in the services.

Finally, change in the baseline hazard over the course of 1991–98 is operationalized for men as a log-quadratic function of integer years elapsed since December 1990 (denoted y): $\log(y + 1) + y^2$. This specification, identified as the best-fitting in the earlier studies, captures the curvilinear trend evident in the annual male entry rates (see fig. 9.2 below). Women's entry rates followed a different temporal pattern, jumping (aside from entry to professional self-employment) in 1993, then exhibiting no discernible trend. A simple dummy for the first two years of the observation period (1991–92) fit better than the log-quadratic specification for women.

I estimate three models for exit from self-employment. The baseline model includes a linear age term, a dummy variable for women, a restricted set of education dummies (1c/2a, 3a, and 3b, which contrast different levels of specialized education to general secondary or less), dummies for trade/catering/services and construction, and dummies for form of self-employment. I then expand the model by incorporating dummy variables for professional father, employer (vs. individual self-employed), and CPSU membership, as well as the three locality measures, a trend variable (y^2 provided the best fit), duration of the current self-employment spell (in years), and a dummy variable identifying left-censored spells (which began prior to December 1990, the outset of the observation window).

CHARACTERISTICS OF THE SELF-EMPLOYED

The education, earnings, and employer status of each category of self-employed and the equivalent categories of dependent employees at the time the data were collected shed some initial light on distinctions among the categories (table 9.1). Self-employed professionals of both genders have somewhat lower educational attainment than hired professionals, but they are still more than twice as likely than average to have a college education. The situation is the reverse for the other categories of self-employment. If anything, the qualified (among women) and unqualified self-employed have lower than average educational attainment. However, their educational attainments generally exceed those of the equivalent dependent employees. These descriptive statistics suggest that the relationship between self-employment and education is not straightforward.

The relationship between self-employment and earnings is quite clear: mean earnings of each category of the self-employed are higher than the overall average, and substantially higher than the earnings of the equivalent category of dependent employees. For both sexes, the professionally self-employed enjoy the highest average earnings of all, followed by the qualified self-employed. Among men, even the unqualified self-employed

TABLE 9.1
Characteristics of Self-Employed and Dependent Employees in Russia, January–March 1998

	Professional		Qualified		Unqualified		
	Self	Dependent	Self	Dependent	Self	Dependent	Overall
Self-employment and de-pendent employment							
All							
N	21	614	65	794	33	950	2,477
Percent	0.8	24.8	2.6	32.1	1.3	38.4	
Men							
N	15	194	46	398	13	396	1,062
Percent	1.4	18.3	4.3	37.5	1.2	37.3	
Women							
N	6	420	19	396	20	554	1,415
Percent	0.4	29.7	1.3	28.0	1.4	39.2	
Education (column %)							
All							
Ed1a–2b	4.4	2.0	33.5	32.6	30.3	34.3	25.6
Ed2c	23.4	9.9	21.0	22.7	22.1	32.1	23.1
Ed3a	26.1	31.6	22.8	35.8	34.7	27.6	31.2
Ed3b	46.1	56.5	22.8	8.9	12.9	6.0	20.1
Men							
Ed1a–2b	5.8	0.0	37.7	37.8	40.8	37.8	31.6
Ed2c	19.4	12.1	16.4	24.7	16.7	24.7	23.7
Ed3a	29.7	23.0	18.3	28.7	26.6	28.7	25.6
Ed3b	45.1	64.9	27.7	8.8	15.9	8.8	19.1
Women							
Ed1a–2b	0.0	3.2	20.6	26.0	21.3	28.4	19.9
Ed2c	35.8	8.6	35.1	20.2	26.7	34.1	22.6
Ed3a	15.0	36.7	36.5	44.9	41.7	30.7	36.6
Ed3b	49.2	51.6	7.8	9.0	10.3	6.8	20.9
Mean earnings (rubles, pre-vious month)							
All	5,336	812	2,168	668	918	632	775
Men	6,481	1,046	2,662	786	1,259	771	989
Women	996	669	820	512	642	498	561
Hired employees (%, self-employed only)							
All		44.4		25.4		11.1	24.5
Men		47.6		27.1		6.3	25.3
Women		33.3		21.1		15.0	23.0

TABLE 9.1 (*continued*)

	Professional		Qualified		Unqualified		
	Self	Dependent	Self	Dependent	Self	Dependent	Overall
Most common occupations (self-employed only)							
Men	Mgr., business svcs.		Buyer			Shop/stall salesperson	
			Mgr., whl/ret				
	Mgr., manufacturing		Trade			Taxi driver	
	Mgr., operations		Sales, tech. and commercial			Building caretaker	
Women	Accountant		Buyer			Stall salespersons	
			Mgr., whl/ret				
	Teacher		Trade			Office clerk	
	Mgr., construction		Nurse			Street vendor	

earn more than professional employees, while unqualified self-employed females earn slightly less than hired female professionals. The "returns" to self-employment within each occupational category are lower for women.[13] This might help explain why women are less likely to enter self-employment than men.

In any case, the descriptive statistics confirm that self-employment—even unqualified self-employment—is a path to relative material success in Russia. Unlike in other countries, where they represent a marginalized faction of the labor force, even the unqualified self-employed enjoy average earnings that approach or exceed those of professional/managerial employees. This may reflect the precipitous decline in real earnings that Russian employees experienced throughout the 1990s, as well as the prevalence of wage arrears at the time of the survey. Also, many dependent employees in Russia continued to receive substantial benefits through their employers, such as housing, childcare, subsidized meals, insurance, and even vacation facilities. These benefits may well offset, to some degree, the earnings advantages of the self-employed—particularly for those categories of self-employed with the lowest earnings advantage. Despite these qualifications, the data clearly indicate that in early 1998 self-employment—even unqualified self-employment—represented a relative path to material success in Russia. Whether it remains so now that the Russian economy has grown for three consecutive years (beginning in 1999) can be determined only with future research.

Not surprisingly, self-employed professionals are the most likely to hire employees, and individual self-employment is by far the norm among the qualified and nonqualified self-employed. Gender differences among the self-employed in the hiring of employees are most pro-nounced among professionals and the unqualified, but women have the advantage in the latter category. The most common occupations within each form of self-employment suggest some notable gender differences: managerial occupations in business and manufacturing predominate among professional males, while professional women are most likely to be accountants or educators. Commercial activities predominate among the qualified for both genders, but women also provide medical assis-tance, and some skilled trades are also among the qualified (bricklayers/stonemasons among men, seamstresses among women). The male un-qualified are more likely to drive taxis or take care of buildings, while women do routine office work or sell items as street vendors.

Self-Employment and the Life Cycle

The life cycle graph (fig. 9.1) demonstrates that self-employment is most concentrated among males in their mid-twenties to late-thirties. For Russian men the effect of age would appear to be curvilinear, as is often observed in advanced economies. But the peak comes at a relatively early age in Russia, so the effect is, in essence, negative for more than half of the working life cycle.[14] This may partly reflect a cohort effect: younger generations of Russians were not exposed to Soviet-era socialization and thus be may more inclined to take up self-employment. Also, they face greater obstacles on the labor market (Gerber 2002b).

Among women, the age effect on the overall probability of being self-employed is nearly linear and negative, starting at age 25. This conceals interesting variations by form of self-employment. Analysis of the equiv-alent life-cycle figures, broken down by types of self-employment (not shown), reveals that there is no professional self-employment whatsoever within the SEIAR sample among women under 29. Thus, the gender gap in rates of the most lucrative form of self-employment is greatest early in the life cycle. On the other hand, within the 18–28 age range women's probabilities of qualified and unqualified self-employment approach or exceed men's, only to fall behind thereafter. Among those in their thirties and forties, the gender gap is greatest for qualified self-employment, the most common form. Overall, the gender gap is lowest for the least re-warding form, unqualified. Russian women's disadvantages regarding self-employment appear even starker when we examine the different forms of self-employment separately.

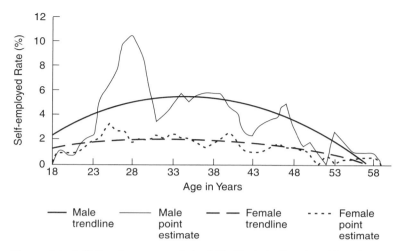

Figure 9.1: Self-Employment and the Life Cycle in Russia, 1991–97

ENTRY TRENDS

Among men, transition rates to self-employment overall (fig. 9.2) and to each form of self-employment (not shown) increased during the first years following the demise of the Soviet system, then declined after 1995 or 1996.[15] The patterns are succinctly represented by second-order polynomial trend lines fit to the observed yearly data points. This curvilinear trend most likely reflects a secular increase in self-employment due to an initial expansion of opportunities to become self-employed and spiraling macroeconomic push factors, which are eventually offset by dynamic selection on unobserved variables (Gerber 2001b). As those who are especially prone to become self-employed do so and thereby leave the risk set, the unobserved propensity in the still-eligible population declines.

Trends in women's rates of entry are less clear. There is some indication that entry to unqualified and, perhaps, qualified self-employment increased after 1992. Consistent with the life-cycle patterns, gender differences in entry rates are generally greater for entry to professional and qualified self-employment, and they are minimal where unqualified self-employment is concerned.

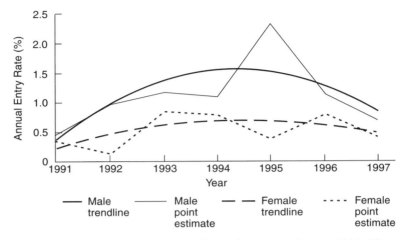

Figure 9.2: Annual Shift Rates to Self-Employment in Russia, 1991–97

Multivariate Results

Binary Entry Models

Age, employment status, and industry of employment all have significant effects on the log-odds of entering some form of self-employment for both men and women (table 9.2). More so in Russia than elsewhere, self-employment is the province of the young. The positive age effect turns negative at the relatively young age of 33 for men, and for women the effect is monotonic and negative. Russians of both sexes who (at the start of a year) are unemployed or out of the labor force are more likely to enter self-employment (during the course of the year) than those who are employed. These effects are stronger for women, suggesting that the labor market offers them fewer opportunities. Dependent employment in trade, catering, and personal services and (for men) in construction increases the probability of entering self-employment. This is typical: self-employment in these industries is fairly common in Western societies, and we can infer that employees gain skills and contacts that facilitate their becoming self-employed. The development of the service sector is a hallmark of Russian capitalism, aptly characterized by Burawoy (1997) as *merchant capitalism*.

For men, education appears not to have any significant effect, net of these variables and the additional variables incorporated in both the baseline and expanded model.[16] The absence of significant education effects is surprising, because earlier analyses of the same data found that college and specialized secondary education (3b and 3a) both significantly

TABLE 9.2
Discrete-Time Hazard Models of Entry to Any Form of Self-Employment[a] in Russia

| | MEN | | | | WOMEN | | | |
| | Baseline | | Expanded | | Baseline | | Expanded | |
	B	SE	B	SE	B	SE	B	SE
Age (−18)	0.086	0.04	0.083*	0.04	0.048	0.05	0.044	0.05
Age (−18)^2/100	−0.290*	0.12	−0.274*	0.12	−0.223	0.14	−0.210	0.14
Education (Ed1a–2b)								
Ed2c	0.024	0.38	0.011	0.38	0.635	0.51	0.656	0.51
Ed3a	0.370	0.36	0.301	0.36	0.924#	0.48	0.939*	0.48
Ed3b	0.392	0.47	0.334	0.46	1.002*	0.50	1.103*	0.50
Current employment (dependent un-qualified worker or missing occupa-tion)								
Dep. professional	−0.070	0.44	0.021	0.43	0.365	0.53	0.353	0.54
Dep. qualified	−0.466	0.36	−0.481	0.36	1.176*	0.50	1.214*	0.50
Unemployed	2.083**	0.44	2.037**	0.46	3.247**	0.60	3.148**	0.60
NLF	1.638**	0.40	1.696**	0.40	2.765**	0.51	2.675**	0.51
Father's occupation (unqualified worker)								
Professional	1.046**	0.37	1.048**	0.41	−0.379	0.37	−0.390	0.36
Qualified	0.056	0.32	0.057	0.32	−0.488	0.35	−0.485	0.35
Farmer	0.055	0.49	0.013	0.50	−2.017#	1.07	−2.089#	1.08
Trade/catering/ services	1.647**	0.42	1.669**	0.42	1.471**	0.41	1.444**	0.41
Construction industry	1.096**	0.34	1.089**	0.35	0.974	0.78	1.014	0.78
Log(year + 1)			1.697**	0.52				
Year^2			−.063**	0.02				
Post-1992							1.019*	0.42
CPSU*reversal			1.137*	0.46			1.014#	0.60
Oblast unemploy-ment[b]			0.144**	0.05			0.084*	0.04
Oblast service index[b]			0.643*	0.28				
Log(citysize), mean-centered			−0.028	0.07				
Constant	−5.941**	9.51	−7.237**	0.75	−7.318**	0.77	−8.089**	0.80

TABLE 9.2 (*continued*)

	MEN				WOMEN			
	Baseline		Expanded		Baseline		Expanded	
	B	SE	B	SE	B	SE	B	SE
Number of events	88		88		62		62	
Weighted person-years at risk	8,753		8,753		9,877		9,877	
Log-likelihood	−464.95		−448.88		−356.57		−350.73	
Pseudo R^2	.098		.130		.115		.130	

[a] Dummy variables for missing respondent occupation, respondent activity, industry of employment, and father's occupation are included in all models, but not shown.
[b] Variable centered at the annual mean for all oblasts.
# $p < .10$; * $p < 0.05$; ** $p < .01$

raised the hazard rate of entry to self-employment (Gerber 2001b). The discrepancy in findings probably results from several differences in the model specifications and samples analyzed, and from the loss in statistical power resulting from the separate analyses of men and women.[17] Another possibility is that the earlier results reflect the effect of education among women, for whom education has the anticipated positive effect.

Among women, qualified workers have higher odds of entering self-employment than unqualified workers and professionals, net of the other variables. There is no significant effect of occupational category for men. However, men whose father was a professional are nearly three times ($e^{1.05} = 2.85$) more likely to enter self-employment than otherwise similar men whose father was an unqualified worker. Daughters of farmers have substantially lower odds of becoming self-employed, but for women having a professional father has no effect.[18]

If education, occupation, and (to a certain extent) employment status affect self-employment entry more strongly among women than among men in Russia, contextual variables have stronger effects on men: male self-employment entry is more common in regions where the labor market offers fewer opportunities and the service sector is larger. Only the former contextual effect applies to women, and it is lower in magnitude. The baseline hazard varies curvilinearly over time for men, while it increases in 1993 for women.

Communist Party membership had the expected time-varying effects for both men and women in roughly the same magnitude. In the year preceding and following the introduction of market reforms, CPSU members were more likely to enter self-employment, but the effect quickly reversed and grew more negative through 1997 (see note 10). CPSU members who failed to enter self-employment early in the market transition have thereafter been increasingly less likely to do so than non-members with the same traits. This implies that *power conversion* (Róna-Tas 1994) played only a limited and brief role in shaping the new entre-preneurial class in post-Soviet Russia.[19] In sum, although there are some similar effects—age, industry, employment status (to some degree)—there are a number of noteworthy differences in the determinants of self-employment entry among men and women.

Competing Risk Models of Entry

The baseline competing risk models (table 9.3) yield additional insights into the different mechanisms shaping the self-employment opportuni-ties of Russian men and women.[20] Among men, the age effect peaks sub-stantially later—at approximately 41 years—for entry to professional self-employment than for entry to the other forms. Also, male entry to professional self-employment is affected by education in the expected manner. Even obtaining a general secondary degree raises the probability of becoming professionally self-employed (in comparison with lower levels of educational attainment), though specialized secondary (3a) and tertiary (3b) degree have stronger effects.

Male dependent qualified workers are not more likely to enter quali-fied self-employment, but they are significantly *less* likely to enter un-qualified self-employment. Unemployed males are more likely to enter professional or qualified self-employment than those in unqualified de-pendent employment, but the effect of unemployment on entry to un-qualified self-employment is much weaker and nonsignificant. The posi-tive effect of dependent work in construction is limited to entry to qualified and unqualified self-employment, while the positive effect of work in trade, catering, and personal services is limited to the latter.

The competing risk models for women also reveal some varying effects across contrasts. The multinomial model indicates that only college edu-cation significantly increases the odds of entering professional self-employment, which is generally quite rare among women.[21] Specialized secondary and tertiary education both significantly increase women's odds of entering unqualified self-employment. In contrast to the situation for men, qualified dependent employment raises the odds that a women will enter qualified self-employment. For women, dependent work in trade/catering/personal services *hinders* entry to professional self-employment but facilitates entry to qualified and unqualified self-employment. Sim-ilarly, dependent work in construction facilitates entry only to unqualified self-employment, hindering entry to the other two forms.

TABLE 9.3
Baseline Discrete-Time Competing Hazard Model of Entry to Three Forms of Self-Employment in Russia

| | MEN | | | | | | WOMEN | | | | | |
| | Professional | | Qualified | | Unqualified | | Professional | | Qualified | | Unqualified | |
	B	SE	B	SE	B	SE	B	SE	B	SE	B	SE
Age (−18)	0.068	0.07	0.066	0.07	0.208*	0.09	0.246	0.16	0.047	0.08	0.022	0.08
Age (−18)²/100	−0.147	0.17	−0.297	0.23	−0.592*	0.23	−0.561	0.42	−0.244	0.25	−0.181	0.21
Education (Ed1a–2b)												
Ed2c	2.119#	1.15	−0.257	0.54	−0.161	0.61	0	f	0.383	0.65	1.046	0.83
Ed3a	2.659*	1.10	−0.175	0.50	0.525	0.62	0	f	0.329	0.62	1.376#	0.80
Ed3b	2.806*	1.17	−0.245	0.69	0.274	0.75	1.247#	0.74	0.247	0.91	1.258	0.78
Current employment (dependent unqualified worker or missing occupation)												
Dep. Professional	0.182	0.75	0.249	0.69	−0.913	0.79	1.309	0.91	0.641	1.36	0.023	0.46

	Model 1		Model 2		Model 3		Model 4		Model 5		Model 6	
Dep. Qualified	−1.479	1.08	0.121	0.49	−1.307#	0.78	0	f	2.453**	0.78	0.547	0.53
Unemployed	2.443**	0.74	2.244**	0.66	1.582#	0.86	3.588**	1.25	4.357**	1.04	2.626**	0.72
NLF	2.355**	0.72	1.360*	0.60	1.645*	0.75	4.362**	0.96	3.883**	0.88	1.828**	0.57
Father's occupation (unqualified worker)												
Professional	1.059*	0.49	0.969#	0.53	1.081*	0.54	1.717	1.12	−1.856#	1.09	−0.102	0.48
Qualified	0	f	0	f	0	f	−0.102	1.42	−0.733	0.52	−0.230	0.49
Farmer	−0.408	1.09	−1.093	1.05	1.207#	0.67	−32.676**	1.21	−1.327	1.15	−35.132**	0.48
Trade/catering/ services	0.827	0.77	2.049**	0.53	1.284	0.88	−32.150**	0.65	1.431#	0.80	1.529**	0.47
Construction	0.627	0.76	1.090*	0.49	1.464*	0.70	−33.146**	0.90	−34.371**	0.56	1.756*	0.82
Constant	−9.570**	1.52	−6.088**	0.63	−8.138**	1.08	−13.181**	1.90	−8.498**	0.93	−7.692**	1.15
Number of events	17		49		22		5		25		32	
Weighted person-years			8753				9877					
Log-likelihood			−536.92				−400.28					
Pseudo R^2			0.122				0.139					

Notes: F = Coefficient fixed at zero.

[a] Dummy variables for missing respondent occupation, respondent activity, industry of employment, and father's occupation are included in all models, but not shown.

# $p < 0.10$; * $p < 0.05$; ** $p < 0.01$

TABLE 9.4

Expansions of Discrete-Time Competing Hazard Models of Entry to Three
Forms of Self-Employment[a] in Russia

	Professional		Qualified		Unqualified	
	B	SE	B	SE	B	SE
Men						
Log(year + 1)	2.568*	1.10	1.407#	0.78	2.187*	1.07
Year^2	−0.102**	0.04	−0.035	0.03	−0.130**	0.04
CPSU*reversal	0.618	0.76	1.313*	0.64	1.746#	0.91
Oblast unem- ployment[b]	0.061	0.05	0.198**	0.07	0.110	0.10
Oblast service index[b]	0.917#	0.48	0.869*	0.41	−0.036	0.48
Log(citysize), mean- centered	−0.188	0.12	−0.101	0.10	0.328#	0.18
Constant	−11.865**	1.90	−7.601**	0.88	−9.548**	1.39
Log-likelihood	−508.704					
Pseudo R^2	0.169					
Women						
Post-1992	0.795	1.37	0.650#	0.38	1.130**	0.40
CPSU*reversal	−0.937	0.75	1.139	0.79	1.815*	0.81
Oblast unem- ployment[b]	0.134	0.08	0.043	0.04	0.105#	0.06
Constant	−12.825**	2.05	−9.443**	1.28	−9.143**	1.29
Log-likelihood	−390.642					
Pseudo R^2	0.160					

[a] All variables from the corresponding baseline models in table 9.3 are also included, but not shown. Their magnitudes change only to a trivial extent after adding the additional covariates, and in no case are inferences affected.

[b] Variable centered at the annual mean for all oblasts.

# $p < 0.10$; * $p < 0.05$; ** $p < 0.01$

There are some similar patterns across genders and across contrasts within genders. Most strikingly, both unemployment and nonparticipation increase the odds of entry to *all* forms of self-employment for both sexes, though the effects tend to be stronger among women. Among men, the effect of a professional father is significant for each contrast.

The expanded competing risk models reveal that the gender-specific patterns of temporal change in the baseline hazard are fairly uniform across forms of self-employment within each sex (table 9.4). Also, the time-varying effect of CPSU membership pertains only to qualified and unqualified forms of self-employment. This is further evidence against the view that party members parlayed network connections into entrepreneurial opportunities in Russia: at the outset of the transition period, they were more likely than otherwise similar nonmembers to enter the less remunerative forms of self-employment, but no more likely to enter the most. Moreover, even their advantaged access to qualified and unqualified self-employment quickly reversed. It is also noteworthy that the essentially the same CPSU effect obtained for both men and women. In contrast, contextual variables once again appear to exert stronger effects among men. Perhaps surprisingly, regional unemployment most strongly affects entry to qualified self-employment among men, and the size of the regional service sector only increases the odds of men entering professional or qualified forms.

Earlier research (Gerber 2001b) and the descriptive statistics discussed above showed that Russian women enter self-employment much more rarely than men. The separate competing risk models for entry to the different forms of self-employment suggest that the "entry gap" varies depending on the characteristics of the men and women being compared, the form of self-employment, and the point in time. The constants pertaining to each form of self-employment in the male and female competing risk models correspond to the baseline category in each preferred model: 18-year-old non–party members whose fathers were not professionals who have, say, vocational education, work as dependent employees in manufacturing, and live in an *oblast* with an unemployment rate equal to the average for all *oblasts*, assessed in 1991. The differences in constants imply that men with such characteristics were more than four times more likely (in terms of odds) to enter qualified self-employment than women in 1991, but only about half as likely to enter professional or unqualified self-employment. But women's advantage in entry to the latter forms was short-lived: by 1992 the male/female odds ratios were 2.6, 10.9, and 14.3 for the baseline hazard. Thereafter, the male advantages fluctuated in magnitude but remained substantial in all years and for each form of self-employment, with one exception: women gained ground on men in entry to unqualified self-employment and actually had a higher baseline hazard in 1997.

Altogether, based on the baseline hazards the gender gap has clearly been greatest for entry to qualified self-employment, high for entry to professional self-employment, and lowest—even disappearing—for entry to unqualified. This is not surprising if we recall that qualified self-employment offers the lowest earnings returns for women, while unqualified self-employment offers the lowest returns for men (see table 9.1). Thus, women have relatively less incentive to enter qualified self-employment and men have relatively less incentive to enter unqualified self-employment.

Gender differences in the effects of education, prior dependent occupation, and nonemployment also lend insight into the overall gender gap in entry to self-employment. A university degree increases men's odds of entering professional self-employment by a factor of 16.5, while it increases the same odds for women by a factor of only 4.4. On the other hand, the effect among women of qualified employment, which increases their odds of entering qualified self-employment by a factor of 11.7, might mitigate the entry gap. But women are substantially less likely to be in qualified employment than men (19.9% vs. 28.5% in January 1998).

This difference in the effects of qualified employment could reflect the different skill mix of male and female qualified employees. The vast majority (82.5%) of men in *qualified* occupations are in class VI, which traditionally has enjoyed relatively favorable wages in Russia. This helps explain why male qualified dependent workers are especially unlikely to enter unqualified self-employment. In contrast, female qualified employees are far more likely to be technicians or auxiliary professionals (combined, 63.8%), who are traditionally poorly paid and also possess the types of skills that can serve as the basis for professional or qualified self-employment. Thus, poor wages and working conditions "push" female qualified employees into self-employment more strongly than male qualified employees, and female qualified employees typically have skills that are better suited to professional self-employment than the typical skills of male qualified workers. Finally, the effects of unemployment and nonparticipation are considerably stronger for women than for men, which, as noted above, probably reflects the less favorable labor market opportunities faced by women in post-Soviet Russia (Gerber 2002b). These differences in effect magnitudes tend to ameliorate the entry gaps, as women are more likely to be nonparticipants (19.3% vs. 13.2% in early 1998), though they are slightly less likely to be unemployed (5.4% vs. 7.6%).

EXIT FROM SELF-EMPLOYMENT

Analysis of exit from self-employment provides additional evidence of women's disadvantage: for self-employment overall (fig. 9.3) and within each form of self-employment (not shown), women's cumulative survival rates quickly fall behind men's. Women's lower rates of entry to self-employment are compounded by their higher rates of exit. Perhaps, however, their more frequent failure at self-employment stems from gender

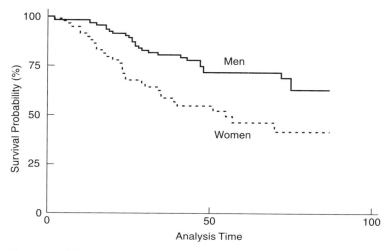

Figure 9.3: Kaplan-Meier Survival Functions by Sex, Self-Employment Spells, Beginning January or Earlier in Russia

differences within the self-employed on other variables that influence exit from self-employment.

In fact, multivariate analysis of the factors influencing exit confirms that women have higher exit rates than men, even controlling for the other variables in the baseline and preferred models (table 9.5). According to the preferred model, at any point in time the odds that a self-employed women will exit are 2.5 times higher than the odds that a self-employed man with identical values on the other variables will.

Education, age, industry, city size, period, and duration in state also significantly affect survival in self-employment. Preliminary analysis revealed the optimal specification of education: Russians with vocational training (1c and 2a), specialized secondary, and college education are less likely to leave self-employment than otherwise similar Russians with 1ab, 2b, or 2c. This pattern implies that specialized skill, rather than the quantity of education, is what matters most for survival in self-employment. Age has a negative and linear effect on survival, further evidence that in Russia self-employment is mainly the province of the young. This is not a function of retirement, as spells ending in retirement are omitted from the exit analysis. Those whose ventures are in the typically volatile trade/catering/services have higher exit rates, as do residents of larger cities (perhaps because there are more opportunities for dependent employment in larger cities).

The baseline exit rate increased sharply during the period in question,

TABLE 9.5
Discrete-Time Hazard Models of Exit from Self-Employment in Russia

	Baseline Model		Expanded Model		Preferred Model	
	B	SE	B	SE	B	SE
Age (-18)	0.028*	0.01	0.032*	0.02	0.037*	0.02
Woman	0.615*	0.30	0.760*	0.36	0.885*	0.35
Education (Ed1ab/2bc)						
Ed1c/2a	-0.821	0.55	-1.283*	0.57	-0.949#	0.54
Ed3a	-0.479	0.36	-0.801#	0.47	-0.711	0.44
Ed3b	-0.468	0.35	-0.779*	0.40	-0.825*	0.40
Current industry (manufacturing/ extraction or not employed)						
Trade/Catering/ Pers.Svc.	0.523	0.34	0.572	0.36	0.593#	0.32
Construction	0.475	0.51	0.150	0.50		
Form of self-employment (unqualified)						
Professional	-0.276	0.42	-0.237	0.51		
Qualified	-0.617#	0.34	-0.595	0.41		
Father professional			-0.525	0.35		
Has employees			0.056	0.40		
CPSU member			-0.273	0.55		
Oblast unemployment[a]			0.030	0.05		
Oblast Service Index[a]			0.250	0.43		
Log(citysize), mean-centered			0.220#	0.10	0.237**	0.08
Year^2			0.078**	0.02	0.077**	0.02
Years in self-employment			0.246#	0.14	0.217#	0.12
Pre-1991 Spell			-1.350*	0.62	-1.254*	0.57
Constant	-2.699**	0.56	-5.012**	0.97	-5.780**	0.81
Log-likelihood	-179.813		-149.961		-154.742	
Weighted person-years	534		534		534	
Pseudo R^2	0.061		0.213		0.192	

[a] Dummy variables for industry of employment and father's occupation are included in the appropriate models, but not shown.
# $p < 0.10$ * $p < 0.05$ ** $p < 0.01$

which helps explain why cross-sectionally observed self-employment rates have increased slowly in Russia. The probability of exit increases the longer one has been self-employed, but net of the negative duration dependence there is a strong and significant pre-1991 effect: Russians who were self-employed at the outset of the observation window have 29.2 percent the odds of exiting of otherwise similar Russians who entered self-employment after 1990. This most likely reflects unobserved heterogeneity: those who survived in self-employment until the observation window presumably score higher on some unobserved attributes that favor survival in self-employment than a randomly selected sample of self-employed would.[22]

CPSU membership does not affect survival in self-employment: the *power conversion* process that shaped entrepreneurial success in postsocialist Hungary according to Róna-Tas (1994) does not operate in Russia. Nor do form of self-employment (net of the expanded model variables), regional economic conditions, or having hired employees (vs. being individually self-employed) influence exit rates in Russia. Of course, it is possible that the effects on exit of gender, education, age, and industry vary by origin state and that the effects of other covariates vary by gender, but there are too few cases to provide robust tests, and it is hard to develop strong a priori hypotheses about the nature of such differences.

Conclusions

The detailed analyses reported add several nuances to the main findings reported in Gerber (2001b). First, by disaggregating the self-employed by gender and by form of self-employment, we can claim more confidently that each form of self-employment represents a path to relative material success for both genders. Although professional self-employment clearly yields the highest returns for both men and women, qualified and unqualified self-employment also bring average earnings greater than or equal to the earnings of dependent professionals and managers. The unqualified self-employed, male or female, do not represent a marginalized faction of the labor force in Russia. In some sense, almost the entire labor force could be viewed as "marginalized" in 1998, but in relative terms the self-employed earn more than all groups of dependent employees.

Russia's exceptionally strong barriers to entering self-employment—including lack of access to capital, weak laws and legal infrastructure to protect property rights and enforce contracts, burdensome and unstable tax and regulatory regime, rampant official corruption, and organized crime (Gerber 2001a)—may indirectly account for the relatively high earnings of the unqualified self-employed in Russia. Such barriers could deter all but those who stand to gain the most from self-employment from entering in the first place and make it especially difficult for all but the most adept to survive.

Education plays an important role in the path to *professional* self-employment for both sexes. For men, academic secondary, specialized secondary, and tertiary schooling all increase the odds of entering professional self-employment. For women, only tertiary education has a significant effect, and its magnitude is weaker. However, specialized secondary and tertiary education also positively influence Russian women's entry to unqualified self-employment, while education does not shape men's entry to either qualified or unqualified forms. Earlier findings (Gerber 2001b) of positive, relatively linear effects of education on entry to self-employment in general could pertain only to women.

Net of the other variables analyzed, prior dependent occupation has only minimal effects on entry to self-employment in Russia. Women employed in qualified occupations have higher odds of entering qualified self-employment. Men thus employed have lower odds of entering unqualified self-employment. In contrast, workforce status has strong effects for both sexes: the unemployed and those out of the labor force are substantially more likely to enter all three forms of self-employment. "Push" factors evidently play a more important role in the paths to self-employment in Russia than do enabling factors associated with occupation-specific skills and resources. While we might expect such push factors to operate on the odds of entering qualified and unqualified self-employment, it is surprising to observe such effects pertaining to entry to professional self-employment as well. Women's labor market disadvantages might explain the greater magnitude of the workforce status effects for them.

Gerber (2001b) found that in Russia the offspring of professionals are more likely to enter self-employment, suggesting that Soviet-era professionals and managers passed on motivations, social connections, and skills associated with their future self-employment. According to the current analysis, which uses only father's occupation to measure the effect of family background, this holds for all three forms of self-employment, but only for men. Perhaps the cross-gender influences of parental occupation are weaker than the within-gender influence. In any case, the alternative specification does provide some evidence that where entry to self-employment is concerned, parental professional/managerial status could substitute for parental proprietor status in countries where the latter does not exist. The current analyses also generally supported earlier findings regarding the effects of age, industry of current employment, regional labor market conditions and service-sector size, Communist Party membership, and trends in entry over the course of the 1990s.

The separate analyses by gender of entry to self-employment in Russia both confirmed the sizable gender gap and showed that the magnitude of the gap varies by form of self-employment, time, and other characteristics that affect self-employment. In brief, the gender gap grew dramatically in the early years of the transition, then receded somewhat, even reversing by 1997 for unqualified self-employment. The magnitudes of coefficients suggest that the gap in overall entry to self-employment is greater among the offspring of professionals and lower among the unemployed and nonparticipants in the labor force. The gap in entry to professional self-employment is greater among those with secondary education or higher, while the gap in entry to unqualified self-employment is lower among those with specialized secondary or tertiary degrees. The gap in entry to qualified self-employment is nonexistent or reversed among those employed as qualified dependent employees. Thus, in the context of broad female disadvantages in access to self-employment—a path to material success in post-Soviet Russia—we find a complex pattern of variation in the magnitudes of gender gaps in entry rates. More detailed analysis and explanation of the specific patterns should await their replication with additional data.

The analyses of self-employment exit demonstrate that in Russia women are less successful at self-employment than otherwise similar men, insofar as survival in self-employment adequately measures "success." The gender difference in survival rates could account for some of the gender gap in self-employment entry. If women discount their expected earnings in self-employment by the probability of failure, their higher failure rates would dampen their incentives for becoming self-employed, relative to those of men, just as their lower expected returns (relative to men's) do. In particular, women who are employed may prefer the security associated with their current jobs over the risks and uncertain returns of a venture into self-employment.

Apart from gender, the effects of education and the noneffect of CPSU membership on survival in self-employment merit attention. The specialized skills acquired through lower vocational education, specialized secondary, and tertiary schooling appear to be resources that facilitate success at self-employment. Human capital is an important ingredient in the recipe for survival at self-employment. In contrast, CPSU membership has no effect on survival in self-employment, and its effect on entry is initially positive, then turns negative (in 1993). These findings suggest that where self-employment is concerned, *market transition theory* (Nee 1996; Cao and Nee 2000) has more relevance for Russia than *power con-*

version theory: human capital, not political connections or network ties, enhances both access to and survival in self-employment.

We began with the observation that self-employment is a newer and less widespread phenomenon in Russia than in any of the other countries analyzed in this volume. Both factors—its novelty and its rarity—might explain why entry to the various forms of self-employment appears to be rather weakly structured by the variables whose effects we have examined. Nonetheless, many of these variables did exert effects that are broadly similar to those found in other countries. Research on self-employment in Russia is also, perforce, new and relatively rare. As Russia's transition proceeds and more data sources become available, it will be especially important to re-examine how age, gender, education, current activity, industry of employment, family background, time, and contextual variables affect access to self-employment opportunities and survival in self-employment. Future studies will do well to distinguish the three forms of self-employment and test for gender differences in the effects of other variables.

NOTES

The author acknowledges financial support for data collection from the (United States) National Science Foundation (SBR-9729225), a Short-Term Travel Grant from IREX, and support for writing in the form of a National Academy of Education/Spencer Foundation Post-Doctoral Fellowship. Address correspondence to Prof. Theodore P. Gerber, Department of Sociology, University of Wisconsin, Madison, WI 53705. E-mail: tgerber@ssc.wisc.edu.

1. I am able to deduce "contract work for a firm" from a question, addressed to all respondents for each spell of (self- or hired) employment regarding the size of their current employer. In the vast majority of cases (84%), individually self-employed respondents indicated that they were the sole employees. A contract worker for a firm would logically indicate one of the other response categories (2 to 20, 21 to 50, etc.).

2. The figures are for *small enterprises*, which are defined as commercial organizations in which government bodies and nongovernment institutions each hold less than a 25 percent ownership stake and the number of employees does not exceed specific limits: 100 for industrial firms, 60 for scientific concerns, 50 for wholesale trading concerns, 30 for retail trade, and 50 for other types of firms (Goskomstat Rossii 1998:326).

3. Annual "snapshots" of the retrospective SEIAR data capture well-known developments in Russia during the 1990s, such as the growth of private-sector employment and the redistribution of the work force from manufacturing to services. These snapshots, which I omit here to save space but can be found in Gerber (2001b), therefore suggest the data are reliable. For details on sampling

procedures, refusal rates, quality control, and the exact questions used to construct the employment histories, see Gerber (1999).

4. Students who are not in their final year of schooling are excluded on the grounds that they are not really at risk for entering self-employment, and their highest level of education attained may mismeasure the level attained in a year when they were in school but did not finish. The risk set includes respondents who reported being engaged in an "other" activity at the start of a given year and those who were employed but in a *missing* occupation. These origin states are represented by separate dummy variables, in order to preserve the integrity of the baseline origin state. Because no substantive interpretation can be attached to these effects, I do not present the relevant coefficients. I use the same approach for missing data on father's occupation and respondent's industry.

5. I calculated postsampling weights to reproduce within the sample the gender*age*urban residence*education distribution in the population. I dropped 32 respondents whose histories could not be reliably prepared due to incongruities or missing data.

6. The extension of the risk set to include those who entered self-employment during the course of a particular year is necessary not only to increase the statistical power of the analyses, but also because there are six cases where respondents both entered and exited self-employment within one calendar year. Limiting analysis of self-employment exit to respondents who are self-employed at the start of a year would discard important information and bias estimates of the effect of duration on exit.

7. I omit marital status and spousal variables because the information is available only for the time of data collection. The quadratic term for the age effect did not improve model fit for women (based on the likelihood-ratio test), so I omit it.

8. This is not surprising, because in the Russian context lower vocational education has long been considered an undesirable outcome reserved for future manual workers, and there is little to differentiate lower vocational programs that include a general secondary education from those that do not.

9. All the education categories except 3b and the *qualified employee* category had to be fixed at zero for the entry to professional self-employment vs. nonentry contrast. However, some of these categories have significant effects on other contrasts, so fixing them at zero for all contrasts would sacrifice substantive information. The solution was to estimate the professional vs. nonentry contrast separately from the other two contrasts, using different specifications for the two sets of estimates, then adding the log-likelihood statistics.

10. Preliminary analyses revealed no significant effects in the binary models and many sampling zeros in the multinomial models associated with other industry categories.

11. Specifically, the *reversal* variable is coded as follows for 1991–97: $+1.3$, $+0.3$, -0.2, -0.7, -0.9, -1.2, -1.2. A positive, statistically significant coefficient—say $_{CPX}$—on the product of this variable and a dummy for CPSU membership implies positive effects of CPSU membership equal to $1.3*_{CPX}$ in 1991, $.3*_{CPX}$ in 1992, and negative effects equal to $-.2*_{CPX}$ in 1993, $-.7*_{CPX}$ in 1994, etc.

12. *Oblasts* (regions) are the largest territorial subunits of the Russian Federa-

tion, roughly equivalent in scale and, at least formally, political autonomy to American states. Of the eighty-nine *oblasts* that constitute the federation, forty-one are represented in the data. *Oblast*-level data are obtained from Goskomstat (1998). See Gerber (2001b) for descriptive data on the *oblasts*. Unemployment figures for 1991 had to be extrapolated, since they are not available. The *oblast* measures are centered at their annual means, and the logged city size is centered at the overall sample mean.

13. Using the observed earnings of the self-employed as a measure of the returns to self-employment probably overstates those returns due to the partial endogeneity of self-employment with respect to earnings. More sophisticated procedures to take account of the selection effect on the earnings of the self-employed would take us well beyond the focus of this paper.

14. It should be kept in mind that these figures reflect the combined effects of age on both entry to and exit from self-employment.

15. The recency of self-employment as a phenomenon in Russia justifies using calendar time as the main metric for assessing temporal patterns in rates of entry to self-employment rather than individual exposure durations. Because nobody was effectively exposed to the risk of self-employment until about 1988 at the earliest, it makes little sense to view the risk as a function of duration in current (non-self-employment) state.

16. For both binary and multinomial analyses, I report trimmed versions of the expanded models, where the nonsignificant additional variables are removed.

17. The earlier study included additional control variables (in particular, a control for parental CPSU cadre status and more extensive contextual measures), disaggregated the NLF and CPSU categories, constrained all effects to be the same for men and women, and excluded from the risk set those in the military and those in school who did not leave school during the current year. Lastly, Gerber (2001b) employed continuous-time rather than discrete-time analysis, which probably reduced measurement errors and thus increased the precision of parameter estimates.

18. Gerber's (2001b) measure of family background incorporated information from both parents. Thus, a pattern of weaker cross-gender effects of parental occupation may obtain. This hypothesis should be examined in future studies of the determinants of self-employment entry using different data, as the present data set is fairly heavily burdened by the analyses I have already undertaken.

19. For further discussion of how CPSU members fare in Russia's market transition, see Gerber (2000a, 2001c); Róna-Tas and Guseva (2001).

20. I undertook minor trimming of the baseline and expanded competing hazard models—fixing some effects at zero based on preliminary results or estimation considerations—to make the pattern of effects easier to interpret.

21. Only one woman with a specialized secondary degree (3a) entered self-employment during the observation window, and none with less. This required the effects for CASMIN categories 2c and 3a to be fixed at zero in order to obtain reasonable estimates of the education effect for professional self-employment.

22. However, excluding the pre-1991 entrants in the models does not significantly alter parameter estimates (results not shown). The dummy variable denot-

ing left-truncated observations adequately appears to capture the unobserved heterogeneity, which does not appear to be correlated with the observed measures in the model.

REFERENCES

Arum, R. 1997. Trends in male and female self-employment: Growth in a new middle class or increasing marginalization of the labor force? *Research in Stratification and Mobility* 15:209–38.

Arum, R., M. Budig, and D. S. Grant II. 2001. Labor market regulation and the growth of self-employment. *International Journal of Sociology* 30:3–27.

Aslund, A. 1995. *How Russia became a market economy*. Washington, DC: Brookings.

Barkhatova, N. 2000. Russian small business, authorities, and the state. *Europe-Asia Studies* 52:657–76.

Blasi, J. R., M. Kroumova, and D. Kruse. 1997. *Kremlin capitalism: Privatizing the Russian economy*. Ithaca: Cornell University Press.

Boyco, M., A. Shleifer and R. Vishny. 1995. *Privatizing Russia*. Cambridge: MIT Press.

Burawoy, M. 1997. The Soviet descent into capitalism. *American Journal of Sociology* 102: 1430–44.

Cao, Y., and V. G. Nee. 2000. Comment: Controversies and evidence in the market transition debate. *American Journal of Sociology* 105:1175–88.

Gerber, T. P. 1999. *Survey of employment, income, and attitudes in Russia*. Codebook, Technical Report and Machine-Readable Data File. Ann Arbor: University of Michigan Inter-University Consortium for Political and Social Research.

———. 2000a. Membership benefits or selection effects? Why former Communist Party members do better in post-Soviet Russia. *Social Science Research* 29: 25–50.

———. 2000b. Regional migration dynamics in Russia since the collapse of communism. Paper presented at the annual meeting of the Population Association of America in Los Angeles.

———. 2001a. *The development of self-employment in Russia*. Policy Memo 186. Program on New Approaches to Russian Security, Council on Foreign Relations.

———. 2001b. Paths to success: Individual and regional determinants of self-employment entry in post-Communist Russia. *International Journal of Sociology* 31:3–37.

———. 2001c. The selection theory of persisting party advantages in Russia: More evidence and implications. *Social Science Research* 30:653–71.

———. 2002a. Joining the winners: Self-employment and stratification in post-Soviet Russia. In *The new entrepreneurs of Europe and Asia: Patterns of business development in Russia, Eastern Europe and China*, ed. V. Bonnell and T. Gold, 3–38. Armonk, NY: M. E. Sharpe.

———. 2002b. Structural change and post-socialist stratification: Labor market transitions in contemporary Russia. *American Sociological Review* 67:629–59.

Gerber, T. P., and M. Hout. 1998. More shock than therapy: Employment and income in Russia, 1991–1995. *American Journal of Sociology* 104:1–50.

Gimpelson, V., and D. Lippoldt. 2001. *The Russian labour market: Between transition and turmoil.* New York: Rowman & Littlefield.

Goskomstat Rossii (The State Committee on Statistics of the Russian Federation). 1998. *Regiony Rossii, 1998* (Regions of Russia, 1998). Moscow: Goskomstat.

———. 1999. *Maloe Predprinimatel'stvo v Rossii* (Small business in Russia). Moscow: Goskomstat.

———. 2000. *Rossii v Tsifrakh, 2000* (Russia by numbers, 2000). Moscow: Goskomstat.

Hanley, E. 2000. Self-employment in post-communist Eastern Europe: A refuge from poverty or road to riches? *Communist and Post-Communist Studies* 33:379–402.

Jones, A., and W. Moskoff. 1991. *Ko-ops: The rebirth of entrepreneurship in the Soviet Union.* Bloomington: Indiana University Press.

Kalleberg, A. L., and K. T. Leicht. 1991. Gender and organizational performance: Determinants of small business survival and success. *Academy of Management Journal* 34:136–61.

Kolodko, G. W. 2000. Transition to a market and entrepreneurship: The systemic factors and policy options. *Communist and Post-Communist Studies* 33:271–93.

Loscocco, K. A., and K. T. Leicht. 1993. Gender, work-family linkages, and economic success among small business owners. *Journal of Marriage and the Family* 55:875–87.

Loscocco, K. A., and J. Robinson. 1991. Barriers to women's small-business success in the United States. *Gender and Society* 5:511–32.

Nee, V. 1996. The emergence of a market society: Changing mechanisms of stratification in China. *American Journal of Sociology* 101:908–49.

Radaev, V. 2002. Entrepreneurial strategies and the structure of transaction costs in Russian business. In *The new entrepreneurs of Europe and Asia: Patterns of business development in Russia, Eastern Europe and China,* ed. V. Bonnell and T. Gold, 191–213. Armonk, NY: M. E. Sharpe.

Róbert, P., and E. Bukodi. 2000. Who are the entrepreneurs and where do they come from? Transition to self-employment before, under and after communism in Hungary. *International Review of Sociology* 10:147–71.

Róna-Tas, Á. 1994. The first shall be last? Entrepreneurship and communist cadres in the transition from socialism. *American Journal of Sociology* 100:40–69.

Róna-Tas, Á., and A. Guseva. 2001. "The Privileges of Past Party Membership in Russia and Endogenous Switching Regression," *Social Science Research* 30:641–52.

Russell, R., and R. Hanneman. 2000. The use of part-time employees and independent contractors among small enterprises in Russia. *Research in the Sociology of Work* 9:187–208.

Shelomentsev, A. G. 2001. Personnel policy at industrial enterprises of the Ural Region. *Problems of Economic Transition* 43:79–87.

Szeleńyi, I. 1988. *Socialist entrepreneurs: Embourgeoisement in rural Hungary.* Madison: University of Wisconsin Press.

Van Selm, B. 1998. Economic performance in Russia's regions. *Europe-Asia Studies* 50:603.

Walder, A. 1996. Markets and inequality in transitional economies: Toward testable theories. *American Journal of Sociology* 101:1060–73.

Wharton, A. S. 1989. Gender segregation in private-sector, public-sector, and self-employed occupations, 1950–1981. *Social Science Quarterly* 70:923–40.

Xie, Y. and E. Hannum. 1996. Regional variation in earnings inequality in reform-era urban China. *American Journal of Sociology* 101:950–92.

Zhou, X. 2000. Economic transformation and income inequality in urban China: Evidence from panel data. *American Journal of Sociology* 105:1135–74.

CHAPTER TEN

Self-Employment in Italy:
Scaling the Class Barriers

Paolo Barbieri and Ivano Bison

SELF- AND EXTRA-farm employment has once again become of interest to sociologists and economists in Italy, as well as in other developed countries. This is a consequence of both high growth rates in the last two decades (compared with a constant decrease in waged work) and the fact that many of the new occupations available in the post-Fordist labor market are, to some extent, independent. Like other Mediterranean countries, Italy has always had a strong tradition of independent work, even when agricultural self-employment is excluded. This large presence of small and microeconomic activities has long been interpreted, in the light of the functionalist theory of modernization, in terms of productive traditionalism, economic marginality, and global residuality. Political science, on the other hand, has interpreted the phenomenon in terms of the behaviors and expressions of particularistic and socially conservative petty bourgeois classes. But the new forms assumed by self-employment have also given rise to debate among labor market analysts and sociologists about the connections between self-employment and issues like welfare reform and the management of the new social risk (marginality, working poor, exclusion, insider/outsider society), which—even in a country as traditional as Italy—are spreading.[1]

This chapter examines the determinants of nonfarming self-employment over two decades (1980–1997). This was a period of particular importance for Italy, since it saw both the crisis of the Fordist mode of production, with the concomitant revival of the small and medium-sized flexible specialized firm, and the growth of a service economy that outstripped manufacturing not only in terms of total employment, but also in net employment growth.

After illustrating the close link between labor market analysis and the evolution of self-employment, and a brief glance at the debate on independent work in Italy with particular regard to the "new type of self-employment" and its related issues, we sum up our working hypothesis. Then we give details about the data and method used and discuss the changes in self-employment composition and attitudes. Finally, we turn to the mechanisms that induce individuals to enter, remain in, and finally exit independent work. The chapter concludes with a summary of the findings in light of current discussion on precarization and polarization in the labor market.

Why Is the Self-Employment Rate So High and Growing?

Compared to the European Union (EU) average, Italy has been historically characterized by a high degree of self-employment: from 1958 to 2000, the average Italian nonagricultural self-employment rate was twice as high as the OECD rate (23.1 vs. 11.8). Various explanations for the phenomenon have been put forward. For at least a decade, numerous analysts endorsed the mainstream thesis of the neoliberal labor economists who used an attractive but spurious bivariate correlation between the two macroquantities to read the growth of self-employment as related to the existing degree of employment protection legislation (EPL), operationalizing the latter in terms of OECD standard EPL indexes. This thesis was first put forward at the beginning of the 1990s (Grubb and Wells 1993) and, thanks to its immediate simplicity, was constantly reiterated thereafter to affirm the proposition that the greater the degree of employment protection, the more the tightness of the labor market gives rise to self-employment, the only form of employment not subject (or subjectable) to the foibles of waged work. Soon after the thesis of labor market rigidity was proposed, however, it was contradicted by empirical research in both Europe and Italy. We cite in particular, for the international context, the studies by Robson (1997, 1998, 2000) and Blanchflower (1998), subsequently considered by OECD (2000); and for Italy, studies that have emphasized the profoundly autochthonous roots of self-employment in independent artisan nonmarginal work, and the new employment opportunities provided by the growth of a postindustrial service economy (Rosti 1987; Sestito 1989; Barbieri 1998a, 1999, 2001, 2003a). Together with the composite nature and marked heterogeneity of self-employment in Italy (Barbieri 1999), it has been shown that a thorough explanation of the evolution of self-employment cannot ignore the interactions between the existing background of traditional, small, artisan activities and the economic consequences of the post-Fordist restructuring of the industrial system (delocalization, outsourcing, reorganizing, and downsizing). Nor can the explanation neglect the economic and developmental prospects of specialized innovative microactivities, where actors endowed with managerial skills and innovative capacity are able to create personalized strategies for achievement through the market. Some data will clarify the matter: in 1996, according to the Italian Census Bureau, the total number of firms in activity approximated 3.5 million, with an average size of 3.9 employees. About 95 percent of Italian companies employed fewer than ten workers. This testifies to the importance of small and very small firms in the Italian productive system. Indeed, the average size of Italian manufacturing firms was 7.7 in 1991, 6.5 in 1996, and 8.6 in 2001. With regard to services, the same averages were 3.3 and 2.9 (2001 data for services are not yet available). Last but not least, one should also consider that wages in small firms (those with fewer than ten employees), in which 49.1 percent of dependent employment is concentrated, are 44.4 percent lower than they are in bigger companies (with over 250 employees): 13,900 euros, compared with 25,000 euros per year, while the "value added per worker/ hourly labor cost" ratio is quite similar between small and larger firms: 2.2 in small firms (<10) and 2.5 in bigger ones (>250). This is evidence that a large part of small and very small firm competitiveness is based mainly on labor cost compression (Istat 1999).

These observations are matched by the findings of labor economists (Cappellari 1999) concerning low-wage mobility in the Italian labor market and the compression of lower wages of dependent employees. In Italy, real wages have been constantly decreasing since the early 1990s, while during the previous decade, the wage compression caused by the system of industrial relations in place at that time had penalized the dependent, skilled, labor force (Locke 1995). Interestingly, Cappellari reports that lower-paid waged workers are more likely to enter self-employment than higher-paid ones, with probabilities ranging from a minimum of 2.69 to a maximum of 3.68 according to the specifications of the model (hourly/monthly wages; bottom quintile/third decile as the threshold for low-paid employment definition).

As pointed out by other case-studies similar to the Italian one with regard to the structural conditions favoring self-employment growth (see chapter 12 of this volume), the prevalence of small-sized enterprises, often family-based, can be taken as a signal of the structural lack of career opportunities for a large number of waged workers. This is supported by research on the characteristics of the Italian system of social stratification. In their analysis of intergenerational class mobility in various European countries, Schizzerotto and Pisati (1999) found that the proportions of manual waged workers (aged up to 45) who had entered self-employment from skilled manual work were 18.1 in Italy, 8.4 in Germany, 12.6 in Great Britain, and 11.4 in Sweden. When entries from unskilled manual work were also considered, the Italian rate was again consistently higher: 20.9 compared with 11.7 in Germany, 9.6 in Great Britain, and 8.0 in Sweden.

We may thus state that different but converging structural determinants of Italian self-entrepreneurial employment can be brought to bear on certain important issues:

- the new economic opportunities becoming available as a result of the post-Fordist transformation of the productive structure
- the highly fragmented productive arrangement, which obviously reduces the degree of social mobility in the (salaried) labor market
- the concomitant (labor) price competition strategies practiced by small firms, which depress income mobility
- the ceiling effect produced by rigid national wage settings

All of these factors considered, self-employment emerged as a viable option—probably the main one—for intragenerational social and income mobility by individuals endowed with limited human capital but broad work experience and an entrepreneurial propensity for risk-taking.[2]

New Forms of Self-Employment?

As pointed out in the previous section, Italy's high self-employment rates have been long regarded from the point of view of the sociopolitical behaviors of the middle classes, among which is the small, autonomous, petty bourgeoisie (Pizzorno 1980). Today, a new feature of self-employment may be that, together with quantitative growth, polarization is taking place, between skilled self-employment (intellectual work no longer being subject to the subordination typical of dependent Fordist employment) and secondary (*b-series*) self-employment of the manual kind, where low or no skills are required. This is exactly the type of social phenomenon that has been identified in the literature with the "new service proletariat" (Esping-Andersen 1993).

The possibility that Italy is undergoing a process of professional polarization in the independent labor force[3] characterized by extremely flexible labor markets, similar to that noted in other countries (Arum 1997, 2001), is a matter of heated debate in Italy. The likelihood that, in view of a set of institutional and productive characteristics that make the Italian labor market one of the most segmented among OECD countries, a secondary marginal and precarized (self-employment) labor market is gaining ground in parallel to the primary, well-protected one has been suggested by various authors (for a review, see Bologna and Fumagalli 1997). The thesis that new self-employment is a source of potential exclusion supports the view that the "targeted and partial deregulation" of the labor market (Esping-Andersen and Regini 2000) introduced in the 1990s has given rise to new formally autonomous but economically dependent occupations that are in fact subordinate and substantially precarized (e.g., solo self-employed, labor only subcontractors, pseudo-self-employed). These occupations, it is alleged, are job traps for those endowed with scarce personal resources (human and social capital), and therefore excluded from the "stable" job opportunities of insiders, who are still relatively well protected (OECD 1999). Since insiders in Italy today correspond to the dependent labor force regularly employed in secure jobs—that is, adult male breadwinners (Reyneri 2002)—the outsiders most at risk of joining a secondary "autonomous-precarized" labor market are young people and women, those with no professional experience, those who are low skilled, and/or those who are poorly educated.

Moreover, a precarious occupational circuit entrapping workers should exhibit a large number of transitions between unemployment and precarious, unskilled self-employment, as a consequence of what has in the literature been called the growing "individualization" of employment relationships. This process, although it does not exclusively concern unskilled jobs, nonetheless hits them particularly hard (Beck 1992, 2000; Sennet 1998). The process, which the precarization thesis of new self-employment seems to assume quite uncritically, would entail the high flexibilization of employment relationships, the increased circulation between unemployment and marginal employment, and the reduced centrality of work as a factor in identity-building, with the consequent fragmentation of individual biographies. However, previous surveys have shown that transitions between unemployment *strictu sensu* and self-employment are rare, and that they have not increased among the cohorts entering the labor market in recent years (Barbieri 2001).[4]

After a description of the data and measurement instruments, we shall try to give better specification to the evolution of self-employment in Italy over the last two post-Fordist decades. In particular, we shall seek to verify whether the sharp upskilling of self-employment and the slow (and still uncertain) growth of poorly qualified autonomous positions are necessarily combined with its precarization, or whether instead the changing composition of the professional structure of self-employment does not imply a parallel underlying process of precarization. A further reading of the phenomenon based on the postmodern, individualizing approach would consider the classical variables of social stratification (e.g., the individuals' social origins, their human capital, and their family members' as well as their own present or previous occupational statuses) as less relevant to the analysis of the new forms of self-employment. An interpretation in terms of the changing composition of the professional structure of self-employment, on the other hand, considers the typical heterogeneity of Italian self-employment to be one of its structural characteristics, and part of its evolution, and therefore regards the mechanisms of social stratification as also relevant in the segmentation of self-employment. Class of origin, human capital, and occupational status stand out as crucial variables with which we may analyze the components of the polarization observed and shed light on its structural determinants.

To sum up, we have stressed the composite nature of self-employment in Italy, its deep autochthonous roots in the artisan- and small-firm-based national productive structure, and the revival of the small and medium-sized flexible specialized firm following the crisis of the Fordist mode of production. This revival has been paralleled by an expansion of the (independent) service economy. We have shown that this fragmented economic structure, combined with rigid national wage setting, has reduced the chances of social and income mobility for a large part of waged workers, who are often endowed with mid-low formal education but with valid industry-specific skills that are quite portable on the independent labor market. We have also set out the thesis most frequently used to explain self-employment dynamics in Italy, recalling both the degree of dependent employment protection and the postindustrial individualization and precarization of labor. As the former aspect has already been discussed elsewhere (Barbieri 2001), we shall now examine the determinants of self-employment in the past two decades, checking whether evidence for self-employment precarisation can be found.

Data, Methods, and Variables

The analysis is based on the Italian Households Longitudinal Survey (ILFI) carried out in 1997 by the University of Trento on a national representative sample of 9,874 individuals belonging to 4,457 households. The survey contains retrospective information on various dimensions of the subjects' life cycles, of which their employment histories were the most thoroughly surveyed. Here, the population at risk is constituted by all individuals aged 18–60 who moved in and out of self-employment between 1980 and 1997. Neither farmers/agricultural laborers nor family workers have been included in the analysis. The decision to exclude (self-declared) family workers, despite their importance in the Italian self-employment structure, was taken for a substantive reason: family workers could, in fact, bias the likelihood and speed of transitions into self-employment because they enter their family businesses directly after leaving the educational system. On average, in fact, family workers are younger and have less labor force experience than self-employed: their exclusion, therefore, enables us to focus on core self-employment.

The observation window between 1980 and 1997 is probably best suited to capturing the most recent transformations of self-employment in Italy. Although this procedure may pose problems for analysis, for instance with respect to the number of transitions that can be analysed, this observation window was chosen to enable comparative analysis among all the chapters in this volume.[5] In a sense, it represents the smallest common denominator. The same applies to the use of a discrete-time axis. The units of analysis are yearly person spells, examined by using discrete-time techniques for event history-data (Allison 1984; Yamaguchi 1991). As a matter of fact, this decision to focus only on yearly person spells within the reported observation window implies right *and* left censoring of the spells. While right censoring is not a problem in a longitudinal analysis, left censoring may be problematic. We shall deal with this specific aspect when presenting the models, as we control for left censoring.

The empirical analysis in the following section will explore transition into and out of self-employment. All of the models are based on discrete-time transition rate models using logistic regressions and multinomial logistic regressions, respectively. They all control for a dummy variable of the year (not reported in the tables), to allow the baseline transition rate to vary over time. Specifically, we shall investigate entering self-employment in general, undistinguished according to destination state (table 10.3); entering different types of self-employment (table 10.4); leaving self-employment (table 10.5), and finally leaving self-employment distinguished according to the different kinds of self-employment (table 10.6). We distinguish three types of self-employment: professional and managerial self-employment (EGP I and II); skilled self-employment (EGP IIIa, V, VI); and unskilled self-employment (EGP IIIb, VIIa). This distinction is particularly important in the Italian case because it enables closer specification of self-employment composition and highlights the changes that have taken place in the structure of independent work in recent decades. The models include two kinds of independent variable: time-constant and time-varying (Blossfeld and Rohwer 1995). Furthermore, we distinguish between micro covariates (i.e., those directly referring to individuals) and macro covariates, which were added to the individual data set and refer to macro dimensions. We used the previous year's annual national unemployment rate and the previous year's annual GDP index, measured at constant prices (100 = 1913). A continuous measurement was adopted with regard to age. A squared term was also inserted to control for quadratic trends. Education was measured at the beginning of the relative spell, and it was coded according to the CAS-MIN scheme (König, Lüttinger, and Müller 1988; Shavit and Müller 1998) into seven levels, as follows: (1) up to compulsory schooling (*scuole elementari e medie*, 1ab); (2) postcompulsory vocational qualification (*scuole professionali*, 1c); (3) secondary qualification, vocational (*istituti professionali*, 2a); (4) technical (*istituti tecnici*, 2b/2c-voc); or (5) general (*licei*, 2c); (6) lower tertiary certification (*diploma universitario*, 3a); (7) higher tertiary certification (*laurea*, 3b). The reference category was compulsory schooling (1ab). Time-constant social origin was also controlled for in all models. Social origin was coded as follows: professional and managerial positions; skilled positions; unskilled positions, which represent the reference category; and farmers (small proprietors and agricultural labourers). Self-employment origins were controlled for by a dummy variable. The models also controlled for marital status and partner's occupational position. The variable recording both of these items specified the following positions: unmarried, widowed, or separated (reference category); partner is self-employed; partner is a waged worker; partner is a family worker; partner is unemployed or not in the labor force. Previous industrial branch specifies the sector of the respondent's last occupation: public sector; finance and business services; transport and communications; wholesale, retail, and hotels; building; or mining and manufacturing (the reference category).[6] The models used to estimate transitions into self-employment also controlled for the respondent's previous occupational status, distinguishing between professional and managerial waged work; skilled waged work; unskilled waged work; first job search; unemployed (former worker); not in the labor force (reference category). Finally, five additional covariates were considered in the additional models: a measure for the time since the actual beginning of the spell until the 1980 left censoring, which enabled us to control for the real duration of the spells considered; the number of spells spent in waged work and/or in self-employment during the previous work career (its entire length); as well as the number of previous unemployment spells. Only in the additional models for transitions out of self-employment was a possible period effect controlled for by inserting two specific dummy variables: period 1986–91 and period 1992–97. Period 1980–85 was used as the reference category.

Self-Employment as a Precarious State?

In what follows, we shall give a preliminary description of the change in composition of self-employment over recent decades. Figure 10.1 reports the share of self-employment divided by gender and three professional levels: professionals and managers, skilled, and unskilled positions. The historical series considered in figure 10.1 date back to the 1960s. Given the nature and the characteristics of self-employment in Italy, historical series limited to the 1980s and 1990s alone might have excessively flattened the trends, thereby hiding social and productive phenomena that have a longer time span.

In fact, our data show that, since the end of the 1970s, a change has

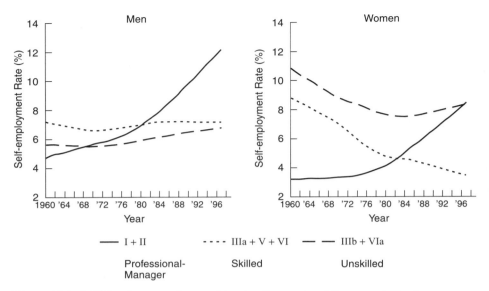

Figure 10.1: Self-Employment Composition by Occupational Status and Gender in Italy, 1960–97

taken place in the professional structure of the independent labor force in Italy. Some trends are particularly visible. First, one notes a net increase in high professional, service-class self-employment, together with a parallel growth, though much less rapid, of autonomous positions with poor or no qualifications—the latter have slightly increased in recent years after a long period of decline. Besides being similar for the two genders, these trends in self-employment have grown more marked since the end of the 1970s, namely, during the period coinciding with the final demise of the Fordist mode of production in Italy (and with the observation window considered). Rather stable for men, though with a net decrease for women, is the component of qualified and artisan self-employment.

In conclusion, we may state that although there is some evidence for increasing polarization within the self-employed, the data point only very restrictedly to a growth of unskilled positions that would support an interpretation of a precarizing "service proletariat."

To delve further into the question of the increasing precarization and/or polarization of self-employment in the course of postindustrial change, we explore one aspect of precariousness, namely, the temporal insecurity of job positions. Figure 10.2 represents the Product Limit Estimates (Kaplan-Meier) curve for survival in self-employment positions, for job

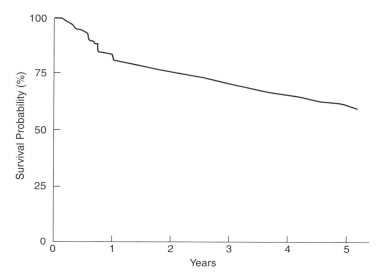

Figure 10.2: Exits from Self-Employment in Italy, Episodes Started between 1980 and 1992

episodes that began between 1980 and 1992, to allow for five years of observation, given that our data set ends in 1997. The graph illustrates only the first five years of self-employment activity, namely, the period during which mortality rates should be most concentrated, according to the precarization hypothesis.

We see that, on average, the survival curve remains quite high: five years after startup, almost 70 percent of Italian self-employed still survive in their position.[7]

Table 10.1 disaggregates the survival analysis for the different occupational positions, differentiating between self-employed and waged workers. Since all transitions analyzed in this case were toward a destination state markedly different from the initial one (e.g., from unemployment or waged worker to self-employed or vice versa), the comparison of survival times in the state of origin between self-employed and waged workers can be reasonably supported.[8] Reported in the table are the medium and median times (in months) of survival in employment spells beginning after 1980 (in order to avoid all possible risks connected with left censoring).

We find that the self-employed are definitely more stable in their professional positions than are waged workers. Only waged women, professionals, and managers are slightly more stable when compared with their female self-employed counterparts (the difference is nonsignificant). As

TABLE 10.1
Product Limit Estimates (Kaplan-Meier) of Surviving in Current Occupational Position

	Self-employed				Waged workers			
	Men		Women		Men		Women	
	Mean	Median	Mean	Median	Mean	Median	Mean	Median
Professionals/ managers	127.5	138	93.4	55	96.9	66	99.3	61
Skilled	122.3	125	98.7	75	84.0	52	78.2	38
Unskilled	103.3	79	92.0	62	64.6	25	53.9	17

Source: ILFI 1997
Note: Data are for job episodes beginning after 1980.

expected, the medium and median times of surviving in the initial professional position decrease with the lowering of the skill level. But not even
in the case of the unskilled do the times recorded give an impression of
such high turnover rates as to create job carousels between unskilled self-
employment and unemployment/non-labor force participation. In this
sense, we can hardly speak of precarious, unstable positions, even with
regard to the unskilled self-employed.

Moreover, those who appear to be most at risk of job carousels are
unskilled waged workers, especially when the median times of surviving
in the job spell are considered.

Still, in descriptive terms, the data on survival times in the occupational position seem to suggest that self-employment has not, in the last
twenty years, constituted a transitory and contingent experience in the
life course. If an area of precarization does exist, as regards job quality,
the security and protection of employment and its duration and stability,
it is not to be found in self-employment.

This finding is borne out by the data in table 10.2, which further characterize the attitudes of the self-employed toward their occupations. It
should be borne in mind that an important corollary to the individualization theory and to the self-employment precarization hypothesis is that
work is losing its importance as a source of social identity and personal
growth. Obviously, this should also come about as a result of the marginality of the work experience (in terms of duration, contents, and stability) in individual life cycles. Fortunately, sociology has a long and robust tradition of empirical studies on attitudes and meanings relating to
employment. The data in table 10.2 are explicit: the first row gives the
percentages of the self-employed who declare that they would be reluctant to give up their current job should they be offered an equivalent
position as a dependent worker. The last two indicators represent two, by

TABLE 10.2
Attitudes of the Self-Employed Regarding Their Occupations in Italy
(in percent)

	Professional level		
	Professionals/ managers	Skilled	Unskilled
Not keen on changing job	86.8	78.6	77.1
Close work involvement	77.9	71.4	60.0
Distressed (GHQ)[a]	39.7	35.7	60.0

Source: Barbieri 2003b.
[a] Index of Psychological Distress, General Health Questionnaire

now standard, indicators in the sociological literature on labor force attitudes: the index of work involvement and the GHQ index of psychological distress (Gallie et al. 1998; Whelan, Hannan, and Creighton 1991). All the data show that the Italian self-employed are closely attached to their work, and to the autonomy that it allows, even in professional and occupational conditions that we would unhesitatingly call suboptimal, poorly qualified, or highly stressful and unsatisfactory, working conditions that would at any rate not induce us to expect such close commitment to work (much lower values, in fact, are recorded among dependent workers).[9]

Though limited and mainly descriptive, these indexes reinforce the picture of a self-employed world that does not match the postmodern idea of isolated individuals detached from their professional activities, monads at risk in a fragmented society itself at risk. Work for the self-employed is seemingly not a marginal or transitory period in their life courses; rather, it is a powerful source of identity, and therefore a primary element in the self-building process.

DETERMINANTS OF SELF-EMPLOYMENT

After this first description of the situation of self-employed persons in Italy, we now turn to the determinants of self-employment. To provide a differentiated picture of the forces structuring this status, we shall investigate both transition into and exit from self-employment. The results given above suggest that there are different pathways into autonomous work for men and women. Accordingly, the models are estimated separately for both genders. Following the inherent time-structure, we shall begin with entry into self-employment.

Paths into Self-Employment

Table 10.3 gives details on the chances of entering self-employed job positions in general. As noted above, the results are based on discrete-time transition rate models. Obviously, transitions into self-employment can occur from different kinds of origin states. We take this feature into account by including the various origin states among the covariates. Specifically, we distinguish waged work (EGP I and II); waged work (EGP IIIa, V and VI); waged work (EGP IIIb, VIIa, the reference category); first-job seeker; former worker, unemployed; not in the labor force. We find that the self-employed are mainly men and adults (the age effect is quadratic), and that the largest share enter self-employment directly from the first-job search or via periods of unemployment. If the self-employed have some work experience, it has mainly been acquired in the building, trade, and financial services sectors. Central to structuring access to self-employment is social origin. Membership in the petty bourgeoisie and in those professions endowed with specific qualifications positively influence the decision to set up one's own business. In contrast, farming origin reduces this tendency. Although not always significant, a family business nonetheless proves to be important for self-employment access: having a partner in self-employment or in a family-based business increased the speed of entry into self-employment for our subjects. Here it is the role of strong ties and close kin social capital which intervenes, thereby revealing that one of the mechanisms underpinning the social foundations of self-employment in Italy is the familial environment.

The already-mentioned heterogeneity of Italian self-employment emerges very clearly: differences by gender and certain well-marked parameters (e.g., education, sector) highlight the existence of various underlying structures of self-employment that are sometimes markedly different from each other. It is therefore advisable to investigate these different forms of self-employment separately, which we shall do in table 10.4. First, however, we discuss a slightly extended model: model B in table 10.3 yields more detailed explanation and further specification of the baseline model presented in model A. It allows the verification of macro and contextual effects that have not been considered previously. We note first that the length of the pre-1980 spells (*timeself*), namely, the period before left censoring, has a mildly negative effect on the speed of transition, one that is rarely statistically significant. That the amount of time spent in a given state of origin exerts a certain "stickiness" by keeping workers in their original position is certainly nothing new. However, the finding that the significance of the specific parameter is almost never sufficiently robust (not even in the following analysis, see also tables 10.4, 10.5, 10.6) shows that the decision to keep a fixed observation window, with simultaneous acceptance of left-censored cases, is not a major problem for the sociological interpretation of the phenomenon observed.[10] This confirms the results of previous analysis on the same topic (Arum 2001). In addition, we control for previous job history to evaluate whether and how entries into self-employment are tied to an individual's previous work experience. Although affected by the binomial structure of the transitions analysis, which fails to grasp the marked heterogeneity of self-employment types and developments, this additional insight into individuals' work career is nevertheless quite informative. In particular, we note the positive and significant effect of the number of previous self-employment spells, for both genders: those who were self-employed before have once again a greater propensity to become self-employed. The positive effect of previous self-employment periods therefore may suggest the existence of a carousel among self-employment and unemployment spells. For this "carousel" hypothesis to be validated, however, the number of previous unemployment spells should also be positive.[11] Not only is this not the case, but the parameter for previous unemployment spells is always negative and significant. This finding is interesting in light of the previously mentioned theory of the precarization and individualization of labor relationships, and its assumption of high turnover between unemployment and (in this case self-) employment, which is not confirmed by our data. An alternative interpretation of the positive effect of previous self-employment experience focuses on the role of social capital. This "push" effect of previous self-employment spells—which, as we shall see when analyzing the subsequent multinomial models (table 10.4), proved to be a rather general pattern for entries into all three types of self-employment—seems to be verified not only for the Italian case but, more appropriately, for entrepreneurial, small firms in many countries. In the Taiwanese case, this was explained by familiarity with self-employment, either through strong ties or through one's own work experience, both of which are factors that reduce fears concerning risks and uncertainty and help build the amount of social capital required to make the transition. An interpretation that emphasizes the embeddedness of self-employment determinants in the wider social background of individuals can be proposed for the Italian case as well, in the light of the high value that social capital proves to have for the Italian self-entrepreneurial activities (Barbieri 2003).

With respect to previous work experience as a waged worker, we find that—partially in antithesis to the effect of self-employment spells—the number of episodes of dependent employment displays a negative effect, which is particularly significant for women. Since this parameter will be explained better by the following multinomial analysis, we will not comment further on it here.

TABLE 10.3
Transitions into Self-Employment: Binomial Logistic Regression in Italy

	All	Men	Women	All	Men	Women
Sex: (ref: men)	−0.746***			−0.704***		
Age	0.095***	0.075***	0.121***	0.119***	0.074***	0.181***
Agesq	−0.003***	−0.002***	−0.003***	−0.004***	−0.003***	−0.005***
Education (ref: 1ab)						
Education: 3b	−0.129	0.097	−0.553**	−0.162	0.197	−0.785***
Education: 3a	−0.065	0.257	−0.573*	−0.171	0.258	−0.742**
Education: 2c	0.003	0.332**	−0.430**	−0.052	0.355**	−0.552***
Education: 2b	−0.150	−0.190	−0.011	−0.167*	−0.148	−0.088
Education: 2a	−0.115	0.128	−0.546**	−0.149	0.145	−0.657**
Education: 1c	−0.024	−0.216	0.281	0.062	−0.097	0.300*
Father's occupational status (ref: unskilled)						
Professional	0.531***	0.436***	0.630***	0.496***	0.346***	0.716***
Skilled	0.178**	0.198*	0.154	0.174**	0.121	0.315**
Farmer	−0.232**	−0.195	−0.356**	−0.345***	−0.309**	−0.359**
Father self-employed	0.331***	0.433***	0.174	0.267***	0.365***	0.140
Previous occupational status (ref: unskilled wagework)						
professional/managerial wagework	0.206	0.068	0.371	0.179	0.078	0.274
skilled wagework	0.067	−0.056	0.321	0.066	−0.049	0.231
First job seeker	1.662***	1.466***	2.013***	1.338***	1.258***	1.415***
Unemployed	1.456***	1.474***	1.453***	1.250***	1.252***	1.230***
NLF	0.069	0.270	0.186	0.057	0.278	0.059

Previous occupational branch (ref: mining, manuf.)

	(1)	(2)	(3)	(4)	(5)	(6)
Public sector	-0.722***	-0.795***	-0.577**	-0.721***	-0.793***	-0.558**
Finance, business	0.255*	0.493***	-0.568	0.153	0.422**	-0.729**
Transport, communication	-0.942***	-1.182***	-0.140	-0.881***	-1.119***	-0.094
Trade	0.448***	0.511***	0.241	0.391***	0.452**	0.209
Construction	0.515***	0.481***	0.388	0.403**	0.372**	0.451
Partner's occupational status						
Waged worker	-0.538***	-0.444***	-0.636***	-0.510***	-0.500***	-0.536***
Self-employed	0.088	0.377**	-0.140	0.081	0.285	-0.072
Family worker	0.908***	0.557*	1.350***	0.837***	.646*	0.955**
Unemployed/NLF	-0.925***	-0.741***	-2.012***	-0.761***	-0.653***	-1.631***
Timeself				-0.015	0.001	-0.029*
Number of waged work positions				-0.064***	-0.025	-0.145***
Number of self-employment episodes				0.156***	0.159***	0.149***
Number of unemployed episodes				-0.290***	-0.227***	-0.379***
GDP				-0.049	-0.045	-0.063
Unemployment Rate				0.179***	0.112	0.29**
Constant	-5.184***	-4.859***	-6.447***	-6.311***	-4.980***	-8.768***
R^2	0.144	0.136	0.165	0.186	0.172	0.221
N	85,559	42,800	42,759	85,559	42,800	42,759

$* p < 0.05$, $** p < 0.01$, $*** p < 0.001$

TABLE 10.4
Transitions into Self-Employment: Multinomial Logistic Regression Models in Italy

	Professional/managers			Skilled			Unskilled		
	All	Men	Women	All	Men	Women	All	Men	Women
Sex: female	-0.922***			-0.536***			-0.557***		
Age	0.142***	0.103***	0.222***	0.052**	0.066**	0.065*	0.071***	0.057**	0.074**
AgeSq	-0.003***	-0.002***	-0.005***	-0.002***	-0.003***	-0.004*	-0.002***	-0.002***	-0.002*
Education (ref.: 1ab)									
education: 3ab	0.733***	0.845***	0.509*	-1.749***	-1.655**	-2.200***	-1.769***	-1.028**	-2.988***
education: 2abc	0.569***	0.705***	0.317	-1.046***	-0.990***	-1.312***	-0.179	-0.368**	-0.046
education: 1c	0.421**	0.050	0.984***	-0.013	-0.152	0.110*	-0.620**	-0.577*	-0.837**
Father's occupational status (ref: unskilled)									
Professional/ manager	0.958***	0.902***	1.069***	-0.089	-0.143	-0.035	-0.169	-0.681**	0.153
Skilled	0.414***	0.553***	0.209	0.331***	0.237	0.580**	-0.268*	-0.307	-0.208
Farmer	-0.518***	-0.517**	-0.519	-0.195	-0.136	-0.339	-0.161	0.051	-0.501*
Father self-employed	0.219***	0.501***	-0.291	-0.146	-0.251	0.059	0.886***	0.860***	0.883***
Previous occupational status (ref.: un-skilled wagework) Waged worker: EGP I, II	0.258	0.112	0.692*	0.404	0.245	0.636	-0.845**	-0.997**	-0.376

Waged worker: EGP IIIa, V, VI	−0.306	−0.307	−0.304	0.937***	0.882***	1.002**	−0.451**	−0.778**	0.138
First job seeker	1.874***	1.737***	1.867***	1.525***	1.278***	1.892***	1.535***	1.129***	2.064***
Unemployed	1.383***	1.347***	1.136***	1.494***	1.684***	1.191**	1.651***	1.433***	1.862***
NLF	−0.126	0.081	−0.497	0.217	1.028**	0.261*	0.253	−0.296	0.743**
Previous occupation branch (ref: mining, manuf.)									
Public sector	−0.967***	−0.532**	−2.064***	−0.231	−1.060**	0.447	−0.632**	−1.107**	−0.339
Finance, business	0.504**	0.748***		−0.083	0.267		−1.151*	−1.214	
Transport, communication	−1.295***	−1.270***	−0.599	−1.061**	−1.454**	−0.816	−0.234	−0.694	−0.286
Trade, hotels, restaurants	0.545***	0.532***	0.397	−0.456	−0.260	−1.543	1.010***	1.069***	0.639
Construction	0.268	0.353	—	0.427	0.411	—	0.869**	0.484**	—
Partner's occupational status (ref: other)									
Waged worker	−0.593***	−0.623***	−0.676***	−0.559***	−0.142	−1.088***	−0.427*	−0.378	−0.360*
Self, family worker	0.082	0.416**	−0.410	−0.324	−0.138	−0.457	0.655***	0.734***	0.743**
Unemployed, NLF	−1.104***	−0.969***	−1.793***	−0.427***	−0.209	−1.548**	−1.109***	−0.880***	−2.364***
Intercept	−6.096***	−6.084***	−6.895***	−5.206***	−5.452***	−5.546***	−5.384***	−5.060***	−6.286***

TABLE 10.4 (continued)

	Professional/managers			Skilled			Unskilled		
	All	Men	Women	All	Men	Women	All	Men	Women
Timeself		−0.028	−0.033		0.014	−0.037		0.028	−0.01
Number of previous jobs as waged worker		−0.054*	−0.184**		0.054**	−0.107*		−0.081**	−0.13*
Number of previous jobs as self-employed		0.139***	0.177***		0.178***	0.068		0.203***	0.15***
Number of previous unemployment spells		−0.288**	−0.562**		−0.173	−0.262		−0.142	−0.21
GDP		−0.076	−0.172		−0.232	−0.272		0.136	0.29
Unemployment rate		0.154	0.332*		0.352*	0.380*		−0.071	0.10
Intercept		−6.690***	−8.537***		−6.987***	−6.703***		−5.082***	−9.89***

Fitting values	All individuals	Baseline model		Additional model	
		Men	Women	Men	Women
R^2	0.161	0.159	0.188	0.193	0.237
Number of valid observations	85,559	42,800	42,759	42,800	42,759

* $p < 0.05$ ** $p < 0.01$, *** $p < 0.001$

Finally, the two macro variables considered, GDP at constant prices and yearly unemployment rate, display highly diversified effects. While the former is devoid of significance (but slightly negative), the unemployment rate is positive; but again only for women, whose recourse to self-employment therefore seems more affected by adverse economic conditions.

Greater clarity is required at this point. We must observe the internal diversity in the composition of self-employment in Italy so that the underlying structural dynamics are brought out. So far the analysis of transitions into self-employment has revealed features typical of the Italian self-employment structure, while others relating to its intrinsic heterogeneity have been obscured by the fact that the different paths into self-employment have been considered jointly. Table 10.4 therefore analyzes the paths into the three already-mentioned self-employed positions. We find first that, even when disaggregating by professional composition, self-employment in Italy again proves to be male-dominated: the coefficient according to gender is always unfavorable to women, and significant. Moreover, age affects female entries into self-employment more than it does male entries: the effect of age for women, in fact, is always higher in the models distinguished by gender. The analyses of the paths into self-employment, once these have been distinguished by professional type, confirm the fundamental importance of at least two of the variables used by the "classical" analysis of social stratification (education and social origin) in establishing self-employment polarization. Secondary and tertiary education is capital for self-employed professionals and freelancers, while as regards the remaining two employment positions it is compulsory education that proves to be most important. Interestingly, vocational education of lower level (1c) shows a positive and significant value for transitions into service-class self-employment. The coefficient is particularly strong and significant for women. This supports our hypothesis that self-employment has indeed been a source of upward social mobility for less-educated individuals. It is also worth noting that education generally protects against entry into unskilled self-employment: not only does tertiary education have a strong negative effect, but also secondary education, both general and technical (2abc), and vocational education (1c) prevent entry into poor, autonomous working positions.

It is thus evident that unskilled autonomous positions are almost exclusively occupied by the less educated, and that education does indeed constitute one of the main factors responsible for the segmentation of self-employment in Italy, although it is not the only variable with a significant role in this segmentation process: social origin exerts equally important effects, which can be analyzed both as the effect of having a father who is also self-employed, and as the effect of class of origin. As already seen in table 10.3, the models presented in table 10.4 illustrate that being of self-employed origin increases children's chances of entering a similar kind of independent employment, be it simply by joining, or starting with, their father's business. The models presented in table 10.4, divided by the professional position entered, afford better understanding of this trend: most influenced by self-employment origins are independent professionals/managers and unskilled autonomous workers. The two extremes of our self-employment typology therefore appear to have some sort of "structural stickiness" that affects the professional experience of self-employed descendants.

With regard to class of origin, to be noted is the strong effect of a service-class father (EGP I–II), whether a manager or a professional, on the chances that his children will themselves become self-employed professionals. Indeed, higher social origins (father in service classes I and II) also prevent children from experiencing downward social mobility within the self-employment world. The effect is strong and significant for men in particular. The same applies to the children of skilled and qualified fathers (EGP IIIa, V, VI), who, via self-employment, either experience some upward social mobility by joining independent service class positions or—in the worst cases—remain "stable on the diagonal" in their father's class. Ultimately, having had an unskilled father increases the likelihood that the offspring will follow him into unskilled self-employed positions, according to the classical mechanism of class segregation and social closure. The relevance of social origin, with its inheritance effect of social class position, therefore still yields better understanding of the real, effective, determinants of self-employment in Italy.

Further considerations arise from observations of the parameter relative to the previous occupational status of the subject. Previous job history and occupational positions are highly informative and statistically significant for predicting the kind of self-employment that will be entered. As will be seen from table 10.4, self-employment can originate both from professional/skilled waged work and from the area of non-employment. However, the dynamics of entry differ according to the origin state: in one case (entrants from salaried EGP IIIa, V, VI positions), we have workers endowed with professional skills who become self-employed; in the other (entrants from nonemployment), paths into self-employment are apparently less determined by previous work experience.

Transitions from waged to self-entrepreneurial work are more frequent and more rapid for professionals and managers (in particular for women belonging to the service class), and for qualified workers of both genders, for whom the qualification attained and labor force experience developed over the years act as an evident preselection or self-selection factor. This can be seen from the positive and significant value of the parameter associated with transition from skilled employed positions to qualified self-employed ones. Previous work experience, especially in skilled or service-class positions, also has a rather important effect, especially for men, in preventing transitions into unskilled self-employment.

Therefore, a large "reservoir" of self-employment consists of the dependent occupations typical of the service class, and of the skilled working classes (manual or nonmanual). As regards the latter, the transition originates in skilled dependent occupations in the industrial and manufacturing sectors, usually (table 4.A) after a professional career comprising episodes of waged and/or self-employed work essential for the acquisition of labor force experience, human capital, and professional skills, as well as social contacts and relational resources (Brüderl and Preisendörfer 1998).

Nonetheless, in Italian self-employment, a second "reservoir" seemingly outlined by our data consists of the area, not at all insignificant, of those who are out of work. When compared with waged workers, the parameters of these groups are always higher. Despite the high values, however, these effects do not necessarily mean that those who are out of work have a general propensity to become self-employed; rather, they have higher mobility rates than other workers. While transitions from first-job search to professional self-employment, for the better educated, can be partly explained in terms of the intergenerational transmission of privileged positions in the free-professions labor market,[12] the case of transitions to skilled and unskilled self-employed positions from the non-employment area is somewhat peculiar. The nonemployment area includes all first-job seekers, former workers currently unemployed, as well as all periods spent off work by seasonal workers. The latter, in particular, have for decades constituted a highly distinctive component of self-employment and "pseudo-self-employment" in Italy. This is not so much the case, or at least no longer so much the case, in agriculture, but rather, increasingly, during the years considered, in the sector of trade, tourism, hotels, and restaurants. A further feature of seasonal workers is their "inactivity periods" between seasonal job spells, which have been reported as unemployment or NLF. Since they constitute a large proportion of the "nonemployed," one can argue that a significant part of the unemployment/NLF effect is explained by their "waiting time" between job spells as formally self-employed workers. The positive effect of the number of self-employment spells, which is shown in table 10.4, in fact, supports this interpretation,[13] as does the positive and significant effect of the NLF coefficient for males in transition to skilled self-employment. The same NLF effect in the case of women seemingly pushes them more toward unqualified positions.

Among the previous occupational branches, a clear effect—as we saw also in table 10.3—is displayed both by business services (finance, business) in the case of transitions into service class self-employment positions and by consumer services (trade, hotels, restaurants) and construction, which exert a significant influence in pushing (mainly men) toward unskilled self-employment positions. It is once again evident that both the new freelance/managerial highly skilled professions and the traditional consumer and building activities best characterize the structure of Italian self-employment.

Partner's occupational status yields some last observations of a certain interest in characterizing the processes of self-employment entry. A feature shared by all the occupational categories considered is that persons without a partner are generally more willing to undertake the risk of transition toward self-employment. Contrary to what one might expect, the presence of an employed partner—which usually means a steady source of income because at least one member of the household has "a link to the (occupational) welfare system"—does not support transitions to self-employment; on the contrary, the effect is always negative and significant. Since there are no substantial differences between men and women with regard to this specific effect, one may presume that it is not an "effect of familiar responsibility" that discourages the running of self-entrepreneurial risk by the head of household, but simply greater freedom in taking their own decisions by singles. The same also happens when the partner is nonemployed, although in this case the discouraging effect is stronger for women than for men.

Interestingly, having a partner who is a family worker has a positive effect only in the case of transitions toward forms of unskilled self-employment. This is indicative of how self-employment in poorly qualified activities (small cleaning enterprises, general and/or personal services, mainly manual activities of microenterprises) is often organized as a family business.

Overall, however, the presence of a partner seems to discourage, rather than facilitate, the running of self-entrepreneurial risk. Although it is generally true that "it takes two to tango," this does not hold for self-employment, unless it is unskilled self-employment, which comes in couples, so to speak.

Our findings with regard to entries into self-employment can be summed up in three distinct points. First, the determinants of self-employment in Italy are still the classical stratification variables: education, family and social origin, and labor market experience. Second, these structural determinants of self-employment also play an important role in defining the different types of self-employment and the pathways along which individuals become freelance professionals or craftspeople or unskilled autonomous workers. Third, individuals' job histories must also be considered when evaluating the different mechanisms that regulate entries into the different types of self-employment. We may accordingly maintain that self-employment trajectories are path dependent—different origin states do, in fact, matter in explaining different outcomes.

Paths Out of Self-Employment

Understanding the mechanisms giving rise to the current stock of self-employment also requires analysis of the mechanisms involved in leaving this status. We therefore now turn to the second part of the question. Who leaves self-employment? Table 10.5 illustrates the paths out of self-employment. Table 10.6 adopts a finer-gauge grid of analysis and distinguishes exit rates according to the different forms of self-employment.

We begin with brief discussion of the general pattern of exit from autonomous jobs. Those who leave self-employment are mainly women, the young (the effect of age is quadratic), and in general those who are less qualified, that is, those who have possibly been unable to use self-employment as a channel for professional and personal advancement. The data in table 10.5 yield further information of specific interest. Those leaving self-employment are mainly workers with a general secondary education (2c), the descendants of the small agricultural bourgeoisie (an opposite effect is exerted by the urban petty bourgeoisie), and all those who have had unstable work careers, as indicated by the positive signs of the three covariates measuring the number of waged work, self-employment, and unemployment spells. Thus, instability also reproduces with self-employment.

Interestingly, having a partner now seems to significantly reduce the speed of transition out of self-employment, whatever the occupational status of the partner. As all the employment characteristics of the partner (including nonemployment) show similar effects of stabilizing the person's self-employment, these indicators probably depict more general conditions of the life situation of individuals who have partners. The phase of the life cycle in which an individual has formed his or her own (more or less) stable family is also the one in which he or she has achieved a certain stability in his or her professional life. This may account for the strong "stabilizing" effect of having a partner, which is obviously stronger when the partner also works in the family business, as the high coefficient for the partner being a family worker clearly demonstrates.

Oddly enough, economic well-being, as approximated by GDP at constant prices, augments self-employment instability. As the economic cycle improves, there seem to be increased opportunities for individuals to

TABLE 10.5
Transitions Out of Self-Employment: Binomial Logistic Regression Models in Italy

	Model 1			Model 2		
	All	*Men*	*Women*	*All*	*Men*	*Women*
Sex: female	0.364***			0.442***		
Age	−0.062***	−0.061***	−0.062**	−0.107***	−0.118***	−0.099***
AgeSq	0.002***	0.002***	0.001**	0.002***	0.002***	0.001***
Previous self-employment status (ref: unskilled)						
Professional/ manager	−0.214**	−0.261**	−0.152	−0.356***	−0.405***	−0.265**
Skilled	−0.415***	−0.344**	−0.499***	−0.391***	−0.358**	−0.387**
Education (ref: 1ab)						
Education: 3b	−0.215	−0.220	−0.200	0.135	0.161	0.085
Education: 3a	−0.288	−0.383	−0.426	0.063	−0.094	−0.047
Education: 2c	0.336**	0.535***	−0.037	0.497***	0.680***	0.071
Education: 2b	−0.044	0.102	−0.206	0.095	0.304**	−0.203
Education: 2a	−0.153	0.116	−0.665**	0.005	0.263	−0.526*
Education: 1c	0.084	0.266	−0.198	0.184	0.438**	−0.094
Father's occupation status (ref: unskilled)						
Professional/ manager	0.161*	0.184	0.118	0.228**	0.221	0.254
Skilled	0.071	0.063	0.107	0.176*	0.151	0.245
Farmer	0.325***	0.410***	0.157	0.396***	0.427***	0.302
Father Self-employed	−0.298***	−0.462***	0.045	−0.264***	−0.427***	0.078
Last Occupational branch (ref: mining, manuf.)						
Other services	−0.245**	−0.165	−0.415**	−0.298**	−0.128	−0.564***
Wholesale, retail, hotels	−0.623***	−0.522***	−0.772***	−0.597***	−0.555***	−0.704***
Construction	−0.279**	−0.193	−4.655	−0.301**	−0.189	−4.479
Partner's occupation status (ref: other)						
Waged worker	−0.548***	−0.631***	−0.562***	−0.487***	−0.634***	−0.365**
Self-employed	−0.566***	−0.550***	−0.705***	−0.577***	−0.608***	−0.629***
Family worker	−2.185***	−2.221***	−2.336***	−2.059***	−2.065***	−2.338***
Unemployed/ NLF	−0.723***	−0.686***	−1.071***	−0.590***	−0.567***	−0.895***

TABLE 10.5 (*continued*)

	Model 1			Model 2		
	All	*Men*	*Women*	*All*	*Men*	*Women*
Timeself				0.008	0.008	0.026**
Number of previous jobs as waged worker				0.076***	0.068***	0.101**
Number of previous jobs as self-employed				0.161***	0.168***	0.151***
Number of previous unemployment spells				0.175**	0.294***	0.025
GDP				0.985***	1.123***	0.825***
Unemployment rate				0.045	0.068	—
Period exiting self-employment (ref: 1980–85)						
1986–91				−1.666***	−2.145***	−0.939***
1992–97				−2.854***	−3.560***	−1.836***
Constant	−1.651***	−1.754***	−0.997**	−9.272***	−10.118***	−7.721***
R^2	0.148	0.085	0.085	0.169	0.179	0.155
N	12,992	9,253	3,739	12,992	9,253	3,739

* $p < 0.05$ ** $p < 0.01$, *** $p < 0.001$

leave their independent positions in the market. The effect of GDP is stronger for men than for women. We shall return to this point when commenting on models in table 10.6 and 10.6.

Last but not least, the period effect, inserted as a control variable in the second model presented in table 10.5, reveals a sustained decrease in paths out of self-employment between the 1980s and 1990s. This is a significant finding because it contradicts the hypothesis of a growing outflow from self-employment. Conversely, the marked diminution of this outflow signaled by the period effect indicates that neither self-employment instability nor self-employment turnover is increasing, as the precarization theory hypothesizes. As already seen in the case of self-employment inflows, however, the development of self-entrepreneurial paths is quite different, given the heterogeneous composition of independent work. Therefore, to specify the underlying structure of Italian self-employment better, as well as the dynamics of its components, we must refer to models that analyze outflows from self-employment distinctly by professional type (tables 10.6, 10.6).

TABLE 10.6
Transitions Out of Self-Employment: Multinomial Logistic Regression Models in Italy

	Professional/manager			Skilled			Unskilled		
	All	Men	Women	All	Men	Women	All	Men	Women
Sex (ref: males)	0.350***			0.424**			0.254*		
Age	−0.053**	−0.046*	−0.054	−0.092***	−0.107***	−0.072*	−0.073***	−0.066*	−0.096**
AgeSq	0.001**	0.002**	0.001	0.002***	0.002***	0.001	0.002***	0.002**	0.002**
Education (ref: 1ab)									
Education: 3b	−0.367**	−0.426**	−0.497	0.215	1.467	−0.592	−5.089	−7.965	−4.637
Education: 3a	−0.427	−0.550	−0.637	0.059	0.202	0.670	−3.857	−5.49	0.480
Education: 2c	0.244	0.422**	−0.359	0.823**	1.374*	0.628	0.329	−0.594	−0.107
Education: 2b	−0.348**	−0.328	−0.434	0.183	0.409	−0.480	0.392*	0.996***	−0.239
Education: 2a	−0.559	−0.173	−1.433**	−0.001	0.257	−0.755	0.162	0.217	0.521
Education: 1c	0.181	0.239	0.012	−0.204	0.134	−0.579	0.501*	0.644*	—
Father's Occupation status (ref: unskilled)									
Professional/manager	0.014	0.238	−0.199	0.465*	0.081	1.479***	0.342*	0.209	0.501**
Skilled	0.052	0.213	−0.109	−0.096	−0.420*	0.749**	0.269*	0.496*	0.180
Farmer	−0.076	0.018	−0.007	0.308*	0.232	0.641*	0.599***	0.716***	0.247
Father self-employed	−0.275**	−0.319**	−0.073	−0.367**	−0.583***	0.145	−0.165	−0.540**	0.351*
Last Occupational Branch (ref: mining, manuf.)									
Other services	0.221	0.079	0.440	−0.281	−0.096	−0.885***	−0.803***	−1.197***	−0.696***

Wholesale, retail, hotels	−0.270	−0.308	−0.226	−0.535**	−0.359*	−1.070**	−1.022***	−1.530***	−0.853***
Construction	0.348	0.337	−5.660	−0.210	−0.197	—	−0.873***	−1.256	
Partner's Occupation Status (ref: other)									
Waged worker	−0.825***	−0.778***	−1.075***	−0.487**	−0.721**	−0.108	−0.244*	−0.448*	−0.222
Self-employed	−0.429**	−0.433	−0.660***	−0.918***	−0.572*	−1.284***	−0.633**	−0.971**	−0.524**
Family worker	−1.958***	−2.065***	−2.098**	−5.514	−5.411	−1.242**	−2.277***	−2.322***	−2.517**
Unemployed, NLF	−0.902***	−0.835***	−1.559***	−0.443**	−0.377*	—	−0.766***	−0.945***	−0.615**
Constant	−2.012***	−2.080***	−1.673*	−1.828***	−1.879***	−0.841	−1.379***	−0.867	−1.141*
TimeSelf	0.000	−0.000	0.020	0.028**	0.044**	0.034	0.003	−0.009	0.035*
Number of previous jobs as waged worker	0.080***	0.067**	0.228***	0.106***	0.133***	0.089	0.058*	0.062	0.065
Number of previous jobs as self-employed	0.144***	0.147***	0.157***	0.177***	0.170***	0.355*	0.396***	0.574***	0.196***
Number of previous unemployment spells	0.280**	0.503***	−0.742**	0.158	0.030	0.084	0.219**	0.258	0.241*
GDP	0.624***	0.557**	0.776**	1.513***	2.015***	1.310***	1.146***	1.706***	0.818**
Unemployment rate	0.145	0.174	0.065	0.016	0.108	−0.260	−0.160	−0.153	−0.164
Period exiting self-employment (ref: 1980–85)									
1986–91	−1.426***	−1.462***	−1.324**	−2.463***	−3.892***	−0.896	−1.546***	−2.656***	−0.479
1992–97	−2.618***	−2.500***	−2.694***	−4.197***	−6.083***	−2.187**	−2.169***	−4.196***	−0.282
Constant	−7.301***	−6.876***	−7.725***	−13.466***	−17.449***	−9.543***	−8.843***	−12.220***	−6.946***

TABLE 10.6 (continued)

Fitting values	All		Men		Women	
	Baseline model	Additional model	Baseline model	Additional model	Baseline model	Additional model
Professional-managers						
R^2	0.104	0.175	0.104	0.175	0.138	0.214
N valid observations	5,581	5,581	4,002	4,002	1,579	1,579
Skilled						
R^2	0.069	0.157	0.081	0.190	0.143	0.198
N valid observations	3,912	3,912	2,982	2,982	930	930
Unskilled						
R^2	0.157	0.266	0.210	0.348	0.133	0.235
N valid observations	3,499	3,499	2,269	2,269	1,230	1,230

* $p < 0.05$ ** $p < 0.01$ *** $p < 0.001$

The models in table 10.6 confirm that leaving self-employment is more frequent among women than among men, and among young people than among older workers. Thus far, these have been the most common features of the various transitions examined. As in the case of self-employment inflows, institutional factors play a specific role in structuring the paths out of the self-employment configurations. High education level (3a and 3b) protracts the stability of free professionals' self-employment; the same effect, for the same category of self-employed, is exerted by secondary technical education (2a, 2b). General secondary education (*Licei*, 2c) seems to favor abandonment of the origin state of self-employment, an effect that—though not always statistically significant—concerns all kinds of independent positions, but in particular professional males and skilled workers.

Finally, to be noted is that technical and vocational secondary education pushes unskilled autonomous workers out of their unqualified positions, probably by allowing them to enter employment of a higher quality, whether this is qualified wage work or self-employment at a higher skill level.

Social origin is the second dimension noted as influencing subjects' work careers. Also in the case of transitions out of self-employment, the father's profession proves to be an influential variable. Note the negative effect on outflow for those with self-employed origins. The effect is common to all self-employed categories considered, and generally significant. Having been born and growing up in a tradition of self-employment produces a higher degree of attachment to an independent occupational position. At the macro level of structural mechanisms, this effect of social class immobility is well recognized as a characteristic peculiar to the petty bourgeoisie. Nonetheless, shifting our focus to the micro level of social mechanisms, this finding supports the interpretation proposed with regard to the influence of family and kinship relations, which constitute the environment that "socializes" individuals to self-employment, and provides them with self-employment-specific social capital resources.

With regard to the remaining structural determinants of self-employment dynamics, one notes that the occupational sector also exerts an important influence on the paths out of autonomous work positions (table 10.5). The effect is negative with regard to the reference category constituted by mining and manufacturing, in which self-employment is always more unstable. In table 10.6, where the paths out of self-employment are modeled separately by type of origin, the greater instability of industrial self-entrepreneurial activities is confirmed, and statistically significant for paths out of skilled and unskilled positions.

Leaving self-employment from both the service and construction sectors therefore appears to be more unlikely than exiting from industry—a

branch that does not record such high turnover rates with highly fragmented and carousel-type self-entrepreneurial career courses.[14] These
sectors are particularly significant in the case of the unskilled self-
employed, considering that if a service proletariat (Esping-Andersen
1993) does exist among the low qualified self-employed, their self-
employment status is undoubtedly more stable and enduring than that of
industrial artisans.

Finally, the variables relative to the individual's employment career and
labor force experience (number of previous spells as a waged worker in
self-employment, or the number of previous experiences of unemployment) as illustrated in the model in table 10.6, are quite interesting, as
they show—for all kinds of self-employment independently of gender—a
positive effect on outflow transitions. Since age is controlled for, these
variables primarily indicate the level of instability and mobility in the
preceding career, indicating that people with more unstable previous careers also spend less time in self-employment episodes. Therefore, far
from testifying to the increased instability of self-employment in Italy,
the variables in question show who spends relatively more or less time in
self-employment once they enter their independent positions. In fact, as
a general rule, self-employment is highly stable in Italy.

As regards the two macro variables introduced, their explanatory capacity is reversed when compared with the inflow models previously analyzed. The unemployment rate loses significance as a proxy for labor
market conditions, while the opposite holds for GDP, the proxy for more
general macroeconomic conditions, which therefore seems to accelerate
transitions out of self-employment when positive.

Finally, controlling for period effect shows that paths out of self-
employment decreased from 1980 to the end of the 1990s. This effect is
significant for all three kinds of self-employment considered, independently of gender. Only for unskilled women is the effect of the period
not significant, although it is always, as expected, negative.

FINAL CONSIDERATIONS

We have analyzed the dynamics of self-employment in Italy during the
last twenty years. As highlighted, the period observed is particularly significant with regard to both the demise of the Fordist mode of production and the rise of the service economy and the parallel changes that
have taken place in the labor market.

The sustained self-employment growth recorded in the past two decades has induced many observers to interpret these changes in light of
neoliberal economic theory, which criticizes the excessive protection of

dependent employment. When this proved inadequate, an interpretation focused on postmodernist theories was proposed. The latter assumes an underlying process of life-course individualization that parallels the increased precarization of work careers, with a consequent loss of centrality not only of the Fordist idea of a lifelong secure job, but above all of work as a dimension that structures both individuals and society.

The postmodern approach to social life tends to reject the importance of the mechanisms that structured social stratification in Italy in previous decades: family, education, social origin, and employment status. Self-employment and its rapid growth in the 1980s and 1990s are therefore taken to be a signal that a "new" criterion of organizing work and social reproduction is replacing the "traditional" mechanisms of social stratification. We began by recalling the marked heterogeneity of self-employment in Italy, still today partly rooted in traditional and premodern activities, destined to survive for a long time, and partly arising from the economic and technological innovations that transformed the OECD economies from mass production to flexible production systems, thereby producing an economic and productive environment more favorable to small firms and microentrepreneurial activities. We then observed that self-employment is composed mainly of adults, men, skilled, and professional workers with long work experience, embedded in relational circuits well-endowed with social capital, the vital resource for the survival of self-entrepreneurial activities. We showed that such survival protracts itself for extended periods of time, thereby gainsaying hypotheses or scenarios that forecast an increase in self-employment turnover and precarization. We concluded that the Italian self-employed worker is much more similar to an individual rooted in his or her own status, well convinced of his or her professional choice, and well grounded in his or her personal strategy of individualistic mobilization than to a precarized outsider, regardless of the kind of activity or the level of qualification attained.

In addition to analyzing self-employment composition, we have also identified the social stratification cleavages that still segment Italian self-employment. This segmentation, we have claimed, rather than indicating the precarization or balkanization of independent work, is taking the form of the sustained growth of highly qualified independent positions (free professionals in the service class), slightly counterbalanced by a weaker growth of poorly qualified and unskilled (mainly female) self-employment, while a stable quota of qualified artisan work still survives, mostly limited to skilled men.

This polarization process appears to be strongly shaped by the traditional cleavages of social inequality, which therefore do not lose their causal importance in predetermining individuals' life courses as well as their occupational and professional destinies. Human capital, family background, social class, labor market status, and experience still prove to be solid and robust determinants of self-employed and self-entrepreneurial positions. Therefore, as shown by our analysis, the thesis of the "end of work," of the "corrosion of character," of the growing precarization in the labor market and of postmodernity seem not to furnish a proper understanding of the composition and dynamics of Italian self-employment. The sharp increase in service-class independent positions is the main phenomenon displayed by the evolution of Italian self-employment during the last two decades, and the effects of vocational training and low technical education for entries into professional self-employment and of the professional skills accumulated in previous waged work for entries into skilled self-employment testify that self-employment has played an important role in enabling mid-low educated individuals to scale the class barrier in Italy.

Nonetheless, the possibility that an increasing process of self-employment polarization is taking place in the Italian labor market, as signaled by the growth of autonomous unqualified positions, should be taken seriously. This scenario, in fact, both raises new problems and imposes new kinds of social risk, thus burdening a part of the independent labor force already less or not at all protected by a public welfare system primarily intended to safeguard dependent workers.

While the old and new professional self-employed are protected against social risks by their strong market position, as well as by their ascribed social belongings, the unskilled self-employed are, in the Italian "subprotective" welfare regime, undoubtedly those most vulnerable to the new social risks. That, however, is a different story.

NOTES

For helpful comments on earlier drafts, we thank Walter Müller. The usual disclaimers apply.

1. As elsewhere in Europe, self-employment in Italy incorporates a large variety of categories, including both individuals well furnished with human and social resources and those who are poorly educated and socially isolated. Small and micro entrepreneurs and business proprietors, professionals, and artisans are generally referred to as "self-employed," as well as unskilled autonomous workers, both manual and nonmanual. Given that no strict legal definition of self-employment exists, it is usually defined in opposition to dependent employment, which is characterized by a set of criteria, normally well defined by labor legislation dating back to the Fordist period (i.e., the 1960s and 1970s), according to the main characteristics of the Fordist model of work and production (Supiot 2001).

Therefore, the "new forms" of atypical or pseudo-independent jobs are often "embedded" in self-employment. This problem defining independent activities is mirrored in the current data sets: survey data rely mainly on respondents' self-definition of their labor market status. The specific legal arrangements of work contracts are usually not surveyed, and the only way to get at indications of the diversity of self-employment arrangements is by looking at either determinants of self-employment or sectoral and occupational patterns.

2. More difficult, as well as questionable, is the assessment of the impact of public and state policies tailored to support or encourage self-employment growth. State support for business startup, although scarce in terms of quantity of resources, and uncertain in policy aims, has lasted almost two decades and is mainly targeted at young unemployed and women in disadvantaged areas in southern Italy. In 1986 Law 44/1986 was introduced to help young people develop business plans, and to give them additional support in technical training and business administration. Following in its footsteps, Law 608/1996 offers public support, in the form of subsidized loans, technical assistance, training courses, and vocational programs, to (young) people willing to set up their own (small) business. Targeting women, the so-called positive actions for women's entrepreneurship (Act 215/92 1997) offer access to reduced-rate financing and capital grants to create or modernize a business. Still unclear is the impact on self-employment growth of Law 196/1997, which encourages enterprises and informal (or pseudo self-employed) workers to "rise to the surface" of the legal and formal economy. The real impact of these programs and active labor market policies is hard to assess. No real monitoring has been done to evaluate the efficacy of public support in the subsidized firms' survival rates. Recent studies, however, have shown that mainly educated, mid-high social origin claimants benefited more readily from this form of state-subsidized self-entrepreneurship (Barbieri 2003a).

3. An analogous trend is not apparent among waged workers.

4. According to the European Community Household Panel 1994 data, transitions between self-employment and unemployment are also limited. Between 1993 and 1994, paths in and out were 0.8% in Italy, compared with 2.1% in Germany and 4.2% in Great Britain (Barbieri 1998).

5. In addition, the period covered also reduces problems concerning the reliability of retrospective data (Elias 1996; Gershuny and Hannan 1997).

6. The previous industrial branch classification was reduced in the multinomial models.

7. We stress that we are dealing with survival rates in self-employment status, which does not necessarily mean surviving in the same business.

8. The outcome could have been different if transitions had also considered passages among subsequent spells but with the same employment status (i.e., from self-employed to self-employed versus from waged work to waged work). In this case, there would have been a greater risk of a self-employment spell resulting from unification of subsequent adjacent self-employment spells. However, given that in the analysis shown in table 10.1 the destination states are radically different from the origin states, the said risk does not exist. We also point out that in the retrospective ILFI records, all spells are one month or longer, which also enables the recording of brief and transitory unemployment passages.

9. These results are also meaningful when other data sets are considered, e.g., Eurobarometer 1996, which allow for similar (but not identical) comparisons, and which allow GHQ and work involvement indexes to be compared between self-employed and waged workers. The self-employed appear to be less stressed than waged workers, and definitely more committed to and involved with their jobs.

10. To clarify the point, we reiterate that we used yearly person spells falling inside a fixed observation window (1980–7). By analyzing only yearly person spells since 1980, we left room for left-censoring of careers that started before 1980 but were considered as having formally started in 1980. This could be criticized: to shorten the length of the spell theoretically can affect the transition rate. To control for the length of the "previous spell," we inserted a variable that simply reports that length until the beginning of the observation windows (1980). As we show, the choice of keeping the observation windows fixed did not raise particular problems.

11. This is also due to the fact that, according to the common research guidelines, we considered subsequent self-employment spells, if not interrupted by periods of unemployment or in waged work, as constituting a unique episode of self-employment.

12. A specific interaction (not shown here) was added to the model to test the hypothesis of intergenerational transmission of high self-employment positions. Graduate descendants of professional self-employed fathers have better chances of becoming professionally self-employed after leaving the educational and training system, that is, from first-job search. This is a quite reasonable result, given the way that the market of the free professions is currently structured in Italy. It is extremely closed and protected, left to self-regulation by the professional corporations themselves, whose concern is to restrict and to select entries as much as possible. This mechanism of corporatist regulation favors he offspring of professionals, who take the place of their fathers as notaries, lawyers, doctors, chemists, and so on. This is how the classical liberal service class professions reproduce themselves by enacting a strategy of social boundary-marking intended to prevent, as far as possible, entry by outsiders (Weber 1922).

13. This interpretation is also supported by the fact that, in the complete model shown in table 10.4, the effect of being a first-job seeker loses all significance in the case of transitions to unskilled self-employment positions, while the parameter for unemployment maintains all its causal relevance, for both genders. The complete model is available, as usual, on request.

14. In Italy, firm turnover rates for the 1980–90 period were 15.5 for manufacturing; 29.0 for construction; 21.1 for wholesale, retail, hotels; and 14.0 for business services (Contini 2002). This trend remains valid when only small and micro activities are considered.

References

Allison, P. D. 1984. *Event history analysis: Regression for longitudinal event data.* Beverly Hills: Sage Publications.

Arum R. 1997. Trends in male and female self-employment: Growth in a middle class or increasing marginalization of the labor force? *Research in Stratification and Mobility* 15:209–38.

———. 2001. Entrepreneurs and laborers: Two sides of self-employment activity in the United States. Ms.

Barbieri, P. 1998a. Lavoro autonomo "di seconda generazione": problemi e prospettive. *Polis* 2.

———. 1998b. Regolazione istituzionale e redistribuzione dello stigma. *Rassegna Italiana di Sociologia* 2.

———. 1999. Liberi di rischiare: Assetti istituzionali ed individualizzazione dell'offerta di lavoro autonomo. *Stato e Mercato* 2.

———. 2000. Social capital and exits from unemployment. In *Welfare regimes and the experience of unemployment in Europe*, ed. D. Gallie and S. Paugam. Oxford: Oxford University Press.

———. 2001. Self-employment in Italy: Does labor market rigidity matter? *International Journal of Sociology* 31:38–69.

———. 2003a. Capitale sociale e sviluppo locale: un'analisi microrelazionale di una politica attiva del lavoro. *Sociologia del Lavoro* 1.

———. 2003b. Social capital and self-employment: A network analysis experiment and several considerations. *International Sociology*. 18(4).

Barbieri, P., I. Bison, and G. Esping-Andersen. 1999. Italy: Laggard postindustrial society or a great historical u-turn? Paper presented at the European Consortium for Sociological Research meeting, Mannheim, 7–8 September.

Beck, U. 1992. *Risk society: Towards a new modernity*. Beverly Hills: Sage Publications.

———. 2000. *The brave new world of work*. Malden, MA: Polity Press.

Blanchflower, D. G. 1998. Self-employment in OECD countries. Paper presented at the CILN Conference, Ontario.

Blossfeld, H., and G. Rohwer. 1995. Techniques of event history modeling: New approaches to causal analysis. Mahwah, NJ: Lawrence Erlbaum.

Blumberg, B., and G. Pfann. 2001. Social capital and the uncertainty reduction of self-employment. IZA Discussion Paper 303.

Bologna, S., and A. Fumagalli, eds. 1997. *Il lavoro autonomo di seconda generazione: scenari del postfordismo in Italia*. Milan: Feltrinelli.

Brüderl, J., and P. Preisendörfer. 1998. Network support and the success of newly founded businesses. *Small Business Economics* 10.

Cappellari, L. 1999. Low-wage mobility in the Italian labour market. *Warwick Economics Research Paper Series* 531.

Coleman, J. S. 1990. *Foundations of social theory*. Cambridge: Harvard University Press.

Contini, B. 2002. *Osservatorio sulla mobilità del lavoro in Italia*. Bologna: Mulino.

Elias, P. 1996. Who forgot they were unemployed? In *Working Papers of the ESRC Research Centre on Micro-social Change* 97-19. Essex: University of Essex.

Esping-Andersen, G., ed. 1993. *Changing classes: Stratification and mobility in post-industrial societies*. Beverly Hills: Sage Publications.

Esping-Andersen, G., and M. Regini, eds. 2000. *Why deregulate labour markets?* Oxford: Oxford University Press.

Gallie, D., et al. 1998. *Restructuring the employment relationship*. Oxford: Clarendon Press.

Gallie, D., and S. Paugam. 2000. *Welfare regimes and the experience of unemployment in Europe*. Oxford: Oxford University Press.

Gershuny, J., and C. Hannan. 1997. Unemployment: Blame the victim? *Working Papers of the ESRC Research Centre on Micro-social Change* 97-23. Essex: University of Essex.

Grubb, D., and W. Wells. 1993. Employment regulation and patterns of work in EC countries, *OECD Economic Studies* 21.

Hall, P. A., and D. Soskice, eds. 2001. *Varieties of capitalism: The institutional foundations of comparative advantage*. Oxford: Oxford University Press.

Istat. 1999. *Struttura e competitività del sistema delle imprese industriali e dei servizi*. Rome: Istat.

———. 2000. *Rapporto Istat* (Istat Report). Rome: Istat.

König, W., P. Lüttinger, and W. Müller. 1988. A comparative analysis of the development and structure of educational systems: Methodological foundations and the construction of a comparative educational scale. *CASMIN Working Paper* 12. Mannheim: University of Mannheim.

Locke, R. M. 1995. *Remaking the Italian economy*. Ithaca: Cornell University Press.

OECD. 1992. *Employment outlook*. Paris: OECD.

———. 1994. *Employment outlook*. Paris: OECD.

———. 1999. *Employment outlook*. Paris: OECD.

———. 2000. *Employment outlook*. Paris: OECD.

Pizzorno, A. 1980. *I soggetti del pluralismo: classi, partiti, sindacati*. Bologna: Mulino.

Reyneri, E. 2002. *Sociologia del mercato del lavoro*. Bologna: Mulino.

Robson, M. T. 1997. The relative earnings from self and paid employment: A time series analysis for the UK. *Scottish Journal of Political Economy* 44.

———. 1998. The rise in self-employment amongst UK males. *Small Business Economics* 10.

———. 2000. Does stricter employment protection legislation promote self-employment? Ms. Durham: University of Durham, Department of Economics and Finance.

Rosti, L. 1987. L'occupazione indipendente in Italia: stock e flussi. *Economia e Lavoro* 4.

Schizzerotto, A., and M. Pisati. 1999. Pochi promossi, nessun bocciato: La mobilità di carriera in Italia in prospettiva comparata e longitudinale. *Stato e Mercato* 56.

Sennet, R. 1998. *The corrosion of character: The personal consequences of work in the new capitalism*. New York: Norton.

Sestito, P. 1989. Alcune note sull'occupazione indipendente in Italia. *Economia e Lavoro* 3.

Shavit, Y., and W. Müller, eds. 1998. From school to work: A comparative study of educational qualifications and occupational destinations. Oxford: Clarendon Press.

Supiot, A. 2001. Beyond employment: Changes in work and the future of labour law in Europe. Oxford: Oxford University Press.

Università degli Studi di Trento e Istituto Trentino di Cultura. 1997. *Indagine Longitudinale sulle Famiglie Italiane*. File dati su supporto magnetico.

Weber, M. 1922. *Wirtschaft und Gesellschaft*. Tübingen: Mohr.

Whelan, C. T., D. F. Hannan, and S. Creighton. 1991. *Unemployment, poverty and psychological distress*. Dublin: Economic and Social Research Institute.

Yamaguchi, K. 1991. *Event history analysis*. Beverly Hills: Sage Publications.

CHAPTER ELEVEN

Entry into and Exit from Self-Employment in Japan

Hiroshi Ishida

THE SELF-EMPLOYED and their family workers have long been a substantial and dynamic component of the post-war Japanese economy. The rapid economic development of the 1960s and early 1970s transformed small businesses: the number and proportion of nonagricultural self-employed increased, and many experienced increased profits and made technological improvements and other investments (Kiyonari 1990). Small businesses, which include the self-employed, family workers, and small employers and employees in firms with less than three hundred employees, make up more than two-thirds of the Japanese labor force. The self-employed constitute 11 percent of the total labor force, and family workers account for another 3 percent, according to the 2000 Japanese Census. The proportion of self-employed among all workers was at its highest (26 percent) in 1950, and it has been continuously declining since then. The decline is primarily due to the reduction of self-employment in agriculture, but there has also been a decline in nonagricultural self-employment since 1980. Despite the declining trend, self-employment is considered an active sector in the Japanese economy.

The self-employed are composed of a variety of people in the labor market, and this chapter will attempt to show their diversity. The chapter is organized as follows. First, I will describe the sociolegal context of self-employment in Japan. I will also review previous research on self-employment and show how the chapter builds on and expands on previous work. Second, I will explain the data set, statistical methods, and variables used in the analyses. Third, I will present detailed descriptive accounts of self-employment activities in Japan, both government statistics and micro work-history data. Fourth, I will examine the determinants of entry into and exit from self-employment, using survival curves and multivariate event history models. Finally, I will discuss the interpretations and implications of the major findings from the multivariate analyses.

The Sociolegal Context of Self-Employment in Japan

The Small and Medium Enterprise Basic Law, enacted in 1963, is probably one of the most important and systematic governmental regulations related to small business in Japan (Kiyonari 1990). It defines small enterprise owners as those who employ less than five workers in wholesale, retail, and service industries, and those who employ less than twenty workers in manufacturing and other industries. These owners are often considered self-employed, although the Small and Medium Enterprise Basic Law does not use the phrase "self-employed." The 1999 amendment to the law stated that government policies aimed to support the diversification and growth of independent small and medium-sized enterprises by promoting business innovation and new business startups, strengthening the management base of small and medium-sized enterprises, and facilitating adaptation to economic changes (Small and Medium Enterprise Agency 2002).

Various policies of both the national and local governments offered support to small and medium-sized firms, including financial assistance in the form of loans and other subsidies, development of human resources and technology among small and medium-sized firms, and tax benefits for owners of small and medium-sized enterprises. Financial assistance comes primarily from the three major government agencies that are responsible for providing long-term loans for capital investment and short-term financing such as bill discounting: the National Life Finance Corporation (3.2 trillion yen), the Japan Finance Corporation for Small Business (1.9 trillion yen), and Shoko Chukin Bank (1.9 trillion yen). The amounts in parentheses indicate total planned loan investments in 2002 (Small and Medium Enterprise Agency 2002). In addition, financial assistance is provided to encourage the creation of new small businesses, including a new startup loan program which was established in January 2002 and administered by the National Life Finance Corporation. It provides loans of up to 5.5 million yen to small business without the need for collateral or guarantors.

To promote innovation and human resource development, eight national support centers established by local governments offer advisory services and consultations with legal experts and organize training seminars for business management. There are special budgets in the national government for assisting the development of new technology, the commercialization of technological innovation, and business innovation using information technology among small firms.

Some government regulations were intended to restrict the entrance of large-scale firms into the market. For example, the Large-scale Retail

Stores Law was enacted in 1974 to protect small-scale shop owners. Large retailers planning to open a new store were required to notify the government office and participate in an adjustment process that was designed to consider the interests of local small retailers and consumers. However, the law was modified during the 1990s and eventually abolished in June 2000, allowing easier expansion by large retailers, including foreign businesses. Nonetheless, it contributed greatly to the proliferation and persistence of small-scale neighborhood stores in Japan in the 1970s and 1980s (Upham 1993; Schoppa 1997).

Small business owners are eligible for various tax benefits. Unlike employees, whose income tax is automatically deducted from their income, the self-employed report their own income, and are able to deduct a variety of business expenses, including advertising, depletion, depreciation, insurance, rent, repairs, taxes, travel, utilities, and wages. When there is loss from business, the self-employed may deduct the loss from income in the following three years. In addition, when gross sales are less than 30 million yen, the self-employed are exempt from paying sales tax. Tax incentives are also provided under the "Angel tax system," to encourage personal investors ("angels") to invest in small business. These tax benefits greatly aid the operation of self-employed businesses in Japan (Ministry of Labor Women's Bureau 1999).

Previous Research

Economists have been concerned with the role of self-employment in the Japanese economy for some time. Two prominent themes in the study of small business in Japan are apparent. First, small businesses in manufacturing are often involved in a complex web of subcontracting relationship with parent firms. Subcontracting arrangements are typically embedded in long-term social relations, rather than short-term spot transactions (Sako 1992). Subcontracting arrangements also stimulated the emergence of a flexible and innovative form of specialization, because parent firms recognized the need for specialty suppliers. Research on subcontracting relationships thus attracted the attention of economists as well as sociologists of organization and economy (e.g., Piore and Sabel 1984; Nishiguchi 1994; Orru, Biggart, and Hamilton 1997). Second, labor economists were particularly interested in studying how skills are developed in small firms. Koike (1981, 1988, 1994) showed that small firms offer training to their employees and that employees accumulate skills while working on a series of different but related jobs in the workshop. This acquisition of skills often enabled employees of small firms to embark upon their own self-employed business.

More recent studies by economists on self-employment reported the importance of access to capital in the rate of entry into self-employment. Using the National Consumption Survey, Genda (Genda, Ishihara, and Kanbayashi 1998; Genda and Kanbayashi 2001) empirically shows a positive association between the value of household assets and the chances of the household being self-employed. Abe and Yamada (1998) also point out that homeownership is related to the emergence of self-employment among middle-aged and older workers. These studies show the role of assets in predicting entry into self-employment.

Recent sociological studies on social mobility have examined intergenerational stability in self-employment (Hara and Seiyama 1999; Hashimoto 1999, 2000; Jeong 2000, 2002). Ishida (1993, 2000, 2001; Ishida, Goldthorpe, and Erikson 1991) claims that Japanese class origin and class destination distributions in the 1970s and 1980s contained a higher proportion of nonfarm self-employment than the same distributions in other industrial nations, and that the urban self-employed were heavily recruited intergenerationally from both farm and nonfarm self-employed. The relative propensity of intergenerational inheritance among the self-employed was also high compared with other classes. Jeong (2000, 2002) points out that intergenerational inflows from nonfarm self-employment into urban self-employment have increased in recent cohorts, thereby increasing the barriers to entry from other classes.

Studies focusing on career mobility (Seiyama et al. 1990; Hara and Seiyama 1999; Y. Sato 2000) have addressed the question of entry into self-employment during the worker's career. Hara and Seiyama (1999: 82) show that there is a clear path for blue-collar employees working in small and medium-sized firms into manual self-employment, and another path for white-collar employees working in a firm of any size to white-collar self-employment. These studies show the importance of firm size and skill level (blue-collar versus white-collar) in predicting entry into self-employment in Japan.

A number of social surveys specifically targeted at self-employed workers have recently become available in Japan. The most important among these is a series of surveys conducted by the National Life Finance Corporation (NLFC), a government financial institution that has provided a small fund for use by small business. The NLFC has been conducting surveys since 1969 of self-employed who used their funds to start a new business. Because the surveys do not include those who never applied for funds or those whose applications were rejected, the samples inevitably overrepresent the successful self-employed. The results of the surveys, nonetheless, offer an unusually rich description of the conditions and attitudes of the self-employed. The most recent survey in 1999 (National Life Finance Corporation Research Institute 2000), which includes a sample of 1,600 new businesses in all major industrial sectors, shows that 87 percent of entrepreneurs are men. It also shows that a third of the self-employed opened their business while in their thirties, 30 percent in their forties, and 19 percent in their fifties. The founding of a new business is less frequent among very young and very old people.

In the same survey, over 70 percent of entrepreneurs reported that they had worked in small firms with fewer than fifty employees prior to entry into self-employment. Most of the entrepreneurs (85 percent) already had experience in the kind of work they began as self-employed, and they averaged fourteen years of work experience. The three most popular reasons for embarking upon a new business were (marking more than one answer was possible): (1) "to have autonomy and discretion" (47 percent); (2) "to prove my ability" (40 percent); and (3) "to make good use of my previous work career" (33 percent). The improvement of income ("to receive more income than employees") was chosen by only 12 percent. The average startup cost was 17 million yen (about 150,000 U.S. dollars), more than twice the annual salary of an average employee. The average proportion of one's own funds in the startup costs was 31 percent. The main source of alternate funding, other than the NLFC, is "parents, siblings, and relatives" (35 percent), followed by "private financial institutions" (19 percent). About 20 percent of entrepreneurs began their new business alone, and 53 percent had one to four employees at the time of the startup of the new business.

The results of the survey reveal that the self-employed who recently began a new business tended to be ambitious and independent middle-aged men who had previously worked in small firms. Case studies attached to the survey results (National Life Finance Corporation Research Institute 2000) suggest that entry into self-employment was planned well in advance, with previous employment used for preparatory training. These entrepreneurs also used their extensive relationships with relatives and contacts built up during their previous experience to reduce risks and to raise capital.

This study builds on the accumulated knowledge of previous research but expands earlier work in four respects. First, it pays direct attention to occupational divisions among the self-employed. Some previous work distinguished self-employment by industrial sector, but the distinction among professional/managerial, skilled, and unskilled types of self-employment is unique to this study. As shown in the other studies in this volume, these three types represent a variety of forms of self-employment activity in advanced economies, ranging from highly specialized and profitable professional self-employed to the marginalized and often inefficient unskilled self-employed.

Second, it examines both entry into and exit from self-employment using rich work-history data. None of the research discussed above has addressed the question of what determines exit from self-employment. Third, this study uses multivariate analyses of the determinants of entry into and survival in self-employment. In particular, it evaluates the relative impacts of social background on entry into and exit from self-employment. Previous surveys often lacked measures of social background and thus could not investigate the role of social background in self-employment. This study, in contrast, incorporates two measures of social background: the father's self-employment status and the father's occupation. The importance of father's self-employment in entry into self-employment has been pointed out by researchers who analyzed the same national social mobility data set used in this study (Hashimoto 1999, 2000; Ishida 2000, 2001; Jeong 2000, 2002). They show a strong tendency toward intergenerational reproduction of self-employment in postwar Japan. However, these studies do not examine the mechanism of entry into self-employment.[1] This study will take advantage of the rich retrospective work history records of the nationally representative sample to assess the effects of the various factors that determine the chances of entry into and exit from self-employment. For example, it will examine the relative effects of social background, education, and prior labor market characteristics on entry into self-employment.

Finally, this study aims to contribute to the cross-national comparison of entry into and exit from self-employment. The setup of the analyses in this study closely follows the guidelines proposed by Müller, Lohmann, and Luber (1999, 2000), and the results should be comparable to those reported in other chapters. In this respect, it is important to emphasize a significant addition to the otherwise comparable analyses. As pointed out by Koike (1981, 1994) and many others, small firms provide the basis for the accumulation of skills that can eventually be used for becoming independent and self-employed. Our analyses of the Japanese data, therefore, include the effect of firm size on entry into and exit from self-employment. We will examine the role of small firms in facilitating the transition from employee to self-employed.

DATA AND METHODS

This chapter uses the 1995 Social Stratification and Social Mobility (1995 SSM) National Survey conducted in Japan in November 1995 (Hara and Seiyama 1999).[2] The survey is drawn from a sample of Japanese residents between the ages of 20 and 69. The 1995 SSM consists of three different samples, each using different questionnaires; this study uses Survey A, which asked the respondents for their entire work histories.

The response rate for Survey A was 65.8 percent, and the total sample size is 2,653. No weight factor is given by the researchers who conducted the survey, so our analyses are based on a nonweighted sample.[3]

To make our analysis comparable to those of other countries, we restrict the age range of the respondents to those between 20 and 60 years of age. We also exclude respondents who were engaged in agricultural occupations or worked in the agricultural industry. We will present analyses using data covering the period of 1980 to 1995 (for comparisons with other countries), and use data for the entire sample (which will give us a much larger sample size and more stable estimates).

We constructed person-year files using the entire work histories of the respondents. When either the starting year or the ending year is missing, that segment is excluded. When there are multiple entries into self-employment by the same individual, each entry is treated as a separate event. In the entire data set, there are 293 entries into self-employment, which can be broken down by type: 54 in professional/managerial self-employment, 208 in skilled self-employment, and 31 in unskilled self-employment. For the period since 1980, 125 entries into self-employment were observed: 38 into professional/managerial self-employment, 74 into skilled self-employment, and 13 into unskilled self-employment.

We use discrete time event-history models (Allison 1984; Blossfeld, Hamerle, and Mayer 1989). These models allow us to include time-varying covariates in the equation (Yamaguchi 1991; Powers and Xie 2000). Using the person-year file, simple logistic regression models are used to estimate the effects of various independent variables on entry into and exit from self-employment. For the analysis of entry, respondents who were employed, family workers, piecemeal workers, housewives, unemployed, and others who do not have an occupation are at risk. For the analysis of exit, respondents who were self-employed are at risk. Furthermore, for the analysis of entry, we use a multinomial logistic regression model to estimate competing risks of becoming professional/managerial self-employed or skilled self-employed (as compared to the risk of not entering these two categories). Because the number of entries into unskilled self-employment is small, we do not distinguish unskilled self-employment as a distinct destination and instead treat them as censored cases.

We briefly describe below the variables used in our event history analyses. Our dependent variable, self-employment, is determined by a question on employment status. Respondents who reported being "self-employed" are automatically assigned self-employment status. Respondents who reported being part of the "board of directors, and top management" in a firm with less than thirty employees are also assigned self-employment status. This is because the "employment status" question allowed the response of "board of directors, and top management" in addition to "self-employed," "general employees," "part-time employees," "dispatched employees," "family workers," and "piecemeal workers." Some self-employed, especially those who employ others, are likely to select the category of "board of directors, and top management."[4]

Following guidelines proposed by Müller, Lohmann, and Luber (1999, 2000), we restrict our analyses to nonagricultural self-employment, which is further differentiated into three distinct subcategories. Professional/managerial self-employment is composed of respondents who are classified in categories I and II of the Erikson-Goldthorpe-Portocarero (EGP) schema (Erikson, Goldthorpe, and Portocarero 1979; Erikson and Goldthorpe 1992). Skilled self-employment is composed of respondents who are classified in EGP categories IIIa, V, or VI, and unskilled self-employment is composed of those who are classified in EGP categories IIIb or VIIa. We classify self-employed respondents based on their reported occupation, exactly the same way as we do for the respondents who were employees.[5]

The respondent's education is based on CASMIN educational categories (Müller et al. 1989; Shavit and Müller 1998), and the procedure follows exactly the same schema proposed for the Japanese version (Ishida 1998).[6] There are four CASMIN categories: 1abc (minimum compulsory level), used as the base reference category; 2c (high school graduates); 3a (two-year junior college graduates); and 3b (four-year university graduates).

To represent social background, father's occupation and father's self-employment status are constructed. The detailed occupation code of the father's main employment is converted into one of four occupational categories: professional/managerial (EGP categories I or II), skilled (EGP categories IIIa, IVab, V, or VI), farm (EGP categories IVc or VIIb), unskilled (EGP categories IIIb or VIIa), and no occupation. "Unskilled occupation" and "no occupation" are used together as the base reference category. Father's self-employment is a dummy variable constructed using the employment status of the father's main occupation during his career, and developed in the same way as the respondent's self-employment status.

Three sets of time-varying variables are created. First, four categories representing occupation in an "origin state" are constructed. Using information about the respondent's career prior to self-employment, the type of occupation is classified into one of the four categories: professional/managerial (EGP categories I or II), skilled (EGP categories IIIa, IVab, V, or VI), unskilled (EGP categories IIIb or VIIa), and no occupation. The base reference category is, again, the combination of the unskilled and "no occupation" groups. The second set is composed of seven categories of industry classification in origin state, that is, employment prior to entry into self-employment. The detailed Japanese SSM industry codes are converted to NACE70 industrial codes (Eurostat 1996). By collapsing some of the NACE codes, the following categories are created: mining (NACE70 major code C), manufacturing (D), construction (F), traditional services (G and H), transportation and communication (I), finance and business service (J and K), and other services (L through Q). Mining and manufacturing together serve as the base reference category. The third time-varying variable is firm size in origin state. The size of the firm in the origin state is broken down into very small (fewer than 30 employees), small (30–99 employees), and large (100 or more and public sector). The base reference category is the large firm.

For the analyses of exit from self-employment, the origin state refers to self-employment, and we distinguish three types (professional/managerial, skilled, and unskilled), with unskilled as the base reference category. Self-employment is also differentiated according to the industry categories discussed above. With regard to firm size, we use a dummy variable representing solo employment—that is, self-employed working on their own account, without employing others. An additional variable is included in the analyses of exit from self-employment. Duration in self-employment (in years) is included as an independent variable. Finally, demographic variables are included in the analyses of both entry and exit: a "female" variable, which is a dummy variable indicating that the respondent is a female; an "age" variable, which is computed as the respondent's age minus 18; and an "age squared" variable which is a square of "age" variable.

Descriptive Analyses

This section first reviews government macro statistics related to the labor market conditions of the self-employed and dependent employees. The second part uses the 1995 SSM survey and presents a descriptive picture of the self-employed by occupational type.

Figure 11.1, based on Japanese censuses, shows that the number of nonagricultural self-employed increased dramatically from 4.1 million in 1960 to 6.6 million in 1980. However, from 1980 to 2000, the number of nonagricultural self-employed gradually declined to about 5.6 million. The change in relative size of nonagricultural self-employed parallels the change in absolute numbers. The proportion of the nonagricultural self-employed in the total labor force was 9.5 percent in 1960, reached a peak of 11.9 percent in 1980, and declined to 8.8 percent in 2000. According

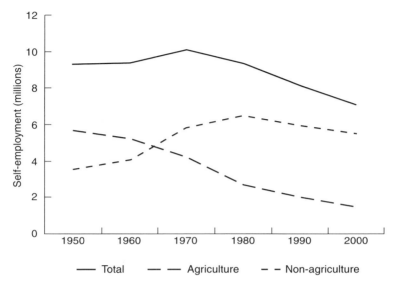

Figure 11.1: Number of Self-Employed by Type of Self-Employment by Year in Japan

to the OECD (OECD 2000:158–61), only a few countries experienced a decline in self-employment in the 1980s and 1990s: Japan, Denmark, and France. Furthermore, Japan is the only country that experienced a decline for both men and women (Genda and Kanbayashi 2001:30). Genda and Kanbayashi (2001) conclude that the declining real value of the household assets during the postbubble economy contributed to the reduction of self-employment in Japan.

When we examine the income distribution of the self-employed and employees in the nonfarm sector (figure not shown), we find that the self-employed are clearly represented more in the lower income groups, especially in the lowest group, with an income of less than 500,000 yen per year. However, the proportion of the self-employed who had more than 15,000,000 yen, the highest income bracket, is greater (2 percent) than that of employees (1 percent). In other words, although the distribution of income among the self-employed is skewed toward the left (lower end), compared with that of employees, a greater proportion of the very wealthy is found among the self-employed than among employees. Income distribution among the self-employed, therefore, is probably more unequal than among employees. Genda and Kanbayashi (2001:32) report that the gini coefficient for the income distribution among the self-employed is 0.454, while the same coefficient among the regular employees is 0.320, according to the results of the Income Redistribution Survey report.

With regard to working hours (figure not shown), the self-employed and family workers tend to work longer hours than employees. More than 20 percent of the self-employed (22 percent) and of family workers (21 percent) work more than sixty hours per week, compared with only 9 percent of employees. The modal category among employees is between thirty-five and forty-two hours (37 percent), while the mode among the self-employed and family workers is the longest category (sixty hours or more).[7]

Government macro statistics presented thus far do not distinguish self-employment into our three types, so we shall now examine the 1995 SSM data. Tables 11.1A and 11.1B present male and female occupational distributions of self-employed and dependent employees by education, industry, and social background, for the pooled data from 1980 to 1995. The unit of analysis is the person-year spell, and the numbers are based on nonagricultural respondents aged 18 to 60. All self-employed (combining tables 11.1A and 11.1B) can be classified into one of the following occupation types: professional/managerial (16 percent), skilled (74 percent), and unskilled (10 percent). The similar occupational distribution for all dependent employees is professional/managerial (23 percent), skilled (51 percent), and unskilled (27 percent). The self-employed are clearly more represented in skilled occupations than in unskilled occupations, while the proportion of the professional/managerial occupation is slightly higher among dependent employees.

An examination of the actual occupations of the self-employed may be instructive here. Those who report their occupation as managers, members of boards of directors, and holders of other upper-level positions constitute 45 percent of the professional-managerial self-employed. They are probably owners of small-scale enterprises and consider their occupations to be the management of employees and their firms' business. The second largest group among the professional-managerial self-employed is "private teachers," comprising about 16 percent. They seem to engage in a variety of teaching activities, including private lessons of piano and traditional Japanese instruments and private tutoring for entrance exam preparation. Two groups, "designers" and "engineers," tie for third at 8 percent each. Lawyers and accountants together comprise another 8 percent.

The skilled self-employed are composed of three main groups. By far the largest group consists of retail and wholesale shop owners (24 percent). If we add restaurant and noodle shop owners (12 percent), these shopkeepers amount to more than a third (36 percent) of all skilled self-employed. A related category consists of those who describe themselves as cooks and beauticians/barbers (7 percent). The second largest group is construction-related work (15 percent): carpenters, plasters, bricklayers, and others. The third largest group is composed of skilled workers in production (11 percent), such as metal processor, machinery fitter, vehicle mechanic, electrical fitter, or machine tool operator. The unskilled self-employed are engaged in a variety of nonskilled occupations. There are two large groups: (1) those who are engaged in personal service-related occupations (23 percent), such as domestic housekeeping service workers and service workers in entertainment, and (2) semiskilled production workers (23 percent), such as paper makers and soy sauce makers. In addition, there are automobile drivers (15 percent) who are most likely independent truck and taxi operators.

Returning to tables 11.1A and 11.1B, we examine the relationship between education and the type of self-employment. A strong association between education and occupational type is found. If men completed only minimum compulsory education or high school education, they are more likely to be engaged in skilled or unskilled self-employment. About two-thirds of the professional/managerial self-employed are graduates of the institutions of higher education (CASMIN categories 3a and 3b), while only 12 percent of the skilled and 8 percent of the unskilled self-employed achieved similar levels of education.[8] The same pattern characterizes women, but the concentration of the highly educated in the professional/managerial occupation is more conspicuous among women.

The type of self-employment and the respondent's industrial sector are also associated. Professional/managerial self-employed are concentrated in the "other service" industrial sector, which includes education, health, public, and personal services (other than financial and real estate). This concentration is greater than the corresponding percentage of professional/managerial employees: 71 percent of professional/managerial self-employed are in "other services," while only 59 percent of professional/managerial employees fall in the same broad sector.[9] The skilled self-employed are more likely to be found in construction and traditional services, such as wholesale and retail. Once again, the concentration among the skilled self-employed is higher than among skilled employees: 64 percent of the skilled self-employed are in construction or traditional services, while only 25 percent of skilled employees work in these sectors. The unskilled self-employed are more evenly spread across different industrial sectors than are other self-employed workers. The same tendency is found among unskilled employees.

Another association exists between social background and type of self-employment. The self-employed, regardless of occupational type, have a much higher proportion of fathers who were self-employed (69 percent), compared with all employees, regardless of occupational type (47 per-

TABLE 11.1A
Male Occupational Distribution of Self-Employed and Dependent Employees in Japan, 1980–95 (in percent)[a]

	Self-employment				Dependent employment				N of row (% in Row)
	Prof.	Skilled	Unskilled	Total	Prof.	Skilled	Unskilled	Total	
Education[b]									
1abc	1.1	27.0	3.7	31.8	4.0	34.3	29.9	68.2	3,472 (26.1)
2c	1.7	15.2	1.7	18.6	15.9	44.7	20.8	81.4	6,413 (48.2)
3a	9.7	9.1	0.0	18.8	45.6	30.9	4.7	81.2	340 (2.6)
3b	5.6	8.1	0.8	14.5	44.7	35.7	5.1	85.5	3,089 (23.2)
Industry sector (NACE classification)									
Manufacturing (C,D,E)	0.7	7.6	1.9	10.2	20.5	51.0	18.3	89.8	3,861 (29.0)
Construction (F)	2.4	31.7	1.6	35.7	11.4	30.3	22.6	64.3	1,679 (12.6)
Traditional service (G, H)	1.6	39.3	0.8	41.7	10.7	35.1	12.5	58.3	2,485 (18.7)
Transport, communication (I)	0.0	1.2	2.1	3.3	12.9	34.8	49.0	96.7	1,352 (10.2)
Finance, business service (J, K)	3.0	15.4	4.2	22.6	13.6	51.4	12.4	77.4	623 (4.7)
Other service (L–Q)[c]	6.8	8.3	2.8	17.9	35.7	34.0	12.3	82.0	3,314 (24.9)
Father's self-employment[d]									
Other employment	1.0	10.4	1.0	12.4	25.4	42.0	20.2	87.6	5,921 (46.0)
Self-employment	4.2	21.7	3.0	28.9	16.1	36.7	18.3	71.1	6,963 (54.0)

Father's occupation[d]								
Professional	8.4	11.2	0.6	20.2	41.7	27.7	10.4	79.8	2,325 (18.9)
Skilled	1.4	21.0	0.9	23.3	19.3	44.3	13.1	76.7	4,566 (37.2)
Unskilled	2.1	11.1	6.2	19.4	12.0	36.8	31.9	80.7	2,010 (16.4)
Agriculture	1.2	19.0	2.6	22.8	13.8	37.4	26.1	77.3	3,382 (27.5)
Time period[e]								
1980–87	2.5	16.6	2.0	21.1	19.4	40.8	18.7	78.9	6,559 (49.3)
1988–95	2.8	16.3	2.0	21.1	21.1	38.4	19.5	79.0	6,755 (50.7)
% in column	2.7	16.5	2.0	21.2	20.2	39.6	19.1	78.9	
N of column	402	2,144	266	2,812	2,700	5,259	2,543	10,502	13,314

[a] Pooled data, 1980–95, ages 18–60. The unit of analysis is person-year spells.

[b] CASMIN educational classification (Müller et al. 1989) was used to define the educational categories.

[c] Other service included health, education, public administration, personal/domestic services, etc.

[d] Father's self-employment status and father's occupation are based on his main employment.

[e] Years as of the starting date of the job spell.

TABLE 11.1B
Female Occupational Distribution of Self-Employed and Dependent Employees in Japan, 1980–95 (in percent)[a]

	Self-employment				Dependent employment				N of row
	Prof.	Skilled	Unskilled	Total	Prof.	Skilled	Unskilled	Total	(% in row)
Education[b]									
1abc	0.0	8.3	1.3	9.6	6.5	38.6	45.3	90.4	1,820 (21.8)
2c	0.7	6.3	0.9	7.9	12.4	53.2	26.4	92.0	4,776 (57.3)
3a	4.3	2.2	0.3	6.8	30.5	47.6	15.1	93.2	1,000 (12.0)
3b	14.0	2.4	0.0	16.4	49.0	30.3	4.2	83.5	736 (8.8)
Industry sector (NACE classification)									
Manufacturing (C,D,E)	0.0	2.3	0.0	2.3	3.2	69.3	25.3	97.8	2,249 (26.9)
Construction (F)	0.0	12.4	0.0	12.4	0.4	56.9	30.2	87.5	225 (2.7)
Traditional service (G, H)	1.3	9.1	1.1	11.5	2.3	38.3	47.8	88.4	2,023 (24.2)
Transport, communication (I)	0.0	9.0	1.2	10.2	6.7	67.7	15.4	89.8	344 (4.1)
Finance, business service (J, K)	0.0	1.3	4.8	6.1	3.5	60.9	29.6	94.0	460 (5.5)
Other service (L–Q)[c]	5.0	6.3	0.7	12.0	40.0	32.3	15.6	87.9	3,045 (36.5)
Father's self-employment[d]									
Other employment	2.8	4.5	0.4	7.7	19.7	49.4	23.3	92.4	4,279 (54.1)
Self-employment	1.7	7.4	1.5	10.6	13.3	45.0	31.1	89.4	3,630 (45.9)

Father's occupation[d]								
Professional	7.0	8.0	0.0	15.0	23.7	47.3	14.1	85.1	1,403 (19.0)
Skilled	2.1	5.8	1.6	9.5	19.4	45.6	25.5	90.5	3,092 (41.9)
Unskilled	0.0	5.5	0.0	5.5	13.9	52.2	28.4	94.5	1,164 (15.8)
Agriculture	0.0	3.5	1.0	4.5	10.6	45.6	39.3	95.5	1,723 (23.3)
Time Period[e]								
1980–87	1.9	6.0	0.6	8.5	16.4	48.8	26.3	91.5	3,761 (45.1)
1988–95	2.3	5.9	1.1	9.3	16.6	46.3	27.9	90.8	4,585 (54.9)
% in column	2.1	5.9	0.9	8.9	16.5	47.4	27.2	91.1	
N of column	178	494	71	743	1,376	3,958	2,269	7,603	8,346

[a] Pooled data, 1980–95, ages 18–60. The unit of analysis is person-year spells.
[b] CASMIN educational classification (Müller et al. 1989) was used to define the educational categories.
[c] Other service included health, education, public administration, personal/domestic services, etc.
[d] Father's self-employment status and father's occupation are based on his main employment.

cent). There is a gender difference in the transmission of self-employment status: men generally have a much higher rate of inheritance than
women. Among the male self-employed, the highest inheritance rate is
found in professional/managerial occupations (83 percent), while the
highest rate among the female self-employed is found in unskilled occupations (78 percent). It is worth noting that the proportion of self-
employed fathers is higher in Japan than in many other nations, and this
reflects in part the fact that the Japanese government historically provided more financial assistance to small business and had extensive policies to protect the domestic self-employment sector.

There is also a tendency for occupational inheritance. For both males
and females, professional/managerial self-employed are more likely to
have a father who was engaged in professional/managerial occupations
than other occupations, and the skilled self-employed are more likely to
have a father who was engaged in skilled occupations than other occupations. With regard to the unskilled self-employed, men are more likely to
have a father with the same occupation, while women are more likely to
have a father who was engaged in skilled occupation. The comparison of
self-employment and dependent employment indicates that the extent of
occupational inheritance of professional/managerial occupation is much
stronger among the self-employed than among employees.

Finally, tables 11.1A and 11.1B report the size of self-employment by
occupational type for the period of 1980–87 and 1988–95. Consistent
with the figures shown in the government macro statistics, there is no
clear tendency toward growth in the total self-employment sector, but
the professional/managerial and unskilled self-employed showed slight
increases at the expense of the skilled. Overall, unlike many other industrial nations, Japan did not experience significant expansion of the self-
employed sector in any occupational group in the 1980s and early 1990s.

Multivariate Analyses

In this section, I report the findings of our multivariate analysis in the
following order. I first examine the determinants of entry into self-
employment, followed by the determinants of exit from self-employment. For each outcome, I show Kaplan-Meier survival curves and present the results of discrete time logistic regression and (for entry
analyses) discrete time multinomial regression.[10]

Figure 11.2 shows Kaplan-Meier survival curves estimating cumulative
likelihood of entry into all types of nonfarm self-employment among
men and women. Respondents who were self-employed were excluded
from the analyses. Respondents who were employees, family workers,

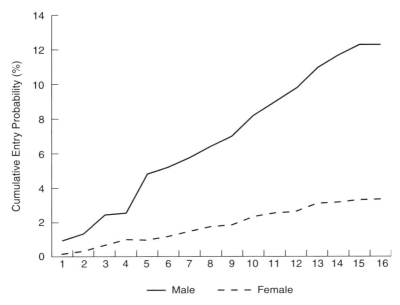

Figure 11.2: Kaplan-Meier Survival Curves Estimating Cumulative Self-Employment Entry Likelihood in Japan

unemployed, or had no occupation (including housewives and househusbands) were considered at risk to become self-employed. Because our comparative setup focuses on the period of the 1980s and 1990s, figure 11.2 is based on observations since 1980. It is clear from the figure that men are more likely to become self-employed than are women. This gender difference emerges after about five years of "waiting time" before becoming self-employed. "Waiting time" can mean participating in the labor market as an employee, being unemployed and not participating in the labor market (e.g., housewives), or some combination of the above. The entry rates are very low and increase by a constant amount among women. Among men, the entry rates are always higher than those of women, and there seems to be a jump after five years.

The same Kaplan-Meier survival curves—this time using observations of all the data including those prior to 1980 (figure not presented)—show that the rates of becoming self-employed seem to increase after fifteen years of waiting time among men, and after twenty years among women. Furthermore, the gender difference widens as waiting time increases. In other words, both men and women face an increased likelihood of entering self-employment after fifteen or twenty years, but the accelerated rate is higher among men. It should be noted that many women who enter self-employment after being at risk for more than twenty years are housewives who do so directly or through the route of part-time employment. Many Japanese women still withdraw from the labor market after marriage or childbirth and return to the market after children grow up, producing an M-shaped curve of labor force participation by age, with higher participation when younger and older, but much less in child-raising years (Brinton 1993). When they re-enter the labor market, they face great difficulties in finding a full-time job comparable to what they held prior to leaving the labor market (Shirahase 1995; Seiyama 1999). Therefore, it is not surprising to see that some women seek self-employment as a means of re-entering the labor market on a full-time basis.

Table 11.2 provides results for simple logistic models of paths into all types of nonfarm self-employment. The first column, labeled "all observations since 1980," refers to the observation window between 1980 and 1995. There were a total of 125 entries into self-employment during this period. Since the number of events (that is, entries into self-employment) is relatively small, we present the results for simple logistic models using all observations in the data set. This observation window refers to the period between 1938 and 1995, which provides a total of 293 events. The overall picture that emerges from the two results is very similar, although the magnitude of the effect and the significance level are sometimes different. We therefore discuss the results of the two columns at the same time.

Females are less likely to move into self-employment than males. The gender gap is highly significant and substantial: men are about three times (using observations since 1980) to four times (using all observations in the data) more likely to become self-employed than women. We have already seen this gender gap in the survival curves, but the multivariate analyses confirm that the gender difference remains even after controlling for social background, education, age, and prior labor market characteristics. In other words, the advantage enjoyed by men with respect to transition to self-employment is not explained by men's better education and prior labor market characteristics.

There is a curvilinear effect of age on entry into self-employment. Although the effects of age and age-squared are not significant in the first column, it is probably safe to conclude that there is an inverted U-shaped relationship between age and entry into self-employment.[11] This relationship implies that the chances of entry into self-employment are low at the early stage of the life cycle, increase when individuals are middle-aged, and decrease again late life. The chances of becoming self-employed are not uniform across the life cycle, and they show nonlinear change.

TABLE 11.2
Entry into All Types of Self-Employment in Japan since 1980

	All observations since 1980		All observations in the data	
Female	− 1.119**	(0.232)	− 1.450**	(0.159)
Age	0.013	(0.034)	0.043*	(0.021)
Age squared[a]	− 0.050	(0.081)	− 0.147*	(0.059)
Education (*ref: 1abc*)				
2c	− 0.272	(0.255)	− 0.421*	(0.146)
3a	0.154	(0.426)	0.058	(0.276)
3b	− 0.237	(0.335)	− 0.405*	(0.218)
Father's occupation (*ref: unskilled, no occupation*)				
Professional	1.099**	(0.363)	0.650**	(0.231)
Skilled	0.252	(0.345)	0.053	(0.212)
Farmer	− 0.381	(0.395)	− 0.291	(0.233)
Father self-employed	0.961**	(0.223)	0.711**	(0.149)
Occupation in origin state (*ref: unskilled, no occupation*)				
Professional	0.076	(0.333)	− 0.204	(0.235)
Skilled	0.466*	(0.238)	0.310*	(0.146)
Industrial sector in origin state (*ref: mining, manuf.*)				
Construction (F)	0.932**	(0.338)	0.636**	(0.224)
Traditional service (G/H)	1.033**	(0.261)	1.130**	(0.162)
Transport, communication (I)	− 0.655	(0.612)	− 0.658	(0.341)
Finance, business service (J/K)	0.644	(0.436)	0.416	(0.331)
Other service (L–Q)	0.474	(0.280)	0.476*	(0.185)
Constant	− 6.166**	(0.528)	− 5.528**	(0.288)
Number of observations	23,878		46,066	
Number of events	125		293	
Pseudo R^2	0.078		0.080	
Log likelihood	− 676.8		− 1544.0	
Firm size in origin state (*ref: 100+ and public*)				
Very small (less than 30)	1.710**	(0.267)	1.653**	(0.175)
Small (30–99)	0.552	(0.349)	0.514*	(0.241)
Number of observations	17,393		34,323	
Number of events	125		293	
Pseudo R^2	0.102		0.102	
Log likelihood	− 576.1		− 1328.8	

Note: Standard errors are in parentheses.

[a] The coefficient for age squared is multiplied by 100 for ease of presentation.

* $p < 0.05$ ** $p < 0.01$

Educational attainment does not increase the likelihood of entering self-employment. Since the effect of education is estimated after controlling for prior labor market characteristics, it is possible that the effect is mediated by these characteristics. To test this possibility, we estimated a reduced form equation model using only education and social background as independent variables for observations since 1980. The effects of educational categories were still not significant. This is probably one of the most interesting findings of the analyses of entry into self-employment. Contrary to the studies in some industrial nations, including those in this volume, Japanese education does not seem to facilitate the transition into self-employment. If anything, the coefficients using all observations in the data set suggest that education lowers the chances of entry into self-employment. High school graduates and university graduates are less likely to enter self-employment than those with minimum compulsory education. I will take up this finding again later in the chapter, and discuss the possible reasons and implications.

Social background affects the likelihood of entry into self-employment. Individuals whose father was engaged in professional or managerial occupation are two (using all observations) to three times (using observations since 1980) more likely to move into self-employment than those with a father who was an unskilled worker or did not work. Additionally, father's self-employment has a significant and substantial effect on entry into self-employment. People with a self-employed father are about two times more likely to become self-employed. It should be noted that these effects are net of demographic factors, education, and prior labor market characteristics. In other words, the gross effects of social background, both direct and indirect, are much larger than those reported in the table.

Labor market characteristics prior to becoming self-employed are associated with the chances of entry into self-employment. Two sets of characteristics are considered in our analyses: the type of occupation and the type of industry in which the respondents were engaged as an employee in the previous year. When the respondents did not work prior to entry into self-employment, they are included in the base reference category. Individuals who worked as skilled workers are more likely to move into self-employment than those who worked as unskilled workers or those who were not in the labor market during the previous year. Accumulated skills from the workplace appear to increase the chances of becoming self-employed. Employees in the construction and traditional service (such as wholesale, retail, hotel, and restaurants) sectors are also more likely to enter self-employment. Both of these sectors are characterized by a high proportion of small-scale, often family-operated, firms. According to the 1997 Employment Status Survey (Statistics Bureau, 1998), 85 percent of employees in the construction industry and 72 percent of employees in the wholesale and retail trade industry (including restaurants) worked in small firms (with one to nine employees). In other words, there are plenty of examples of self-employed workers in these sectors, and work experience here seems to have the same kind of effect as does the acquisition of skills in other sectors.

The last section of table 11.2 presents selected results of running simple logistic models with two firm-size dummy variables added to the original equation.[12] I present only the coefficients for the two dummy variables: the "very small" firm (fewer than 30 employees) and the "small" firm (30 to 99 employees). The reference category includes medium-sized and large firms as well as the public sector. It is clear from the two samples (either using observations since 1980 or all observations in the data) that individuals who worked in a very small firm in the previous year are more likely to enter self-employment than those who worked in medium-sized or large firms or in the public sector. Prior experience in a very small firm, regardless of industry or occupation, increases the chances of entry into self-employment. Because these small firms are usually managed by the self-employed, exposure to an environment run by a self-employed manager probably increases the chances that one will enter self-employment. It is also possible, of course, that limited promotion opportunities in small firms encourage employees to seek self-employment as a way of advancing their career.

The inclusion of firm size variables also changes the effects of other variables in the equation (not shown in the table). Most noticeably, the effect of the construction industry is substantially reduced and becomes nonsignificant. Similarly, the effect of the traditional service industry is reduced by a large amount, although it remains significant. This implies that it is not experience specific to the construction industry that induces entry into self-employment, but rather the experience of working in a very small firm, because the construction industry, as shown above, is dominated by small firms.

Table 11.3 shows the results of multinomial regression models by distinguishing two types of self-employment. It is a competing risk event-history model. We did not include unskilled self-employment as a possible destination because there were very few cases of entries into unskilled self-employment, and entries into unskilled self-employment are treated as censored observations. We will focus on the difference in the determinants of entry into professional/managerial self-employment and into skilled self-employment. As noted below, the pattern observed in table 11.2, which treated all entries into self-employment identically, is more visible among the skilled self-employed than among the professional/managerial self-employed because the number of entries into skilled self-employment is much higher.

Females are less likely to move into either professional/managerial

TABLE 11.3
Entry into Two Different Types of Self-Employment in Japan since 1980

	All observations since 1980				All observations in the data			
	Professional		Skilled		Professional		Skilled	
Female	−0.793*	(0.420)	−1.391**	(0.321)	−0.906*	(0.353)	−1.610**	(0.199)
Age	−0.092	(0.057)	0.103*	(0.051)	−0.025	(0.046)	0.093**	(0.028)
Age squared[a]	0.216	(0.129)	−0.289*	(0.127)	0.096	(0.109)	−0.327**	(0.085)
Education (ref: 1abc)								
2c	−0.245	(0.616)	−0.205	(0.311)	0.112	(0.493)	−0.481**	(0.166)
3a	0.761	(0.701)	−1.205	(1.057)	1.369*	(0.556)	−0.805	(0.479)
3b	0.204	(0.681)	−0.215	(0.439)	0.337	(0.557)	−0.598*	(0.268)
Father's occupation (ref: unskilled, no occupation)								
Professional	1.752*	(0.762)	0.788	(0.469)	0.933*	(0.504)	0.734*	(0.299)
Skilled	0.330	(0.784)	0.149	(0.411)	−0.347	(0.526)	0.317	(0.265)
Farmer	−1.195	(1.032)	−0.530	(0.478)	−1.914	(0.750)	0.114	(0.287)
Father self-employed	0.878**	(0.362)	1.097*	(0.305)	1.106**	(0.307)	0.516**	(0.181)
Occupation in origin state (ref: unskilled, no occupation)								
Professional	1.713**	(0.647)	−2.497*	(1.054)	1.426**	(0.513)	−1.247**	(0.428)
Skilled	0.806	(0.620)	0.538*	(0.298)	0.560	(0.478)	0.484**	(0.171)

Industrial sector in origin state (ref: mining, manuf.)								
Construction (F)	0.748	(0.687)	1.060*	(0.424)	0.583	(0.657)	0.602*	(0.254)
Traditional service (G/H)	−0.265	(0.678)	1.376**	(0.333)	0.393	(0.468)	1.268**	(0.186)
Transport, communication (I)	—[b]		−0.524	(0.761)	—[b]		−0.905*	(0.435)
Finance, business service (J/K)	0.271	(0.805)	0.729	(0.588)	0.575	(0.666)	0.310	(0.412)
Other service (L–Q)	0.610	(0.445)	0.292	(0.433)	0.630	(0.385)	0.285	(0.243)
Constant	−7.545**	(1.121)	−7.170**	(0.704)	−8.154**	(0.801)	−6.112**	(0.356)
Number of observations	23,878		23,878		46,066		46,066	
Number of events	38		74		54		208	
Pseudo R^2	0.143		0.173		0.121		0.149	
Log likelihood	−631.9		−538.7		−1451.0		−1238.2	

Firm size in origin state (ref: 100+ and public)								
Very small (less than 30)	1.118*	(0.457)	2.208**	(0.416)	1.924**	(0.391)	1.643**	(0.218)
Small (30–99)	0.237	(0.541)	0.988*	(0.534)	0.051	(0.531)	0.673*	(0.290)
Number of observations	17,393		17,393		34,323		34,323	
Number of events	38		74		54		208	
Pseudo R^2	0.173				0.149			
Log likelihood	−538.7				−1238.2			

Note: Standard errors are in parentheses.

[a] The coefficient for age squared is multiplied by 100 for ease of presentation.

[b] There are too few cases to estimate the parameters.

* $p < 0.05$ ** $p < 0.01$

self-employment or skilled self-employment than are males. The disadvantage of entering self-employment faced by women remains, regardless of the type of self-employment. The curvilinear effect of age, observed in table 11.2, is present only among the skilled self-employed. The lack of age effects for entry into professional/managerial self-employment suggests that this route is unaffected by one's place in the life cycle, and its chances are more or less constant throughout the working career. In contrast, the chances of entry into skilled self-employment are highest at the middle of the working career.

Educational attainment does not increase the chances of entry into professional/managerial self-employment. The only exception, which is observed in the sample using all observations, is the effect of junior college. Junior college graduates are predominantly women, and the significant effect suggests that women with a junior college diploma are more likely to enter professional/managerial self-employment than women who have achieved only compulsory education. The effect of junior college is consistent with the finding that many female professional/managerial self-employed are private teachers.

Educational attainment seems to reduce the chances of entry into skilled self-employment. In the sample created using observations since 1980, all of the effects of education are negative, although none are significant. The other sample, created using all observations, displays effects that are again all negative, but significant for high school and university graduates. These effects suggest that people with the minimum level of compulsory education are more likely to enter skilled self-employment than are people with more education. We will discuss later the reasons for the negative association between education and self-employment.

Social background affects the chances of entry into both types of self-employment. Father's self-employment exerts a strong and significant effect on entry into both professional/managerial and skilled self-employment; this is clear evidence of intergenerational transmission of self-employment status. Individuals with a professional/managerial father are more likely to become professional/managerial self-employed, although there does not seem to be an inheritance of the skilled occupation itself.

The likelihood of entry into professional/managerial self-employment is substantially increased when the respondents engaged in professional/managerial work prior to entry into self-employment. Similarly, the likelihood of entry into skilled self-employment is increased when the respondents worked as skilled workers in the prior year, although the same likelihood decreased when the respondents worked as professional/managerial employees in the prior year. With regard to the effect of the type of industry in which the respondents worked prior to entry into self-employment, there is no significant effect on entry into professional/ managerial self-employment, while previous work experience in construction and traditional service industries increases the chances of entry into skilled self-employment. The industry effects evident in the analyses of entries into all types of self-employment, therefore, come from the effects on skilled self-employment.

The effects of firm size, shown at the bottom of the table, are significant for entry into both professional/managerial self-employment and skilled self-employment. Prior work experience in a very small firm that employs fewer than thirty employees increases the likelihood of entry into both professional/managerial and skilled self-employment. In addition, prior work experience in a small firm employing thirty to ninety-nine employees also increases the chances of entry into skilled self-employment. As we have seen for entries into all types of self-employment, the inclusion of firm size as a variable substantially reduces the effects of industry on entry into skilled self-employment. Furthermore, the significant negative effects of education on entry into skilled self-employment, observed in the sample using all observations in the data, disappear completely after controlling for firm size. In other words, the finding that respondents with only compulsory education are more likely to enter skilled self-employment can be explained by these respondents' entry into self-employment through working in small firms. Small firms, therefore, act as a key gateway for feeding people into self-employment in Japan.

We next examine the pattern of exit from self-employment. Respondents who are considered at risk for this set of analyses include those who were self-employed since 1980 (in the case of analyses using observations since 1980), and those who were self-employed at any time during their working career (in the case of analyses using all observations). Figure 11.3 presents Kaplan-Meier survival curves for exit from professional/managerial self-employment and for exit from skilled self-employment.[13] Due to the small number of cases, exit from unskilled self-employment is not considered. The stability seen in these two categories is roughly equal for approximately eight years. After that, the professional/managerial self-employed have a lower survival rate than do the skilled self-employed. However, if we take a long-term perspective by analyzing the two survival curves drawn from a sample using all observations in the data (not shown), the difference between the survival rate of professional/managerial self-employed and skilled self-employed is quite small for nearly eighteen years; the professional/managerial self-employed show a higher survival rate than do skilled self-employed after that. Overall, there does not seem to be a great difference in survival rates between the two types of self-employment. When Kaplan-Meier

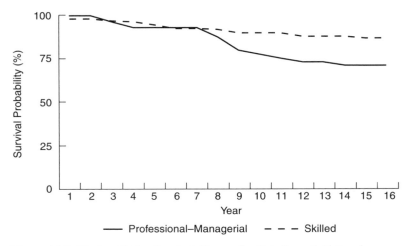

Figure 11.3: Kaplan-Meier Survival Curves for Exit from Self-Employment in Japan

survival curves for exit from all types of self-employment are compared between men and women (not shown), the gender difference is not large either. Self-employed men show slightly lower survival rates than do women, especially after ten years.

Table 11.4 presents the results of simple discrete time logistic models predicting exit from all types of self-employment. We did not conduct separate analyses by type of self-employment, or by gender, because of the small number of events. Instead, gender and type of occupation are included as independent variables. Because the number of events in the sample of observations since 1980 is also quite limited, we will focus on analyses that use all observations in the data, especially when interpreting the significance of coefficients.

Females show a higher risk of leaving self-employment than do males. Although survival curves suggest a slightly lower rate of exit from self-employment among females, the net effect of the female variable after controlling for other factors seems to be positive in the multivariate analyses. Therefore, women are disadvantaged not only in the chances of entry into self-employment, but also in the risk of leaving self-employment. The effects of age and age-squared are significant, suggesting a U-shaped relationship between age and the likelihood of exit from self-employment. As individuals age, and presumably accumulate experience, they show a decreased risk of failure in self-employment, though their risk of exit increases when they become elderly, probably because of retirement.

TABLE 11.4
Exit from Self-Employment in Japan since 1980

	All observations since 1980		All observations in the data	
Female	0.267	(0.463)	0.642*	(0.304)
Age	−0.207**	(0.067)	−0.132*	(0.041)
Age squared[a]	0.375**	(0.144)	0.196*	(0.100)
Education (ref: 1abc)				
2c	0.059	(0.475)	−0.217	(0.301)
3a	0.269	(0.914)	0.016	(0.649)
3b	0.112	(0.703)	−0.511	(0.562)
Father's occupation (ref: unskilled, no occupation)				
Professional	1.423	(0.857)	0.730	(0.524)
Skilled	0.991	(0.813)	0.678	(0.462)
Farmer	1.295	(0.863)	1.106*	(0.493)
Father self-employed	−1.285**	(0.416)	−0.926**	(0.301)
Occupation in origin state (ref: unskilled)				
Professional	−0.559	(0.802)	−0.282	(0.555)
Skilled	−0.778	(0.641)	−1.065**	(0.368)
Industrial sector in origin state (ref: mining, manuf.)				
Construction (F)	−0.030	(0.582)	−0.586	(0.409)
Traditional service (G/H)	−0.751	(0.553)	−0.615	(0.342)
Transport, communication (I)	−0.091	(1.129)	0.023	(0.616)
Finance, business service (J/K)	—[b]		−1.475	(1.077)
Other service (L–Q)	−0.829	(0.623)	−1.033*	(0.423)
Self-employment duration	−0.003	(0.023)	0.009	(0.020)
Constant	−1.310	(1.193)	−1.605**	(0.610)
Number of observations	3,091		5,662	
Number of events	40		78	
Pseudo R^2	0.097		0.081	
Log likelihood	−173.1		−350.4	
Firm size in origin state (ref: with employees)				
Solo self-employment	0.315	(0.442)	0.327	(0.282)
Number of observations	3,091		5,662	
Number of events	40		78	
Pseudo R^2	0.098		0.083	
Log likelihood	−172.9		−349.8	

Note: Standard errors are in parentheses.
[a] The coefficient for age squared is multiplied by 100 for ease of presentation.
[b] There are too few cases to estimate the parameter.
* $p < 0.05$ ** $p < 0.01$

Educational attainment does not affect self-employment stability. The effects of CASMIN educational categories are not significant, and the direction of the effects is not even consistent in the two samples. Furthermore, the gross effects of education in the reduced form equation are not significant either (not reported in the table), so we are fairly certain that the likelihood of departure from self-employment is not influenced by education. Therefore, self-employment activities, either entry or exit, are largely independent of educational attainment in Japan.

The father's self-employment status has a substantial and significant effect on the chances of exit from self-employment. When fathers are self-employed, there is a strong intergenerational effect on the stability of self-employment. Self-employed fathers are able not only to provide financial assistance, but also to pass on entrepreneurial skills and networks to sons and daughters. Therefore, having a father who is self-employed is beneficial both at the startup stage (entry into self-employment) and in the survival stage. When the fathers are farmers, the likelihood of exit from self-employment is further increased, presumably because these fathers have limited resources to assist their children.

The occupational type of self-employment affects the likelihood of survival in self-employment. Skilled self-employment, as opposed to unskilled self-employment, reduces the risk of exit. This is probably related to the fact that skilled self-employment is by far the largest type in the sample.[14] The type of industry in which the self-employment activities took place does not affect the stability of self-employment, with the exception of the "other services" category, which includes education, health, public service, and personal services. The self-employed in this category are less likely to exit from self-employment than those in the mining or manufacturing sector. The industrial context of self-employment as a whole, however, does not seem to have any noticeable impact on the survival of self-employment. An additional variable measuring duration in self-employment is also included as an independent variable, though it seems to have little effect. Durability in self-employment does not ultimately lead to a lower chance of departure.

Finally, as in the case of the analyses of entry into self-employment, firm size is added to the original equation. I include a dummy variable called "solo self-employment," representing the independent self-employed working on his/her own account without employing others. The purpose of this inclusion is to test whether independent self-employed working alone are more vulnerable and subject to a higher risk of failure than are self-employed who employ others. The results indicate that solo self-employment does not have any effect on the risk of exit from self-employment. I have also tried to evaluate whether there is a difference between small- and large-scale self-employment in their survival chances (not reported in the table) and have found no difference.

DISCUSSION

The results of Kaplan-Meier survival analyses and discrete time event-history models present a number of important findings characterizing the pattern and the determinants of entry into and exit from self-employment in Japan. In this section, I will concentrate on three findings that clearly stand out and discuss their interpretation and sociological implications. These findings are that in Japan: (1) educational attainment neither increases the chances of entry into self-employment nor reduces the risks of exit from self-employment; (2) small firms play a decisive role in providing access to self-employment entry; and (3) an intergenerational transfer of self-employment status is clearly evident.

One of the most interesting and perhaps surprising findings of our analyses deals with the lack of any positive effect of Japanese educational attainment on self-employment. In Japan, in contrast to the results from many other industrial nations, educational attainment does not increase the likelihood of entering self-employment. This absence is especially conspicuous when one considers the fact that there are no gross positive effects of education on self-employment activities without controlling for other variables.

There are several possible explanations for the absence of a positive association between educational attainment and entry into self-employment. The most obvious candidate is the measurement of education. The effect of education may be underestimated because I have not used a refined enough measure of education. For example, if I had taken into account the difference in academic and vocational tracks in high school education, I might have detected a positive effect for vocational track on entry into skilled self-employment. Or if I had considered the quality of higher education, I might have encountered a positive effect for attending a high-quality institution on the entry into professional/managerial self-employment. However, the sample was too small to further break down the educational categories, and consequently, it would have been difficult to detect significant effects in the multivariate analyses.

Rather than resorting to measurement issues, I am inclined to believe that the lack of a positive association between education and the chances of entry into self-employment in Japan is real. To begin with, the highly educated are probably not attracted so much to the risky option of opening up a new business, given the well-established route of internal promotion in large firms. Self-employment often involves long working hours, and there is large income variation among self-employed. The highly educated must be prepared to take the risk of losing a seemingly secure position when they enter self-employment. There are also reasons for enabling those who have not attained a high level of education to pursue a career path in self-employment. The educational level of the average Japanese is generally high by cross-national standards (Cummings 1980; Rohlen 1983), and educational achievements indicated in science and mathematics test scores also surpass those in many other nations (Lynn 1988). A lack of education may become a significant barrier to entry into self-employment, especially in advanced industrial economies where literacy, good work habits, and ability to adapt to new technology are essential elements for success in self-employment. The high average level of educational attainment among Japanese ensures that there is a large pool of well-educated potential entrepreneurs who possess many qualities essential to becoming a successful self-employed. It is possible, therefore, that even people with only compulsory education are already equipped with the necessary work habits and qualities, and that the difference in education does not affect the likelihood of entry into self-employment.

To reinforce the above explanation, I call attention to the only significant effect of education observed in the analyses (among the sample using all observations in the data): respondents with only compulsory education were more likely to enter skilled self-employment. There is a negative association between educational attainment and the chances of entry into skilled self-employment. The key to understanding the negative effect of education lies in the kind of firm in which people with low education are employed. People with minimum compulsory education typically find jobs in smaller firms, and workers in small firms are much more likely to become self-employed than are those in large firms, regardless of their education and prior labor experience. In other words, low education feeds people into small firms, providing them with the skills and networks which, in turn, are essential for opening a new business. Workers in small firms who have only the minimum level of education, therefore, still obtain essential skills before entering the labor market and are probably ready to seize the opportunity to move into self-employment when given the chance.

The second finding of note is the relationship between small firms and entry into self-employment. The chances of entry into both professional/managerial and skilled self-employment are increased substantially if the respondents previously worked in a very small firm employing fewer than thirty people. The likelihood of entry into skilled self-employment is also increased if the respondents worked in a small firm employing thirty to ninety-nine employees. Work experience in small firms, therefore, leads to successful entry into self-employment.

This suggests that small firms offer training and that workers accumulate skills necessary for self-employment. Koike (1981, 1988, 1994) painstakingly documented that Japanese small-scale firms rely on training programs that are set up within the company to train their employees, and that very few workers in small firms acquired their skills externally. Skills are formed and accumulated by working on the job, especially by experiencing different but related jobs in the workplace (Whittaker 1997). However, compared with large companies, the extent of production and the scale of workshops are more limited in small companies, so the range of skills that can be obtained in training is likely to be somewhat narrow.

One might argue that the skills offered by small firms are less relevant than the poor labor conditions—such as low wages, poor fringe benefits, and limited promotion opportunities—that push workers to leave and start business. As opposed to workers in small firms, workers in large firms do not perceive the need, at least in terms of labor conditions, to become independent. This is only half right. Even if worse labor conditions in small firms are a good explanation for departure from the firm, they do not explain the reasons for starting a new business. Entry into self-employment requires more than unfavorable working conditions. Indeed, in the survey conducted by the National Life Finance Corporation (National Life Finance Corporation Research Institute 2000) cited at the beginning of this chapter, the most popular reasons for starting a new business reported by self-employed involve the realization of skills and abilities, and the attraction to being independent and autonomous, rather than unfavorable working conditions of the previous employment.

Along with providing extensive training, employers of small firms sometimes encourage independence among their workers. For many employers, especially in the manufacturing, construction and service sectors where subcontracting arrangements with smaller enterprises are abundant, an employee's decision to shift toward self-employment is not necessarily an unwelcome development (Kiyonari 1990). Subcontracting takes the form of first-tier, second-tier, and third-tier relationships, and self-employed are located at the bottom of the subcontracting hierarchy (Sako 1992). Owners of small companies may subcontract part of their contracts with the parent company to solo self-employed. Small-scale enterprises in manufacturing produce parts for parent firms (which can also be small business) by long production runs of a single item or by using specialized skills. In the service industry, the self-employed who work as subcontractors find their niches in locational advantages and personalized/customized services. The relationship between parent firms and self-employed operating small business can be simple and symbiotic, but it can also become a more complex one involving ongoing and mutually dependent cooperation (Nishiguchi 1994).

In addition to skill formation, the work experience generated in small firms allows employees to observe closely the activities of the employers who are often self-employed. It thus gives them the unique opportunity to study the operation of the business while on the job, because the scope of the business is relatively small and the interactions with the owner frequent. This provides a distinct advantage in developing the knowledge necessary to create one's own firm. A survey of the self-employed conducted by the Tokyo Labor Research Institute (1992) asked how the self-employed obtained the necessary knowledge and experience in order to manage their business. The overwhelming majority (68 percent) responded that they obtained it from their previous employment. Furthermore, social ties cultivated through former employers, former customers, and industry colleagues can provide access to capital, markets, and other resources that are key factors in starting up a new business and in remaining a competitive actor in the market (Patrick and Rohlen 1987). Social networks are crucial to minimizing the costs of information and to reducing the uncertainties of fraud and unreliability. New business opportunities and investments are often channeled along social connections. The relatively confined and intimate social relationships surrounding small firms are probably conducive to generating a favorable environment for entry into self-employment.

The final striking finding in Japan that deserves special attention relates to the persistent effect of the father's self-employment status on both the chances of entry into self-employment and the chances of survival in self-employment. What is the mechanism of the effect of the father's self-employment on the next generation's self-employment activities? The most obvious link can be found in the direct inheritance of the father's small business. Sons and daughters might have been employees or, more likely, family workers in the father's business, and perhaps they succeeded him gradually on the job, or suddenly took over the business due to the father's death or illness. Whether planned or unplanned, the direct inheritance of a family business represents the most extreme manifestation of the effect of the father's self-employment. Since the survival probability is higher for an established small business than for a newly formed enterprise, inheriting the father's small business implies less risk of failure than opening a new company. The direct inheritance of business, therefore, affects the chances of both entry into and exit from self-employment.

The transfer of capital from the father's generation to the children's generation can help the emergence of new entrepreneur activities. The survey of self-employed conducted by the Tokyo Labor Research Institute (1992) pointed out that inheritance from fathers (presumably at the time of the father's death) enabled some self-employed to begin their own businesses. Inheritance from a self-employed father often involves the transfer of capital in the form of land, shops, and other assets, and these assets must have facilitated the path for sons and daughters to invest in a new self-employed business. The assistance from the father does not have to be in the form of inheritance. Self-employed fathers can financially assist sons and daughters by lending money or labor. Self-employed fathers also have better access to information about financial opportunities for small businesses than fathers who are employed by others, and they can offer a few pieces of wise advice. The influence of the father's self-employment, therefore, is not limited to the startup of a new business but extends also to the survival of the small business.

Just as employees in a small firm can learn knowledge about the operation of the business from their employer, children of the self-employed almost certainly benefit from the opportunity to learn from their self-employed fathers how to run a small business. Learning involves not only knowledge and information but also personality traits, such as independence, autonomy, and willingness to take risks, which are often considered to be important ingredients for success in self-employment (Tachibanaki 1994). Children of the self-employed may have internalized these values and other skills relevant to operating a small business when they were growing up. Socialization into an environment that is conducive to self-employment can take place early in the childhood. The mechanisms through which the father's self-employment status influences the next generation's self-employment activities, therefore, are comprehensive, ranging from the direct inheritance to subtle socialization process of values.

Conclusion

Self-employment in Japan, as in many other nations, involves diverse and heterogeneous groups. Educational levels are clearly different between the professional/managerial self-employed, on the one hand, and the skilled and unskilled self-employed on the other. Three occupational types of self-employment are distributed across different industrial sectors. The Japanese self-employed tend to work longer hours, many of them under less favorable working conditions than those who work in large firms or the public sector. There is a greater inequality of income among the self-employed than among employees. However, the self-employed do not seem to have a strong sense of discontent or unfairness (National Life Finance Corporation Research Institute 2000). They are ambitious and highly motivated individuals who have a strong desire to become independent and prove their ability.

Japanese self-employment, nonetheless, is characterized by features that are different from those of other nations. First, there is no trend of growth in the self-employment sector in the 1980s and 1990s. Both the number and proportion of nonagricultural self-employed declined in the 1980s and 1990s. Second, traditional skilled self-employment continues to be the dominant type of self-employment. Third, the chances of entry into and exit from self-employment are not affected by education. Fourth, small firms that attract people with low education act as a gateway to self-employment. In Japan, two mechanisms for accumulating skills that are essential to running a small business seem especially significant: training in small firms and socialization in the home environment of self-employed. If these small-scale firms survive the recent Japanese recession, they will continue to provide important avenues into self-employment.

However, there are recent trends which seem to discourage the emergence and survival of self-employment in Japan. Sato (1998, 2000) claims that people do not value the inheritance of a family business as much as they used to in contemporary Japan. Furthermore, the declining real value of household assets following the collapse of the bubble economy in the mid-1990s contributed to threatening the financial stability of small businesses and increasing the barriers to entry into self-employment. Although there were new policies to assist in the startup of small businesses in the 1990s, personal finance remains the most important ingredient when founding a small business, and in surviving self-employment activity (Genda and Kanbayashi 2001).

The sudden downturn in the economy in the late 1990s appears to have accelerated the declining trend of the self-employment sector that began in the 1980s. At the same time, it should be remembered that small business probably plays an important stabilizing role during recession, by reducing the overt unemployment that would otherwise escalate. The future of self-employment in Japan over the long run will be largely affected by economic and demographic forces, such as changes in demand and market competition, and the gentrification of the population. The self-employment sector is most likely to persist and provide a strong basis for the Japanese economy, especially offering employment opportunities for the aged population.

Notes

The author is grateful to the members of the Self-Employment in Advanced Economies Project, in particular to Richard Arum, Ted Gerber, Lohmann Henning, Silvia Luber, Walter Müller, and Kuo-Hsien Su, the participants of the economic sociology seminar at the University of Michigan; to Hikaru Fukanuma, Yuji Genda, Mark Mizruchi, Hiroki Sato, Noriyuki Takahashi, and Yu Xie for their comments and suggestions; and to Tom Blackwood and David Leheny for their editorial assistance.

1. Ishida, Müller, and Ridge (1995), however, showed that the inheritance of self-employment is largely independent of educational attainment in Japan.

2. I would like to thank the 1995 SSM Survey Research Committee for allowing me to use the 1995 SSM Survey. For details of the survey, see Hara and Seiyama (1999: appendix) and T. Sato (2000: appendix).

3. However, the comparison of the age distribution of the 1995 SSM survey and that of the census shows that younger people are less represented in the survey.

4. Our definition of self-employment is similar to those used in government surveys. For example, the Japanese Census uses the following categories for the question of employment status: "employees," "directors and top management," "self-employed employing others," "self-employed without employees," "family workers," and "piecemeal workers." However, as discussed above, our definition of "self-employed" includes those who selected the category of "board of directors and top management" employing less than thirty employees because some self-employed, especially those who incorporated their business, are likely to report themselves as "directors" of the firm even though they employ only a small number of workers. Since the Small and Medium Enterprise Basic Law defines small enterprise owners as those who employ less than five workers in the wholesale, retail, and service industries, and those who employ less than twenty workers in manufacturing and other industries, we used the cutoff point of thirty employees (the closest cutoff point available in the survey questionnaire) to capture small business owners who identified themselves as board of directors.

5. Shopowners and restaurateurs are assigned to skilled self-employment, rather than to professional-managerial self-employment.

6. However, there are small differences in the educational categories used in this chapter and the earlier version. Ishida (1998) distinguished high school graduates who had additional postsecondary (not tertiary) education as category 2d. This study does not distinguish 2d because the number was too small. Furthermore, category 2c in this study is the same as category 2bc in Ishida (1998). This is because respondents who completed high school education are considered to hold "full maturity certificates" (see Shavit and Müller 1998; Brauns and Steinmann 1999).

7. These figures are based on the distribution of hours worked per week among the self-employed, family workers, and employees in Japan, reported in the 1997 Employment Status Survey (Statistics Bureau 1998). The sample is restricted to those who worked more than two hundred days in the previous year. Self-employed as well as employees and family workers include both nonfarm and farm workers.

8. These figures are based on tables that use column percentages. These tables are not reported in this paper.

9. Again, the figures related to concentration are not in the tables reported in the chapter.

10. The author gratefully acknowledges the assistance of Ku-Hsien Su in running survival curves and event-history models.

11. It will become apparent that the curvilinear relationship is real, even among observations since 1980, when we examine the effect of age and age-squared by type of self-employment.

12. Because the firm size variable was missing in some observations, the total number of spells is reduced, although the number of events (entries into self-employment) is not affected.

13. The Japanese survey asked retrospective questions about the respondents' work history, so it probably led to underreporting of short, unsuccessful self-employment spells, thereby overestimating self-employment survival, especially during the first year of self-employment activities.

14. Almost two-thirds of the events are exits from skilled self-employment.

REFERENCES

Abe, M., and A. Yamada. 1998. Chukoreiki niokeru dokuritsu kaigyo no jittai (Emergence of new business among the middle and old-aged). *Japanese Journal of Labor Studies* 452:26–40.

Allison, P. D. 1984. *Event history analysis*. Beverly Hills: Sage Publications.

Blossfeld, H., A. Hamerle, and K. U. Mayer. 1989. *Event history analysis*. Hillsdale, NJ: Erlbaum Associates.

Brauns, H. and S. Steinmann. 1999. Educational reform in France, West Germany and the United Kingdom: Updating the CASMIN Educational Classification. ZUMMA Nachrichten 44:7–44.

Brinton, M. C. 1993. *Women and the economic miracle: Gender and work in postwar Japan*. Berkeley: University of California Press.

Cummings, W. K. 1980. *Education and equality in Japan*. Princeton: Princeton University Press.

Erikson, R., and J. Goldthorpe. 1992. *The constant flux: A study of class mobility in industrial societies*. Oxford: Clarendon Press.

Erikson, R., J. H. Goldthorpe, and L. Portocarero. 1979. Intergenerational class mobility in three Western European societies. *British Journal of Sociology* 30:415–41.

Eurostat. 1996. *Eurostat Yearbook 1996*. Luxembourg: Office for Official Publications of the European Communities.

Genda, Y., M. Ishihara, and R. Kanbayashi. 1998. Jieigyo gensho no haikei (The decline of the self-employed). *Chosa Kiho* (Research Quarterly of the NLFC Research Institute) 47:14–35.

Genda, Y., and R. Kanbayashi. 2001. Jieigyo gensho to sogyo shiensaku (The decline of the self-employed and policies to support new business). In *Koyo seisaku no keizai bunseki* (Employment Policies and Economic Analyses), ed. T. Inoki and F. Ohtake, 29–74. Tokyo: University of Tokyo Press.

Hara, J., and K. Seiyama. 1999. *Shakai kaiso: yutakasa no nakano fubyodo* (Social stratification: Inequality in an affluent society). Tokyo: University of Tokyo Press.

Hashimoto, K. 1999. *Gendai nihon no kaikyu kozo: riron, hoho, keiryo bunnseki* (Class structure in contemporary Japan: Theory, methods and quantitative analysis). Tokyo: Toshindo.

———. 2000. Sengo nihon no nominso bunkai (The breakdown of the farm class in postwar Japan). In *Nihon no kaiso shisutemu 1—kindaika to shakai kaiso* (The stratification system in Japan 1: Modernization and social stratification), ed. J. Hara, 109–34. Tokyo: University of Tokyo Press.

Ishida, H. 1993. *Social mobility in contemporary Japan*. Stanford: Stanford University Press.

———. 1998. Educational credentials and labor market entry outcomes in Japan. In *From school to work: A comparative study of educational qualifications and occupational destinations*, ed Y. Shavit and W. Müller, 287–309. Oxford: Clarendon Press.

———. 2000. Sangyo shakai no nakano nihon (Japan among industrial societies). In *Nihon no kaiso shisutemu 1—kindaika to shakai kaiso* (The stratification system in Japan 1: Modernization and social stratification), ed. J. Hara, 219–48. Tokyo: University of Tokyo Press.

———. 2001. Industrialization, class structure and social mobility in postwar Japan. *British Journal of Sociology* 52:579–604.

Ishida, H., J. H. Goldthorpe, and R. Erikson. 1991. Intergenerational class mobility in post-war Japan. *American Journal of Sociology* 96:954–92.

Ishida, H., W. Müller, and J. Ridge. 1995. Class origin, class destination and education: A cross-national study of industrial nations. *American Journal of Sociology* 101:145–93.

Jeong, H. S. 2000. Jieiso no senzen to sengo (The self-employed class before and after World War II). In *Nihon no kaiso shisutemu 1—kindaika to shakai kaiso* (The stratification system in Japan 1: Modernization and social stratification), ed. J. Hara, 65–88. Tokyo: University of Tokyo Press.

———. 2002. *Nihon no jieigyoso* (Self-employment in Japan). Tokyo: University of Tokyo Press.

Kiyonari, T. 1990. *Chusho kigyo dokuhon* (Reader on small and medium-sized firms), 2nd ed. Tokyo: Toyo Keizai Shinposha.

Koike, K. 1981. *Chusho kigyo no jyukuren* (Skills in small and medium-sized firms). Tokyo: Dobunkan.

———. 1988. *Understanding industrial relations in modern Japan*. London: Macmillan.

———. 1994. *Nihon no koyo shisutemu* (The Japanese employment system). Tokyo: Toyo Keizai Shinposha.

Lynn, R. 1988. *Educational achievement in Japan: Lessons for the West*. London: Macmillan.

Ministry of Labor Women's Bureau. 1999. *Kiso kara manabu jyosei notameno kigyo manyuaru* (A manual for women entrepreneurs). Tokyo: Jyosei Rodo Kyokai.

Müller, W., H. Lohmann, and S. Luber. 1999. *Self-employment in Advanced Economies Project Summary*. Mannheim: University of Mannheim.

———. 2000. Minutes from First Workshop on Self-Employment in Advanced Economies, Libourne, France, 10 May.

Müller, W., P. Luttinger, W. Koning, and W. Karle. 1989. Class and education in industrial nations. *International Journal of Sociology* 19:3–39.

National Life Finance Corporation Research Institute. 2000. *Shinki kaigyo hakusho* (White paper on newly opened business). Tokyo: Medium and Small-size Firm Research Center.

Nishiguchi, T. 1994. *Strategic industrial sourcing: The Japanese advantage.* New York: Oxford University Press.

OECD. 2000. *Employment Outlook.* Paris: OECD.

Orru, M., N. W. Biggart, and G. G. Hamilton. 1997. *The economic organization of East Asian capitalism.* Thousand Oaks: Sage Publications.

Patrick, H. T., and T. P. Rohlen. 1987. Small-scale family enterprises. In *The Political economy of Japan, Volume 1: The domestic transformation*, ed. K. Yamamura and Y. Yasuba, 331–84. Stanford: Stanford University Press.

Piore, M. J., and C. F. Sabel. 1984. *The second industrial divide.* New York: Basic Books.

Powers, D. A., and Y. Xie. 2000. *Statistical methods for categorical data analysis.* San Diego: Academic Press.

Rohlen, T. P. 1983. *Japan's high schools.* Berkeley: University of California Press.

Sako, M. 1992. *Prices, quality and trust: Inter-firm relations in Britain and Japan.* Cambridge: Cambridge University Press.

Sato, T. 1998. Hikoyosha no shokugyo saiseisan to kaiso-kaikyu ishiki (Reproduction of employees and their status-class consciousness). *Japanese Journal of Labor Studies* 455:40–49.

———. 2000. *Fubyodo shakai nihon* (Japan as an unequal society). Tokyo: Chuokoron Shinsha.

Sato, Y. 2000. Kodo seicho no hikari to kage (Light and shadow of rapid economic development). In *Nihon no kaiso shisutemu 1: kindaika to shakai kaiso* (The stratification system in Japan 1: Modernization and social stratification), ed. J. Hara, 137–60. Tokyo: University of Tokyo Press.

Schoppa, L. J. 1997. *Bargaining with Japan: What American pressure can and cannot do.* New York: Columbia University Press.

Seiyama, K. 1999. Josei no kyaria kozo no tokusei to doko (Characteristics and trends of women's career structure). *Japanese Journal of Labor Studies* 472:36–45.

Seiyama, K., et al. 1990. Shokureki ido no kozo (The structure of career mobility). In *Gendai nihon no kaiso kozo 1—shakai kaiso no kozo to katei* (The stratification structure in contemporary Japan, Volume 1: Structure and process of social stratification), ed. A. Naoi and K. Seiyama, 83–108. Tokyo: University of Tokyo Press.

Shavit, Y., and W. Müller, eds. 1998. *From school to work: A comparative study of educational qualifications and occupational destinations.* Oxford: Clarendon Press.

Shirahase, S. 1995. Diversity in female work: Female part-time workers in contemporary Japan. *American Asian Review* 13:257–82.

Small and Medium Enterprise Agency. 2002. *The White Paper on small and medium enterprises in Japan.* Tokyo: Japan Small Business Research Institute.

Statistics Bureau, Management and Coordination Agency, Japanese Government. 1998. *1997 Employment status survey: Results for Japan.* Tokyo: Statistics Bureau, Management and Coordination Agency, Japanese Government.

Tachibanaki, T. 1994. *Raifu saikuru to shotoku hosho* (Life-cycle and income guarantee). Tokyo: NTT Press.

Tokyo Labor Research Institute. 1992. *Jieigyosha no kyaria to shuro* (Career and work among self-employed). Tokyo: Tokyo Labor Research Institute.

Upham, F. 1993. Privatizing regulation: The implementation of the Large-scale Retail Stores Law. In *Political dynamics in contemporary Japan*, ed. G. Allinson and Y. Sone, 264–94. Ithaca: Cornell University Press.

Whittaker, D. H. 1997. *Small firms in the Japanese economy*. Cambridge: Cambridge University Press.

Yamaguchi, K. 1991. *Event history analysis*. Newbury Park, CA: Sage Publications.

CHAPTER TWELVE

On One's Own: Self-Employment Activity in Taiwan

Wei-hsin Yu and Kuo-Hsien Su

SELF-EMPLOYMENT HAS been one of the major activities of postwar economic development in Taiwan. Despite the increase of wage and salaried employment that accompanied industrialization, more than one-fifth of the labor force in Taiwan, a comparatively large proportion among industrial societies, remained self-employed until the mid-1990s (see Yu 2001b: table 9.1). Furthermore, the average number of employees per establishment declined from 8.6 in 1981 to 7.6 in 1996 (DGBAS 1982, 1997). This was the result of a greater increase in the number of establishments, rather than a change in the size of the labor force during this period. This trend implies a somewhat steady labor flow into self-employment over the last two decades, despite the fact that the labor force in the agricultural sector shrank by nearly 10 percent. Not only do these facts present an evident challenge to earlier assumptions that wage employment would absorb most of the labor supply, and that self-employment would inevitably decline and disappear as the economy advances (see Portes and Benton 1984, or chapter 1, this volume, for references), but they also speak to the importance of studying self-employment activity in Taiwan.

Like other types of employment, self-employment results from a match of supply-side characteristics with structural opportunities enabled by the demand side. This chapter aims to tell the story of such a match for the case of Taiwan. First, we emphasize the macro-level opportunity structures in Taiwan that encourage entry into self-employment, in order to explain the unusually high percentage of self-employed labor force in Taiwan compared with other economies with a similar level of development. Looking at Taiwan in a cross-national context, we are forced to ask why self-employment was a more popular option in this national labor market than in Western countries and in Japan (see the figures in chapter 1 of this volume). Following previous studies that associate self-employment activity with macro-level opportunity structures in the labor market (Arum, Budig, and Grant 2000; Blau 1987; De Soto 1989; Portes and Benton 1984; Steinmetz and Wright 1989; Piore and Sabel 1984; Waldinger 1986), we consider the propensity of becoming self-employed in Taiwan as a reflection of a particular macro-level opportunity structure that enables self-employment activity to flourish. Thus, this study aims to contribute to an understanding of the persistence of self-employment in industrial economies.

With respect to the labor supply side, individual attributes and resources such as ethnicity, gender, human capital, and personal ties have been found to impact entry into and exit from self-employment in various countries (e.g., Bates 1999; Portes and Jensen 1989; Sanders and Nee 1996; Waldinger 1989; Yoon 1991). Previous studies on self-employed women in Taiwan show that this group does not necessarily possess less human capital, despite great heterogeneity within the group (Simon 2000; Yu 1999, 2001b). Moreover, individual attributes that aid in the acquisition of social capital, such as kinship networks, geographical origins, or previous work experience, determine one's entry into self-employment to a great extent (Ka 1993; Simon 2000; Yu 2001b). This study will also examine determinants for entry into and exit from self-employment among individuals, while supplementing previous research by depicting detailed individual trajectories to and from self-employment for each job episode.

We will also address heterogeneity in Taiwanese self-employment processes. Research on self-employment in industrial societies often notes great heterogeneity within this category (e.g., Arum 1997; Arum, Budig, and Grant 2000; Jurik 1998; Yu 2001b). Not only do determinants for moving into and out of self-employment vary for different types of self-employment (e.g., unskilled, skilled, and professional self-employment), but paths into self-employment and the relevant outcomes of the activity also differ between men and women, as previous studies suggest (Boden 1996, 1999; Morokvasic 1991; Carr 1996; Yu 2000, 2001a). Therefore, this chapter will also explore the similarities and differences in individual attributes, occupational characteristics, survival chances, and exit patterns among unskilled, skilled, and professional self-employment, as well as gender differences.

Macro-Level Trends

The rapid expansion of the workforce, together with the proliferation of small businesses focusing on exports, created ample opportunities for self-employment in Taiwan in the postwar period. Small-scale enterprises began to flourish, particularly in labor-intensive industries such as textiles, processed food products, leather goods, wood products, and paper products, after the state shifted its development strategy from import substitution to export-led growth in the late 1950s (Cheng and Gereffi 1994). The total number of establishments doubled within a decade: from 216,300 in 1966 to 426,500 in 1976. By 1996, the number of establishments had reached 866,500, with an average of 7.6 employees per establishment. In the meantime, the labor force rose from 2.89 million in 1953 to 9.38 million in 1999, as a result of both industrialization and population growth. Throughout the period, there was a constant and significant proportion of nonwage employees, including the self-employed, within the labor force. As of 1999, some 5.4 percent of the labor force listed themselves as employers, 16.3 percent as self-employed workers, and 7.7 percent as unpaid or irregularly paid family workers (DGBAS 2000).

Despite the growth of self-employment in absolute terms, the percentage of self-employed has remained relatively stable over the past two decades. Figure 12.1A traces the changes in labor force composition for men from 1980 to 1999. The greatest change in the labor force has been a shift from agriculture to the service sectors. Although agricultural production was the prime engine of Taiwan's economic development in the early 1960s, the annual growth rate in farm production has steadily declined over the past three decades. There has been a downward drift for the labor force in the agricultural sector from 20 percent in 1980 to 10 percent in 1990. However, the employment shares in the industrial sectors remained relatively stable for both dependent employees and the self-employed. The most remarkable change took place in the service sector, where dependent employees increased their share by 8.8 percent and the self-employed by 3 percent.

Figure 12.1B shows changes in the female labor force. In addition to the downward trend in agriculture, the percentage of women employed in the industrial sector has also steadily declined since 1987. The two sectors together decreased their share of total employment by 24.4 percent. At the same time, female workers in the service sector increased their share to a similar extent; workers employed by the service sector rose from 15.6 percent in 1980 to 37.2 percent in 1999. Because female self-employment was predominantly located in the service sector, the shift of employment toward this sector has had a positive influence on the growth of female self-employment. While the share of female self-employment in the industrial sector remains small and more or less constant, the proportion of the self-employed in service industries has increased from 6.8 to 8.6 percent for women.

SCALE OF ECONOMY AND SELF-EMPLOYMENT

The scale of economy in Taiwan has a great impact on easing the entry into self-employment, partially as a result of state policy in the early

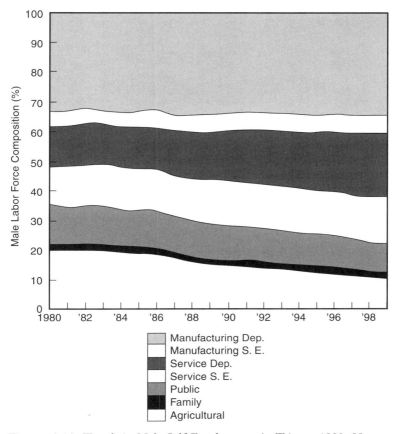

Figure 12.1A: Trends in Male Self-Employment in Taiwan, 1980–99

stages of economic development. Previous research has noted an unusually large number of small, mostly family-owned businesses and highlighted their significant role in the postwar economic development of Taiwan (Cheng and Gereffi 1994; Deyo 1989; Galenson 1979). In comparing Taiwan to its East Asian counterparts Japan and South Korea, several scholars argue that the Kuomintang regime, in order to defend its legitimacy, as well as secure its dominance on the island after the civil war in 1949, intentionally sponsored the establishment of small enterprises and caused a unique organizational structure that consisted of mostly small- to medium-sized family businesses widely dispersed all over the island (Cheng and Gereffi 1994; Hamilton and Biggart 1988; Noble 1998). The regime's fiscal policy of high interest rates, preference for short-term loans, and unsupportive attitude for markets in equity capital (e.g., the stock market), along with nonfavorist economic plans

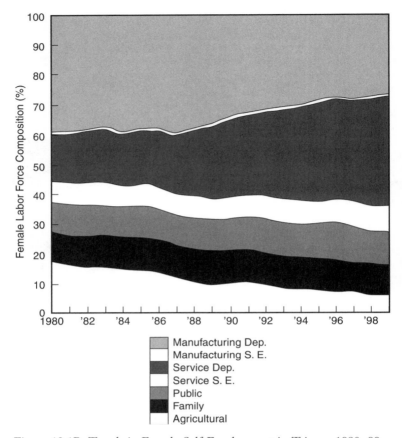

Figure 12.1B: Trends in Female Self-Employment in Taiwan, 1980–99

that encouraged competition, constrained the amount of capital available for individual businesses, and therefore impeded the growth of large enterprises (Hamilton and Biggart 1988).

Furthermore, Shieh (1991, 1992a, 1992b) argues that the unique arrangement of manufacturing processes in Taiwan has provided a niche for small and even very small establishments. Rather than incorporating mass production lines in large-scale factories, the process to manufacture goods in Taiwan involves many small establishments that contribute a simple part or task required for making the end product. The concentration on light and labor-intensive industries during the early decades of Taiwan's economic development allowed for arrangements of production that divided the overall process into many simple tasks, and these tasks were subcontracted to self-employed or home-based piece workers and very small establishments. Thus, with these arrangements of production, an establishment can start and survive with relatively little input of skills and financial capital. Furthermore, with the help of subcontracting systems, a family-based establishment can simply mobilize family members to carry out the small and simple tasks in the whole production process (e.g., Ka 1993; Lu 2001).

Regardless of the reasons why small businesses flourish, there is no debate that the industrial structure in Taiwan has been characterized by a small scale of economy and relatively low capital requirement for business establishments. To illustrate, 33.8 percent of the Taiwanese labor force was employed in firms with fewer than ten employees, while in the United States only 11.8 percent of the labor force was in establishments of the same scale in 1996 (DGBAS 1997; US Department of Commerce, Bureau of Census 2000). The scale of economy remains comparatively small when we compare the figures for Taiwan with other East Asian countries, such as Japan and South Korea. For example, 55.2 percent of the Taiwanese labor force was working in firms of fewer than twenty-nine employees in 1995, whereas the percentages were 32.9 percent and 25.3 percent for Japan and South Korea, respectively (see Brinton 2001: table 1.5).

This particular economic structure has great implications for workers and their working lives. It eases the entry into self-employment and encourages the notion that "black hands (i.e., blue-collar workers) becoming bosses (by becoming self-employed)" was a possible path of upward mobility for manufacturing workers (Shieh 1989, 1992a). Furthermore, the large number of small businesses and subcontracting jobs leads to a large proportion of female workers participating in economic activities as unpaid or irregularly paid family enterprise workers or home-based piece workers (Ka 1993; Kao 1999; Li and Ka 1994; Lu 2001; Yu 1999, 2001b). Other research also shows that the small scale of the Taiwanese economy facilitates female self-employment and therefore empowers the women in the society (Simon 2000).

While the macro-level economic structures lower the threshold and smooth entry into self-employment, Taiwanese workers are not solely *pulled* into self-employment. A proper explanation of individuals' choice of self-employment needs to take into account the alternative—namely, dependent, paid employment. Studies in other countries often attribute the concentration of self-employment to overly rigid structures associated with dependent employment due to state regulations or employment practices in large firms (Arum, Budig, and Grant 2000; Aldrich and Waldinger 1990; Cheng 1997; De Soto 1989; Morokvasic 1991). Structural constraints maintained by the state or leading firms in the economy *push* certain groups of workers, such as immigrants or minorities, into self-employment, as the barriers to dependent employment for these groups are particularly high.

We argue that Taiwan exemplifies a very different perspective on the connection between state or market regulations and self-employment. To be specific, while in various advanced economies self-employment is a response to rigidities imposed by state regulations or private firms, self-employment in Taiwan is a reaction to a weakly regulated private sector that does not provide proper labor compensation and sufficient job stability. It was not until the late 1980s that the Labor Standard Law was first enacted. The law mandated that employers were required to provide basic protections (e.g., minimum wages, workplace safety, upper limits of working hours, annual leave, maternity leave) and health insurance for employees, but covered only certain industries and firms beyond a certain size. The Labor Standard Law later expanded its coverage, but it is still inadequate and does not cover all in the labor force.

Furthermore, dependent employment in the private sector generally does not provide much more fringe benefits than self-employment, due to the state's policy. Most firms in the private sector do not have a pension plan or other fringe benefits for employees, since it is not required. The state does, however, require employers to partially bear the costs of their employees' employment and medical insurance, to ensure the state's provision of a lump-sum payment upon retirement and medical care for workers. However, these benefits are also available for self-employed workers through occupational unions, and the premiums for people who obtain insurance in this way are only slightly higher, as the state subsidizes part of the cost. In addition, the Employment Insurance Regulations exempted owners of businesses of fewer than ten employees from providing employment and health insurance for their employees until 1988. Based on the statistics from 1988, nearly 40 percent of the dependently employed were no better off than the self-employed, as far as fringe benefits were concerned, before the regulations changed (DGBAS 1989). Currently the exemption still applies to owners of firms of fewer than five employees.

With respect to job security, the small-establishment-based economy implies relatively high job instability for dependent employees, although in the postwar era, layoffs and large-scale layoffs in particular have been unusual because of labor shortages and economic prosperity (Tsay 1995; Yu 1999). In addition, while the birth of a small business is not difficult, the death of small businesses is also common. Small and very small establishments simply do not have the capacity to survive economic fluctuations. Hence, the lives of small establishments are likely to be shorter than individuals' working lives. Furthermore, there is little legal protection against employee dismissal and defiance of explicit or implicit employment contracts.[1] Both the authoritarian Kuomintang regime and the disproportionately large percentage of small- to medium-sized enterprises in the economy caused labor unions to play inactive roles in protecting private sector employees (Cheng and Gereffi 1994; Huang 1999). Thus, there has not been a considerable advantage for private-sector employment as compared to self-employment, with respect to job stability. This is particularly the case for unskilled workers, whose chances in the labor market are relatively poor.

Moreover, the prevalence of small-scale, family-owned businesses indicates blocked mobility for a large number of dependent employees; career ladders are already limited by the size of many businesses, and nonfamily members seldom reach the management level in small- to medium-scaled family-owned businesses. Thus, Shieh (1989) argues that becoming self-employed is considered the only way to break these low ceilings. Yu (1999, 2000, 2001b), using two different sources of survey data, also finds that self-employment has the potential to bring greater financial returns to education than dependent employment in the private sector. Therefore, the economic structures and low degree of state regulations create relatively high risks and little upward mobility for dependent employment. Such structures push those workers who most likely possess low human capital and skills and would not benefit from dependent employment into self-employment. This explains why the proportions of unskilled to skilled self-employment were noticeably greater than in all other countries examined in this volume (see figures 12.1A and 12.1B).

It is worth noting that we consider self-employment a response to the macro-level opportunity structures facilitated by the unique organizational structures in Taiwan, and we disregard the cultural explanation that there is a preference for being a leader in a small group rather than a follower in a large one, as expressed in the Chinese saying: "It is better to be a rooster's beak than a cow's tail." The insufficiency of this cultural explanation is evident in Hong Kong and Singapore, two other Chinese societies that contributed to the "East Asian Economic Miracle" but had only about 10 percent of the labor force in self-employment in 1995, while the percentage was as high as 22 percent in Taiwan for the same year (see Yu 2001b, fig. 9.1). The preference for becoming a "rooster's beak" in Chinese culture is certainly not strong enough to explain the exceptionally high proportion of self-employed workers in Taiwan.

Self-Employment and Social Capital

In spite of the push and pull forces at the macrolevel, not everyone is able to become self-employed. The startup capital may be low, but previous research suggests that social networks or personal ties are the major determinants for entering and surviving self-employment (Ka 1993; Yu 2001b). Social connections to other self-employed people increase exposure to this type of employment and enhance the likelihood of considering self-employment as a career option. In Ka's case study of very small establishments in the textile industry in Taipei, help from strong ties such as families and friends was often identified as the reason for entering self-employment in this industry (Ka 1993). Similar to the findings from studies of immigrants and self-employed in the United States, close friends and family members from the same rural area moved to urban areas together and began small businesses in the same neighborhood, taking over various parts of the production process in Taiwan (Ka 1993; see also Aldrich and Waldinger 1990; Waldinger 1986, 1989). Strong ties also allow small establishments to mobilize labor with a high level of flexibility, which reduces costs and helps cope with economic fluctuations. Previous research shows that the exploitation of family labor is usually a key to survival for small businesses (Ka 1993; Kao 1999; Li and Ka 1994; Lu 2001). The capability of mobilizing family labor implies social capital and is demanded by many types of self-employment, particularly those that involve low skills.

Following existing literature, this chapter stresses the importance of family-based social capital on entry and retention in self-employment. Social capital is defined as the strong ties that have the potential to increase one's access to either information or cheap labor for self-employment activity. We hypothesize that workers who have strong ties to self-employment activity are more likely to become self-employed themselves and to succeed in this activity. Even though previous research also suggests that weak ties from previous work experience and acquaintances in the same business increase the survival rate for self-employment by reducing uncertainty and smoothing information flows (Yu 2001b), we will not emphasize this aspect of social capital, as we do not have the necessary network data to examine this hypothesis in this chapter.

Growing Heterogeneity and Gender Differences

Heterogeneity is one feature that has been noted frequently by researchers on self-employment (e.g., Arum 1997; Yu 1999). Unlike dependent employment, self-employment exists in environments with much greater uncertainty. Job schedules, returns to labor, as well as work content are all less standardized for self-employment than for dependent employment. Just as there are differences in worker characteristics and labor outcomes for wage or salaried employees across occupations and industries, there are differences among the self-employed. In fact, self-employed workers are likely to be an even more heterogeneous group, given their job characteristics and work conditions: a dentist operating his or her own clinic and a street vendor selling hot dogs are both considered self-employed.

With respect to this heterogeneous feature of self-employment, existing research shows that Taiwan is no exception. Studies on Taiwan demonstrate that there are great variations in skill levels, work orientations, and motivations for labor force participation among self-employed women (Simon 2000; Yu 1999, 2001b). Yu (1999, 2001b) also shows that the usual determinants for earnings for dependent employment, such as work experience, on-the-job tenure, and occupations, do not predict the earnings of the self-employed well, and that there is greater variation in earnings within the self-employed than within wage or salaried employees. The diversity within this group makes it difficult to determine earnings based on human capital characteristics. Taking this into account, we divide self-employed workers by the skill level of their occupations (i.e., professional, skilled, and unskilled self-employment) and examine the different dynamics within self-employment activity. If the heterogeneity hypothesis holds, we should find great differences in the determinants for entering and exiting professional, skilled, and unskilled types of self-employment.

With respect to differences in self-employment processes, many studies show that men's and women' paths to and experiences of self-employment differ (e.g., Arum 1997; Carr 1996; Loscocco and Leight 1993; Yu 2001a). Hence, gender also determines self-employment experiences. Previous studies on Taiwan show that upon separation from wage or salaried employment, men are much more likely to turn to self-employment than women; a good proportion of women become family enterprise employees rather than self-employed workers (Yu 1999). Among those who become self-employed, men are much more likely than women to employ workers in their establishment, and a good number of self-employed men have their spouse participating in their business as an unpaid or irregularly paid family enterprise worker. This is rarely the case for self-employed women (Kao 1999; Li and Ka 1994; Lu 2001; Yu 1999). Female self-employment also yields lower financial returns than male self-employment in Taiwan, after controlling for human capital and job characteristics (Yu 2000). Self-employed women, however, are more likely to remain in the labor force than their counterparts in dependent employment, despite marriage, childbearing, and child rearing (Yu 2001a, 2001b). "Being one's own boss" apparently permits married women to cope with family-work conflicts much better than dependent employment. Family cycles, in contrast, do not affect Taiwanese men's decision to participate in dependent or self-employment (Yu 2001a). All of these findings indicate that gender is a major determinant of self-employment experiences and outcomes, just as it is for dependent employment.

DATA AND METHODS

Data for the analyses in this chapter are drawn from part 2 of the 1996 Taiwan Social Change Survey, which included a nationally representative sample of 2,831 respondents aged 25–60, based on a multistage cluster sampling design.[2] Each respondent was asked to provide retrospective work histories for up to fifteen jobs, all of which had to be the primary ones of the time, and to have lasted at least one month. However, the survey requested detailed information only on respondents' most recent seven jobs and the first job. Within the sample, less than 1 percent of the respondents reported more than eight jobs. We are therefore able to reconstruct complete work histories for the vast majority in the sample, despite the missing information for those respondents who had more than eight jobs. We exclude the 105 respondents who have never worked and 21 respondents with incomplete job spells or missing demographic information. Because we are primarily interested in nonfarm job transition, we also exclude all employment spells in agricultural occupations or industries. This procedure yields 2,570 respondents; all individuals in the final sample had at least some working experiences in nonfarm sectors prior to 1996. The average number of jobs reported is 2.8 per respondent, with a standard deviation of 1.6 jobs. Based on the starting and ending age of each job spell, we construct a person-year file that extends from 1980 to 1996. For each respondent in the sample, the person-year file begins when the respondent turns 18 years old. The final sample consists of 37,427 person-year spells, with an average of 14.86 spells per respondent.

The survey asked respondents to identify for each job spell its employed or self-employed status. We believe that these self-reported results are consistent with the legal definition of self-employment provided by the state. For example, both measurements would consider owners of incorporated enterprises as self-employed. Nonetheless, the percentage of the self-employed in the labor force in the data is greater than the percentage in the labor statistics published by the government of the same year (DGBAS 1997, 31.4% for the former, 22.3% for the latter). One reason for this discrepancy is the wider age range in the government labor statistics (from age 15 onward), and the underrepresentation of self-employed among the relatively young and relatively old. The other reason is that our survey data, as compared to government reports, are better at capturing informal self-employment activity, which is believed to contain a sizeable proportion of the labor force in Taiwan (Yu 2001b).

The measurement of our dependent variables and all independent variables in the baseline models follows the research design specified in chapter 1 of this volume. Hence, educational qualification is measured on the CASMIN scale with five categories (Müller et al. 1989; Shavit and Müller 1998): (1ab) completed up to nine years of compulsory education; (2c vocational) high school graduates with a vocational emphasis; (2c general) completed senior high school; (3a) completed junior college; (3b) four-year university graduates. Two-digit Taiwanese Standard Industrial Codes were converted into the six categories of NACE industrial coding (Eurostat 1996): (1) manufacturing, mining, water/gas/electricity (C/D/E); (2) construction (F); (3) wholesale, retail (G/H); (4) transportation and communication (I); (5) finance, business service (J/K); (6) public administration, personal/domestic service (L-Q). We use the EGP class schema to classify father's and respondent's occupations into three major categories: professional/managerial (EGP I, II), skilled (EGP IIIa, V, or VI), and unskilled (EGP IIIb, VIIa) (Erikson, Goldthorpe, and Portocarero 1979; Erikson and Goldthorpe 1992). Due to a lack of detailed information, respondent's education and spouse's employment status are presumed to be constant, estimated by those reported at the time of interview. Respondent's age is measured as of the starting date of each spell. We use father's occupation and employment status when the respondent was 15 years old as a measure of socioeconomic background.

In addition to the starting and ending age of each job spell, our survey data consist of detailed information on individual work experiences and work conditions, including employment status, industry, occupation, and employer characteristics. We are therefore able to include several time-varying, work-related covariates in our extensive models. Our variable "number of job spells," which reflects one's labor force experiences, is measured by the number of job episodes that one had experienced since the first job. "Self-employment experience" measures cumulative years in self-employment prior to the current job spell. In addition to the measure of firm size, we introduce a few variables representing career opportunities and job stability in order to test our hypothesis that blocked mobility leads to self-employment. The measures of work characteristics are: (1) opportunities for promotions ("Do people of a similar rank to yours still have chances for promotion?"); (2) whether the work place is unionized ("Was there a union in your workplace?"); (3) job security ("If you wanted to, could you stay at your job for as long as you like?"); (4) the existence of internal labor markets ("Was it more likely for your company to hire a person of your rank from within or outside of the company?"); and (5) business group affiliation ("Was your organization an affiliate of a large-scale business group?"). All of the above are dummy variables except for "promotion opportunities," which is measured on a Likert scale from one to four. All extended models also control for two macroeconomic time-varying covariates: change in unemployment rate and percentage of the service sector. Unemployment rate is measured as a gender-, education-, and industry-specific annual national rate. Percentage of the service sector, which estimates interindustry differences in labor demand, is simply the share of employment in the service sector of a given year.

Following the research design of this cross-national comparative project (chapter 1), we first use logistic regression in an event-history approach to estimate the effects of various independent variables on the likelihood of transition to self-employment, treating all types of self-employment as a single category. We then adopt discrete competing-risk models to examine the processes by which individuals move into the three different types of self-employment. Respondents who are considered at risk for transition to self-employment must have been at least 20 years old, not self-employed, and not in agricultural industries or occupations as of 1979. With respect to the analyses of separation from self-employment, we use only logistic regression analyses because the total number of exits from each category of self-employment is too small to model competing risks.

DESCRIPTIVE FINDINGS

To properly describe self-employed workers in Taiwan, we first compare the characteristics of the self-employed to dependent-employed workers in our sample (table 12.1). The unit for the descriptive statistics is the person-year, not the individual, so these results are weighted by the number of spells that a respondent had in our sample. In general, self-employment was highly concentrated in establishments with less than ten employees, while dependent employees were more evenly distributed across medium- and large-sized firms. Skilled and unskilled self-employment consisted of mostly small-sized, family-owned businesses. Some 80 to 95 percent of these spells involved establishments employing fewer than five employees, mostly irregularly paid family members.[3]

Moreover, the industrial distribution of nonfarm self-employment differs for men and women. For men, professional self-employment is concentrated highly in manufacturing; skilled self-employment in construction; and unskilled self-employment in traditional services and transportation. For women, we find more than 85 percent of unskilled self-employment spells and nearly 60 percent of professional self-employment spells in traditional service industries. The largest group of skilled self-employed workers was in personal services.

The most common occupations for male professional self-employed were executives and directors (55.5%) and managers and administrators (11.5%). In contrast, skilled self-employment for men consisted mainly of construction contractors (23.5%), construction and maintenance painters (11.3%), and machinery mechanics or fitters (9.0%). Furthermore, the mostly likely occupations for unskilled self-employment among men were shop salespersons and demonstrators (37.5%), motor-vehicle drivers (15.7%), street vendors, stall and other market salespersons (12.4%), and housekeeping or restaurant service workers (11.3%). For women, the largest groups for professional self-employment are executives and directors (29.8%), followed by managers and administrators (19.1%), while skilled self-employment included occupations such as hairdressers, beauticians, and workers providing other personal services (45.9%); tailors, dressmakers, and garment trade workers (22.7%); and accounting, bookkeeping clerks, and security brokers (7.5%). As for female unskilled self-employment, the main categories are shop salespersons and demonstrators (37.2%), housekeeping and restaurant service worker (25.6%), and street vendors, stall or other market salespersons (12.4%).

With respect to educational attainment, professional self-employed workers had higher education on average than dependent employees, while unskilled self-employed workers had less education than dependent employees. This is to some extent consistent with the skills required for these different types of employment. However, both professional and unskilled self-employed workers had somewhat less educational attainment compared with their counterparts in dependent employment. The results are consistent with our arguments that self-employment provides an alternative route of upward mobility for those whose opportunities are relatively limited as wage or salaried employees in the private sector. Surprisingly, educational attainment among the skilled self-employed was not higher than among the unskilled self-employed: over 70 percent of skilled self-employment spells in our sample were associated with no more than nine years of compulsory education. The government statistics in the same year revealed a similar pattern: 69.1 percent of male own-account workers and 71.3 percent of female own-account workers had received only minimum education (DGBAS 1997). This result suggests that many of the skills needed for skilled self-employment are acquired from previous work experiences rather than in school.

Despite the prevalence of family business in Taiwan, the rate of family inheritance was not particularly high, as far as the descriptive statistics are concerned. Compared with dependent employees, self-employed men

TABLE 12.1
Characteristics of Self-Employed and Dependent Employed in Taiwan, Pooled Data, 1980–96 (in percent)

| | Male | | | | | | | Female | | | | | | | | |
| | Self-employed | | | Dependent | | | | Self-employed | | | Dependent | | | | Number | |
Industry	Prof.	Skill	Unskilled	Prof.	Skill	Unskilled	Total	Prof.	Skill	Unskilled	Prof.	Skill	Unskilled	Total	in row	%
Manufacturing (C/D/E)	41.5	28.9	15.4	38.0	41.5	49.9	38.0	23.4	23.8	6.0	15.3	49.6	56.9	41.0	10,786	39.2
Construction (F)	7.6	43.1	0.1	4.6	32.2	5.2	16.8	5.3	3.6	0.0	1.4	6.4	3.8	3.9	3,224	11.7
Traditional service (G/H)	21.4	10.4	63.9	5.8	5.7	8.6	14.6	59.6	4.7	85.3	8.4	12.3	15.4	19.3	4,532	16.5
Transport/communication (I)	2.4	0.4	16.4	5.8	7.0	16.7	9.0	0.0	0.9	1.3	1.8	3.7	5.3	3.6	1,889	6.9
Business service (J/K)	11.8	2.9	0.0	10.5	3.1	2.5	4.5	0.0	6.1	1.1	8.4	6.6	4.1	5.4	1,333	4.8
Other service (L–Q)	15.2	14.4	4.3	35.3	10.5	17.0	17.1	11.7	61.0	6.2	64.7	21.3	14.5	26.8	5,765	20.9
Education 1ab	23.9	71.8	68.3	5.0	53.0	61.7	47.7	19.1	75.0	72.8	6.0	35.3	66.0	47.4	13,116	47.6
2c (vocational)	16.1	17.5	17.7	20.4	24.0	25.9	21.7	5.3	17.4	19.0	20.6	35.5	23.6	25.8	6,439	23.4

															Total N	Total %
2c (academic)	8.4	4.5	7.3	4.3	6.0	3.8	5.2	17.0	2.5	4.0	3.9	6.0	3.5	4.4	1,356	4.9
3a	30.0	4.2	5.4	27.7	11.4	6.1	12.9	40.4	2.8	3.4	35.6	13.8	5.5	13.0	3,557	12.9
3b	21.6	2.0	1.3	42.6	5.6	2.5	12.4	18.1	2.3	0.8	33.9	9.4	1.4	9.3	3,083	11.2
Father self-employed	28.2	28.0	24.0	20.2	17.4	17.5	20.6	67.0	19.8	21.6	29.9	22.9	20.5	23.2	5,960	21.6
Annual Income																
Mean	1,057	567	582	583	353	299	446	717	394	415	419	257	201	275	3,800	
Median	600	420	400	500	300	265	360	600	300	360	380	207	180	216	3,800	
Weekly work hours	52.1	52.5	61.7	48.6	49.4	51.4	51.4	58.7	55.2	61.3	45.2	48.6	50.0	50.2	4,052	
Firms Size																
1 person	13.2	38.0	55.9	0.0	2.2	1.5	12.8	1.1	49.9	40.9	0.1	1.8	1.5	7.9	2,771	10.9
2–4	15.5	39.1	31.0	2.8	16.0	8.3	15.9	13.8	33.0	53.6	2.4	9.2	8.4	13.4	3,802	14.9
5–9	18.2	14.3	10.0	4.0	14.2	12.7	11.3	51.1	11.6	3.0	8.1	13.8	10.5	10.8	2,836	11.1
10–29	36.5	7.6	2.2	10.3	18.5	17.4	14.0	5.3	4.6	2.5	14.1	22.1	17.1	15.9	3,763	14.7
30–99	15.1	1.0	1.0	14.3	11.0	18.2	11.1	8.5	0.8	0.0	18.7	16.4	16.7	14.3	3,159	12.4
100–499	1.6	0.0	0.0	21.8	11.4	14.3	11.2	20.2	0.0	0.0	21.3	16.9	23.1	17.3	3,476	13.6
500+	0.0	0.0	0.0	46.8	26.7	27.5	23.8	0.0	0.0	0.0	35.4	19.8	22.7	20.3	5,708	22.4
Column N	740	2,048	1,984	3,478	4,679	3,697	16,626	94	643	979	1,790	3,377	4,042	10,925	27,551	
%	2.7	7.4	7.2	12.6	17.0	13.4	60.3	0.3	2.3	3.6	6.5	12.3	14.7	39.7		

Source: 1996 Social Change Survey, Taiwan

Note: The units of analysis for industries, education, father's self-employment and occupation, and firm size are "person-year." The units of analysis for weekly work hour and wage are "person-job."

had a slightly higher proportion of fathers who were also self-employed, but the difference was not significant. Self-employed women in professional occupations, however, were somewhat unique in this perspective, as 67 percent of female professional employment spells were linked to fathers who were self-employed. This finding indicates that women's entry into professional self-employment is closely tied to their family conditions. Facing relatively high entry barriers, women who entered professional self-employment were likely to have done so through the direct inheritance of a family business.[4]

Across all three occupational types, the earnings for the self-employed were, on average, higher than their counterparts in wage or salaried employment. But this is not without a sacrifice: self-employed workers worked longer weekly hours than dependent employees. The differences were particularly large for unskilled occupations. The average hours of work per week for the unskilled self-employed exceeded sixty hours, which was ten hours more than the dependent employees in unskilled occupations worked. Gender differences in hours worked also reveal an interesting pattern. While female dependent employees generally worked fewer hours than their male counterparts, self-employed women in professional and skilled occupations worked longer hours than self-employed men in the same occupations.

The previous discussion has described the characteristics of self-employed workers in Taiwan. To further our understanding of self-employment processes in Taiwan, we use the Product-Limit method developed by Kaplan and Meier to estimate the survivorship functions for different types of self-employment (Blossfeld, Hamerle, and Mayer 1989). The survival function gives the probability of "surviving" (remaining in self-employment) during a specific time period $t_{(j)}$, given that a self-employed person has not yet left his or her status by time $t_{(j-1)}$. The slope of the survival curves thus indicates an approximate rate of separation from self-employment at different time points.

Figure 12.2 plots the survival functions of self-employment by gender and by types of self-employment. Compared with the other countries examined in this volume, self-employment in Taiwan is relatively stable. The five-year survival rate was 86 percent for men and 80 percent for women. Nevertheless, the fact that we have been making use of retrospective data, where short unsuccessful spells are often not reported, is also likely to contribute to the stability in our estimates. The comparison between male and female survival curves shows that self-employed men were less likely to exit than self-employed women (logrank test $\chi^2 = 16.51$, p $<$ .000). While men still had an 80 percent survival rate after ten years in self-employment, the survival rate for women dropped to 64.1 percent. The pattern of the Kaplan-Meier curves among different

Male

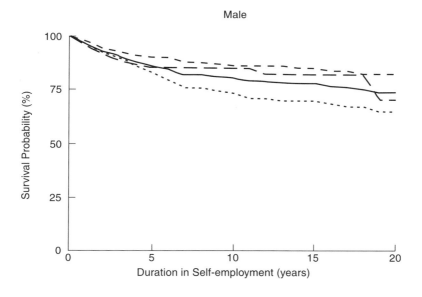

Female

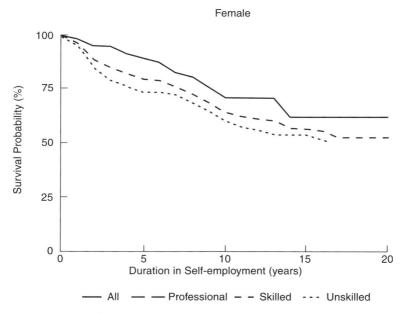

——— All — — Professional – – Skilled - - - Unskilled

Figure 12.2: Kaplan-Meier Survival Function for Exit from Self-Employment in Taiwan

types of self-employment is also interesting. Skilled self-employment is more stable than unskilled, for both men and women. Furthermore, for self-employed men in professional and skilled occupations, most exits occurred during the first five years, whereas the downward part of the step function continues for at least ten years in self-employment for females.

In summary, the descriptive findings show that the self-employed differ from wage and salaried employees in a number of respects. Self-employed workers are generally less educated and more likely to be engaged in small-scale, family-owned businesses with their spouses. They also work longer hours but with higher earnings and are more concentrated in a few industries and occupations. Father's employment status is correlated with one's choice of self-employment, but a closer examination is required to determine the impact. Moreover, among those in self-employment, the highest exit rate was observed among unskilled workers. Our explanation is that the higher resource requirement and sunk-cost investment among skilled and professional self-employed create a greater propensity for retention, compared to unskilled self-employment. Finally, the descriptive findings indicate that not only do women encounter greater obstacles upon entering self-employment, but they are also less likely to succeed in self-employment than their male counterparts.

Multivariate Analyses

Tables 12.2–12.4 show the results from the logistic and multinomial logit models; we examine both entry into and exit from self-employment for all respondents, as well as for male and female respondents separately, with an event-history approach. Tables 12.2 and 12.4 include both baseline and extensive models, with the latter including additional variables concerning mostly one's previous work conditions. It is important to note that for the entry models (tables 12.2 and 12.3), we examine entry into self-employment without regard to original status (including unemployment and being in school), within the period 1980–96. Such job movement also has to occur after a respondent turned age 18 to be taken into account, since our person-year data excluded time periods before age 18 for each respondent. Those who were self-employed before or at age 18, or before 1980 and remained so throughout our examination period, would not be considered at risk of entering self-employment because they were already self-employed in our selected person-year sample. As a result, our analyses on the entry into self-employment censor 208 respondents. Thus, discrepancies between the descriptive statistics in table 12.1 and the results of the following analyses may exist, because the two samples are not exactly the same.

Table 12.2 predicts entry into self-employment among all respondents during the period of 1980–96. There is an interesting contrast in table 12.2 between the logistic models that predict one's movement into self-employment, which treat self-employment as a single category, and the multinomial models that estimate competing risks of turning into professional, skilled, and unskilled self-employment. The findings are consistent with our argument that self-employment is a category of great heterogeneity, and that the paths to self-employment vary for different types of self-employment. For example, in the baseline logistic model, the coefficients for the effect of education suggest that highly educated people are less likely to become self-employed (panel 1). The multinomial logit model (baseline), however, shows that educational attainment is *positively* associated with entry into professional self-employment but has a negative effect on entry into unskilled self-employment.

Comparison between the single-event and competing-risk models also shows that the contribution of family-based social capital to self-employment activity varies across different types of self-employment. Father's self-employment status serves as a good predictor *only* for entry into unskilled self-employment, even though the effect in the former model is positive and significant. Likewise, while having a spouse in family employment, usually working for one's own business, has positive effects on entry into self-employment in the single-event logistic model, the competing-risk multinomial logit model shows that this is the case only for professional and unskilled self-employment, but not for skilled self-employment. We argue that it is because unskilled self-employment tends to use exploitation of family labor as a way to reduce costs and increase labor flexibility. Hence, having a spouse working for the enterprise increases one's chance of being self-employed in unskilled occupations. In contrast, professional self-employed may not need the spouse's labor. But, since this type of self-employment tends to yield high returns, provides relatively great time flexibility, and renders relatively high status for family members in the enterprise, it attracts one's spouse to the enterprise. For skilled self-employment, whether the spouse works for the family enterprise may be neither necessary for the business nor beneficial for the spouse and therefore has no significant effect.

The baseline models in table 12.2 also show strong gender effects on entry into self-employment, particularly with professional self-employment. The gender effects remain in the extensive models. Women are less likely than men to become self-employed, after controlling for social background, human capital, previous job characteristics, and macro-level economic changes. Despite an increase in female self-employment in the service industries (figure 12.1A), men continue to predominate in the self-employment sector in Taiwan. Women are even more unlikely to

TABLE 12.2
Logistic and Multinomial Logit Coefficients on Entry into Self-Employment in Taiwan

	All	Prof.	Skilled	Unskilled	All	Prof.	Skilled	Unskilled
Education								
2a	0.18	0.79+	0.37	0.04	0.21	0.91	0.69*	-0.10
2b	0.39+	1.55**	0.31	0.25	0.34	1.47*	0.63	0.09
3a	-0.04	1.91**	-0.05	-0.95**	0.08	2.23**	0.39	-0.99**
3b	-0.60*	1.28*	-0.68	-1.31**	-0.42	1.80**	-0.17	-1.31**
Female	-0.98**	-2.27**	-0.74**	-0.81**	-0.97**	-2.15**	-0.69**	-0.83**
Age	0.12**	0.25**	0.09+	0.11**	0.12**	0.23**	0.05	0.11**
Age squared	-0.00**	-0.01**	-0.00*	-0.00**	-0.00**	-0.01**	-0.00*	-0.00**
Father's employment (*ref: unskilled*)								
Professional/managerial	0.14	0.66+	-0.14	0.02	0.13	0.74*	-0.16	0.04
Skilled	-0.02	0.30	-0.03	-0.13	-0.08	0.23	-0.08	-0.20
Farmer	0.14	-0.21	0.17	0.23	0.12	-0.05	0.17	0.21
Family worker	0.44	0.20	0.85	0.29	0.23	-0.21	0.76	0.15
No job/no information	-0.18	-0.52	0.22	-0.36	-0.27	-0.26	0.07	-0.44
Father self-employed	0.34*	-0.01	-0.04	0.63**	0.26+	-0.04	-0.19	0.58**
Employment status in origin state (*ref: unskilled*)								
Professional/managerial	0.06	0.41	0.21	-0.33	0.10	0.52	0.28	-0.25
Skilled	0.02	-0.31	1.14**	-0.40*	0.03	-0.21	1.17**	-0.36+
Not working	0.38*	0.33	1.15**	0.24	-0.17	0.47	0.51	-0.31
Industial sector in origin state (*ref: manufacture*)								
Construction (F)	-0.38+	-0.40	-0.31	-0.39	-0.59*	-0.85	-0.68+	-0.52
Traditional service (G/H)	0.26	0.71+	0.41	0.08	-0.02	0.19	0.07	-0.07
Transport, communication (I)	0.08	-1.20	0.34	0.35	0.19	-1.35+	0.62	0.41
Finance, business service (J/K)	0.06	-0.15	-0.05	0.26	-0.09	-0.18	-0.18	0.12
Other service (L–Q)	-0.43*	-1.53**	0.19	-0.27	-0.32	-1.48**	0.38	-0.20

Employment of spouse (*ref: no partner*)

Employee	−0.35*	−0.04	−1.11**	−0.15	−0.27	0.10	−1.13**	−0.07
Self-employed	0.50**	1.41**	−0.68	0.62**	0.53**	1.45**	−0.78+	0.70**
Family worker	1.62**	2.68**	0.90	1.62**	1.58**	2.73**	0.61	1.68**
Not working	−0.14	−0.07	0.16	−0.34	−0.02	−0.12	0.24	−0.21
Number of job spells					0.00	0.07	0.04	−0.01
Self-employment experience (in years)					0.26**	0.49*	0.22*	0.25**
(Self-employment experience)^2					−0.02**	−0.05	−0.01	−0.02*
Unemployment rate					0.08	0.14	0.03	0.12
% service sector					2.43+	0.92	0.54	4.49*
Firm size (under 5)								
5–9					−0.04	0.10	−0.60	0.19
10–29					−0.19	−0.10	−0.82*	0.03
30–99					−0.39	−0.73	−1.24**	0.12
100–499					−0.58*	−0.80	−1.25**	−0.23
500+ or government					−1.30**	−1.94**	−2.36**	−0.52
No information					−0.27	−1.09	−0.86+	−0.22
Union					−0.33*	−0.19	−0.69*	−0.20
Possibility of promotion					0.14*	0.37**	0.12	0.05
Job security					−0.49**	−0.11	−0.28	−0.68**
Promotion from within					−0.24	−0.61+	0.03	−0.25
Business group affiliation					0.45**	0.06	1.16**	0.20
Number of children under 5					0.05	−0.16	0.11	0.07
Intercept	−4.66**	−8.21**	−6.29**	−5.01**	−5.40**	−9.46**	−6.19**	−6.64**
Number of observations	30,939	30,939	30,939	30,939	30,939	30,939	30,939	30,939
Number of events	386	67	103	216	386	67	103	216
Log likelihood	−1962.2		−2242.1		−1914.2		−2173.7	
Pseudo R^2	0.055		0.087		0.078		0.114	

Source: 1996 Social Change Survey, Taiwan

+ $p < 0.10$ * $p < 0.05$, ** $p < 0.01$

enter professional or managerial self-employment. These effects are consistent with our descriptive findings.

The extensive models in table 12.2 have not changed the effects of the variables in the baseline models much. We still observe considerable differences in determinants for entry into the three types of self-employment. Moreover, the expansion of the service (and sales) sector since 1980 has increased the likelihood of entering only unskilled self-employment, which included a disproportionate number of low-skilled service and sales occupations, but not the other two types. The characteristics of previous jobs and their relevant opportunities for upward mobility also affect the odds of entering professional, skilled, and unskilled self-employment differently, but we will discuss these variables in the analysis by gender, as their effects are gender-specific. Likewise, we will discuss the variable that signifies family responsibilities and number of children under age 5 in a later section.

There are still several results worth mentioning in the extensive models in table 12.2. First, the coefficients in the extensive models further show that previous experience with self-employment has positive effects on entry into all three types of self-employment, even though the magnitude varies. We argue that previous exposure to self-employment activity reduces one's fears of the risk and uncertainty involved in self-employment, not to mention increasing one's knowledge and information base for succeeding in self-employment. Moreover, those who have had experience in self-employment may have established the "right" social networks that increase information flow and lower the cost of self-employment activity. For example, previous experience as a dependently employed hairstylist familiarizes one with certain customers and suppliers of relevant products for the business. Thus, one can establish one's own hair salon based on these social networks. Nonetheless, our lack of network data makes this connection between previous self-employment experience and social capital mainly suggestive.

Second, father's self-employment affects only entry into unskilled self-employment, while father's employment in professional or managerial occupations, self-employed or not, positively affects one's entry into professional self-employment. We argue that these effects are consistent with our social capital hypothesis, where the different characteristics of professional, skilled, and unskilled self-employment need to be taken into account. For unskilled self-employment, having close family ties, including father and wife, in self-employment increases one's exposure to this activity and allows the possibility of mobilizing family labor at low cost. However, for professional self-employment, access to cheap labor is less important. Father's employment in professional or managerial occupations helps movement into professional self-employment because it enhances one's access to the professional and managerial networks necessary for successful professional self-employment. The results also reveal that family-based social capital does not have significant impact on entry into skilled self-employment in Taiwan.

Table 12.3 displays results from the extended models in table 12.2, while separating the analyses for male and female respondents to obtain a more specific picture of the gender effects in self-employment. The differences in the self-employment dynamics for professional, skilled, and unskilled self-employment remain in the analyses among male respondents. The model that estimates competing risks of entry into the three types of self-employment for men also finds that not only does education have opposite effects for entry into professional and unskilled self-employment, but alternative career opportunities also have similar results. Opportunities rendered by previous jobs are positively associated with entry into professional self-employment, yet negatively connected with entry into unskilled self-employment. For example, the self-reported possibility of being promoted at the previous job positively contributes to one's movement into professional self-employment, whereas poor previous work conditions such as a non-unionized workplace and low job security increase the likelihood for entering skilled and unskilled self-employment. This shows that professional self-employment is for those men who possess relatively great human capital and promising careers and choose to take risks in search of greater returns. This somewhat fits our usual image of business entrepreneurs.

The story for men in unskilled and skilled self-employment, in contrast to professional self-employment, is completely different. Generally, those men who have less education and undesirable jobs that permit little security and union protection, and yet have been exposed to self-employment through either a father or a spouse, are most likely to shift into unskilled self-employment. The case is less extreme for entry into skilled self-employment. However, it is also true that those men whose previous jobs were in smaller firms and unprotected by labor unions were likely to move into skilled self-employment. Along with the descriptive finding that the percentage of unskilled and skilled self-employment is exceptionally high compared with other economies examined in this volume, these results support our argument that the relatively large proportion of self-employed workers in Taiwan should be considered a response to an unregulated private sector and low protection for dependent employment in an economy composed of mostly small- to medium-sized enterprises.

Previously working at a business-group affiliate has a strong positive effect on men's entry into skilled self-employment, but not on other types of self-employment (table 12.3). This is somewhat surprising because a job at a unit affiliated with a large business group may mean

TABLE 12.3
Logistic and Multinomial Logit Coefficients on Entry into Self-Employment in Taiwan by Gender

	Male				Female		
	All	Prof.	Skilled	Unskilled	All	Prof./Skilled	Unskilled
Education (1ab)							
2a	0.31	0.93	0.69+	0.07	0.03	0.87	−0.26
2b	0.42	1.41+	0.62	0.31	0.20	1.03	−0.02
3a	0.31	2.17**	0.51	−0.87*	−0.68	0.38	−1.18+
3b	−0.40	1.36+	0.04	−1.41**	−0.35	0.82	−1.06
Age	0.15**	0.14	0.09	0.18**	0.08+	0.15	0.06
$(Age)^2$	−0.01**	−0.01*	−0.00+	−0.01**	−0.00+	−0.01+	−0.00
Father's employment							
Professional/managerial	0.31	0.50	−0.05	0.41	−0.26	0.26	−0.53
Skilled	0.15	−0.01	0.12	0.16	−0.38	0.17	−0.59+
Farmer	0.18	−0.07	0.21	0.39	0.09	0.20	0.06
Family workers	0.11	−0.22	−0.19	0.64	0.49	1.52*	−0.19
No job/no information	−0.01	−0.35	−0.00	0.17	−0.83+	0.23	−1.50*
Father self-employed	0.25	−0.37	−0.16	0.81**	0.35	0.07	0.45+
Employment status in origin state							
Professional/managerial	0.14	0.70	−0.09	−0.07	−0.27	0.60	−0.55
Skilled	−0.18	−0.19	0.89*	−0.67*	0.53*	1.36*	0.24
Not working	0.09	−0.02	0.54	0.15	0.13	0.52	0.19
Industrial sector in origin state							
Construction (F)	−0.60*	−0.87	−0.48	−0.66	−0.08	−34.16	0.45
Traditional Service (G/H)	−0.07	0.31	0.16	−0.36	0.15	−0.11	0.30
Transport, communication	0.24	−1.21	0.46	0.55+	−0.21	0.38	−0.56
Finance, business service	−0.02	−0.03	−0.11	0.28	−0.19	−0.69	−0.03
Other service (L-Q)	−0.97**	−2.08**	−0.98	−0.36	0.33	0.76	−0.07

Employment of spouse (no partner)

	(1)	(2)	(3)	(4)	(5)	(6)	(7)
Employee	0.00	0.14	-0.92+	0.29	-0.52+	-1.02*	-0.22
Self-employed	1.30**	1.71**	0.25	1.37**	0.15	-0.75	0.56+
Family worker	1.79**	2.92**	0.84	1.77**	1.51**	0.57	1.97**
Not working	0.26	0.29	0.58	0.01	-0.51	-0.68	-0.31
Number of job spells	0.04+	0.08	0.01	0.05	-0.03	0.01	-0.04
Self-employment experience (in years)	0.35**	0.52*	0.50**	0.17	0.15+	0.09	0.29*
(Self-employment experience)^2	-0.03**	-0.05	-0.04*	-0.02	-0.01	0.00	-0.02
Unemployment rate	0.02	0.07	-0.02	0.02	0.12	-0.02	0.18
% service sector	2.29	0.29	0.39	4.25+	3.43	-0.30	4.50
Firm size (under 5)							
5–9	-0.16	-0.13	-0.91+	0.05	0.06	-0.35	0.25
10–29	-0.14	-0.05	-0.80+	0.18	-0.40	-1.22+	-0.06
30–99	-0.58+	-0.97	-1.53*	0.06	0.01	-0.71	0.36
100–499	-0.55+	-0.57	-1.37*	-0.00	-0.67	-1.81*	-0.09
500 + or government	-1.52**	-1.71*	-2.91**	-0.76	-0.65	-1.93*	0.04
No information	-0.25	-1.04	-0.60	0.22	-0.50	-34.78	0.21
Union	-0.56**	-0.38	-0.92*	-0.47+	0.12	-0.19	0.21
Possibility of promotion	0.14+	0.32*	0.21	0.02	0.17	0.16	0.17
Job security	-0.63**	-0.09	-0.50	-0.95**	-0.25	0.06	-0.36
Promotion from within	-0.21	-0.59	0.12	-0.21	-0.26	-0.41	-0.22
Business group affiliation	0.49*	-0.04	1.38**	0.31	0.18	0.65	-0.09
Number of children under 5	-0.10	-0.26	0.00	-0.07	0.25*	0.33	0.22+
Intercept	-5.73**	-8.01**	-6.12**	-7.22**	-6.79**	-7.14**	-7.74**
Number of observations	14,073		14,073		16,866		16,866
Number of events	240	58	67	115	146	45	101
Log likelihood	-1081.9		-1255.6		-794.8		-857.9
Pseudo R^2	0.110		0.144		0.052		0.077

Source: 1996 Social Change Survey, Taiwan
+ p < 0.10 * p < 0.05 ** p < 0.01

better pay and better chance of promotion, compared with a job at an independent firm that is likely to be very small. It seems contradictory to our other result that men who enter skilled employment are those who had experienced bad jobs in the private sector. However, we argue that large business groups are particularly likely to outsource skilled work. Previous affiliation increases the odds for a skilled self-employed worker to subcontract such work from a large business group. Hence, previous affiliation with a large business group enhances the survival chances for a skilled worker in self-employment, as well as lowering entry barriers.

To answer why this is not the case for entry into professional self-employment, we need to keep in mind that only those who possess relatively high human capital are likely to enter professional self-employment. Highly educated men with abundant skills at an affiliated unit of a large business group have great opportunities for moving up within the business group, unlike midlevel workers with modest skills. Given that large business groups are the only kind of organizations that adopt internal labor markets and have high enough ceilings for upward mobility in Taiwan, where small- and medium-sized enterprises prevail, those men who are capable of taking advantages of internal labor markets become less likely to leave.

Panels 5–7 in table 12.3 are the results of applying similar models to the female sample. Because women are still less likely than men to become self-employed, the number of cases in our female sample who had shifted into self-employment is rather small. This leads to less robust results than those for the male sample. We also have to combine professional and skilled self-employment in the analyses because there are not enough cases of women who entered professional self-employment in the given period to provide stable results. Nevertheless, some of the coefficients are in similar directions as those for the male sample. For example, previous work experience in skilled occupations increases the chance of entering skilled self-employment. Father's self-employment also contributes to a woman's entry into unskilled self-employment, although the effect is not very significant. It is worth noting that even though the descriptive findings suggest that a high percentage of women in professional self-employment were from self-employed families (see table 12.1), there is no significant effect of father's self-employment on entry into professional or skilled self-employment. This is partly because the number of women moving into professional employment is quite small.

It is interesting that husbands who are contributing family workers have a positive effect on entry into unskilled self-employment, but not into skilled self-employment. Even though there is no direct evidence that husbands in family employment were contributing to their wife's business, there were a good number of cases in which the husband was reported as a family worker when the wife identified herself as the owner of the business, despite the fact that in the national statistics, the percentage of men in family employment was extremely small (see fig. 12.1A). Thus, gender relations in small, low-skilled, family-owned establishments are not fixed: either the husband or the wife may be reported as the owner, with the spouse reported as a family worker, depending on who is classifying the self-reported status, while in reality the couple runs the business as a partnership. Lu's (2001) ethnographic work on the "boss's wife" and small family businesses supports this observation. For women's entry into skilled self-employment, however, whether the husband is self-employed or in family employment has no effect, but previous experience in skilled occupations does have a large and positive effect. These findings are similar to the findings for men.

Few of the work-related variables in table 12.3 show meaningful effects for women. Whether a woman had great opportunities for upward mobility with the previous job, how secure the previous job was, or whether the previous workplace was unionized all have insignificant effects. Nonetheless, we would like to mention that the effects for the number of children under age 5 appear positive for entering self-employment, though the effects become less stable when looking at entry into the different types of self-employment separately. These are consistent with previous findings that women's self-employment is less likely a decision based on career concerns, but more likely one related to family responsibilities, as compared to their male counterparts.

The last table for our multivariate analyses, table 12.4, provides results for predicting separation from self-employment. In the baseline model on all respondents, we observe that women are far more likely to leave self-employment than their male counterparts. The effect remains in the extensive model for all respondents. It is worth noting that these models do not set any limit on the destinations after leaving self-employment, so a large proportion of women may leave self-employment upon withdrawal from the labor force. In addition, for married women, the gender roles that assume that husbands are the major income provider for the household, and that female earnings are supplementary, allow women to quit even when there is no other job opportunity. Despite such gender effects, relatively successful women, namely, women in professional self-employment, are much less likely to leave self-employment than their male counterparts.

It is worth noting that having a father or a spouse in self-employment or a spouse in family employment makes exit from self-employment less likely. This supports our social network argument that strong ties in self-employment, regardless of whether they serve as contributing family workers, increase the survival rates of self-employment. Furthermore,

TABLE 12.4
Logistic Regressions on Exit from Self-Employment in Taiwan

	All	Male	Female	All	Male	Female
Education (1ab)						
2a	0.38⁺	0.28	0.75*	0.21	0.24	0.13
2b	0.48	0.53	0.81	0.34	0.52	−0.02
3a	0.45	0.21	1.01⁺	0.21	−0.06	0.33
3b	0.24	0.08	0.81	0.09	−0.09	−0.24
Female	0.75**			0.76**		
Age	−0.05	0.09	−0.17**	−0.05	0.09	−0.15*
Age squared	0.00	−0.00	0.01**	0.00	−0.00	0.01**
Father's employment (unskilled)						
Professional/ manager	−0.40	−0.54	−0.34	−0.39	−0.59	0.11
Skilled	0.14	0.23	0.07	0.09	0.24	−0.00
Farmer	−0.67**	−0.51⁺	−0.88*	−0.71**	−0.64*	−1.09**
Family worker	−0.40	−0.92	−0.13	−0.42	−0.92	0.66
No job/no information	−0.59	−0.77	0.26	−0.54	−0.72	0.27
Father self-employed	−0.31	−0.55⁺	0.12	−0.34	−0.62*	0.02
Employment status in origin state						
Professional/ managerial	−0.44	−0.20	−2.21*	−0.51	−0.35	−1.86
Skilled occupation	−0.27	−0.14	−0.42	−0.30	−0.23	−0.32
Industrial sector in origin state						
Construction (F)	−0.76⁺	−0.89*	0.24	−0.68⁺	−0.84⁺	1.86
Traditional service (G/H)	0.13	0.21	−0.12	0.17	0.28	−0.34
Transport, communication (I)	0.39	0.55		0.47	0.70⁺	
Finance, business service (J/K)	−1.81⁺	−1.24		−1.79⁺	−1.22	
Other service (L-Q)	−0.46	−0.32	−0.74	−0.40	−0.14	−1.00*
Employment of spouse (no partner)						
Employee	0.05	−0.01	0.04	0.03	−0.04	0.10
Self-employed	−1.12**	−1.16**	−1.14**	−1.13**	−1.02*	−1.09**

TABLE 12.4 (*continued*)

	All	*Male*	*Female*	*All*	*Male*	*Female*
Family worker	−2.72**	−3.25**	−1.76[+]	2.74**	3.36**	−1.87[+]
Not working	−0.51*	−0.55[+]	−0.77	−0.45[+]	−0.48	−0.59
Duration in s.-e. spell	−0.12**	−0.25**	0.02	−0.12**	−0.27**	0.02
(Duration in s.-e. spell)^2	0.00**	0.01**	−0.00	0.00**	0.01**	−0.00
Labor market experience (in years)				−0.02	−0.05	−0.04
Self-employment experience (in years)				−0.00	0.00	−0.07
Unemployment rate				0.01	−0.26	0.24
% service sector				5.07*	4.60	4.43
Firm size (under 5)						
5–9				0.40	0.84**	−0.57
10–29				0.08	0.40	−2.72*
30–99				0.26	0.16	0.69
No information				−0.27	−0.16	−0.42
Intercept	−2.09**	−2.65**	−1.07[+]	−4.13**	−3.97**	−2.93
Number of observations	6,488	4,772	1,716	6,488	4,772	1,716
Number of events	171	98	73	171	98	73
Log likelihood	−709.9	−425.7	−265.5	−704.8	−418.2	−259.5
Pseudo R^2	0.102	0.109	0.112	0.108	0.124	0.129

* $p < 0.05$, ** $p < 0.01$

one's own duration in self-employment also helps male self-employment survival. The longer a man has been self-employed, the less likely he is to leave this employment status. Our explanation is that self-employment experience by itself increases one's skills and social connections in a business and increases the survival rate. However, this variable does not determine women's exits from self-employment. We suggest that this gender difference may be affected by the generally greater odds for women to exit self-employment than for men.

The coefficients for firm size on departure from self-employment are also worthy of note. Among self-employed men, those who own firms of five to nine employees are more likely to exit from self-employment than owners of very small establishments with fewer than five employees who are usually all family members. For the other categories of firm size, the signs of the effects are also positive, but not statistically significant, for predicting men's exits from self-employment.[5] These findings show that owners of enterprises that hire people outside of the family have to bear greater and more regular labor cost than those who do not, and therefore they would need to end the business when the profits are insufficient. In contrast, the very small businesses that employ close family members can survive for a relatively long time as the labor cost can be reduced to zero if necessary. It is also possible that exits from self-employment for men who hire five to nine employees are the consequences of acquisitions by larger firms, when establishments of this size are successful.[6] Moreover, many establishments with five to nine employees are in retail sales or personal services (e.g., coffee shops, convenience stores, beauty salons), where large franchises prevail, so the exits may also result from quitting one's own enterprise to join a franchise of a similar kind.

DISCUSSION

This chapter unfolds the story of self-employment in Taiwan in three perspectives: macro-level opportunity structures, influences of individual social networks, and heterogeneity within self-employment activity. In an earlier section we presented the macro-level economic structure in Taiwan and argued that we need to understand self-employment activity in this context. The state-led economic development in the postwar era, the concentration of light and labor-intensive industries, and the unique arrangements of production all contributed to an economic structure that consists of a large number of small to medium-sized establishments and subcontracting systems that help perpetuate small-scale establishments. These economic settings have consequently lowered the threshold for entry into self-employment. However, we argue that it is the other side of this economic structure that causes the majority of self-employed to choose this path.

The economic and legal context in Taiwan leads to relatively low gains from dependent employment in comparison with self-employment. As stated previously, over half of the labor force in Taiwan worked in firms with fewer than thirty employees in 1996. Small enterprises fail easily, permit little upward mobility from within, and cannot afford adequate fringe benefits or long-term pension plans for employees. It is also difficult for the state to force the majority of small firms to provide employment benefits because such action could induce bankruptcy, not to mention that these firms are usually small enough to absent themselves from state regulations. As a result, the poor work conditions that low-skilled workers encounter in the weakly regulated private sector push them into self-employment. Our multivariate analyses support this argument. The results show that poorly educated workers, particularly male workers who were employed in nonunionized workplaces and not offered long-term employment, are likely to move into low-status self-employment. Even though our analyses also show that the profile for self-employed workers in professional occupations is remarkably different, we should keep in mind that what makes self-employment activity unique in Taiwan is the large percentage of low-skilled self-employment. Thus, our argument that an unregulated private sector causes the unusually large proportion of self-employed in the labor force in Taiwan is validated.

Regarding the relevance of social capital to self-employment activity, our results support the hypothesis that strong ties in self-employment are important in determining paths to self-employment, despite different dynamics for professional, skilled, and unskilled types of self-employment. Close family ties in self-employment also help retention. In addition, strong ties smooth the entry into professional self-employment in a somewhat different way: father's employment in professional and managerial occupations helps promote access to social networks in high-power positions and therefore makes it easier to survive this type of self-employment.

Our analyses also show that heterogeneity is indeed one of the major features of self-employment in Taiwan. While nonprofessional self-employment is a response to poor alternatives in the labor market for those individuals who possess relatively few resources, professional self-employment is a result of utilizing high-quality human and social capital in search of great financial returns. There are also considerable differences between male and female self-employment dynamics. Our comparisons between male and female self-employment dynamics show that the former are highly affected by variables that estimate work conditions and career opportunities, whereas the latter are much less sensitive to these variables, yet modestly influenced by child-rearing responsibility.

Furthermore, women are much less likely to become self-employed, all else held constant, but much more likely to exit self-employment than men. This is to say that self-employment is still to a great extent a male-dominated economic activity. However, it is important to note that when women have entered professional self-employment, however difficult this process was, they are likely to be exceptionally persistent in continuing such businesses. All these findings indicate that gender is an important determinant of self-employment dynamics.

CONCLUSION

The persistence of self-employment points to the importance of studying this economic activity. One's involvement in self-employment is determined by both individual attributes and macro-level opportunity structures, which could either propagate or suppress this activity. Using the Taiwanese case, we have created an alternative framework for understanding the effects of macro-level opportunity structures on individual level decisions around self-employment. While it is often noted that self-employment activity flourishes when state regulations are strong, the case of Taiwan shows the opposite to be the case. When state regulations are *too weak*, there are not sufficient protections for low-skilled workers in the private sector, and this lowers the incentives for remaining dependently employed. Meanwhile, the small-scale economy of Taiwan has lowered the capital requirement and made entry into self-employment relatively easy. A low-skilled worker whose opportunities of finding a decent, well-paid, stable job as a wage employee are so poor that there is little risk involved in moving into self-employment. Thus, we argue that self-employment activity also flourishes in economies that are full of small to medium-sized establishments, which the state finds difficult to regulate.

Furthermore, once the economic settings create a niche for self-employment activity, the existing number of self-employed would further perpetuate this activity in the economy because individuals in the existing enterprises can deliver social capital to the next generation and smooth entry into self-employment for the latter. We have shown that the kinship networks and personal ties connected to self-employment activity are important for entry into self-employment. The relevance of social networks to self-employment increases the likelihood that this activity will persist in the economy. The macro-level trends for the last two decades have proved this to be true (figs. 12.1A and 12.1B).

In addition to the persistence of self-employment activity, the growth of heterogeneity within self-employment is foreseeable in Taiwan. We have shown considerable differences in self-employment dynamics between professional and nonprofessional, as well as between male and female, self-employment. Recent economic development in Taiwan has been characterized by a shift from labor-intensive to skill-intensive industries and the expansion of service and sales industries. On the one hand, the increasing share of skill-intensive industries is likely to lead to the growth of highly educated entrepreneurs who establish enterprises with their knowledge and professional skills. On the other hand, our analyses show that the expansion of the service sector since the 1980s has increased only the odds of entering unskilled self-employment. This is because many unskilled occupations in self-employment, by definition, are for the purpose of providing personal services at a rather low skill level. Given these two consequences of the economic transformation, we expect further polarization within self-employment activity. Therefore, while self-employment as an economic activity is likely to persist in the economy, the direction of economic development will have an effect on self-employment activity by enlarging the gap in worker characteristics and outcomes within it.

Finally, this study provides an insight into self-employment activity and gender equality at work. Even though self-employment activity in Taiwan is still dominated by men, and the number of women entering professional self-employment is extremely small, our results suggest that those women who are in professional self-employment are more likely to succeed and remain in this status than women in nonprofessional self-employment. Thus, while Simon (2000) argues, based on his ethnographic study, that any type of self-employment has the potential to empower women by creating their social identities outside of marriage, career opportunities for women in professional self-employment are particularly good.

This different propensity of women to remain in different types of self-employment calls for further studies that include a larger sample of self-employed women. We will then be able to better examine the different meanings and implications of professional and nonprofessional self-employment for women. It is unfortunate that we have neither enough cases to examine the obstacles for women entering professional self-employment, nor sufficient information on gender discrimination in professional and nonprofessional self-employment. It is also unknown whether the barriers to professional and managerial positions are equally high for women in dependent employment and self-employment. These are all important issues for further research on gender and self-employment. Finally, future studies also need to pay special attention to how the types of self-employment activity interact with women's work commitment, family roles, and status attainment in society.

NOTES

1. Legal protection for dependent employment was virtually absent until the late 1990s. For example, it was not until 1999 that the law for compensation for involuntary unemployment was enacted.

2. This survey is also part of the 1997 East Asia Social Survey, a three-society (Taiwan, South Korea, and coastal China) comparative project conducted in 1996–97. We acknowledge Academia Sinica for providing us with the survey data.

3. Self-employed workers in our data, in particular male ones, were much more likely than their counterparts in dependent employment to have spouses who were reported as family enterprise workers. Thus, we infer that many of these self-employed workers in very small establishments have their spouses work

with them. Within the sample, 23.5 percent of the respondents did not have a spouse at the survey time, 34.8 percent had dependently employed spouses, 11.8 percent had self-employed spouses, 3.5 percent had spouses that were family enterprise workers, and 26.4 percent reported that their spouses did not have a job at the time.

4. The descriptive findings show that father's occupation was weakly associated with entry into self-employment for men, but the association was stronger for women. Overall, 27.2 percent of the person-year samples had an unskilled father, 12.3 percent professional, 16.3 percent skilled, 35.0 percent agricultural, and 9.3 percent other (family workers, no job, no information, etc.).

5. The firm size effects differ on women's exits from self-employment: the ones who own enterprises with 10–29 employees are extremely unlikely to leave self-employment. As this firm size effect shows in the extensive model, the negative effect of being in professional or managerial occupations on women's separation from self-employment, however, becomes smaller and insignificant. In fact, women in professional self-employment in our sample were mostly owners of small- to medium-sized firms, firms with 10–29 employees. A likely explanation is that these women are exceptional in the way that they have been capable of resisting gender discrimination and reaching their positions. Consequently, they are more likely to survive than other women in self-employment, and less willing to move into dependent employment, which rarely promotes women to equivalent status. However, as the number of women in this category is quite small ($N = 8$), we are uneasy about conclusions drawn from these results.

6. However we suspect that the acquisition explanation is less likely in this case. Until the late 1980s, the state-controlled banking systems and inactive capital market made it difficult to mobilize enough funds for acquisitions. Thus, acquisitions have been rather uncommon in Taiwan.

REFERENCES

Aldrich, H., and R. Waldinger. 1990. Ethnicity and entrepreneurship. *Annual Review of Sociology* 16:111–35.

Arum, R. 1997. Trends in male and female self-employment: Growth in a new middle class or increasing marginalization of the labor force? *Research in Stratification and Mobility* 15:209–38.

Arum, R., M. Budig, and D. Grant. 2000. Labor market regulation and the growth of self-employment. *International Journal of Sociology* 30:3–27.

Bates, T. 1990. Entrepreneur human capital inputs and small business longevity. *Review of Economics and Statistics* 72:551–59.

———. 1999. Exiting self-employment: An analysis of Asian immigrant-owned small businesses. *Small Business Economics* 13:171–83.

Biggs, T. S. 1988. Financing the emergence of small and medium enterprise in Taiwan: Financial mobilization and the flow of domestic credit to the private sector. *Discussion Paper No. 15*, The Employment and Enterprise Policy Analysis Project.

Blau, D. M. 1987. A time series analysis of self-employment in the United States. *Journal of Political Economy* 95:445–67.

Blossfeld, H., A. Hamerle and K. U. Mayer. 1989. *Event history analysis: Statistical theory and application in the social sciences.* Hillsdale, NJ: Lawrence Erlbaum.

Boden, R. J. Jr. 1996. Gender and self-employment selection: An empirical assessment. *Journal of Socio-Economics* 25:671–82.

———. 1999. Flexible working hours, family responsibilities, and female self-employment: Gender difference in self-employment selection. *American Journal of Economics and Sociology* 58:71–84.

Brinton, M. C. 2001. Married women's labor in East Asian economies. In *Women's working lives in East Asia*, ed. M. C. Brinton, 1–37. Stanford: Stanford University Press.

Carr, D. 1996. Two paths to self-employment: Women's and men's self-employment in the United States, 1980. *Work and Occupations* 23:26–53.

Cheng, L., and G. Gereffi. 1994. The informal economy in East Asian development. *International Journal of Urban and Regional Research* 18:195–219.

Cheng, M. M. 1997. Becoming self-employed: The case of Japanese men. *Sociological Perspectives* 40:581–600.

Chou, T. 1995. Taiwan. In *Financial systems and economic policy in developing countries*, ed. S. Haggard and C. H. Lee, 56–75. Ithaca: Cornell University Press.

Cumings, B. 1987. The origins and development of the northeast Asian political economy: Industrial sectors, product cycles, and political consequences. In *The political economy of the new Asian industrialism*, ed. F. C. Deyo, 44–83. Ithaca: Cornell University Press.

De Soto, H. 1989. *The other path: The invisible revolution in the Third World.* New York: Harper and Row.

Deyo, F. C. 1989. *Beneath the miracle: Labor subordination in the new Asian industrialism.* Berkeley: University of California Press.

DGBAS (Directorate General of Budget, Accounting and Statistics, Executive Yuan), Republic of China. 1982. *Report on 1981 Industrial and Commercial Census Taiwan-Fukien Area, the Republic of China.*

———. 1997. *Report on 1996 Industrial and Commercial Census Taiwan-Fukien Area, the Republic of China.*

———. 2000, 1989. *Yearbook of Manpower Survey Statistics, Taiwan Area Republic of China.*

Erikson, R., and J. Goldthorpe. 1992. *The constant flux: A study of class mobility in industrial societies.* Oxford: Clarendon Press.

Erikson, R., J. Goldthorpe, and L. Portocarero. 1979. Intergenerational class mobility in three Western European societies. *British Journal of Sociology* 30:415–41.

Galenson, W. 1979. The labor force, wages, and living standards. In *Economic growth and structural changes in Taiwan*, ed. W. Galenson, 384–447. Ithaca: Cornell University Press.

Hamilton, G., and N. W. Biggart. 1988. Market, culture, and authority: A comparative analysis of management and organization in the Far East. *American Journal of Sociology* 94 Supplement: 52–94.

Huang, C. 1999. Labor militancy and the neo-mercantilist development experience: South Korea and Taiwan in comparison. Ph.D. dissertation, University of Chicago, Department of Sociology.

Johnson, C. 1987. Political institutions and economic performance: The government-business relationship in Japan, South Korea, and Taiwan. In *The political economy of the new Asian industrialism*, ed. F. C. Deyo, 136–64. Ithaca: Cornell University Press.

Jurik, N. C. 1998. Getting away and getting by: The experiences of self-employed homeworkers. *Work and Occupations* 25:7–35.

Ka, C. 1993. *Market, social networks, and the production organization of small-scale industry in Taiwan: The garment industries in Wufenpu* (in Chinese). Taipei: Institute of Ethnology, Academia Sinica.

———. 1999. *The economic activities and social meanings of the "boss's wife" in small and medium-sized enterprises in Taiwan* (in Chinese). Taipei: Linking Press.

Li, Y., and C. Ka. 1994. Sexual division of labor and production organization in Wufenpu's small-scale industries (in Chinese). *Taiwan: A Radical Quarterly in Social Studies* 17:41–81.

Loscocco, K. A., and K. T. Leicht. 1993. Gender, work-family linkages, and economic success among small business owners. *Journal of Marriage and the Family* 55:875–87.

Lu, Y. 2001. The "boss's wife" and Taiwanese small family business. In *Women's working lives in East Asia*, ed. M. C. Brinton. Stanford: Stanford University Press.

Morokvasic, M. 1991. Roads to independence: Self-employed immigrants and minority women in five European states. *International Migration* 29:407–19.

Müller, W., et al. 1989. Class and education in industrial nations. *International Journal of Sociology* 19:3–39.

Noble, G. W. 1998. *Collective action in East Asia: How ruling parties shape industrial policy*. Ithaca: Cornell University Press.

Piore, M. J., and C. F. Sabel. 1984. *The second industrial divide: Possibilities for prosperity*. New York: Basic Books.

Portes, A., and L. Benton. 1984. Industrial development and labor absorption: A reinterpretation. *Populations and Development Review* 10:589–611.

Portes, A., and L. Jensen. 1989. The enclave and the entrants: Patterns of ethnic enterprise in Miami before and after Mariel. *American Sociological Review* 54:929–49.

Sanders, J. M., and V. Nee. 1996. Immigrant self-employment: The family as social capital and the value of human capital. *American Sociological Review* 61:231–49.

Shavit, Y., and W. Müller. 1998. *From school to work: A comparative of educational qualifications and occupational destinations*. Oxford: Clarendon Press.

Shieh, G. 1989. Putting out system: A comparative historical overview (in Chinese). *Taiwan: A Radical Quarterly in Social Studies* 2:29–69.

———. 1991. Network labor process: The subcontracting networks in the manufacturing industries of Taiwan (in Chinese). *Bulletin of the Institute of Ethnology Academia Sinica* 71:161–82.

———. 1992a. *"Boss" Island: The subcontracting network and micro-entrepreneurship in Taiwan's development*. New York: Peter Lang.

———. 1992b. Invisible factory: Subcontracting points and homeworkers in Taiwan (in Chinese). *Taiwan: A Radical Quarterly in Social Studies* 13:137–60.

Simon, S. 2000. Work and gender in Taiwan: Between patriarchy and the marketplace. *Anthropology of Work Review* 21:19–23.

Steinmetz, G., and E. Olin Wright. 1989. The fall and rise of the petty bourgeoisie: Changing patterns of self-employment in the postwar United States. *American Journal of Sociology* 94:973–1018.

Tsay, C. 1995. Taiwan: Labor shortage. In *Asian NIEs and the global economy*, ed. G. L. Clark and W. B. Kim. Baltimore: Johns Hopkins University Press.

U.S. Department of Commerce, Bureau of Census. 2000. *Statistics of U.S. Businesses*. Washington, DC: Government Printing Office.

Waldinger, R. 1986. *Through the eye of the needle: Immigrants and enterprise in New York's garment trades*. New York: New York University Press.

———. 1989. Structural opportunity or ethnic advantage? Immigrant business development in New York. *International Migration Review* 23:48–72.

Yoon, I. 1991. The changing significance of ethnic and class resources in immigrant business in Chicago. *International Migration Review* 25:303–31.

Yu, W. 1999. Unequal employment, diverse career paths: Gender stratification in Japan and Taiwan. Ph.D. dissertation, University of Chicago, Department of Sociology.

———. 2000. Gender, labor market structures and forms of employment: Earnings inequality in Japan and Taiwan. Paper presented at the American Sociological Association Annual Meeting in Washington, DC.

———. 2001a. Crossing the line: Gender differences in job shifting to nonstandard employment in Japan and Taiwan. Paper presented at the American Sociological Association Annual Meeting in Anaheim, CA.

———. 2001b. Taking informality into account: Women's work in the formal and informal sectors in Taiwan. In *Women's working lives in East Asia*, ed. M. C. Brinton, 233–62. Stanford: Stanford University Press.

CHAPTER THIRTEEN

The Reemergence of Self-Employment: Comparative Findings and Empirical Propositions

Richard Arum and Walter Müller

SEYMOUR MARTIN LIPSET and Reinhard Bendix in *Social Mobility in Industrial Society* (1959) observed that "statistics on the small proportion of self-employed at any one time conceal the fact that many more than the present number have owned their own business at some time in the past, and many more will do so in the future." Lipset and Bendix suggested that "self-employment is one of the few positions of higher status attainable by manual workers" and that while "most of those who try it apparently fail does not change the fact that they do try" (Pp. 180–1). Reviewing the topic four decades later, what has changed? Is contemporary self-employment still characterized by high failure rates? Does it continue to provide access to high-status occupations for manual workers disadvantaged by lower levels of educational attainment? As women increasingly participate in the labor force, are their self-employment dynamics similar to men? How are families implicated in this process? We believe that these questions are best answered in a comparative framework that examines self-employment similarities and differences across diverse economic and social settings. Specifically, while the process of self-employment entry and survival has much in common across industrialized societies, differences in labor market regulation and the importance of family-based social capital affect varying aspects of self-employment, including its determinants, levels, and form.

In this concluding chapter, we will work to make sense of the myriad findings provided in the detailed case studies found earlier in the book. We will begin by briefly reviewing the theoretical framework advanced in the introduction to guide understanding of self-employment dynamics and its relationship to determinants such as education and family background. Next, we will discuss cross-national similarities and differences in findings and advance a series of empirical propositions or generalizations about self-employment designed to summarize our results and to guide future research on the topic. Finally, we will conclude our work by exploring the theoretical and policy implications of the identified patterns and associations more generally.

ANALYTIC ORIENTATION

We reiterate that our theoretical stance assumes that—given existing structural constraints, variation in individual-level resources, and differences in personal preferences and tastes—individuals become and stay self-employed when the relative advantages are higher than in dependent employment. In other words, one must analyze separately the processes leading into self-employment and the factors that then keep individuals in such enterprises. To understand fully the conditions promoting self-employment, however, one should consider entry and exit results simultaneously, since the amount of individuals in any form of self-employment is affected by both inflow and outflow rates. Given this theoretical orientation, event-history modeling of determinants of entry and exit probabilities is an analytical methodology well suited to capture the logic and dynamic character of self-employment.

While we do not have adequate cross-national data to allow adequate empirical modeling in economic terms of benefits and costs that underlie individuals' choices between the alternatives of self-employment and dependent employment, we rely instead on identification of the individual and institutional conditions that affect positively or negatively the choices producing self-employment. On the individual level, both for entry into and exit from self-employment, the models examine a set of core resources that can be expected to crucially affect the likelihood of entering self-employment and of surviving in these enterprises. Basically these resources are those related to either human capital (education, work experience) or family embeddedness (inheritance and spousal support). From our perspective, not only are resources useful for direct substantive deployment in the process of becoming and staying self-employed (e.g., financial resources to open a firm, knowledge of markets and processes to maintain a business, network ties to develop an organization), but as importantly resources can affect decision-making processes *indirectly* through social-psychological mechanisms. Specifically, individual-level resources can alter preferences and tastes, as well as change an individual's assessment of the possibility of success relative to the risk of failure. In making these decisions, individuals do not simply compare average earnings in dependent and self-employment activity, but rather likely consider their *expected* earnings and appreciate the extent to which there is greater variation in self-employment rewards than in income from dependent work. Given the well-known fact that individuals tend to overestimate their abilities and thus their likelihood of success, variation in resources likely leads to upwardly biased individual estimation of the possibilities for entrepreneurial returns and thus overcrowding of markets with high potential earnings (Frank and Cook 1996). As a counterweight to this, however, most individuals are also risk averse and would therefore prefer to avoid the uncertainty attached to self-employment activity if relatively satisfactory and stable dependent employment was already secured.

For entry into self-employment, another core individual-level element considered in the models refers to the specific occupational-employment position of the individual facing the decision. Two aspects are particularly important: first, whether individuals consider self-employment from conditions of being employed in dependent work or from conditions of not working but searching for employment (being either unemployed or at present not in the labor force); second, for those employed, the specific nature of the job they have, given the resources they command, evidently should strongly affect the evaluation of self-employment alternatives—in particular, how easy the transition into self-employment would be in the area of one's specific work competences, and whether movement into self-employment may constitute an option for occupational advancement. We will discuss these elements in more detail below.

In principle, individual-level conditions and resources can be expected to operate in similar ways in modern societies. However, institutional and other contextual conditions—such as particular political interventions or formal requirements for setting up one's own business—can affect the availability of resources, the opportunities to engage in self-employment, as well as the relative advantages attached to involvement. Variation across countries in these conditions should then lead to variation in self-employment, both in the factors affecting entry and survival as well as in the resulting overall levels and form of self-employment. In this chapter, we scrutinize cross-national variation along two dimensions: the extent to which a society is characterized by labor market regulation and the degree to which family-based social capital is prevalent. While we emphasize these two factors in the present study, other conditions that may also contribute to cross-national variation are discussed in the introductory chapter and in the country studies included in the volume.

Our eleven countries were grouped into several categories based on the two dimensions of particular interest here. Germany, France, and the Netherlands were identified as *corporatist states* with relatively high levels of labor market regulation and low levels of family-based social capital. The United States, Australia, and the United Kingdom were labeled *neo-liberal economies* and shown to have relatively low levels of both labor market regulation and family-based social capital. *Postsocialist societies*, represented in our study by Russia and Hungary, were characterized as having moderate levels of labor market regulation and low to moderate levels of family-based social capital. A final set of countries was argued to share a higher reliance on family-based social capital than other countries in the study, but to vary among themselves in the extent to which their labor markets were regulated: Japan and Italy have relatively strong employment protection legislation; Taiwan only recently has made efforts to provide such safeguards for employees.

Comparative Findings and Empirical Propositions

In all country analyses, we were able to utilize longitudinal data that allowed dynamic entry and exit modeling. In terms of inflow, all country chapters model entry with a discrete time competing risk model—given that the competing risks of entering professional-managerial, skilled, and unskilled self-employment are all quite small and the reference categories relatively large and stable, interpretation of coefficients is fairly straight-forward. In terms of exit, survival analyses were conducted for the different forms of self-employment under investigation. To capture the effects of resources and institutional conditions described above, variables (such as social origin, education, prior employment, industrial sector, age, family context, gender) were included in individual-level models and measured similarly for all country-specific analyses with only a few exceptions. However, while the models and the variables used in the different country studies in general are well comparable, estimates can be affected by the fact that data sources relied on either longitudinal panel designs or retrospective methodologies—which would in particular affect estimates related to the presence of self-employment of short-term duration. Slight differences in measurement strategies were also unavoidable given other data limitations (discussed in chapter 1). While small differences in magnitudes of effects should thus not be overinterpreted, we were able to identify broad patterns of effects that are common to practically all countries and significant variation in some effects across the theoretically defined sets of countries studied in the project. We take this as indication that we have identified factors responsible both for the general pattern of self-employment dynamics as well as for differences observed between countries. We highlight these findings below by setting them off as italicized empirical propositions intended to summarize the results of the present study and guide future research.

In the meta-analysis of the results obtained in the country case studies, we first assess the findings concerning the evolution of self-employment in terms of the composition found in the different (professional-managerial, skilled, and unskilled) categories of self-employment that we have distinguished. Is self-employment becoming more heterogeneous, and how do the different countries vary in this respect? This descriptive analysis is mainly based on measurement of the relative size of the different groups and their change over time. We then will evaluate in turn how various individual resources and workers' occupational-employment position affect entry and survival in self-employment.

Self-Employment Heterogeneity

P₁. *Self-employment has developed into a more heterogeneous employment type with increases prevalent in professional-managerial and unskilled occupations, but declines in traditional forms of petty bourgeois and skilled self-employment.* Self-employment includes workers in different kinds of work and in different conditions of economic well-being and social standing. Traditionally, however, the dominant form of self-employment was petty-bourgeois self-employment of craftsmen, small shopowners, proprietors, and others working on their own in skilled occupations. How did the composition of self-employment change in the course of the growth of service economies and the "renaissance" and recent stabilization of self-employment? Figure 13.1 identifies rates of self-employment in the three different occupational categories for men and women by national setting at the close of the twentieth century. While all countries examined continue to have significant numbers of individuals in traditional craft-based self-employment or related small-scale proprietorship, in the vast majority of countries self-employment now occurs predominately in other areas—that is, in professional-managerial or unskilled occupations. Figure 13.1 also suggests that while overall self-employment rates vary across countries, in all societies significant numbers of individuals continue to engage in these economic activities. Women have a relatively similar pattern as men across countries, but with generally lower concentrations in professional/managerial occupations (Italy as an exception) and higher concentrations in unskilled occupations (Germany, UK, and Hungary as exceptions). The figure overall demonstrates the heterogeneous character of self-employment both within and across countries, and for men and women.

P₂. *In terms of cross-national variation, labor market regulation manifests a curvilinear relationship with pressures for self-employment highest at either end of the continuum, particularly for professional-managerial forms of the activity; societies with higher levels of family based social capital have higher rates of self-employment, particularly traditional inherited petty bourgeois and also marginal unskilled self-employment forms.* The occupational composition of self-employment varies significantly and follows a pattern associated with conceptualization of cross-national variation along the two dimensions of labor market regulation and family-based social capital. We provide formal identification of these statistical associations in table 13.1, which

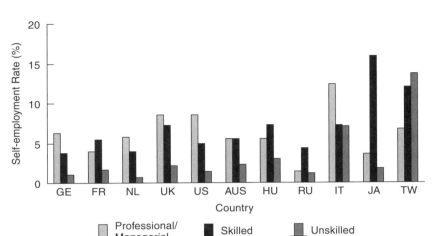

Figure 13.1A: Male Self-Employment

provides results for a regression of the percentage of women and men in self-employment categories on our indicators of labor market regulation and family-based social capital. In order to identify a parsimonious expression of the curvilinear effects of labor market regulation for this analysis, we operationalized the OECD measure of labor market regulation for this regression by mean centering the variable at zero and squaring. Our two measures of state (i.e., labor market regulation) and familial

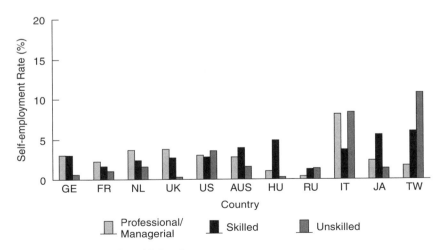

Figure 13.1B: Female Self-Employment

Table 13.1

Self-Employed Men and Women Regressed on Indicators of Labor Market
Regulation and Family-Based Social Capital (in percent)

	All	Professional/ managerial	Skilled	Unskilled
Male self-employment rates				
Labor market regulation	0.26	0.82	−0.17	0.05
(distance from mean)	(1.51)	(4.18)	(0.99)	(0.20)
Family-based social capital	0.85	0.19	0.85	0.71
	(4.97)	(0.99)	(4.94)	(2.87)
Adjusted R^2	0.71	0.62	0.70	0.38
Female self-employment rates				
Labor market regulation	0.44	0.79	−0.18	0.30
(distance from mean)	(2.27)	(3.69)	(0.79)	(1.27)
Family-based social capital	0.72	0.15	0.73	0.70
	(3.72)	(0.73)	(3.15)	(2.99)
Adjusted R^2	0.62	0.54	0.46	0.45

Notes: N = 11, standardized coefficients, *t*-statistics in parentheses. Labor market regulation measured as OECD Employment Index (mean-centered at zero and squared for regression analysis); family-based social capital measured as percentage of adults aged 25–59
living with parents in household.

variation in national setting had significant power in predicting levels of
self-employment: the R-squared for predicting the overall self-employment rate was 0.71 for men, and 0.62 for women; the R-squared ranged
from 0.38 to 0.70 for predicting self-employment levels separately for
our three occupational groupings. Self-employment rates in general were
largest in countries where family-based social capital was most pronounced. Family-based social capital had particularly strong effects on
nonprofessional self-employment forms. Labor market regulation had
pronounced effects on professional-managerial occupations, with both
low and high extremes of labor market regulation creating greater prevalence of such activity.

In terms of specific countries, traditional petty bourgeois, skilled, and
unskilled marginal self-employment is particularly prevalent in Taiwan,
Italy, and Japan—the societies characterized by high levels of family-
based social capital (Japan's large concentration of skilled and low-level
unskilled self-employment is partially related to occupational coding of
noodle shop owners and similar enterprises as skilled; see chapter 11). In
both corporatist and neoliberal states, self-employment is relatively more
pronounced in professional/managerial occupations than in other countries. However, also in Italy, professional/managerial self-employment is

TABLE 13.2
Self-Employment Activity that Employs Others, by Category and Country
(in percent)

	Professional/managerial	Skilled	Unskilled
Corporatist states			
Germany	59.9	71.9	52.6
France	49.9	52.9	37.1
Netherlands	46.7	40.2	19.2
Neoliberal states			
United Kingdom	47.9	17.3	25.2
United States	60.7	43.9	13.5
Australia	50.9	47.9	28.6
Postsocialist states			
Hungary	47.6	22.2	12.3
Russia	44.5	25.8	10.9
Other states			
Italy	40.7	28.8	21.4
Japan	74.8	79.9	67.4
Taiwan	77.4	41.7	23.8

high, and this may be due to Italy's pronounced labor market regulation. While we would expect higher rates of professional self-employment in Japan given the extensive labor market regulation found there, it is possible that in Japan the traditional reliance of firms on internal labor markets, lifelong employment, and hierarchical within-firm control has discouraged the outsourcing of professional work and services with the exception of select industries embedded in particular regional economies there. In the postsocialist countries with moderate levels of labor market regulation, self-employment is less professional/managerial and more nonprofessional. Marginal unskilled self-employment is by far the smallest segment of self-employment in all countries except those with high levels of family-based social capital (the deviation of Japan probably being due to coding).

Table 13.2 identifies the heterogeneous character of self-employment by using a different approach. Here we identify the percentage of self-employment that is associated with individuals hiring other workers for their enterprise. In most of the countries, professional-managerial self-employment is associated with the highest rates of employing others. Exceptions are the two corporatist states Germany and France and also Japan, in which high rates of employing others are not as strongly tied to professional-managerial activity (in these countries, skilled self-employment is actually the most likely type of self-employment to employ others). Rates of employment of others by self-employed individuals are lowest for individuals in unskilled self-employment in all countries (except the UK, likely due to the high rates of subcontracted marginal self-employment found in construction). In several countries (UK, Italy, and the two postsocialist societies), employment of others is low in both skilled and unskilled enterprises. Female self-employment is more likely not to involve hiring others than male self-employment (results not shown). In most of the countries (exceptions are Germany and Japan), less than 50 percent of all self-employed hire other workers. These findings suggest that policies crudely equating self-employment with entrepreneurial activity and job creation are clearly naïve and unwarranted. Self-employment does not necessarily lead to the creation of small firms in every occupational form, nor in all national settings (for related evidence, see Brüderl and Preisendörfer 2000).

While distinguishing self-employment by occupational categories demonstrates the heterogeneous character of this activity within and between countries, a related and evident interest is the determination of whether the heterogeneous character of self-employment is increasing or decreasing in these societies. One indicator of growing heterogeneity in self-employment would be identification of increases in the most and least desirable forms of the activity—that is, growth both in professional-managerial and unskilled occupations at the expense of traditional petty bourgeois skilled self-employment. Figure 13.2 attempts such an analysis with the limited time series data available in our comparative study. In spite of the fact that historical comparison time points for our national case studies are often measuring only a decade of recent change, a clear pattern emerges. Figure 13.2 provides a scatter-plot with the x-axis measuring the overall change in the rates of self-employment in the data and the y-axis measuring the change in occupational composition of self-employment over the same time period.[1] The scatter-plot provides clear evidence that in most countries professional-managerial as well as unskilled occupations are increasingly common relative to traditional craft-based skilled self-employment. The scatter-plot also suggests that this is particularly true in settings where self-employment has been increasing most. Skilled self-employment has been growing in only two countries. One can conclude from this figure that over time, self-employment is becoming increasingly more heterogeneous in terms of a growing polarization of occupational quality and type.[2] This is true for both men and women analyzed separately as well as for the overall pattern of self-employment in pooled data where women often play an increasing role.

Over time self-employment has become increasingly female primarily as a result of women's increasing participation in the labor market more

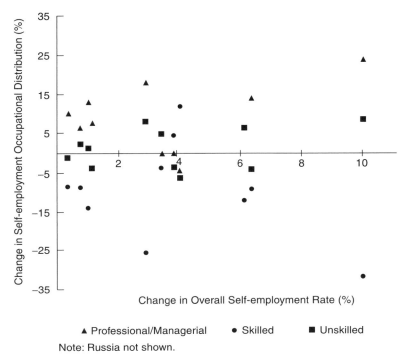

Figure 13.2: Self-Employment Growth and Self-Employment Occupational Composition

generally. The increasing presence of women in self-employment has implications about the character and heterogeneity of self-employment because self-employment quality is usually lower for women relative to men. Figure 13.3 provides suggestive data illustrating differences in the quality of self-employment by gender. Specifically, we identify the extent to which female self-employment is more likely solo (i.e., not to employ others) and to occur in unskilled occupations relative to male self-employment. In most countries, we find pronounced gender disparities in these areas, the few exceptions to this are likely due to general under-reporting of certain categories of unskilled self-employment, particularly female domestic work or, in the case of England, specific labor market policies encouraging high rates of male unskilled self-employment in certain activities. Since female self-employment is often of relatively short duration, the increasing presence of women in these positions creates not only growing heterogeneity, but also increasing instability within self-employment as a whole.

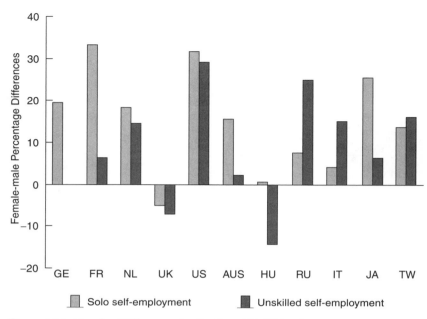

Figure 13.3: Gender Differences in Quality of Self-Employment

The extent to which self-employment no longer can be equated simply with traditional inherited petty bourgeois status is identified further in descriptive results shown in table 13.3. The results identify the extent to which self-employed men and women (considered separately) had a father who was also self-employed. In Japan and Italy, more than half of self-employment occurs in an occupational position that is inherited from parent to child. In most other countries, only approximately one-third of self-employment has this intergenerational character.[3] Given that father's—and not mother's—self-employment is measured, sons are found to inherit their occupational position more often than daughters in most of the countries.

While self-employment status in most countries thus is not intergenerational in character, self-employment positions are also now relatively unstable intragenerationally as well. In examining survival curves that were presented in the country-specific chapters, although some variation is associated simply with variation in data sources (e.g., retrospective or panel data), self-employment was overall quite unstable. In a typical country where annual panel data was available, between one-third and one-half of those entering self-employment had already discontinued their involvement in the activity within three years.

Table 13.3
Self-Employed with Self-Employed Fathers, by Gender and Country
(in percent)

	Men	Women	Pooled
Corporatist states			
Germany	16.8	10.5	14.7
France	32.6	26.2	30.9
Netherlands	41.8	27.8	37.1
Neoliberal states			
United Kingdom	26.0	30.8	27.7
United States	8.9	7.5	8.4
Australia	31.6	20.1	27.1
Postsocialist states			
Hungary	2.4	18.6	6.6
Russia			
Other states			
Italy	48.2	56.0	50.7
Japan	73.7	51.9	69.2
Taiwan	27.7	26.8	27.4

Note: Russia not estimated.

So far we have summarized descriptive results identifying broad characteristics of self-employment in the last two decades of the twentieth century, the occupational composition of the group, the growing heterogeneity of its composition, and other indicators that document a rather limited stability of the status, both from generation to generation and in the course of individuals' working lives. We also have seen substantial variation across countries in several of these respects and related such variation to labor market characteristics and family patterns prevailing in the countries. This is probably as much as one can do with the kind of cross-sectional indicators used so far. Such indicators, however, are not sufficient to uncover the underlying logic that structures individual choices to become or remain self-employed. The strength of our comparative research project lies in being able to move from these simple associations to a more complex examination of determinants of entry and exit dynamics in an event-history framework. Specifically, we are able to identify not simply whether a factor such as father's self-employment is associated with the likelihood of self-employment, but why these associations appear: does father's self-employment facilitate entry, or is it related to a greater stability of the activity once an individual has begun such an enterprise? Entry and exit event-history analysis provides an analytic technique whereby one can distinguish between factors associated with each of these two related, but distinct processes.

Education

Education is a core resource in modern societies and strongly influences entry into advantageous class positions. However, in several respects self-employment has been understood as functioning at odds with such a bold conception of the role of education in the process of class and status attainment. Social mobility research has repeatedly emphasized that the role of education in the intergenerational reproduction of social class position depends upon the type of social class to be reproduced (Robinson and Kelly 1979; Kerckhoff, Campbell, and Trott 1982; Robinson 1984). In contrast to other class positions, access to self-employment is one of the main instances in which parental social class affects children's class destination not mediated through their educational attainment, but rather through direct inheritance of parental socioeconomic position (Yamaguchi 1983; Ishida, Müller, and Ridge 1995). Also self-employment has been understood and shown as an alternative path of social advancement for individuals who lack educational credentials required for bureaucratic careers. Nevertheless, in other research, human capital has been found to facilitate successful business startups (Brüderl, Preisendörfer, and Ziegler 1992, 1996). What do we learn from our comparative findings on these contrasting views?

P₃. *Education, particularly tertiary and vocational, provides individuals with human capital skills that are transferable between either self-employment or dependent employment and thus facilitates movement into desirable forms of self employment; education has ambiguous effects on self-employment exit in that it increases the likelihood of entrepreneurial success but also is associated with improved opportunities to transition back into desirable forms of dependent employment.* Figure 13.4 presents logit estimates of tertiary education effects relative to primary education for models of entry into and exit from all forms of self-employment run on longitudinal data in the different countries studied. Logit effects can be translated into odds ratios through the exponential computation [e^{bx}], such that a logit effect of 1.0 in this figure is equivalent to an estimate that individuals with tertiary education, net of other covariates in the model, are 2.7 times more likely than those with primary education to either become or remain self-employed.

Our results suggest that tertiary education matters in general more for entry than for survival. We believe that the limited effect on survival is likely due to the fact that educational resources can be used either to remain successfully in self-employment or alternatively to enter desirable forms of dependent employment. While prior research on small firms

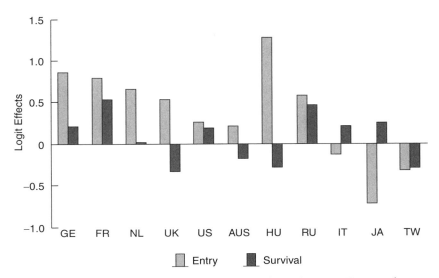

Figure 13.4: Effects of Tertiary Education on Self-Employment Entry and Survival

suggests that the educational level of the enterprise's founder consistently has strong associations with organizational survival, this is not clearly the case in our study given that we include not just small firms but also solo self-employment such as unskilled itinerant activity and professional free-lancing, which is often used in a more limited fashion during gaps occurring between jobs in regular dependent employment careers.

The strong positive effects of tertiary education on entry likely reflect that in certain industrial sectors and activities (e.g., professional freelancing and traditional liberal professions), human capital is the most important resource required for self-employment. Education also likely produces increased preferences and tastes for autonomy found in self-employment (see, e.g., Abbott 1988 on professional opposition to bureaucratic regulation). In addition, tertiary education likely increases self-employment entry by affecting an individual's assessment of his or her likely chances of self-employment success and thus facilitating greater personal confidence in assuming entrepreneurial risk.

While in general education clearly matters more for self-employment entry than for survival, additional analysis shows that we have to consider education effects in even more discrete ways: specific kinds of education matter for specific forms of self-employment. Figure 13.5 examines the extent to which tertiary education is related to professional/managerial self-employment entry and the degree to which secondary vocational education is associated with entry into skilled occupations (in both these cases educational effects are estimated relative to primary education). This more specific analysis reveals considerably stronger education effects (consider scaling of the vertical axis in figures 13.4 and 13.5). Workers with more education are much more likely to enter self-employment than workers with low qualifications, whereby each level of education is tied to self-employment at a more or less corresponding occupational level. It should be stressed that the strong education effects on self-employment entry result from models in which parental self-employment and parental professional employment are controlled. This suggests that tertiary education in particular is a powerful resource that facilitates individuals taking up self-employment, and additional tertiary education expansion thus potentially may support further self-employment growth.

P_4. *Education effects on self-employment dynamics are greatest in countries with lower levels of family based social capital and with higher levels of labor market regulation.* Figures 13.4 and 13.5 both suggest considerable cross-national variation in effects of education. Educational effects on entry are highest in corporatist states where self-employment entry often entails significant credential barriers. Education appears to play a less prominent role in countries higher in family-based social capital (i.e., Italy, Japan, and Taiwan). In these countries, tertiary education effects on professional/managerial self-employment are considerably weaker; there are no consistent effects of secondary vocational education, and in general tertiary education associations with self-employment overall are negative rather than positive. These latter findings, however, most likely are largely compositional results related to the relatively small share of professional and the large proportions of traditional petty bourgeois, skilled, and unskilled self-employment in these countries, that provide relatively greater opportunities for workers with low education to become self-employed.

Work Experience and Occupational Position

P_5. *Entry into self-employment takes place at midcareer; postsocialist countries vary from other countries in their associations between age and self-employment.* In most countries individuals who both have acquired sufficient levels of human capital and financial resources required for self-employment success, as well as those possessing sufficient years of expected future earnings to make initial investments in this activity worthwhile are most likely to enter self-employment. The national case studies find consistent evidence of the effects of work experience (operationalized in terms of age and age-squared) on self-employment entry and exit (not shown here with figures). In all countries other than those undergoing postsocialist

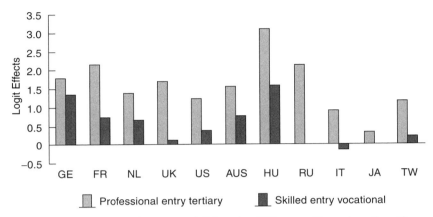

Figure 13.5: Tertiary and Vocational Education Effects on Entry into Specific Self-Employment Categories

transformations, associations between age and self-employment entry and exit have a curvilinear pattern. The age when individuals were most likely to enter self-employment varied, but typically was the early forties. Transition into self-employment thus typically occurs only after a lengthy period of preparation and accumulation of experience, financial assets, and other resources.

In the postsocialist countries, conditions differ. In these countries, young adults have very high rates of entry and continuation in self-employment. In Hungary, self-employment entry was most likely to occur, particularly in nonprofessional occupations, when men and women were in their twenties (see chapter 8). The Russian case is relatively similar to the Hungarian one. Self-employment was most likely to occur for men in their late twenties and early thirties, and slightly earlier for women. Gerber (chapter 9) argues that young adults in Russia are more inclined than their elders to engage in self-employment because they have encountered significant difficulties locating desirable dependent employment and have also been less exposed to Soviet-era socialization that stigmatized capitalist entrepreneurial activity.

P6. *Prior occupational position and industrial sector define the labor market opportunity structure and constraints that an individual faces. While entry into self-employment is associated with stability in terms of occupational status, transitions into self-employment are more likely among workers with prior employment in service and construction industries.* When considering options to move into self-employment, workers are unlikely to make the transition when a choice would be associated with occupational downgrading. Individuals moving into self-employment are therefore expected to keep at

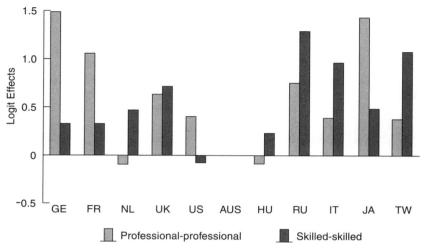

Figure 13.6: Occupational Stability on Entry

least the occupational status level of their previous employment. In contrast, Shavit and Yuchtman-Yaar (2001) as well as others have suggested that entry into self-employment might be pursued as a strategy for upward mobility in cases where career advancement in dependent work is blocked. The country studies provide only limited evidence of this latter alternative. Instead, we find that the predominant pattern in all countries is that self-employment is associated with stability in terms of career occupational status. Figure 13.6 identifies the extent to which individuals move from prior professional-managerial dependent occupations into professional-managerial self-employment and the extent to which movement occurs from prior skilled dependent employment into traditional petty bourgeois, skilled self-employment (in both cases estimates are made relative to individuals having moved into these positions from prior unskilled dependent occupations). Our findings suggest that individuals move into horizontally equivalent occupational forms of self-employment. Horizontal career transitions are much more likely than upward moves into higher-level self-employment. We uncovered only very limited evidence of upward mobility in the case of unskilled dependent employment into skilled self-employment and no clear evidence of occupationally downward mobility into self-employment (results not shown here). Results for occupational stability are fairly consistent across national setting. Our findings also suggest that individuals move into equivalent and familiar industrial sectors—where experience and knowledge have previously been acquired. As is well documented by prior research,

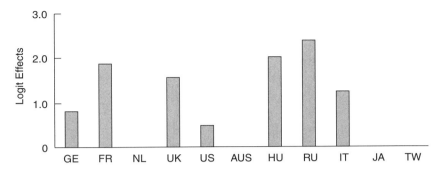

Note: Not estimated for Netherlands, Australia, Japan and Taiwan.

Figure 13.7: Effects of Unemployment on Self-Employment Entry

certain industrial sectors are particularly conducive to self-employment activity regardless of national setting. Construction and service self-employment has lower financial barriers for firm startup than manufacturing. The country studies consistently show higher rates of transitions into self-employment among dependent workers employed in these sectors, underlining thus the core significance of entry-level market opportunity structures for transitions into self-employment.

P₇. *Unemployed individuals have relatively higher incentives to move into self-employment than dependent employees with similar characteristics—individuals use self-employment as a refuge from unemployment if facing significant obstacles in securing traditional dependent employment opportunities.* Figure 13.7 partially addresses the relationship between individual-level unemployment and self-employment entry—a topic commonly subject to both social policy and empirical debate. The figure provides consistent evidence (in the seven countries where data permitted analysis) of significant inflow into self-employment from previously unemployed individuals. These high inflow rates are likely a reflection of the fact that unemployed individuals face very different situations when considering self-employment entry. While those in dependent employment have to leave a job that they hold to become self-employed, the unemployed are instead actively searching the market looking for alternatives to their current undesirable situation. Our results suggest that at the micro-level unemployed individuals are indeed more likely than others to become self-employed—they must simply forgo the possibility of finding a dependent job in the future to enter self-employment immediately. Note, however, that these results do not necessarily imply that unemployment and self-employment rates are correlated at a macrolevel. Higher overall rates of unemployment produce a greater number of unemployed individuals more likely than others to become self-employed but simultaneously are likely also associated with greater reluctance of those in dependent employment to leave secure jobs, dampening of an overall interest in establishing businesses during the period of economic difficulties, and increased existing entrepreneurial failure.

The significant role of occupational position in individual decisions related to self-employment is also suggested by considering how our different self-employment occupational categories vary in terms of exit likelihood. Figure 13.8 identifies how much more likely individuals are to survive in professional-managerial and skilled (as compared to unskilled) self-employed enterprises. In most countries traditional petty-bourgeois skilled self-employment is the most stable form of this activity. Given increasing heterogeneity and the decline of petty-bourgeois skilled self-employment enterprises, individual involvement with self-employment in the future will thus be more transient and short-lived in terms of an individual's life course. This change will likely have significant economic, social, and political consequences associated with it. Variation in stability across our occupational categories of self-employment is lowest in corporatist states where credential barriers to entry (and thus closure) are greatest and most diffusely shared across occupational groupings; in corporatist states selectivity into self-employment is uniformly high (for example, recall in table 13.3 how corporatist countries have relatively high rates of employment of others in unskilled self-employment).

Family Embeddedness

P$_8$. *Family support, provided in terms of either direct inheritance of parental self-employment position, other parental support, or spousal assistance and involvement in the enterprises, are significant individual-level resources that encourage an individual's decision to both become and remain self-employed. Such family resources have greater saliency for self-employment entry and exit dynamics in countries with high levels of family-based social capital than in other societies.* Intergenerational inheritance of self-employment is one of the most stable findings in studies of father-to-son social reproduction of class position. For all countries examined in our study, the results consistently confirm the well-known intergenerational stability of self-employment. The focus, however, on the role of spousal involvement in the dynamics of self-employment entry and exit adds further substantial detail on the family embeddedness of self-employment. Familial experience and involvement in self-employment can provide not only direct material transfers supportive of the activity, but also indirectly a transmission of entrepreneurial dispositions, knowledge, and networks. We first summarize the findings on intergenerational relations and then turn to the spousal component of self-employment activity.

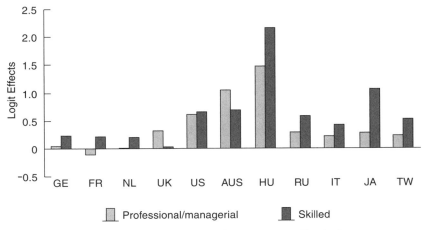

Figure 13.8: Effects of Self-Employment Occupation on Survival

Figure 13.9 identifies the extent to which father's self-employment is related to an individual's likelihood of becoming self-employed and remaining in that state. The figure identifies a broad pattern of relatively consistent positive effects on both entry and survival. In most countries effects on entry are strongest. This means that parental background and support is of particular relevance to encouraging initial involvement in self-employment. Effects on survival, however, are considerably larger in

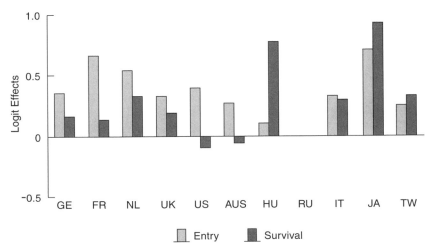

Figure 13.9: Effect of Father's Self-Employment on Entry and Survival

countries with greater reliance on family-based social capital: in these countries intergenerational relationships are likely characterized by more enduring and pronounced patterns of mutual responsibility and reciprocity. In two out of three of the neoliberal countries where an ethos and ideology of individual self-reliance is most pronounced (Australia and the United States), father's self-employment has no discernable effects net of other covariates on individual's survival in self-employment: for those following in father's footsteps, self-employment in these settings is a case of "sink or swim"—similar to the widely experienced conditions of organizational uncertainty shared by other entrepreneurs in the "at risk pool."

Shifting discussion of family effects to the role of spousal influence, figure 13.10 identifies (in the seven countries where data permitted analysis) the effects of prior spousal self-employment on individual's likelihood to become or remain self-employed. Spousal activity in all countries influences self-employment likelihood and supports the contention that "self-employment often comes in twos." The pattern of cross-national variation in spousal effects is largely similar to the variation found for the effects of father's self-employment on entry and survival (see fig. 13.9 above). In countries with greater prevalence of family-based social capital, spousal effects are more pronounced on survival than entry, the opposite is the case elsewhere. Taken together, the results highlight the extent to which self-employment is embedded in family relationships—both intergenerational as well as matrimonial. These factors tend to work in similar ways within, but vary across, countries studied. It is worth emphasizing that while family effects are found for entry everywhere, the associations remain more pronounced on survival rates in countries with more prevalent family-based social capital than elsewhere. While education has been found to matter somewhat less in countries with higher levels of family-based social capital, family-related factors appear indeed to matter more.

Gender

P9. *Women—since they differ from men in their relative resources, opportunities, and constraints—have distinctly different patterns and determinants of self-employment.* While most of our analytic discussion has concentrated on the effects of education, occupational position, and family relationships as the most salient individual-level resources affecting decisions related to self-employment entry and exit, it is worth discussing in detail the extent to which gender also structures self-employment activities. Recall from our discussion of heterogeneity in self-employment above that self-employment overall is becoming increasingly characterized by

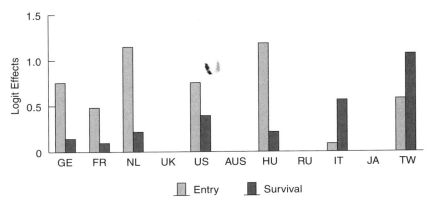

Note: Effects of spousal self-employment not estimated
for United Kingdom, Australia, Russia and Japan.

Figure 13.10: Effect of Spouse's Self-Employment on Entry and Survival

female involvement, often as a solo enterprise in activities of relatively low quality and short duration.

Table 13.4 identifies the extent to which male and female self-employment is associated with father's self-employment. The estimates in the table are odds ratios calculated from descriptive data—they are not event-history estimates identified net of covariates as is the case with the last several findings discussed in this chapter. Nevertheless, the table suggests that intergenerational inheritance is high everywhere for men, but not for women where data suggest significantly lower rates, sometimes even lower than one. This finding is consistent with prior stratification research that has pointed to lower female inheritance of self-employment. In Taiwan inheritance is unexpectedly low given that it is a country we have characterized as being high on the dimension of family-based social capital, but this relatively low association is because barriers to self-employment entry are also minimal and have led to large inflow of individuals (including those without self-employed fathers) into this activity, particularly in unskilled occupations. As the chapter on Taiwan emphasizes, entry into self-employment is relatively open and many attempt through such access to escape the vagaries of unprotected dependent labor. England unexpectedly has higher rates of female intergenerational inheritance than male, because of a large uninherited inflow into nonprofessional self-employment for men (this is most likely related to the high rates of self-employment in construction industries for reasons described more fully in chapter 5).

The extent to which men in general have significantly higher rates of

TABLE 13.4
Odds Ratio of Self-Employment for Respondents with Self-Employed Fathers
Relative to Self-Employment for Respondents with Fathers Not Self-Employed,
by Gender and Country

	Men	*Women*
Corporatist states		
Germany	1.9	0.9
France	3.7	2.5
Netherlands	2.6	1.3
Neoliberal states		
United Kingdom	2.0	2.7
United States	2.3	1.7
Australia	1.9	0.9
Postsocialist states		
Hungary	1.7	1.1
Russia		
Other states		
Italy	2.4	1.5
Japan	3.7	1.5
Taiwan	1.3	1.3

Note: Russia not estimated.

entry and stability in self-employment is identified in figure 13.11. For
all countries, the findings suggest that the generally observed smaller
presence of women in self-employment is primarily due to their lower
likelihood of starting self-employment, and less to lower rates of survival than men, once they have become self-employed. Still, in most
countries, men also stay longer in self-employment than women. The
exceptions are France (which models exit likelihood with more covariates than elsewhere), Hungary (where the exit coefficient is not significantly different from zero), and Australia (where survival rates net of
occupational composition and other factors are slightly lower for men
than women). The effects of gender are smallest in the United States
and Australia, perhaps because of relatively less gender structuation of
labor markets, higher rates of female labor force participation, and
more pronounced defamilialization in these societies. This interpretation is largely conjecture, however. It also remains unclear, why in the
Netherlands gender effects are quite small. Further research is thus required to identify the mechanisms producing the observed patterns of
cross-national gender variation.

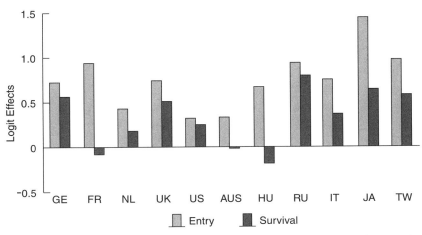

Figure 13.11: Effects of Male Gender on Self-Employment Entry and Survival

THEORETICAL AND POLICY IMPLICATIONS

The research in this project has identified both commonalities as well as significant cross-national variation in self-employment. Overall self-employment rates have become largely stable with only slight increases or decreases in the years immediately leading up to the end of the twentieth century; this stability in the prevalence of self-employment followed a long period of historic decline and a brief window in the mid-1970s to mid-1980s of small but consistent growth. While trends in self-employment rates have thus apparently stabilized, we have identified increasing heterogeneity within this employment sector. As traditional petty bourgeois and craft-based self-employment continues to decline, professional-managerial as well as unskilled self-employment has expanded in many countries. Since there are significant differences in the stability of self-employment across these occupational categories, increases in many of these new self-employment forms are associated with rising career instability. It is worth emphasizing that given the growing heterogeneity of self-employment, this instability cannot be equated simply with firm failure, as it can also result from individual reassessment of the relative rewards of continuing in the activity instead of moving back into dependent employment.

We also found considerable consistency in the effects of individual level resources (i.e., education, occupational position, work experience, and family relationships). In general these effects were more pronounced on entry than exit but remarkably consistent across countries—the differences largely were simply in magnitude not direction. Our analysis was also better able to identify factors such as traditional human capital and family resources as determinants of entry rather than exit likelihood, because self-employment stability at the enterprise or individual-level is likely influenced more by additional environmental influences, such as localized or firm-specific economic conditions.

In terms of cross-national variation, our study identified variation across three traditional political regime types (neoliberal, corporatist, and postsocialist states) as well as along two conceptual dimensions (labor market regulation and the level of societal prevalence of family based social capital). In countries where family-based social capital is more sa-lient as a principle of social organization (i.e., Italy, Taiwan, and Japan), self-employment in general occurs at a higher rate and is more concen-trated in traditional petty bourgeois, skilled, or unskilled enterprises than elsewhere. In these societies, we also found that educational effects were slightly smaller and that family-based resources (i.e., fathers or spouses that were self-employed) had a more lasting and continuing influence on self-employment stability than in other countries. Labor market regula-tion was also associated with self-employment level and compositional forms. Self-employment overall was encouraged in societies with both low and high levels of regulation. In societies with low levels of regula-tion (e.g., Taiwan and the neoliberal states), self-employment often ap-pears as a relatively attractive alternative compared to unregulated dependent employment; in these economies, we found unskilled self-em-ployment particularly prevalent. Taiwan is unique in our study as far as high family-based social capital with relatively low labor regulation, but this might be related to their stage of economic development. It is possi-ble, but not demonstrated, that other developing countries might have similarities with the Taiwanese case.

In corporatist states with higher levels of labor market regulation, we found that self-employment forms often had less variation in internal characteristics than elsewhere; for example, self-employment more con-sistently involved the employment of other workers regardless of occupa-tional category. In addition, educational credentials typically had slightly stronger effects on entry and exit likelihood in corporatist states than in other countries. Lastly, we found that in postsocialist societies self-employment was concentrated less in professional-managerial activities than elsewhere; as the history of re-emergent self-employment is still short in these countries, few entrepreneurs are in a position to employ others and young individuals are particularly likely to become and re-main self-employed.

Increasing heterogeneity is associated with growth of short-term in-volvement with the activity; this means that although self-employment is not necessarily expanding dramatically in terms of its proportional presence in the larger economy, it is significantly expanding its role in individual life courses as greater numbers of individuals increasingly have some involvement with the activity over their work careers. As individual involvement in self-employment is now more varied—that is, some individuals look to the activity as a temporary state and others invest and commit themselves more seriously to longer-term involvement—the character of those self-employed at any one point in time are quite heterogeneous and diverse in their orientation and backgrounds. Women in general are an increasing proportion of the self-employment sector. This growing presence of women increases heterogeneity and affects self-employment character in many ways: female self-employment stability is significantly lower than male self-employment; it is concentrated in unskilled occupations to a greater extent than for men and is less likely to employ others.

In terms of ascription and achievement, while we have found that education and other forms of human capital have a significant role to play in entering and remaining in various forms of self-employment activity, inheritance has persisted as a source for self-employment recruitment. Evidence of significant education and training effects suggests that establishment of particular types of occupationally relevant educational training can facilitate individual entry into self-employment activity. In Italy, for example, small firm growth has been promoted by regional state policies that have provided extensive occupational training in certain industries and locations.

As professional occupations increase their role in the self-employment sector, education increasingly becomes important, relative to direct effects of intergenerational inheritance, and in a manner similar to the role that education plays in providing entry into dependent professional occupations. While human capital influences on self-employment have emerged quite clearly, so too have factors persisted that are related to the embeddedness of self-employment in family relationships, particularly in societies characterized by high degrees of family-based social capital. Spousal involvement can facilitate entry into and support of stable forms of self-employment generally, as can prior parental self-employment.

While increased heterogeneity and instability within self-employment is consistent with sociological accounts that have emphasized globalization and the spread of neoliberal policies, our research design does not allow a direct test of the extent to which these factors are related to changes in self-employment. However, our findings about the curvilinear relationship of labor market regulation and self-employment suggest that neoliberal policies that reduce labor market rigidities can create relative incentives for individuals to move from dependent employment to self-employment (particularly in nonprofessional forms), but state policies enhancing employment protections can also produce greater incentives for businesses to outsource production and subcontract with small firms and professional self-employed individuals. Policy recommendations that have associated reduction of labor market regulation with both the promotion of entrepreneurialism and job growth have ignored the complexities of considering simultaneously what are at times contradictory incentives for individuals as opposed to existing firms.

Our use of dynamic event-history modeling has demonstrated the importance of recognizing that the existence of self-employment is related to two distinct processes: entry and exit decisions. Certain determinants of self-employment, such as social origin and spousal self-employment, in general have cumulative effects influencing both entry and exit processes. Other factors, such as education, have particularly pronounced effects on entry, but much weaker effects on stability. In addition, our dynamic modeling highlighted the extent to which self-employment activity is unstable and often of short duration, particularly for unskilled occupations and women.

Our findings overall provide a critique of postmodern claims related to self-employment (see, e.g., Hakim 1998). Postmodern arguments about the transformation of self-employment, while consistent with increases in professional, marginal, and temporary self-employment, ignore the extent to which traditional self-employment has persisted and that professional self-employment is also often of considerable duration. Self-employment is indeed becoming more heterogeneous as these social commentators have suggested; but self-employment is not exponentially expanding, unlikely to threaten seriously the existence of dependent employment in traditional firms, nor to become fully dominated by subcontracting, freelancing, and temporary work. We believe that increasing heterogeneity within self-employment also should be understood not simply as the emergence of "new forms" of work, but rather with a clear recognition that these activities are likely quite similar to those found in earlier historic periods when self-employment was also heterogeneous and included a large portion of very marginal activities. Rather than interpreting current forms of self-employment as new and unprecedented, we thus prefer to raise pointedly the possibility that, in contrast, the historical anomaly was instead the dramatic—but temporally short-lived—disappearance of these marginal forms during the expansion of twentieth-century mass industry, ascendancy of trade unionism, and related comparatively desirable conditions found in dependent work. Given the historically unusual conditions found in dependent employment in advanced economies in the decades following World War II, the relative incentives for self-employment were exceptionally low.

Our results also have political implications. In terms of social policy, our findings should serve to caution those policymakers who advocate promoting entrepreneurialism as a simple economic panacea. We find these policy schemas of relatively limited merit, since self-employment today often no longer employs others nor does it always involve individuals who likely even aspire to developing firms into large-scale enterprises. At best policies directed at moving unemployed individuals into self-employment should be understood as temporary stopgap solutions. More generally, our identification of a continued decline in traditional petty bourgeois self-employment also has broader political implication. Given that self-employment is no longer simply dominated by inherited and relatively stable traditional forms of petty bourgeois self-employment, this social grouping can no longer simply be understood as a politically conservative force. Even if the relative level of self-employment has shown slight increases and then relative stability, the growing heterogeneity and change in composition has likely transformed the role and potential of self-employment for coordinated and significant political action in advanced societies. Specifically, self-employment today is often solo, increasingly female, and occurring more often than previously in both liberal professions as well as in domains historically associated with the lumpen proletariat. Declining stability and declining long-term and full-time involvement in business concerns of one's own have likely led to a reduction in support for traditional forms of voluntary association and civic participation as the growing number of marginal and more temporarily self-employed are ill-suited and relatively less inclined to embrace such roles. Given the declining intergenerational stability and increased heterogeneity of self-employment, the structural basis for petty bourgeois class organization and political participation have weakened. It would be increasingly difficult for the group to organize itself—or even become conscious of itself—as a class.

NOTES

1. Change in overall self-employment rate is simply calculated as the percent self-employed time-2 minus percent self-employed time-1. Change in occupational composition is similarly calculated as percent of self-employment in a particular occupational category time-2 minus the percent of self-employment in that category time-1. Note that the observed time-spans vary as a feature of limitations to country-specific data.

2. The decrease in skilled occupational self-employment in most of the countries we examined is occurring at a rate higher than the decrease in skilled dependent self-employment. The average decrease is 10.9 percentage points for self-employed compared with 3.4 percent for dependent employment (excluding the

exceptionally pronounced case of Hungary from the analysis, skilled self-employment decreases by 5.8 percentage points compared with 3.6 percentage points for dependent employment).

3. The inheritance rate appears particularly low in the United States because the data source identifies only self-employed businessmen and not self-employment more generally as a category for father's occupation.

REFERENCES

Abbott, A. 1988. *The system of professions: An essay on the division of expert labor.* Chicago: University of Chicago Press.

Brüderl, J., and P. Preisendörfer. 2000. Fast growing businesses: Empirical evidence from a German study. *International Journal of Sociology* 30:45–70.

Brüderl, J., P. Preisendörfer, and R. Ziegler. 1992. Survival chances of newly founded business organizations. *American Sociological Review* 57:227–42.

———. 1996. *Success of newly founded firms: An empirical study of prospects and risks of start-ups.* Berlin: Dunker and Humboldt.

Frank, R., and P. Cook. 1996. *Winner take all society.* New York: Free Press.

Hakim, C. 1998. *Social change and innovation in the labor market.* New York: Oxford University Press.

Ishida, H., W. Müller, and J. M. Ridge. 1995. Class origin, class destination and education: A cross-national study of ten industrial nations. *American Journal of Sociology* 101:145–93.

Kerckhoff, A., R. T. Campbell, and J. M. Trott. 1982. Dimensions of educational and occupational attainment in Great Britain. *American Sociological Review* 47:347–64.

Lipset, S. M., and R. Bendix. 1959. *Social mobility in industrial society.* Berkeley: University of California Press.

Robinson, R. 1984. Reproducing class relations in industrial capitalism. *American Sociological Review* 49:182–96.

Robinson, R., and J. Kelly. 1979. Class as conceived by Marx and Dahrendorf: Effects on income inequality and politics in the United States and Great Britain. *American Sociological Review* 44:34–58.

Shavit, Y., and E. Yuchtman-Yaar. 2001. Ethnicity, education and other determinants of self-employment in Israel. *International Journal of Sociology* 31:59–91.

Yamaguchi, K. 1983. The structure of intergenerational occupational mobility: Generality and specificity in resources, channels and barriers. *American Journal of Sociology* 88:718–45.

Contributors' Notes

Thomas Amossé is a research fellow at the National Institute of Statistics and Economic Surveys (INSEE) in Paris. His main areas of interest are occupational structures, labor market transitions, and employment relations.

Richard Arum is professor of sociology and chair of the Department of Humanities and Social Sciences in the Professions, New York University. His research on education includes *Judging School Discipline* (Harvard University Press, 2003), and on stratification, contributions to *Inequality by Design* (Princeton: Princeton University Press, 1996). He has published peer-reviewed articles in *American Sociological Review, Criminology, Annual Review of Sociology, International Journal of Sociology*, and *Sociology of Education*. His research has received funding from the National Science Foundation, the National Institute of Justice, the National Academy of Education, and the Spencer Foundation.

Paolo Barbieri received his Ph.D. in sociology at the University of Trento and is currently teaching economic sociology as an associate professor at the University of Milan-Bicocca. His main research interests deal with labor market studies in comparative perspective, analysis of the relationship between welfare and labor markets, analysis of new forms of precarious employment, and labor market segmentation. His recent publications include "Social Capital and Exits from Unemployment" and "Gender and the Experience of Unemployment: A Comparative Analysis," in *Welfare Regimes and the Experience of Unemployment in Europe* ed. Duncan Gallie and Serge Paugam (Oxford: Oxford University Press, 2002); "Male Self-Employment in Four European Countries: The Relevance of Education and Experience across Industries," *International Journal of Sociology* (2001) 30:3 (with S. Luber, H. Lohmann, W. Müller; and "Self-Employment in Italy: Does Labor Market Rigidity Matter?" *International Journal of Sociology* (2001) 31:1.

Peter Bates is a research fellow at the Institute for Employment Studies (IES), University of Sussex, with six years experience in policy research. His main areas of interest include examination of participation in postsecondary education, exploration of labor market transitions among the self-employed, and investigation of the impact of new technology on employment.

Ivano Bison teaches statistics for the social sciences at the University of Trento. His main research interests are methodology, computer science, longitudinal data analysis and sequence analysis. His recent work includes "Unemployment and Cumulative Disadvantage in the Labour Market" (with R. Layte, H. Levin, and J. Hendrikx), and "Unemployment, Welfare Regime and Income Packaging" (with G. K. Esping-Andersen), both in *Welfare Regimes and the Experience of Unemployment in Europe*, ed. D. Gallie and S. Paugam (Oxford: Oxford University Press, 2000).

Boris F. Blumberg holds a MBA from Mannheim University, Germany, and a Ph.D. in sociology from Utrecht University, the Netherlands. Currently, he is employed as a senior researcher at the Business Investment Research Center (BIRC) and as assistant professor in the Department of Organization and Strategy, both at Maastricht University, the Netherlands. His research interests are rooted in the interfaces between management science, economics, and sociology and include self-employment, entrepreneurship, and social network theory.

Erzsébet Bukodi is head of section of social stratification within the Department of Social Statistics of the Hungarian Central Statistical Office, Budapest. She finished her Ph.D. in sociology in 2002 on marriage timing and homogamy in Hungary. Her research interests also involve educational inequalities and different aspects of life-course analysis. She is a participant of a research project aiming to develop a new social indicator system in Hungary. Her recent studies have been published in *European Sociological Review*, and in *Careers of Couples in Contemporary Societies*, ed. H.-P. Blossfeld and S. Drobnic (Oxford: Oxford University Press, 2001).

M.D.R. Evans is a senior research fellow at the Melbourne Institute, University of Melbourne (Australia). On the topic of self-employment, she has previously published "Immigrant Entrepreneurship: Effects of Ethnic Market Size and Linguistically Isolated Labor Pools" in the *American Sociological Review*, and "Professional Commitment: Myth or Reality?" *Research in Social Stratification and Mobility* (with Edward O. Laumann). Her primary research interests include work, family, immigration/ethnicity, inequality, and values. She has published more than 100 refereed articles. Her publications for 2002 include a number of works co-authored with Jonathan Kelley: *Australian Economy and Society: Volume 1: Education, Work, and Welfare* (Federation Press); "National Pride: Survey Data from 24 Nations," *International Journal of Public Opinion Research*, which won the World Association of Public Opinion Research's Worcester Prize.

Theodore P. Gerber is associate professor of sociology at the University of Wisconsin, Madison. He received his Ph.D. in sociology from the University of California, Berkeley, in 1995. His research focuses on social stratification, education, migration, and political processes in contemporary Russia.

Dominique Goux is the head of the division of employment statistics at the National Institute of Statistics and Economic Surveys (INSEE) in Paris. She is also professor of applied econometrics at the Ecole Normale Supérieure de la rue d'Ulm.

Paul M. de Graaf is associate professor at the Department of Sociology, Nijmegen University, the Netherlands. His research interests include the sociology of education, social stratification and mobility, life-course research, and the sociology of the family.

Hiroshi Ishida received his undergraduate education in both Japan and the United States and continued his graduate work at Harvard University where he obtained his Ph.D. in sociology in 1986. He was a research fellow at Nuffield and St. Antony's College, University of Oxford, in 1985–88, working on a project of comparative social mobility. From 1989, he moved to Columbia University where he was an assistant and later a tenured associate professor in the Department of Sociology and the East Asian Institute. He published *Social Mobility in Contemporary Japan* in 1993 and worked on research projects on the relationship between education and the labor market, and on career trajectories and promotion patterns in Japanese and U.S. organizations. He has been a professor of sociology at the Institute of Social Sciences, University of Tokyo, since 1999. Since his return to Japan, he has been writing in Japanese and has co-authored the prize-winning *Schools, Public Employment Offices, and the Labor Market in Postwar Japan* (2000) and co-edited *Secondary Data Analysis in Social Research* (2000).

Henning Lohmann worked as research fellow at the Mannheim Centre for European Social Research (MZES, University of Mannheim) and is currently working at the University of Cologne. Selected publications include "Income, Expenditure and Standard of Living as Poverty Indicators—Different Measures, Similar Results?" Schmollers Jahrbuch. *Journal of Applied Social Science Studies* (2001) 121:2 (with Hans-Jürgen Andreß and Gero Lipsmeier); "Male Self-Employment in Four European Countries: The Relevance of Education and Experience Across Industries," *International Journal of Sociology* (2000) 30:3 (with Silvia Luber, Walter Müller, and Paolo Barbieri).

Silvia Luber worked as a research fellow at the Mannheim Centre for European Social Research (MZES, University of Mannheim) in Germany. She finished her Ph.D. in sociology in 2003 on self-employment in Germany and Great Britain. Currently she is a special assistant for the vice president for planning and development and the chancellor's office at the University of Mannheim.

Nigel Meager is deputy director of the Institute for Employment Studies (IES), University of Sussex, and director of employment policy research at IES. His personal research interests include the evaluation of active labor market measures, international comparisons, the employment of disadvantaged groups (including disabled individuals), and the role of self-employment in the economy.

Walter Müller is professor of sociology at the University of Mannheim and director of the Mannheim Centre for European Social Research (MZES). His present research relates to the comparative study of the social structure of European societies, in particular on the development of educational systems, labor markets, and occupational structures, and on their implications for social stratification in advanced industrial societies. Selected recent publications include *From School to Work. A Comparative Study of Educational Qualifications and Occupational Destinations* (Oxford: Oxford University Press, 1998) (with Yossi Shavit); "Class Cleavages and Party Preferences in Germany Old and New," in *The End of Class Politics? Class Voting in Comparative Context* ed. Geoff Evans (Oxford: Oxford University Press, 1999); "Male Self-Employment in Four European Countries: The Relevance of Education and Experience across Industries," in *International Journal of Sociology* (2000) 30: (with Silvia Luber, Henning Lohmann, and Paolo Barbieri); "Social Mobility," in *International Encyclopedia of the Social & Behavioral Sciences* (Amsterdam: Elsevier, 2001).

Péter Róbert is associate professor at the Department of Sociology at the Eötvös Lóránd University, Budapest. He is also a senior researcher at the Social Research Center (TÁRKI). His research interests are in the field of social stratification and mobility with special focus on educational inequalities and life-course analysis. He is also doing research on life-style differentiation, attitudes toward inequalities, and political preferences. His recent articles have been published in *European Sociological Review, International Review of Sociology*, European Societies and H.-P. Blossfeld-S. Drobnic (eds.): *Careers of Couples in Contemporary Societies*, ed. H.-P. Blossfeld and S. Drobnic (Oxford: Oxford University Press, 2001).

Joanna Sikora received her Ph.D. in 2001 from the Australian National University and then worked as a research Fellow at the Melbourne Institute, University of Melbourne (Australia). She is now a Lecturer at the Australian National University. Her primary research interests focus on economic attitudes in industrialized countries. Recent publications include "Is Corruption Necessary for Upward Mobility? Perceptions from 26 Nations in 1999/2000," *Australian Social Monitor*, and (with Jonathan Kelley) "Attitudes to Private and Public Ownership in East and West: Bulgaria, Poland, Australia, and Finland, 1994–1997," *Soviet and Post-Soviet Review.*

Kuo-Hsien Su is associate professor in the Department of Sociology at National Taiwan University. He received his Ph.D. in sociology from Columbia University. His research interests include organizational demography and human resource practices in small and medium-sized firms. He has co-authored, with Hiroshi Ishida and Seymour Spilerman, "Educational Credentials and Promotion Chances in Japanese and American Organizations," *American Sociological Review*, 1997.

Wei-hsin Yu is assistant professor at the Institute of Sociology, Academia Sinica, Taiwan. Her research interests include gender stratification, labor markets, and comparative sociology. Her current work continues her University of Chicago doctoral dissertation research that compared labor markets and women's work trajectories in Japan and Taiwan. She also studies nonstandard work arrangements, self-employment activity, and the informal sector, with emphasis on their relevance to gender inequality in East Asian societies.

Index

Abe, M., 351
ACCRE. *See* Aide aux Chômeurs Créateurs ou Repreneurs d'Enterprise
Acs, Z. J., 105
age of the self-employed: in Australia, 214–15, 225, 230, 232–34, 236; cross-national analysis of, 440–41; in France, 87–89, 94; in Germany, 38, 47, 50–51, 63, 66; in Hungary, 254–55, 269; in Italy, 333, 339; in Japan, 352, 366, 372, 374; in the Netherlands, 121; in Russia, 288–90, 293, 299; in the United Kingdom, 138–40, 151, 156; in the United States, 94, 180, 191, 196–97. *See also* work experience and self-employment
Aide aux Chômeurs Créateurs ou Repreneurs d'Enterprise (ACCRE), 78, 92
Amossé, Thomas, 27
Arum, Richard, 9, 281
attitudes of the self-employed: in Australia, 219, 234, 237; in Italy, 320–21
Audretsch, D. B., 105
Australia, 203, 234–37; data and methods for analyzing self-employment in, 212–14, 237–38n1; descriptive statistics of self-employment in, 214–21; entry into self-employment in, 222–30, 237; exit from self-employment in, 221–22, 230–33; globalization and marketization in, 235; institutional context of self-employment in, 204–6; labor market regulation and family-based social capital in, 19–20; marginalization hypothesis applied to, 225–26, 235–36; rates of self-employment in, 203; requirements to establish a new business in, 19; research regarding self-employment in, 206–11

Barbieri, Paolo, 29
Bates, Peter, 27, 148–49
Bates, T., 95, 109
Beck, U., 241n36
Bendix, Reinhard, 5, 426
Bennett, R., 209

Bison, Ivano, 29
Blanchflower, D. G., 82, 311
Blau, David, 175
Blau, Peter, 5–6, 8
Blossfeld, H., 252
Bluestone, B., 171
Blumberg, Boris, 27
Brüderl, J., 109
Bryson, A., 136
Budig, M., 281
Bukodi, Erzsébet, 28
business organizations. *See* firms

Campbell, M., 138
Capellari, L., 312
Carroll, G. R., 107
Casey, B., 168n1
categorization/definition of self-employment: in Australia, 212–13; conceptualization in occupational terms, 5–9; in France, 77, 80, 100–101; in Germany, 37; in Italy, 342–43n1; in Japan, 349, 383n4; in the Netherlands, 109–10; in the United Kingdom, 135–36; in the United States, 172
class and self-employment, 108; education and, 438; intergenerational mobility, 108–9, 312–13; in Italy, 330; in Japan, 351; in the Netherlands, 113–14, 121–27, 130–31; the petty bourgeoisie (*see* petty bourgeoisie); political orientation and, 6–8. *See also* family and self-employment
Communist Party membership: market transition theory, 277–78, 303–4; power conversion theory, 278, 293, 301, 303–4; self-employment in Hungary and, 251, 260–61, 265, 271, 282; self-employment in Russia and, 284, 292–93, 297, 301, 303–4
contractors, independent. *See* independent contractors
corporatist states, 19–22, 428. *See also* France; Germany; Netherlands, the
Cox, D. R., 94